STUDIES IN THE HISTORY
OF CHRISTIAN MISSIONS

R. E. Frykenberg
Brian Stanley
General Editors

D1596166

STUDIES IN THE HISTORY
OF CHRISTIAN MISSIONS

Judith M. Brown and Robert Eric Frykenberg, *Editors*

Christians, Cultural Interactions,
and India's Religious Traditions

Robert Eric Frykenberg

Christians and Missionaries in India:
Cross-Cultural Communication since 1500

Susan Billington Harper

In the Shadow of the Mahatma: Bishop V. S. Azariah
and the Travails of Christianity in British India

D. Dennis Hudson

Protestant Origins in India:
Tamil Evangelical Christians, 1706-1835

Brian Stanley, *Editor*

Christian Missions and the Enlightenment

Kevin Ward and Brian Stanley, *Editors*

The Church Mission Society and World Christianity, 1799-1999

Christians and Missionaries in India

Cross-Cultural Communication since 1500

WITH SPECIAL REFERENCE TO
CASTE, CONVERSION, AND COLONIALISM

Edited by

Robert Eric Frykenberg

Associate Editor

Alaine Low

WILLIAM B. EERDMANS PUBLISHING COMPANY
GRAND RAPIDS, MICHIGAN / CAMBRIDGE, U.K.

ROUTLEDGECURZON
LONDON

© 2003 Wm. B. Eerdmans Publishing Co.

Published jointly 2003 by
Wm. B. Eerdmans Publishing Co.
255 Jefferson Ave. S.E., Grand Rapids, Michigan 49503 /
P.O. Box 163, Cambridge CB3 9PU U.K.
www.eerdmans.com
and by
RoutledgeCurzon
11 New Fetter Lane, London EC4P 4EE
RoutledgeCurzon is an imprint of the Taylor & Francis Group

Printed in the United States of America

07 06 05 04 03   7 6 5 4 3 2 1

Library of Congress Cataloging-in-Publication Data

Eerdmans ISBN 0-8028-3956-8

British Library Cataloguing-in-Publication Data

A catalogue record for this book is available fron the British Library.

RoutledgeCurzon ISBN 0-7007-1600-9

Contents

109886

Contents

Contributors

Peter B. Andersen is Associate Professor in the Sociology of Religions in the Department for the History of Religion, University of Copenhagen. He wrote his doctoral thesis on the Santals in India and has conducted statistical investigations on religious change and modern religious movements in Denmark.

Michael Bergunder is Lecturer in Ecumenics and Religious Studies in the Theological Faculty, University of Halle. His research has focused on the Pentecostal movement; modern esotericism; religion and society of modern South India, especially Tamilnadu; and the Tamil-speaking diaspora. He is working on the Theosophical Society and its impact on the religious history of India and the West.

Marine Carrin, an anthropologist, is director of research with the CNRS at the Centre d'Anthropologie, Toulouse. Among her recent publications is *Managing Distress: Therapeutic Cults in South Asia.* She is currently working on a book on Santal ritual discourse, and she has also published on the Bhuta cults and related themes in South Canara, India. With H. Tambs-Lyche she is finishing *Another Orientalism,* on the cultural encounter between missionaries and Santals.

Penelope Carson is an independent historian based at Malvern College in Worcestershire, England. Her main areas of interest are the East India Company's religious policy and the interaction between Christianity and indigenous religions and cultures. She has published numerous articles and reviews on these themes. Her most recent publications are "Golden Casket or Pebbles and Trash? J. S. Mill and the Anglicist/Orientalist Controversy," in *J. S. Mill's*

Encounter with India, edited by M. Moir, D. Peers, and L. Zastoupil, and "The Religious Establishment and Toleration, 1698-1833," in *Christian Missions and the Enlightenment,* edited by Brian Stanley.

Gunnel Cederlöf is Research Fellow in the Department of History and the Department of Cultural Anthropology and Ethnology at Uppsala University, Sweden. Her main field of research is the nineteenth- and twentieth-century social history of South India. She is the author of *Bonds Lost: Subordination, Conflict and Mobilisation in Rural South India c. 1900-1970,* and she is currently doing research in the field of environmental history for a project entitled *Claims and Rights: Processes of Negotiation over Nature in India.*

Susanne Foss is head of section at the Faculty of Humanities, University of Copenhagen. She completed her master's thesis in 1999 on the subject of discourse on immigrants and ethnic minorities in Denmark.

Robert Eric Frykenberg is Emeritus Professor of History at the University of Wisconsin-Madison. His works include *Guntur District, 1788-1848: A History of Local Influence and Central Authority in India.* His edited works include *Christians, Cultural Interactions, and India's Religious Traditions.*

Eleanor M. Jackson studied at the Universities of Birmingham, United Kingdom, and Heidelberg, Germany, before serving as a missionary in Madurai, South India, and Serampore, Bengal. She is now a Senior Lecturer at the University of Derby, United Kingdom, and an Anglican lay minister. Her principal work to date is *Red Tape and the Gospel: A Life of Dr. William Paton (1886-1943).* She is currently writing a life of Lesslie Newbigin. She is the editor of the *Question of Woman: The Collected Writings of Charlotte von Kirschbaum* and *God's Apprentice: The Autobiography of Bishop Stephen Neill.*

Heike Liebau studied Indian languages and literatures at Tashkent University and completed her Ph.D. at Halle University, on linguistic studies of German missionaries in India. Her current research, on Indian Christians and Christian education in the Madras Presidency, is being done in collaboration with the Department of History of South Asia, at Humboldt University, Berlin, and the Center for Modern Oriental Studies, Berlin. She is also writing a book on conversion and social change, focusing on the role of Indian middlemen in mission history. Recent publications include: "Tamilische Christen im 18. Jahrhundert als Mitgestalter sozialer Veränderungen: Motivationen, Möglichkeiten und Resultate ihres Wirkens," in *Akteure des Wandels. Lebensläufe und Gruppenbilder an Schnittstellen von Kulturen,* edited by Petra Heidrich and Heike Liebau; "Zwischen Hinduismus und Christentum. Veränderung sozialer und religiöser Bindungen im Süden des vorkolonialen Indie," in *Aneignung und Abgrenzung in der Globalisierung,* edited by Henner Fürtig; and "Über die Erziehung 'tüchtiger Subjekte' zur Verbreitung des Evangeliums. Das Schulwesen der Dänisch-Halleschen Mission," in *Missionsgesellschaften als globale Organisationen,* edited by Artur Bogner, Bernd Holwick, and Hartmann Tyrell (forthcoming).

Iwona Milewska is an assistant professor in the areas of Sanskrit grammar and didactics and classical literature in the Indian Department, Institute of Oriental Philology, Jagiellonian University, Krakow, Poland. Her previous publications include "Sanskrit Studies in Krakow," in *Cracow Indological Studies,* volume 1, ed. Przemyslaw Piekarski et al., and "Two Modern Film Versions of the Mahabarata: Similarities and Differences between an Indian and a European Approach," in *Composing a Tradition: Concepts, Techniques, and Relationships,* ed. Mary Brockington and Peter Schreiner.

An Honorary Research Associate at the University of Sydney, **Geoffrey A. Oddie** is the author of a range of books and articles on South Asian History. These include studies of Protestant missionaries, Hinduism, and religious conversion movements, mostly during the nineteenth century. Among his more recent works are *Popular Religion, Elites and Reform: Hook-Swinging and Its Prohibition in Colonial India, 1800-1894* and *Missionaries, Rebellion and Proto-Nationalism: James Long of Bengal, 1814-87.* He is currently working on Protestant missionary constructions of Hinduism in the nineteenth century.

Indira Viswanathan Peterson is a Professor in the Department of Middle East and Asian Languages and Cultures at Columbia University. She specializes in Sanskrit and Tamil literature. She is author of *Poems to Siva: The Hymns of the Tamil Saints* and editor for Indian literature, *Norton Anthology of World Masterpieces.* Her most recent research is on literature and culture in eighteenth-century South India.

Avril A. Powell is Senior Lecturer in the History of South Asia at the School of Oriental and African Studies, University of London. Her recent publications include "Modernist Muslim Responses to Christian Critiques of Islamic Culture, Civilization, and History in Northern India," in *Christians, Cultural Interactions, and India's Religious Traditions,* edited by Judith M. Brown and Robert Eric Frykenberg, and *Muslims and Missionaries in Pre-Mutiny India.*

Paula Richman is the Irvin E. Houck Professor of Religion at Oberlin College. She is the author of *Extraordinary Child: Poems from a South Indian Devo-*

tional Genre and *Women, Branch Stories, and Religious Rhetoric in a Tamil Buddhist Text,* and the editor of *Questioning Ramayanas: A South Asian Tradition* and *Many Ramayanas: The Diversity of a Narrative Tradition in South India.*

Jayeeta Sharma was born in Assam and studied at Guwahati, Delhi, and Cambridge. She is currently completing her dissertation, "The Making of Modern Assam: 1826-1935," at the University of Cambridge. Her previous research was on caste and religious identities among Dalit groups. Her other areas of interest range from a study of dance as a focus for national imaginings to the connections between contemporary anthropological knowledge and contemporary nationality movements in Northeast India.

Harald Tambs-Lyche is professor of ethnology at the Université de Picardie — Jules Verne, Amiens. He is the author of *London Patidars* and of *Power, Profit, and Poetry: Traditional Society in Kathiawar, Western India.* He is also the editor of *The Feminine Sacred in South Asia.* He is also finishing, with M. Carrin, *Another Orientalism,* which examines the cultural encounter between Santals and missionaries.

Richard Fox Young is the Elmer K. and Ethel R. Timby Associate Professor of History of Religions at Princeton Theological Seminary. His research interests focus on the history of encounter between Christianity and various religions of Asian origin, especially Hinduism and Buddhism; the place of Christianity in non-Western pluralism; and contemporary understandings of interreligious dialogue.

CHAPTER ONE

Introduction: Dealing with Contested Definitions and Controversial Perspectives

ROBERT ERIC FRYKENBERG

Not surprisingly, the pervasive assumption that Christianity in India is noth-ing more than a Western, European, or "colonial" imposition is again open to challenge.[1] Nevertheless, despite this being so, many of those who think and write about India all too often forget, or else are unaware of the fact, that Christianity has always been, in some measure, a non-Western religion; that in India this has always been so; and that there are now more Christians in the "non-West" (Africa and Asia) than in the West. Recognizing that, until very recently, most studies of Christians in India have been heavily Eurocentric, both in content and in tone, chapters contained within this volume attempt to subject this long-standing bias to closer scrutiny and provide perspectives that are more Indocentric. Realizing that many more studies, yielding deeper and wider understandings, of many different Christian communities in India will be needed before a truly comprehensive history of Christianity in India can be written, each chapter here is an attempt to address some particular as-pect of cultural cross-contact and communication with special reference to

1. Roger E. Hedlund, ed., *Christianity's Indian: The Emergence of an Indigenous Com-munity* (Delhi, 2000), covers a wide range of perspectives on many different Christian communities, from ancient Thomas Christians to various local tribal Christian communi-ties. Each essay emphasizes the essentially Indian character of Christianity in India.

With due apologies to those who study Christians in other parts of India, evidence, exam-ples, and illustrations in this introduction are largely restricted to South India, which is best known to the author.

Christians in India. Subjects addressed range from histories of Sanskrit grammar and modern scientific knowledge to histories of populist Pentecostalism, Urdu polemics, and Tamil poetry.[2]

Interestingly, relationships between India's Christians and questions about caste, conversion, and colonialism have always been complex and convoluted. Simplistic conflations between Christians and colonialism, conversion, or caste have almost invariably resulted from confusing complex forms of *dual identity*. These have themselves reflected confused manifestations of cultural ambiguity and ambivalence, not to mention manifold verities within each Christian community of India. Exactly how such confusions have come about has needed to be studied more closely. The common thread running through all of the studies presented within this volume is an argument that, despite intrusions from the West and from Christians of the West, from cultures that were alien and foreign, most Christians of India have continued to retain their own distinct cultural identities. These identities have remained, in most respects, clearly and predominantly Indian.

Communication, lack of communication, and failures of communication lie at the very heart of every chapter presented in this volume. Failures of communication, as we know, can be accidental or inadvertent. Failures can also be due to ineptitude or ignorance. There are times, however, when barriers to communication have been deliberately erected. When this has happened, special ciphers or codes of encryption have served to inhibit or restrict the free or full flow of information, either partially or totally. Miscommunication, misinformation, or obfuscation, in such circumstances, are not mere accidents. Secrecy has been the form, and the name, for the purposeful prevention of communication or for the deliberate withholding of information. As a barrier to communication, this has often arisen from attempts to create or retain special preserves of power. Even when full and accurate communication has been intended, there have been occasions when access and tools to do so were not adequate or available, when communication has been far from perfect.

Christians, from their earliest beginnings some two thousand years ago, have always been obliged to communicate their faith and to convey the Word of God to others. The "mission" of accurately communicating the gospel, of spreading it to the far ends of the earth, was and is an imperative. This mission, as enjoined and made mandatory for all true believers, has never been rescinded. Since, in India, this imperative has always extended beyond the

---

2. Questions that are posed within this volume, for the most part, emerged out of papers presented at European Conferences of Modern South Asian Studies in Copenhagen (August 1996) and Prague (September 1998).

constraints of caste and culture, the "alien" and "intrusive" features of communication, as the quintessential missionary activity, have always been, in some measure, unavoidable.

Yet, at the same time, essential as it has always been to communicate the Word of God to all mankind, Christianity, unlike other major religious traditions, has never possessed a single "sacred language." Despite attempts to the contrary, no single tongue nor script has ever been allowed to achieve or hold a privileged status above all others, at least for very long. Rather, as reflected in the historic episode known as the "Day of Pentecost," when the apostles "began to talk in many different tongues, as the Spirit gave them power of utterance" so that among devout Jews in Jerusalem "from countries every nation under heaven, each heard what was spoken *in his own language*,"[3] every language has held the potential of being sacred. Since language itself is viewed as a gift of God, by implication all languages and all cultures have been, in a theological sense, potentially equal. All have been "redeemable." Each individual or community and, by inference, each vehicle of communication is a part of "creation in progress." As such, each has been capable of becoming more perfect and pure (or sacred). In the words of Yale Professor Lamin Sanneh, "Christianity triumphs by the relinquishing of Jerusalem or any fixed universal centre, be it geographical, linguistic or cultural, with the result that we have a proliferation of centres, languages and cultures within the Church. Christian œcumenism is a pluralism of the periphery with only Christ at the centre."[4] His words echo those of Bishop Vedanayagam Azariah of Dornakal who, in 1932, wrote: "The religion of Christ is one of the most dynamic factors in the world. It always bursts its boundaries, however strong and rigid those boundaries may be. It refuses to be confined to any one race, class, or caste. It seeks to embrace all."[5]

Refining Concepts and Definitions

Problems related to communication remain close to the very heart of the task of conveying the Christian message within each of the world's cultures. For

---

3. Acts 2:4-6, 7-12 from *The New English Bible: The New Testament* (New York, 1961). Italics added.

4. Lamin Sanneh, "Mission and the Modern Imperative: Retrospective and Prospect: Charting a Course," unpublished paper (ca. 1993).

5. Quoted in Susan Billington Harper, *In the Shadow of the Mahatma: Bishop Azariah and the Travails of Indian Christianity* (London and Grand Rapids, 2000) from V. S. Azariah, "The Communal Award," *Guardian* 10.31 (8 September 1932): 368 and reprinted in *Dornakal Diocesan Magazine* 9.10 (October 1932): 10-13.

this reason, the pivotal concepts, or sets of concepts, used within chapters of this volume will be no more useful than the sharpness with which they are defined. As tools of analysis, definitions are descriptions that identify and de-limit precise properties or explain exact meanings of given words, terms, and phrases and of the concepts and entities that they purport to represent. Con-cepts, as abstractions, each contain a general idea or notion, an "invented" re-ceptacle or formation of thought. Well-defined concepts are the essential tools that make clear communication possible. Even when arbitrarily set, they can serve as benchmarks, as heuristic devices, or as instruments by which one can measure or understand things more precisely. Thus, however abstract or apparently reductive or simplistic some definitions may seem to be, they are elements of conceptual apparatus without which it is difficult to attain en-lightenment or achieve broader understandings. Without them, assessments of events concerning relations between various kinds of cultures within India become impossible. For our purposes, among various specific sets of con-cepts that are of special concern, what it is meant by the term "Christian" needs to be defined. Without a baseline definition of what it means to be "Christian" — both in the sense of a delimiting adjective and in the sense of an identifying or named entity (or noun) — understanding of relations within cultures and between communities of India becomes impossible. Thus, for purposes of this volume, distinctions need to be made: between things "Christian" and things "colonial"; between things "Christian" and "caste" or other elements deeply imbedded or institutionalized within "Hindu" culture; and between what is "Christian" and "conversion" (or "proselytism").

Controversies over the Terms "Christian," "Christians," and "Christianity"

As already indicated, much depends upon whether a concept is used as a modifying adjective, something that qualifies something else, or whether that concept is used as denoting a primary noun (namely, as a subject or object). When used to modify something else, the word "Christian" is a term of di-minishment.[6] It is subject to something else and is subordinated to it. Things "Christian" — Christian missions, Christian individuals, Christian institu-tions, or Christian activities — pertain to things concerned with or defined

6. David Jeffrey, *Newsletter of the Institute for Advanced Christian Studies* (Madison, Wisc., November 2000), feature article, pp. 1-3.

4

by faith in a person and in the gospel (or "good news") delivered to his followers. As a term of identity, "Christian" pertains both to belief and to relationship with the person at the center of that belief. Things Christian are subordinate — to Jesus the Messiah (Christ) and to his commands. This identifying subordination can be either individual and personal or institutional and communal. Followers are commanded to spread "the good news" about "the faith."[7] This faith itself is a "gift."[8] This news, in essence, was and is this: that each person is made in the likeness of God (however tainted that likeness may have become); that each person is of such intrinsic worth as to prompt a divine act of redemption (atonement by God-in-Christ in the sacrifice of himself); and that divine grace thereby enables anyone to gain direct access to an everlasting relationship with God. This news, carried in heart and mind, expressed by every tongue and pen, is at the core of what Christian means. To be Christian embodies this subjection.

"Christianity"[9] (and Christian missions), therefore, in basic theological and historical terms, has consisted of individualized and institutionalized expressions of such belief. It embodies both commitment and obligation. It is the continuous, ongoing, and still unfinished work by God within the heart and mind of each person and within the culture of every people. This work, carried out through the agency of imperfect human beings, both as individuals and as institutions, is an ongoing process. In every age and in every place on earth, persons converted or turned around by the agency of God's Spirit have been obliged to carry this message to those who have not yet received it. This obligation, as embodied in the Great Commission, is deemed to be *the* ultimate Christian mandate. As such, it still remains in force. The history of things Christian consists of attempts to understand exactly how well this imperative has or has not been carried out within the contexts of mundane human affairs.

Yet, one of the most lingering, persistent, and stubborn misperceptions, both in India and in the West, is the notion that Christianity is essentially European and that European religion has traditionally been Christian. Of course, neither of these notions is true. Contradictions arising from such misconceptions are so manifold that they need hardly be elaborated upon further. It is sufficient to be reminded that the long westward movement from Antioch by which peoples of Europe gradually became Christian was far from

---

7. A mandate recorded both by Mark (15:15) and by Luke (Acts 1:8).

8. Eph. 2:8-9.

9. The term "Christianity" is full of ambiguity and subject to such misunderstanding that, like the term "Hinduism," it has no single or precise meaning. The adjective alone, like the adjective "Hindu," is required for precise analysis here.

complete as late as 1500; and also that, in the ante-Nicene centuries, a no less significant eastward movement was carrying the Christian faith to peoples of Persia, India, and China, as also to peoples of Africa. Christianity in the non-Western world was already strong long before the Great Councils began to codify the institutions of a Latin Christian culture. Developments in the West in no way mitigated or nullified the various forms of Eastern Christianity that had already become established. It is also important to remember that, by the very time that Christianity in Europe was becoming, at least for a time, *the* religion of the West, its very ascendancy in the West was already beginning to go into retreat — and that this retreat came largely as a result of influences from the non-Western world. Thus, reference points for perceptions about the future of Christians in the world now seem to lie, more and more, in Africa and Asia (if not also in Latin America). Meanwhile, the stereotype of Christianity as Western continues to survive and to be repeated, over and over. Such being the case, if the full story about the nature of Christians in history is to be properly understood, scholars need to more fully explore the entire complex of different Christian cultures, each with its own separate history, among every people of the world.

Controversies over "Colonialism" and Its Conflations

"Colonialism" is a modern concept. Indeed, it has become common within the historiography of India only during the past forty years. As such, it is now far removed from the original root term used in ancient times within the contexts of Roman imperial history.[10] As it is now commonly used, and in many ways misused, as also neatly simplified within the Marxian lexicon, and as then spread within the secular academy (in arts, humanities, and social sciences), media, and government, the term itself has become a synonym for coercion, domination, and exploitation, especially and often specifically, of peoples everywhere by peoples and institutions of the West. It also denotes oppression by any "alien" and "foreign" forces or rulers (again, especially by Western: European and American oppressors). Its meaning has been further expanded, moreover, so as to imply acts of oppression by ruling elites of any

10. The Roman (Latin) "colony" *(colonia)* was a settlement of Roman citizens in a hostile or newly conquered country. The word applied to a Greek *apoikia*, a settlement of "people [far] from home" as an independent, self-governing *polis* or "city-state." In modern usage, it refers to a settlement in a new country, a body of settlers forming a community connected to their parent state, or a number of people of one nationality residing in a foreign city or country (*SOED* [Oxford, 1959], p. 343).

kind and in any circumstance, but especially those within, or stemming from, the capitalist West.

Colonialism, in short, is more of a rhetorical device than a precise, scientific tool. It is part of a technology for denigrating, shaming, and shunning. It applies to anything that is perceived to be politically incorrect. Anything perceived as a form of institutionalized (or systemic) inhumanity can be so labeled, whether or not there is evidence that this is or was actually so. Anything seen as "damage" inflicted by one group of humans upon another group of humans, either individually or institutionally, often by use of demeaning stereotypes about "lesser" forms of human life, or even upon the life or breath of an inanimate ecological environment itself, is seen as suffering from colonialism. The term, obviously, has become a convenient device for labeling, demonizing, or assigning collective guilt. It has thereby, ironically, itself become an instrument of oppression, a way to bring shame upon whole categories of peoples and cultures; or, conversely, a way to abuse close colleagues and family members. In short, the term has become an epithet of choice. As such, it is a vehicle of and for sweeping condemnation. For many within the scholarly community and within society, "colonialism" is the ultimate term by which one can characterize what the West or North (America and Europe) has done to the East (Asia) and/or to the South (Africa and Latin America). Oddly, despite its broadly rhetorical vagueness, the concept continues to be employed as if it were a precision tool or a scientific instrument.

As applied to India (or South Asia generally), the terms "colonial," "colonialism," and "colonialist" have now become *the* pejorative devices or epithets of choice. While especially applicable for demonizing all things "British," the terms have also been extended so as to include things American and European (or Western). In relation to Christianity, Christian mission, or even to all things Christian, the term has been useful for categorically demonizing or epitomizing evil and exploitation, for assigning guilt, or for categorizing anything deemed to be "anti-national." Christian "colonialism," in other words, is a manifest form of oppression of the weak (East and South) by the strong (West and North). Its essence is to be found in charges of forced conversion and proselytization. In the historiography of modern India, both as practiced in the East *and* in the West, the grip of the conceptual apparatus related to the perspective of this term remains firm. Use of the term in this way against Christians in India may not have started with Gandhi. Yet, ever since Gandhi attacked Bishop Vedanayagam Azariah in 1937 and called his action, in attempting to evangelize by bringing the gospel to outcaste Malas and Madigas of Dornakal, "anti-national," the term has been used to implicate Indian Christians as being alien, anti-national and unpatriotic, or subject to forces from outside of India. The view that Christians in India, one and all, are man-ifestations of colonialism has remained pervasive, if not dominant, ever since. Despite inner and outer historical contradictions, the assumptions lying be-hind the use of this rhetorical device have driven out of fashion those more useful and precise meanings connected to the term. Ironically, long after methods of materialist (Marxian) analysis have ceased to be ascendant, the perspective embodied in this concept has remained dominant in India. It is part of a Eurocentric lexicon used by scholars and journalists, for a worldview ideology (in its Marxian forms). As such, the term represents a point of view, a perspective, which many academics and thinkers, both of the West and of the non-West, hold dear. Given the elite origins of such historiographic per-spectives, both in India and in the West, it is hardly surprising that scholars of Indian history, both within India and in the world at large, have long casually conflated Christianity with colonialism.

At the same time, it is important to note that there are some grounds for such conflation. This cannot be denied. Indeed, as we shall see within this vol-ume, there is evidence enough to support some instances of such a conflation and to show that, in specific or occasional instances, the conflation has been fully justified. What is more at issue here is an axiomatic conflation. This "perspective from above" that is still fixed within current fashions within the academy, both in casual public discourse and historiography, has tended, in one way or another, to deny legitimacy or recognition to the critical or serious study of India's Christians in general, and of missionaries in particular. This conflation, indeed, has assumed a kind of sacrosanct quality: it is a truism that none dare question and about which no more need be said. It represents an attitude that some chapters within this volume either bring into question or subject to closer scrutiny.

What is argued here is that, while the "colonialism-conflation theory" represents part of a much larger reality, it is far from the whole story, and it is a subject on which the last word has yet to be uttered. What is challenged is the implicit assumption, now almost axiomatic as it is enshrined in the canon of much contemporary historiography, both within academic institutions and among many historians who focus attention upon India, that missionary movements need not be taken seriously and that they have had relatively little to do with general history of events in modern India. What has also been im-plied, therewith, are the views that missionary records hold little of conse-quence or utility and that they are hardly worth more than a passing, perhaps scornful, glance. One may even wonder at times whether, for many South Asianists in the West also, especially in America, the subject of Christians in India and Christian missions is not all but closed. That this strong negative

8

bias may now perhaps be softening, if only a little, in no way diminishes the blindness arising out of what has for so long been the prevailing situation.[11] To call this situation into question, along with the academic shunning it has engendered, is still tantamount to challenging enshrined truth and to assaulting the canons of verity.

The often all too casual conflation of Christianity and colonialism, sometimes crudely blunt or simplistic and sometimes bereft of empirical evidence, seems to have inhibited efforts to find more balanced understandings. Significant elements in the history of Christians in India, and much in Indian history itself, have to be ignored in order to cherish this perspective. The conflation presumes that an alien religion could somehow be "foisted" upon "hapless natives" and that this could be done in defiance of rational choice. It presumes that mindless people in India meekly suffered a forced imposition; and, moreover, that forced conversion was the deliberate device officially sanctioned by a callous and heartless Raj. It assumes that, without the agency of British rule and without the institutions of the Indian Empire, neither Christians nor Christian institutions such as Christian missions could ever have survived in India.

For reasons such as these, it is necessary to recount how Christianity in India first came into existence and how India's Christians and their cultures, at various times and under very different circumstances, became firmly established. It is important to demonstrate how indigenous or "Indianized" the Christian cultures in India were. It should be appreciated, however, that the emergence of Christian institutions in India occurred long before the arrival of Europeans *(Farangis)* and long before the Raj. Christians and Christian missions in India, in other words, have as much claim to being considered "Indian," indigenous, and products of cultures that have arisen within the continent as any other socio-religious institution within the subcontinent.[12] If most origins of Christians in India were never, even in any remote or retrodictive sense, "colonial," it is also important to understand the measure to which what is Christian in India never has been, in any sense, "Western" or "European." Prior to the coming of modern missionaries, both foreign and

---

11. It may now be, however, that attention has begun to shift toward Christianity and to missions. If so, perhaps this is partly as a result of rising forces of oppression, especially fundamentalist movements and events since the destruction of the Babri Masjid in December 1992. Such events have evoked concern for the future of constitutional governance, human rights, rule of law, secularism, and tolerance.

12. Every culture is a human construction. Unlike what is found or given, culture is formed out of resources of "nature." "Culture," so defined, reflects the ambiguities, both in aspects of *imago dei* and in more "demonic" and destructive actions.

native, Christians had been in India for a long time. Thereafter, successive waves of distinctively different Christian cultures became established in India. These, increasing variegated and complex in form, have traditionally been identified as falling into three successive categories: first, Orthodox (Thomas, or Syrian); second, Catholic (Roman); and third, Evangelical (and Protestant). A brief survey, exploring the complexity of these distinctive categories and their cultural origins, is provided in chapter one and serves as a contextual framework for the chapters that follow.

Controversies over Caste, Community, and Dual Identity

Perhaps the biggest, most ceaseless, and most continuous of all ongoing arguments and conflicts that have brought about mutations within Christian groups in India, regardless of whether they were Catholic or Evangelical, Anglican or Dissenter, Mar Thoma or Syrian, conservative or liberal, are those that have centered in or swirled around some issue relating to caste. Indigenous cultures and processes of acculturation have highlighted such conflicts. Indeed, it is difficult to find any time in the history of Christians in India when caste has not been a burning issue. No problem has remained more persistent or enduring. No group of Christians in India seems to have been immune. This is one problem that has never gone away, one that still hangs in the air, bringing dissension and strife wherever it is found. Dimensions of this problem, in intricate permutations that never seem to dissipate, both historical and theological, seem limitless, such that a sweeping hypothesis may be suggested: namely, that every single Christian community that has ever existed in the subcontinent or that continues to exist, sometimes in a fossilized form but just as often in some altogether different or in some revitalized new form, has suffered from what, for want of a better term, can be called "caste" troubles.[13] In theological terms, issues of unity and diversity, of polarity and universality, can be seen in seemingly paradoxical contradictions. In historical terms, processes of ceaseless challenges to acceptance within the fold of a common humanity, in its fullest sense, have contended with processes wherein damages have been suffered by people who have been rejected or

---

13. The neatest and simplest definition for the word *caste,* a Portuguese derivative from *casta* for "breed," is the Indic or Sanskrit term *jat* or *jāti,* meaning "birth" (anything that is born, be it butterfly or elephant) or "birth-group" or "birth-community." Too often it is compounded and confused with the term *varna* (lit. "color"). In Brahmanical sociological thinking, *varna* is an abstract concept that might best be translated as "category" or "class."

stigmatized by other people who claim, ironically, to hold the same faith. Faith and family, in this sense, have formed pluralistic foundations of dual identity within which, since time immemorial, Christians in India have had to struggle.

In attempting to address this complex issue of faith and family and caste and culture, India's Christians have also had to deal with the presence and influence, if not the pervasive power and pressure, of missionaries and, to a lesser degree, of what may be called "missionary colonialism." All missionaries, whether "foreign" or "native" ("indigenous" or "domestic"), are and have always been, by definition, agents of change.[14] They have been, by nature, disturbers of the peace and enemies of the status quo. Their actions were and are intrusions. Intrusions are disturbing. Christians and non-Christians alike are averse to disturbances.

Clashes between alien influences and indigenous institutions, therefore, have also always been more than simply religious or theological in nature. Cultural, political (including ecclesiastical), and material issues have been at stake. If and when "alien"[15] missionaries have been opposed by prevailing political regimes dominant in territories within which they worked, then alien Christians and indigenous Christians have tended to find common ground and could look to each other for mutual solace and support. Yet, if and when alien Christians (even if few in number) and alien rulers have come from the same culture and ethnicity — even if and when such rulers have been indifferent to religion — or if and when missionaries and rulers have found common ground or have become inextricably linked politically, then indigenous Indian Christians have found themselves, in lesser or greater degree, marginalized, if not oppressed. If they have not been marginalized, this has been because they were obliged both to collaborate and to submit to domination. This, like many of the non-Christian neighbors surrounding them, Indian Christians have tended, quite understandably, to resent.

In both theological and historical terms, therefore, caste has never been

---

14. They also have been, for the most part, "beyond caste" or "outside caste" and, since the nineteenth-century arrival of egalitarian principles from Europe, opponents of caste.

15. It should be emphasized at this point that the meaning of "alien" or "foreign" in the Indian context is neither simple nor clear cut. "Alien" or "foreign" does not simply apply to something from outside the subcontinent. Rather, these adjectives apply from one part of India to another. Thus, a Tamil missionary who worked among Telugus, and certainly a Tamil missionary in Assam or Bihar, would also have been alien, in some measure. These categories, in other words, are not absolute but require subtle gradation and measurement.

just a simple matter of birth *(jāti)*. It has also been a matter of culture, including elements of language, social relations, taste, and style.[16] The views of two early-nineteenth-century Vellālar Christians of Thanjāvur, Muttusami Pillai and Vedanāyakam Sāstri, one a Catholic and the other an Evangelical Lutheran, serve to illustrate and to crystallize one central question concerning contradictions inherent in tensions of dual identity arising out of persistent caste consciousness. The question posed was somewhat as follows: How is it possible that a compassionate, just, and rational God could provide a single, uniform, and universal salvation for all of humankind, with access available for each and every single person in the world, on the grounds of redemption through the atoning blood of a single person; and how could such a provision be made for a single and universal humanity that, despite the sameness and universality of its essential nature, continued always to contend with realities of the existence on earth of so many broken shards of diversity among various kinds of human beings, and of so many manifestly complex and distinctly different kinds of castes, communities, and cultures?

For both of these gifted Tamil Vellālar Christians, devout believers that they were, there could never be such a thing as *a "Christian" in the abstract or in general.* Christians, either as individuals or as members of a community, could only be known and understood in concrete, local, and specific terms. They could experience, and be experienced or described, only in nonabstract terms: each Christian was (and is) a person with a reality and specificity of face and name and place, with a specificity of birth and blood (*vamsha:* lineage), with specific gifts of tongue and language, and with characteristics of culture, elements of education, and standards of style and taste (or lack of style). In other words, for these Christian thinkers, the concept of a common, "generic" (or primordial) humankind could only be a metaphysical abstraction, a philosophical category created by the human mind for purposes of sophisticated intellectual activity. For these Tamil Christian thinkers, the same kind of perspective could also be applied to all stories about human origins and all stories about the social significance of birth, caste, pollution, social ranking, and status.

Thus understood, for those who gathered around the Lord's Table (namely: Communion, the Eucharist), different peoples could only, at best, *sit*

16. Whether or not "caste" and the modern "caste system" is a by-product of colonialism or of Brahmanical collaboration is an issue that is not addressed (or answered) here. See Nicholas Dirks, "The Invention of Caste," *Social Analysis* 25.1 (1989): 42-52; idem, "Castes of Mind," *Representations* 37 (1992): 56-78; and idem, "The Conversion of Caste," in *Conversion of Modernities: The Globalization of Christianity,* edited by Peter Van der Veer (New York, 1995), pp. 115-37.

together separately. Fellow believers could only enjoy "spiritual unity" within a context of a social diversity that allowed different peoples to live separately; and, thus, to enjoy different degrees of status, wealth, and wisdom. So also, if they wished, Christians were free to organize themselves hierarchically according to earth-bound resources and distinctions such as caste (in India) or class (in Europe). In his "Dialogue on the Difference of Caste" (*Jātiyacara-campavinai,* 1824), Vedanāyakam described how, within a single building of worship, European Christians could sit on benches; Vellālar Christians, on grass mats; Paraiyar Christians, or low-caste Christians, on the bare (dirt or stone) floor; and women (together with children), separately from the men — each according to his or her own particularity and peculiarity of conditions, circumstances, essential needs, requirements, and status.[17] None of these concrete or "earthly" circumstances were to be seen as being immutable or irrevocable. Change in social ranking and status was certainly possible, but this was only seen as coming slowly, and sometimes painfully.[18]

Despite earlier generations of missionaries who had tried not to foist European culture upon Tamil congregations, fully realizing that some Tamil gentry lived more elevated lives than *Farangi* (European) merchants and soldiers whose drunken debaucheries often blackened the name of Christ in India, the fresh and new cultural attitudes that arrived from postrevolutionary America and Europe radically altered the dynamics of missionary activity in India. Dreamers and visionaries, seeking to fulfill what they saw as a divine injunction concerning doctrines of common humanity, were convinced that ideals about intrinsic equality were to be more than mere metaphysical abstractions. They were determined that, for the sake of human progress, social distinctions among Christians in India should be obliterated: cream and skimmed milk should no longer be separated but should be mixed and made whole. Implicit within these ideals were agendas that, in theological terms, challenged the very notion of caste and advocated its total abolition among India's Christians. This would not be the first, nor the last, call for all to worship together, sit together in public sanctuaries, eat bread together from the

17. In Vedanāyakam Sāstri's St. Peter's Church in Thanjāvur, different castes also sat in different corners, or quadrants, of the nave and transept, as had been their custom for generations, ever since the time of Christian Friedrich Schwartz.

18. See D. Dennis Hudson (*Protestant Origins in India: Tamil Evangelical Christians, 1707-1835* [Grand Rapids and Richmond, 2000]), who refers to British Library, Oriental Books and Manuscripts (Cat. No. OR 11,742), where the work is transliterated "*Jati-tiruttalin Payittiyam,* etc. (Tamil)" and " '*Saditeratoo*' By Vedenayaga Sastree, the Evangelical Poet" (Tanjore, 1829) ["The Foolishness of Amending Caste"]. Also referred to in Sāstri's "Dialogue . . ." as *Jāti-ārasan-bhāvanai* (1824).

same dish, drink together from the same cup, sing together the same songs, sit together in the same school-rooms, share together in doing the same work, and even bring together in matrimony persons whose backgrounds, birth, and blood were not the same. The very idea of mixing and confusing men and women was seen as especially abhorrent and shocking. Such forced together-ness could only cause social turmoil.

What made the controversy of the 1820s to 1850s even more aggravating was the arrival in South India of an especially aggressive generation of Angli-can missionaries. After more than a century of Lutheran missionary effort (under the auspices of the Royal Danish–Halle Mission and the Society for the Promotion of Christian Knowledge [SPCK]), ecclesiastical dominion over Tamil congregations was abruptly turned over to the Church Missionary Society (CMS) and the Society for the Propagation of the Gospel in Foreign Parts (SPG). Thus, by fiat and without prior consultation, over twenty thou-sand mostly Evangelical Lutheran Tamils found themselves "converted" into Anglican Protestants. Suddenly they found themselves forced to read from different translations of the Bible, sing from a strange hymnbook, and recite from an unfamiliar Book of Common Prayer. More disturbing, caste customs and practices were to cease: "New missionaries tried to force all castes or na-tions of this country to be of one caste and to make them eat and drink to-gether and to have those of higher and lower castes connected to each other in marriage."[19]

Caste controversy also divided Europeans. Bishop Reginald Heber, shortly before his sudden death (in Tiruchirapalli), defended caste-segregated public worship among Tamil Christians from missionaries who wished to see caste abolished. He argued that Indian Christians of different castes had long been seated separately, that Black Christian slaves in America regularly worshipped separately in their own chapels, and that Christian servants of the rich in Eu-rope normally sat in separate galleries.[20] In 1830, however, Daniel Wilson, the new Bishop of Calcutta, reversed Heber's ruling. A CMS missionary from Germany who attempted to defend Tamil Christians from Anglican domina-tion was summarily dismissed. A Lutheran with Pietist (Moravian) leanings, he had not only ordained Tamils whom he had trained at his seminary in

19. Hudson, *Protestant Origins,* p. 129.

20. Reginald Heber (Archdeacon of Madras and Late Domestic Chaplain to His Lordship), letter, 21 March 1826, Madras Public Consultations/Proceedings (hereafter MPC/P) TNA: 620: 1155-67, para. 2-5; "The Humble Petition of Native Tamil Protestants of Vepery Congregation," 7 March 1834: MPC/P TNA: 619: 830-741, para. 2-3. Thomas Robin-son, *The Last Days of Bishop Heber* (London, 1830), pp. 321-25: Bishop Heber to the Rev. D. Scheivogel, Chillumbrum, 21 March 1826.

Tirunelveli but had gone so far as to openly question apostolic succession.[21] Here, indeed, was an instance of cultural and ecclesiastical, or "colonial" domination. Non-Anglican missionaries, especially those who were not British, vigorously resisted actions of the Anglican missionary societies (the CMS and the SPG). In Thanjāvur, George Uglow Pope and other High Church (SPG) missionaries attempted to "reform" the famous schools that Christian Friedrich Schwartz had founded and where Vedanāyakam Sāstri and his followers had taught for over sixty years, even calling upon government officials to publicly flog and imprison "Hindu Christians" for refusing to abandon caste rules.[22] When Vedanāyakam Sāstri, the renowned leader of the Vallalar Tamil (Evangelical) Christian community of Thanjāvur, long-time head of the modern school system and recognized former poet-laureate of Rajah's court, was removed from all positions of leadership, he and his followers vigorously resisted.[23] Along with petitions sent to the government of Madras, he published pamphlets publicly accusing the new missionaries of committing four cruelties: (1) tampering with Tamil scripture, replacing old versions with their own translations; (2) trying to combine Pallar and Paraiyar Christians (both from the lowest level castes) and every other people into one caste by excommunicating from the Lord's Supper any who refused to abandon caste customs; (3) restricting festive celebrations by prohibiting the use of flowers at weddings, funerals, and similarly important occasions; and (4) removing Tamil lyrics and music from worship services and other festive events.[24]

21. C. T. E. Rhenius, *The Church: Her Daughters and Handmaidens, Her Pastors and People, &c.* (Tinnevelly, 1834; London, 1835), book review by Archdeacon of Madras. J. Rhenius, ed., *Memoir of the Rev. C. T. E. Rhenius, Comprising Extracts from his Journal and Correspondence, with Details of Missionary Proceedings in South India* (London, 1841). C. T. E. Rhenius's son was the editor.

22. G. U. Pope (*The Lutheran Aggression, A Letter to the Tranquebar Missionaries, regarding "Regarding Their Position, Their Proceedings, and Their Doctrine"* [Madras, 1853]) listed failings of "Hindu" Christians of Tanjore. Pope, apparently dismissed from Tanjore, as he was previously from a school in Nazareth (Tinnevelly District) and as he was later from schools in Bangalore and Ootacamund, for mistreatment of boys, ended his career at Oxford (Balliol) as a renowned Tamil scholar. His imperious letter (dated 14 October 1853) and actions caused great offense.

23. Petitions and "Humble Addresses" from Soodra Christians, complaining of beatings, imprisonment, and so on item 8; 18 April 1834 (para. 5): MPC/P 620: 1155; item 5, 24 June 1834: MPC/P 622: 2146-55, report Tanjore Resident (A. Douglas); and item 5, 27 February 1835: MPC/P 633: 961-68, containing petitions from Devasagayam, Trichilvay, Nullathamby, David Pillay, and six other Christians at Tanjore. Yet when Bishop Wilson (Calcutta) scolded the government (9 May [item 3] 1834: MPC/P 621: 1471-76 in TNA) for interfering "in purely spiritual matters," he was roundly rebuffed.

24. Hudson, *Protestant Origins,* pp. 148-51.

Ironically, at the very time that Pope's actions were stirring controversy in Thanjāvur, another controversy erupted when Robert Noble, a CMS missionary in Masulipatam, was attacked by missionaries for focusing attention solely on Brahmans, to the exclusion of other peoples.[25] Roman Catholic missionaries also were scarcely any more of one mind about caste observances and practices among Indian Christians than they had been in previous centuries.[26] French missionaries along the Coromandel were more ready to respect existing caste and cultural norms; Irish missionaries were more opposed; and Italian missionaries were more evenly divided.[27]

Elsewhere, when large-scale mass movements of conversion later took place among *āvarna* (lit. "colorless," polluting, or untouchable) communities in Telugu country at the end of the nineteenth century, controversy over caste consciousness again reared its head. Here also, Mālas and Mādigas, both communities equally *āvarna (dalit,* or *panchama)* at the lowest level of the caste hierarchy, refused to mingle or to "break bread" together (and still do not do down to this day).[28] Each birth group *(jāti)* kept its own distinct sacred story, each with its own *vamshāvali,* each telling how its own particular lineages had emerged from the mists of antiquity into the light of Christian faith, and telling of how it had survived many assaults upon its distinctive identity.

It seems clear that missionaries, as change agents, fully understood and taught practical procedures and provided tools, which they thought necessary for survival within difficult social environments of modern India. Occasionally, when pressed, they would even strive to "protect" local Christians and to further their interests, especially when trouble arose over the hostile laws or over conflicts with Hindu or Muslim neighbors. In doing so, Western missionaries sometimes clashed with colonial authorities while, at other times, they also utilized or exploited those same authorities. The success of their efforts depended largely upon the personal chemistry and dynamics of a given situation. The evidence clearly shows the caste-culture question was never resolved, and caste conflicts among Christians never disappeared. In-

25. John Noble, *A Memoir of the Rev. Robert Turlington Noble, Missionary to the Telugu People of India* (London, 1853).

26. For summary assessment of Catholic missions during previous centuries, see ch. 1 below.

27. Kenneth Ballhatchet, *Class, Caste and Catholicism in India 1789-1914* (Richmond, 1998). Kenneth Ballhatchet and Helen Ballhatchet, "South and Southeast Asia," in *Oxford History of Christianity,* edited by John McMannern (Oxford and New York, 1990, 1993), ch. 14, pp. 511-20.

28. John C. B. Webster, *A History of Dalit Christians in India* (San Francisco, 1992).

deed, as already mentioned, evidence also indicates that no mass movement of evangelization in India ever occurred that was brought about or led by a European or "foreign" missionary.[29] In the quaint language of Vedanāyakam Sāstri, as he reviewed the evangelizing efforts that he witnessed during the early nineteenth century, it took "an elephant to catch an elephant" and "a quail to catch a quail."[30]

Controversies over Conversion, Forced Conversion, and/or Proselytization

Conversion, as already mentioned, is an essential part of what defines Christian faith. The same concept, and what it ostensibly designates, has recently become a bone of contention within the politics of contemporary India. Charges continue to be made that the poor and helpless of India are being forced, against their wills, to convert to Christian faith and Christian identity and that they convert only to obtain desperately needed essentials of life, health benefits, or basic education for their children. Charges of proselytism are being leveled at Christian evangelists and missionaries, virtually all of whom are Indian citizens. In order to put such charges into proper perspective, it is necessary to see how both terms "conversion" and "proselytism" are viewed, both in the light of Christian theology and in that of formal pronouncements made by ecclesiastical institutions. It is also important to understand how, from a sociological and political perspective, there are grounds for using the term in an entirely different way. The result is that, since there are at least two broad schools of interpretation, the term itself has become a bone of contention, controversy, and confusion.

At the risk of some oversimplification, people in India identifying themselves as Christian can be seen as in at least two groups. First, there are Christians of India who are Christians by birth. By self-definition and by the definition of others, their identity is publicly acknowledged. While they may or may not hold basic doctrines or observe basic rituals essential for reinforcing such claims, they are viewed as Christians by non-Christian communities that surround them, regardless of personal belief or behavior. How they first became Christian, or how they first became converted, whether as a group or

29. Alvin T. Fishman, *For this Purpose: A Case Study of the Telugu Baptist Church* (Madras, 1958); idem, *Culture Change and the Underprivileged: A Study of Madigas under Christian Guidance* (Madras, 1941).

30. "Twelve Arguments of the Divine Songsters"; Hudson, *Protestant Origins*, p. 155.

as individuals, is part of their history, as seen in the story of each lineage. Such Christians retain their identity, not only by virtue of creeds and rituals, such as basic sacraments (e.g., baptism, Eucharist), but by birth into a Christian community. As such, they can be categorized as Christian on the basis of socio-anthropological evidence, in the same way that any other caste or class or community in India would be identified.

Second, there are some Christians of India who are Christians by virtue of commitment, or conversion, and, therewith, by virtue of having made a profession of faith. These are Christian because they claim to have become converted, either as individuals or as parts of a community (or family). Conversion,[31] based upon a life-changing experience or series of experiences, often culminating in clear decisions or dawning self-consciousness, can be defined, very basically: it is an event that results in turning or being turned around from one condition or direction to another, and from one identity or orientation to another. At heart, this turning requires some minimal quantum of self-understanding and volition, some minimal changing of beliefs, some minimal changing to faith (and identification). Radical conversion is a drastic, rapid, or total turning around leading to a completely changed life. It is a metamorphosis. For this reason the term denotes — and, for some, this is understood in some mystical sense — a "rebirth" or "second birth" (again change from one condition to another), while, for others, the term also denotes salvation or liberation.

In theological terms, conversion is an internal or inward event; it is what happens *within* a person or a group.[32] The event of turning around, or the metamorphosis known as conversion, is so named because it is also seen as resulting from more than mere human volition alone. While not denying the importance of human agency and free will, conversion in orthodox Christian thinking ultimately depends also upon divine agency. It is something God does, not just something done by mankind alone (either in individual or institutional terms). Thus defined, the expression "forced conversion" is an oxymoron. What a person feels, thinks, and wills, in the deepest sense, cannot

31. The *OED* and *SOED* define the term in several senses: turning or transposition of subject and predicate, properties and ratios, and so forth; a spiritual turning to God or change of form or properties, condition, or function; and a translation or change of one thing into another, substituting one thing for another; "the fact of being converted to a religion."

32. For a useful analytical summary and definition, tracing "conversion" to the Hebrew *shub* and Greek *epistrophē*, see the entry by J. W. McClendon, Jr., and C. J. Conniry, Jr., "Conversion," in *The Oxford Companion to Christian Thought,* edited by Adrian Hastings et al. (Oxford, 2000), pp. 136-37.

be "forced" by any external power, whether by beatings, tortures, deceptions, or enticements.

In sociological terms, changes in religious identity and religious behavior are events that can be observed, described, and measured. What cannot be reduced into empirical data can sometimes be attributed to epiphenomenal events, false consciousness, or simple fantasy. Conversion, in this sense, may also be explained by factors other than vocal claims about inner convictions concerning truth or falsehood. In human sciences, an explanatory framework, often in narrative form, can serve to link changes in human behavior with questions about rational or irrational choice. While correlations do not prove causation and while vexing questions about the direction of causation often remain, correlational or scientific investigation is seen as relevant. The point is this: namely, what is often labeled as "conversion" may sometimes have less to do with an inner change or a theological event and may, alternatively, be based upon more mundane decisions rising out of rational choices and self-interest. Conversion, in this sense, does indeed become an event that has social, economic, and political ramifications.

Another name for forced conversion is proselytization.[33] As far as historic Christian thinking and ecclesiastical declarations are concerned, neither form of activity is legitimate, valid, or moral. Attempts to induce changes in religious identity, by any means, are seen as unethical and spurious. Merely external changes, without inner transformations of heart, mind, and will, do not count as being truly Christian, in any proper sense. Not only are such forms of conversion viewed as less than truly genuine, in an emotional, spiritual, or theological sense, they are also immoral and stupid, in any this-worldly, social, or political sense.[34] Nowadays sometimes seen as loathsome spiritual predators, those who engage in this kind of behavior have been defined in the West as follows:

> As for proselytism, the Geneva-based World Council of Churches, grouping *inter alia* the largest Orthodox, Lutheran, and Anglican communities, defined it in 1961 as "a corruption of Christian witness," which

33. Historically, a proselyte (Latin: *proselytus*) was a Gentile convert to the Jewish faith. Generally, it is anyone who has come over from one opinion, belief, creed, or party to another. Proselytization is the action or process of making one or more proselytes. The meaning has become much more invidious in recent times.

34. As such, and especially as promoted by the BJP Government of India and its Hindutva or Sangha Parivar allies, "conversion" has become a hot button issue during the last two or three years. See feature articles in *The Hindu* (25 and 26 January 1999), entitled "The Conversion Bogie."

used "cajolery, bribery, undue pressure, or intimidation, subtly or openly, to bring about seeming conversion." Similarly, the Roman Catholic Church defined proselytism in Vatican II as "a manner of behaving contrary to the spirit of the Gospel, which makes used of dishonest methods to attract [persons] to a community — for example, by exploiting their ignorance or poverty."[35]

In other words, most Christians in the world today seem to be in agreement about the negative aspects of this concept. More recently, in 1991, the World Council of Churches and the Vatican produced a joint statement that echoed sentiments expressed in previous statements.[36]

Contending Historical Perspectives

For Christians of India, the story of the past century has been a story of contending perspectives over issues related to the controversial concepts and definitions described above. As the nineteenth century came to an end, some missionaries, influenced by the post-Darwinian cultural climate, repeatedly confused "conversion" with "civilization" as worthy goals, and then went on to exalt and extol Brahmanical civilization. Among upper-class, intellectually eclectic, theologically liberal missionaries, such as William Miller of Madras Christian College, the downward filtration theory of Alexander Duff was replaced by the upward fulfillment paradigm as a way of explaining why Western missionaries had not seen more conversions among the high-caste elites of India. The Christian task was not so much to pray (and strive) for the conversion of people as to permeate Indian society with Christian values. To accomplish this, Christians were now seen as needing to influence those Hindu elites who were taking to Western education in droves. The biblical injunction of the Great Commission notwithstanding, conversion, as such, was no longer seen as such a worthy goal.

Since much in the life and conduct of Hindus and Muslims was found to be highly praiseworthy, a new strategy was articulated by J. N. Farquhar.[37] All

35. Jonathan Luxmoore and Jolanta Babiuch-Luxmoore, "New Myths for Old: Proselytism and Transition in Post-Communist Europe," *Journal of Ecumenical Studies* 36.1-2 (Winter-Spring 1999).

36. John Wilson, "Proselytizers," *Books & Culture* (May/June 2000), p. 3. Editorial.

37. Summarized in Stephen Neill, *A History of Christian Missions* (Harmondsworth, Middlesex, 1964), pp. 358-59. J. N. Farquhar (*The Crown of Hinduism* [Oxford, 1913]) epitomized his "fulfillment hypothesis." Cf. Eric J. Sharpe, "J. N. Farquhar, 1861-

religions were now to be seen as, in some measure, divinely inspired. Since Hinduism was now seen as already leading Indians towards Christian faith, missionaries had only to devote more effort to "dialogue" and "mutual understanding." This kind of thinking, sometimes called "fulfillment theory," gained wider acceptance among theological liberals. It was put forward both in the Parliament of World Religions at Chicago in 1892[38] and in the World Missionary Conference at Edinburgh in 1910.[39]

Among some Indian Christians also, the same spirit of an accommodating and acculturating theological liberalism gained headway. In Bengal, as in North India and Western India, where there were relatively fewer Indian Christians and where there were proportionately more Brahman Christians, the same message emerged. Anglican Krishna Mohan Banerjea argued, in 1875, that Hindus could become Christians without having to abandon their own cultural or social traditions. Kali Charan Banerjea's Calcutta-based Christo Samaj, formed in 1887, required neither liturgy nor clergy. Upadhyaya, a Brahman Catholic, donned the ochre robes of a *swami* and declared that one could be both a Hindu and a Christian. In Maharashtra, where the prominent Brahman Christian poet, Narayan Vaman Tilak, founded a Christian ashram in 1917, an Anglican Christo Seva Sangh (Christian Service Society) was also established. Only in Madras, where the National Church had been founded in 1886, did such efforts fail to survive beyond the 1920s.[40] In short, while saying that Christians in India should be Indian in culture, these later thinkers were, in many respects, saying something very different, something much less orthodox, than what Vedanāyakam Sāstri or Roberto de

1929: Presenting Christ as the Crown of Hinduism," in his *Mission Legacies* (Maryknoll, N.Y., 1994), pp. 290-96.

38. Eric J. Ziolkowski, "Heavenly Visions and World Intentions: Chicago's . . . World Parliament of Religions (1893)," *American Culture*, 13 (1990): 11-12; J. H. Barrows, *The World's Parliament of Religions* (Chicago, 1983).

39. Brian Stanley, "Church, State, and the Hierarchy of 'Civilization': The Making of the Commission VII Report, 'Missions and Governments,' Edinburgh 1910" (Edinburgh, April 1998), http://office3.divinity.cam.ac.uk/carts/cwc/PosPaper.htm and NAMP/CWC Position Paper 70; idem, "Missionaries Observed, Observing, and Unobserving: V. S. Azariah at Edinburgh 1910," Yale-Edinburgh Mission Studies Conference, Edinburgh, July 2000.

40. See Ballhatchet and Ballhatchet, "South and Southeast Asia"; Neill, *Christian Missions;* and Malcolm J. Nazareth, "Reverent Narayan Vaman Tilak: An Interreligious Exploration," 2 vols., Ph.D. dissertation, Temple University, Philadelphia, 1998. See also Y. Vincent Kumarados, "Creation of Alternative Public Spheres and Church Indigenization in Nineteenth-Century Colonial India," in *Christianity Is Indian: The Emergence of an Indigenous Christianity,* edited by Roger E. Hedlund (Delhi, 2000).

Nobili would have had in mind, even when they used some of the same words.

Theologically more conservative and pragmatic missionaries from lower levels of society in America, Canada, Britain, and the rest of Europe, tending to work within and come from an entirely different cultural ethos, were often ignored by upper-caste Indian Christians and upper-class Western missionaries in India. Radical Nonconformists in Britain, already conscious that Methodism was no longer as much of a working-class movement as it had once been, sensed a dangerous loss of spiritual fire. For them and for others, theological liberalism was a more serious problem than either caste or culture in India. Such missionaries, from whatever country they came, criticized those whom they now saw as having failed to deliver the full gospel message and who only prepared high-caste Hindus for lucrative careers while, at the same time, neglecting the plight of poorer, low-caste Christians, failing to help them to overcome cultural, economic, and social disabilities. Officers of the Salvation Army, arriving in the 1880s, while theologically conservative, abandoned European clothes, furnishings, food, and even music. They took Indian Christian names and adopted as many elements of Indian culture as possible in order to identify themselves with the downtrodden.[41] Meanwhile, Pandita Ramabai, the Brahman widow who had won such renown in Calcutta for her high learning and had then become a Christian while in Britain, and who had been fêted among high-society women's missionary circles in the eastern states of America, turned away from social elites and rationalizing theologies of the West. She ended up drawing support among Pentecostals and expanding the reach of her Mukti Mission for female orphans and widows to child-widows from more downtrodden castes.[42] Among Catholic and Thomas Christians also, similar kinds of critical concerns developed, with similar divergences and similar expansions into new kinds of educational ventures.

As war clouds gathered over Europe, doubts about theological liberalism began to appear among more conservative Christian thinkers. Theological views darkened after the First World War and became darker still during and after the Second World War. Chief among the missionary critics was the Dutch thinker, Hendrik Kraemer. Looking at resurgent forms of anti-Christian Islamic militancy, he took a Barthian theological position. His *Christian Message in a Non-Christian World* (London, 1938) reminded Christians that their faith

---

41. Solveig Smith, *By Love Compelled: The Salvation Army's One Hundred Years in India and Adjacent Lands* (London, 1981).

42. Padmini Sengupta, *Pandita Ramabai Saraswati: Her Life and Work* (New York, 1970).

was fundamentally and intrinsically different. With war again looming over Europe, his views were heeded by many who attended the International Missionary Conference at Tambaram, just south of Madras, in 1938. Christian faith, he argued, was not just a man-made religion but came from God, as a gift of divine grace. In all religions, even within Christian religion, certain elements were merely human in origin. It was crucially important to know where the differences lay and how to make clear distinctions.

Meanwhile, among Roman Catholics also, old controversies continued. Some, over rites of different kinds, such as Latin and "Malabari" or Syriac (as well as Chinese), went back many centuries. While Pope Benedict XIV (in 1744) had held that Catholics of high and low birth alike should hear the same mass, take the same communion, and meet in the same building at the same time, Jesuits in South India had erected little walls and opened different doors for the high and the low castes. In problems over training clergy, rival Catholic jurisdictions, *Padroado* and *Propaganda Fide,* often favored separate castes. The Mukkavan fisherfolk petitioned Rome asking how, if a fisherman could be the first Pope, they should not be considered worthy enough for clerical training and ordination. One Apostolic Delegate, in 1902, pointed out that, while no descendants of de Nobili's Brahman converts remained in the Church, many descendants of Paravas converted by St. Francis Xavier remained faithful. If anything, problems of caste and culture seemed to become more and more formidable.

Mass movements of conversion, with whole villages becoming Christian, such as had occurred at the end of the eighteenth century and again in the late nineteenth century among both Evangelicals and Catholics, became a focal point of nationalist concern and opposition in the twentieth century. Such movements were severely criticized by higher-caste Hindus, including Mohandas Karamchand Gandhi. Gandhi went so far as to openly chastise India's first Indo-Anglican Bishop, Vedanāyakam Azariah, accusing him of betraying the nation for his leadership of mass conversions in Dornakal. Untouchable communities, denied access to temples, common wells, or other facilities enjoyed by clean-caste peoples, had hitherto hardly counted as being "Hindu." The charge that such converts were only motivated by material considerations was refuted by Indian Christians. Advocates of mass conversion argued that all human motives are mixed and that imperfect motives need not nullify the genuineness of conversions. For despised peoples who desired a fuller life for themselves and their children, self-improvement and progress could hardly be considered unworthy, ignoble, or unpatriotic.[43] Vedanāya-

43. Sundararaj Manickam (*The Social Setting of Christian Conversion in South India*

kam Azariah was himself the son of a Nādar Christian village pastor from Tirunelveli whose forebears had been lowly Shānars. His consecration as Bishop of Dornakal in 1912 and his subsequent leadership of a mass movement among Telugu speakers symbolized the ongoing consequences of work begun by Tranquebar, Thanjāvur, and Tirunelveli disciples of Schwartz, Satyanāthan Pillai, and Vedanāyakam Sāstri a century earlier. Azariah and others like him represented an ongoing process of evangelization and Indianization that would continue to grow among India's Christians and their leaders during the later twentieth century.[44]

Chapter Descriptions

The chapters presented in this volume are attempts to address some of the misconceptions and misperceptions that have clouded historical understandings of Christianity and missions in India. The chapters are arranged, first and as much as is possible, so as to conform to a chronological or sequential framework, covering the period from the year A.D. 1500 to the present; and, second, as far as possible, so as to show their affinities by linguistic region, moving roughly from south to north. The second chapter provides an overview, briefly sketching the multiple origins of the hundreds of separate Christian communities that have emerged within the subcontinent. It begins with events linked to the Thomas Tradition of A.D. 52[45] and then traces the subsequent waves of arrival and/or development of Orthodox (Syrian) Christians prior to 1500, of Roman Catholics after 1500, of Evangelicals (Protestants) after 1700, and of Pentecostals since 1900. Chapter three, by Iwona Milewska (Jagiellonian University, Krakow), provides a brief and insightful description of the earliest of Sanskrit grammars to be produced by European scholars in India, beginning with Jesuits such as Thomas Stevens, who came to Goa in 1579. Most chapters thereafter pertain to events that occurred during and after the rise of the Raj, first under the East India Company, then under the Crown, and finally under national regimes.

Chapter four, by Heike Liebau,[46] analyzes the pivotal role played by those

---

[Wiesbaden, 1971]) examines the impact of the Wesleyan Methodist efforts in the Trichy-Tanjore area, especially with reference to mass movements among Dalits, from 1820-1947.

44. Harper, *Shadow of the Mahatma*.

45. This date, A.D. 52, is the formally and officially accepted date of the Tradition, with his ministry of twenty years ending in martyrdom at Mylapore, in A.D. 72.

46. Originally entitled "Unrecognized Scholars: The Role of 'Native Informants' in the Research Work of German Missionaries in Eighteenth Century South India."

who were Indian go-betweens or middlemen in eighteenth-century South India (namely, Tranquebar, Thanjāvur, and Tirunelveli).[47] Without these native informants, known by manifold terms, such as "catechist," "village pastor/teacher," or simply "helpers" (to use common labels), it would have been impossible for European missionaries to have accomplished much. Indeed, as will be indicated, there has never been a single major movement of genuine Christian conversion in India (or elsewhere), certainly no mass movement, in which a pivotal role of leadership was not played by an extremely influential, and often very gifted, native agent (as "change-agent"). Without such a person playing the crucial role of cultural broker, without the initiating inspiration and dynamic of the *dubash,* it is doubtful whether many conversions would have occurred.[48] It is important to note, in this connection, that most of the hundreds of Indian Christian agents whose careers became linked to the Tranquebar Mission worked *outside* of the Danish settlement of Tranquebar, within the noncolonial and precolonial princely or warlord domains in Thanjāvur, Tiruchirapalli, Tirunelveli, and Travancore.

The next two essays, in order of sequence, pertain to cultural encounters and influences — contacts and conflicts as well as forms of acculturation — that occurred within two of these princely states of South India. Chapter five, by Indira Viswanathan Peterson, is a study of the transmission of Enlightenment philosophies and sciences from Halle (in Germany) to Tranquebar and Thanjāvur. Attention is focused on two extraordinarily gifted Tamil leaders, one a Christian scholar-writer and the other a highly educated Hindu king, both of them classmates and disciples *(sishiyas)* of the same aged German *Raja-Guru.*[49] The approach taken is that of a specialist in Sanskrit and Tamil literature who, at the same time, has delved into the German and Danish archives in Halle and Copenhagen. Slightly later in sequence was the coming to the Hindu kingdoms of Cochin and Travancore (Thiruvanthakode, with its capital at Trivandrum or Thiruvananthapuram), both now incorporated into the State of Kerala, of English Evangelical missionaries of the Church Missionary Society (CMS).[50] The cultural encounter that occurred is described

47. Known, generally, as *dubashi,* literally, "two-language" person or "interpreter"; later, any "agent" or "broker." Other terms, used with different connotations, were *baniya* ("banian") and *vakil'* ("agent" or "broker").

48. A later example of such a *dubash* is the three-volume *Diary of Savariraya Pillai: Tamil Village Schoolteacher: 1834-1876,* translated by David and Sarojini Packiamuthu, edited by R. E. Frykenberg (London and Grand Rapids, forthcoming).

49. The redoubtable Christian Friedrich Schwartz (d. 1798) had been in India since 1750.

50. Even before their arrival, a radical movement had already begun, partially in-

in chapter six by Penelope Carson. Her approach, as an imperial historian, has a somewhat more Eurocentric perspective than that of Indira Peterson; and what she describes is a less happy sequence of events, involving colonial confrontation with indigenous institutions, both Christian and Hindu. Interestingly, despite many traumatic conflicts suffered in the past, the population of Kerala today is among the most highly advanced and literate (98 percent), as well as venturesome, in all of South Asia. Malayali-speaking people are among the most energetic and opportunistic of all competitors, taking plum positions in every profession and in government service within India and rising to the forefront of Indian diaspora throughout the world.[51]

In chapters seven, eight and nine, attention moves northward, to Bengal and the upper Gangetic Plain. Geoffrey A. Oddie examines how British Protestant missionaries first studied and came to understand "Hindu" religious customs, institutions, and texts; and how, in consequence, they contributed to the construction of modern "Hinduism." He also shows how, in so doing, these missionaries contributed to the rise of a clear "Hindu" self-consciousness and of a manifest self-understanding among Brahman elites, not only among the *bhadralog* (gentry) of Bengal but also among elites in other parts of the subcontinent. Richard Fox Young pursues the course of such developments further by exploring similar events that were occurring elsewhere, either at the same time or perhaps slightly later. He describes how Indian intellectuals, mostly Brahmans, tried to grapple with the challenges that modern science posed for their own traditional worldviews, especially as these were being conveyed to them through institutions being set up and run by younger generations of British officials, as well as missionaries. He shows how Indian thinkers were able to make distinctions between the claims of science and the claims of theology, religion, and philosophy coming from the West.

Chapter nine is the only essay that deals with interactions between Chris-

---

spired by the influence of a mendicant missionary from Germany. See *Ringeltaube, The Rishi: The Pioneer Missionary of the London Missionary Society in Travancore* (Sheffield, 1902). These letters and journals were collected and arranged by William Robinson, who was a missionary in Salem. The book was produced for the celebration centenary of Ringeltaube's 1804 arrival. *Rishi* is a sage, made more-or-less divine through disciplined abstraction and mortification. The seven principal *rishis* are: Agastya, Angirasa, Gautama, Kasypa, Pulasthya, Markandaya, and Vashishta. To these Ringeltaube was added by his Hindu friends.

51. What events in the past could have brought about such a radical transformation among Christians, Hindus, and Muslims alike? is a historical question yet to be satisfactorily answered.

tians and Muslims. Avril A. Powell has carefully examined the career and thought of the Reverend Maulvi 'Imad ud-din. She has tracked these from his early life to his conversion; and thence from his ordination as a clergyman to his work as an evangelist. He sought, by means of persuasion and scholarly argument, to convince the *ashraf* and other members of his prestigious class within the Muslim community that his newfound faith rested upon truths that could bring any person closer to God. Since relationships between Christian convert theology and Hindu religious philosophy have received considerably more scholarly attention than has the study of Muslim Christian theology, especially as found within Indian contexts (in contrast to such studies that focus on the Middle East), Powell's close examination of the writings of 'Imad ud-din adds a entirely and refreshingly different dimension to the other perspectives on Christian cultural encounters contained within this volume. This is especially so since 'Imad ud-din, like Vedanāyakam Sāstri, was one of the more prolific converts to Christian faith.

Much attention has been focused, over the past forty years, upon the role of missionaries in the Bengal renaissance. Until now, however, almost no attention has been devoted to how the Hindu gentry of Assam entered into the modern world. Thanks to work being done by Jayeeta Sharma, we now know much more. In chapter ten, she clearly portrays how, through the medium of print, American Baptist missionaries in nineteenth-century Assam influenced the culture of Assam. They did so particularly through articles on a wide range of topics dealing with modern life, science, and thought that for nearly forty years (1846-82) they published in their periodical *Orunodoi.* Despite their arduous efforts and fervent prayers, missionaries saw very few if any converts among the Assamese people. While their work failed to ignite faith in the Christian message, the impact of this missionary periodical upon the culture of Assam in matters more mundane was profound. By the time the American missionaries turned their attention to tribal peoples, especially the Nagas, the culture of Assam no longer benefited from or needed them.

The story of the turning of India's tribal peoples towards the Christian gospel constitutes another dimension within the highly complex and multiplex pattern of Christian presence that has yet to be fully comprehended. Conversions have occurred among dozens, or scores if not hundreds, of distinct tribal peoples. What seems to have facilitated this process is that, while they are the oldest and most aboriginal *(adivāsi)* of all India's roughly three thousand ethnically distinct peoples (castes and tribes), most had remained virtually untouched by those processes of Sanskritization (Hinduization) or Islamization that, in one way or another, had brought "untouchable" *(āvarna, panchama,* or *dalit)* peoples "into the fold"[52] (or into thralldom) of those in control of the more dominant cultures.[53]

While numerous studies of various *adivāsi* (aboriginal or "tribal") Christians have been made or are currently in progress, the purposes of this volume are well served by two chapters that focus upon one such people, the Santals. Santals are approached from two angles and two disciplines: anthropology and history. Each study serves as a vector on the other, and together they provide, to change the metaphor, a two-eyed or stereoscopic perspective. Chapter eleven, by Marine Carrin and Harald Tambs-Lyche, delves deeply into the tribal roots of Santal culture and the Pietistic roots of the missionary movement coming out of Norway. This leads them to historical understandings of the Santali Christian culture and institutions that, at different times and in various ways, came into conflict with the alien and European cultures brought to India by missionaries. Chapter twelve, by Peter B. Andersen and Susanne Foss, criticizes recent anti-Orientalist discourse analysis in the works of such writers as Edward Said and Ronald Inden, as well as Salman Rushdie's fictional work, *The Satanic Verses,* and claims that hegemonic imperialism lies behind Western scholarship on India. Drawing upon empirical data in materials on the Santals after 1855, found in both official and missionary records, they argue that the Santals suffered a status of "double otherness" separating them both from colonial rulers and from the indigenous majority. Postmodernist anti-Orientalist scholarship, in Andersen's and Foss's opinion, has led to untenable oversimplification.

At the top of the social hierarchy among Christians of Kerala were people of one community whose families (as is typical among most elite families), consciously and conscientiously sought to preserve records, traditions, and understandings of their lineages as far back into the mists of antiquity as possible. Some from the most ancient of these Syrian or Thomas (Jacobite) communities,[54] such as the Malankara Nazranies, have been able to count and name up to seventy and eighty successive generations of *kattanars* (priests), intermingled with occasional family members who became *catholicos* and *metrans* (prelates and metropolitans; bishops or ruling elders). Even among

52. For a postmodern perspective on this subject, see Gauri Viswanathan, *Outside the Fold: Conversion, Modernity, and Belief* (Princeton, 1998), and reviews thereof.

53. For a journalistic but highly interesting and penetrating travelogue into some of these communities, see Charlie Pye-Smith, *Rebels and Outcastes: A Journey through Christian India* (London and New York, 1997).

54. Distinctions between these separate communities and their branches, which number at least a half dozen, including various Orthodox, Catholic (Latin and Syrian rite), and Mar Thoma branches, are too complex and confusing to elaborate here.

families of more recent converts, some tracing their lines back only one or two hundred years, the custom of keeping and maintaining a family history, as a traditional lineage or *vamshāvali (vaṃçāvali)*, is very strong.[55] One such history, collected and compiled by Eleanor M. Jackson, is found in chapter thirteen. What she presents, in modern format, is the story of the Sattianadan family. This family, emerging out of the mass movements of radical conversion that shook villages in the Tirunelveli Country during the 1790s, left Palayamkottai and settled in Madras in 1863. Her narrative reconstruction differs from traditional accounts, however, by giving special attention to prominent women of the family and their literary accomplishments.

At the opposite end of the social spectrum, in late nineteenth- and twentieth-century South India, came further outbreaks of popular resistance from those seeking social justice in the face of opposition from entrenched elites. A number of studies of such movements indicate the importance of caste, in combination with conversion, as a vehicle for social mobilization. This can be seen, especially among peoples at the very lowest levels of society where the motor for such mass movements of social change, in numerous instances, was fueled by radical religious conversions within whole communities or villages. In chapter fourteen, Gunnel Cederlöf looks at the strivings for dignity, recognition, self-esteem, and socioeconomic improvement among two such peoples in the highlands of Coimbatore District. Here, peoples of the two major local castes who sought upward mobility through conversion were the Paraiyar (locally calling themselves Adi-Dravida) and the Madhari. Yet, at the same time, members of each caste also held those of the other caste in contempt. Arguments between them almost invariably revolved around issues of precedence and over which of them ranked lower in the social order (or *varnāshramadharma*). Thus, if members of one caste became Christians, those of the other caste would either refuse to become Christians or, if they did, would only join Christians of their own caste and Christians of another mission. Accordingly, Wesleyan Methodists (MMS) served Paraiyar Christians; and Evangelical Lutherans, supported by the Church of Sweden Mission (CSM), Madhari Christians. Increasingly, most of the trained Christian workers from these missions who helped them to improve their lives, such as Bible women, evangelists, health providers, missionaries, pastors, teachers, and development experts, were themselves Indian. Closely studying the

---

55. A truly remarkable example was presented to me in Palayamkottai (December 1998). See Shaku Devagnanam and Manuel Aaron, *Patti Heritage: A History of the Patti Family during the 19th and 20th Centuries* (Madras, 1997). It runs 384 pages and has many biographical entries on each page.

methods of these two missions over a forty-year period, as found in their respective records, Cederlöf has been able to compare processes of social mobilization within these two Christian communities. Within wider contexts of growing local enterprises and demands for increasing labor force mobility, she has examined contrasts between the "outcomes" of Madhari conversions and conversions among Paraiyar people.

Perhaps the largest and most dynamic of the Christian mass movements currently sweeping the world have been those that can be categorized as Pentecostal (in various forms and under various banners). Nowhere have such movements been more pronounced than in many countries of Africa, Asia, and Latin America. In India, nearly a century ago, Pandita Ramabai Saraswati became involved with such a movement; but this had its origins and roots not in Azuza Street (Los Angeles) but in her Mukti Mission near Poona (Puné).[56] No one has studied Pentecostal movements in India more comprehensively, deeply, or extensively than Michael Bergunder.[57] In chapter fifteen, he focuses upon the remarkable career of Paulaseer Lawrie, alias Shree Lahari Krishna (1921-89), a Pentecostal faith healer and evangelist.

Finally, chapter sixteen turns to the embedding of the "Baby Jesus Story" within the heart of modern Tamil literary culture. Paula Richman elucidates this theme by examining one example, coming from a long-standing genre of Tamil poetic tradition, called the *pillaittamil*. Several Tamil Christian poets have found the *pillaittamil* an appropriate literary mode in which to express their love for Jesus. She has selected the work of one of them, Arul Cellatturai, whose *Iyecupiran* [Lord Jesus] *Pillaittamil* was published in 1985. She shows how the tradition of praising the infant Jesus that began in Europe during the early Middle Ages has now become an integral part of Tamil cultural tradition. The author whose work she examines, Cellatturai, so admired ancient Sangam poetry that he wanted the poetry of his own time to be more like the verses of ancient times. Her study shows how such ambitions came to fruition.

Conclusion

The usual charge made against volumes of this sort, that their contents are uneven, in one way or another, is one that can be accepted. In the present

56. Gary B. McGee, "'Latter Rain Falling in the East': Early-Twentieth-Century Pentecostalism in India and the Debate over Speaking in Tongues," *Church History* 68.3 (September 1999): 648-65.

57. Michael Bergunder, *Die südindische Pfingsbewegung im 20. Jahrhundert* (Frankfurt, 1999).

case, moreover, this charge is certainly true from a number of perspectives. Whether seen in terms of coverage, discipline, size, or weight, the contents of this volume are highly uneven. Only one essay focuses upon Catholic Christians of India; and only one on Pentecostals. Only one chapter deals with a convert from Islam, an Indo-Islamic, whose subsequent lifelong preoccupation lay with questions of how better to bring the gospel to former fellow Muslims. Not even one chapter is devoted to the complexities of Syrian/ Thomas Christian culture. Most of the chapters tend focus on Indian Christians and on missionaries who were Evangelical or Protestant; most deal with events in the nineteenth and twentieth centuries; and most also concentrate, in one way or another, upon Hindu culture and Hindu responses to Christian influences; or, alternatively, upon peoples in non-Hindu communities, such as *adivāsi* tribals and *āvarna (dalit)* castes, who have been oppressed (or ignored) by dominant Hindu elites and who, in consequence, decided to become Christians. At the same time, there has been a consistent effort on the part of various contributors to exclude Eurocentric or Western perspectives as much as possible. While this effort may not have been entirely successful — indeed, the very fact that most contributors are from the West would make it unlikely that they would achieve perfectly Indocentric perspectives — and while even attempting to do so may itself constitute a bias that some might find questionable, the very conscious effort of trying to avoid falling into a Eurocentric trap contributes to a kind of calculated unevenness.

Finally, one can easily see that this volume is uneven more because of circumstances than because of design. One can, after all, seldom pick and choose all the contributions needed to give a work like this a neat balance. Circumstances do not work out that way. Hence, what is presented here is an attempt to provide samples, of various kinds, of the complex and confusing problems that any serious scholarly study of the history of Christians and missionaries in India can encounter. It is fortunate that, especially in Europe at this time, there are as many specialists in South Asian studies as there are whose research, in every discipline and particularly in history, has focused upon interactions between Christians, including Christian missionaries, and the many complex cultural contexts and situations within which they have lived and worked over the past five centuries.

In this connection, the authors of chapters found in this volume are grateful to the organizers of several biennial meetings of the European Conference on Modern South Asian Studies, in Copenhagen, Prague, and Edinburgh, for the occasions and opportunities that these afforded for critical scholarly discussion and interaction. The editorial committee, consisting of R. E. Frykenberg, G. A. Oddie, and R. F. Young, ably assisted by Dr. Alaine Low, appreciate the commendable patience and long-suffering of all collaborating authors. Were it not for the wonders of e-mail technology, the long distances separating the contributors and the long times of waiting for the completion of editorial work would have been even longer — lines of communication stretched from Sydney and Tokyo to London, and Uppsala and the United States. They are also grateful to officers of Pew Charitable Trusts whose support of various research projects connected with aspects of the history of Christianity in India with special reference to cross-cultural communication within Hindu-Muslim environments have undergirded publication of this volume.

CHAPTER TWO

Christians in India:
An Historical Overview of Their Complex Origins

ROBERT ERIC FRYKENBERG

The westward movement of the Christian message and mission from Antioch
is much better known than the eastward movement by which the same message was carried down the valley of the Euphrates to Babylon and then,
steadily, further and further eastward until it took root among Arabs of the
sea, among Persians in the domains of Zoroastrian rulers, and onward, both
by land and by sea, to peoples of India and China.[1] Too often we forget that
Christianity became the official religion of Armenia well before it became official in Rome. All of this happened beyond the eastern edge of the Roman
Empire. It radiated out from a tiny principality of Osroene, and its capital of
Edessa.[2] Its vehicle of conveyance was not primarily Hellenistic, but Semitic
— the cultural matrix out of which Christian thought itself had originated.
Its language was Syriac, not Greek; and its concerns related more to cosmic
struggles between Darkness and Light than to concepts and categories of
Greek philosophy.[3]

1. H. J. W. Drijvers, *East of Antioch: Studies in Early Syriac Christianity* (London,
1984); Robin E. Waterfield, *Christians in Persia: Assyrians, Armenians, Roman Catholics and
Protestants* (London, 1973).

2. William Cureton, ed. and trans., *Ancient Syriac Documents Relative to the Earliest
Establishment of Christianity in Edessa and the Neighbouring Countries, from the Year after
Our Lord's Ascension to the Beginning of the Fourth Century* (Amsterdam, 1967).

3. For more on this perspective, see Andrew F. Walls, "Eusebius Tries Again,
Reconceiving the Study of Christian History," *International Bulletin of Missionary Research*
24.3 (July 2000): 105-11.

Earliest Christians of India

Long antedating the arrival of Christianity in western or central Europe (where missionaries of Celtic and Slavic cultures carried their message to remotest corners of the West), there were communities in India now known as "Thomas" (or "Syrian") Christians. Whatever dating is accepted for their arrival, there can be no doubt that forms of Christian presence and tradition became established along Indian shorelines during the earliest (ante-Nicene) centuries of the Christian era. Thomas Christians firmly believe themselves to be descended from converts of the Apostle Thomas. They claim he arrived in A.D. 52 and was martyred in Mylapore (near St. Thomas Mount, Chennai/ Madras), about A.D. 69. When confronted by skeptics, they often point out, perhaps whimsically, that there is as much evidence to support the coming of Thomas to India as there is for the coming of Peter to Rome, and they claim that equal status should be accorded to both apostolic traditions.[4]

Historical self-understandings of Christian communities in India, like those of royal communities of India, trace descent from ancient times. They have their own *itihasa-puranas*, *kāvyas*, and *vamshāvalis*, their own ballads and bardic songs, their own oral or literary traditions, and their own copper or stone inscriptions and palm-leaf documents, as well as artifacts.[5] These tell them how the Apostle arrived at the court of Gondaphar, the Indo-Greek who ruled the upper Indus (A.D. 19-45); how he landed in Malabar; how he healed the sick, won converts, established congregations, and undertook missions to China; and how, in the end, he died a martyr in Mylapore *(Maila-pur)*.[6] Lyric sagas — the *Margam Kali Pattu*, the *Rabban Pattu*,[7] and the *Thomma Parvam* — tell of "The Coming of the Way of the Son of God" and of early settlements at Malankara, Chayal, Kokamangalam, Niranam, Paravur

---

4. Leslie W. Brown, *The Indian Christians of St. Thomas: An Account of the Ancient Syrian Church of Malabar* (Cambridge, 1956); A. E. Medlycott, *India and the Apostle Thomas: An Inquiry with a Critical Analysis of the Acta Thomae* (London, 1905). James Hough, *History of Christianity in India*, 5 vols. (London, 1839-60), is a useful but dated source, as is John W. Kaye, *Christianity in India* (London, 1855).

5. "Literature As a Source of History: Interview with David Shulman," *Frontline* 17.11 (27 May to 9 June 2000): http://www.the-hindu.com/fine/fl1711/1711250.htm. "So basically . . . there is a natural and intuitive distinction between reports that are meant to be factual and reports that are not considered factual; the latter may be true but not factual."

6. B. A. Figredo, *Bones of St. Thomas and the Antique Casket at Mylapore* (Madras, 1972).

7. Henry Hosten, *The Song of Thomas Rabban* (Madras, 1931); cf. his *Antiquities from San Thome and Mylapore* (Madras, 1936), a book on the traditional site of the martyrdom and tomb of the Apostle Thomas. P. J. Podipara, *The Thomas Christians* (Madras, 1970).

(Kottakkayal), Palayur, and Quilon. From such places, some of the oldest lineages of leaders *(achāryas* and *gurus)* are descended. One epic relates how Thomas left a self-propagating and self-sustaining community of seventeen thousand — 6,850 Brahmans, 2,800 Kshatriyas, 3,750 Vaishiyas, and 4,250 Shudras. Dozens of families, claiming Brahman and Nayar lineage, trace their clerical authority as *kattanars* (pastors) or *metrans* (bishops or elders) to Thomas. They recite *vamshāvalis,* naming fifty, sixty, or seventy generations of successive officeholders. Stone crosses, inscriptions, and monuments, preserved by *kattanar* families and villages, commemorate events dating from the earliest Christian centuries and are evidence of ancient antiquity.[8]

Syriac materials from antiquity — apocryphal gospels, epistles, chronicles, church documents, and familial aphorisms — provide further literary evidence. Some sources are attributed to the Apostle Thomas himself, or to several Thomases, and to his successors. The oldest narrative of Christian missionary work in India is found in the *Acts of Thomas.* This document, of unknown origin and provenance, surviving today only in Syriac versions of fourth-century Edessa, can be traced to the second century.[9] While it is a romantic tale, it rests upon solid historical events: an Indo-Greek king named Gundaphorus, the monarch who ostensibly commissioned the Apostle to build him a palace, did indeed reign in the Indus Valley from A.D. 19 to 45.[10] Descriptions in Strabo and the *Periplus;* artifacts of Roman colonies dug up along the coasts of India; tales told by Indian merchants and scholars mixing in marketplaces and academies of Egypt[11] (with Greeks and Arabs, Jews and

8. S. G. Pothan, *The Syrian Christians of Kerala* (New York, 1963).

9. This, one of the oldest surviving narrative accounts of any congregation, links Thomas with India. The Babylonian or Chaldean congregations of Edessa were caught in the war between Parthia and Rome. Claiming apostolic legitimacy comparable to that of Antioch and Rome, they "published" works, such as the Abgar legend of Judas Thomas, their version of the *Acts of Thomas,* and others (e.g., Ephrem of Nisibis's [d. 373] hymn stressing links between believers of Edessa and India). G. Bornkamm, "The Acts of Thomas," in *New Testament Apocrypha,* vol. 2, edited by E. Hennecke (London, 1965). J. K. Elliott, ed., "The Acts of Thomas," *The Apocryphal New Testament: A Collection of Apocryphal Christian Literature in an English Translation* (Oxford and New York, 1993 [1924]), which has revised bibliographical references and indexes. A. F. J. Klijn, *The Acts of Thomas: Introduction, Text and Commentary* (Leiden, 1962).

10. For descriptive analysis of nineteenth-century coin finds and their provenance, see Alexander Cunningham, *Journal of the Asiatic Society of Bengal* 23 (1854): 679-712; and A. E. Medlycott, *India and the Apostle Thomas.* See the bibliography in Avadh Kishore Narain, *The Indo-Greeks* (Oxford, 1957).

11. Other non-Indian writings about early Christians in India date from the second century. In Alexandria, the gifted Jewish-Christian named Pantaenus (mentor of Clement and Origen), wrote of preaching Christ "to the Brahmans and philosophers"; and, accord-

Syrians, Armenians and Persians); Sanskrit and Tamil literary references to huge *Yavana* (Greek) ships laden with glass, gold, and horses coming to trade for gems, ivory, pepper, and exotic animals or birds (e.g., peacocks); and Greek workmen employed to build a Chola palace-temple — these are but a few well-known items of actual contemporary evidence dating from the time in which the Thomas story took place. While they do not confirm its historicity, they do give the tale plausibility.

During later centuries, *metrans* (metropolitans, or *catholicos*) were appointed and sent to India by patriarchs of Antioch, Babylon or Edessa, and Armenia. Arrivals of Christian refugees, settlers, and traders on the western shores, both before and after the rise of Islam, are documented by certified deeds confirming endowments, gifts, and privileges that were granted them by local kings, inscribed on copper, stone, and palm-leaf, and then embellished by oral traditions. One tradition tells how, in A.D. 293, a great persecution occurred within the Chola kingdom (Cholamandalam, on the east coast); how seventy-six families fled and settled among Christians of Quilon; how some were led astray by a Tamil Shaiva (presumably *bhakti*) guru, or *pandaram;* and how disputes arose over rites of smearing ashes on the forehead and venerating the five products of the cow. Another narrative, recorded on copper plates and stone inscriptions and dating A.D. 345 (shortly after great persecutions of Christians within the Persian Empire), tells how an Armenian merchant-banker named "Thomas of Jerusalem" (or "Thomas of Kana") was honored by Cheraman Perumal with specific grants of land that stipulated high social status. Syriac documents, translated by Mingana, further confirm this event.[12] They indicate that the Catholicos of Babylon sent "Thomas of Jerusalem" (alias "Thomas of Kana") and that, upon his arrival at Malankara, he was accompanied by a bishop, deacons, and an entire community of men, women, and children. Documents such as these suggest that Christians were widely sought after and highly valued, especially for their ability to generate general prosperity where they settled.

The character of ancient Christian communities that evolved in early times seems to have remained, for the most part, largely aristocratic. Hindu in

---

ing to Eusebius, he went to India. Jerome also mentioned "Brahmans." Jewish communities (dating back to the first Exile) already settled along the coasts of India were joined by more Jews after the destruction of Jerusalem in A.D. 70 (and in A.D. 136). Christian and Jewish communities were well settled along the shores of the subcontinent from the second century onward.

12. *The Early Spread of Christianity in India* (Manchester, 1926) [The John Rylands Library]; extract in George Menachery, ed., *The Nazranies* (Thiruvananthapuram, 1998), pp. 509-12.

culture, Christian in faith, and Syrian (or Nestorian) in doctrine, liturgy, and ecclesiology, they added to an already complex structure of castes. With an occupational, ritual, and social ranking mainly as merchant-rulers, they seem to have stood at the top of a Brahmanically prescribed class system (*varnāshramadharma,* or [four-color] *chaturvārnya*). While not all Christian cultures were of uniform rank and while not all Christians enjoyed equal status, not all being of the same caste (*jāti*) or lineage (*vamsha*), all seem to have possessed features that were distinctly native to the land. All, in that sense, seem to have been "Hindu."[13]

Some of the most exclusive Christian communities were known as "southists."[14] These people, claiming a pure lineal descent from Thomas of Jerusalem, wore tonsures (shaven heads with tufts of hair), comparable to *dvija* or "twice-born" castes of India and to certain medieval monks in the West. Known as Malankara Nazaranis,[15] they ranked with Nayars in enjoying close relations with Brahmans. Their dwellings (*tharavād*), their rituals for removing pollution (from *ghee* to *ghur*), and their food, drink, and utensils were also comparable. In the marriage ceremonial, a husband put a *thāli* around his bride's neck and invested her with a "marriage cloth." In rules for interdining and intermarriage, as also for disposal of dead bodies, Nayars and Nazaranis were linked. Christian merchant-bankers and traders, like Nayars, traveled with the protection of their own skilled regiments of warriors. These warriors were trained in the same traditional martial arts and sciences (*kalāri-pāyat*) as were used by Nayar overlords. According to the *Villiarvattom Pāna,* Malankara Nazaranis whose settlements were scattered across Kerala even formed a separate "little kingdom" of their own. With their domains stretching north and south along the coast, they eventually moved from their capital at Mahadevapatnam ("Port of the Great God"), on the island of Chennamangalam, to Udayamperur in order to avoid Arab depredations. The Church and Kingdom of Udayamperur (Diamper), built by the Raja of Villiarvattom (ca. A.D. 510), survived until after the coming of the Portuguese. Even after betrayal led to a partial conquest of the kingdom, remnants of Malankara partisans continued to resist *Farangi* subjugation.

For more than a thousand years and, indeed, perhaps as long as fourteen

13. K. L. Anantakrishna Ayyar, *Anthropology of the Syrian Christians* (Ernakulam, 1926).

14. Jacob Kollaparambil, *The Babylonian Origin of the Southists among the St. Thomas Christians* (Rome, 1992).

15. George Menachery, ed., *Indian Church History Classics: The Nazranies* (Thiruvananthapuram, 1998), vol. 1 (of projected series of three). This contains texts, bibliographical information, illustrations (photographs), and maps.

to fifteen centuries, waves of migration brought fresh infusions of Christian merchants and missionaries, refugees and settlers to Indian shores. They came from Roman Egypt; from Mesopotamia and Syria; from Zoroastrian Parthia; from Persia after *dar-ul-Islam;* from Europe as pilgrims (such as those mentioned in the Anglo-Saxon Chronicle) or travelers; from Central Asia (especially after the Mongol conquests); and, finally, from Armenia (from whence a nearly ubiquitous Christian presence found a respected place within the durbars of Turkish and Mughal rulers, a presence that has endured into the present century).[16]

However isolated and weakened the Church of the East became, it continued to exist in India long after the virtual disappearance of Christians from other parts of Asia.[17] While this presence remains largely unexplained, one or two factors may partially explain the gradual decline and disappearance elsewhere.[18] First, within those forms of Indian, Syrian, and Persian Christianity that flourished in the East, forms that had come out of Antioch, Babylon, and Edessa, an enormous communication gap seems of have opened up between clerical leadership and ordinary believers. Syriac, a form of Aramaic, remained the language of the Church. As the exclusive preserve of the learned and literate clerics, it served as the only vehicle through which doctrine and liturgy could be transmitted from generation to generation. Yet, in Persia, India, China, and other lands of the East, Syriac could never be the mother tongue for the common, nonclerical peoples. Efforts to translate scriptures, sermons, hymns, and learned discourses into common languages seem never to have become effective. As a consequence, the language of the Church remained largely foreign and beyond the reach of any except a small clerical elite. Since all peoples tend to have a great affection for, and affinity to, the beauty of their own languages, especially their mother tongues, the failure of Eastern Christians to use their already rich literary traditions for purposes of faith, other than for formal rituals of worship and for scholarship and recitation of doctrinal creeds, seems to have left an enormous residual ignorance, a gulf that could not easily be bridged.

16. In the manuscript records of the Madras High Court, there are letters by a prelate in Armenia in the eighteenth century, begging Robert Clive to arbitrate in local disputes between Armenians over the legitimacy of an ecclesiastical succession within the Armenian Church of Madras.

17. George Mark Moraes, *A History of Christianity in India, from Early Times to St. Francis Xavier: A.D. 52-1542* (Bombay, 1964). S. G. Pothan, *The Syrian Christians of Kerala* (New York, 1963).

18. Robin E. Waterfield (*Christians in Persia: Assyrians, Armenians, Roman Catholics and Protestants* [London, 1973], pp. 30-32) makes these suggestions.

Second, Christianity in the East not only became increasingly, if not predominantly, monastic and celibate (in normative social doctrine), but it also became isolated from Christianity of the West. As a consequence, very little was known in the West about the daily life of the ordinary Christian believers in Eastern lands. While Eastern Christians embarked on amazing and extraordinary missionary ventures, to Central Asia and to islands beyond, most of the faithful of the East became increasingly isolated and relegated to the exclusion from essentials of Christian belief. Doctrinal disputes persisted, something that virtually ceased in the West after the canon and the creeds had been settled by the great Councils. Strict celibacy became equated, at least among the clergy, with spirituality, and even with eternal salvation. Traditions of family purity and lineages in India may have further isolated Christians of India from Christians elsewhere, as also from other peoples of India. According to one fourth-century Persian sage (Aphrate), all Christians fell into two categories: they were either "Offspring of the Covenant" *(Bar Qiyama)* or they were "Penitents." Only persons dedicated to an ascetic and celibate life could be baptized. Those not so inclined were denied baptism. This "Manichaean" separation of Christians, between elites and masses and between dwellers in the Light and those in Darkness, weakened the Christian communities in Asia. Such weaknesses were exacerbated during times of prolonged persecution. Strict rules against improper marriage and baptism, improper fasting and prayer, vows of poverty, simplicity of food and garb, ceaseless study, and prolonged silence may also have had alienating consequences. Islamic rule brought further persecution. This, along with elitist "renunciations" from the world, may well have prompted more Christians (along with Zoroastrians) to abandon Persia for India.[19] Islam, initially averse to asceticism and elitism alike, strove to obliterate distinctions between the religious specialists and ordinary people. Thereafter, among Christians of the East, only Armenian Christians, venturing out of their homelands and strongholds to the north and west, seem to have thrived in Islamic lands of the East.[20]

19. Waterfield, *Christians in Persia*, pp. 30-32.

20. A footnote to these events was recorded in far off England. See Anne Savage, trans. and coll., *The Anglo-Saxon Chronicles* (New York, 1983), p. 97. It is recorded for A.D. 883 that monks "Sigehelm and Aethelstand conveyed alms that the king vowed to send thither . . . to St. Thomas and St. Bartholomew in India." Some may quibble over what was meant by "India," but long journeys of that nature occurred and travelers moved in both directions.

Catholic Christians in India

European (*Parangi* or *Farangi;* from the Perso-Arabic for "frank") Christians came to India in 1498. Coming in the wake of Vasco da Gama's arrival, the earliest of these new arrivals were not just Catholic. They were Roman Catholic. Priests and missionaries who accompanied fleets that set out from Lisbon each year fanned out across parts of India, seeking converts and establishing monastic institutions. Increasingly blending ideals of a ruling medieval Christendom with those of the Renaissance and Counter-Reformation, these *Farangi* missionaries eventually disturbed older Christian institutions in India. After early reports confirmed the existence of a strong Christian presence along the southwestern shores, attempts were made to gain ecclesiastical control over all Indian Christians. Where Portuguese rule became established, in such enclaves as Goa, Daman, Diu, and Mumbay, European clerics engaged in aggressive, disruptive, and destructive actions. These actions can certainly be described as having been "colonial" in the current sense (as defined in the Introduction). Yet, in time, steady resistance from indigenous institutions gradually undermined colonial domination so that its impact was mitigated. The *Padroado,* reflecting the ecclesiastical authority and patronage of the Portuguese Crown, strove to remain autonomous and free of Papal interference. Such resistance not only continued but seems to have increased after the union of Portugal with Spain, when Portugal itself became a "colony." Along the littoral fringes of the Indian Ocean Basin, outside areas of Portuguese rule, where *Farangis* intermarried with native Indians and settled down, the ecclesiastical sway of Rome was further undermined. However much it tried, *Propaganda Fide* in Rome never succeeded in fully imposing its authority upon this "Eastern Rome" located in Goa, nor upon Indian Christians.[21]

Initially, in 1502, Indian Christian leaders of Cochin sought for help in dealing with predators. The European newcomers discovered that prior to the seizure of Cochin by its Hindu raja, Christians had ruled Udayamperur (also soon known as Diamper, or Vyampur). Now it was all they could do to keep the Raja of Cochin and Zamorin of Calicut at bay. Never quite strong enough to gain lasting security from local rajas, Christian merchants offered the prospects of bringing much of the local spice trade over to the Portuguese. Yet, when they presented Vasco da Gama with an ornamented staff, he misinterpreted their gift as a token of submission. Nevertheless, an alliance between the *Catholicos* (or Patriarch) of Babylon and the Portuguese was eventually

---

21. A. Mathias Mundadan, *A History of Christianity in India,* vol. 1: *From the Beginning up to the Middle of the Sixteenth Century* (Bangalore, 1982).

concluded. Mar Jacob, *Metran* of Ankamāli (1504-49), wrote to the Pope in 1523, confirming the alliance. Local parades, with gospel, cross, candles and canticles, consecrations, ordinations, and sacraments before high altars, were jointly celebrated.

As explorers, friars, merchants, or soldiers of Portugal who continued to travel along the shorelines and to penetrate ever more deeply into the interior, they uncovered and gathered increasing amounts of data and engaged in arguments over the nature of the masses of new information they were gathering. Eventually, from data sent to Goa, Lisbon, and Rome, estimates concerning the exact number of Thomas Christians in India increased from 70,000 to over 200,000. Native Christians in India were seen as holding positions of prominence in some sixty towns and villages along the shorelines and their adjacent uplands, living in territories ruled by some twenty rajas and a multitude of petty warlords. The area they inhabited was called the *Serra*.[22]

However, harmony between European and Indian Christians did not last. The struggle that ensued lasted for centuries. Tensions gradually mounted and eventually led to the conquest and capitulation of a splinter group of Indian Christians. Metran Mar Abraham refused to ordain some fifty students trained in the Jesuit seminary at Vaipikkottai. The dispute centered in Catholic objections to Malayalam and Syriac theology and liturgy and attempts to correct books and eradicate Nestorian heresy. Thomas Christians saw that their whole way of life as being endangered. Told that their rejection of images — a practice that had for so long made them distinct from Hindu communities surrounding them — was heresy, that customs handed down to them by their forebears were unacceptable, and that their family ceremonies and traditions were an abomination, they strenuously objected. The Archbishop of Goa (Menezes) sailed down to Cochin and confronted their *Metran* (George of the Cross). A large and menacing crowd, led by their *metran*, *panikkars* (fencing masters) with drawn swords, fifty *kattanars*, and three thousand armed retainers, openly opposed him. When church sanctuaries were forcibly opened, people refused to abandon them. When libraries were destroyed and heretical texts burned, books were hidden. When secret agents were sent to watch and report every move the *Metran* made, extremists countered with an attempt to kill the prelate. Indignation reached its peak on 20 June 1599, when the Archbishop convened the Synod of Diamper. At this

---

22. A. Mathias Mundadan, *Sixteenth Century Traditions of St. Thomas Christians* (Bangalore, 1970); Joseph Thekkedath, *History of Christianity in India*, vol. 2: *From the Middle of the Sixteenth Century to the End of the Seventeenth Century* (Bangalore, 1982); vol. 3 (Bangalore, 1982), pp. 24ff. for numbers of Christians.

event, ceremonially opened amid colorful pomp, with processions and choral masses of great solemnity, a group of "properly trained" and "submissive" Catholic *kattanars* were formally ordained. Anathema was then pronounced against the Patriarch of Babylon or any *metran* who might dare to oppose Rome. Claims equating the legacy of the Apostle Thomas with that of Peter were condemned. As loud voices, marshaled in advance, shouted down all opposition, doctrines that had been held for twelve hundred years were cast aside.[23]

Yet, Roman Catholic ascendancy was never left unchallenged. No sooner had Menezes returned to Europe and celebrated his "victory of the faith" than more struggles with Thomas Christians erupted. These were incessant, going on year after year and century after century (down into our own time). Leaders rising out of the powerful Pakalomarram family, in which nephews had succeeded celibate uncles for untold generations, employed carefully cultivated and specialized ancient skills of silent subversion — bending without breaking and ceaselessly dissimulating, evading, hiding, manipulating, and undermining Catholic authority. The struggle went on for fifty years. One European prelate after another was worn out trying to subdue recalcitrant Thomas Christians. Local Christian leaders devised every conceivable kind of stratagem and subterfuge to defend their ancient institutions. Eventually, on 3 January 1653, anti-Catholic *kattanars* met in solemn assembly at Koonen Cross of Mattanceri. There, and later at Vaipikkottai and Manat, they swore an oath never to again accept any *Farangi* prelate or any *metran* imposed upon them from outside the Eastern Church. From that day onward, to the present day, the Malankara Church has marked the event as that grand moment when their community recovered its full independence. Some Thomas Christians then determined to go even further. Since a Portuguese blockade denied them access to patriarchs of Syria, so that no new *metrans* could be sent, they decided to consecrate their own. This action, they determined, required only a solemn "laying on of hands" by twelve *kattanars*. On 22 May 1653, for the first time in their long history, Thomas Christians installed their own High *Metran*. Parambil Tumi (or Archdeacon Thomas) became India's first native archbishop, and took the title Mar Thoma I.[24]

23. Michael Geddes, *The History of the Church of Malabari from the Time of Its Being First Discover'd: Giving an Account of the Persecutions and Violent Methods of the Roman Prelates, to Reduce Them to the Subjection of the Church of ROME, Together with the SYNOD OF DIAMPER, Celebrated in the Year of Our Lord 1599. With Some Remarks upon the Faith and Doctrine of St. Thomas Christians. Done out of Portugeze into English* (London, 1694).

24. Thekkedath, *Christianity in India*, 2:32-140, 101.

In vast areas of the continent beyond the reach of Portuguese power, *Farangi* missionaries ventured into the courts of the *rayas* of Vijayanagara, the palaces of the *nayakas* of Cinji, Madurai, and Thanjāvur, the durbars of the Grand Mughals of Agra and Delhi, and the *mahals* of subordinate subadars and sultans in Hugli, Machlipatinam, or Surat. In doing so, they manifested an entirely different kind of Catholic presence. In Madurai, Roberto de Nobili proclaimed himself to be a "twice-born" Roman Brahman; and in the Coromandel domains of Ramnad, Sivaganga, Thanjāvur, or Vellore, John de Britto and Constanzo Guiseppe Beschi left a lasting legacy as scholars of Sanskrit and Tamil literature. In the imperial durbars of the north, missionary physicians, scientists, and technicians rendered service and were rewarded with privileges and perquisites. As in China, Jesuits built libraries and won reputations for scientific knowledge. They privately employed correspondents (*jawabnavis*: lit., "back-writers") who sent information and news reports from each corner of the countryside.[25]

While several monastic orders became involved in missionary activities, some of the most important carriers of Catholic influence beyond coastal enclaves under European rule were Jesuit. In archives of what was once Shambhagannur Monastery, records yet to be exploited detail this story. Small communities of new converts that came into existence, often from elite or high-caste families, remained largely encapsulated within prevailing cultural and social structures. Among movements known to have occurred, the most famous was the conversion of fishing communities, Paravas and Mukkuvars, along the shorelines. For the Paravas, this event was as political as it was spiritual. When this proud and venturesome seafaring folk who engaged in fishing, pearl diving, trading, and piracy felt threatened by Arab sea power and Nayaka land power, they turned to the Portuguese for protection and adopted the Christian faith in order to strengthen bonds of mutual obligation. A formal delegation led by Vikrama Aditha Pandya, their *jāti thalavan* (caste headman) came to Goa; and the Portuguese recognized their strategic importance and the prospect of gaining access to lucrative pearl revenues. After a furious battle at Vedālai (1538), Paravas enjoyed a time of unprecedented prosperity.

At that point, however, Paravas were Christian only in name. They knew next to nothing about their new faith until Francis Xavier landed on the

---

25. Today the media provides bankers, merchants, and scholars with information. At that time the division between news reporting and intelligence gathering and "spying," as now defined, had yet to be clearly drawn. C. A. Bayly (*Empire and Information: Intelligence Gathering and Social Communication in India, 1770-1820* [Cambridge, 1996]) brilliantly explores the intricacies of such processes, albeit for three centuries later.

Fisher Coast. With no knowledge of Tamil, he and three Tamil-speaking assistants walked from village to village, building prayer houses, baptizing children, and drilling people in rote recitations of the Lord's Prayer, *Ave*, the Creeds, and the Commandments. These were to be recited aloud every morning and evening. Attempts were made to install a *kanakkapillai* (catechist/accountant) for each village to keep track of births, deaths, and marriages for each lineage *(vamsha)*, for family solidarity. When families from other communities — Karaiyars, Shānars, Kaikolars, Pallars, and Paraiyars — asked for baptism, they too were drawn into the fold. When Mukkavars on the western Fisher Coast also asked to be included, ten thousand more were baptized (in late 1844). Parava and Mukkuva Christian identity set by Xavier and strengthened by his *Padroado* successors remained firm for more than four and half centuries.[26]

These shoreline Christian communities retained their autonomy. Their religion, while Christian, remained conspicuously Hindu or Nativistic. Ceremonials, rituals, and social structures also remained *jāti* (birth and caste) oriented. The *jāti thalavan* of all Paravas ruled as their "little king," leading processions to the Great Church or Mother Church *(Periya-Koyil* or *Māda-Koyil)*, where the Virgin or Our Lady of Snows was enshrined as a cultic patroness comparable to any tutelary *avatar* of *Mahādevi* (e.g., Minakshi, Kali, and others). From his throne situated just below her statue, the "little king" would rise to unveil her image, adorn it with garlands and jewels, and celebrate family ceremonies and marriages. At the festival of the Golden Car each year, an event lasting ten days, thousands of people would drag the huge-wheeled vehicle bearing the Virgin ("Mother of God") on its annual *Rath Yātra* through the streets of Tuticorin, doing so to the beating of drums, chanting of hymns and prayers, and festooning of garlands. Rituals of Parava Christianity had the approval of the *Padroado*, but not of Jesuits, nor of *Propaganda Fide* in Rome.[27]

What happened in Madurai, not far from Tirumal Nayak's palace, did not win easy approval from either the *Padroado* or *Propaganda Fide*. Where Francis Xavier dealt with the lowest, polluting segments of Tamil society on the Fisher Coast, Robert de Nobili dealt with the highest and purest. In the shadow of the four towering gateways *(gopurams)* of the ancient Minakshi-Sundareswarar Temple, where thousands came each day and where throngs

26. Georg Schurhammer, *Francis Xavier: His Life, His Times (Franz Xavier, sein Leben und seine Zeit)*, 4 vols., translated by M. Joseph Costelloe (Rome, 1973-82).

27. Susan K. Bayly, "A Christian Caste in Hindu Society: Religious Leadership and Social Conflict among the Paravas of Southern Tamilnadu," *Modern Asian Studies* 15.2 (1981): 203-34.

of students from far corners of the land flocked, a young aristocrat of Italy settled in 1606. Here, with Vishvāsam, Malaiyappan, and Shivadharma, his guru, he become a scholar-missionary. His aim was to become thoroughly Brahmanized, to avoid any word or deed that might give offense and to gain a complete mastery in Sanskrit and Tamil learning *(veda)*. Acquiring fluency in texts of the Agama and the Alvar and Nayanar poets, scrupulously abstaining from all pollution from defiled or tainted things (e.g., flesh), subsisting only on one simple meal a day, and wearing the "sacred thread" of the "twice-born" *(dvija)* along with the ochre robe of a *sannyāsi,* he engaged Vedanta philosophers in public conversations and won a following of converts and disciples (including his guru). His manifesto, inscribed on palm-leaf and posted on his house, declared: "I am not a *parangi.*[28] I was not born in the land of the *parangis,* nor was I ever connected with their [lineages]. . . . I come from Rome, where my family holds a rank as respectable as any *rajas* in this country." By cutting off all links with crude, beef-eating, alcohol-drinking barbarians from Europe, de Nobili, the "Roman Brahman," identified himself as Indian and became known by the name Tattuwa-Bhodacharia Swami.[29]

Catholic learning established in Nayaka Madurai, epitomized by its repository of rare manuscripts at Shambhaganur Monastery, reached its zenith with the work of the Italian Jesuit Constanzo Guiseppe Beschi (1680-1747). This sage, known as Viramāmuni Swami or as Dharrya Nāthaswami, left classical (Sangam) epics, philosophical treatises, commentaries, dictionaries, grammars, translations, and tracts for Hindu Christians and non-Christians alike. Such scholarship put him in the forefront of Tamil scholarship. His *Tembāvani,* an epic of 3,525 tetrastichs of 30 cantos, his commentary on the *Tiruvalluvar* Kural, and his public disputations with scholars *(achāryas)* and mendicants *(padārams)* won renown. The grandeur of his entourage matched that the Shankaracharya. Clothed in a long tunic bordered in scarlet and robed in pale purple, with ornate slippers, purple-and-white turban, pearl and ruby earrings, bangles and rings of heavy gold on his wrists and fingers, and a carved staff of inlaid ivory in his hand, he sat in his sumptuous palanquin upon a tiger skin, with attendants fanning him, holding a purple silk parasol surmounted by a golden ball to keep the sun from touching him. With attendants marching before and behind him lifting high a standard of spread peacock's feathers (symbolizing Saraswati, goddess of wisdom), he

28. By *parangi* he obviously meant "Portuguese" rather than "European" (common soldiers had become notorious).

29. Vincent Cronin, *A Pearl to India: The Life of Roberto di Nobili* (London, 1959). Thekkedath, *History of Christianity,* 2:212-80.

displayed all the marks of regal authority. Chanda Saheb, Nawab of the Carnatic, honoring him in his durbar, bestowed the title of "Ismattee Sannyasi" upon him, presented him with the inlaid-ivory palanquin of his grandfather, and appointed him *diwan,* a position that also awarded him a tax-exempt estate *(inām)* of four villages worth 12,000 rupees income per year. Thereafter, when Beschi ventured on any journey, his "circuits, assuming the pomp and pageantry of a potentate, included *chobdars, sawars* [horsemen], caparisoned steeds, *hurcarrahs* [informers/messengers/spies], *daloyets* [shield-carrying spearmen], *nowbuts* [kettle drums] and fife, and tents."[30]

Clearly, a high degree of indigenizing acculturation characterized Catholic Christianity in India. After the Portuguese arrival in 1498 and the establishment of their *Estado da India,* Catholic orders under the *Padroado* of Goa enjoyed considerable autonomy. Often free of control from either Rome or Lisbon, they manifested a considerable transcultural adaptability. From their monastic and collegiate citadels, missionaries went into the countryside beyond spheres of Portuguese rule. While expanding clerical domains and newly won converts, sometimes at the expense of ancient Christian communities, included whole communities along southern shorelines and a high-profile learned tradition, Catholics failed to make significant inroads in Mughal India. Yet, in the centuries that followed (and right down to the present), the earliest and strongest expressions of indigenous Christianity anywhere in the subcontinent, in both ideological and institutional forms, survived in those communities that still claimed and accepted the apostolic tradition of St. Thomas as the historic basis for their origin and as the doctrinal basis for their ecclesiastical authority. Among these, as found today, are the Orthodox Syrian Church (in two branches), the Independent Syrian Church of Malabar (Kunnamkulam), the Mar Thoma Church, the Malankara (Syrian Rite) Catholic Church, the (Chaldean) Church of the East, and the St. Thomas Evangelical Church (or factions thereof), along with at one time the Church Missionary Society (CMS) segments within the Church of South India. From the sixteenth century onward, all of these communities or branches thereof interacted with or evolved in connection with branches of the Roman Catholic Church. Some answered, in varying degrees, to the Portuguese patronage of the *Padroado Real* in Goa or to the Papal Office of the *Congregatio de Propaganda Fide* in Rome.

---

30. [Revd.] L. Besse, *Father Beschi, of the Society of Jesus: His Times & His Writings* (Trichinopoly, 1918), pp. 35-49. Muttusami Pillai, *A Brief Sketch of the Life and Writings of Rev. Father C. J. Beschi, "Honorifically" Surnamed* Viramāmani *("Great Champion Devotee")* (Madras, 1840).

Evangelical Christians in India

In 1706, at the very time that the Viramāmani Swami (Constanzo Guiseppe Beschi) was about to have such a profound impact upon Tamil learning at its highest levels, German Evangelical missionaries began to arrive to Tranquebar.[31] Their arrival set in motion a complex chain of events that moved Christians of India in a radically different direction. Their arrival coincided with the decline of Indo-Islamic and rise of European power, so that what was "Christian" increasingly became confused with what was "European." Out of turmoil of the eighteenth century, an all-embracing Indian Empire emerged. With the coming of William Carey to Bengal in 1793, transcultural interactions, conversions, and transformations in India increased. As the modern missionary movement gained momentum, Evangelical and Catholic institutions spread until, by the twentieth century, they were reaching tribal peoples in the remotest corners of frontier areas. These events had profound consequences for Hindu and Muslim cultures. Imperial India was eventually challenged by the Indian National Congress (led by Gandhi and Nehru) and the All-India Muslim League (led by Jinnah). The politics of protest and the politics of competitive communalism thus engendered led to the Partition of the Raj in 1947 and left the subcontinent broken. Thereafter, under the successor states of India and Pakistan (from which Bangladesh broke in 1971), Burma, Sri Lanka, and Nepal, the momentum of religious changes increased. Despite the swift decline and disappearance of Western missionaries, increasingly radical religious movements and cross-cultural transformations led to the rise of strident fundamentalisms of many different kinds. Some of these, in turn, have now begun to challenge the very existence of Indian Christianity in its manifold forms. Much of this entire, highly complex, process began in Tranquebar, Thanjāvur, and Tirunelveli.

A mingling of Enlightenment thought and Evangelical Pietism led to the sending of two young Germans as the first Evangelical (non-Catholic or "Protestant") missionaries to India. Behind their coming lay the sufferings of the Thirty Years War (1618-48) and the Pietist movement (or "Second Refor-

---

31. The term "Evangelical" is used here instead of the term "Protestant" — indicating, thereby, its German/Danish rather than Anglo-American roots. Terms such as "Orthodox," "Catholic," and "Evangelical" have broader, more positive (historical and theological) connotations than "Protestant." "Evangelisch" is still the standard term for German Lutherans although some Lutherans do use "Protestant," especially in reference to personal conversion and individualistic faith. "Evangelical" is also a post–Second World War term that has come into usage for Anglo-American Protestantism, including those who are now commonly regarded as "Evangelicals."

mation"), which also led to the Evangelical Great Awakening in Britain and America.[32] Moravian refugees fleeing from persecution; Count Zinzendorf's shelters for refugees at Herrenhut; Professor August Hermann Francke's educational innovations at Halle University; and private collaborations between pious royal cousins, Queen Anne of England and King Frederick IV of Denmark — these are but a few elements that brought about a new kind of ecumenical voluntarism and the forming of an altogether new kind missionary collaboration.[33] Formation of state-sponsored agencies, such as the SPCK (Society for Promoting Christian Knowledge) in 1698, the SPG (Society for the Propagation of the Gospel in Foreign Parts) in 1702, and the Royal Danish Mission served as a prelude to the rise of even more thoroughly voluntary forms of missionary activity a century later. These agencies reflected the latest and most advanced ideas about education, science, and technology. New methodologies developed at Halle were already beginning to bring rapid changes to northern Germany. Francke set forth his unprecedented dictum — that proper belief required biblical understanding, that proper biblical understanding required literacy, and, hence, that universal literacy and practical education were duties incumbent, in a very fundamental sense, upon all true believers, in simple obedience. Every single human being should be enabled to read in his or her own mother tongue and each should also possess a useful manual skill. For early Evangelicals, the *Kindergarten* and the *Kunst und Wunder Kammer* were to be the twin engines of literacy and laboratory whereby the gospel of Christ was to be spread to the remotest corners of the world. This radical ideal, of carrying basic literacy, practical numeracy, and modern science to all people everywhere, possessed revolutionary possibilities. It was this ideal that came to India in 1706.

Bartholomäus Ziegenbalg and Heinrich Plütschau landed at Tranquebar (Tarangambadi). This seaport, close to rich lands of the Cauvery Delta, had been leased to Danish merchants by Raghunath Nayaka of Thanjāvūr in 1620. Dutch chaplains of Jan Company, Abraham Rogerius and Philip Baldaeus, had already explored and written about Hindu cultures, and a tiny Brahman-Christian community of believers may already have existed in Jaffna. The

32. F. Ernest Stoeffler, *The Rise of Evangelical Pietism* (Leiden, 1971); idem, *German Pietism during the Eighteenth Century* (Leiden, 1973).

33. John Foster, "The Significance of A. W. Boehme's [Böhme's] 'The Propagation of the Gospel in the East,'" *Oecumenia* (1968). Böhme was the German chaplain to Prince George of Denmark, Queen Anne's husband, sent to the English court from the Halle Pietist professor, August Hermann Francke. Bartholomaeus Ziegenbalg, "Preliminary Discourses Concerning the Character of Missions . . . ," in *The Propagation of the Gospel in East,* ed. with introductory notes by A. W. Boehme (London, 1709, 1710, 1718).

young German missionaries who arrived in July 1706, however, encountered hostility from the outset. The local Danish trading establishment, fearing anything that might endanger profits, harassed, persecuted, and even imprisoned one of them. Yet, being university educated, they were soon able to demonstrate their usefulness, if only as teachers for children of the Danish residents. Soon thereafter, they applied themselves to mastering local languages, setting up schools for native children, printing vernacular textbooks, and training local teachers. At the same time, they collected and studied as many manuscripts as they could. Small congregations of Tamil Christians were formed, and Tamil disciples were trained as pastors and teachers. Each convert was trained to take up some practical responsibility. As trained Tamil teachers and pastors proliferated, plans were made to apply and extend the Halle system of education to the entire Tamil countryside.[34]

What made this venture distinctive was the level and volume of its scholarly accomplishment. Unlike efforts of Beschi, which aimed at capturing the respect of the cultural elite, this mission aimed at providing universal literacy for the common and lowly. Extremely gifted in languages, Ziegenbalg not only mastered Tamil in its classical and colloquial forms but also made exhaustive comparisons between palm-leaf manuscripts and books in his huge collection to ascertain and distinguish varieties and idioms. Dedicated to making written Tamil available to all ordinary people, he was the first scholar to complete a Tamil translation of the New Testament. This work, however crude the attempt may have been, was printed in 1715. As early as 1709, as he became increasingly amazed at the depth and quality of Tamil learning and wisdom, he produced his most notable work. *Genealogy of the Malabarian Gods* (manuscript completed in 1713) sought to show what Hindus believed.[35] This disturbed Europeans. Francke, who responded by writing that "Missionaries were sent out to extirpate heathenism, and not to spread heathenish nonsense in Europe," failed to see that sharing the gospel required deep understanding of Hindu culture.[36]

Ziegenbalg's second major accomplishment was his planting in India of the Halle ideal of the Charity School *(Dharmappallikkuduam')*. This symbol-

---

34. Erich Beyreuther, *Bartholomaeus Ziegenbalg: A Biography of the First Protestant Missionary in India, 1682-1719*, translated by S. G. Lang and H. W. Genisichen (Madras, 1956).

35. Daniel Jeyaraj, "A Genealogy of the Malabarian Gods," Ph.D. dissertation, Halle University, 2000.

36. Daniel Jeyaraj, *Inkulturation in Tranquebar: Der Bertrag der frühen dänisch-halleschen Mission zum Werden einer indisch-einherimischen Kirche (1706-1730)* (Erlangen, 1996).

ized the Francke vision of bringing basic literacy to every human being, in that person's mother tongue.[37] Between 1728 and 1731, as models of this new kind of school multiplied, they caught the eye of Rajanayakam, a *servaikāran* or captain of the palace guard at Thanjāvur. He, his brother, and fellow soldiers soon became instrumental in bringing the first such school into that kingdom and in obtaining a royal land-grant *(inām)* from the raja for its support. Another high-born Vellālar became the first Tamil Evangelical pastor to be fully ordained as a pastor for congregations within the Thanjāvur kingdom. The most outstanding Europeans to succeed Ziegenbalg were Benjamin Schultze (Madras, 1727-43) and Philip Fabricius (Madras, 1740-91). Schultze initiated modern studies of Telugu, compiling a dictionary, producing a grammar, collecting manuscripts, and translating the Gospels. Fabricius strove to perfect works that Ziegenbalg had begun by producing a Tamil grammar (in English), an English-Tamil dictionary, and new translations of both Old and New Testaments — a work that Vedanāyakam Sāstri was later to extol as "the gold translation of the immortal Fabricius."[38]

The most renowned of all precolonial and noncolonial Evangelical missionaries of eighteenth-century India was Christian Frederick Schwartz. By the time of his death in 1798, he had spent forty-eight years in continuing and unceasing service.[39] Adept in Tamil, Telugu, Marathi, Persian, Sanskrit, Portuguese, and European tongues, both modern and classical, he gained fame as a preacher, teacher, schoolmaster, diplomat, and statesman, ending his career as Protector-Regent, *Raja-Guru,* and "Father" to Serfoji, the Maharaja of Thanjāvur. His disciples, whom he trained and then called "Helpers," were sent far and wide across South India — from Tranquebar to Tiruchirapalli, to Thanjāvur, to Tirunelveli, and even to Kanyakumari (Cape Comorin) and Travancore — and extended the reach of Tamil Evangelicals as never before. That all this occurred during times of ceaseless war, famine, and human suffering makes his story all the more astonishing. All of this was done, more-

37. D. Dennis Hudson, *Protestant Origins in India: Tamil Evangelical Christians, 1706-1835* (Grand Rapids and London, 2000), pp. 20-21, 93-94, 101.

38. E. Arno Lehmann, *Es begann in Tranquebar* (Berlin, 1955); and abridged English translation, *It Began in Tranquebar* (Madras, 1956). Johannes Ferdinand Fenger, *History of the Tranquebar Mission, Worked out from the Original Papers,* translated by Emil Francke (Tranquebar, 1863), with biographies of ninety-eight Evangelical Lutheran missionaries in India.

39. Hugh Nicholas Pearson [Dean of Salisbury], *Memoirs of the Life and Correspondence of the Reverend Christian Frederick Swartz, to Which Is Prefixed, a Sketch of the History of Christianity in India,* 2 vols. (London, 1834-); Wilhelm Germann, *Missionar Christian Schwartz — Sein Leben und Wirken aus Briefen des Halleschen Missionsarchives* (Erlangen, 1870).

over, in the face of opposition to Indian Christians and missions from the English East India Company and during the time when Company forces were inexorably extending British rule over much of the subcontinent. Among the most notable of Schwartz's disciples, the stories of two, Satyanāthan Pillai and Vedanāyakam Sāstri, are especially noteworthy.

Satyanāthan Pillai came from a high-born Vellālar family of Thanjāvur. He became an ardent disciple despite strong domestic opposition. As one of Schwartz's most energetic assistants, he became a pastor to Christians within the East India Company's military garrison at Vallam. In 1771, when Company forces destroyed the church in Thanjāvur, seven miles away, he also became pastor to the city congregation. The progress of church growth at that time was almost invariably linked "to the mobility of Christians, and especially of Christian soldiers in the armies of the Company and of the local rulers."[40] Thus, when Sāvarimuthu Pillai, a Vellālar Evangelical who was employed as a sepoy in the garrison at Palayamkottai in Tirunelveli, wrote to Schwartz (first in 1769 and again in 1771), begging for someone to serve as pastor among Tamil Christians settled in Tirunelveli, and when an affluent Brahman widow at Palayamkottai also wrote to Schwartz asking him to visit the congregation, he eventually made the long journey to see things for himself. In 1778, when Schwartz came to Palayamkottai, he baptized and christened the widow "Clorinda." She and a local catechist were put in charge of the congregation. With occasional help from a visiting Vellālar pastor named Rayappan, a Charity School was opened. When she offered to endow the building of a *pukka* prayer-school hall, Schwartz sent Satyanāthan Pillai to serve as the first permanent resident pastor-teacher of the fledgling congregation. In 1790 Satyanāthan was recalled to Thanjāvur to receive full formal ordination. He was then commissioned as the first Tamil Evangelical missionary, before being sent back to his post in Tirunelveli. In 1799, he was joined by a newly commissioned disciple named David Sundarānandam.

Sundarānandam, the first person from the Shānar (now Nādar) community to have been converted, was clearly a charismatic, if not revolutionary, leader. Under his influence, whole villages became Christian. Yet, as thousands of Shānars flocked to embrace the new faith, they incurred the wrath of local landlords. At the instigation of disturbed landlords, warlords *(palaiyakarans)* "plundered, confined, and tortured Christians," destroying their chapel/schools and burning their books. During the years 1799 to 1806, thousands of Christians lost everything they possessed, some being stripped of their clothes and sent into the jungle to die. Eventually their fiery leader, David Sundarānandam, disappeared, perhaps poisoned.

---

40. Stephen Neill, *History of Christianity in India* (Cambridge, 1984), 1:53.

Yet, in the face of persecution and martyrdom, movements of mass conversion to Christianity continued to break out. (At various times during the nineteenth century, whole villages often would turn Christian *en masse*.) In desperation, a "Village of Refuge" was established. Called Mudalur or "First Village," the innovation was so successful that others soon followed — namely, Megnanapuram, Dohnavur, Jerusalem, Galilee, Sawyerpuram, Suviseshapuram, Anandapuram, and Nazareth. Mutual care societies for those fleeing their homes were formed. As numbers of Christians doubled, and sometimes tripled (in every decade), institutional infrastructures proliferated. Schools to provide basic literacy for all, colleges and seminaries to train leaders, and hospitals and various self-help voluntary and welfare societies to care for the sick and the poor, the widows, and the orphans were established. In short, Tirunelveli Evangelicals transformed the entire area, bringing about a profound change in local culture and society.[41]

The most renowned of all Schwartz's helpers, however, was to be Vedanāyakam [Pillai] Sāstri, who was born in Palayamkottai. Schwartz noticed him among the children of the Vellālar Christian poet, Devasahayam Pillai, during his visit to the area in 1785. The remarkable gifts of this twelve-year-old so impressed him that he asked Devasahayam to let him adopt the lad and take him to Thanjāvur for training. Vedanāyakam soon became a master-teacher, writer of renown, and headmaster of one of the three modern schools that Schwartz had built. These schools, endowed by the rajas of Thanjāvur, Shivaganga, and Ramnad, were models of the educational ideals developed by Professor Francke a century earlier in Halle. Their mixed Tamil-English curriculum, while using biblical and Christian texts, also conveyed the very latest developments in Enlightenment principles, sciences, and technologies, something available nowhere else in India at that time. They became so renowned for pedagogical excellence that the Company's directors in London offered an annual subsidy if the schools could also help to meet the rising demand for trained recruits within the burgeoning Madras Presidency. Not surprisingly, Maratha Brahman families vied with each other to get their sons admitted. Youths from these three schools soon filled high-level cadres of the Company governments in South India.

41. Robert Caldwell, *Records of the Early History of the Tinnevelly Mission* (Madras, 1881); R. E. Frykenberg, "The Impact of Conversion and Social Reform upon Society in South India during the Late Company Period: Questions concerning Hindu-Christian Encounters, with Special Reference to Tinnevelly," in *Indian Society and the Beginnings of Modernisation: c. 1830-1850*, edited by C. H. Philips and Mary Doreen Wainwright (London, 1978), pp. 187-243.

One dazzling symbol of scholarly and scientific achievement in Thanjāvur was the construction of the Saraswati Mahal Library within the palace of the Maharaja. Within this building, begun by Schwartz himself, the old classmates Serfoji Raja and Vedanāyakam fulfilled their fondest dreams. Collections of rare manuscripts and books were preserved; and scientific instruments were placed within the Saraswati Mahal's own "Cabinet of Arts and Wonders."[42]

Vedanāyakam's Sāstri's main historical significance, however, lies in the powerful contributions to Tamil literature and, especially, to Tamil Christian thought that came from his pen. His masterful works in classical Tamil poetry and his equally creative works in modern Tamil prose remain his most enduring legacy. The corpus of this writing is astonishing, not only for its volume but for its depth, range, and subtlety. The range of modern and scientific subjects on which he wrote — astronomical, geographical, biological, and such — is truly astonishing. His use of the *kuruvanci* genre — the play about a wandering [woman] soothsayer [or fortuneteller] — conveyed profound expositions of fundamental elements underlying human society in relation to everlasting verities. The *Bethlehem Kurvanchee,* a presentation of the gospel story in verse, uses various well-known Tamil modes of tunes, tones, and tempos within the framework of this standard art form and employs well-known idioms to symbolize essential truths. The story is about the ultimate union between the Lord *(Nathan)* as Bridegroom, and the Church, portrayed either as "Virgin Daughter of Zion" or as "Bride of God" *(Devamohini).* This relationship gradually emerges as a consequence of the actions of Faith Foretold *(Visvasa kuruvanci),* the wife who is a wandering prophetess, and of Reason Conveyed *(Gnanachinnakkan),* the husband who, as a birdcatcher and fisherman (or preacher/teacher/catechist), goes out to "capture" souls and present them to the Lord. The husband is under obligation *(dharma)* to cast his net of knowledge, which is the Word of God *(Veda)* in order to bring his catch of birds or fish (metaphors for mankind) as gifts to his Lord and Savior, who is King Jesus, the Son of God. First, however, he must also confront and defeat evil. He must vanquish the devilish and wandering Thief *(Kallakuravan).* Works such as this, composed by Vedanāyakam in 1800 and revised in 1820 for presentation among Chistian congregations, received wide popu-

42. Indira Viswanathan Peterson, "The Cabinet of King Serfoji of Tanjore: A European Collection in Early Nineteenth-Century India," *Journal of the History of Collections* 11.1 (1999): 71-93; and her "European Science and German Missionary Education in the Lives of Two Indian Intellectuals of the Eighteenth Century: The Cabinet of Curiosities *(Kunstkammer)* in Halle and Thanjavur," paper presented to the 14th European Conference on Modern South Asian Studies, Copenhagen, August 1996.

lar acclaim.[43] Vedanāyakam's career as a renowned Tamil poet and writer eventually culminated in his being made court poet-laureate by his old classmate, Serfoji, the Maharaja of Thanjāvur. Thereafter, provided with a stipend and land on which build a house, the title *Sāstri* was affixed to his name.

The pathway blazed by Vedanāyakam was followed by H. A. Krishna Pillai. Pillai, another Thanjāvur Vellālar, also spent his life teaching in one of the model schools. His greatest work, the epic *Irakshaniya Vāttirikam,* is a poetic rendering of Bunyan's *Pilgrim's Progress.* Set within the context of Tamil culture, it demonstrated how conversion to Christianity could occur without doing violence to any of the most hallowed modes of classical Tamil literature.[44]

Christians of nineteenth- and twentieth-century India were continually overshadowed by the increasing military, administrative, and technological presence of an increasingly enormous imperial system. Yet, despite the profound influence of the Raj, Indian Christians themselves continued to control and develop their own institutions. The gospel was interpreted in new ways and extended to new peoples, reaching ever lower strata of society, seeking out peoples in ever more remote jungle areas, and touching more women and children. Help for peoples in want — people hitherto neglected, impaired, diseased, or relegated to exclusion and oppression — entered increasingly into Christian consciousness. Expanding notions of humanity radically suggested that all people, no matter what their birth, color, or condition, should be equal to each other, not just intrinsically in the sight of God, but in circumstances of life on earth. Expanding vision required new agendas and new laws. As equal access to basic protections and basic needs of food, health, education, and opportunity were sought, Christian responsibility mandated more radical and revolutionary changes in society.

Christians and Missionaries under the Raj and After

Hostility toward Christians and Christian missions long remained a predominant feature of government policy under the Raj. The logic of power under

43. "*Bethlehem Kuṟuvañci* of Vedanayaka Sastri of Tanjore: The Cultural Discourses of an Early Nineteenth-Century Tamil Christian Poet," in *Christians, Cultural Interactions, and India's Religious Traditions,* edited by Judith M. Brown and Robert Eric Frykenberg (Grand Rapids and London, 2002), pp. 9-36.

44. D. Dennis Hudson, "The Life and Times of H. A. Krishna Pillai (1827-1900): A Study of the Encounter of Tamil Sri Vaishanava Hinduism and Evangelical Protestant Christianity in Nineteenth Century Tirunelveli District," Ph.D. dissertation, Claremont Graduate School, 1979.

the Company rested, after all, on the hard realities of social structures under-girding the imperial system and foundations of support from Hindu elites. Most of the some three hundred thousand soldiers of the Raj came from high-caste families that held lands and status in the villages. Most of the ap-proximately three hundred thousand civil servants of the Raj came from twice-born communities, such as Brahmans and Kayasthas. Most of the tens and tens of thousands of proper *(pukka)* temples, some them of enormous size, strength, and antiquity, were under the care of native servants of the Raj. In many ways, at least unofficially, therefore, the Company's Raj was indeed a Hindu Raj.

This being so, it is hardly surprising that official attitudes toward India's Christians and toward missionaries were often less than cordial. Exceptions tended to be opportunistic and pragmatic. As urgent needs arose, Chris-tians "on the ground" would readily be exploited by British officials. Sub-ventions, for example, were paid to Roman Catholic Vicars Apostolic in Bombay for Catholic missionaries to serve as chaplains for Irish soldiers in India; and, under SPCK auspices, German missionaries of the Royal Danish Mission were also employed as Company chaplains. After 1792, pressures of the Evangelical lobby in the British Parliament enabled missionary chap-lains to enter the Company's service in India.[45] Thus, Catholic and Evangel-ical (Protestant) missionaries alike would be called upon to serve as mili-tary chaplains, school teachers, or diplomatic emissaries (as when C. F. Schwartz attended the durbar of Hyder Ali and Tipu Sultan in Mysore). At the same time, Indian Christians and missionaries also often tended to fare better in territories outside of direct Company control (e.g., under the Velama Nayakas of Madurai, the Marava Tevars and Setupatis of Ramnad and Sivaganga, the Kallar Tondaimans of Pudukottai, the Nayar Raja Vermas of Travancore, the Maratha Rajas of Thanjāvur, and others). In British-controlled districts, appeals of persecuted Christian villagers to the Company's Court of Directors during the late eighteenth century often fell on deaf ears.[46] Only after the 1813 Charter Renewal Act mandated that,

45. Almost all of these, "pious chaplains" such as David Brown, Claudius Buchanan, Daniel Corrie, James Hough, Henry Martyn, and Thomas Thomason, had been trained by Charles Simeon at Cambridge. Cf. John C. Bennett, "Charles Simeon and the Evangelical Anglican Missionary Movement: A Study of Voluntarism and Church-Mission Tensions," Ph.D. thesis, University of Edinburgh, 1992, pp. 291-367.

46. Extract of a General Letter from the Court of Directors to the Government of Fort St. George (Madras Public Department, 23 January 1805): Madras Public Consulta-tions/Proceedings [MPC/P] (16 July 1805); and letter from Madras Board of Revenue to Collector in Zillah Ramnad (14 August 1805) concerning petitions from Christian inhabit-

henceforth, British missionaries be allowed to work in British India, albeit by permit, did official attitudes begin to soften. Even so, covert forms of official resistance to missionaries never fully disappeared (neither under the Raj nor under postcolonial regimes).

The "Father of the Modern Missionary Movement," in the eyes of Anglo-Saxon Protestants, was William Carey.[47] An Evangelical who came from the "lower" or "mechanics" class (originally a shoemaker before becoming a preacher), he became so inspired after reading about German Evangelicals in India that he initiated a voluntarist movement. He did this by appealing directly to grassroots believers whose Christian faith had been revived during the Evangelical Awakening (or Great Awakening in America). His pamphlet, *An Enquiry into the Obligations of Christians to Use Means for the Conversion of Heathens* (1792), made such an impact that, within months, in 1792, the Baptist Missionary Society (BMS) was formed, and he himself was bound for India (surreptitiously, aboard a Danish vessel). Other voluntary societies, such as the London Missionary Society (LMS) of 1795 and the Church Missionary Society (CMS) of 1799, soon followed. Some societies were formed on the other side of the Atlantic and in other countries. Once formed, contributions were solicited and overseas agendas were drawn up for the sending forth of missionaries to the far corners of the world. Since the Company still refused entry of missionaries into its territories, Carey himself encountered many difficulties. Not until the Danish Governor at Serampore (Srirampur) allowed him and two newcomers (Joshua Marshman and William Ward) to reside in a Danish settlement (under Danish passports) did the mission become established, and not until he was hired to teach Indian languages at Fort William College did Carey gain free entry to Calcutta.[48] Even so, a long pamphlet war had to be fought in Britain.[49] This called for combined efforts of

---

ants in villages of Tinnevelly pleading for relief from cruelties (being placed in stocks and fetters and exposed to scorching sun due to prejudice of public servants against Christians): "The Humble Peitition of the Christian Inhabitants in the Zillah of Tinnevelly, to the Rt. Hon. The English Houses of Parliament," translated from Tamil, in *Memorial of the Church Missionary Society . . . in Reference to the Renewal of Powers to the Hon. East India Company* (London, 27 May 1853), app. C, pp. 72-78, is indicative of a long lingering official antipathy.

47. Timothy George, *Faithful Witness: The Life and Mission of William Carey* (Birmingham, Ala., 1991).

48. E. Daniel Potts, *British Baptist Missionaries in India, 1793-1837: The History of Serampore and Its Missions* (Cambridge, 1967). Brian Stanley, *The History of the Baptist Missionary Society, 1792-1992* (Edinburgh, 1992).

49. Jörg Fisch, "A Pamphlet War on Christian Missions in India, 1807-1809," unpublished paper, Universität Bielefeld, 1983.

prominent Company directors (Charles Grant,[50] John Shore [Lord Teignmouth], and others) and powerful "Claphamite" friends in Parliament (Wilberforce, Thornton, and others), in alliance with the Free Trade lobby. Only then was what, since 1792, had been known as the "Pious Clause" reinserted into the Company's Charter (Renewal) Act of 1813. Thereafter, missionaries who were still denied entry to India could at least appeal directly to the Board of Control.

Officials in London and in India still had good reason for caution. What they feared most was any action that might reflect European arrogance, hubris, and tactlessness, anything that might lead to disorder.[51] They did not hesitate to summarily expel any European, whether public official or missionary, whose activities might endanger "public" security or provoke social unrest. Thus, when combined outcries of Hindu reformers and Christian missionaries for the abolition of female infanticide and widow burning aroused public opinion in Britain so that legislative action had to be taken, and when this, in turn, aroused furious reaction from the Hindus of Calcutta, the government had reason for concern.[52] Again, when devout ("Pietistic") servants of the Company, both civil and military, launched a formal protest expressing outrage against official involvement in idolatrous practices, the government reacted with ruthless severity. It did not hesitate to censure, dismiss, and expel even high officials, such as the Lord Bishop of Madras, George Spencer, and the Commander-in-Chief of Madras, Lt. General Sir Peregrine Maitland.[53]

---

50. After his "Damascus Road" type of conversion in India, Grant had retired and, as a member and sometime chair of the Company's Court of Directors, devoted the remaining years of his life to missionary causes. See Ainslie T. Embree, *Charles Grant and British Rule in India* (New York, 1962).

51. Some Company officials and prominent public figures laid blame for the Vellore Mutiny of 1806 upon the "proselytizing zeal" among Christians. They did this despite the fact that British missionaries had still been forbidden entry into Company-ruled territories until 1813. This charge was later to resurface after the Great Rebellion (Mutiny) of 1857.

52. Great Britain, *Parliamentary Proceedings* (7 July 1832): ["The Sacred Petition (1827)"] "From Hindoo Inhabitants of Bengal, Behar, Orissa . . . to a Committee of the Lords of His Majesty's Most Honorable Privy Council (11 May 1831): Public Record Office: vol. 213 (1832), facs. 404-19. Registers (P.C.2): Suttee Committee Reports.

53. Right Rev. the Lord Bishop of Madras to the Right Hon. Sir Frederick Adam, K. C. B., Governor in Council, Fort St. George, Transmitting a Memorial . . . : MPC/P, 11 October (No. 60) 1836. TNA [formerly Madras Record Office]: 656: pp. 4862-4959 [4864-66]. Government of India to Government of Madras, 15 February (No. 1) 1837: MPC/P (TNA: 663: pp. 873-88); and 25 April (Nos. 12-15) 1837: MPC/P (666: pp. 2237-46). *Letters of Lieutenant General Sir P. Maitland . . . Late Commander-in-Chief of Madras on the Compulsory Attendance of the British and Native Christian Troops at Idolatrous and Mahomedan Festivals* (London, 1841). The Anti-Idolatry Connection League, welcoming protesters de-

State management of temple endowments and ceremonial functions, involving tens of thousands of *pukka* temple institutions; state protection of Hindu pilgrimage sites and traffic; state honor guards and parades at Hindu festivals *(melas)*, requiring attendance of Christian soldiers (in violation of their consciences); state enforcement of forced corvée labor, requiring tens of thousands of persons, including Christians, to pull great Temple Cars *(Rath Yātras)*, a hazardous risk that invariably led to some being crushed to death beneath giant wheels; and state blindness to the plight of tens of thousands of temple "dancing girls" *(devadasis)* whose forced servitude consigned them to perpetual prostitution — these were matters in which the state would brook no opposition.[54] Indeed, any action deemed to be insulting to Hindu and Muslim feelings, such as use of such epithets as "devilish" or "heathen," could lead to severe reprimands, penalties, and, even sometimes, to ejection from the country. In one notorious case, the governor of Madras, the Marquis of Tweeddale, was formally censured in the 1840s for injudicious use of the term "heathen" in official communications.[55] Thus, aggravating actions by some missionaries, occasionally abetted by sympathetic officials, especially when reflecting attitudes of condescension and especially when coming from upper-class or High Church missionaries, tended merely to increase already tense church-state relations in India.[56]

After the Charter Act of 1813 allowed foreign missionaries into British India, government attitudes toward missionaries continued to be cautious and pragmatic. It was only after many generations of missionary teachers and physicians, both male and female, had come to India in increasing numbers and after missionary schools, colleges, and hospitals had proliferated across

---

ported from India, published over a dozen pamphlets, such as *A View of the British Connexion with Idolatry in the Madras Presidency* (London, 1841), no. 6; copies may be found in the British Library.

54. For details of state involvements see Chandra Y. Mudāliar, *The Secular State and Religious Institutions in India: A Study of the Administration of Hindu Public Trusts in Madras* (Wiesbaden, 1974); R. E. Frykenberg, "The Silent Settlement," in *Land Tenure and Peasant in South Asia*, edited by R. E. Frykenberg (New Delhi, 1977), pp. 37-57; and Franklin A. Presler, *Religion under Bureaucracy: Policy and Administration for Hindu Temples in South India* (Cambridge, 1987).

55. R. E. Frykenberg, "Conversion and Crises of Conscience Under Company Raj in South India," in *Asie du Sud, Traditions et changements: VIth European Conference on South Asian Studies, Sevres 8-13 juillet 1978*, edited by Marc Gaborieau and Alice Thorner (Paris, 1979), pp. 311-21.

56. Susan Billington Harper (*In the Shadow of the Mahatma: Bishop V. S. Azariah and the Travails of Christianity in British India* [Grand Rapids and London, 2000], pp. 99-115) provides an overview of such relations.

the length and breadth of India that official attitudes began to soften. Even then, after thousands of missionaries had come to India — with dedicated professionals and volunteers of some fifty Protestant and sixty Catholic societies from all over the world (e.g., America, Canada, Australia and New Zealand, and countries of Scandinavia and Southern Europe) spending most of their lives for what, at least in their own eyes, was seen as a calling in the cause of a needy humanity — official attitudes and responses in India still showed a certain ambivalence.

Each new generation of missionaries coming from the West tended to represent different countries and cultures of Europe and America. Some newer missionaries arrived with more recent ideological attitudes, reflecting more liberal theologies and radical ideologies. Each new wave also tended to add its own new form of intergenerational strife. Newer and younger missionaries from abroad, coming from new and younger missionary societies, and often from different countries in the West, tended to look for vacant places in order to work among as yet "unreached" peoples. The latest to arrive tended to move into the remotest areas or into contact with yet "untouched" tribal (*adivāsi,* aboriginal) peoples or into contact with ever lower or more "untouchable" rungs of the social ladder — into places where ritually polluted people had long been viewed, by Hindu tradition, to be *āvarna* or "sub-human" and into places where people had been all but "abandoned." Among such peoples — peoples not yet Sanskritized or Islamicized, people eager to escape conditions in which they had lived for ages untold — spectacular results were recorded. So much was this so, for example, that huge numbers of Badigas, Bheels, Khasis, Khonds, Mizos, Mundas, Nagas, Santals and scores of other peoples became Christian. These groups often became Christian, with no previous knowledge of Sanskritic Hindu culture, and without having experienced any self-conscious sense of Indian identity, at least in any strict sense. These circumstances, indeed, may also have hindered such groups from becoming fully homogenized, integrated, or nationalized within the larger, more dominant societies of the subcontinent.

By the late nineteenth and the twentieth century, long after the Company had ceased to exist and into the twilight years of the Raj, the government of India still had little reason for enthusiasm toward missionaries (especially foreign missionaries). At no time in the history of India did anything like a majority of missionaries in India, whether British or non-British, show a predisposition in favor of colonialism. Several reasons for this may be suggested. First, missionaries with precolonial, noncolonial, and anti-colonial attitudes have always outnumbered those British missionaries who might have gone so far as to even think of making India an Establishment fiefdom within Anglican Christendom. Second, the very fact that so many European Catholic missionaries were non-British (French, Italian, Irish, and so on) and that so many Evangelical or Protestant missionaries were not British tended to make missionary opposition to colonialism more pronounced. Third, opposition to the Raj tended to increase in direct proportion to the increase in free, nondenominational and unfettered forms of voluntarism. This was so because voluntarism, especially in faith mission or para-church forms, drew more and more recruits, along with more financial support, from successively lower and lower strata (and/or cultural levels) within Western societies. As more missionary recruits came from nondenominational or faith societies, their activities also tended to remain well beyond the control of mainline denominations and beyond the established systems of ecclesiastical control that such denominations, or that state-churches, possessed. Indeed, it can be found that, at every stage during political struggle for self-determination and self-rule (swaraj), forces of anti-imperial nationalism within India received broad, substantial, and sympathetic support from Western missionaries. Such missionaries as Allan Hume (American Marathi Mission, who was one of the founders of the Indian National Congress) and Charles F. Andrews (SPG, Cambridge Mission to Delhi), as well as Verrier Elwin, J. N. Farquhar, E. Stanley Jones, Edward Thompson, and Amy Carmichael, were among the more prominent. Many of them were friends and supporters of Gandhi. These were, however, but a few of the hosts of other missionaries who, either openly or covertly, sympathized with or rendered aid to the cause of national independence for India. Numbers of sympathizers, even among Anglican missionaries, were much larger than have yet been counted.

After Independence in 1947, attempts to put down obstreperous resistance to national intrusions or interference in the lives of local tribal peoples caused many troubles, some of which led to continual insurrection and warfare. As a result, blame for mass conversion movements fell increasingly upon missionaries, especially foreign missionaries. Such blame tended to be accompanied by charges that all conversions had been forced and that crude inducements, such as food, health benefits, and literacy, were used to bribe hapless people who were already desperate and disadvantaged. Reactionary forces from within the larger dominant societies within both India and Pakistan made conversion of any kind, much less conversion to Christianity, into a political issue, if not a public offense. Thus, just as it was a policy under the Raj, from Company times into the 1930s and 1940s, to intern and expel "alien" missionaries on grounds of their being a risk to internal security, so it has been a policy in the years since 1947 for governments to look with suspicion upon all missionaries. As a result, numbers of foreign missionaries rapidly dwindled, until they are now almost entirely gone. At the same time, however, thousands of indigenous missionaries have arisen to take the places of the departed foreign missionaries.

The last but most important of all reasons not to conflate or confuse Christian missions with Western colonialism rests, very self-evidently, in the essential participation, power, and presence of India's own Christians. While deeply influenced by Roman Catholics and Evangelicals, substantial numbers of Thomas Christians never submitted to domination. Moreover, one can never overlook the fact that among all Christian missionaries who worked in India, it was the Indian Christians, those who served as "indigenous" or "native" missionaries — for example, catechists, pastors, teachers, Bible-women, and such — who did most of the work and who accomplished most of the truly significant results. India's own Christian leaders always far outnumbered those who came from abroad and made by far the greatest overall impact within societies of India. Thus, while Europeans provided much useful support, especially in matters institutional and intellectual, there never was any major movement of conversion, certainly no mass movement, in which the primary impetus was not Indian.

CHAPTER THREE

First European Missionaries on Sanskrit Grammar

IWONA MILEWSKA

Purusasya vag rasah.
[The essence of man is speech.]

Thus says the *Chandogya Upanisad* (I: 1, 2). If we follow this statement, we must agree that the meeting between people from any unknown, discovered, or rediscovered culture is, or should be, based on the knowledge and understanding of language. Language is, after all, the basic tool of expression and communication among human beings.

The Sanskrit language and its literature was first discovered by Europeans in the time of Alexander the Great. Yet it was not until the first European missionaries came to India that Sanskrit was rediscovered and described in a detailed way. It took Europeans a long time to find teachers who were willing to share their knowledge of Sanskrit. That being so, the European way toward understanding Sanskrit was not an easy one and was complicated by the special character of this sacred language. For ages, "foreigners" were not allowed to even hear about Sanskrit. They were treated as barbarians *(mleccha);* and most of the Brahmans did not want to teach them Sanskrit. However, the Europeans were initially more interested in languages spoken by local people, such as Marathi or Tamil. Only later, after reflection, did they become interested in trying to deal with Sanskrit: the language of the sacred texts of the Indian people, the language of religion and culture, the language used by limited circles of upper classes in Indian society, and the language that was one of the main keys to understanding India. Quite rapidly Europeans, and especially missionaries, realized that the knowledge of Sanskrit would be as indispensable as the knowledge of modern languages for any good understanding of the Indian people and for purposes of communication rather than confrontation.

The first European missionaries, from Franciscan and Dominican orders, reached India in the sixteenth century. Yet the first descriptions of Sanskrit came from the Jesuit missionaries who reached India later, at the turn of six- teenth and the seventeenth century. The person who noticed the similarities between Indian and European languages was the English Jesuit, Thomas Stephens (Stevens) (1549-1619). He came to Goa in 1579. In a letter to his brother, written on 24 October 1583 in Latin, he observed: *Linguae harum regionum sunt permultae. Pronunciationem habent non invenustam et compositione latinae grecaeque similem; phrases et constructiones plane mirabiles. Literae syllabarum vim habent, quae toties variantur quoties consonantes cum vocalibus, vel mutae cum liquidis combinari possunt.* [There are many languages used in these countries. Their speech is not without charm; in composition it resembles Latin and Greek; phrases and construc- tions are worthy of our respect. The letters signify syllables, and they have as many shapes as there are possible combinations of consonants with vowels.][1] His observation is not as well known as that made by a Welshman, William Jones. In his famous third "Anniversary Discourse," presented at the meeting of Asiatic Society of Bengal on 2 February 1786, he announced that he had found a similarity between Sanskrit, Greek, Latin, German, Celtic, and Per- sian languages. His words were to become the basis for studies in comparative linguistics. Jones said:

> The Sanskrit language, whatever be its antiquity, is of a wonderful struc- ture; more perfect than the Greek, more copious than the Latin, and more exquisitely refined than either, yet bearing to both of them a stronger affinity, both in the roots of verbs and in the forms of gram- mar, than could possibly have been produced by accident; so strong in- deed, that no philologist could examine them all three, without believ- ing them to have sprung from some common source, which, perhaps, no longer exists: there is a similar reason, though not quite so forcible, for supposing that both the Gothick and the Celtick, though blended with a very different idiom, had the same origin with the Sanskrit; and the old Persian might be added to the same family, if this were the place for discussing any question concerning the antiquities of Persia.[2]

1. J. C. Muller, "Recherches sur les premieres grammaires manuscrites du sanscrit," *Bulletin d'Etudes Indiennes* 3 (1985): 125.
2. F. Edgerton, "Sir William Jones," in *Portraits of Linguists: A Biographical Source*

What is often now forgotten is the fact that Jones's observation was made two hundred years after Thomas Stephens sent his letter to France. This was not the first, nor the last, time when ideas would have to wait a long time before being rediscovered and then made available to the broader public.

Another important figure in the history of the European endeavor to know Sanskrit was an Italian Jesuit, Roberto de Nobili (1577-1656). Active in the region of Pondicherry about 1620, he left two fundamental books to posterity: *Informatio de quibusdam moribus nationis indica* [Information about some customs of the Indian nation], written in 1613 and only republished in 1972; and *Narratio fundamentorum quibus Madurensis Missionis institutum caeptum est et hucusque consistit* [The lecture about the basic rules of Madure Mission], written in 1618-19, republished in 1971.[3] In these works, he describes the traditional Indian division of branches of science; and, in first place among these, he mentions grammar — *Siabda Siastram*. De Nobili, in his books, includes several citations in Sanskrit. His was a very particular form of behavior while in India. He tried to be "an Indian among the Indians," to speak local languages, to wear native clothes, to live in an Indian way, and to be an Indian sage *(rishi,* or *sanyasin)* rather than an European priest. For this de Nobili was strongly criticized. Yet, while attacked by his superiors, it is he who is still often called "the first European Sanskrit scholar."[4]

The European who first truly described Sanskrit in a detailed way, however, was Father Heinrich Roth (1620-68). Also a Jesuit, he spent ten years in Goa and Agra, between 1650 and 1660. His grammar, written in Latin most probably between 1660 and 1662, was produced after six years of learning Sanskrit from local pandits. It is the first-known, complete European grammar covering all major grammatical topics. It remained for many years in manuscript form only and was published finally in 1988 by A. Camps.[5] Father Roth was also the person who gave five plates with the Sanskrit alphabet to

---

Book for the History of Western Linguistics, 1746-1963, edited by Thomas A. Sebeok (London, 1966), 1:5-6.

3. Edited by S. Rajamanickam as *Adaptation* in a translation of J. Pujo (Palayamkottai, 1971) and as *On Indian Customs* in a translation of the editor (Palayamkottai, 1972).

4. W. Halbfass, *India and Europe: An Essay in Philosophical Understanding* (Delhi, 1990), pp. 38-43.

5. H. Roth, "Grammatica linguae Sanscretanae Brachmanum Indiae Orientalis, 1660-1662," in *The Sanskrit Grammar and Manuscript of Father Heinrich Roth S.J. (1620-1668),* facsimile edition of Biblioteka Nazionale, Rome, MSS.OR. 171 and 172 with an introduction by A. Camps and J. C. Muller (Leiden, 1988).

Athanasius Kircher, the author of *China Illustrata,* printed in Amsterdam in 1667. This was, most probably, the first European publication of the *nagari* alphabet. Roth's grammar, entitled *Grammatica linguae Sanscretanae Brachmanum Indiae Orientalist* [The grammar of the Sanscrit language of the Brahmans of East India] consists of five chapters: *De Ortographia, De Declinationibus Nominum, De Coniugationibus Verborum, De Verbalibus seu krdamtah,* and *De syntaxi huius Linguae.* It is enlarged by a short *Appendix ad universam grammaticam.*

Chapter 1 lists and describes the sounds of Sanskrit — namely, the vocals and consonants, grouped according to the place of articulation. This shows the most common ligatures and depicts rules of external and internal *sandhi,* giving samples for various rules. It ends with the definitions of Indian technical grammatical terms.

Chapter 2 describes paradigms of nouns, adjectives, and pronouns. It gives the division for vowel and consonant declinations and the list of possible case-endings. It also describes numerals and gives details about the rules of their derivation.

Chapter 3 presents Sanskrit verbs. It speaks about roots, about *parasmaipadam* and *atmanepadam,* about ten classes, about the system of tenses, moods, and endings and gives paradigms, with ten main classes in indicative, optative, imperative, and imperfect. It also describes *passivum, intensivum, denominativum, desiderativum,* and *causativum* and enlists some forms described as anomalies.

Chapter 4 gives information about participles, infinitives, gerunds, and other forms.

Chapter 5 discusses syntax and, in an appendix, describes adverbs. It presents functions of cases and explains the system of compounds (*avyayibhava, tatpurusa, dvandva, bahuvrihi, karmadharaya* and *dvigu* being discussed).

The appendix of this grammar gives thirty-seven kinds of metric stanzas together with examples. Roth added two Sanskrit manuscripts to his grammar. These were: *Pancatattvaprakaāa* of Venidatta and *Vedantasara* of Sadananda.

The content of Roth's grammar makes it highly probable that Roth's teacher was using the Sanskrit grammar entitled *Sarasvata Vyakarana* by Anubhuti Svarupacarya. It is possible that Roth may also have known the work of Vopadeva from the thirteenth-century version entitled *Mugdhabodha.*[6]

---

6. R. Hauschild, "Zum Inhalt der drei Handschriften Roths," *Zeitschrift für Missionwissenschaft und Religionswissenschaft* 53 (1969): 195-202.

When one looks closely at Roth's grammar and compares it with descriptive grammars written by Europeans in later years, what is striking is the completeness of his description. In most of later European descriptive grammars we find the same choice of grammatical topics, arranged in a very similar or identical order, the same choice of examples, and a very similar method of presentation. Roth's grammar, however, is a Sanskrit grammar. It is based on Indian sources but arranged in a way that would, in our times, be characteristic for descriptive grammars written for classical European languages like Greek and Latin. These grammars were then used for teaching purposes. Such a method of presentation was to be the dominant feature of most of the Sanskrit grammars prepared by Europeans from that time onward. This is so, even if it was most probably not Roth's grammar that established the canon for such works. His descriptive approach was to remain unknown for nearly three hundred years. In the form of a manuscript, it has had to await rediscovery in the late twentieth century.

In the seventeenth and eighteenth centuries Europeans acquired much more information about India and Sanskrit. Many missionaries went to India, and many of them, as a side interest, avidly studied languages. The Dutch missionary Abraham Roger (d. 1649), who was in India between 1630 and 1647, left a work entitled *Open Deure tot het verborgen Heydendom* [The open door to the hidden paganism]. This was published in 1651 in Leiden. In it he included the translation of *Trisataka* by Bhartrhari. Another renowned missionary scholar was the German Pietist from Halle, Benjamin Schulze (d. 1760). He, according to R. Hauschild, is the author of an unpublished manuscript "Grammatica Granthamica seu Samscridamica."[7]

A French Jesuit, J. F. Pons (1688-1752), went to India in 1726 and spent most of his time in Bengal. There he gathered a huge collection of Sanskrit manuscripts and sent 168 of them to the Bibliotheque Royale in Paris in 1733. Number 13 in this collection is a priceless manuscript (since all other manuscripts have their prices mentioned), which is probably the work of Pons himself. This is a Sanskrit grammar entitled "Rudiments de la Langue Samskretane en Latin." The work was most probably the major source of information about Sanskrit for such famous later linguists as A. L. Chezy (1733-1832) and Friedrich Schlegel (1772-1829).[8]

According to J. C. Muller, there is one more work on Sanskrit grammar, perhaps also written by Pons, entitled, "Codex chartaceus quo continentur

7. R. Hauschild, "Notes on the Content of the Three Manuscripts of Heinrich Roth," in *Sanskrit Grammar and Manuscripts of Father Heinrich Roth S.J.*, p. 13.
8. Muller, "Recherches," p. 135.

Grammatica et dictionarium linguae samscretanicae."[9] Written in Bengali characters, it consists of five chapters:

Chapter 1, *De litteris,* has different arrangements of the alphabet as proposed by Indian grammarians, a division of sounds into groups according to the place of articulation, vowel gradation, and *sandhi.*

Chapter 2, *De pronominibus,* has lists of pronouns, their paradigms, and descriptions of their functions.

Chapter 3, *De declinatione nominum,* contains general rules and forty-six paradigms of declination.

Chapter 4, *De conjugatione verborum,* generally describes verbs. It gives lists of endings, discusses moods and system of tenses, augments, infixes, and secondary verb roots. It also gives the list of verb roots according to the classification of Vopadeva.

Chapter 5, *Paradigma conjugationis primitivum,* contains the complete paradigm of the root *kr* and an incomplete one of *bhu.*

In its choice of topics and the order of presentation, this grammar is similar but not as complex as the work done by Heinrich Roth. It was most probably based on Vopadeva's *Mugdhabodha.* J. F. Pons was also the author of part of the letters edited by J. B. Halde in a series entitled *"Lettres edifiantes et curieuses."* This series is rich in information concerning India. In one of the letters, in 1740, Pons wrote:

> La grammaire des brahmanes peut etre mise au rang des plus belles science; jamais l'analyse et la synthese ne furent plus heureusement employees que dans les ouvrages grammaticaux de la langue samskrt ou samskroutan. Il me parait que cette langue, admirable par son harmonie, son abondance et son energie, etait autrefois la langue vivante dans les pays habites par les premiers brahmanes.[10]

J. E. Hanxleden (1681-1732) was another Jesuit whose stay in southern India, in Malabar from 1699 to 1732, bore fruit in a work on Sanskrit grammar. Information about his grammar, however, came from works of other authors, who mention Hanxleden's name and ascribe different titles to his grammar (e.g., "Grammatica Granthamia seu Samscrdumica," "Grammatica Grando-

---

9. Jean Filliozat gives the title of this manuscript as "Grammatica sanscritica cui adjunctam est Dictionarium Amara Kocha inscriptum, latine partim interpretatum auctore incerto. Voces sanskriticae litteris Bengalicis (non Devanagaricis) exaratae sunt" in his article "Une grammaire sanscrite du XVIIIe siecle et les debuts de l'indianisme en France," in *Laghu-Prabandhah: Choix d'articles d'indologie* (Leiden, 1977), p. 278.

10. Muller, "Recherches," p. 134.

nica," or "Sidharubam seu grammatica samscredamica"). The manuscript has
not been found, nor precisely described.[11]

It is very probable that Hanxleden's grammar was the basis for the work
that, until not a long ago, was treated as the oldest European work dealing
with Sanskrit grammar, namely, the *Sidharubam seu Grammatica Samscridamica. Cui accedit Dissertatio historico-critica in linguam Samscridamicam,
vulgo Samscret dictam.*[12] The author of this work was a Carmelite of Croatian
origin named Paulinus a Sancto Bartholomaeo (1748-1806), also known as
Filip Vesdin or J. Ph. Wessdin.[13] He was in India between 1776 and 1789,
mainly in Kerala. His first Indian language was Malayalam. Perhaps this may
explain his use of the Grantha alphabet in a description of Sanskrit. His work
includes a long general introduction concerning Sanskrit *Dissertatio
historico-critica in linguam Samscridamicam.* In this he discussed the position
and role of Sanskrit in India and compared it with that of Latin in Europe. In
1804 Paulinus published an enlarged version of this grammar entitled
Vyacarana seu locupletissima Samscridamicae linguae institutio. Neither of
these works is in fact a grammar; they are theoretical introductions to grammatical topics. Paulinus wrote many other books about Indian religions, culture, geography and history.[14] He strongly criticized his predecessors and
contemporary researchers; and he was criticized by them. One of his critics
was Anquetil du Perron, who, about one of Paulinus books, wrote:

> This passage proves that the Missionary has not read the theological and
> philosophical books composed by the Indians, and that he probably did
> not know more Sanskrit than from what he found in the dictionaries of

11. As M. Winternitz (*A History of Indian Literature* [Delhi, 1981], 1:7) describes
"Grammatica Granthamia seu Samscrdumica," it looks strikingly similar to the work by
Benjamin Schulze mentioned above; "Grammatica Grandonica" or "Sidharubam seu
grammatica samscredamica" are the titles ascribed to it by Muller ("Recherches," p. 132).

12. Paulinus a Sancto Bartholomaeo, "Sidharubam seu grammatica samscridamica
cui accedit dissertatio historico-critica in linguam samscridamicam vulgo Samscret
dictam in qua huius linguae existentia, origo, praestantia, antiquitas, extensio, maternitas
ostenditur, libri aliqui ea exarati critice recensentur, et simul aliquae antiquissimae
gentilium orationes liturgicae paucis attinguntur et explicantur," in L. Rocher, *Paulinus
Bartholomaeo a Sancto, Dissertation on the Sanskrit Language: A reprint of the original Latin
text of 1790, together with an introductory article, a complete English translation, and an index of sources by Ludo Rocher* (Amsterdam, 1977).

13. M. Jauk-Pinhak, "Some Notes on the Pioneer Indologist Filip Vesdin (Paulinus a
Sancto Bartholomaeo)," *Indologica Taurinensia* 12 (1987): 129-37.

14. The specification of these works is in the introduction to Rocher, "*Paulinus,*" pp.
ix-xi.

the Propaganda, translated into some European language, and in the works of his confreres which have been deposited in the library.[15]

He was also criticized by the British for his "incompetence" and in response he called them "The English in Calcutta."

The knowledge and understanding of Sanskrit among Europeans was far from perfect in these times. Paulinus, in his "Sidharubam," gathered the names that were used for Sanskrit by many different researchers, and even this list shows how far from precise Europeans were. Names given by Paulinus were as follows: Hanscret, Sanscroot, Samscroustam, Samscroudam, Samskretam, Samscretan, Sanscreet, Grandon, Samscret, Sanscrit, Shanscrit, Samscrit, Samskrdam, Samscrit, Samscredam.[16]

For a long time, there was a "European" way of coming to knowledge and understanding of Sanskrit. The first attempts at this had, however, already been made, and the period between 1660 and 1790 left some valuable grammars of Sanskrit by European missionaries.

If we try to summarize and identify the main characteristics of the first European descriptions of Sanskrit grammar, we must acknowledge that:

> All the grammars described above were prepared with the help of Indian pandits. It was they who were the major sources of information for European missionaries, and without them none of these works could have been accomplished.
>
> All were most probably based on secondary grammars and commentaries to major Indian Sanskrit grammars. However, they came from the Panninean tradition of grammar (they were not based directly on works of *Panini* or *Patañjali,* and so forth, but upon secondary grammars such as Vopadeva's and *Anubhuti Svarupacarya*).
>
> All were repreprared or rearranged by European missionaries, who tried to apply to them European methods of descriptive grammars used for classical European languages (Latin, Greek).
>
> None followed Indian ways of presentation.
>
> All were written in Latin.

The final result was a Sanskrit essence in a European form.

---

15. Rocher, *"Paulinus,"* p. xiii.
16. Rocher, *"Paulinus,"* pp. 81-82.

CHAPTER FOUR

Country Priests, Catechists, and Schoolmasters as Cultural, Religious, and Social Middlemen in the Context of the Tranquebar Mission

HEIKE LIEBAU

From 1705 until the beginning of the nineteenth century the Danish-Halle Mission, better known as the Tranquebar Mission after the main locality of their activity, sent fifty-six missionaries from Europe to the Coromandel Coast of India.[1] During this time the Tranquebar Mission employed approximately five hundred Indians, including at least nine ordained country priests,[2] and more than two hundred catechists, schoolteachers, and assistants.

1. On 29 November 1705 Bartholomäus Ziegenbalg (1682-1719) and Heinrich Pluetschau (1677-1747) left Copenhagen to start mission work in India. See Arno Lehmann, *Alte Briefe aus Indien* [hereafter *AB*] (Berlin, 1957), p. 33; letter by Ziegenbalg, Tranquebar, 5 September 1706 to v.d. Linde. August Friedrich Caemmerer (1767-1837) arrived in Tranquebar on 14 May 1791. See *Neuere Geschichte der Evangelischen Missions-Anstalten zur Bekehrung der Heiden in Ostindien*, vol. 1 (Halle, 1776); vol. 6 (Halle, 1825) [hereafter *NHB*], 41st. Stueck [hereafter St.], p. 405. He died in 1837, the last missionary of the Tranquebar Mission. See Arno Lehmann, *Es begann in Tranquebar* (Berlin, 1956), p. 305.

2. Lehmann (*Es begann*, p. 261) mentions fourteen ordained country priests within the Tranquebar Mission but only six by name. Their names and dates of ordination are: Aaron

An article based on my contribution at the 14th European Conference on Modern South Asian Studies in Copenhagen was published in 1998: Heike Liebau, "Missionary Encounters: Interaction between Indian Mission Servants, European Missionaries and Local Populations in 18th Century South India" in *Essays on South Asian Society, Culture and Politics II*, edited by Bernt Glatzer (Berlin, 1998).

This chapter deals with this special group of South Indian Christians. The first section characterizes these "national" workers, describes the different fields of work, and examines the recruitment policy of the Tranquebar Mission. On the assumption that the identity of these intermediaries changed within the context of altering relations, connections, subordinations, and loyalties, the second section will be concerned with changes in the social position of local mission agents within the mission context, and in their behavior towards different classes within the population. One aspect is how converts looked for associations between the new faith and elements of local tradition that would enable them to become Christians, which would be acceptable to the European missionaries and, at the same time, enable them to remain Indians in the eyes of the local population. Against this background, the third section will deal with the role of Indians as assistants and informants to German missionaries in eighteenth-century southeast India.

The questions that must be borne in mind are: Who were the Indians that acted as informants? What kind of dialogue took place? Who dominated this dialogue? How did the Indians reflect their own society?

Establishment of the Mission, Fields of Work, and Recruitment Policy

After a plan to found a mission station in Africa failed, the Danish king, Friedrich IV (1671-1730), had the idea of opening a mission station in the territory of the Danish trade colony around Tranquebar (Tarankampati).[3] The Danish court priest, Franz Julius Lütkens (1650-1712), found the first two missionaries, Bartholomäus Ziegenbalg and Heinrich Plütschau. Both were former students of the Francke Foundations in Halle.[4] After their ordination as priests in Copenhagen, on 11 November 1705[5] they left for India and reached Tranquebar on 9 July 1706.[6]

(1733), Diogo (1741), Ambrosius (1749), Philipp (Pulleimuttu) (1772), Rajappen (1778), Sattiananden (1790), Abraham (?), Wedanayagam (? d. 1812), and Adeikalam (ca. 1812).

    3. For names of Indian persons and places, I adopt the spelling of the mission records. Where possible the modern common version or the Tamil spelling is given in parentheses.

    4. For the history of the Francke Foundations see August Hermann Francke, *Segensvolle Fußstapfen: Geschichte der Entstehung der Halleschen Anstalten von August Hermann Francke erzählt* (Giessen, 1994).

    5. *AB*, p. 33, letter from Tranquebar to v.d. Linde, 5 September 1706.

    6. *Der Königlich-Dänischen Missionairen aus Ost-Indien eingesandte Ausführliche*

Tranquebar and the surrounding territories had been a Danish colony since 1620, when the Danish admiral, Ove Gedde (1594-1660), and the *nāyak* Ragunātha (1600-1633) of Thanjāvur signed a treaty according to which the Danes were permitted to build a fort in Tranquebar.[7] When the Danish-Halle Mission began its work, there were approximately eighteen thousand people living in Tranquebar — Hindus, Muslims, and (Catholic) Christians.[8]

For the first few years the missionaries limited their activities to the territory of the Danish East India Company. As early as 1709, however, they founded a mission garden in Poraiyar near Tranquebar. In 1728 the missionary Benjamin Schultze (1689-1760) left Tranquebar and established a new mission in Madras, which came under the guidance of the Society for Promoting Christian Knowledge in London.[9] Until 1753 the Raja of Thanjāvur prohibited European missionaries from propagating Christianity in his territory. After that date Christian Friedrich Schwartz (1726-98) established mission stations on this territory in Thanjāvur, as well as on the territory of the Nawab of Carnatic in Tiruchchirāppalli.

European missionaries depended on local assistants to organize missionary work among the South Indian population. These people not only played an essential role with regard to religious activities but, living with the missionaries, often had enormous influence on missionary understandings of local circumstances. The missionaries used various terms to describe this group: "workers of the nation" *(Arbeiter der Nation)*, "national assistants" *(Nationalhelfer)*, "national workers" *(Nationalarbeiter)*, or "native assistants" or "helpers" *(eingeborene Helfer)*.[10]

The group of "national workers" included accountants, bookbinders, printers, washermen, and cooks, as well as country priests, catechists, school-

---

Berichte, Halle 1710-1760 (Hallesche Berichte) [hereafter *HB*], 6th *Continuation* (part of the *Hallesche Berichte* [hereafter *Cont.*]), p. 218; letter from Tranquebar, 25 September 1706; *AB*, p. 39.

7. The treaty is published in Eberhard Schmitt, ed., *Wirtschaft und Handel der Kolonialreiche. Dokumente zur Geschichte der europäischen Expansion* (Muenchen, 1988); or *Tarangampadi*, occasional paper brought out in honor of the visit of His Excellency Mr. Poul Schlueter, the Prime Minister of Denmark and Mrs. Lisbeth Schlueter on the occasion of their visit to Dansborg Museum, Tarangampadi, on 17 January 1987.

8. *AB*, p. 35, letter 5 September 1706. See also, Stephan Diller, *Tranquebar — die Stadt an der Brandung: Dänischer Handelsstützpunkt, Kronkolonie und europäischer Freihandelsplatz (1620-1845)* (Bamberg, 1993), p. 20. He says that the number of inhabitants in Tranquebar and the surrounding villages grew from 7,557 in 1702 to 20,000 during the eighteenth century.

9. *HB*, 26th *Cont.*, Vorrede §XI.

10. The term nation *(Nation)* stood for the Tamil people *(Das Volk der Tamuler)*.

teachers, and other assistants. While the first group, the so-called "workers in the external institutions" *(Arbeiter in den äußeren Anstalten)*[11] did not play a large role in mission reports, there are detailed descriptions of the second group, the so-called "workers of the word" *(Arbeiter am Wort)*,[12] such as country priests, catechists, schoolteachers, and assistants. This second group numbered more than two hundred during the 150 years of Tranquebar Mission activities. My interest is concentrated on these individuals because of their position within the mission hierarchy and because of their own activities.

A few words are necessary about the sources available in various, mainly European, archives.[13] The question is whether there are authentic (genuine) documents produced by native agents or merely texts written by European missionaries about their native helpers. The volume of information on local mission agents differs from missionary society to society. With regard to the Tranquebar Mission the information, including authentic documents, is fairly comprehensive. First of all, there are statistical surveys on the number of native mission workers, classified according to their locality and working position. Second, parts of the monthly working reports presented by country priests, catechists, and teachers were translated by the missionaries and printed in "Der Königlich-Dänischen Missionarien aus Ost-Indien eingesandter ausführlichen Berichten erster Theil . . . bis siebenter Theil"[14] and "Neuere Geschichte der Evangelischen Missions-Anstalten zur Bekehrung der Heiden in Ostindien."[15] Several original manuscripts of working reports, written on palm leaves, are deposited in Copenhagen and in London.[16] The archives also contain letters written by local catechists and country priests. Missionary reports, diaries, and letters reveal a considerable amount about their local assistants. Detailed life stories of native individuals are given, especially on the occasion of ordination or death. In January 1802 the *dubash* Daniel Pullei (1740-1802), who had very close connections with the Tranquebar Mission, died. We would not know so much about this important person, who for many years had acted as a language

---

11. *HB*, 33rd *Cont.*, p. 870, "Von den Anstalten der Mission, und von derselben Arbeitern überhaupt."

12. *HB*, 33rd *Cont.*, p. 870, "Von den Anstalten der Mission, und von derselben Arbeitern überhaupt."

13. Archives of the Francke Foundations (Archiv der Franckeschen Stiftungen, Halle); National Archives (Rigsarkivet, Copenhagen), Society for Promoting Christian Knowledge.

14. *HB*, Halle, 1710-60.

15. *NHB*, Halle 1/1 1770–8/95 1848.

16. For these sources see Daniel Jeyaraj, *Inkulturation in Tranquebar: Der Beitrag der frühen dänisch-halleschen Mission zum Werden einer indisch-einheimischen Kirche (1706-1730)* (Erlangen, 1996), pp. 25-29.

teacher for several missionaries, had the missionary Christoph Samuel John (1747-1813) not asked him to relate his life story. John wrote down the story that was then printed after Daniel Pullei's death.[17]

Native agents were chosen by the missionaries. There was a special need for language teachers and translators. In the fifth *Continuation of the Hallesche Berichte* we find the first statistics on local workers, which included schoolmasters, assistants, and catechists.[18]

Various methods of recruitment were employed. There were a number of people who were directly descended from Hindu families and deeply rooted in traditions of local Indian religious beliefs, especially in the early days of missionary activity. Working as language teachers or translators, they often remained Hindus. Others, like the missionaries, were active in propagating Christianity, having converted to the new religion. They were educated in one of the mission schools for which missionaries chose the candidates according to their ability, piety, and caste affiliation. A change of religion for these people not only was often synonymous with the loss of their social environment (extended family, village community, affiliation to a certain caste) but, at the same time, would obviously lead to a break with important elements of their previous everyday life (i.e., naming within Indian traditions, eating habits, clothes, and festivals). For this reason missionaries felt a special responsibility for the material welfare of their native assistants.

A second group from which native agents were recruited were Roman Catholic families.[19] It is well known that a Christian population existed in Tranquebar before the arrival of the Lutheran missionaries.[20] Although no exact figures exist on the number of Catholics who converted to Protestant Christianity,[21] it may be assumed that the interest of local Catholics in com-

17. *Archiv der Franckeschen Stiftungen/Halle, Missionsarchiv (Missionary Archives; part of the Archives of the Francke Foundations in Halle)* [hereafter AFrSt, MA], I K 5:16, "Kurzer Lebenslauf des Daniel Pullei, Erster Königl. Gouvernements Dolmetscher welcher im Schwarzen Gericht und Vorsteher der Christl. Missions Gemeine in Tranquebar." See also *NHB*, 62nd St., pp. 166-81.

18. *HB*, 5th *Cont.*, pp. 185-216.

19. In a letter of 1728 Christian Friedrich Pressier (1697-1738) only mentioned Roman Catholics who had changed their faith and converted to the Lutherans, but not Hindus or Muslims (*HB*, 27th *Cont.*, p. 220).

20. Hugald Grafe, "The Relation between the Tranquebar Lutherans and the Tanjore Catholics in the First Half of the Eighteenth Century," *Indian Church and History Review* (1967): 41-58.

21. An exception to this is the Thanjāvur congregation with statistics on the number of Roman Catholic converts. From 1773 to 1800 in Thanjāvur 808 Roman Catholics converted to the Lutheran faith (*NHB*, 59th St., p. 944).

municating with the new Christians in their region was enormous. With the employment of the catechist Rajanaikken (1700-1770) at Thanjāvur in 1728[22] and with the later opening up of Thanjāvur to foreign missionaries in 1753,[23] systematic efforts to reach and convert Catholics began. As adherents to Catholicism they already possessed knowledge of Christianity. Their meetings with Tranquebar missionaries offered them a new approach to Christian belief that involved contradictions to their former ideas of Christian faith. Thus, although these people did not "change" their religion, "only" their denominational affiliation within the same religion, consequences were often painful. Rajanaikken, who was a descendant of a Roman Catholic family, worked as a catechist mainly among Roman Catholic Christians. At the same time, however, he and his family suffered persecution and violence from Roman Catholics.[24]

The third group of native agents recruited consisted of Protestant Christians of the second and subsequent generations who had been specially trained for some task from the time when they entered school. In time this group became more and more significant. The missionaries stressed that, first of all, members of Protestant Christian families had to become catechists or be ordained.[25] Having been in missionary service, Indian families wanted their children to grow up in the same tradition. Children took part in mission life at an early age. In 1748, Curupadam, the son of the first country priest, Aaron (1698-1745), became an urban catechist in Tranquebar.[26] Two sons of the catechist Matthaeus (1732–ca. 1805), Arulappen (ca. 1752–1805) and Christian, also became catechists.[27] In a few cases one can trace the development of a catechist family over two or more generations.

Corresponding to the personal position that each native agent occupied within the hierarchy, each also had a clear and strict sphere of responsibilities and duties. First of all, there were common duties for each post. In addition to these general responsibilities, each native agent had to undertake special duties that depended on his place of work, "his" own congregation, and his own individual abilities. The "native workers" were divided into ordained country

22. *HB*, 28th *Cont.*, p. 316.

23. In 1753 Johann Christian Wiedebrock (missionary from 1736 to 1767 in Tranquebar) held the first public service in Thanjāvur (*HB*, 80th *Cont.*, Halle 1756, p. 1212).

24. *HB*, 26th *Cont.*, p. 810.

25. *HB*, 33th *Cont.*, p. 881, Ausführlicher Bericht von der gegenwärtigen Verfassung des Evangelischen Missions-Wercks zu Trankenbar. Anno MDCCXXXII.

26. *HB*, 69th *Cont.*, Vorrede.

27. *NHB*, 58th St., pp. 852-57.

priests (or pastors), different types of catechists, schoolteachers, prayer leaders, and assistants.

The ordained country (pastoral) priests were specially trained to perform religious duties and ceremonies in their region of work. They had full religious responsibility for their congregations such as preaching in churches and celebrating Holy Communion. Country priests were also allowed to baptize new local converts after examining them. In special circumstances, persons could be baptized without examination as in the case of the old or the sick, if they wished to become Christians just before they died. In such cases, baptism could also be performed by a catechist or even by an assistant.[28]

The procedure for selection from a small group of good candidates was very rigorous and searching. After each candidate had been examined, the best, or the most suitable of them, would be elected by a secret vote. Catechists were trained at a special school founded in 1716.[29] A catechist was to be a person who should be grateful to God. He should discharge his duties out of love for God, that is, he was expected to carry out his duties properly. His behavior was expected to be exemplary because he would be observed by Christians and non-Christians alike. He should work continually among the Indian people in his locality. He should not quarrel with Christians or "heathens" but should talk to everybody in a consistently peaceful and modest way.[30]

There were different types of catechists depending on their assigned places of work, whether as a urban catechist *(Stadtkatechet)* or as rural catechist *(Landkatechet)*; and, according to their position and rank within the mission hierarchy, whether as a "high catechist" *(Oberkatechet)* or a "low catechist" *(Unterkatechet)*. A catechist had to perform many different functions.[31] A variety of practical tasks were involved in looking after local Christians and in seeking the conversion of non-Christians. Each catechist was responsible for the population of a particular locality. The territorial sphere of missionary activity was thus divided into several *Missionskreise* (mission districts). In 1716 the following congregations are mentioned: the Tamil urban congregation in Tranquebar, the Portuguese urban congregation in Tranquebar, and the rural congregations in the Mayavaram, Thanjāvur, Madevipatnam, and Marava dis-

28. On 8 July 1753 the assistant Nattam baptized a man who was terminally ill (*HB*, 80th *Cont.*, p. 1137). Three years later the catechist Muttu (?-1777) baptized a widow (*HB*, 85th *Cont.*, p. 29).
29. *HB*, 13th *Cont.*, p. 22.
30. For the characteristics of a catechist, see *HB*, 26th *Cont.*, pp. 1-3.
31. *HB*, 26th *Cont.*, pp. 1-3.

tricts.[32] Around 1740 the congregation of the Marava district was divided into the Tiruppalātturai and Kumbakkonam congregations.[33]

Catechists had a pastoral duty to look after the Christians within their territory. They had to go to wherever Christians were living and then try to care for them, solve problems, settle quarrels, end disagreements, and discipline or punish offenders. To practice the Christian faith, a catechist had to hold regular prayer hours in his house and repeat the catechism every morning and evening. Every Sunday he had to pray with the whole congregation and read parts of the Bible to them. A catechist was authorized to teach Christian children, helping them to attain literacy and giving instruction both to converts and to people who wanted to consider becoming Christians. A newborn child of Christian parents had to be brought to Tranquebar in order to be baptized by the missionaries. Only if the child's life was in danger were the catechists allowed to perform baptism themselves. The responsibility of a catechist for his congregation also covered the social and religious practices of local Christians. He had to make sure that Christians did not partake in "heathen" religious ceremonies, such as smearing their bodies with holy ashes or taking part in Hindu *yatras*. If Christians left their territory as a social protest, the catechist had to follow them and persuade them to return to their houses. Sattianaden (1783-1815) had to comply with the following regulations: If someone wanted to be converted, he was not authorized to promise them anything but was to inform the missionaries about that person's wishes. If Roman Catholics talked to him, he could tell them about the "only truth" but was not to pursue them, since Catholics did not pursue Lutherans in order to convert them.[34]

Rajanaikken, the Thanjāvur catechist, had the following special tasks: If a member of the Roman Catholic Church were to announce his intention of converting to Lutheranism, he had to be given time to think it over. Rajanaikken was requested to write down information, on palm-leaf *(ōlai)* pages, about the person and their reasons for wishing to change from one religious community to the other, and he was then to send it to the missionaries for further investigation. If, in Rajanaikken's opinion, somebody seemed suitable to be a catechist, he was to offer his opinion to the missionaries but to make no promises.[35]

Before a native mission worker could become a catechist, he often had to

---

32. *HB*, 33rd *Cont.*, p. 870; *Archiv der Franckeschen Stiftungen/Halle* [hereafter *AFrSt*], 2 a 2:7.

33. *HB*, 58th *Cont.*, p. 1513.

34. *HB*, 26th *Cont.*, pp. 1-3.

35. *HB*, 26th *Cont.*, p. 15.

have gained experience as a schoolteacher or as an assistant.[36] Assistants were assigned to catechists, to country priests, or to missionaries, in order to take over various special, particularly practical, tasks.

Positions Occupied by National Workers
within the Mission and within Local Society

In the period when the Tranquebar Mission was active, the number of Indian mission workers and assistants increased in proportion to the growing congregations in Tranquebar and the surrounding areas. While most of the work in Tranquebar itself could be carried out by resident European missionaries, for pastoral care or for reaching potential converts people in the rural areas, native workers were essential. The Tranquebar missionaries explained the necessity of incorporating local agents in the missionary service, stressing their superior knowledge of local languages, customs, and living conditions and, especially, the growing number of Christians in rural areas needing attention. To a certain extent political considerations prevented local European missionaries from expanding their own work beyond Tranquebar. The Tranquebar missionaries were, for example, not permitted to act in the territory of the Thanjāvur kingdom until the 1750s.[37]

The Tranquebar Mission was highly organized, functioning as a strongly defined hierarchical system. European missionaries had authority and control over the "national workers" whom they trained and then employed. In monthly written or verbal reports, each of the local mission workers gave a detailed description of what had happened in that worker's locality. After they had received new instructions from the missionaries, workers would once again leave Tranquebar for their work places. At first the missionaries, catechists, and assistants usually visited places together. Then the native agents were instructed how to look after the population of these villages. They would reside permanently in the district where they worked and periodically visit different villages to explain the "message" or "good news" (gospel) and Christian doctrines. Missionaries demanded, and expected, obedience of their local assistants; and, in cases of disobedience, they sometimes reacted with harsh punishment.

36. Lehmann, *Es begann*, p. 251.

37. In 1728 Rajanaikken became the catechist of the Thanjāvur region (*HB*, 26th *Cont.*, p. 12). European missionaries had started to visit Thanjāvur periodically from the 1750s (*HB*, 53rd *Cont.*, p. 1212). Christian Friedrich Schwartz began to live there permanently only in 1778.

The group of national workers did not form a homogeneous community. Country priests had authority over the catechists, while schoolmasters and assistants ranked below both priests and catechists. National workers, as employees, were financially dependent on the organized missionary institution to which they had committed themselves. How much they were paid depended on their position within the mission hierarchy. In 1725 Benjamin Schultze gave a detailed list of wages for all mission workers for that period. According to him a catechist received 136 Rthl. (Reichstaler, currency); a schoolmaster, 36 Rthl.; an accountant/writer *(kaṇakkappiḷḷai)*, 28 Rthl.; and a Telugu schoolmaster, 25 Rthl.[38] Usually, mission workers were paid in kind and in cash.[39]

Highly visible to the local population, native Indian mission workers acted on behalf of the European Christian mission. Sometimes they were accompanied by Europeans. Even country priests wore clothing, like a uniform, similar to that worn by the missionaries. They brought palm leaves and books for their teaching of the Christian faith. The native missionary workers had to manifest a certain authority toward the local people, on the one hand; but, on the other hand, they had to remain close enough to local people to be accepted by them, to be identified with them, and to win and hold their confidence. Attitudes of different social classes toward this special group of Indian workers depended on circumstances. For members of Christian congregations and individuals who sought conversion, Indian catechists and country priests represented an authority permanently in touch with the European missionaries at the main mission stations. Every native agent acted upon special instructions, each according to his individual abilities and to conditions of the field in which he was working. Catechists were in charge of the Christian congregations and peoples living in their separate villages. They were permitted to exercise discipline or punishment upon village Christians in cases of disobedience or if they continued practicing Hindu traditions. Such a case was reported where two catechists punished a Christian who had painted his face with Hindu religious symbols.[40]

One may suppose that the attitudes of non-Christians toward converts in general, and toward mission assistants in particular, would be characterized by disapproval and by acts of persecution. Against this background we need to try to assess encounters between Indian Christian mission agents and persons within the local Indian non-Christian populations among whom they

---

38. *AFrSt, MA,* I H 3, p. 15.
39. *AFrSt* III J 3, accounts of Madras and Cuddalore.
40. *NHB,* 53rd St., p. 408.

resided and worked. The question as to why it was necessary for Indian non-Christians to get in touch with missionary agents needs to be addressed. Different interests, forms of indifference, and rejection found on both sides required some form of resolution. After all, the main reason for native agents to associate with non-Christians was to realize their hope of seeing "heathens" converted. Therefore, they were expected to keep in touch with local people and to talk to them about all the vicissitudes of life. Most non-Christians, however, had no particular or urgent reason for association with mission native agents. There were always exceptions, of course. Hope for support in the case of financial difficulties or disease; conversion of a family member; and the existence of Christian congregations, schools, or hospitals in the neighborhood might lead to encounters with mission workers. Interest in Christians and their institutions could be positive or negative depending on individual circumstances and local situations. Native agents were often sent to their own native villages to work. Where family members did not hold to any Christian faith, they would be cautious and distrustful of Christian relatives who came to them. There exist, however, several descriptions of cases of open violence against missionary workers involving their families or villagers. Two native assistants, Ignasi (?-1770) and Canagappen, for example, were arrested by village inhabitants when they tried to bring a group of Hindus to Tranquebar for education.[41] Sometimes the whole family of a catechist or missionary assistant would be persecuted even though the other family members had not changed their religious identity. Anger toward the Indian mission servants was often directed not so much against their Christian faith as against the Christians who had been discourteous had hurt the religious feelings of local Hindus.

Thus, on 8 September 1769, the lower catechist in the Kumbakkonam district, Sinappen (?-1772), a brother of the above mentioned Rajanaikken, was asked by the head of the village Padtisuram to give medicine to a sick Hindu.[42] When, on 11 October 1769, Sinappen was asked to speak at the burial ceremony of a drowned man who had belonged to the local *chettiar* (mercantile) caste,[43] powerful local Hindus expected gifts from the district catechists as a sign of respect at assuming responsibility for such an important assignment. Sinappen was punished for not giving a present to the local *nāyak* (ruler), Tondaman-peddaiatschi, in December 1763.[44]

41. *HB*, 67th *Cont.*, p. 1142.
42. *NHB*, 4th St., p. 446, "Diary of the Tranquebar missionaries from the second half of 1769."
43. *NHB*, 4th St., p. 459.
44. *HB*, 100th *Cont.*, p. 427.

Giving up one's original name for a Christian one was an important indicator of changing religious identity. One significant result of baptism was the granting of a Christian name to a new convert. Since the original name of a local person represented that person's former faith, it could not be used when that person became a Christian. Degrees of relationship, honorary titles, occupation, or profession are constituent parts of a Tamil name, which usually also indicate caste or sectarian identification. Because of this, missionaries were sometimes unable to give each convert a biblical or "Christian" name. Often, a baptized person could not be sent back to his village with a biblical name, since everyone would continue to use his original Tamil name.[45] The missionaries therefore began to look for Tamil equivalents of Christian and biblical names, and since in the course of translating the Bible into Tamil missionaries had coined Tamil equivalents to sacred biblical and Christian names, the process was not difficult.[46] Among the 157 native agents registered by name in the records of the Tranquebar Mission, as many as one-third were known by European names, with five having both a European and a Tamil name. The remaining native agents were known by Tamil names. These were composed with such suffixes as *-appan* (or *-appen*, "father" = 22), *-das* ("servant" or "slave"), *-mutthu* (or *-muttu, "pearl"* = 13), or *-nadan* (or *-nāden* or *-nāthan*, meaning "lord," "master," or simply "man" = 9) and prefixes such as *satya-* (meaning "truth").

As with Tamil names, items of clothing indicated the strata of the society to which a man or a woman belonged. As a symbol conveying Christian authority, dress was not an insignificant matter, either for Indian country priests and catechists or for European missionaries. The European missionaries of the Tranquebar Mission wore black robes with a collar similar to, and typical of, those worn by the clergy in Europe. In the beginning they even wore wigs. When he needed a new wig, Johann Philipp Fabricius (1711-91) asked authorities in Germany to send him a smaller and lighter one.[47] When the first Indian minister, Aaron, was ordained in 1733, the mission had to make a decision regarding his dress. Aaron wore a long gray closed robe without collar, tied together with two cloth belts, a turban, and Indian slippers typical of those worn by notables.[48] The Tamil catechist probably wore clothes in accordance with his social rank and class. In one pictorial illustra-

---

45. Diary of Schawrirajen from 1796 (*NHB*, 52nd St., p. 336).

46. Jeyaraj, *Inkulturation*, pp. 254-56.

47. Wilhelm Germann, *Johann Philipp Fabricius: Seine fünfzigjährige Wirksamkeit im Tamulenlande und das Missionsleben des achtzehnten Jahrhunderts daheim und draußen* (Erlangen, 1865), p. 96, remark 2.

48. *HB*, vol. 6a, copperplate engraving on the inside cover.

tion of a Tamil catechist dating from around 1730, the subject is wearing wooden slippers and a canvas cloth held together around his hips, with one end of the cloth either placed on his arm or wrapped over his shoulder.[49] In 1801 Christian David, a catechist in Thanjavur and a minister/priest from Jaffna, was instructed to wear clean national dress. "Sie müssen Sorge tragen, in Ihrem Äußern anständig zu erscheinen, und bis auf weitere Verordnung und auf besondere Erlaubnis die weiße Musselinkleidung tragen, die bey Ihrer Nation üblich ist."[50]

After some time in India and having learned from experience with the local people, missionaries gradually realized that their guiding principles would have to change. From the very beginning in India, European missionaries were confronted with the caste system. Although the idea of caste was incompatible with their Christian doctrine, missionaries had to deal constantly with this phenomenon. Most of the baptized Indians and most of the native mission servants were of low castes.[51]

When examining the motives of converts who, as descendants of Hindu families, decided to change their religion, one has to consider their caste origins, level of education, and socioeconomic condition. In propagating the Christian faith among the local Indian peoples, early Danish-Halle missionaries tried to forbid caste differences within the new Christian congregations. Forced to ignore caste differences, Christians were asked to sit side by side during worship and to drink out of the same cup during Holy Communion. Bartholomäus Ziegenbalg, who condemned the caste system for its oppression and inequality, showed a great interest in understanding its underlying rules and structures in South India. Under his supervision, caste was considered part of the Hindu religious system, and, as such, it was to be fought against. Yet everyday experience, observation, and practice showed that the caste system was also a social, civil, and cultural institution and that, as such, it could not be completely ignored. Even Benjamin Schultze, generally regarded as more opposed to caste differences than other missionaries, had to accept the existence of caste among Christians as an inescapable and undeni-

49. For the illustration see *HB*, 31st *Cont.*, unpaginated pages at the end of the continuation. For the explanations see *HB*, 31st *Cont.*, p. 748.

50. *NHB*, 60th St., p. 1085, "Instructions given to Christian David by the governor of Colombo, Friedrich North," 4 February 1801.

51. Editor's Note: What constituted or defined "low" could be problematic. Brahmans defined Vellalars, the former elite rulers and upholders of the proud culture of Tamils, as *sudras* even though they were anything but that, and they certainly cannot be confused with *paraiyar* or lowest of "polluted" or "untouchable" peoples. It took early Europeans some time to sort such things out.

able fact. In 1732 he explained problems resulting from building a Christian church in Madras where there was a limited amount of available space: namely, that pariah Christians could not sit far enough away from higher caste Christians.[52] As a rule, converted Indians continued to see themselves as still belonging to a caste. As "caste" Christians, they would return to their native villages and retain contact with relatives who remained Hindus.

Missionaries had to bear in mind the original castes, and differences between castes, even in matters relating to a social hierarchy of native agents within the mission organization. Catechists and assistants were usually appointed to work in their own native villages. Indeed, even when they were exposed to assaults, violence, and persecution in their home villages, those were the places where they were most likely to find acceptance and where they were most able to keep closest contacts. On 29 September 1768, for example, an old Christian woman lying on her deathbed wanted only Rajanaikken at her side because he was a member of the *paraiya* category of castes.[53] The other local catechist, Arulappen, from a different caste, was not even allowed to enter the humble place where she was dying.[54] Devanesen (ca. 1728-88), one of the schoolmasters and catechists in Thanjavur and Tiruchchirappalli, belonged to the *sudra* category of castes. When his wife and children were expelled from their family home by Hindu family members, they received help from the village headman, or ruler.[55]

Most converts belonged to the *paraiya* category of castes, but Christian Friedrich Schwartz baptized a number from the *sudra* category, most of them Vellalar, especially in Tiruchchirappalli. He needed the help of a catechist, therefore, who belonged to a specific *sudra,* namely, Vellalar, community.[56] Although the caste affiliation of a native agent is not given in every such case, documents often indicate the caste (or at least the category of castes) of the individual. One has to consider, among other things, relationships within the group of native assistants as a whole and the relationship of these to the

---

52. *HB,* 33rd *Cont.,* pp. 990-91.

53. Editor's Note: One of the peculiarities of mission records is their simple categorization of most non-Brahman upper-caste Tamils as *sudra* — the fourth and lowest category of castes within the Brahmanical "color-coded" rankings system known as *varnashramadharma* — and lumping all lowest castes, which were outside of the Brahmanical system and had no color *(āvarna)* as being *paraiya* even though *paraiya* is a distinct caste.

54. *NHB,* 2nd St., pp. 185-86.

55. *HB,* 101st *Cont.,* p. 504, "report given by Rajanaikken and Dewanesen from 1764."

56. *HB,* 33rd *Cont.,* p. 882. See also *NHB,* 4th St., p. 422, 3 July 1768.

structure of the society in which they were active. A prayer leader *(Vorbeter)* working among *paraiyas* had surely to belong to one of the *paraiya* castes. European missionaries in India were forced to realize that the upholding of caste differences was one of the ways in which Tamil Christians could maintain and strengthen their Tamil Christian identity.

Influences of Native Agents on Missionary Ideas about Society and Religion in South India

Both missionary work and the creation of "missionary knowledge" about South India was, to a large extent, dependent on collaboration with native peoples and, particularly, with the missionaries' native agents.

German missionaries had been sent to India to teach Christianity. When they arrived they had their own ideas about mission work that were based on their own religious and intellectual understandings, as well as on instructions given by August Hermann Francke (1663-1727) and his successors, or by the mission board in Copenhagen. These missionaries believed in the necessity of bringing the Christian message to the "heathens," such as their own forebears had once been. They were convinced that Christianity was the only true religion for all. With conviction as to the superiority of their message, missionaries did not have very clear notions about the religious beliefs or practices of those they called "heathens." Through their everyday mission work in India, however, they adopted ideas that were often diametrically opposed to their earlier ways of thinking. Missionary life left them caught between adaptation and differentiation, between refusal and acknowledgment, and between sympathy and contempt.

Viewing the discovery and production of knowledge about Indian society as a process of dialogue, Eugene F. Irschick has written: "What this process suggests is that we can no longer presume that the view of local or what became Indian society was a product of an 'imposition' by the hegemonic colonial power onto a mindless and subordinate society. . . . The research presented here questions this claim that knowledge is constructed by willed activity of a stronger over a weaker group. It suggests, instead, that changed significations are the heteroglot and dialogic production of all members of any historical situation, though not always in equal measure."[57] C. A. Bayly thinks that "European and indigenous discourses both played a role in the construction of modern India. European knowledge may have been hege-

---

57. Eugene F. Irschick, *Dialogue and History* (Delhi, 1994), p. 8.

monic, but it was never absolute. The creation of colonial knowledge was a dialogic process."[58] Considering the role of Indian informants in the process of gathering knowledge within the Tranquebar Mission, it can be stated that the creation of missionary knowledge was also a process of dialogue between missionaries and informants. In the missionaries' view, mission work meant the transfer of Christian values and beliefs to a non-Christian population. They took the view that knowledge of the people, of their social order, their traditions and languages, was necessary in order to be successful in missionary efforts. The missionaries explored and described the missionary field as an alien world to the home churches and peoples in Europe in order to obtain support and money for their work. If they were to succeed, they needed local people as informants or assistants. These people could be both Christians and non-Christians. Examining the different contexts in which local people could become informants or assistants in the service of European Christian missionaries, it becomes obvious that studies that were carried out by missionaries would have been unthinkable without the work of native informants and assistants.

The most frequent practice was that Indians became traveling companions. It is well known that missionaries traveled constantly in order to preach the gospel. Usually they were accompanied by indigenous people well acquainted not only with the places they were visiting but with the varying climates and natural phenomena they would encounter, the local people, their character, languages, habits, and the social structure of their society. Locals were more than just carriers. They were consultants. Often, they were called "helpers." Thus, when the missionaries Schwartz and Daniel Zeglin (1716-80) visited the Raja of Thanjavur in 1759, they were accompanied by the Indian country pastor named Diogo (ca. 1705-81). He made efforts to contact the local people, and he arranged accommodation for the missionaries in a local weaver's house.[59]

In some cases, instead of accompanying missionaries, local assistants had to go to particular regions on their own, ahead of the missionaries or without any missionary presence, either to explore unknown places for future mission activity or because Europeans could not go for reasons of climate, political or religious circumstances, or matters of health. When traveling beyond the frontiers of the Danish colony in the local kingdom of Thanjavur, these "foreigners" had to ask the local raja for permission to enter their domains. For-

58. C. A. Bayly, *Empire Information: Intelligence Gathering and Social Communication in India, 1780-1870* (Cambridge, 1996), p. 370.

59. *HB*, 91st *Cont.*, pp. 790-808, "Reisediarium nach Tanschaur im Jahr 1759."

eign missionaries were not permitted to propagate the gospel in Thanjavur kingdom until 1753, but from 1728 onward Rajanaikken acted alone in this region on behalf of the German missionaries.[60]

The role of "translator" has always been considered that of the classic intermediary. He had to express ideas given in one language to a person speaking another language. In contrast to the African context, however, where translators were usually casual laborers such as traders or soldiers,[61] Europeans in India could use the existing system of *dubashes* that had been developed since the Muslim period.[62]

The missionaries of the Tranquebar Mission took advantage of this, at least at the beginning, when they had insufficient knowledge of the local language. In 1707 Ziegenbalg reported on Arhagappen or Aleppa (1660-1730), the former chief *dubash* for the Danish East India Company who had been suspended. Aleppa had a knowledge of various European languages: German, Dutch, Danish, and Portuguese.[63] Although he remained a Hindu until his death, he maintained close links with the Tranquebar missionaries. Because of these connections and his support for Ziegenbalg during the latter's arrest in 1708/9, he and members of his family were arrested and expelled from Tranquebar.[64]

The *Königliche Gouvernementsdolmetscher* (first royal translator of the government), the *dubash* Daniel Pullei,[65] attended the mission school in Tranquebar and worked as a servant for the missionaries David Poltzenhagen (1726-56), Petrus Dame (1731-66), and Ole Maderup (1711-76) before he himself became a translator of the new governor Hermann Jacob Forck (1760-61). As well as occupying this position, Daniel Pullei was a member of the so-called "black court"[66] in Tranquebar and chairman of the "Malabar" (eigh-

60. *HB*, 26th *Cont.*, p. 12.

61. Trutz von Trotha, *Koloniale Herrschaft: Zur soziologischen Theorie der Staatsentstehung am Beispiel des "Schutzgebietes Togo"* (Tübingen, 1994), p. 188. Editor's Note: See also Lamin Sanneh, *Translating the Message: The Missionary Impact on Culture* (Maryknoll, N.Y., ca. 1989).

62. Francis Buchanan mentioned three different castes of *dubashes* in the Madras region (Francis Buchanan, *A Journey from Madras through the Countries of Mysore, Canara, and Malabar*, 3 vols. [Madras, 1988 (1807)], 3:466).

63. *AB*, p. 59, letter to an unknown person, 22 September 1707.

64. Kurt Liebau, "Die Malabarische Korrespondenz von 1712/13 und das Bild der Tamilen vom Europäer," *asien, afrika, lateinamerika* 25 (1997): 53-73.

65. Heike Liebau, "Indische Angestellte in der Dänischen Kolonialadministration während der sozialen Unruhen in Tranquebar und Umgebung im Jahre 1787," *Asien, afrika, lateinamerika* 25 (1977): 111-26.

66. This court settled differences among the local population under supervision of the Danish government.

teenth-century term for Tamil) Christian congregation in Tranquebar. Until his death he remained in contact with the missionaries, especially with Christoph Samuel John, to whom he told his life story.[67] In the initial stages of missionary work there was an urgent need for translators to serve in order to make contact with the native population. Later, when the missionaries had sufficient knowledge of the language themselves, the classic translator lost some of his importance, but not entirely. It is clear that the connections and the influence of the *dubashes,* as well as their position within the local society, remained indispensable for the missionaries.

In order to master the local language, which was their most important working instrument, missionaries needed language teachers. Usually these people could only speak their mother tongue and no second language. Although they were often not able to explain the rules of grammar, they could help the missionaries to understand local idioms and practice pronunciation. Only a few missionaries could learn the basics of the Tamil language before going to India. Most of them were dependent on the help of teachers in India. As language teachers, Indians were sometimes in a position to make demands on the missionaries. Schawrirajen (ca. 1756-?), town catechist and school-teacher in Tranquebar, refused to teach Tamil to the new missionary, Lambert Christian Fuerchtenicht (Tranquebar, 1799-1802), who arrived in Tranquebar in 1799. In his letter to Christoph Samuel John and Johann Peter Rottler (1749-1836) dated 1 May 1800, he complained about Fuerchtenicht's excessive drinking and unpunctuality.[68] Translators and language teachers lived with the missionaries, either in their houses or at least on missionary territory. This contact usually lasted for quite a long time, often for several years. To some extent these people were also engaged in translating Christian literature into Tamil. In this position they could exert significant influence. Peter Maleiappen (1700-1730), who had accompanied Ziegenbalg on a journey to Europe from 1714 to 1716, worked for several years with the missionary Benjamin Schultze. They translated parts of the Bible into Tamil together. This would seem to indicate that Maleiappen must have had a good knowledge both of German and of the Bible.[69] Besides this, he translated Christian

---

67. *AFrSt, MA,* I K 5:16, "Kurzer Lebenslauf des Daniel Pullei"; *NHB,* 62nd St., pp. 166-81.

68. *Rigsarkivet (National Archives), Copenhagen* [hereafter *RA*], Missionskollegiet 9i.

69. Kurt Liebau, "Die ersten Tamilen aus der Dänisch-Halleschen Mission in Europa: Vom Objekt zum Subjekt kultureller Interaktion?" in *Fremde Erfahrungen: Asiaten und Afrikaner in Deutschland, Österreich und der Schweiz bis 1945,* edited by Gerhard Höpp (Berlin, 1996), pp. 9-28.

literature into Tamil on his own. In his diary, Schultze mentioned that Maleiappen had translated Wilken's *Communion Book*.[70] Checking the books of the mission library in 1731, Christoph Theodosius Walther (1699-1741) mentioned some books that had been translated with the help of Maleiappen. These are listed in chapter 4: "die recension der von hiesigen Evangelischen Missionarien nach und nach verfaßten Olesbücher." Among the works translated with the help of Maleiappen are "Differentia da Christandade" by Johann Ferreira (from Portuguese into Tamil) and *A Short Refutation of the Principal Error of the Church of Rome* (London, 1714).[71]

In their attempt to supply missionaries with the information or material they needed, Indian assistants could fall back on existing networks and former contacts. This was so when Ziegenbalg sent several writers to rural areas to collect Tamil literature from Brahman widows. "Jedoch habe ich derenthalben [der Bücher, H. L.] meine Malabarischen Schreiber viele Tage-Reisen weit ins Land schicken müssen die allenthalben dergleichen Bücher bey den verwitweten Brahmanens Weibern ausgeforschet, u. selbige von ihnen um einen geringen Preiß gekauffet haben."[72]

In addition to these relations the Tranquebar Mission set up its own information network. Christian catechists and schoolteachers, who lived with the congregations in the surrounding villages, were expected to report regularly on the situation of the local Christians and on other events in their villages. These reports were usually presented in written form. Parts were translated and published in the *Hallesche Berichte (HB)* and *Neue Hallesche Berichte (NHB)*. The most interesting category of native informants were those who helped the European missionaries by their specialist knowledge of a subject of particular interest to the missionaries, for example, natural sciences, medicine, history, religions, literature, and philosophy.

The creation of knowledge about local societies has always been a constituent part of missionary activity in India. Some useful research has been done on grammars and dictionaries for various Indian languages as well as on studies of religious, literary, or philosophical matters by European missionaries, but little regard has been paid to some missionaries' interest in natural sciences: geography, medicine, zoology, or botany. It was not just sheer curiosity that caused missionaries to dig deeper into the structure of religion and nature. They had to demonstrate the necessity of missionary work among the

---

70. *AFrSt*, d 16 a, "Diary of Benjamin Schultze," 14 July 1720.

71. *Det Kongelige Bibliotek (Royal Library), Copenhagen* [hereafter *KB*], Ny kgl. p. 589 c, 4E.

72. *AB*, p. 77, Ziegenbalg to J. F. Lütkens in Copenhagen, 22 August 1708.

"heathen." They tried, therefore, to show the "otherness" and singularity of Indian people that they hoped to overcome by missionary activity. At the same time, missionaries had to demonstrate or estimate the chances of successful missionary work with a particular local community. To this purpose they looked for universal human elements that unified all mankind, showing that Indians, like all human beings, were worthy of being reached and baptized. In the missionary reports, one can find two kinds of views: descriptions of the Indian population as "poor and blind heathens" in need of the gospel and expressions of respect for Indian cultural achievements and the highly skilled craftsmen of South India. Although it is difficult to assess the influence exercised by native assistants and local informants on the research by missionaries in the Tranquebar Mission, it can be assumed that individual helpers played a much greater role in translation and research than has been hitherto known or accepted.

The first missionary, Bartholomäus Ziegenbalg, used a local poet and an accountant/writer to help him read Tamil books. The poet told him about the time and circumstances of the story. If there were new words and phrases, the writer wrote them down and the poet explained them.[73] In 1708 Ziegenbalg translated the Tamil book on behavioral norms and everyday ethics or *ulakanāti* into German with the help of a young Tamil poet, probably Christian Friedrich (ca. 1685–after 1733).[74] In the preface, Ziegenbalg described his debt to Christian Friedrich for the translation. While Ziegenbalg gave a word-by-word translation of each verse, Christian Friedrich made the necessary comments that were absolutely essential for comprehension of the work. "Ich bin mir aber nicht anders bewußt, als daß ich alle malabarischen Worte gantz accurat in meine Muttersprache übersetzt habe, ohne daß ich fast bey einer jedweden Regel eine kurtze Erklärung geschrieben, so, als wie selbige mir von dem jungen malabarischen Pöeten ist gesaget worden, den ich dazumahl bey mir hatte."[75]

One method of gathering interesting information on Tamil society was correspondence with knowledgeable people. Although correspondence between missionaries and Indian people was much less than that between missionaries and European scholars, missionaries carried on some interesting correspondence. In the Tranquebar Mission the most famous letters were published under the title *Malabarische Korrespondenz* from 1714 to 1717.[76] This

---

73. *AB*, p. 77, Ziegenbalg to J. F. Lütkens in Copenhagen, 22 August 1708.
74. His Tamil name was Kanabadi Wattiar (the singing teacher).
75. *KB*, Oriental Department. Cod tamul 5.
76. *HB*, 7th *Cont.*, pp. 337-504. *HB*, 11th *Cont.*, pp. 871-959.

consists of ninety-nine letters representing answers of Brahmans to questions asked by the missionaries Johann Ernst Gruendler (1677-1720) and Bartholo-mäus Ziegenbalg.[77] Aleppa, the former chief *dubash* of the Danish East India Company, later Ziegenbalg's translator, used his contacts, information, and communication network to establish contact with the Brahmans.

In the later years of the Danish-Halle Mission we do not find a compara-ble correspondence for a long period. This does not mean, however, that no exchange of letters took place. From time to time missionaries mentioned that they received letters from representatives of the local population, but as a rule, these letters were never translated or sent to Europe. Undoubtedly, the exchange of views in that period was mainly in the form of verbal communi-cation. And, unlike the *munazara* in North India during the nineteenth cen-tury,[78] these early discussions were usually not recorded.

During the second half of the eighteenth century both the direction and intensity of the missionaries' scientific interest underwent significant changes. Whereas at the beginning of the work of the mission, religion, lan-guage, literature, and philosophy dominated, this changed to a broader inter-est in natural sciences such as botany, zoology, or astronomy. This research was not only time-consuming but also very expensive. In the 1780s one of the most active missionaries in this field, Christoph Samuel John, made several requests for greater financial and material support for missionary research to be carried out parallel to religious activities.[79] August Friedrich Caemmerer, the last missionary of the old Tranquebar Mission, tried to learn Sanskrit with the help of a Brahman teacher with whom he had interesting discussions on local religious beliefs and traditions.[80] Local informants, in such cases, were not so much middlemen who mediated between two different parties as informants who decided autonomously what information should be passed on. They were, to some extent, their own masters.

Native people were motivated to act as informants for European mission-aries because they themselves were Christians and wanted to help spread Christianity; because they could make money or gain important positions by so doing; and/or because they were well-educated themselves and wanted the

77. For further information see: Liebau, "Malabarische Korrespondenz," p. 54; Kurt Liebau, ed., *Die Malabarische Korrespondenz: Tamilische Briefe an deutsche Missionare: Eine Auswahl* (Sigmaringen, 1998).

78. Avril A. Powell, *Muslims and Missionaries in Pre-Mutiny India* (Richmond, 1993).

79. *RA*, Missionskollegiet 9g/1781-1792, Ch. S. John, "Einige Vorschläge die Mißion betreffend," Tranquebar, 20 February 1784; and Ch. S. John, "Pro Memoria für neue Missionarien," Tranquebar, 27 October 1784.

80. *NHB*, 52nd St., p. 353.

missionaries to get an accurate picture of their society. Sometimes the names and descriptions of the work of these Christian informants are known. Some of them became famous as poets or translators of Christian literature, such as Daniel Pullei or Maleiappen. As Christians, they had no problem with informing or teaching their European co-religionists about things that were needed or deemed necessary. As Hindus, however, they had to fear hostility from local people, particularly where religious themes were concerned. Hindu informants, in such circumstances, often remained anonymous. Among the non-Christians were educated Brahmans, or other knowledgeable people, who were interested in the Europeans and their religion and who wanted the Europeans to be correctly informed about the religion and culture of India. Unlike the Christians, non-Christian informants took a greater risk in providing Europeans with information.

Conclusion

Throughout Indian history, all foreigners, whether travelers, traders, or diplomats, have been dependent on the support and cooperation of sections of the local population in order to achieve their aims. However, unlike *dubashes* and brokers in the field of trade, native agents in the European missions have rarely come to the attention of historians.[81] This special group of Indian Christians differs from the rest of the Christian community because of their close connection with, and direct dependence on, the Europeans. Comparing this group with other groups of intermediaries such as *dubashes* in political affairs or Indian brokers in trade matters, it is obvious that acting as intermediaries and "cultural brokers" between Europeans and Indians, between European Christians and Indian Christians, and between Indian Christians and local Hindus and Muslims, native mission agents permanently crossed social and religious borders. They worked in an atmosphere of tension and played their roles differently, according to their individual capabilities or social status. They tried to compensate for some of the consequences of conversion by making compromises with, and syntheses of, the different worlds in which they lived. The encounter between European missionaries and Indian assis-

81. For brokers in trade affairs, see Sinappah Arasaratnam, *Maritime Trade, Society and European Influence in Southern Asia, 1600-1800* (Aldershot, 1995). For research on religious middlemen see Henriette Bugge, *Mission and Tamil Society: Social and Religious Change in South India (1840-1900)* (Richmond, 1994), pp. 79-110; Dick Kooiman, *Conversion and Social Equality in India: The London Missionary Society in South Travancore in the Nineteenth Century* (Amsterdam, 1989).

tants is not simply a linear history of conquest or control by missionaries over their hapless "subjects," as if they were disposable "objects." While they were working together, they depended on each other and also controlled and influenced each other. Activities on the Indian side seem to have been remarkably strong, especially with regard to the struggle for symbols and social status. As local authorities, native agents influenced the knowledge that the missionaries acquired about Indian society and the Hindu religion. Intensive research on Indian societies, languages, and religions would have been impossible without the contributions of these native "helpers." A more thorough study of this phenomenon needs to be carried out, breaking down rigid categories of hierarchy that seem to show the missionary as a dominant leader and the native worker as a humble, unskilled person trying to assist his teacher.

In the perceptions of local Tamil people, these native agents were a numerically small elite, close to the locals but with broader ranging circles of activity and influence, through their contacts with Europeans. The "native agents" of the Tranquebar Mission, although closely attached to European missionaries, continued to be strongly influenced by their local cultures and strong social bonds. They incorporated a large part of their "Indian life" into their "Christian life" after baptism. European missionaries had to take this fact into account when they stipulated the conditions and norms of cooperation and collaboration. Each of these Indians had specific abilities that qualified them to become informants for the Europeans. Besides their special knowledge, their information networks were the most significant factor for the Europeans. Often they had long experiences in dealing with Europeans and therefore were able to explain local circumstances in a way understandable to Europeans.

This chapter has challenged the paradigm of the missionary as "master" and the native assistants as "victims," individuals without ideas of their own. In research on missionaries in India, for too long scholars have concentrated on missionary activity, as seen through the eyes of the missionaries themselves, and have neglected the significant role of the local assistants and informants.

CHAPTER FIVE

Tanjore, Tranquebar, and Halle: European Science and German Missionary Education in the Lives of Two Indian Intellectuals in the Early Nineteenth Century

INDIRA VISWANATHAN PETERSON

The introduction of English-language education in India in the nineteenth century has received much attention from scholars, as have the scholarly activities of British Orientalists and missionaries, especially in the context of British colonial rule. It is only recently, however, that studies have begun to appear on science in modern education in India, and these have focused mainly on a critique of the dissemination of European science as a colonialist project. Little has been said about Indian agency in the encounter with Western science, and little research has been done on European science (or on English-language education) in India during the eighteenth century, when British colonial hegemony had not yet fully entrenched itself in the subcontinent. The few available studies suggest that the modes of Indian contact with European science in this earlier period do not quite fit the generalizations that have been made about science and education in India in the latter half of the nineteenth century.

This chapter examines the enthusiastic and creative responses to European science expressed by two south Indian intellectuals who were educated by German missionaries in the late eighteenth century. The attitudes and achievements of these two show the late eighteenth century as a period in which the possibilities for Indians for creative intellectual engagement with European ideas were of a different order from those of the late nineteenth century. In addition, the discussion attempts to provide insights into the complicated intersections of religion, science, and Enlightenment ideologies in eighteenth-century Europe.

King Serfoji II (1777-1832) and the Tamil poet Vedanāyakam Sāstri (1774-1864), both of the kingdom of Tanjore (Thanjāvur), were important in the history of South India. Serfoji, a prince of the western Indian Maratha dynasty that had ruled Tanjore from the late seventeenth century, oversaw a great flowering of literature and the arts in Tamil, Maratha, and other Indian languages that flourished in Tanjore. The king is remembered for his initiatives in Western education and his lifelong interest in European arts and sciences. Well before the systematic establishment of British education in South India, Serfoji founded free public schools that provided Western education in several Indian languages, designed new curricula, and published textbooks for the schools. He practiced European-style experimental science and tried to synthesize European and Indian systems of learning in medicine.

Celebrated as the "Evangelical Poet of Tanjore," Vedanāyakam Sāstri was the first major Protestant Christian poet in the Tamil language, with more than 120 literary works on Protestant religious themes to his credit. He taught Western astronomy and mathematics at the Tanjore mission school and wrote innovative poems and plays in which he incorporated "lessons" in several Western systems of scientific knowledge, including astronomy and anatomy. The nearly five hundred hymns (jnana-kirttanai) that Sāstri wrote were very popular with the Tamil congregations. The poet also gave public performances of his longer poems in the form of musical-dramatic discourses.

The careers of King Serfoji and Vedanāyakam Sāstri reflect a lively engagement with indigenous literary and cultural forms as well as with European knowledge systems and education, and especially with European scientific traditions. This particular configuration of shared interests resulted from the early education of both men under German missionaries associated with the Danish-German Protestant mission in Tranquebar near Tanjore, as well as to the personal impact of their common mentor, the illustrious German missionary statesman, Christian Friedrich Schwartz (1726-98).[1] By 1706 when Bartholomäus Ziegenbalg, sponsored by the king of Denmark, had established the first Protestant mission in India in the small Danish territory of Tranquebar (a.k.a. Tarangambadi) on the Coromandel coast near Tanjore,

1. Jesse Page, *Schwartz of Tanjore* (London, 1921); W. Germann, *Missionar Christian Friedrich Schwartz: Sein Leben und Wirken: Aus Briefen des Halleschen Missionsarchivs* (Erlangen, 1870).

Pietist missionaries from Halle in Germany[2] had lived and worked in southern India and had maintained close contact with the kings of Tanjore. By the late eighteenth century, several of them (including Schwartz) were receiving some of their financial support from the Society for Promoting Christian Knowledge (SPCK), a British missionary agency (founded 1698), and had served as chaplains and educators in Madras, Tanjore, and elsewhere in South India. A trusted friend of King Tuljaji of Tanjore, Schwartz had worked in the provincial centers of Tanjore and Trichinopoly and had represented the English East India Company in its diplomatic negotiations with the Muslim rulers of the Carnatic during the Mysore Wars.

Sāstri, the son of Devashayam Pillai of Tirunelveli, a Roman Catholic of Hindu Vellāla origin who eventually converted to Protestantism, joining what was known as the Evangelical church, was taken to Tanjore by the Rev. Schwartz in 1785 when he was eleven years old. After a period of instruction on a personal basis with Schwartz, the boy attended the mission's school in Tanjore. In 1789 the missionary sent him to the theological seminary for Indian catechists at the Danish-German mission headquarters in Tranquebar. There, in addition to theology, Sāstri studied astronomy, anatomy, and mathematics with the Halle missionary Christoph Samuel John (1747-1813), and possibly with the missionaries A. F. Caemmerer and J. P. Rottler as well. In 1794, at the age of nineteen, he was appointed to the headmastership of the Tamil school Schwartz had established in Tanjore for training Indian catechists. There he taught mathematics and astronomy. In 1829, when Sāstri lost his post in the school because of controversies with the missionaries over matters of Tamil Christian practice, King Serfoji made him court poet. Sāstri then wrote one of his most interesting poems, incorporating material from the European sciences, for Serfoji. His commission at court was terminated at the king's death in 1832.[3]

In 1787, at the death of King Tuljaji of Tanjore, the ten-year-old Prince Serfoji's claim to the Tanjore throne was contested by rivals. The English East India Company, by then a key player in South Indian politics, intervened in the Tanjore succession controversy and eventually espoused Serfoji's cause, thanks to the mediation of Schwartz, whom Tuljaji had appointed as his adopted son's guardian. From 1793 to 1797 the young Serfoji was educated in Madras by Schwartz and his colleague, the missionary W. Gericke. Under the

---

2. On German Pietism see J. Ernest Stoeffler, *German Pietism in the Eighteenth Century* (Leiden, 1973).

3. Noah Jnanadikkam, *Tancai Cuviceta Kavirayar Vetanayaka Sastriyar* [The Life of Vedanāyakam Sāstri, the Evangelical Poet of Tanjore] (Thanjāvur, 1899).

English Company's aegis, he was restored to the Tanjore throne in 1798. Within a year of his accession, however, the king was compelled to sign a treaty with the Company. This effectively limited his authority to the fort and city of Tanjore, the Company becoming the de facto ruler of the Tanjore kingdom. Serfoji devoted the rest of his life to social, intellectual, and cultural projects.

Historians of the Tanjore Maratha kingdom and the Tranquebar Mission have noted the influence of the charismatic Schwartz and Western education on Serfoji and Sāstri. What has not been noticed is that the Hindu king and the Christian poet also shared an interest in European science. Contemporary European visitors to the Tanjore court left approving notices of Serfoji's serious study and practice of a number of European sciences (including astronomy, natural history, and chemistry). A recent evaluation of Sāstri's poetry includes some discussion of his use of material from various sciences in his long poems, but to date no study exists of the sources and implications of Sāstri and Serfoji's interest in European science, and the integral role it played in their intellectual lives.

Serfoji and Sāstri were among the earliest Indians to receive systematic education in Western science as part of European schooling. This education resulted in a lifelong, creative engagement with science in the contexts of learning, teaching, and cultural activity for both. Their responses to European science bear the strong imprint of particular developments in late seventeenth- and early eighteenth-century German Pietist thought regarding science as the methodical investigation of nature. Eighteenth-century European ideologies of the learning and practice of science — what may be characterized as "Enlightenment" ideas and ideals — were mediated for Serfoji and Sāstri by the educational philosophy propounded and put into practice by the eminent German Pietist theologian and educator August Hermann Francke (1663-1727), in the forms in which they received it through their early education with Schwartz and other German missionaries.

From its inception, the Danish Tranquebar Mission was staffed by German missionaries trained at the Pietist schools and the seminary founded by Francke at the end of the seventeenth century in the German city of Halle-on-the-Saale. The Tranquebar Mission was the first Protestant one in India, and the British colonial community patronized the Halle missionaries in its early days. In South India the Halle missionaries had overseen European (especially English-language) education in Madras and the provinces from as early as 1717, beginning with schools established with the sponsorship of the Society for the Propagation of the Gospel. Despite British authority and patronage, Francke's complex of educational institutions in Halle, surviving even today under the name of the Francke Foundations *(Franckesche Stiftungen)*, remained the spiritual and intellectual headquarters of the Tranquebar Mission and its German missionaries throughout its history. For Francke's philosophy, science and theology stood in an integral relationship to each other, and science education was centrally important to the educational ideals of the Francke Foundations, where the missionaries received their theological and pedagogical training. In Madras, Tranquebar, and elsewhere, the German missionaries put Francke's educational ideals into practice in modified form. Thus, both Serfoji and Vedanāyakam Sāstri were educated through a variant of the Halle curriculum, with an emphasis on a particular kind of science education. Before examining the careers of the two men, it is important to understand the role of science in Francke's educational philosophy and its practice in the Francke Foundations.

Science and Pedagogy in the Halle Pietist Curriculum

August Hermann Francke was both a leader of Pietist theology and a pioneer in education in eighteenth-century Europe. His interest in education and his pedagogical theories were an important part of his formulation of Pietist religion and arose out of his conception of the true Christian life. In contrast to the Lutheran Orthodoxy of his time, Francke rejected all dogma, defining true theology as "living religion," that is, convictions arising from personal religious experience, centering on love of God and one's fellow men. His definition of the true Christian life focused not on articles of belief but on a variety of ideas and activities that would contribute to the building of Christian character. Francke argued that only a universally accessible and practically oriented education, based on the principle of *das Nützliche*, "the useful," would facilitate the making of Christians on the above-described model. With this goal in mind, in the 1690s Francke founded an "orphan-house" *(Waisenhaus)* for boys and girls, which quickly grew into a complex of schools and related institutions.

The most innovative aspect of Francke's educational system, in addition to its universal accessibility, was its emphasis on active, experiential learning, especially learning through studying and handling actual objects in the sciences and in the technical professions. The Halle complex included a printing press, a bookshop, and a pharmacy, at which students were apprenticed, and which were working concerns that helped support the schools. However, Francke's principle of "utility" transcended mere vocational training. Practical training was intended not simply to enable students to secure a livelihood but to serve as a direct way of knowing God through working with real-life objects for real-life purposes, and for the good of one's fellow men.

The study of nature was an essential component of the curricula of all of Francke's schools. Students were required to spend one or two hours a week in the practice of what we might call "hands-on" or laboratory science. Francke prescribed the practice of geometry by measurement, the study of applied mathematics and physics with the use of instruments, and astronomy by using celestial globes and observing the sky. The pupils learned anatomy through dissection and the manipulation of a skeleton and conducted experiments to study the physical properties of the elements; they grew and studied plants in a botanical garden and used them in the service of the pharmacy. In the late seventeenth century, Francke's schools were unique in possessing this scientific curricular complex.

At the center of the Halle institutions' science curriculum was a *Kunst- und Naturalienkammer* (Cabinet of Natural History and Arts), a room dedicated to the systematic investigation of objects from nature and culture through collection, observation, classification, and the use of instruments.[4] The theological objective of practical learning in Francke's curriculum emerges most clearly in the context of science study in the *Kunst- und Naturalienkammer* at the *Franckesche Stiftungen*. The institution of the Cabinet of Natural History or Cabinet of Curiosities, which was very popular in seventeenth-century Europe, was founded on the philosophy of natural or physical theology in which the empirical study of nature was seen as a major path to the knowledge of God's works and his power and glory. To collect specimens from nature and art *(res naturales* and *res artificiales)*, classify them, and study them with the help of appropriate instruments was to apprehend firsthand the wisdom of God manifested in the works of his creation. The design of the *Kunstkammer* as a representation of the whole world within a single room, combined with its encyclopedic scope and emphasis on classification, was an attempt to image the completeness and order of God's creation. Theoretical works often cited Noah's ark as the model for the *Kunstkammer,* and at least one famous British collection was actually named "The Ark."

While a room dedicated to the study of science had existed in the Francke school complex as early as 1698, in 1739 (twelve years after A. H. Francke's

4. On museums see Oliver Impey and Arthur MacGregor, eds., *The Origin of Museums: The Cabinet of Curiosities in Sixteenth- and Seventeenth-Century Europe* (Oxford, 1985). The account of scientific learning in Francke's schools that follows is based on Thomas J. Müller, "Der Realienunterricht in den Schulen August Hermann Franckes," in *300 Jahre Erziehung in den Franckeschen Stiftungen zu Halle* (Halle, 1997), pp. 43-65.

death), a *Kunst- und Naturalienkammer* (hereafter Francke *Kunstkammer*) designed according to the prescription in C. F. Neickel's *Museographia* (1727), a popular book on *Kunstkammer* design, was built on the top floor of the main building *Waisenhaus,* or of the *Franckesche Stiftungen,* at the symbolic heart of the school complex. Built by the renowned engraver and Halle University technician Gottfried August Gründler, twelve display cabinets, each devoted to a particular kind of exhibit or field of study, were symmetrically arranged along the walls of the rectangular room. The cabinets devoted to *Naturalien (res naturales)* contained fossils, mollusks, zoological specimens preserved by various methods, conches, and so on, organized according to the Linnaean classification (just four years after the publication of Linnaeus's work and within a year of its translation into German). The cabinets meant for *Kunst (res artificiales)* contained mathematical and mechanical models, ethnographic curiosities, writing instruments, and paintings. There was also a manipulative skeleton and other models and instruments for scientific study. At the center of the room stood two gigantic armillary spheres representing the world systems of Copernicus and Tycho Brahe, symmetrically flanked by celestial and terrestrial globes and models of biblical topography (the Holy Land, the city of Jerusalem, Solomon's temple, the tabernacle). On either side was an apothecary's table *(Apothekentisch),* with drawers for storage and display and surface space for demonstrations. Paintings, including portraits of noble benefactors, completed the layout. The room was meant to reflect as clearly as possible the idea of the macrocosm, a vision of God's creation in encyclopedic fullness, with Heaven, Earth, the topography of the Bible, and representatives of all the species of Nature and the works of man forming a totality. As in all well-designed *Kunstkammer,* the activities of study, observation, and experiment in the Halle cabinet were organically connected with a library, a botanical garden, and an observatory.

The distinctive features of the Francke *Kunstkammer,* however, were its centrality in the Halle Pietist school curriculum, its universal accessibility, and its use in practical and professional training for the students. Open to poor and rich students of all ages and levels in Francke's orphan schools and to the general public, the collection was not like the private ones, or even ones at the universities and learned societies, which were meant exclusively for study by scholars and a few privileged individuals. The empirical studies conducted in the Francke *Kunstkammer* were meant to educate the young. They were linked to training, production, and transactions in the pharmacy, press, and bookshop run by the poor pupils. Although other Europeans (contemporaries and colleagues of Francke, in particular) had advocated educational experiments that included an element of theologically based scientific study,

Francke and his followers in Halle were unique in linking the *Kunstkammer* ideal, empirical investigation of nature, and universal and practical education in such a thorough and systematic manner. For very particular reasons, motivations that did not always coincide with those of the rational thinkers of the Enlightenment, the Halle Pietists became leaders in the Enlightenment enthusiasm for pushing back the frontiers of scientific learning. Wherever they went, the Halle missionaries carried with them the ideal of universal education, with experimental and observational science as a crucial component, and the *Kunstkammer* as the blueprint for scientific study.

Although studies in a *Kunstkammer* did not figure as an actual component in the education of Schwartz's Indian protégés, the *Kunstkammer* idea served them as an important model of and metaphor for a coherent universe. In his Tamil poems Vedanāyakam Sāstri expounded new classificatory systems and taxonomies, new approaches to natural history, and a new cosmology in a Pietist Christian theological context. In addition to commissioning poems and studies dealing with the European sciences, Serfoji actually practiced several of these sciences. His activities as an amateur scientist in a room dedicated to the purpose of empirical study consisted of collection, classification, observation, and experimentation. The king of Tanjore created for himself a cabinet of arts and sciences, a *Kunstkammer* on the Halle model. What were some of the factors that contributed to the enthusiasm and ease with which Serfoji and Sāstri embraced Western science in the premodern Indian environment, and what are some of the issues raised by the style and content of their responses?

Interpreting European Education in Eighteenth-Century Tanjore

I use the phrase "European science" to connote a range of phenomena and ideas that were the focus of scientific education in eighteenth-century Europe. These include several distinct scientific disciplines as they emerged from older and broader concepts such as "philosophy" or "natural philosophy," and, more generally, the foundation of these disciplines in the empirical approach to scientific investigation propounded by Francis Bacon. As a Hindu king in the eighteenth century, Serfoji would have been familiar with the Hindu cosmologies and views of the natural world taught in the *Shastras* (treatises on various disciplines) and *Puranas* (cosmological and mythological texts). Although educated in a Pietist context, Sāstri lived in a new Tamil Protestant community that had roots in the dominant Hindu (especially Shaiva Vallala) culture, and was deeply conversant with the worldview of this culture.

With the strengthening of rule by Islamic dynasties, especially the imperial Mughals from the sixteenth century onward, Islamic science, with strong rationalistic and empirically oriented aspects, had become an important scientific tradition in India. Mughal rulers from Babar to Jahangir vigorously patronized scientific investigation and were themselves practicing naturalists and amateur scientists. European science itself was not new to Indian inquirers. The Portuguese, Dutch, and Danish trading interests, along with Jesuits, had brought new streams of both Christian thought and Western science to India well before the eighteenth century. Nevertheless, neither Islamic science nor the Christian and Western ideas brought by these earlier European groups appear to have resulted in the kind of major paradigm shift that we see in the attitudes of the two Tanjore intellectuals in the eighteenth century concerning the nature and functions of scientific investigation and knowledge.

Serfoji and Sāstri's response to European science appear to be unusual even in the context of the contemporary encounter of Indian intellectuals, mainly pandits (traditional Indian scholars) and scholars, with European systems. The encounter of Indian scholars with European learning took place in the course of collaboration with European administrators and Orientalists. In the case of Western scientific ideas, the response of the pandits was characterized by resistance to the empirical method and to the European cosmologies that threatened to displace indigenous ones. As Richard Fox Young has shown, in Malwa and Ceylon, for example, at first Indian scholars rejected and spoke against European science in the form of the heliocentric cosmology, and indigenous ideas were only slowly displaced or synthesized through discussion, debate, "conversion," informal advocacy, and the gradual assimilation of European ideas.[5]

Unlike the pandits of Sehore and Ceylon, Serfoji and Sāstri did not encounter Western science as isolated doctrines or dogma; they underwent a systematic European education in which scientific investigation formed an important part of a coherent curriculum of learning. It was not until an entire generation of young Bengali men had been educated in the colonial British curriculum in Calcutta, the metropolis of British India, that Ram Mohan Roy and others would clamor for the "Baconian learning," in opposing the efforts of traditionalist Indians and British Orientalists to promote traditional Indian learning and the Indian cosmologies that Thomas Babington Macaulay would dismiss as astronomy that would move girls at an English boarding school to laughter, and geography, made up of seas of treacle and

5. Richard Fox Young and S. Jebanesan, *The Bible Trembled: The Hindu-Christian Controversies of Nineteenth-Century Ceylon* (Vienna, 1995).

seas of butter. As a prince from the South Indian provinces, and a boy deprived of the traditional education that would normally have been tendered to a member of the royal family, Serfoji appears to have assimilated European cosmologies easily, and with little or no resistance, compared to other Indian princes of major status who came into contact with Europeans.

At the beginning of the nineteenth century, the training of the young men of the rising Indian middle classes of metropolitan Calcutta was directly guided and shaped by the cultural and political agendas of the British colonial authority. In contrast, the Halle missionaries were mainly in charge of the curriculum in which Western learning was disseminated in Madras and provincial South India. The mediation of the Halle educational ideals appears to have allowed for a more individualized and intellectually oriented response to European learning, at least in the case of privately tutored pupils such as Serfoji and Sāstri. Schwartz, the principal mentor for both men, showed no particular interest in the sciences, but passed on to his protégés, who revered their mentor with great filial affection, the spirit of the Halle Pietist curriculum.

John, Rottler, and Caemmerer, the Halle missionaries who taught Sāstri at Tranquebar and kept in touch with Serfoji during his reign, must have been important models for their Indian students in the dedicated pursuit of science. All three were active naturalists.[6] John collected mollusks, and Rottler had a botanical collection that he sent to the great herbarium of King's College in London (it was later transferred to Kew Gardens). All three corresponded with learned societies in Halle and elsewhere in Europe and sent specimens from their collections to the *Kunst- und Naturalienkammer* at the *Franckesche Stiftungen*. In fact, John's "excessive" emphasis on natural historical and "secular" studies in the Tranquebar mission school became a matter of controversy among the authorities in Halle.[7] Throughout his "reign" under British supervision, the Tanjore king kept in close touch with British and other European naturalists and learned societies that were proliferating in Madras. As the achievement of an "enlightened," that is, European-educated Indian ruler, Serfoji's own scientific pursuits gained the notice of amateur collectors and experimentalists in these circles, and the king was eventually elected a member of the Royal Asiatic Society in Britain.

Serfoji and Sāstri appear to have flourished at a unique moment in the Indian encounter with European science. The kind of creativity and initiative

---

6. See C. S. Mohanavelu, *German Tamilology: German Contributions to Tamil Language, Literature, and Culture During the Period 1706-1945* (Madras, 1993), p. 151.

7. Anders Nørgaard, *Mission und Obrigkeit: Die Dänisch-hallesche Mission in Tranquebar 1706-1845* (Gütersloh, 1988), pp. 195-98.

with which they approached European science rapidly became unthinkable in the context of the British colonial educational system that became entrenched in India from the 1830s onward. As Deepak Kumar has demonstrated, all through the nineteenth and early twentieth centuries, the teleology of colonialism allowed Indians to receive little more than "a low form of scientific and technical education under controlled conditions," with no opportunities for fundamental research.[8]

Sāstri's response to European science is remarkable for its innovative synthesis of the Pietist theological-scientific perspective with indigenous Tamil idioms and ideals. Equally creatively, Serfoji reinterpreted and harmonized the new sciences in Indian contexts of learning, action, and performance, deftly discarding their Pietist underpinnings. Despite these differences, the Hindu king and the Christian poet responded to European science in shared Indian cultural discourses, exemplified especially in poetry as a form of expression. Drama, dance, and opera were the preeminent forms of artistic and literary production in early-nineteenth-century Tanjore, and Serfoji was the principal patron of these arts. Poetry and mnemonic verse were important traditional media through which Indian scholars taught and learned the sciences, and it is entirely appropriate that both Serfoji and Sāstri chose to teach science through poems and plays, which were meant primarily for memorization, recitation, and public performance, in an era when print culture had not quite replaced the vibrant oral traditions of the Indian arts and sciences.

It is very important to place Sāstri and Serfoji's passion for Western science in the context of the significant contribution they made to the flowering of indigenous cultural expression at a time of transition from the premodern to the modern in colonial India. Serfoji is known as the promoter of a dynamic and distinctively South Indian culture in Tanjore, in a program that included the development of classical canons in dance and music and the preservation of classical Sanskrit learning. In addition to establishing a great library (Sarasvati Mahal), and commissioning poems and plays, he was a major benefactor of the great Hindu temple of Tanjore. At the Sarasvati Mahal library and the Tanjore palace, European books nestled side by side with Indian-language manuscripts. Serfoji also tried to synthesize European medicine with Indian medical systems.

Sāstri's career reflects an equally passionate concern for the assertion of indigenous cultural values and discourses, in this case, those of the Tamil elites of South India. Not only did Sāstri refashion and domesticate German Pietism in terms of Tamil poetic forms and ideals, he engaged in major dis-

8. Deepak Kumaar, *Science and the Raj, 1857-1905* (Delhi, 1995).

putes with the missionaries whenever he and his compatriots in the Tamil congregation felt that Tamil cultural practices and values were being threatened by the imposition of alien ideas. Śāstri's controversies with the missionaries pertained to issues ranging from the observance of caste rules in church to the appropriate use of the Tamil language in Bible translation and the propriety of singing Tamil hymns in church. The poet's fiercely independent spirit and his outspoken condemnation of European impositions on his own culture cost him his job. Both Serfoji and Śāstri are celebrated not as agents of Westernization but of an Indian cultural blooming. Their response to science was part of a complex assertion of cultural autonomy and creativity, and for them science became an integral part of a pioneering construction of an indigenous cultural tradition for the modern era in original and vital ways.

The next section seeks to interpret and contextualize the use of the content and methods of European natural history, astronomy, and geography in two major works of Vedanāyakam Śāstri and in a long poem attributed to Serfoji. The analysis of the poems is followed by a discussion of the streams of eighteenth-century European thought that appear to be refracted in them, especially through specific concepts: the classification of species, the Copernican world system, the terrestrial globe, and, encompassing these, the idea of the *Kunstkammer*. I end with a brief treatment of Serfoji's lifelong activity in science in the light of the amateur practice of science in eighteenth-century Europe. Here I suggest that the Indian king had, through his own initiative, created for himself an environment for scientific study that shared the philosophical foundations of the European *Kunstkammer*, a "room of wonders," but also that, by the end of his life, he had moved beyond the *Kunstkammer* and into the realm of modern scientific investigation.

The missionary educational enterprise in South India is documented in the published reports[9] and unpublished diaries, registers, and other writings of the Tranquebar missionaries. A reasonably complete assessment of the prince's education and his continuing intellectual activities will require a thorough study[10] not only of British colonial and other administrative and institutional documents, British and German missionary records, and the Tanjore Maratha government's palace records, but also of Serfoji's personal collection of books, the great library he established, and their connections with European learning. Here I can do no more than report on the glimpses I have had of the "translation" of Francke's educational philosophy and meth-

---

9. *Berichte ausfuhrlicher Missionsanstaltungen in Ostindien (Hallesche Berichte).*
   10. Sifting through this material, which has only recently become accessible to non-German scholars, is a formidable and long-term task.

ods over a hundred years in the Indian environment, based largely on my readings in the *Hallesche Berichte,* some missionary letters and diaries, British records and travelers' accounts, and Indian language materials related to Tanjore, Serfoji, and Vedanāyakam Sāstri, both literary and archival.

Natural History, Copernican Astronomy, and Geography in Three Indian Poems

Jnanat Tachchanatakam [Drama of the Architect of Wisdom; *DAW*] and *Bethlehem Kuravanji* [Fortune-Teller Play of Bethlehem; *BK*],[11] two major works of Vedanāyakam Sāstri, abound in material related to the European sciences of anatomy, botany, natural history, astronomy, and geography. The latter is a *tour de force,* a dramatic poem written in the *kuravanji* (fortune-teller play), a very popular eighteenth-century dance-drama genre. *Devendra Kuravanji* [Fortune-Teller Play of Indra, King of the Gods], a *kuravanji* drama in the Maratha language, is attributed to King Serfoji II himself.[12] Both poems are devoted in part to an exposition of the Copernican universe and a modern geography of the world.

The Species Classified: Vedanāyakam Sāstri's Version of Noah's Ark

Vedanāyakam Sāstri's *Drama of the Architect of Wisdom* (or *Divine Architect*) is a long narrative poem relating the creation and flood narratives from the book of Genesis in the Bible. The poem is divided into seven quasi-autonomous sections: The Creator; Noah's Boat (or Ship) Song; The Ark of the Covenant; One Caste (in this section Sāstri argues that the castes are by nature separate but equal creations of God); The Works of the Architect of the Universe; The Song of Joy; and The Bronze Serpent. *Novavin Kappal Tamil,* "Noah's Boat Song" (NBS), the narrative of Noah and the ark, was written for Serfoji and premiered at his court in 1830. Unlike the fortune-teller play and the majority of Sāstri's works, the poem as a whole has no generic model in Tamil, but its

11. Vedanāyakam Sāstri, *Bethlehem Kuravanji* (with a preface by E. Vedabothagam) (Tanjore, reprint of 1820 edition). Sāstri, *Petlakem Kuravanji* [*Bethlehem Kuravanji*] *and other works* [*Nanattacca Natakam, Nanavula, Aranatintam, Nana Antati*] (Madras, 1964).

12. Serfoji II, *Devendra Kuravanji: A Drama in Marathi Giving the Geography of the World in Songs, By Serfoji Rajah,* edited by Tyagaraja Jatavallabhar, Saraswati Mahal Series no. 18 (Tanjore, 1950). Madras, Oriental Manuscripts Library.

individual sections are modeled after popular Tamil genres. "Noah's Boat Song," for instance, is framed in a popular folk-song genre *(kappal pattu),* and the language, meters, music, and poetic and devotional conventions of all the segments are characteristically Tamil.

The poet presents a number of metaphors in *DAW,* beginning with that of God as the divine architect of the universe. The dominant metaphor of the first two segments of the poem, however, is the enumeration and naming of things, classificatory schemes drawn from the sciences of anatomy, natural history, and geography. In part one, "The Creator," Sāstri describes the divine Architect building the city that is the universe, according to a great plan that applies to the minutest detail. Describing human bodies as mobile "abodes" built by God for housing souls, Sāstri launches into a sort of anatomy and physiology lesson, a catalog of all the bones, blood vessels, and muscles in the body. Identifying 249 bones in the body, he declares, in a typical verse:

> Listen to my count, and check your own!
> There are twenty-seven bones in the palate,
> nineteen in the mandible,
> one bone in the nose,
> five in each cheek.

The catalogs in NBS, the section on Noah's ark, cover the flora and fauna of Tamilnadu. Sāstri's Noah has to examine more than ninety species of trees in the Tamil land before he reaches the cypress, which God identifies as the tree out of whose wood ("gopher wood") the ark must be made. The catalog of creatures that go into the ark comprises ninety-four species of animals (including three species of goats, and six of mice and rats) and ninety-three species of birds. The species are named at length, and the list is enlivened by poetic figures such as alliteration and onomatopoeia, as in this description of the last birds entering the ark: four species of *cittu* (sparrow), named in alliterated, rhymed words, imitate the great noise of the gathered birds.

In the next catalog Sāstri lists the insects known in the Tamil region, including eighteen species of wasp and several species of lice. The rest of the segment is devoted to the supplies necessary for life and culture that are loaded into the ark: food and drink, the objects and implements of work and study. Noteworthy is the remarkably complete catalog of the varieties of rice that the Tamil Noah takes with him, not surprisingly, since rice is the staple of the Tamil diet. These same varieties of rice were named by the missionaries in a report they sent back to Halle. Finally, as the ark floats on the flood, the narrator describes more than one hundred species of fish.

Several of Sāstri's catalogs in NBS have no basis in the Genesis narrative of Noah's ark. At the same time, they express both a Tamil and a distinctly Christian worldview. Catalogs are an important component of epic, ballad, and other kinds of Indian narrative poetry, written and oral. The catalogs in NBS are thus examples of an ancient poetic convention. For Sāstri, however, the enumeration of species in the context of cosmic creation is also essentially linked with a seminal concept underlying images of creation in ancient Indian religions, including the Vedic myth of Purusha, the primeval cosmic man (*Rig Veda* X.90), from whose dismemberment the human, natural, and celestial orders are created, in parallel and organic relationship. These orders include caste (*jāti*, "birth"), a fundamental identity-marker and paradigmatic ordering principle in Indian society and culture.

Yet, the form, content, specific contexts, and intention of Sāstri's catalogs set them apart from traditional Indian ones. First, the catalogs in NBS are meant to be systematic, comprehensive, and precise, not just *suggestive* (by illustration) of plenitude or infinitude, as poetic catalogs, and catalogs in Indian creation myths, are apt to be. The Evangelical poet names the species because he wishes to name and classify *all* of them, to catalog and classify as much of God's creation as is known to man. This desire to provide a *complete* list of species is premised on the biblical idea of an omnipotent creator God as the active author of every aspect of creation, down to the individual species. This very completeness of the Christian image of creation contrasts with the assumptions of the major Hindu theories of creation, which are related in compendia of sacred myths called the *Puranas*. The *Purana* myths of creation are told in a number of narratives, each of which gives a different account of the agents, actors, and processes of creation, and few of which involve an active creator God figure.[13] Indeed, premised on a vision of infinite space, multiple world systems, vast, recurrent cycles of time, and the manifestation of the sacred in myriad potent forms, Hindu creation myths stress infinitude, pervasion, process, transformation, spontaneity, and impersonal agency. There is neither a single creator nor a historic act of creation, and "underlying this scheme of continuous creations and dissolutions appears to be a pulsating view of the universe in which matter and energy are periodically transformed into each other."[14]

In an interesting synthesis, the Tamil poet names only the species that he knows from his Tamil environment (this is a characteristic of Tamil poetry

13. Cornelia Dimmitt and J. A. B. van Buitenen, *Classical Hindu Mythology* (Philadelphia, 1978), pp. 15-58.

14. Dimmitt and van Buitenen, *Classical Hindu Mythology*, p. 24.

from about the first to the second centuries A.D.), but he uses the language and the classificatory principles and systems of eighteenth-century European natural history to accomplish the naming. Sāstri's list is based on a new conception of empirical knowledge, drawn from European science, but in a Pietist frame. In the enumeration of the species to the complete extent and detail known to human beings in finite and, if possible, complete terms, Sāstri was expressing the Pietist theological vision of the completeness of God's creation.[15] Indigenous taxonomical principles are thus subsumed by the new paradigm. A last, and simpler, purpose is at work here. Sāstri was interested in science from the point of view of a student and teacher of the new learning, and in this poem he uses the context of the creation to teach the rudiments of European anatomy, botany, and biology to his Tamil Christian audience.

In all these respects Sāstri shares intellectual affinities with the Halle philosophy of education and the Halle missionaries. His teachers were naturalists. In the older, eighteenth-century context of physico-theology, for these missionaries as well as for Sāstri to name the species, and to order them, would have been an epistemic act. According to the physico-theological perspectives that stimulated the study of science at Halle and elsewhere in Europe, one knew the species by classifying them, and thereby knew God through his creation. By the beginning of the nineteenth century, however, physical theology had ceased to be a driving force behind scientific study, and the science of the European Enlightenment based itself on the principle of Rationalism. The *Kunstkammer* was still operative at the Francke Foundations, but that *Kunstkammer* had become an anachronism. John's extensions of his scientific interests into his preaching and evangelical duties in Tranquebar led the Halle headquarters to brand him a "rationalistic" missionary, that is, one who had abandoned the sure ground of Pietist theology. During his long life, Vedanāyakam Sāstri, unlike John and the missionary naturalists, appears not to have engaged in the active pursuit of collection and classification. He continued to express his firm conviction in the early Pietist vision of science as an instrument for knowing God's creation, in an innovative combination of poetry and didacticism, and of the Tamil aesthetic with Christian thought and the discourses and perspectives of European science. How pervasive this combination is in Sāstri's major poems will become clear when we look at the prominent role the disciplines of geography and astronomy played in them.

---

15. The Francke Foundation's *Kunst- und Naturalienkammer* was one of the earliest institutions to organize its collections according to the system Linnaeus propounded in 1735.

The Globe Encompassed in Two Fortune-Teller Plays

A popular dance-drama-musical genre, a *kuravanji* is a play with a stereo-typed plot in which a wandering gypsy fortune-teller *(kuratti, kuravanji)* pre-dicts the happy union of a lovelorn woman pining for the man she hopes to marry or rejoin. The fortune-teller's husband, the bird catcher *(singan)*, is shown catching birds with nets and snares. At the end of the play, the *kuratti* herself rejoins her bird-catcher husband. A noteworthy feature of the for-tune-teller play is the ample opportunity it gives the poet to delineate the na-tive mountain landscapes of the nomadic and tribal *kuravar,* the agricultural landscapes of the lowland towns, and the prosperity of the hero's city and ter-ritory. Such geographic and topographical specificity is a characteristic fea-ture of Tamil literature from the earliest classical period onward.[16]

Composed by learned poets and performed by skilled performers (women court- and temple-dancers), the fortune-teller play is characterized by folk and lower-class characters and elements, but also by classical theologi-cal and mythological themes. Not least among the many points of resem-blance between European comic opera and this Indian genre is its affiliation with classical vocal music. The entire play is composed of songs set to classi-cal melodies and rhythmic patterns. The aristocratic hero of the play is usu-ally either a Hindu god or a king. The genre was popular in the Tamil region in the period, and plays were performed regularly in the courts of noblemen and at temple festivals. Between 1700 and 1830 at least nine *kuravanji* dramas were written at the Maratha court in Tanjore alone, and King Serfoji is him-self the hero of such a play (*Sarabendra Bupala Kuravanji*, ca. 1820), which was enacted at the great temple of the Hindu god Shiva in Tanjore until the middle of the twentieth century. The *kuravanji* genre became popular be-cause its heterogeneous characters, combined with its comic plot and attrac-tive characters, most importantly the charismatic and exotic *kuratti* fortune-teller, mirrored in many ways the pluralistic ethnic and cultural discourses of South Indian society in the eighteenth century. It is likely that poets, mission-aries, and kings chose these popular musical dance-dramas as the vehicle for the dissemination of ideas because they were clearly capable of attracting a wide variety of audiences.

Both *Bethlehem Kuravanji (BK)* and *Devendra Kuravanji (DK)* are didac-

---

16. For a fuller discussion see my "*Bethlehem Kuṟavañci* of Vedanayaka Sastri of Tanjore: The Cultural Discourses of an Early-Nineteenth-Century Tamil Christian Poem," in *Christian, Cultural Interactions, and India's Religious Traditions,* edited by Judith M. Brown and Robert Eric Frykenberg (Grand Rapids, 2002).

tic plays. Vedanāyakam Sāstri's play is, above all, a Christian allegory, deploying the theme of prophecy to narrate the history and foretell the triumphant future of Christianity in the form of a fortune-teller *(kuravanji)* play. The heroine Devamohini ("She who is in love with the Lord"), humankind personified, is hopelessly in love with the Lord of Bethlehem. Faith comes to Devamohini in the form of a female wandering fortune-teller, Jnana-singi ("the fortune-teller with spiritual/doctrinal wisdom"), and predicts that she will become the Bride of Christ. Meanwhile, the preacher and his catechist, as the bird catcher Jnana-singan and his assistant, use the net of the Gospels to trap birds in the form of the peoples of the world. A remarkable feature of Sāstri's drama, however, is a song describing the Copernican system. In narrating his story, the poet teaches, in effect, an alternative to the Hindu cosmography, represented by a combination of European astronomy and geography. In his *DK*, by using the gypsy fortune-teller character to teach European geography and the Copernican system, Serfoji presents the same new cosmography, but in a Hindu mythic-narrative context. It is not clear whether he is indeed the actual author of the book, but there is no doubt that he conceived the work, commissioned it to be executed according to his specifications, and possibly intended it to serve as a children's geography textbook.

According to the proemium to the *BK*, Sāstri worked on the poem during the year 1799 and finished it in its first version in 1800, as a young man of 26. He performed sections of it in Madras and elsewhere in 1809, but revised it later. The version of the play as we now have it dates from 1820. In the preface to the revised edition he says that he revised the drama during the tenure of the Tanjore German missionary Johann Caspar Kohlhoff, son of another parish missionary and also protégé of the Rev. Schwartz. It is not clear what role Kohlhoff played in the revisions, or what exactly the revisions involved. As we shall see, however, at least some of the changes in the poem might have taken the form of corrections and additions to the material on astronomy.

Dancing with the Planets: The Daughter of Zion's Songs of the Copernican World System

In the conventions of the *kuravanji* play the heroine, the woman in love, berates the moon in a song for cruelly directing his "hot rays" at her and making her burn with longing for her lover. In the *BK* song in which the maiden addresses the moon, Devamohini begins the song by telling the moon to stop being conceited, since it is only one of many moons — twenty-four, to be exact, twenty-four satellites created by God:

Earth has one moon, Jupiter (Pon) has four.
Saturn's moons number eight, Tingal's number six,
Uranus has four, Neptune has one —
God made all these twenty-four satellites.

In the remaining verses, the poet refers to episodes in the Bible in which the moon is shown in a subservient position — bowing to Joseph (Gen. 37:9) and being made to stand still by Joshua (Josh. 10:12-13). The purpose of the first verse is, clearly, that of teaching the new discoveries about the satellite moons of planets other than Earth. We know now that Jupiter has twelve moons. Since Sāstri assigns to Pon and Tingal (two names for Jupiter), four and six moons respectively, it is possible that he means them to collectively represent Jupiter's moons. The number eight for the moons of Saturn is close to the nine that we now know. Very little was known about Uranus and Neptune in 1820.

Tevamokini then begins to play ball, in another of the conventional scenes of the *kuravanji* sequence, except that the "balls" she is throwing up in the air are no ordinary balls; they are the planets of the solar system. It should be noted that the "ball play" of the fortune-teller drama resembles a traditional variation of the game of jacks South Indian young women and girls play, tossing up and juggling small seeds or balls *(ammanai)* in complex patterns. While cosmic and religious imagery are an integral part of *kuravanji* poems, Tevamokini's dance in the *BK* is very clearly intended to teach the heliocentric or "Copernican" world system, as opposed to the cosmology of the Hindu *Puranas*:

The daughter of Zion, destined to become the bride
of the One who placed the sun, moon, and stars in space,
marveled at the vast courses of the planets,
and played ball with them — I shall sing of her skillful play!

(*BK*, pp. 57-60)

In the several verses of this song of the girl playing ball, the narrator provides, in sing-song verse, poetic epithets for the planets, facts and figures relating to the celestial bodies. The topics covered include the distance of the planets from the sun (in Indian units called *yojana*, in verse 1, and in "English miles" in verse 5); the rotational period of each of the planets (v. 2); the orbital speed per hour of each planet in English units (v. 3); the orbital period of the planets around the sun, in earth time units (days, hours, minutes, seconds) (v. 4). The information regarding the distances is quite close to those given in modern tables, although the figures indicate that Sāstri is using a unit that is a little more than a modern mile (1.1 or 1.2 miles). The following verse (v. 4), on the orbital period of the planets, is representative:

This is the time the planets take to revolve around the sun:
Mercury — eighty-seven days, twenty-three hours, fourteen minutes,
nine seconds;
Venus — two hundred and twenty-four days, sixteen hours, forty
minutes, twenty-seven seconds;
Earth — one year, twice five hours, forty-eight minutes.

The poem runs through the planets Jupiter, Saturn, and Uranus in similar vein. Like the catalogs of epic poetry, mnemonic verses are common in didactic poems, and certainly in poems that are designed to teach facts and figures; and the songs about astronomy in the *BK* are clearly intended to help the readers memorize rudimentary facts about the solar system. Mnemonic verses are a standard teaching device in Indian scientific texts. Sāstri uses a very traditional means to teach revolutionary facts, to replace the Hindu geocentric universe with a heliocentric one, in relation to the tropical instead of the Hindu sidereal zodiac. The figures he gives are entirely new to an Indian audience since, given the radical difference between the two systems, Indian figures would not have been translatable into Western ones. Poetic elements, including a lilting meter, alliteration and other figures of speech, and the use of a number of traditional epithets and names for the planets, enliven the verses.

In mentioning Uranus and Neptune, Sāstri reveals his knowledge of the latest European discoveries in astronomy. Uranus and Neptune were unknown to Indian astronomers, who did not use telescopes.[17] It is only from European sources that Sāstri could have learned about Herschel's discovery of Uranus in 1781. It is clear that, along with his contemporaries, Sāstri had only the vaguest knowledge of Neptune since he mentions the planet by name only once, in the introductory verse in the moon song. He could not have known Neptune before 1801 since it was only that year that Giuseppe Piazzi's discovery of the asteroid Ceres (followed by the discovery of several of other asteroids) allowed the prediction of another planet beyond Uranus. In fact, the prediction of the existence of Neptune was confirmed only in 1841, and the planet was actually observed only in 1846, by Germans in Berlin. Again, Sāstri's repeated references to the rings of Saturn (he always speaks of Uranus

17. See discussion in Richard Fox Young, ch. 8 below.

as the planet "beyond the rings of Saturn") show a close acquaintance with the features of Saturn as they were being discovered through observation.[18]

The revolutionary nature of Sāstri's assertion of the Copernican system can be understood only in the light of the history of the Hindu view of the relationship between planetary astronomy, the cosmos, and human life, which is dramatically different from the European perspective on these things in the eighteenth century. The astronomy of the *BK* challenged not only facts and figures but an entire worldview and a conception of science in relation to everyday life.

As was the case with other technical subjects in India, astronomy remained an essentially isolated tradition, never to be integrated into general theory of knowledge. Its function was not to discover the truth about the apparent motions of the heavenly bodies or other celestial phenomena but to train experts who could prepare calendars and astronomical tables for use in determining the proper times for religious observances and in operating the various modes of astrology. It was oriented toward these very practical goals and normally eschewed all theoretical considerations. The tradition was one of mathematical computations — their iteration, adjustment, and use — rather than one of observation. Although there was considerable influence from Greek astronomy on the Hindu astronomers during India's medieval period, the influence was not from the mainstream Greek tradition and did not include a close knowledge of Ptolemy. Nor did Islamic astronomy, with its ancient tradition of observational and computational instruments (astrolabes, armillary spheres), directly influence the Hindu astronomers until the seventeenth and eighteenth centuries, particularly under the North Indian Mughal rulers, and especially in the case of a remarkable figure of the Mughal period, the Hindu astronomer-king Sawai Jai Singh, of Jaipur in North India.

Astronomy (Sanskrit *jyotisha, jyotihshastra,* Tamil *sotidam*), in the sense of calculations and prognostications based on planetary movements in relation to the constellations, was covered in Sanskrit *siddhanta* texts and in the south, in their Tamil counterparts, but Hindu cosmology and cosmography were covered in the compendia of sacred myths known as the *Puranas* (in Sanskrit and Tamil). Thus, the knowledge of planetary motions and cosmic phenomena coexisted with a mythic cosmography, in which the earth is a flat-bottomed disc with a golden mountain (Meru) at its center and contains

18. One wonders if the poet added the reference to Neptune in his 1820 revision of the poem, or perhaps in an even later revision? Was the entire segment on the Copernican system added in a later edition? What part did Kohlhoff's advice or injunctions play in these additions and revisions?

seven concentric continents encircled by seven oceans. In this cosmography, situated on a series of wheels above the earth, the celestial bodies are rotated on their axes by the god Brahma with ropes of wind. Astronomers even discussed a spherical earth and assumed such an earth for certain calculations, but they also allowed for the flat-bottomed disc of the *Puranas*. More importantly, astronomical learning was a strictly esoteric tradition. In South as well as in North India, the cosmography of the *Puranas* was the basis of the worldview of the average Hindu, who had no contact with astronomy except in the form of the astrological predictions of the experts.

Before the nineteenth century, nearly all attempts by Europeans to introduce European astronomy, and especially the concept of a heliocentric ("Copernican") universe, had met with intense resistance based on scorn for inconsistency and contradiction of reason and logic and charges of incompatibility with the religious bases of Hindu and Muslim cosmology. Sawai Jai Singh (1688-1743), a stellar figure in the history of Indian astronomy, nearly proved the exception.

Jai Singh built five major observatories, housing large masonry astronomical instruments (several of these have survived in good condition), and possessed major Arabic and Persian astronomical texts, among them Nasir al din's version of Ptolemy's *Almagest,* translated from Persian and Arabic into Sanskrit (1732). While Jai Singh's passion for actual observation was unusual in the Hindu cultural context, we must remember that he was a Mughal feudatory and was well versed in Islamic astronomy, with its stress on instruments and observation. However, Jai Singh, like most Hindu astronomers, was mainly interested in computations and astronomical tables, and the correlation between Indian and European methods for arriving at these computations. Although he appears to have known (and possessed) a telescope, he does not seem to have used it. Last, as a pious Hindu, the king kept his cosmology quite separate from his astronomy. Although Jai Singh was in contact with Jesuits in India and Europe and sent a delegation to Portugal to learn about European astronomy, he does not mention the Copernican system, nor do his observatories and the writings of his court astronomers depart from the assumptions of the Hindu and Islamic astronomical principles and concerns of his time.

Vedanāyakam Sāstri, however, presents the Copernican system precisely as the basis of an alternative cosmology, and as a theory of knowledge based on the empirical observation and study of nature. For him it is important that the figures and the calculations he cites are the results of actual observations of the European astronomers (continually revised, as was the poem itself), and that they should alter one's understanding of the universe, for these continuing discoveries, these new facts and figures, constituted the continuing expansion of the knowledge of God's universe, an expansion that was a celebration of the continuing revelation of the Creator's glory. Sāstri's perspective on the relationships between God, man, and nature is clearly traceable to the ideal of physico-theology that dominated European thought from the Renaissance to the eighteenth century, and that, as noted earlier, Francke had systematically put into pedagogical practice in Halle. It is not surprising that the Tamil Evangelical poet's didactic-poetic works are suffused with Pietistic physico-theology. The mythic cosmography must be rejected and exploded, and the new facts and figures must be memorized in their place, not merely as new mythology in the place of the old but as a scientific-theological cosmography in place of nonscientific mythology. Where scientific exploration and knowledge were a means to the knowledge of God's works, empirical proof and accuracy were crucial, and there could be no tolerance of inconsistencies and inexactitude of fact.

The new cosmology Sāstri was presenting had an essential geographical component as well. As Donald Lach points out, before 1500 "geographical" studies were included in the definition of cosmography, a branch of learning that described and mapped both the heavens and the earth, and not until the middle to the end of the sixteenth century was geography, as an academic discipline, distinct from cosmography, established in Europe.[19] Thanks to Pietist theology, well into the eighteenth and early nineteenth centuries both the Halle institutions and the Tranquebar missionaries continued to use the concept of the pair of globes, the celestial and the terrestrial, to represent the complementarity of the disciplines of astronomy and geography as components of a complete cosmography. In the revised cosmography-geography of the seventeenth and eighteenth centuries, too, the Renaissance separation between the study of nature and "arts" based on mathematics (especially geometry), such as cartography and navigation, had begun to be set aside.

Biblical Geography and World Geography in NBS and the *Bethlehem Kuravanji*

We must return to NBS to see how Sāstri completes his cosmography with an account of a scientific, empirically verifiable (terrestrial) geography. King Serfoji wrote a fortune-teller play largely dedicated to modern geography, and

19. Donald Lach, *Asia in the Making of Europe*, vol. 2: *A Century of Wonder* (Chicago, 1977).

the *BK* contains segments devoted to geography. Thus we turn to the geography lessons of NBS and the two fortune-teller plays.

In NBS, as Sāstri's Noah's ark floats on the flood around all the five continents of the globe, including Australia, the narrator names the major countries and territories on these continents, along with their capitals. Closer to home, even minor ports and towns (Kallik kottai, Velur, Caturanka patnam) appear in the list. The ark floats on and finally comes to rest on Mount Ararat. In Sāstri's poem the voyage of the ark is nothing less than a complete circumnavigation of the terrestrial globe of the eighteenth century, an idea whose implications will be commented on below.

In *BK*, the geographical portions move from a focus on the geography of the Bible lands to the enumeration of the peoples of the world, to a brief description of the continents of the globe. The fortune-teller play is by definition a play about geographies. All fortune-teller plays include detailed descriptions of the mountains and rivers of the land of the poem's hero (a king or a god) as well as of the mountains from which the fortune-teller comes. The nomadic fortune-teller also names the many lands and countries she has visited during her travels. In *BK* the hero's territory consists of the Bible lands, especially Galilee. Nanaccinki names the major and minor hills of the Bible narratives, with descriptive tags — "Eden, the original hill that God gave us, Ararat, Noah's mountain, lofty, cloud-covered Pisgah, from whose summit Moses saw Canaan. Golgotha, the hill of Jesus' passion . . . Meribah, which became a flood of water when Moses struck it with his staff."

In other sections, Jerusalem and the biblical lands and tribes are named in detail, as are the world churches, beginning with the seven churches of Asia. The bird catcher and catechist casts his nets, and birds come from everywhere, on every continent. First, the birds fly over the paddy fields (where the nets have been cast). These birds are people from everywhere, and the fields are their lands, including the Bible lands (the birds fly over Judea, Galilee, Samaria Bethania, Jerusalem, Hebron, Perea, Bethshamesh, Jericho, Bethzaatha, Nain, Tiberias, and also over Salamis, Caesaria, Tabor, and Capernaum just to the north of Tabor). In the "Song of Sighting the Birds" (pp. 136-39) and the "Song of the Birds Arriving" (pp. 139-41), he names, first, the peoples of the world outside India and, then, the communities and tribes of India and South India, using both the traditional and the modern nomenclature. In the "Song of Setting the Snares" (p. 159), the bird catcher–pastor says to his catechist-assistant; "O Nuvan, to gather the Lord's followers from every community all over the world in the Kingdom of Bethlehem's Lord, go to the vast continents of Europe, Asia, Africa, and America and quickly set your snares." The geographical movement is from historical sacred geography to the ethnographies of the immediate present and the glorious future geography of the globe encompassed by Christianity.

In his two "cosmographic" poems Sāstri managed to give expression to the union of science, religion, and didactic intent that he had inherited from the Halle Pietists and from Tamil poetic and cultural traditions. The connection between the various sciences and the world as an object of study, as God's creation, comes across explicitly in the creation context of "Noah's Boat Song." In the *BK*, however, Sāstri also highlights the importance of the historical and ideal landscapes of the Bible lands in the circumnavigable world. A striking metaphor for this unity of vision is perhaps to be discerned in the ideal layout of the *Kunstkammer,* especially as exemplified by the one at the Francke Foundations. In the eighteenth century two large celestial globes, armillary spheres modeling the world systems of Tycho Brahe and Copernicus, stood in the middle of the room, with terrestrial globes on each side. On each side of the globes were placed two tables, each holding a large model of a biblical topographical phenomenon or monument, the Holy Land, and so on. The *Kunstkammer* led to the roof, from which students could observe the sky. Atlases and terrestrial globes were placed elsewhere in the room. In eighteenth-century Tanjore, in his NBS and the *BK,* Sāstri presents a poetic counterpart to the cosmographic vision expressed in the Francke *Kunstkammer.* Yet, the Halle cosmography is not alien to Sāstri's Tamil sensibility, for it fits with ease into the cultural discourses and dominant themes of Tamil poetry embodied in the topographical specificity of fortune-teller plays, among other things.

The Fortune-Teller Play of the King of the Gods: King Serfoji's Textbook of World Geography

Like *BK*, the *Devendra Kuravanji (DK)* is a fortune-teller play with a few variations on the standard plot. This poem pays the merest of respects to the standard love theme of such plays, launching very quickly into the geography lesson, which is its chief concern. The heroine Indrani, Queen of Paradise, consort of the King of the Gods, is awaiting the return of her husband, Indra, in their palace in the celestial city of Amaravati. The arrival of a *burdin* (Marathi equivalent of the Tamil *kuravanji,* a female nomadic fortune-teller, the counterpart of the gypsy women fortune-tellers of Europe) is announced, and Indrani asks her who she is and where she comes from. The "gypsy" woman says that she has come from the top of the golden Mount Meru, the center of the traditional Hindu universe, and has traveled at great speed all over the universe. At once, Indrani says: "Then you must be omniscient. I want to know all about the world's mountains, rivers and countries, I want to learn the geography of the world. Tell me, does the earth revolve around the sun, or does the sun revolve around the earth? Tell me, what is the moon's orbit, and what planets revolve around the sun? What is the diameter of the Earthsphere?" (*DK*, p. 5).

The fortune-teller replies: "You know the cosmology of the *Puranas*. Listen! I shall now tell you a cosmography and geography different from that one" (*DK*, p. 5). She goes to describe the rudiments of the Copernican world system, beginning with: "Like a flaming torch whirled round and round, the sun rotates in place on its own, and not around anything else. But the earth revolves around the sun in a year's time. The sun is a bright star. Many planets revolve perpetually around it, earth among them" (*DK*, p. 6). Indrani asks the visitor to tell her about the continents on the globe, their sizes, the names of all the countries and capitals, and the rivers on these continents. Saying that there are four continents on the globe, the fortune-teller proceeds to name the countries, cities, and so on. The *burdin*'s list is by no means a complete list of the major cities and countries of the world. Like Sāstri in *BK*, she names only four continents, suggesting that perhaps NBS, completed in 1830, is later than *DK* — and *BK* as well — since Sāstri *does* include Australia among the continents around which the ark floats. Serfoji's fortune-teller names the principal countries of Europe, Asia, Africa, and America, going into minute detail in many instances. She seems to know the major kingdoms of Germany and France (e.g., Burgundy). The rivers and towns of Scotland and England are named in some detail, but much space is also given to the details of places in North and South America (Philadelphia in Pennsylvania, St. Augustine and Pensacola in Florida, North Carolina, the islands of the West Indies). At the end of this recital, which is framed in over one hundred songs in a variety of *raga* melodies and *tala* beats and several recitative verses, she predicts Indrani's reunion with her husband, is richly rewarded, and is met by her bird catcher husband, who has abandoned his hunt to come in search of her.

In Serfoji's poem the mythic location of Indra's paradise is merely a take-off point for the elaboration of a verifiable, European-style, modern terrestrial geography, shorn of its Christian cosmographic connotations. Serfoji never traveled abroad but bought and avidly read the abundant literature of his time on the subjects of voyages and exploration. He also had a large collection of all the latest books on geography. We know from the catalog of his personal collection of books (still preserved at the Sarasvati Mahal Library), for instance, that he owned Alexander von Humboldt's accounts of his voyages, *A Geographical and Historical View of the World* (5 vols., 2 sets dated

1810), an *Introduction to Geography and Astronomy* (1791), and several other sets of books on geography (dating from 1788). *DK* itself appears to be one of the books that Serfoji intended to put to use as a textbook for children in the Indian-language schools he had set up. He might even have intended to have it printed at his printing press (equipped with the Devanagari characters for Marathi, Sanskrit, and Hindi), as he had already done for *Aesop's Fables.*[20] Serfoji's image of Indrani, Queen of Heaven, wishing to learn about the cosmos from the wise, exotic, nomadic woman, is surely a very apt and attractive metaphor for the desire of a well-bred, intelligent, open-minded people wishing to cross the frontiers of a new science.

It should not be surprising that, unlike the amateur astronomer king Jai Singh in the seventeenth century, the Hindu king Serfoji could accept and celebrate the Copernican universe in the eighteenth century. Unlike the Mughal feudatory, the Tanjore ruler was not closely familiar with Islamic science and had been educated in an array of Western sciences as part of a coherent curriculum. More importantly, what interested Serfoji was not astronomy *per se* (his preferences were for natural history and physics), but the Baconian experimental and observational biases of eighteenth-century European science. Unlike the pandits of Malwa, whose complex response to the European heliocentric cosmology is examined in Richard Fox Young's chapter in this volume,[21] but each for his own reasons, Serfoji and Sāstri underplay the cognitive dissonance they must have felt between assumptions in the indigenous culture and the views of the universe they were advocating in their poems.

Sāstri bridged the gap with his acceptance of European scientific discourse as an integral part of Pietist theology. Serfoji appears to have had little trouble in simultaneously patronizing large numbers of literary works based on Hindu cosmology and texts advocating the cosmos of European science. In any case, as my discussion of Serfoji's interest in late-eighteenth-century theories in natural history will show, the king accepted a Creator-God or a one-time historical creation. It would also seem, given the broader context of Serfoji's passion for scientific investigation, that he understood that, though the Copernican theory appeared to contradict the evidence of the senses (a point that the pandits of Malwa found contrary to logic), it was premised on more general "natural" laws and principles, which were compatible with the inductive principles employed in all the modern European sciences, including physics and chemistry.

20. Graham Shaw, "The Tanjore 'Aesop' in the Context of Early Marathi Printing," *The Library* 5th series, 33 (1978): 207-14.
21. See below, ch. 8.

Globus Celestis et Terrestris: The Pedagogic Uses
of the Globe in Halle, Tranquebar, and Tanjore

A recurrent symbol and instrument in Sāstri's and Serfoji's poems, and a looming physical presence in the Halle *Kunst- und Naturalienkammer,* is that of the celestial and terrestrial globes, representing astronomy and geography. While the concept of the celestial globe had flourished for centuries in many variations in different communities in Europe, Asia, and the Islamic world, the circumnavigation of the globe was a major turning point in European conceptions of geography, which had a major impact on the making and use of terrestrial globes as instruments of great utility and importance for travelers, to determine terrestrial positions. With Gerard Mercator's *Atlas of 1569* as a landmark, cartography and geography emerged as important new disciplines. Sāstri's Noah's ark's voyage around the world is a graphic depiction of this chain of events, and of the sense of a spherical earth as an experimental, verifiable reality, a concept to be internalized. The same ideas are implicit in *BK* and *DK* as well, with the influence of Mercator's atlas surfacing in the description of the continents. It is possible that in the poems of Serfoji and Sāstri we have the earliest expressions by Indians regarding the combined "lessons" of Copernican or heliocentric astronomy and geography, which they have internalized.

In the 1740s Benjamin Schultze, who became director of the *Franckesche Stiftungen* (1743-60), after several years as a Halle missionary in Madras, reports that the German missionaries in Tranquebar had been provided with a telescope, microscope, thermometer, air pump, and an electrical machine, but that they still needed a large terrestrial globe, as well as a celestial one, in addition to the latest works on natural history, newly invented instruments, and mathematical instruments. From the context of the report it appears that these instruments were intended for the missionaries' own engagement in observation and empirical study, to be reported to Halle.

Several of the Tranquebar missionaries at that time were naturalists and collectors, but missionary letters and reports show that they used at least some of these materials, especially the celestial and terrestrial globes, as illustrative materials in their conversations with Indians to whom they wished to explain Pietist Christianity. Here is an instance of such a pedagogical use of the globes, as reported in the *Hallesche Berichte.* The following excerpt dates from 1756: "A heathen merchant in Cudalur visited us along with several of his relatives and friends, and saw the terrestrial and celestial globes, whereupon, we took the opportunity, first to help them know the Creator through His great and wondrous works, and thereafter, also to talk about His great work of saving, through his only son, Jesus Christ, the race of men who have fallen into sin."

From the late Middle Ages onward, the celestial and terrestrial globes were used in European and Islamic culture and art to express several symbolic meanings, especially those of power and mastery. In the physico-theological thought of the seventeenth and eighteenth centuries, in Europe, the terrestrial and celestial globes were, above all, symbols of the wisdom, omnipotence, and providence of the Creator-God. It is as a vehicle for teaching these ideas that the missionaries used the globes in everyday conversation with their Indian acquaintances and visitors. It is more than likely that they put the globes to similar use in their teaching at the mission schools, and that pupils such as Sāstri first encountered the globes in the context of lessons that combined geography and astronomy with theology. As a teacher of astronomy, too, it is more than likely that the poet himself used globes as instruments in his teaching. Certainly, they serve this didactic purpose in his poems, in which he puts together the celestial and terrestrial globes for a theologically complete vision of the Tamil Pietist universe, in an age in which terrestrial geography and cosmography had become disunited in Europe.

Room for Wonder: Serfoji's Cabinet of Science and the *Kunst- und Naturalienkammer* at the *Franckesche Stiftungen* in Halle

If poetry was the chief arena in which Sāstri articulated his response to science, King Serfoji spent a significant amount of time every day in the pursuit of science. The king's European visitors were very impressed by his close acquaintance with European sciences and arts. In a letter to a friend in England, Bishop Heber wrote of his visit to Tanjore in March 1826, "I have been passing the last four days in the Society of a Hindoo Prince, the Raja of Tanjore, who quotes Fourcroy, Lavoisier, Linnaeus, and Buffon fluently, has formed a more accurate judgement of the poetical merits of Shakespeare than those so felicitously expressed by Lord Byron, and has actually emitted English poetry very superior to Rousseau's epitaph on Shenstone. . . ."[22]

In their accounts of their visits to Serfoji's palace European visitors (these included British residents, Danish and British officers, German missionaries,

---

22. Bishop Reginald Heber, letter to R. Wilmot Horton, quoted in Mildred Archer, "Serfogee, an Enlightened Tanjore Ruler and his Patronage of the Arts," *The India Magazine* 5.2 (January 1985): 12; R. Jayaraman, *The Sarasvati Mahal Library: A Short History and Guide* (Tanjore, 1981).

and gentlemen and gentlewomen travelers) invariably described the large and striking room in which Serfoji housed his collections, pursued his activities in science and art, and received his European visitors. This room clearly reflected the king's response to European science. Readers familiar with European *Kunstkammers* will note that Serfoji's room possessed many of the definitive characteristics of the *Kunstkammer*. In this final part I wish to illuminate both the special affinities of the spirit of his room and the activities he undertook there with the *Franckesche Kunstkammer*, and the ways in which he negotiated the changing world of European science in the nineteenth century.

One of the earliest references to the king's library is in Thomas Robinson's *Last Days of Bishop Heber* (London, 1829), which expands on the account of Bishop Heber's 1826 visit that had been cut short by his sudden death soon after his visit to Tanjore:

> The Rajah received us in his library, a noble room with three rows of pillars and handsomely furnished in the English style. On the one side there are portraits of the Maratha dynasty from Shahjee and Shevaji, ten bookcases containing a very fair collection of French, English, German, Greek, and Latin books, and two others of Mahratta and Sanskrit manuscripts. In the adjoining room is an air pump, an electrifying machine, an ivory skeleton, astronomical instruments, and several cases of books, many of which are on the subject of medicine that was for some years his favorite study. He showed us his valuable collection of coins and paintings of flowers and natural history, with each of which he seemed to have considerable acquaintance, particularly with the medicinal virtues of plants in his "Hortus Siccus." When he took our leave his minister showed us a noble statue of the Rajah by Flaxman. . . . His stables contain several fine English horses; but that of which he is most justly proud, as the rarest curiosity of an Indian court, is an English printing press worked by native Christians, in which they struck off a sentence in Mahratta in the Bishop's presence in honor of his visit.[23]

All the objects that are found in *Kunstkammers* are present in Serfoji's room — skeletons, machines, globes and atlases, astronomical instruments, plant and shell collections, coin collections, paintings and instruments for painting, and

23. Quoted in William Hickey, *The Tanjore Mahratta Principality in South India* (Madras, 1874), p. 123; and Jayaraman, *Sarasvati Mahal Library*, pp. 3-4. Heber's visit took place on 28 March 1826. He was shown round the library on the 30th.

natural history drawings. The last mentioned are particularly important because we know from an album of 117 natural history drawings, which Serfoji presented to the British Resident Benjamin Torin in 1803, that the king used the Linnaean classificatory system for plants, animals, mollusks, and fishes, inscribing the pictures himself with notes from observation and study.[24]

Like the European *Kunstkammers,* Serfoji's room was equipped with a library that had a very large technical section *(Fachbücher).* In 1826, Heber speaks of ten bookcases with books in many European languages, and a technical library with special collections. George Annesley, Viscount Valentia, who had visited Serfoji in 1804, had been shown the same room. At that time, it had only four bookcases, filled chiefly with English books.[25] The catalog of what has survived of Serfoji's personal collection of books (the books themselves are in storage and under conservation, and are currently inaccessible) reveals that he owned the latest editions of the most up-to-date research in botany, physics, chemistry, astronomy, geography, explorations and voyages, medicine, surgery, and natural history. Very few of these books are in languages other than English, but it is significant that many of the books in German relate to the sciences — for example, a German *Natural History of Plants* (1791), and a *Natural History,*[26] both almost certainly dating from Serfoji's school days.

The editor's notes in the *Short Guide* to the Saraswati Mahal Library reveal that the acquisition on books and manuscripts from various sources was meticulously documented in the Marathi Tanjore Palace Records, a close study of which will help establish the chronology of the accession of the titles on European sciences in the collection.[27] In the year 1807 alone, for example, the records indicate that Serfoji purchased a barometer and books on chemistry, mathematics, electricity, and veterinary science. In 1831 the king commissioned Sanji Lakshmanan, a former civil (government) servant of the East India Company, to translate into Marathi all the English works on anatomy in the collection.

The palace records also amply testify to the king's simultaneous interest in the stimulation and recovery of indigenous sciences (including horticulture

---

24. The drawings depicted 30 birds, a falcon hood, 2 bird traps, 28 fishes, 9 reptiles, 12 mollusks. In 1807 Torin presented the drawings to the Library of the British East India Company. Originally accessioned as "The Natural Products of Hindostan painted under the direction of the Raja of Tanjore" in the East India Company's Library in Leadenhall Street, London, Serfoji's Natural History album became part of the holdings of the old India Office Library, London (see Archer, "Serfogee, an Enlightened Tanjore Ruler").

25. Archer, "Serfogee, an Enlightened Tanjore Ruler," p. 11.

26. *A Catalogue of Serfoji's Personal Collection and Other Rare Books* (in English) (Tanjore, 1989), p. 96.

27. Jayaraman, *Sarasvati Mahal Library,* pp. 29-33.

and veterinary medicine), *belles lettres,* and arts. Entries for the year 1827 include accounts for the employment of pandits to write Marathi works on drama and Tamil texts on gynecological medicine, and notations regarding the study of "English medicine" at the newly established Madras College and the purchase of English medical books and surgical instruments for the Tanjore hospital from a British doctor in Madras. These last items of information recall a major point of resemblance between Serfoji's room and the Francke *Kunstkammer* — a direct connection to a medical establishment (in Serfoji's case, a pharmacy and a hospital), a printing press, a library, and school for teaching "the new sciences" *(navavidya).*

For Serfoji, as for the Halle Pietists, the pursuit of science and the activity of collecting became intrinsically connected with the goal of universal education, especially the education of orphans. Among the few personal writings of Serfoji is a poem he had inscribed at the graveside monument of his beloved mentor, Schwartz, hailing him as "Father of orphans, the widow's support." In 1801 the king commissioned (from the eminent sculptor Flaxman) a remarkable marble monument to Schwartz, portraying himself and orphan boys standing at the dying man's bedside. The rhetoric of the poem and the monument was rapidly translated into action in the new schools the king established in and near Tanjore.

In these schools for poor and orphaned boys and girls, called *navavidyakalashala,* the focus of the teaching was on the "new learning" denoting, above all, European science, and the pupils received instruction in English as well as in one of the four modern Indian languages in use in Tanjore (Tamil, Marathi, Persian, and Hindustani). Yet, while the king's educational ideals may have been inspired by his missionary education, the new schools detached the "new learning" from its foreign and Christian contexts, thus offering an unusual alternative to the colonial and missionary schools and their curricula.

The king's initiatives with the printing press, acquired in 1805, and which he had equipped with the earliest fonts for Marathi in India, show his indebtedness to the Halle model. There the *Franckesche Stiftungen*'s press was one of the most important instruments in the dissemination of learning, as well as a center for the training and employment of orphans. In India, until the 1830s, the Tranquebar missionaries printed works for their projects, including Tamil translations of Christian Scripture and catechisms, grammars of Indian languages, and textbooks in sciences.[28] By contrast, Serfoji used his Marathi and

---

28. See E. Arno Lehmann, *Es begann in Tranquebar: Die Geschichte der ersten evangelischen Kirche in Indien* (Berlin, 1965); and Mohanavelu, *German Tamilology.*

Sanskrit press to print secular works for use in his elementary schools, in-cluding *Aesop's Fables.*

Toward a Modern Science: Serfoji and the New Cosmologies

While it is remarkable that Serfoji, on his own initiative, had created a room for scientific study modeled in almost every detail on the eighteenth-century *Kunstkammers* of Europe, more remarkable is his dedication to the *practice* of scientific investigation in the spirit of the Enlightenment quest for knowl-edge. By the end of the eighteenth century *Kunstkammers* had gone out of fashion in Europe, reflecting the increasing specialization of scientific study and the birth of a number of new fields, including biology and geology.

The king was exploring sciences and methods that were hardly in exis-tence when he was being schooled by the missionaries. Serfoji pursued the latest advances in natural historical research, as illustrated by his passion for experiments, and his excellent collection of the works of Lavoisier, Fourcroy, and Buffon, the leading naturalists, chemists, physicists, and cosmologists of the eighteenth century, most of which were published in English translation well after Serfoji's assumption of the Tanjore throne.

The *Catalogue of Serfoji's Personal Collection and Other Rare Books* lists an 1812 English edition in twenty volumes of Georges Buffon's (1707-88) thirty-six-volume *Natural History of the Earth,* which had appeared in the original French between 1749 and 1785, with the last eight volumes appearing posthu-mously in 1804. Also named are Antoine Laurent Lavoisier's (1743-94) *Ele-ments of Chemistry* and a first edition in English (1804) of the pioneering ani-mal and plant chemist Antoine-Francois Fourcroy's (1755-1809) major work, the *General System of Chemical Knowledge,* which appeared in eleven volumes in French in 1801-2 and was published in English translation in 1804.[29] These landmark works were supplemented in the king's collection by popular En-glish manuals on chemistry and experimental science, such as William Henry's *The Elements of Experimental Chemistry* (2 vols.; London, 1818) and Bryan Higgins's *Experiments and Observations* (London, 1786).[30]

Most intriguing of the references above is, perhaps, Serfoji's interest in Buffon. There is reason to think that perhaps Buffon was especially interest-

29. *Catalogue of Serfoji's Personal Collection,* p. 94. Serfoji also owned an earlier work of Fourcroy's, *Elements of Natural History and Chemistry* (London, 1788), which the French scientist had completed prior to his more famous *Philosophy of Chemistry* (1792), which was translated into English in 1795. Fourcroy was Professor at the Jardin du Roi from 1784.

30. *Catalogue of Serfoji's Personal Collection,* p. 94.

ing to the Hindu king because he transformed "natural history" into "a history of nature," departing from the theory of a single historical creation and viewing biology and cosmology as continuous *processes*. As Daniel Boorstin puts it, Buffon "looked for natural causes (events) for the origin (creation) of the earth."[31] Such a view, of course, would have been more congenial to the Hindu king than the Christian view of a single creation.

---

31. Daniel J. Boorstin, *The Discoverers* (New York, 1983), p. 451.

CHAPTER SIX

Christianity, Colonialism, and Hinduism in Kerala: Integration, Adaptation, or Confrontation?

PENELOPE CARSON

In 1813 William Wilberforce, the famous abolitionist and supporter of Protestant missions, told the British House of Commons that missionaries in India were the "most esteemed and popular individuals in the country." He went on to add that "the natives are so tolerant and patient in what concerns their religion that even the grossest imprudence could not arouse their anger."[1] In private letters, however, some missionaries were telling a contrary story, of open hostility and even violence.[2] The cautious, almost antipathetic behavior of the East India Company toward missionary activity was to a large extent due to Company fears of Indian reactions to attempts to convert them. Were there grounds for the Company's caution or was missionary rhetoric correct that conversion would bind rulers and ruled?[3] There are many questions that need to be asked. Was peaceful coexistence between Christians and the wider community in the precolonial period a reality? If harmonious rela-

---

1. *Parliamentary Debates*, 2 June 1813, XXVI, pp. 868-69. See also the letter from E. Parry and C. Grant to R. Dundas, 8 June 1807, Bodleian MSS, Eng.Hist.c.210. Wilberforce was trying to force the East India Company to allow missionaries unrestricted access to India; German agents of the Royal Danish Missionary Society and the Society for the Promotion of Christian Knowledge (SPCK) had been operating in India since the eighteenth century. British missionaries from the Baptist and London Missionary Societies started to enter India in the 1790s.

2. For a detailed discussion see P. Carson, "Soldiers of Christ: Evangelicals and India, 1780-1833," Ph.D. thesis, University of London, 1988, esp. chs. 3, 5, and 8.

3. Carson, "Soldiers of Christ," esp. pp. 43-44.

tions prevailed, what were the factors that enabled this situation to arise? How far was Christianity "inculturated" into the fabric of a common, albeit highly structured, "Hindu"[4] life, and did this amount to what we might regard as socio-cultural integration? To what were converts[5] so attracted that they wished to change religious affiliation, and what did they expect to result from this change? What socio-cultural fissures already existed, and in what way did new fissures develop? Did conflict arise from the mere fact that people became Christian, or were there other factors behind "Hindu"-Christian clashes?[6] Finally, how far was that linkage of Christianity with the colonial powers, such as Portugal and Britain, a factor in promoting the progress of Christians in Kerala? How might such a linkage have been a factor in promoting or retarding the progress of things Christian, especially in Kerala?

These are large and sweeping questions, to which there may not always be simple or clear-cut answers. What happened in Kerala, however, provides an interesting starting point for addressing such questions because it was there that the very earliest Christian communities came into being. How far or for how long they lived together in peace with non-Christians around them is not clear, but that Christians became a part of a "Hindu" culture and society there can be little doubt. For many centuries Christians were regarded as comprising several distinct *jātis* (or separate birth groups) within Kerala's overall caste structure. Every time new groups of people arrived in Kerala from overseas, as they did over many centuries, the existing socio-cultural equilibrium would be disturbed. Among such groups, Christians were not the only newcomers. Jews, Muslims, and even Parsees also arrived on the western coasts of the subcontinent.[7] The arrival of Europeans, first the Portu-

---

4. The terms "Hindu" and "Hinduism" are fraught with difficulties. Originally taken to mean the inhabitants of the Indus valley, the term "Hindu" became used to describe adherents of "Hinduism," a phenomenon that is difficult to describe. As understood today, "Hinduism" describes a Brahamical religion that has gradually evolved from a rich diversity of religious traditions.

5. In this chapter the terms "convert" and "conversion" will be used to refer to the process by which an individual or group assert that a change from one religion to another has been made, whether or not a real "conversion" of heart and action follows or the missionaries accept it as such.

6. It is also a moot point whether there was ever such a thing in India, and especially in Kerala, as a "Hindu fold" or even a "Hindu majority." India has over three thousand different communities that did not intermarry or eat together, while those "twice-borne" categories, deemed "pure" *(savarna)* or "pollution-free" by Brahmans, constitute barely 15 percent of the total population. "Hindu majority" or "majority community" are part of current political vocabulary.

7. As will be shown below, Brahmans, Buddhists, and Jains had also come, many of

guese, then the Dutch, and eventually the British, brought further occasions of challenge and confrontation. By the end of the nineteenth century, perceptions of Christians in Kerala had become increasingly more complex. While the old Christian aristocracy from ancient times retained much of its former cultural strength, influence, and power, many Christian communities had come to be regarded with contempt. In the chapter that follows, an attempt is made to analyze the dynamics of Keralan society in relation to its old and its new Christian communities.

Precolonial Kerala

Kerala is the name identified with a dynasty that apparently ruled during the time of Asoka (269-232 B.C.) and that is associated with a strip of coastal land along the southwestern coast of the subcontinent, lying between the Western Ghats and the Arabian Sea and stretching from Cape Cormorin at the tip of India northward for about 360 miles. This coast was and is popularly known as Malabar. The original inhabitants of Kerala seem to have been of many different "birth" *(jāt)* groups that remained ethnically distinct, whose most dominant language and culture became Dravidian. Whether or not there was a rigid caste system is a matter of debate. Brahmans, Buddhists, and Jains, even perhaps Jews, appear to have arrived sometime in the fourth and third centuries (B.C.).[8] Arguments over these matters remain lively.[9] However, it is known that periodically from the eighth to the eleventh centuries there were inflows of Brahmans from the Deccan. Many of the ancient Hindu temples appear to have been built during this era, and it seems that this also was the time when the Brahmanization of Kerala occurred. As Brahmans gained influence and control, they seem to have "discovered" that many of Kerala's rulers were of "purer lineage" and then persuaded them to undergo rituals "re-admitting" them to *Kshatriya* status within the "color-coded" stratification system apparently constructed by them, known as *varnāshramadharma*. These "little kings" were keen to have Brahmans serving them, both as priests and as advisors and ministers, relishing the symbols and language of caste as useful tools for instilling order in the areas over which they claimed suzerain, if not sovereign, authority. Religious ceremonies, supported by special en-

---

them during the same centuries. The prehistoric "Dravidian" people predated them and supplanted places of dominance previously enjoyed by "aboriginal" *(adivāsi)* peoples.

    8. K. V. Eapen, *A Study of Kerala History* (Kottayam, 1986), chs. 4 and 5, pp. 24-30.

    9. Eapen, *A Study of Kerala History,* p. 30.

dowments, helped legitimate their positions of dominance within each local society.[10] Brahmanism reached a peak of ascendancy after Kerala was conquered by the Chola king, Rajaraja (A.D. 985-1016). Nevertheless, Brahmanism seems not to have been as rigid and predominant as some have thought. Recent research suggests that caste categories, even in Kerala, were not absolute but were reference points "to be negotiated, challenged or reshaped to fit changing circumstances."[11] Caste was a device for providing "patron-client" protection, both for strong and weak. Ritual distance increased and distinctions gradually hardened into ever more elaborate claims of hereditary privilege. However, for many centuries Kerala's rulers seem to have allowed subjects who had other religious systems to live in peace.

By the time of the arrival of the Portuguese in the sixteenth century, Kerala was regarded as already possessing very rigid codes of ritual purity. Among the original and Dravidian inhabitants, only Nayars seem to have managed to negotiate a place for themselves within the "color-coded" system for categorizing differently born peoples. Paraiyar, Ezhavas, Pulayas, and Kuravas, as well as other groups, may already have come to be regarded as beyond the pale of society, as "polluted" or "untouchables" and hence "subhuman" beings. It is ironic that this sea-trading area, having had contact with the Middle East and the West from the early times, should have become a region in which the caste system seems to have flourished with particular rigidity. This would have implications for later movements of conversion to Christian faith.

The presence of Christians in Kerala certainly long predates European arrival, but its origins are unclear. The beginnings of trade with the West are thought to go back at least three or four thousand years. There was already a sizable Jewish community when Christians came; and Christians had long been involved with Indian Ocean trade and commerce by the time Muslims arrived.

There is a very strong tradition, both oral and textual, holding that St. Thomas arrived in India circa A.D. 52 and that he founded seven churches in Kerala. He is also said to have gone to North India and to have then been killed at Mylapore, in what is now the city of Chennai. Many of Kerala's Christians claim descent from early South Indians who were converted by St. Thomas. If this is true, and many scholars acknowledge that the claim is "not

---

10. See S. Bayly, *Saints, Goddesses and Kings: Muslims and Christians in South Indian Society, 1700-1900* (Cambridge, 1989), for a detailed discussion.

11. See S. Bayly, *Caste, Society and Politics in India from the Eighteenth Century to the Modern Age* (Cambridge, 1999), p. 30.

improbable," the presence of Christians probably predates the Brahmaniza-tion of Kerala as well as the introduction of Islam.[12] However, this indigenous Christian culture appears to have been in decline by the fourth century A.D. It was then revitalized with the arrival of more Christians, refugees from perse-cution in Persia. The arrival of Thomas of Cana, a West Asian merchant, is similarly ambiguous, with dates given between the fourth century or the ninth century A.D.[13] It is an indisputable fact that in A.D. 522 Cosmas Indicoplaeste, a rich Alexandrian merchant, found a Christian church in Malabar with its own bishop (who was usually ordained in Persia). This fact leads one to conclude that there was some form of early involvement of the Christians in Kerala with the Persian Church of the East.[14]

Portuguese records also mention the existence of copper plate grants to Christians landing at Malankara in A.D. 345 and similar inscriptions during later rulers.[15] It seems possible, therefore, that the Christian church in Kerala came under some sort of East Syrian supervision from about the fourth cen-tury onward.[16] Copper plates relating to an influx of Persian Christians in the ninth century are still in existence in Kottayam. Much later, in the fourteenth century, a Latin mission was founded at Quilon, the main port; but it did not last for long.[17]

The Christians claiming descent from those converted by St. Thomas also declared that they were descendants of Nambuthiri Brahmans who had been converted to the Christian faith. These "Thomas" Christians also became known as Syrian Christians because of their use of Syriac in the liturgy and their allegiance to prelates from Babylon. Whatever the justice of the claim to Brahman status, there is no doubt that they were regarded at least on a par with Nayars, a caste community that itself claims to have created and helped to established the cultural dominance of Nambuthiri Brahmans who, in turn, claim to have helped to create and establish the ruling power and status of Nayars.[18] Some of these elite Christians, known as Malankara Nazranis, by observing the same rules of ritual purity as the upper-Nayars and differing

12. See A. Mathias Mundadan, *History of Christianity in India: From the Beginning up to the Middle of the Sixteenth Century* (Bangalore, 1984), ch. 1 for a full discussion of the available evidence and current thinking on the subject.

13. Mundadan, *History of Christianity in India*, p. 91.

14. Mundadan, *History of Christianity in India*, p. 99.

15. Mundadan, *History of Christianity in India*, p. 94 for discussion of the various traditions.

16. Mundadan, *History of Christianity in India*, p. 115.

17. Mundadan, *History of Christianity in India*, pp. 130-44.

18. Mundadan, *History of Christianity in India*, pp. 149-50.

little from them in their day-to-day life, even intermarrying with some of them and following the matrilineal marriage and inheritance systems, in effect have been regarded as a subgroup within this caste. Christians took Hindu names and observed many of the same domestic rituals relating to birth, puberty, marriage, and death and became all but indistinguishable from upper-Nayars.[19] Adherence to these rules enabled them to be classed as *savarna,* persons ranked in the "clean" caste category, and hence of high standing in the Hindu moral order.

By the time Nambuthiri Brahmans had consolidated their dominating influence over elites of the area, so-called "foreigners" had long been a vital part of the economy, their settling in Kerala having predated Brahman dominance by many centuries. Brahmanical prejudices against trade and navigation made them happy to leave this to foreigners. Commercial interests fostered a spirit of tolerance, including tolerance for people with other forms of religious practice, together with their communities. It seems not to be known precisely how or why certain Christians and Muslims should have been granted considerable privileges, except for their military and mercantile skills. For the sake of using such skills, one can only assume that Kerala's rulers felt that it would be useful to bind these groups to themselves. Syrian Christians were economically vital to anyone wishing to rule in Kerala. They were a highly mobile occupational and geographical group, whose main occupations were in agriculture, commerce, and military service. They controlled the lucrative pepper industry and in Quilon acted as brokers and port revenue officers. However, it was their military prowess that won them a central place in service to many local rajas. Medieval chiefdoms of Malabar had a distinctive martial culture, known as *kalāripayat,* and powerful warrior communities, of whom Nayars, both Hindu and Christian, formed top-ranked elites. It was very much in the rulers' interests to establish overlordship over this powerful class of communities. Syrian Christians were also a significant presence among these military groups. Estimated at around thirty thousand in 1503, by 1653 their numbers were said by Europeans to have reached two hundred thousand.[20] The presence of Christians among Nayars, one can argue, was the outward sign of their importance to local rulers and within Kerala — a mark of their place within Hindu (or indigenous) society. As far as the Syrian Christians themselves were concerned, it was to their advantage to hold ties of blood and privileged clientage among the ruling lineages. Kerala's rulers bound Syrian Christians to them by ties of ritualized fealty and

19. Mundadan, *History of Christianity in India,* ch. 7, pp. 247-53.
20. Bayly, *Saints, Goddesses, and Kings,* p. 249.

patronage, rewarding them for their services with royal grants of land and other privileges, in ways similar to their ties with Brahmans. The ruler of Venad (Travancore) gave Christians seventy-two rights and privileges usually granted only to high dignitaries, including exemption from import duties, sales tax, and the slave tax. A copper plate grant, dated A.D. 1255, further enhanced the rights and privileges of Kerala's Christians. Kerala's rulers endowed and protected Christian churches in the same way as they endowed and protected Hindu temples. This process, as Nicholas Dirks and Susan Bayly have concluded, was an important function of any ruler.[21] Some Syrian Christians, because of such status, were allowed to enter certain Hindu temples and shrines and to enter streets or ceremonial procession routes connecting sacred sites and temples. In some areas, ties between Hindu Nayars and Syrian Christians were reciprocal, each taking part and having roles at both Hindu and Christian festivals. Well into the nineteenth century, some Syrians were offering sacrificial cocks at the shrines of Nayar warrior goddesses, as well as consecrated food *(prasādam)* offerings.[22] In some places, Syrian churches and Hindu temples were constructed on virtually adjoining sites, and processional regalia was shared. Indeed, up to the end of the sixteenth century, some churches and temples were similarly built and fashioned.[23] Syrian Christian elites were thus incorporated into the networks of churches, shrines, and temples that comprised the domains of each local warlord or ruler. By the sixteenth century, due to long absences of prelates from Syria, certain Christians had come to rely on kings and rulers to adjudicate disputes or to renew the authority of their chief clerics *(metrans)*. These clerics took up the titles and trappings of Malayali lordship.[24] It seems, therefore, that the position of these Syrian Christians amounted to a large-scale cultural and social integration into the wider societal fabric of Kerala. They seem to have succeeded in simultaneously maintaining their corporate identity as Christians and their place as a superior *jāti* within Kerala's caste structure. Their liturgy was in Syriac; their prelates looked to Syria for confirmation; their own hereditary clergy — *kattanars* (pastors) and *metrans* (bishops) — provided local leadership and presided over specifically Christian rituals such as the celebration of Christian feast days and the Eucharist. However, they spoke

21. Bayly, *Saints, Goddesses, and Kings*, p. 249; and N. B. Dirks, *The Hollow Crown, Ethnohistory of an Indian Kingdom* (Cambridge, 1987).

22. Bayly, *Saints, Goddesses, and Kings*, p. 253.

23. Bayly, *Saints, Goddesses, and Kings*, ch. 7, for a detailed discussion of the integration of Hindus and Christians in precolonial Kerala. See also Mundadan, *History of Christianity in India;* and Eapen, *A Study of Kerala History.*

24. Bayly, *Saints, Goddesses and Kings*, p. 257.

Malayalam and followed many codes of purity and domestic rituals common to Hindus of Nayar status. Some of the missionaries who later came from Europe do not seem to have understood the extent to which these mutual obligations were embedded in a distinct Hindu-Christian culture; nor, if they did, would they have been ready to tolerate such a culture. This situation eventually led to much friction.

The Advent of the Portuguese

With the arrival of the Portuguese at the end of the fifteenth century, relations within the wider Hindu community changed, both for the Christian and for the Muslim communities. The most striking feature of Kerala, at this time and perhaps in most times, was the absence of a central unifying power. The region was divided among some fifty distinct principalities, whose "little kings" were ever in relations of mingled tensions and nominal allegiance to a few major rajas: the *zamorin* of Calicut, the *tiruvadi* of Travancore, the *kolathiri* of Cannanore, and later the Raja of Cochin. The income for these rulers came from a combination of land revenues and taxes levied on the pepper trade and on other forest products that were part of the Indian Ocean trading system. The Portuguese wanted to gain greater control of the international trading networks that had long been dominated by merchants and seafarers based at Calicut. To ensure most of the profits from the lucrative spice trade, the Portuguese began to play one powerful ruler against another and bullied the lesser rulers. For the Portuguese to succeed in such an arena, they needed reliable local allies and client groups. Syrian Christians were the most obvious candidates, not only because they ostensibly shared the faith but also because they were skilled both as warriors and as managers of pepper cultivation and commerce. Some Syrians greeted the European newcomers warmly and, in seeking support in struggles with local rajas, especially the Muslim *zamorin* of Calicut, may have sworn to an alliance with the Portuguese king. Such actions seemed to have been interpreted by some Portuguese as an act or promise of fealty.[25] Evidence is unclear whether there were deeper reasons for the Syrian welcome of the Portuguese than the fact that they were fellow Christians. It is possible that, due to the political fragmentation and ceaseless struggles that still persisted at the time, tension over previously granted rights and concern for security led local Christians to welcome the Europeans. A. Mathias Mundadan has found that Christians of Quilon approached Albu-

---

25. See Mundadan, *History of Christianity in India*, p. 266.

querque asking him to restore previously held rights and privileges. The Syrian Christian bishop, Mar Jacob, in 1524 asked the king of Portugal to help with the restoration of lands and privileges in Cranganore.[26] Whatever the situation, its seems clear that Syrian Christians initially regarded the European newcomers as potential allies and that they sought both protection and restoration of "ancient" rights and privileges. Following some of the same methods that the other rajas used to bind different communities to themselves, the *Padroado* sanctioned large sums for the extension and adornment of Syrian churches.

The Portuguese were able to make use of the fragmented political situation to further trading interests and to spread Christianity. Both the ambitious Cochin Raja and Kolathiri Raja of Cannanore, a hereditary enemy of the *zamorin* of Calicut, entered into informal agreements with the Portuguese. In 1452 the Pope had given King Alphonso I authority to "wage war against Saracens, infidels, unbelievers and all other enemies of Christ, whosoever and wheresoever they be" and the right to "invade, occupy seize and subdue their kingdoms," taking possession of their belongings "for the greater glory of the Divine Name."[27] The administration of this authority became known as the *Padroado Real*. The Portuguese, taking this grant of Papal authority to heart in India, committed atrocities against those whom they regarded as the chief enemies of Christ, namely, Muslims. In 1502 they attacked Calicut. Muslims retaliated, and from this time onward there was a gradual militarization among Muslim Mappilas of Kerala.[28] In 1522 local Mappilas massacred Christians after the Portuguese factor had beaten a Muslim. When Mar Jacob, one of the Syrian bishops, persuaded his Christians to sell their pepper directly to the Portuguese, Muslims, deprived of their gains as middlemen in the pepper trade, took revenge by robbing, killing, and burning houses and churches in about 1524.[29] In 1545, following Portuguese use of Tiruvangadi as a base to attack Muslim shipping, Muslims attacked the town and especially houses belonging to Christians. As clashes between Muslim and Portuguese forces became more and more frequent, relations that had existed between Hindus, Muslims, and Christians in previous centuries were severely disturbed.

26. See Mundadan, *History of Christianity in India,* pp. 165-66.

27. J. H. Gense, *The Church at the Gateway of India* (Bombay, 1960), pp. 16-17.

28. See S. F. Dale, *Islamic Society on the South Asian Frontier: The Mappilas of Malabar, 1498-1922* (Oxford, 1980), pp. 46-61. Islam may even have come first to India in Kerala and the Muslim Mappilas may even perhaps be seen as descendants of some of India's first Muslims.

29. Dale, *Islamic Society,* p. 300.

The Portuguese regarded the Syrian or Thomas Christians of India as "imperfect" Christians, who had allowed improper rites and usages to adulterate the "pure" and "true" faith. These pagan practices were abominations that needed to be suppressed. Since the *Padroado Real* granted to Portugal gave rights to ecclesiastical patronage, Portuguese authorities determined to bring the Indian Christians under their jurisdiction and enforce the practices and usages of Latin rites. They established a new series of rites and pilgrimage centers in an attempt to wean the Syrian Christians away from their West Asian patriarchs. Sensing threats to their authority and their flocks in India, they sent increasing numbers of bishops and monks to India at this time. Portuguese-controlled clerics started a seminary at Cranganore in 1541 in a direct attempt to Latinize the Syrians as effectively as possible.[30] The Syrians, for their part, were not prepared to give up their own customs and rites.[31] Results of the new seminary turned out contrary to expectations. The seminary boys who were educated to condemn the old customs and traditions of the community were not permitted to officiate in Syrian churches.[32] The Archbishop of Goa was not prepared to let the matter rest; and in 1599, at the Synod of Udeyamperur (Diamper), he attempted to induce the entire Syrian priesthood, more by foul means than fair, to abjure all non-Catholic doctrines and observances and to swear allegiance to Rome. The Synod allowed Syrian Christian clergy to keep their Syriac liturgy and to continue following their code for avoiding pollution (both of things touched and of distance) so that they might continue to retain their high status in Keralan society. The Synod was not, however, successful in forcing Syrian Christians to toe the line. The veneration of great cult saints carried on, new sacred sites were added, and the hereditary priestly lineages survived. In 1653 there was a general rebellion against Roman Catholic control; and as a result, the Syrian Christian community was deeply and permanently split. The attempted removal of the Church of the East from the authority of the Chaldean patriarch and the imposition of bishops of the Latin rite was very much resented. The Syrian Orthodox section of the community broke off all relations with Rome after 1665. The split was to generate division and violence for at least the next two hundred years, if not longer. One result was that it became even more important for the Jacobite Syrians[33] to rely on the local rajas to help them consolidate their

30. Dale, *Islamic Society,* p. 315.
31. Dale, *Islamic Society,* pp. 282, 287-88.
32. Dale, *Islamic Society,* pp. 339-41.
33. The term "Jacobite" refers here to those Syrian Christians who were originally affiliated with the line of primates known as "West Syrian" or "Jacobite" patriarchs of Antioch. See discussion in Bayly, *Saints, Goddesses, and Kings,* pp. 254-57.

authority by endorsing and supporting their church leaders. Divisions between Syrian Christians practicing Syriac rites and those performing Latin rites were later exploited by Anglican Protestant missionaries in the early years of the nineteenth century.[34]

Apart from trying to entice the Syrian Christian community to Latin usages and to come under Vatican control, European missionaries were also instrumental in bringing about conversions among non-Christian peoples of Kerala. The nucleus of new Christians was formed in Cochin, which served as an administrative center. This was followed by new Christian communities at Cannanore, Calicut, and possibly also Quilon. Few of these converts were Brahmans, many more were Nayars, but the vast majority came from the lowest castes.[35] When Albuquerque offered financial inducements, applications for baptism increased considerably. In Mundadan's opinion, baptism was given with little or no preparation. Intermarriages between converts from different castes were encouraged. By 1527 there were about fifteen thousand Christians in Cochin, of whom about three hundred were Portuguese settlers. The rest were the result of mixed-race relationships. Portuguese efforts to persuade Nayars to convert, again by offering financial inducements, were certainly made. Little is known about how successful they were. Lapses were frequent, perhaps because motives of material gain had been a factor and also because only minimal and superficial instruction or follow-up pastoral care was possible. The previously friendly Raja of Cochin was offended and antagonized by these conversions. High-caste converts lost caste and, considered as untouchables, were driven from their homes and lost their property. This reaction contrasted with the tolerance the raja gave to converts to Islam, who did not lose caste by their conversion, perhaps because Muslim converts did not come from "clean" castes. The raja of Cannanore was similarly unhappy about conversions. In 1507 he wrote to King Manuel of Portugal:

> It is my desire that certain sections of the people in my kingdom whom I and my nayars hold as slaves and who belong to two castes, viz, tines [tiyans] and mucuas, may not be converted to Christianity; nor should nayars and brahmins. The conversion of the slaves will give rise to conflicts between them and my vassals. The nayars derive their income from them and they do not want to lose it.[36]

34. For a full discussion, see Mundadan, *History of Christianity in India,* ch. 10.

35. Mundadan, *History of Christianity in India;* the discussion that follows is based on ch. 7, pp. 348 et seq.

36. Mundadan, *History of Christianity in India,* p. 379.

In 1512 the raja complained to the king that the Portuguese had burned a temple and converted his vassals and that the new converts had stopped paying the customary dues to him. He pointed out that they were still his subjects. In the view of the Portuguese, demands on the new converts were excessive. Yet, at the same time, they could not bring new converts residing in Cochin under direct Portuguese rule, much less recognize them as equals. The new Christian communities needed to be protected, educated, and provided with medical and other facilities,[37] thus placing a burden on the Portuguese treasury.[38] Many such converts became Westernized and isolated. Coming from low-caste backgrounds, they were often looked down upon by other communities. Faced with the financial burden and the raja's warnings, Albuquerque forbade the conversion of "slaves," whether Hindu or Muslim.

The Portuguese first arrived in Kerala at a time of chronic political fragmentation. Many rulers, particularly the *zamorin* of Calicut, were striving against each other to assert their hegemony. During times of political uncertainty the Syrian Christians were open to advances. By turning to the Portuguese, a long process was begun whereby Christians came to be associated with foreigners' rule. Portuguese policies divided Syrian Christians between those who performed rites in Latin and Jacobites and aroused the bitter enmity of Muslims in Kerala, including some who were powerful.[39] By encouraging the conversion of considerable numbers of people, both high and low caste, Portuguese policies antagonized many rulers and notables in Kerala. They profoundly, perhaps even irrevocably, disturbed the social order. What happened, moreover, seems to have occurred during a period when there may have been a further solidifying and ossifying of the caste system.

Syrian Christians, meanwhile, continued to be far more influenced by the local rulers and by local culture than by Europeans. Syrian military skills and commercial links continued to be essential to the expansionist aspirations of the eighteenth-century rajas, especially those of Travancore and Cochin. These skills enabled them to continue to hold on to their privileged roles within society. Indeed, they were especially prominent under the regime of Raja Marthanda Varma (1729-58), in his newly constructed state of Travancore, which became the most powerful state in Kerala. Several thousand Christian Nayars helped him conquer the north and expel the Dutch, who had taken over much of the influence and power in Malabar previously held

---

37. Mundadan, *History of Christianity in India,* p. 390.
38. Mundadan, *History of Christianity in India,* p. 380.
39. See Dale, *Islamic Society.*

by the Portuguese.[40] The state trading monopolies depended to a great extent on Syrian commercial skills. As a result of their help, the most important Syrian families were accorded shares in many of the state rituals. Syrian prelates participated in the installation ceremonies for the new raja. Leading Syrian families were given royal land grants. They continued to be regarded as ritually pure and to be granted rights of access to Hindu sacred space and procession routes, and the Syrian families continued to hold joint shares in local goddess festivals and other Hindu temple rites. This integration was not to continue undisturbed. The right of access to prestigious procession routes was a particularly important status marker in South Indian society, and in the nineteenth century Syrians and Hindus were increasingly involved in religious "honor" disputes that were fought over tokens of caste rank and precedence. The Portuguese had left a difficult legacy for British missionaries.

The Advent of the British

Despite the increasing power of Travancore, the competing rivalries of the Calicut *zamorin* and the Cochin rajas, together with the presence of competing French, British, and Dutch enclaves, amounted to an unstable political situation. This left the way open for Haidar Ali, the Muslim ruler of Mysore (1754-81), to enter the territories of the rajas of Travancore and Cochin. What perhaps made matters more encouraging for Haidar Ali was the fact that, since the end of the fifteenth century, commerce had shifted to northern Kerala, where Muslims had gained a more dominant position, especially those under the *zamorin* of Calicut.[41] Since Mappilas, as fellow Muslims, were regarded as potential collaborators of Haidar, Nayars started to massacre them. There was more to this than issues of feared collaboration, however. The militarization of the Muslim community that, in some measure, had increased in response to Portuguese atrocities had also made it possible for certain Muslim groups to contest the social, economic, and even the political supremacy over Malayali Hindus.[42] The Portuguese had already been able to exploit this virtual state of war on the coast to serve their own ends. By the eighteenth century, violence between Muslims and Hindu rulers and elites of

40. P. Shungoomy Menon, *A History of Travancore* (Trivandrum and Cochin: Government of Kerala, 1983 [1878]), pp. 85-158 (reprint edition prepared by Adoor K. K. Ramachandra Nair). Also see Eapen, *A Study of Kerala History*, ch. 24, pp. 156-64, for a discussion of Dutch rule in Malabar.
41. Dale, *Islamic Society*, p. 15.
42. Dale, *Islamic Society*, p. 4.

ritually superior castes had already become almost endemic, especially in the main Muslim areas of North Kerala. According to Stephen Dale, these strains in Kerala society were partly a result of European entry and partly the result of growing competition between Mappila and Nayar families of noble and royal lineage for social and economic influence. Brahmans and Nayars, rather than rajas, in effect controlled much of the countryside. Moreover, much of the land had been given away by former chieftains or petty rajas as endowments to local temples, so that revenue derived therefrom could be used for the expenses of worship, festivals, schools, and housing for Brahman elites. The *janmi* land holdings held by temples, under no regular obligations to the state, exercised authority over social and ceremonial affairs in their domains. These holdings, which had been acquired by Brahmans, enabled them to have a stranglehold on the countryside.[43] As Dale points out, since rulers were unable to levy taxes upon much of the land, ability to gain revenue from the commerce of the seaports became crucial.[44] Thus, social and economic authority, underpinned by the ritual authority, was confirmed by the Brahmans. In the isolated countryside, moreover, the codes of ritual purity and pollution were much stricter than in the coastal ports.

While Muslims in the north, because of their low ritual status, had previously not been allowed to acquire landed domain *(janmi)* holdings, they were beginning to challenge Nayar dominance of the countryside. Jonathan Duncan, one of the commissioners appointed by the Company in 1793 to set up an administration in northern Kerala (then known as Malabar), reckoned that struggles over rights to landed property were the most common reason for the prevailing and growing communal enmity.[45] Prior to 1766 the outward signs of the struggle were few. In that year, however, after Haidar invaded north Kerala and after his efforts to rule had been thwarted by persistent guerrilla resistance by local Nayar magnates, he ordered that all Nayars be killed. Again, in 1788, after Haidar's son, Tipu Sultan, announced that he intended to force conversion upon infidels and after he also tried to introduce a new land revenue system, tensions between Mappila tenants and Nayar *janmi*

43. See Eapen, *A Study of Kerala History,* pp. 121-27 for a discussion of the *janmi* system. The most astute and acute study of this system is found in William Logan, *Manual of Malabar District,* 2 vols. (Madras, 1887). Also see the *Travancore State Manual* (Trivandrum, 1940), vol. 3, pp. 137-223, 224-46 (ch. 15: "Land Tenures and Land Taxes"); and B. H. Baden-Powell, *The Land-System of British India, being a manual of the land-revenue and of the systems of land-revenue administration prevalent in several provinces,* 3 vols. (Oxford, 1889 and later editions).
44. Dale, *Islamic Society,* ch. 1, pp. 16-18.
45. Dale, *Islamic Society,* p. 92.

holders increased. By the time the Company's armies had expelled Tipu, a state of virtual civil war was raging between Mappilas and Nayars. In the dominions of the former *zamorin*, Mappilas were in de facto control of large areas of the southern districts. Following Tipu's withdrawal, Mappilas were determined to resist attempts of Nayars to recover control of their estates. In 1788, three years earlier, Nayars of south Malabar had risen *en masse* and, led by Ravi Varma, had seized control of the countryside. As Mappilas retaliated, some Nayars and Brahmans had fled south to Travancore.

After his defeat in 1792, Tipu was obliged to cede Malabar, from Mount D'Eli in the north to Cochin in the south, to the East India Company.[46] As allies of the Company, the rajas of Cochin and Travancore were able, by adroit diplomacy, to retain their autonomy and, under revised "subsidiary" or tributary alliances made in 1795, to rule over their domains. In return, and for stipulated payments of tribute, the Company agreed to "protect them" and provide for their security against their foes. A number of insurrections against the Travancore raja, culminating in that of Velu Thampi, the *diwan*, in 1809,[47] were put down before political stability could be established.

After each of these rebellions, the noose of Company control was tightened. While these Malayali rulers retained the right to collect revenues, however, agrarian conflicts and disputes requiring increased internal control continued to exacerbate the problems that the rajas faced. In attempts to find the "hereditary landlords" of Kerala, British officers serving as "advisors" in Travancore helped to make it possible for Brahmans and Nayars to reassert their age-old social and economic dominance within rural society. At the same time, in Company-ruled Malabar, as tenants increasingly contested the rights of the those who were being defined as *janmis* (having hereditary rights over the land), holders of such lands were forced to pay additional taxes and levies. Whether or not tribute demanded by the Company was so high that the Travancore and Cochin princes were soon reduced to penury is debatable. What is not debatable is the fact that such tribute, which was used to pay for Company forces stationed in Travancore and Cochin, forced the rajas to cut military expenditures. This in turn seems to have brought about a gradual disintegration both of the traditional military culture and of organizational structures undergirding royal authority. After the failures of two military re-

---

46. Manifold factors contributed to the war against Tipu. There is no doubt that he was seen as a genuine threat, especially in light of his diplomatic dalliance with Revolutionary France. To interpret direct action against Tipu as an attempt by Britain to gain control of the lucrative pepper trade is far too simple. By then, Company trade within India was being curtailed by actions being taken in Britain.

47. See Eapen, *A Study of Kerala History,* ch. 30, pp. 203-17.

volts, in 1804 and 1808, both states were forced to disband much of their armies. The result of all this was a gradual process of cultural, economic, and social dislocation. Ex-soldiers took to plundering, and the collapse of military spending power brought distress in the region. Yet, for all that, Nayar dominance in the agrarian system, if anything, seems to have grown stronger.

The influence of British rule, indirect as it was within these princely domains, seems to have also opened the door for specifically British Protestant missionary activity. This was to have consequences that would be serious for the welfare of various wings of the Syrian Christian community and, indeed, for Christians in Kerala generally. Colonel Colin Macaulay, an ardent Evangelical, was appointed as the first British Resident (1800-1810). Two Company chaplains, Richard Kerr of Madras and Claudius Buchanan of Bengal, toured Kerala in 1806. They both became greatly excited by the Jacobite Syrian Christians. Kerr reported that, "the service of the Syrian church was performed nearly after the manner of the Church of England, and that such Roman Catholic tenets as were rejected by Anglicans were not held by them."[48] Buchanan also believed that he had found a mainly pure but primitive church that had escaped the debasements of Rome. Like Kerr, he felt that the tenets of the Jacobite Christians were so close to those of the Church of England that he discussed the possibility of union with their *Metran*. The presence of Jews in Kerala and the large numbers of Syrian Christians led him to believe that an era was dawning when the Jews would be converted in preparation for the Second Coming of Christ. He believed the Syrian Christians would prove to be the instrument for the evangelization of India. Buchanan published his views, which had a very wide readership.[49] Unfortunately he seriously underestimated the differences that existed between the Church of England and the Jacobite Syrian Christians. Like the Portuguese clerics, he also failed to understand their attachment to their age-old customs and traditions and their relationship to the wider Hindu community. Similar misapprehensions were later also to lead Colonel John Munro, the next Resident (1810-19), who was also an Evangelical, and British Protestant missionaries who started to arrive in Kerala after 1813, to make decisions that were to damage, in some measure, long-term relationships between Syrian Christians and their Hindu and Muslim neighbors.

Munro arrived during a time of instability and severe turmoil. The young

48. Quoted in J. Richter, *A History of Christian Missions in India,* English trans. (Edinburgh and London, 1908), p. 166.

49. See Claudius Buchanan, *Christian Researches in Asia* (Cambridge, 1811); and Stephen Neill, *A History of Christianity in India, 1707-1858* (Cambridge, 1985), 2:238.

Maharajah had just died (7 November 1810); a power struggle for succession to the regal pillow *(gaddhi)* was in progress; the state's affairs were in shambles; and there was also turmoil over who should be the next *diwan* or chief minister. Rani Gauri Lakshmi Bai, while only twenty when installed as ruler (1810-15), seems to have been both astute and strong minded. Realizing that her power base, in the midst of turmoil and violence, was far from secure and recognizing her need for Company support, she turned to the new Resident in 1811 and asked him to become *diwan*. This put him in the extraordinarily powerful position, of being both *diwan* and Resident at the same time (1811-14).[50]

Munro was closely advised by two or three Maratha Brahmans who had accompanied him to Travancore.[51] Informed that a careful balance was needed between the three elite communities that had historically been powerful in Kerala, he took care to make sure that appointments were evenly divided between local Nambuthiri Brahmans, Nayars, and Jacobite Syrians. He seems to have hoped thereby to strengthen client-patron relationships and thus bind each community more closely to the newly reconstituted princely state of Travancore.[52] He was particularly keen to ensure that the Jacobite Syrians became a client community of the British. Munro told Thomas Norton, a Church Missionary Society (CMS) missionary, that he aimed to accomplish this by granting them privileges, believing that in return the British government would receive "their grateful and devoted attachment on every emergency."[53] That the conversion of India to Christianity would bind rulers and ruled was a staple of British Evangelical rhetoric.[54] Munro also forecast the conversion of the greater part of the Roman Catholics on the coast as a result of attaching the Jacobites to Protestant Christianity and British influence.

On Munro's advice the *rani* was persuaded to bring a considerable number of Jacobite Syrians into government service[55] and to pass a law that a Christian judge should be present in every *zillah* court.[56] All applications for appointments and redress of grievance were to pass through the missionaries.

50. Menon, *Travancore*, pp. 263-73.

51. Gifted persons from this community were, at that time, becoming invaluable as Company administrators throughout South India.

52. Menon, *Travancore*, pp. 273-83.

53. Munro to Norton, 29 May 1817, cited in P. Cheriyan, *The Malabar Syrians and the Church Missionary Society, 1816-40 (Kottayam, 1935)*, pp. 340-41.

54. Carson, "Soldiers of Christ," pp. 43-44, 130.

55. Munro to the Rani, cited in Cheriyan, *Malabar Syrians*, pp. 340-41.

56. Cheriyan, *Malabar Syrians*, pp. 340-41. Thomas Norton of the CMS and Charles Mead of the LMS were appointed as judges to deal with disputes involving Christians. See Mead to LMS, 4 April 1818, CWM MSS, SI (Trav) 1/4/B (Birmingham: Selly Oakes Colleges, CMS Archives).

In 1816 Munro ordered that the missionaries whom he had appointed to act as judges should also act as special advocates on behalf of Syrian plaintiffs. These Christian advocates were told to collect evidence about Hindu officials who were believed to have abused their powers by extorting goods and cash from Syrian Christians.[57] In addition, Munro persuaded the *rani* to grant generous gifts of money, land, and building materials to the Protestant missionaries. Two thousand acres were granted for the support of the Church Missionary Society seminary, and five thousand rupees were given to enable the permanent leasing of paddy fields to support the educational institutions of the London Missionary Society (LMS). Other gains included tax concessions, a memorial from the *rani* granting inheritance rights, and the release of Christians from obligations connected to ceremonies within temples.[58] This was the area where Munro and the missionaries were most determined to "rescue" Indian Christians from what they perceived to be forms of Hindu oppression. They do not seem to have comprehended that Christians could participate in rituals involving idolatry without being under duress.

Resentment against missionaries became equally, if not more, virulent within the Indian Syrian community mainly because of missionary interference in disputes over church property and over local ritual practices. Missionaries of the CMS, patronized by Munro, were instrumental in having a number of churches used by the Syrians who performed Latin rites taken away from them on the grounds that they had originally belonged to the Jacobites.[59] These inept actions mirrored, in part, the arrogant behavior of Roman Catholic missionaries during the ascendancy of the Portuguese several centuries before and stirred up such resentment against the missionaries that one of them told his society that "it was doubtful whether we should remain in the country another month."[60] The balance between the Syrian church leadership and the political system was upset by Munro with significant implications for the status of Syrian Christians in the future.

57. Thomas Norton to the Madras corresponding secretary 14 October 1816, CMS MSS A CI2/E1.

58. See letter from Rani Parvathi to Munro, March 1818, reproduced in Eapen, *A Study of Kerala History*, app. 7, p. xlvi, which makes it clear that pressure was on her to make this donation from state funds: "it is the Colonel's desire that . . . if we of our own accord give the said amount for the maintenance expenses of the Kottayam seminary, it would enhance our reputation in the country and increase the friendship of the Co. towards us."

59. A proclamation issued on 7th Meenam 990 (1815) gave permission to the children of Ezhavas, Channars, and other castes who embraced Christianity to inherit property; see Eapen, *A Study of Kerala History*, p. 235.

60. Norton to CMS, 4 March 1820, CMS MSS C1 2/M1, f. 381.

After Munro left Travancore in 1819, special concessions granted to Syrian Christians seem virtually to have ceased. Missionaries began to feel that the junior officers of the Travancore government made Munro's departure an occasion for harassing Christians. The appointments of nearly three hundred Syrians to public service ended almost immediately. Munro's successor as Resident took steps to curb missionary involvement in local politics.[61] CMS missionaries believed that Christians were suffering under a rapacious, repressive, and inflexible Oriental despotism. They assumed that the Syrian Christians had been singled out for what they regarded as excessive revenue demands, and that at least some of the proceeds obtained would go toward the patronage of idolatry. One of the missionaries, Benjamin Bailey, reported that there were often as many as fifty Christians at a time at the CMS college complaining of oppression, most of whom, however, were poor and "unable to bear the expense of an application to the courts" for redress.[62] It would seem, therefore, that they did not come from elite groups among Kerala Christians. The missionaries thought that their poverty was the result of the state monopolies that they believed had strangled trade and commerce. CMS missionaries, accustomed to special access and privileges that they had enjoyed during Munro's tenure, did not hesitate to petition the new Resident, asking him to do something about injustices. They considered it their duty to stand up for their fellow Christians. Complaints to Colonel McDouall, Munro's replacement, included a list of sixty-two vacant government posts that missionaries believed should be filled by Syrian Christians. They also informed McDouall that Christians "were compelled to give the Sircar grain, sugar and other articles at a quarter to half the price which they themselves can purchase."[63]

CMS missionaries in Travancore do not appear to have recognized that the problems Syrian Christians were facing might have been extemely complex. Syrian Christians in Kerala, along with people from other elite communities, had been under severe pressure since the 1790s. The unstable political situation had led to shifts and dislocations in the economy. There had been a downturn in Malabar's seaborne exports, and the trade routes into the Tamil country had been disrupted. The old tradition of Syrian Christian involvement in commercial activity had led to their being greatly affected by these disruptions. In 1799 a small rebellion against procurement prices within the

61. Cheriyan, *Malabar Syrians*, p. 143.

62. Benjamin Bailey to CMS, 24 March 1820, CMS MSS C1 2M/1, 350.

63. Correspondence Relative to the Missionaries' "Alleged Interference in Secular Affairs," CMS MSS, C1 2/M1, ff. 362, et seq.

state monopoly system may well have been directed, at least in part, at the Christian magnates and officeholders who were most closely associated with the running of the state's commodity monopolies.[64] Missionaries did not appreciate that the British demands for tribute were greatly exacerbating the situation. The Syrians were also hard hit by the loss of their privileged military role in the two states. The group's place in Keralan society was being weakened on two fronts at this time, leading to the distress that the missionaries observed and that their actions accelerated. There is, however, no evidence to substantiate the claim that Christians were being subject to more rapacious demands than other sections of the community as Brahmans and Nayars tried to reestablish their dominance.

Conversion of Low-Caste Christians

The discussion so far has concerned relations between the Syrian Christians and the Resident. While the CMS concentrated its efforts on the Jacobite Syrians and was not yet seeking converts among Hindus and Muslims, the LMS missionaries in Kerala began to work among the Tamil speaking Shanars (Nadars).[65] The Shanars, mostly toddy tappers, were tenants of the Tamil Vellālar and Malayali Nayar elites.[66] In Kerala, Shanar conversions occurred, mainly in the area around Neyoor.[67] In 1818 and 1819, over two thousand inquirers were registered, and a place of worship was being built to hold this number.[68]

Such a social revolution, and the fact that one missionary in Nagarcoil,

64. See Leslie W. Brown, *The Indian Christians of St Thomas: An Account of the Ancient Syrian Church of Malabar* (Cambridge, 1956).

65. The first known mass movement of conversion in modern times began among Shanars twenty years earlier in the Tirunelveli, a Tamil-speaking area adjacent to Kerala.

66. During this time, perhaps due to conversions, Shanars also began a campaign of upward mobility and wished to be known as Nadars, a title that entitled them to more respect. I refer to the group as Shanars as this is how they were commonly referred to by others at the time. See Robert L. Hardgrave, *The Nadars of Tamilnadu: The Political Culture of a Community in Change* (Berkeley and Los Angeles, 1969), for a discussion of the background and struggle for social status of the Nadars, most of whom were in Tirunelveli, adjacent to Kerala, so that much of it is relevant to Kerala.

67. The first LMS missionary, a Pietistic German named Ringeltaube, began working among Shanars in Nagarcoil, in 1806, ten years earlier. *Ringeltaube, The Rishi: The Pioneer Missionary of the London Missionary Society in Travancore* (Sheffield, 1902), letters and journals collected and arranged by William Robinson. He too disappeared.

68. Neill, *A History of Christianity in India*, p. 225.

Charles Mead, was appointed to serve as a judge by Rani Parvathi Rao, stimulated a considerable amount of opposition.[69] Mead reported to his mission directors in London that "evil suggestions, false reports and childish fears" were circulating about these new Christians. He wrote that these Christians were being "robbed" and that converts were being ill-used and falsely imprisoned. Twenty-four other Shanar Christians were falsely charged of assault, and even murder.[70] People of one village had been forced to flee to the mountains for safety. Particular difficulties were also experienced in setting up schools for these Shanar converts. One schoolroom had been burnt down and a schoolmaster imprisoned along with several Christians under his care.[71] Especially great exception was taken when Shanar women dared to start wearing an upper cloth on their bosom, a symbol of privilege only granted to high-caste women. Houses occupied by Christians were surveyed to see if any customary norms or rules about size and convenience had been broken. Such steps were taken to make sure that no Christian convert was living in a house or in a style above his normal station.[72] Threatening language was used to dissuade Christians from going to worship, and men were seized as corvée labor (for "public work"), even on the Sabbath, contrary to a concession that had previously been granted by the Regent, Rani Gauri Parvathi Bai (1815-30). A new royal proclamation required permission for the erection of any new place of worship. Although this was not specifically aimed at Christian places of worship, it was interpreted, by missionaries and officiating magistrates alike, as denying permission for the erection of any new Christian establishment. When one high-caste person in Quilon showed an interest in the Christian faith, he was seized and, after a disturbance between Nayars and new Christians, put in prison for seven years without any public accusation or benefit of trial. Missionaries believed that such action was taken to deter other persons of high caste from embracing Christianity.[73] Parents of high-caste children suspected missionaries had designs to force Christianity upon

69. Menon, *Travancore*, p. 294. She not only allowed missionaries to enter and work in the state in 1816 but contributed five thousand rupees for a "large bungalow in Nagarcoil," "a large Protestant church at Alleppy," and timber for a residence there.

70. C. Mead to LMS, 23 June 1829, CWM MSS SI (Trav) 1/3/D.

71. Report of Quilon Station [1828], CWM MSS SI (Trav) 1/3/A.

72. Reports from the Nagarcoil Station, January-June 1829, CWM MSS SI (Trav), 1/3/C. In geographic, cultural, and social terms, Nagarcoil, briefly under Travancore rule, was not a part of Kerala. The language spoken was Tamil, and it was really more of an southern extension of Tirunelveli Country.

73. Charles Mead to LMS, 12 January 1833, CWM MSS SI (Trav) 2/2/B. CMS Archives.

them and, moreover, resented and feared the giving of any education to the Shanars.[74] By 1829 LMS missionaries were feeling that opposition had extended into virtually every sphere of life and that their labors were being thwarted. They often could not even get ordinary workmen or others to serve them. They placed responsibility for the persecutions squarely on the shoulders of Nayars and the government *(sircar)* officers whom they believed aimed to root out all signs of Shanar Christian presence from the Neyoor district. An LMS missionary, James Thompson, attributed the aversion of government officers mainly to the fact that these new Christians refused "to give bribes." He maintained that because they would not offer bribes, the *sircar* officials represented the Christians as turbulent and disaffected to government and that, under that plea, "no opportunity is let slip to annoy them and the opportunities are frequent."[75] The CMS missionary, Benjamin Bailey, believed that the new raja had "listened to advisers directly opposed to the propagation of Christianity." This, he believed, had aroused "a general feeling of hostility not only to the cause of missions, but even to British authority."[76]

Whatever may have been the rights and wrongs of individual accusations, it is quite clear that Brahmans and Nayars, and perhaps the Syrian Christian gentry also, were determined to maintain their dominant position in society. Robert L. Hardgrave has indicated that a significant number of the Shanars were under the sway of Nayars. Heavily taxed by customary demands and forced to perform corvée labor,[77] their position relative to those they served was reinforced by caste rules and by gradations of ritual purity. As we have already seen, Mappilas had also begun to contest the status quo. Now, another "untouchable" community was demanding rights that had not previously been theirs. Among their most vehement demands was that Shanar women be allowed to wear a breast cloth like high-caste women. Whether or not this protest was a result of outraged Western sensibilities in the early days of protest is not easy to say. An uncovered upper body was a sign of respect rendered by both men and women. The Maharaja of Travancore, and all upper-caste men, would uncover the upper body when in the presence of any deity. It is a moot point whether Shanar women regarded the lack of a breast cloth as a sign of disrespect and shame or as a sign of respect, demanded and involuntarily forced upon them by their lowly position. When some missionary

74. James Thompson to LMS, 5 December 1828, CWM MSS SI (Trav) 1/3/B.
75. Report of the Nagarcoil Station, July-December 1829, CWM MSS SI (Trav) 1/4/A.
76. Benjamin Bailey to Bannister, October 1829, CMS MSS C1 2/M7, 345.
77. Hardgrave, *Nadars*, p. 57; and his "The Breast-Cloth Controversy: Caste Consciousness and Social Change in Southern Tranvancore," *Indian Economic and Social History Review* 5.2 (1968): 171-87.

wives devised a loose jacket for Christian Shanars, Shanar women initially refused to wear it, insisting on the use of the upper cloth as worn by women of
the higher classes. Therefore, the breast-cloth controversy seems to have been
used as a very visible and emotive focus for the struggle of Shanars to improve their social standing rather than as an objection to the lack of an upper
cloth *per se.* Opposition to the wearing of the upper cloth by Shanar women
led to rioting and the burning of chapels and schools. After an attempt was
made on Charles Mead's life, troops had to be sent to the area.[78]

In response to the unrest, the Travancore government issued a proclamation forbidding Shanar women from wearing cloths over their breasts and requiring Christians to perform *palaiyam* service, like any other low-caste community within the population. Christians did, however, succeed in securing
exemption from demands for service on Sundays. As before, places of worship were not to be erected without the permission of the government; nor
were converts to seek redress through petitions made by local missionaries.
Like others, Christians would have to go through the recognized channels.[79]
Yet, despite state decrees, the genie was truly out of the bottle. All Shanar
women, Hindu and Christian alike, began to adopt the upper cloth, and petitions were sent to the Resident concerning its use. The Resident and the Madras government declined to intervene in favor of the Shanars, regarding the
matter as one of local caste usage.[80] In 1859, two hundred Nayars attacked
Christian Shanars at a village near Nagarcoil, beating them and stripping the
upper cloths from the women. Houses were burned and looted. In the face of
such violence, the breast-cloth controversy was finally settled in favor of the
Shanars. Later that same year, a proclamation was issued granting them the
right to wear an upper cloth.[81] In 1865 the right was granted to all peoples of
lower caste. Large numbers of conversions followed in the wake of this social
revolution.

Shanars were not the only untouchable community to convert in large
numbers. In the second half of the nineteenth century, CMS missionaries
began to see large numbers of *pulayas* (agricultural laborers) turning Christian. This group, like the Shanars, was not on the lowest rung of outcaste soci-

78. C. Mead, "A Report of the Neyoor Mission, July 1829," dated 30 June 1829, CWM
MSS (SI (Trav).

79. C. M. Agur, *Church History of Travancore* (Madras, 1904), pp. 843-44.

80. Hardgrave, *Nadars,* pp. 62-63.

81. It is important to remember, here, that the greatest proportion of Nadars, both
Christian and Hindu, lived in the Tinnevelly District of the Madras Presidency (now Tamil
Nadu) and that, as such, their women would already have been setting the standard for
what could be worn.

ety.[82] The conversions of large numbers of outcastes and the way in which missionaries fought for their "rights" sometimes had critical and disturbing implications for relations between the Syrian Christians and the wider Hindu community. Whether such relations deteriorated permanently after the 1850s as a result of missionary interference in support of lower-caste Christian "rights" is debatable. The Madras government ordered the two ruling houses of Cochin and Travancore to cut back on the great festivals of state that still survived, regarding them as a form of "spendthrift indulgence." The missionaries may have had some influence on this decision since they sensationalized and widely publicized accounts of these "heathen" festivals. Reforming elements within the Hindu aristocracy may also have been influential.[83] In the short term, at least, the delicately balanced equilibrium between Syrian Christians and the Hindu community that had been so carefully built up and nurtured over many centuries disintegrated completely when the CMS launched a vigorous campaign through petitions, journals, and pamphlets to gain enhanced rank and standing for any untouchable or low-caste Hindu who converted to Christianity. The missionaries insisted that, once a person became a Christian, he or she should be entitled to all the marks of social and ritual standing held by Syrians, including the right to enter Hindu temple streets and all the other privileged precincts from which they had previously been banned. Missionaries encouraged low-caste and untouchable Christians to press for access to temple streets and procession routes as a sign that they had the same ritual status as the Syrian Christian community. Missionaries saw this as a process of modernization and "uplift." Of course, by the twentieth century, non-Christians of these same castes were demanding the same privileges. As a result of such efforts and interventions, there was usually violence, with clashes and street battles occurring all over northern Travancore and Cochin. Untouchable Christians forced themselves into the presence of Nayars and Brahmans, specifically to pollute them. When beaten or thrown into prison, Christians would claim they were being persecuted for the sake of their faith.[84]

82. See George Oomen, "Strength of Tradition and Weakness of Communication Central: Kerala Dalit Conversion," in *Religious Conversion Movements in South Asia: Continuities and Change, 1800-1900*, edited by G. Oddie (Richmond, 1997), pp. 79-95.

83. This was a time when notable modern *diwans*, from the time of T. Madhava Rao down to that of C. P. Ramaswamy Aiyer, had a profound influence upon the state of Travancore, making them into "model" states. It is hardly an accident that Kerala has the highest literacy (98 percent) and the most highly educated public in India. Nor is it remarkable that later governments have been radical.

84. See discussion in Bayly, *Saints, Goddesses, and Kings*, pp. 294-320; and K. Kawashima, *Missionaries and a Hindu State: Travancore 1858-1936* (Delhi, 1998), pp. 149-98.

The effects of numerous low-caste conversions coupled with demands for various privileges were disturbing for some elements within the Syrian community. Some of them began to be equated, in the minds of their high-caste Hindu neighbors, with people of *avarna* (low-caste or polluting) castes; and they were then treated accordingly. By the mid-1880s, partly as a result also of reactionary (or right-wing) Hindu movements, Syrians were routinely being excluded from Hindu festival sites. Indeed, some of the main religious festivals became a time for provocation and score-settling. During the 1880s and 1890s, there were riots between Hindus and Syrian ("Thomas") Christians. Some of these closely resembled the Hindu-Muslim clashes that were occurring in North India, and Hindu-Christian (Nadar Christian) riots in Tirunelveli. Officials stopped the building of Syrian churches on sites near Hindu temples or near procession streets. There were mob attacks on Syrian Christians who tried to affirm their *savarna* or clean-caste status by approaching Hindu temples. In cases that were taken to court, Christians were invariably charged with provoking the affrays. Christians responded by distancing themselves from "heathen" festivals whereas previously they had been pleased to participate. A chasm between the Syrian Christians and their high-caste neighbors developed. Indeed, Syrian Christian leaders discovered they could be heard more sympathetically in the courts if they could show that they were a dynamic and growing community committed to social action. Their clergy and eminent landholders took to touring major Hindu festivals, denouncing "heathen idolatry" and competing vigorously against each other in order to win over to their own particular subgroups larger numbers of low-caste converts than other groups. In short, relations between increasingly and manifoldly different kinds of Christian communities in Kerala also become more and more fractious.

It is difficult to assess the motivation of the Shanars and other untouchable *(avarna)* castes who converted to Christianity. A desire to improve their temporal position in life seems to have been a significant factor. One missionary wrote how Shanars were "exceedingly ambitious to hold positions of importance and take part in the government of the country."[85] Missionaries helped to provide education and, in some cases, employment. There were many conversions in the wake of the concessions granted to Christians under the Evangelical Residents, Macaulay and Munro. According to Charles Mead, one of the LMS missionaries, one effect of the withdrawal of concessions to Christians was the reversion of hundreds who had converted under the favorable disposition of Colonel Munro.[86] Conversion to Christianity of Shanars

85. Hardgrave, *Nadars,* p. 57.
86. Mead to LMS, 12 January 1833, CWMA SI(Trav) 1/4/A.

and Pulayas seems also to have been regarded as a route comparable to "Sanskritization": raising status by adopting the cultures and customs of higher castes. This may be seen as one reason why the breast-cloth success was so important. Shanars were not necessarily attempting to abolish the caste system so much as to attain a higher status within it. Numerous studies have shown that conversions usually did not occur among the most degraded sections of the population but among those groups that were rising economically and that were determined to carve out a better life for themselves.[87] These groups tended to replicate the caste system with their own social structures. Marriages continued to be endogamous and many "Hindu" customs were kept.[88]

Conversion, however, was more than a way of improving one's status in society. It was also a way of trying to make sense of the pressures resulting from colonial rule and modernization, which threatened traditional ways of life. One needs also to be wary of discounting the existence of conversion in the Evangelical sense of dying to one's previous life (of bondage and sin) and being reborn to a new life in Christ. Richard Eaton and George Oomen have shown how the traditional cosmologies of tribals and untouchable groups became inadequate as a system of "explanation, prediction, and control" in a rapidly changing world.[89] Depending on how the gospel message was presented to them, some individuals and groups came to believe that Christian faith provided a more potent way of dealing with the vicissitudes of life than their previous belief systems. Many wanted to be released from a life of fear of evil spirits, as well as from various forms of social bondage. In times of famine and other distress, faith in Christ could be seen as more powerful and therefore more able to help than faith in former gods and spirits had been. There were mass movements of conversion during the 1860-61 famine and cholera epidemics.[90] This could also work the other way when conversion was not seen to bring the desired results. Dick Kooiman has shown how groups converted in times of crisis and reverted when their condition did not improve.

Whatever the motives for conversion, the new Christian communities of low-caste converts and untouchables found that they did not necessarily un-

87. See, for instance, C. D. F. Mosse, "Caste, Christianity and Hinduism: A Study of Social Organisation and Religion in Rural Ramnad," D.Phil. thesis, University of Oxford, 1986, which illustrates many of the themes that have been discussed here.

88. See also, N. Koshy, *Caste in the Kerala Churches* (Bangalore, 1968).

89. Richard M. Eaton, "Conversion to Christianity Among the Nagas," *Indian Economic and Social History Review* 1.21 (1984): 1-44.

90. The success of the breast-cloth campaign of 1859 may also have been a factor in these conversions.

dergo any transformation in status or identity by virtue of their conversion, although some of them certainly did. They were hived off after baptism into separate churches and congregations of their own. Rarely was there any question of intermingling with the Syrian Christians or other high-caste converts. Hardgrave, Susan Bayly, and K. Kawashima have each shown that once caste Hindus realized that concessions had to be made to aspiring peoples of low caste — or they would gain what they wanted anyway and perhaps also leave the Hindu fold altogether — they began to give ground. The strategy was successful. Many who had previously been converted returned to Hinduism, and the mass conversions of the earlier period began to wane. The case of Kerala illustrates the complexity of the whole question of conversion and its relationship with the wider society.

Conclusion

Some of the questions posed at the beginning of this paper can now be answered. Whether or not, prior to the advent of colonial rule, relations between Christians and Hindus had been peaceful, Christian elites had certainly been integrated into the upper crust of Kerala society. Harmonious relations with Syrian Christians were vital to the local rulers. Thus, while at the same time keeping their own identity as Christians, Syrian or Thomas Christians were nevertheless integrated or "inculturated" within the wider social and cultural matrix. Syrian Christians, in that sense, did not opt out of the indigenous moral order. The case of the Syrian Christians shows that conversion to Christianity did not have to mean a total alienation from the wider, highly segmented social system.[91] Fissures already present may have become more evident with the coming of colonial rule as various groups began to use the situation to further their own ends. By the end of the nineteenth century, as in the sixteenth, seventeen, and eighteenth centuries, the situation was one of stressful and increasing conflict, although in different and disturbing ways. Some British missionaries argued that opposition to Christians was based on antipathy to Christianity *per se*. The coexistence between Christians and Hindus in the precolonial era demonstrates that other factors were at stake. Concessions had long been granted to Christians in Kerala. However, concessions

91. Mosse's study, "Caste, Christianity and Hinduism," n. 89, of a community in Ramnad demonstrates that, in British India also and until well into the twentieth century, Christians and "Hindus" of the same caste were often largely integrated. What happened later when Jesuit priests and certain untouchable castes attempted to improve their status within the caste system is not altogether clear.

granted in Travancore that short-circuited the local judicial and revenue machinery at a time when the Hindu elites of Kerala were losing control over their own positions in society, both because of colonial rule and because of the pressures of a rapidly changing world, led to profound dislocations and disturbances. Munro's control and his support for missionary operations, together with the appointment of two missionaries as judges, had made the presence of British Protestant missions seem to be, at least in the eyes of some, as an arm of the state. What seems to have been even more important was missionary and eventually official support of efforts by low-caste and untouchable peoples to challenge the existing status quo. After conversion, many refused to contribute shares to village festivals or to perform *palaiyam* service. This could be a considerable loss to the village. It also can be seen as demonstrating the missionary's lack of understanding of how participation in such rituals was the visible side of acceptance and status in the wider society. It is significant that the most violent conflicts in Kerala occurred over the breast-cloth controversy and over the right to enter temple precincts. Modernizing administration, including reforms in education, health, revenue, and judicial systems, inevitably destabilized traditional institutions and ways of life. A passion for codification, both Brahmanical and British, served to solidify institutions in ways never before known. As Eaton has argued, colonial rule opened up isolated societies to the pressures, ideas, and opportunities of a wider world. The actions of missionaries sometimes initiated and accelerated the pace of change. However, potential converts had their own views of what they were expecting to gain from conversion. Once converts had begun to challenge the status quo they did so on their own terms. The tragedy for India is that Hindus, in opposing conversion, have succeeded in completing the Brahmanization of India, a process that was taken forward by the British and has succeeded in making the state synonymous with Hinduism. The link between Christians of India and colonial rule has subsequently proved to be an almost insuperable obstacle for the acceptance of India's Christian population as loyal members of the Indian nation and state.

CHAPTER SEVEN

Constructing "Hinduism": The Impact of the Protestant Missionary Movement on Hindu Self-Understanding

"Hindus" and "Hinduism"

In recent years there has been considerable discussion of the origin and development of the idea of "Hinduism." Attention has focused on the role of Catholic missionaries in the discovery and interpretation of texts in the sixteenth and seventeenth centuries, the part played by the British Orientalist scholar-administrators in "the British discovery of Hinduism," and the role of officials in the introduction and development of the census that encouraged the idea that Indians who belonged to different sects and cults could all be classified as "Hindus."[1] Very little attention, however, has been paid to the influence of Protestant missionaries in developing and encouraging the idea that "Hindus," including those who worshipped popular deities, all belonged to a coherent, comprehensive, and unified religious system that could be compared to other systems such as Christianity and Islam.

1. See especially P. J. Marshall, *The British Discovery of Hinduism in the Eighteenth Century* (Cambridge, 1970); Wilhelm Halbfass, *India and Europe: An Essay in Understanding* (New York, 1988), pp. 36-52; Romila Thapar, "Imagined Religious Communities? Ancient History and the Search for a Hindu Identity," *Modern Asian Studies* 23.2 (1989): 209-31; Ronald Inden, *Imagining India* (Cambridge, Mass. and Oxford, 1990), ch. 3; Gunthur D. Sontheimer and Herman Kulke, eds., *Hinduism Reconsidered* (New Delhi, 1997); John Stratton Hawley, "Naming Hinduism," *The Wilson Quarterly* 15 (1991): 20-34; Robert Eric Frykenberg, "Constructions of Hinduism at the Nexus of History and Religion," *Journal of Interdisciplinary History* 23.3 (Winter 1993): 523-50.

It is now well established that the terms "Hindu" and "Hinduism" were categories invented by outsiders in an attempt to interpret and explain the complexities they found in Indian religious and social life. The word "Hindu," as Heinrich von Stietencron has pointed out, is "the Persian variant of Sanskrit *sindhu,* the Indus river, a word applied already in the Avesta both to the river and to the country through which the Indus flows."[2] Thus, for the Persians and later Muslim invaders, "Hindus" were the local or indigenous inhabitants who lived in the vicinity of the Indus river. Later, the meaning of the word was gradually extended to include native inhabitants of the entire subcontinent. The racial/ethnic connotation of the word, as opposed to its later religious or confessional implication and meaning, lingered in the continued but declining usage of the term "Hindu-Christian" to describe Indian Christians in the first half of the nineteenth century.[3] The clear implication of this terminology and usage was that, despite their confessing a different faith, Indian Christians continued to belong to the same race or "nation," the same social set, as other inhabitants and were therefore, in that sense, "Hindus."

As the peoples of India were known as "Hindus," outsiders assumed that they must have characteristics, including religious ideas, in common. This led to an increasingly intensive European search for commonalities and to a conviction, clearly apparent among European commentators in the eighteenth century, that it was possible to locate and discuss a unified system that could be described as "the Hindu religion." For example, in his *History of "Hindustan"* (1768) Alexander Dow refers to "the Hindoo faith" and "the Hindoo religion,"[4] while in a preface to his translation of *A Code of Gentoo Laws,* published eight years later, Nathaniel Halhead also referred to "the Hindoo religion."[5] As a further step towards simplification and rapid reference to the same idea was the term "Hinduism" — a word that was introduced in Bengal-based European comment of the eighteenth century. Charles Grant, a convert to Evangelical Christianity and future Director of the East India Company, used it in correspondence as early as 1787 as well as in his well-known "Observations," written chiefly in 1792.[6] The first missionary who is known to have

2. Heinrich von Stietencron, "Hinduism: On the Proper Use of a Deceptive Term," in Sontheimer and Kulke, *Hinduism Reconsidered,* p. 11.

3. See Hindu comments on "Hindoo Christians" in a petition in Parliamentary Papers, Commons, 1852-53, vol. 27, p. 436. Bishop Robert Caldwell used the term several times in his *Lectures on the Tinnevelly Missions* (London, 1857), pp. 14, 65.

4. Marshall, *British Discovery,* pp. 111, 139.

5. Marshall, *British Discovery,* p. 145. The term "Gentoo" was derived from the Portuguese *gentio,* Gentile. See A. L. Basham, ed., *A Cultural History of India* (Oxford, 1975), p. 473.

6. See references to "Hindooism" in extracts from Charles Grant's correspondence

used the term was the Baptist missionary William Ward, who moved in the same Evangelical circles as Grant (when the latter was in India) and who worked with William Carey and other Baptist missionaries at Serampore near Calcutta from 1799 to 1823. Ward used the term in his diary in 1801. In an entry for June 1800 he noted that one of the Serampore converts was writing a substantial piece against "the whole of the Hindoo System,"[7] and in the following February he referred to the pamphlet being against "Hindooism."[8] Here and in later parts of the diary the word was used as a substitute for "the Hindoo system" or even "the Hindoo superstition."[9]

For most Christians in the early nineteenth century the term signified the existence of an all-embracing religious system that was both the enemy and opposite of Christianity. Indeed, British missionary constructions and representations of "Hinduism," such as those of William Ward, one of the most influential of all missionary writers, had a profound effect on popular attitudes to the Hindu "other" in Britain throughout the nineteenth century. The concept of "Hinduism" incorporating the imagined, suffering, and enslaved "Hindu" was a powerful factor fueling the missionary movement and affecting not only the attitudes of ordinary churchgoers but debates in Parliament and policies of both British and Indian governments. The intention here is not to explore the role of missionaries in creating the Hindu "other" in Britain, but to examine the impact of Christian and especially missionary ideas of "Hinduism" on the "Hindus" themselves. In other words, what part did the missionaries play in helping to develop Hindu self-understanding? How important was the missionary factor as *one* influence in the evolution and construction of various Hindu notions of "Hinduism"?

An analysis of the works of William Ward, Alexander Duff, George

---

in Henry Morris, *The Life of Charles Grant, Sometime Member of Parliament for Inverness-Shire and Director of the East India Company* (London, 1904), pp. 105, 110; and in Oriental and India Office Collection [OIOC] Mss. Charles Grant, "Observations on the State of Society among the Asiatic Subjects of Great Britain, particularly with respect to Morals; and on the means of improving it. Written chiefly in the Year 1792," pp. 74, 87. For the date of the origin of the term, see also J. A. B. Van Buitenen, "Hinduism," in *Encyclopaedia Britannica*, 11th ed. (Cambridge and New York, 1910-11), p. 888, who suggests 1830. W. C. Smith (*The Meaning and End of Religion* [New York, 1964], p. 59) dates "Hinduism" to 1829, and H. von Stietencron (in Vasudha Dalmia and H. von Stietencron, eds., *Representing Hinduism: The Construction of Religious Traditions and National Identity* [Delhi, 1995], p. 75) suggests it was used from the 1820s.

7. Bengal, Serampore College archives, Diary, 29 June 1800.
8. Bengal, Serampore College archives, Diary, 28 February 1801.
9. Bengal, Serampore College archives, Diary, 28 February 1801; 28 February, 14 March, 19 September, and 19 December 1802; 13 November 1804 and 28 September 1805.

Mundy, and other Protestant missionary writers on "Hinduism" in the first half of the nineteenth century suggests that they inherited and reinforced some of the assumptions about "Hinduism" derived from earlier Orientalist scholars.[10] One influential and very basic assumption was about the unity and comprehensive nature of "the Hindu system." This system, the missionaries argued, was created and maintained by Brahmans, primarily, if not wholly, for their own benefit. Furthermore, what appeared to be differences within the religious landscape were only superficially so. Regional variations were largely ignored, and different strategies were used to explain what was assumed to be a relationship between philosophical and popular "Hinduism." The usual argument was that popular religion not only was controlled by Brahmans but exhibited the same "spirit" as philosophical "Hinduism," or, like the latter, was fundamentally pantheistic.

"Hinduism," viewed by these commentators as a holistic objective system, not only had clear boundaries that separated it from other religious systems but like a scientific object had its own particular attributes and character that could be compared in these respects with other forms of faith.[11] While all were agreed in this approach, however, differences of opinion emerged when questions were raised about the nature and relative importance of particular attributes and the overall quality or moral value of "the Hindu system." Was "Hinduism" "a mild and beneficial system" as was often claimed by eighteenth-century European commentators, or was it "evil" and destructive of human welfare? What were its dominant features and how did they affect the life of India's people? It was not only missionary assumptions about the unified nature of Hinduism that affected Hindu ideas of "Hinduism" but also the missionaries' value judgments that provoked strong Hindu reactions and determined, at least to some extent, the way in which "Hindus" themselves reconstructed their own religion.

10. William Ward's work went through three editions in nine years: 1st ed.: *Account of the Writings, Religion, and Manners, of the Hindoos: including translations from their principal works,* 4 vols. (Serampore, 1811); 2nd ed.: 1 vol. (1815); and 3rd ed.: *History, Literature, and Mythology of the Hindoos: including a minute description of their manners and customs and translations from their principal works,* 4 vols. (London, 1817-20). See also Alexander Duff, *India and India Missions including sketches of the gigantic system of Hinduism, both in theory and practice,* 2nd ed. (Edinburgh, 1840); G. Mundy, *Christianity and Hindooism contrasted; or, a comparative view of the evidence by which the respective claims to divine authority of The Bible and the Hindoo Shastrus are supported,* 2nd and enlarged ed. (Serampore 1834).

11. For developing ideas of religion as an objective system that could be compared with objects in the natural world, see especially Peter Harrison, *"Religion" and Religions in the English Enlightenment* (Cambridge, 1990).

Protestant missionary influence and agitation, especially in the first half of the nineteenth century, encouraged a greater sense of being "Hindu" particularly among the Western-educated elites, and it also fostered among Indians the idea that they had their own distinctive, unified, and overarching *religious* system. The sense of being "Hindu" and of needing to play down differences and join together was further encouraged by a fear of conversion to Christianity, which also gave considerable impetus to the process of religious modernization. This included the formation of missionary-type voluntary associations and the adoption of new techniques in defense of what was increasingly felt to be a pan-Indian unified religious tradition. Because of missionary propaganda and the fear of defection to Christianity especially of educated youth, "Hindus" were also under increasing pressure to suppress what the missionaries described as "evil" or unacceptable practices, to redefine the boundaries of "Hinduism" so as to exclude damaging ideas or practice, or to embark on types of reform that would disarm the critics and counter the effects of the missionary activity.

Precolonial Foundations

Before one can assess the impact of missionary activity on "Hindu" views of themselves and their religion, it is necessary to say something about the nature and extent of Hindu self-awareness at the end of the eighteenth century. To what extent was there a consciousness of being "Hindu" during the precolonial period? How far was this feeling supralocal or even India-wide, and in what way, if at all, was it linked with a sense of having a distinctive "religious" identity?

There has been extensive comment on these issues in recent years, and any detailed analysis of the arguments and evidence advanced is not possible here. Suffice it to say that, as a result of the work of a range of scholars, it is now possible to see more clearly general trends and regional variations and to suggest some very tentative conclusions. First, studies such as those of Nainar Jagadeesan, von Stietencron, and Sanjay Subrahmanyam have highlighted the extent of religious diversity and fragmentation that appears to have prevailed among people subsequently described as "Hindus" in different parts of the subcontinent prior to the coming of Islam.[12] Especially well documented is the

12. N. Jagadeesan, *History of Sri Vaishnavism in the Tamil Country (Post-Ramanuja)* (Madurai, 1997), pp. 230-39; Heinrich von Stietencron, "Religious Configurations in Pre-Muslim India and the Modern Concept of Hinduism," in *Representing Hinduism: The*

intensity of the Vaishnavite-Saivite conflict in South India, which, it has been argued, is best thought of as between two mutually exclusive and distinctive "religions." Moreover, not only does there appear to have been an absence of an overall sense of Hindu religious unity during the centuries prior to the appearance of Muslims, but, according to André Wink in particular, when the Muslims first arrived, they collaborated with the locals so that any alliance system that developed tended to cut across the foreign versus indigenous peoples division.[13] In other words, rivalry was between class or special-interest groups rather than between clearly defined religious communities comprising the incoming "invaders" on the one hand and the local people on the other.

There is, however, increasing research that suggests that, after the initial stages of Islamic conquest and settlement in different parts of India, the native peoples (subsequently known as "Hindus") very gradually became conscious that there were general differences between themselves as "insiders," or residents of India, and the foreigners. This process was accelerated by the introduction of what Cantwell Smith has described as the more formal, rigid, and structured form of Islam, culminating in the policies of Aurangzeb in the seventeenth century.[14] Indeed, even before the introduction of these measures that heightened Hindu awareness and helped to undermine the status and position of Hindus within the Mughal administration, there is some evidence that indigenous commentators and writers were beginning to think of themselves as "Hindus." Talbot's work on Telugu inscriptions associated with the rulers of Vijayanagara, Joseph O'Connell's examination of Bengali Gaudiya Vaisnava texts dating from the second half of the sixteenth century, and Balkrishna Gokhale's discussion of Marathi devotional literature produced during the period of Shivaji's conflict with Mughal rulers shows that, during the sixteenth and seventeenth centuries, usage of the term "Hindu" by Hindus was gradually spreading as they began to compare themselves with Islamic intruders.[15]

Construction of Religious Traditions and National Identity, edited by Vasudha Dalmia and H. von Stietencron (Delhi, 1995), pp. 51-81; Sanjay Subrahmanyam, "Before the Leviathan: Sectarian Violence and the State in Pre-Colonial India," in *Unravelling the Nation: Sectarian Conflict and India's Secular Identity,* edited by Kaushik Basu and Sanjay Subrahmanyam (New Delhi, 1996), pp. 44-80.

13. André Wink, *Al-Hind: The Making of the Indo-Islamic World,* vol. 1: *Early Medieval India and the Expansion of Islam 7th-11th centuries* (Delhi, 1900), esp. pp. 196-201.

14. Wilfred Cantwell Smith, "The Crystalization of Religious Communities in Mughal India," in his *On Understanding Islam: Selected Studies* (The Hague and New York, 1981), pp. 177-96.

15. Cynthia Talbot, "Inscribing the Self: Hindu-Muslim Identities in Pre-Colonial

This sense of difference was not always based on what might be described as religious markers — recognition of difference also being based on language, dress, housing, forms of social organization, and so on. O'Connell in his study of the Bengalis' use of the term "Hindu" goes so far as to argue that none of the references to the term really reflects a sense of corporate religious or confessional identity separating Hindus, as a whole, from the Muslims among them. The result of Gokhale's research on the situation in western India during the period of Shivaji's encounter with Mughal rulers is, however, very different. In his study he notes the cumulative effect of Mughal policy on Hindu religious life and practice and the effect this had on Marathi commentators who reflected increasingly their own sense of religious identity and difference that separated them from Muslim opponents. Alongside this research and these developments that are documented especially in Gokhale's study of Hindu responses to the Muslim presence in Maharashtra are comments by "insiders" such as Kabir (1440-1518)[16] and Guru Arjun (1563-1606), who used the terms "Hindu" and "Muslim" in a religious sense but who denied they belonged to either camp.[17]

While this research can hardly be regarded as exhaustive, it does at least suggest that when the missionaries used the term "Hindu" and argued that the Hindus had a distinct religion, these ideas were not always unfamiliar to the Hindus themselves. It is therefore one of the arguments of this paper that Protestant missionary preaching and activity in the early nineteenth century reinforced and further encouraged a trend toward the development of a Hindu religious consciousness that had already begun to grow and was becoming apparent during the precolonial period.

Missionaries and Vernacular Equivalents of "Hinduism"

It was partly through their introduction of new terminology and development of language that the missionaries began to exert pressure and influence

India," *Comparative Studies in Society and History* 37.4 (October 1995): 699; Joseph T. O'Connell, "The Word 'Hindu' in Gaudiya Vaishnava Texts," *Journal of the American Oriental Society* 93.3 (1993): 340-44; Balkrishna Govind Gokhale, "Hindu Responses to the Muslim Presence in Maharashtra," in *Islam in Asia,* edited by Yohanan Friedmann (Boulder, Colo., 1984), 1:146-73.

16. Quoted in Charlotte Vaudeville, *Kabir,* translated from Hindi with introduction and notes (Oxford, 1974), 1:186.

17. Quoted in Harjot Oberoi, *The Construction of Religious Boundaries: Culture, Identity and Diversity in the Sikh Tradition* (Delhi, 1994), p. 57.

Hindu views of themselves. The adoption and use of English by Bengali and other "Hindus" in the early nineteenth century and the influence of key English terms and concepts on the vernaculars were ways in which missionary assumptions and views of the world slowly influenced the attitudes of various classes in India.

The term "Hinduism," implying the existence of some kind of coherent and unified Hindu religious system, was possibly first used in Indian writing in Rammohan Roy's publications in English. Roy who appears to have made his first visit to the Baptist missionaries at Serampore in 1816, collaborated with them for a short period in biblical translation.[18] It was in 1816 that we find one of his first references to "Hinduism" when he complained that "the chief part of the theory and practice of Hindooism, I am sorry to say, is made to consist in the adoption of a peculiar mode of diet," from which the smallest deviation, he argued, resulted in expulsion from caste.[19] Some years later, Rammohan was involved in a bitter debate with the missionaries over Christian doctrine, and in 1823, at the peak of controversy, he contrasted "the mild and liberal spirit of universal toleration, which is well-known to be a fundamental principle of Hindooism" with the indiscreet assaults of Christian writers.[20] On many other occasions, however, instead of generalizing about the whole of "Hinduism," he drew a distinction between the "real Hindooism" and popular belief and practice. For example, in 1817, he declared that "the doctrines of the unity of God are real Hindooism, as that religion was practised by our ancestors, and is well-known even at the present age to many learned Brahmans."[21] In another reference in 1823, he berated missionaries for taking "the popular system of worship adopted by the multitude" (with all its corruptions) as the "standard of Hindooism."[22] Rammohan's adoption and use of the term "Hinduism" in his English writings was followed by an increasing use of the word by the English-speaking *bhadralok* in Bengal in the 1820s and 1830s.[23]

18. E. Daniel Potts, *British Baptist Missionaries in India, 1793-1837* (Cambridge, 1967), pp. 230-44. On Roy see also the Rev. Henry Townley in *Quarterly Chronicle of the LMS,* 1:99-100.

19. *Translation of the Abridgement of the Vedant* (Calcutta, 1816), in *English Works of Rammohan Roy,* 6 parts, edited by Kalidas Nag and Debajyoti Burman (Calcutta, 1945-47), pt. 2, p. 51 (hereafter *EW*).

20. *Brahmunical Magazine,* 4 (Calcutta, 1823), in *EW,* pt. 2, p. 171.

21. *A Defence of Hindu Theism* (Calcutta, 1817), in *EW,* pt. 2, p. 84.

22. *The Brahmunical Magazine* (Calcutta, 1823), in *EW,* pt. 2, p. 185.

23. See, for example, Krishna Mohan Bannerjea's use of the term in a passage quoted in the *Missionary Register* (February 1833), p. 119.

Debates with missionaries, such as that between Rammohan Roy and the Serampore missionaries over the period from 1817 to 1823, and missionary speeches and writings in English were therefore important in acquainting the growing Western-educated elites with the idea of "Hinduism." The same debates were also a powerful factor in the growth and development of indigenous terminology that would express something of the idea of "Hinduism" in the vernacular.[24] According to Wilhelm Halbfass it was the missionaries who, as early as 1801, had chosen the word "dharma" as "the key word for their translations into Bengali"[25] and who juxtaposed the "dharma" of the "Hindus" over against the "true dharma" *(satyadharma)* or Christianity. "Dharma" was also used for the equivalent of "religion" in missionary translations of the Bible and other works into Sanskrit and north Indian languages. In order to meet this challenge Hindu opponents were themselves forced to develop new ways of using "dharma" so that they could compare the notion of "Hindu dharma" favorably with the idea of "Christianity." In other words, "Hindus" were eventually using the term in much the same way as their Christian rivals and in ways that tended to correspond with the foreign and developing concept of "Hinduism."[26]

This change in meaning is certainly borne out by Richard Fox Young, who argues that the term "dharma" was coming to be used more in the sense of "religious creed."[27] The same point was in fact made by the well-known Bengali author and patriot Bankimchandra Chatterji who, writing in his treatise *Dharmatattva* or *The Essence of Dharma* toward the end of the nineteenth century, declared that "the word dharma has been used with different meanings. Several of the meanings have no use for us. The meaning in which you now used the word dharma, that is simply a modern translation of the English word Religion. It is no indigenous thing."[28]

In southern India similar developments in language and terminology, encouraging the idea of the one Hindu religion, took place. The first edition of

24. According to Dermot Killingley there is no equivalent for "Hinduism" in Rammohan's Bengali, "except where he is taking up the terms used by a Christian opponent." Examples of this appear in the *Brahmunical Magazine,* which defended Hindu ideas and attacked Christianity. There Rammohan Roy translates the English term "the Hindoo Religion" as *hindur dharma* or "the dharma of the 'Hindus.'" Personal communication, letter, 15 January 1999.

25. Halbfass, *India and Europe,* p. 340.

26. Halbfass, *India and Europe,* p. 341.

27. Richard Fox Young, *Resistant Hinduism: Sanskrit Sources on Anti-Christian Apologetics in Early Nineteenth-Century India* (Vienna, 1981), p. 34.

28. Quoted in Torkel Brekke, "The Conceptual Foundation of Missionary Hinduism," *Journal of Religious History* 23.2 (June 1999).

the Tranquebar Bible in Tamil (1714) was entitled *Veda-pustagam* [Veda Book], and in subsequent missionary usage and translations the idea of Christianity being the "true veda" or *satyuvedam* was popular.[29] In this situation "Hindus" had little option other than to adopt similar terminology implying parallels between their own "vedam" and Christianity.[30] The term *madam*, "teaching, doctrine or creed,"[31] was also used for "religion." As a synonym for a specific religious system in relation to others, it was combined with the Tamil *Indu* to form *Indu madam*, suggesting, once again, that the "Hindus" had their own distinctive doctrine or religion — their equivalent to the Christian system.

It is apparent from these examples of linguistic developments in both North and South India that the missionaries were encouraging the non-English-speaking as well as the English-speaking classes to think of themselves as belonging to a unified all-embracing "Hindu" system (whether it be called Hindu dharma, *vedum*, or *Indu madam*), a distinctive Hindu religious tradition that could be compared with Christianity or one of the other great religious systems.

"Hinduism" in Missionary Preaching

The idea of a distinctive Hindu religious system, implicit in the term "Hinduism" and encouraged through the work of translation into the vernacular languages, was based on the notion that religions were separate entities. There were many religions including those of ancient Greece and Rome, Christianity, Islam, and Hinduism, and these could be compared as objective systems and, if necessary, placed in an hierarchy according to different principles. In other words, the idea of religious boundaries, of comparison, and of discussing the comparative merits of the different religions was there in Protestant preaching from the beginning.

This comparative approach was apparent in early-nineteenth-century missionary publications intended especially for "Hindus" and Muslims: for example, in George Mundy's work entitled *Christianity and Hindooism Contrasted; a comparative view of the evidence by which the respective claims to di-*

29. Halbfass, *India and Europe*, p. 340.

30. For an example of the use of the term *vedam* in South India see the Rev. J. C. T. Winckler's report on reactions to his preaching in Tinnevelly district in 1830, in *Missionary Register* (May 1831), p. 231.

31. B. F. Tiliander, *Christian and Hindu Terminology: A Study in Their Mutual Relations with Special Reference to the Tamil Area* (Uppsala, 1974), p. 58.

vine authority of the Bible and the Hindoo Shastrus are supported.[32] It was also reflected in works in the vernacular, such as William Smith and C. B. Leupolt, *Din-i-haqq ki tahqiq* [Investigator of True Religion], published in Allahabad in 1842,[33] and Michael Wilkinson's translation of a tract "shewing that Christianity is the only true Religion in the world."[34]

A similar approach was adopted in missionary preaching. Protestant missionaries and Indian Christian workers engaged in extensive public preaching in the cities and villages and on long missionary journeys throughout the countryside. The idea that Christianity was a religion or system with definite boundaries and that "Hinduism" was in that respect comparable with Christianity was a basic assumption that facilitated communication and arguments in favor of what was believed to be the superior Christian position. With two simple models it was relatively easy to compare one with the other. An illustration of this approach was missionary preaching in Benares in the 1830s. The Rev. William Smith of the Church Missionary Society (CMS) (one of the authors of the Urdu work mentioned above), asked one of his Indian assistants to read and explain a Hindi poem containing a brief statement of "the Hindoo, Mussulman, and Christian Religions." After questions were answered, the missionary made "a brief comparison of Hindooism and Christianity," presumably to the advantage of the latter.[35] That this comparative approach was already beginning to affect Hindu thinking is apparent in the Rev. Wilkinson's account of an incident in Gorruckpore a few years earlier. While in conversation with a group of "Hindus" the head pandit of the place arrived; after being introduced to the missionary "as a person disputing the truths of Hindooism," the pandit was asked to satisfy the latter "that the Hindoo Religion was not only true, but the best."[36]

The effect of this comparative approach was to concentrate the listeners' attention on the differences between different systems rather than on differences within. This meant that "Hindus" were encouraged to think that what really mattered was not the differences among themselves but the contrast be-

---

32. George Mundy, *Christianity and Hindooism Contrasted; a comparative view of the evidence by which the respective claims to divine authority of the Bible and the Hindoo Shastrus are supported* (Serampore, 1834).

33. Avril A. Powell, *Muslims and Missionaries in Pre-Mutiny India* (London, 1993), p. 88.

34. *Missionary Register* (March 1833), p. 138.

35. *Missionary Register* (April 1835), p. 205. See also the Rev. Weitbrecht's account of his conversation with the people of Bancoorah in Bengal (*Missionary Register* [February 1833], p. 115).

36. *Missionary Register* (June 1829), p. 281.

tween Hindu teachings on the one hand and Christian teachings on the other. This tendency to gloss over sectarian and other differences between "Hindus" and to treat them as if they were all one is also reflected in the preaching of the Rev. Edward Dent (CMS, Madras) who, according to his own account, told his audience that "all the means which their Vedas propose are vain and fruitless, and can never save their souls. Their sacrifices and offerings; their pilgrimages, both by sea and land, to distant places; their austerities and penances; their ablutions and fastings; and other such observances, could never save them."[37] Here different traditions, rituals, and practices were lumped together and dismissed as of no account alongside the benefits of Christian faith.

Hindu Resentments and Fear of Conversion

The "Hindus" gradual but increasing acceptance of the idea of "Hinduism," a concept incorporating the notion that "Hindus" had their own distinctive and unified Hindu religion was, as we have argued, strengthened by an increasing awareness of foreign religious systems (Islamic and Christian) and by debates with Christian missionaries. Moreover, the sense of being "Hindu" and of having a distinctive religious as well as ethnic identity was not only an "idea." It was also a feeling; and this *feeling* of being "Hindu" in a socio-religious communal sense was greatly intensified by missionary attitudes and aggressive activity. Especially provocative were what "Hindus" perceived as "insults" (missionary attacks on Hindu deities, customs, and culture) and also the reality and increasing fear of conversion.

The style of missionary preaching, at least in the first half of the nineteenth century, was often aggressive and sometimes even inflammatory. Its tone is reflected in Henry Martyn's comments on the Baptist Joshua Marshman's preaching when he remarked that "I feel pain that he should so frequently speak with contempt of the Brahmins, many of whom were listening with great respect and attention."[38] Commenting on the preaching of the Rev. Richards, a CMS missionary at Meerut in the 1830s, one of his colleagues wrote, "Mr. Richards' mode of proceeding was, to attack them [the Hindu audience] on the ground of their own Shasters, continually illustrating the truth of his opinions by Sanskrit quotations, denouncing Idolatry to be folly and sin."[39] Before referring to "the one true God" in his address to villagers near

37. *Missionary Register* (May 1835), p. 245.
38. Potts, *British Baptist Missionaries*, p. 218.
39. *Missionary Register* (June 1830), p. 280.

Ahmednagar in Western India, the Rev. C. P. Farrar of the same society "dwelt briefly and pointedly on the folly of idolatry, and enormities ascribed to the Hindoo gods, and the sin of worshipping them."[40] Likewise when preaching at Paithan in the same presidency the Rev. C. F. Worth (CMS) felt constrained to dwell on the "evils" of the Hindu system by endeavoring to show his audience "the folly of their assertions; the uselessness of their rites; and wickedness of their pride of caste; and the abominable character of their gods."[41] The same confrontational style is also apparent in the preaching of Thomas Cryer, a Methodist preacher, who, while on a visit to the famous temple town of Conjeeveram near Madras, bore testimony against "the abominations of idolatry" and recommended the truth of Jesus Christ.[42]

Though it was recognized increasingly in the light of experience, and also as a result of changes in attitudes toward non-Christian religions, that these methods (including attacks on the listeners' religion) were unfair and counterproductive, this approach still had some vocal support in the latter part of the nineteenth century.[43] Its impact on Hindu audiences is reflected in missionary comments: for example, in the remarks of the Rev. Dixon (CMS, Nassick) that the Hindus were "offended" at his comments,[44] and in the Rev. Dent's confession that "sometimes I receive anonymous letters, which accuse me of having vilified their gods and them, and in which I am threatened and warned not to preach in the streets."[45] On another occasion the Rev. C. P. Farrar explained that after he had spoken to a leading Hindu near Nassick about the "littleness, folly and impurity" associated with the worship of Puranic deities, the man, together with the others, "took his leave."[46]

Growing Fears of Conversion

Possibly more important in raising Hindu consciousness than the sense of resentment, humiliation, and outrage engendered in Hindus as a result of some

40. *Missionary Register* (February 1837), p. 112.

41. *Missionary Register* (August 1842), p. 382.

42. *Missionary Register* (June 1836), pp. 294-95.

43. *Report of the Second Decennial Missionary Conference held at Calcutta, 1882-83* (Calcutta: Baptist Mission Press, 1883), pp. 4-31.

44. *Missionary Register* (April 1837), p. 191.

45. *Missionary Register* (May 1835), p. 245. See also comments by the Rev. C. P. Farrar (CMS) on the effect of missionary preaching on Brahmans near Nassick. *Missionary Register* (February 1834), p. 114.

46. *Missionary Register* (February 1837), p. 116.

of the more outspoken missionary attacks on Hindus and "Hinduism" was a growing fear of conversion, especially among the influential higher-caste and Western-educated elites. Certainly it was this issue that did a great deal to arouse concern, to create a sense of crisis, and to underline the need for Hindus of different sects, cults, and traditions to forget their differences and join together in defense of what was seen increasingly as an overarching dharma, a common religious and social heritage.

(a) Mission Schools and High-Caste Conversion

One source of anxiety and turbulence in the Hindu community was the development of the mission school and the gradual recognition that, contrary to what Rammohan Roy had argued, intelligent high-caste young men were vulnerable to the padres.[47] As has become clearly apparent in detailed studies, the conversion of high-caste individuals, usually young men in mission schools, created enormous upheaval and ferment especially in the cities of Calcutta, Bombay, and Madras in the 1830s and 1840s.[48] As Muhammad Mohar Ali and others have shown, a single instance of conversion was capable of creating widespread panic among parents, relatives, and other members of the Hindu community. One of the more extreme examples of this was the reaction to the conversion of a minor in Nagpur in 1848 when a fifteen to twenty thousand strong deputation waited on the raja and presented him with a petition for the recovery of the boy from the custody of the missionaries.[49] Elsewhere in India, violence, kidnapping, and the institution of legal proceedings was not infrequent. Meetings were convened, students were withdrawn from mission schools, rival Hindu schools were established, and the whole episode was covered at great length in the English-language and vernacular press. What happened in one part of India was therefore reported and usually well known among high-caste Hindus elsewhere. Also relevant and important in the formation of a consciousness among Hindus of belonging to a confessional as well as ethnic community is the fact that, in these circumstances, the young people involved were sometimes forced to state pub-

47. For Rammohan Roy's views see *English Works of Rammohan Roy*, pt. 2 (Calcutta, 1946), p. 188 and pt. 4 (Calcutta, 1947), pp. 43-52.

48. See especially Muhammad Mohar Ali, *The Bengali Reaction to Christian Missionary Activities, 1833-1857* (Chittagong, 1965); R. Suntharalingam, *Politics and Nationalist Awakening in South India, 1852-1891* (Tucson, Ariz., 1974), pp. 35-36; and S. R. Mehrota, *The Emergence of the Indian National Congress* (Delhi, 1971).

49. Mehrota, *Emergence*, p. 43.

licly their reasons for conversion.[50] In this process, and especially in the public domain of legal proceedings, they invariably referred to their religious convictions and the way in which Hindu *religious* beliefs and teachings differed from those of Christians.

(b) Government Policy and Hindu Fears of a Company-Missionary Alliance

In the seventeenth and eighteenth centuries there were two fairly clear models of "church-state" relations on the Indian subcontinent. One was Akbar's model of a tolerant all-inclusive state that recognized the necessity and value of incorporating "Hindus" as well as Muslims into the one integrated system, a state that promoted the idea of a common citizenship for both Muslims and "Hindus." The other was the Portuguese and Aurangzeb's later model of an exclusive state that rejected the idea of an equal citizenship in favor of a policy of active discrimination against "Hindus" and Hindu customs and institutions. During the period when the Company was extending its territories the British not infrequently reassured the local inhabitants that the Company's policy was one of "religious neutrality" and that they had no intention of interfering with the people's sacred customs and institutions.[51] The question, however, was one of trust. Did British officials really believe in religious neutrality? Now that they had secured the empire would they ignore the pledge not to interfere with Hindu rights and customs? Would they not, influenced by missionary pressures, change policy and follow the example of Aurangzeb and the Portuguese?

The first event of considerable importance in raising Hindu consciousness and in increasing fears that the government (in league with Christian missionaries) had embarked on a course of "interference" was legislation banning *sati* in 1829.[52] While Rammohan Roy and his followers condemned the custom and eventually supported Bentinck's legislation, there was considerable opposition to the measure. The government's "interference," which was known to have been encouraged by missionaries, led to the formation of the Dharma Sabha, one of the first defensive Hindu voluntary associations. In their petition to the governor-general opposing legislation, the conservative

50. *Missionary Register* (July 1834), p. 324. *Calcutta Christian Advocate*, 13, 16, 19, 26 April 1851.

51. J. W. Kaye, *Christianity in India* (London, 1859), p. 293.

52. See especially A. F. Salahuddin Ahmed, *Social Ideas and Social Change in Bengal, 1818-1835* (Leiden, 1965), pp. 30-32, 125-26, and text of the Dharma Sabha's memorial.

"Hindus" referred to themselves as defenders of "the Hindoo religion" and were especially critical of Rammohan Roy and his supporters, who they denied had the right to act as its representatives since they had "apostatized from the religion of their forefathers" and had "defiled themselves by eating and drinking forbidden things in the society of Europeans." Fear of conversion and a suspicion that the attempted suppression of *sati* was only the first step in a government-missionary policy of Christianizing Hindu society was therefore compounded by a feeling of vulnerability and a sense that "apostates" were already collaborating with forces outside of Hindu society to undermine and destroy the Hindu religion.

A second development that encouraged a suspicion that the Company and missionaries were collaborating to convert people was Lord Tweeddale's administration in Madras (1842-48).[53] Following on the heels of other official policies that were interpreted as government prejudice in favor of Christianity, it seemed to confirm the "Hindus'" worst fears that the Company's government had, in effect, dropped the policy of religious neutrality and was actively supporting the missionary movement. Widely publicized events of this period were the Tinnevelly riots of November 1845 when Hindu mobs attacked Christian villages, molesting inhabitants, plundering houses, and destroying property.[54] The local magistrate, E. B. Thomas, already suspected of partiality toward Christians, jailed more than a hundred "Hindus." As a result of an appeal to the sessions court in Madras, however, many of the accused were acquitted. The second judge of the court, Malcolm Lewin, compiled a Minute declaring that the Tinnevelly riots were "all imputable to the missionaries, and to the improper support they had received from the local officers of the Government." At this stage in proceedings, Tweeddale, urged on by the missionaries, intervened. The resulting conflict between the judges and the executive culminated in the suspension and subsequent dismissal of Lewin, who very quickly became a martyr. The "Hindus" of Madras presented him with an address, and, in Bengal, the Dharma Sabha, which felt itself called upon to "unite with the Hindoo community of Madras," wrote a letter to Lewin in which they deplored "the attempts which had recently been made at Madras to trespass on the religious privileges of our countrymen in that Presidency."[55]

Tweeddale's handling of the Tinnevelly riots was, however, not the only incident that aroused suspicion among "Hindus" in Madras and elsewhere.

53. Suntharalingam, *Politics and Nationalist Awakening*, pp. 39-45.

54. R. E. Frykenberg, "On Roads and Riots in Tinnevelly: Radical Change and Ideology in Madras Presidency During the 19th Century," *South Asia* ns. 4.2 (December 1981): 34-52.

55. Mehrota, *Emergence*, p. 39.

There was widespread discontent over the open association of officials and missionaries at a time when the Company was withdrawing from the direct administrative oversight of Hindu temples. During the same period, Tweeddale's "Bible Minute" — approving the use of the Bible as a text in English classes in government schools — and other incidents that seemed to show the administration's bias toward Christianity kept the Presidency of Madras in "a state of agitation" that, according to *The Friend of India,* was greater than at any time since the Vellore mutiny of 1806.[56]

A third development, which was perhaps more important for raising Hindu religious consciousness than individual conversions, the banning of *sati,* or Tweeddale's administration, was what became known as the Caste Disabilities Removal Act or Act XXI of 1850. The purpose of the act was to extend provisions (which already applied in the Bengal mofussil) giving Hindu converts to Christianity the right to inherit ancestral property.[57] While missionaries regarded the existing custom that disinherited converts as unfair, "Hindus" viewed it as an automatic consequence of apostasy. The elder son, having opted out of Hindu society, no longer performed the *sharddha* or death ceremonies on behalf of his father and as a result was no longer entitled to inherit the family property.

The publication of the draft act, early in 1845, attracted the immediate attention of "Hindus." In April 1845 "Hindus" describing themselves as "Hindu Inhabitants of Madras" submitted a Memorial to the governor-general-in-council opposing the proposed legislation. They declared that it afforded "strong cause and suspicion that such an innovation is only a prelude to others, [and] that the security in person, property and religion, hitherto ensured to native subjects, is in danger of being taken from them."[58] In Bengal, where the conversion of a youth named Umeschandra Sarkar was already causing great excitement, "Hindus" organized two petitions, one on behalf of the "inhabitants of Bengal, Bihar and Orissa" and another on behalf of Radhakanta Deb and other members of the Dharma Sabha. While explaining their objections they remarked that, in passing the act, the government would be breaching its policy of noninterference with Hindu religious customs and would also appear to be placing "a Government premium on conversion."[59]

Publication of a final draft of the bill in 1849 provoked still greater alarm and dismay as it clearly demonstrated that the government was in no mood

---

56. Mehrota, *Emergence,* p. 40.
57. Ali, *Bengali Reaction,* ch. 6.
58. Mehrota, *Emergence,* p. 39.
59. Ali, *Bengali Reaction,* pp. 122-23.

to listen to Hindu opinion and was determined to proceed with legislation. The proposals were once again attacked in the press and in petitions from both Bengal and Madras, Bengali leaders organizing a Memorial signed by fourteen thousand Hindus of different persuasions.[60] In the Madras Memorial, the "native inhabitants of Fort St. George" stressed their conviction that the legislation had its origin in the Bengal government's desire to lend its aid to "the progress of Christian proselytism."[61] Both the Bengal and Madras petitioners were concerned with a possible government "breach of faith" involving further abandonment of its policy of noninterference. Both show a deep suspicion of government motives, while the Madras Memorial in particular was unusually hostile and threatening in character. If the government were to go along "this path," concluded the Madras petitioners, "it will deserve what it will assuredly attain, the hatred and detestation of the oppressed."

The passing of Act XXI of 1850 was not the end of a growing and increasingly angry protest. A meeting in Bengal condemned the act but failed to move the Court of Directors, and another Memorial, signed by 5,900 persons of Bengal, Bihar, and Orissa, appealed unsuccessfully to the House of Commons. Referring to the outraged feelings of "the Hindoo people," they declared that it was "entirely subversive of Hindoo society" and that it not only encouraged "the spread of religious proselytism," but went "much beyond that object."

The effect of these episodes involving questions of government intervention was cumulative. It was this atmosphere of uncertainty and fear of government-missionary combination that some contemporary observers argued and later historians maintained was a significant factor in the outbreak of the mutiny and civil rebellion of 1857.[62]

The conversion of high-caste students and a growing conviction that the Company was siding with the missionaries in a program of "proselytism" were developments that, if anything, tended to unify Hindus across sectarian, class, and caste divisions. Accounts of anti-conversion rallies in all three Presidencies suggest that disparate social groups and opposing parties, those inclined to social and religious reform as well as those who were more conservative in outlook, joined in attempts to prevent the conversion of Hindu youth.[63]

In addition to the way in which these incidents strengthened the idea that

60. Ali, *Bengali Reaction*, p. 128.
61. U.K. Parliamentary Papers (Commons), vol. 41, 1851, Session Paper no. 176.
62. See, for example, James Lunt, ed., *From Sepoy to Subedar* (London, 1970), pp. 165-66; and M. R. Gubbins, *An Account of the Mutinies in Oudh* (London, 1858), p. 78.
63. Mehrota, *Emergence*, p. 41; Ali, *Bengali Reaction*, p. 73.

all "Hindus" had something in common was the way in which they also heightened the "Hindus" awareness of "hindu dharma" or "the Hindu religion" as an all-Indian phenomenon. C. A. Bayly has drawn attention to the channels of communication and traditions of public debate across caste and community lines that were well developed at the regional level in North India before British rule.[64] Supplementing and building on this preexisting indigenous system was the emergence of a Western-educated reading public and the growth of the English-language press, which greatly facilitated the spread of news at an interregional and all-India level. Information derived from the English-language press was further spread through new, printed, vernacular publications. The development of more effective communications helped to create a sense of India-wide national identity and increased the sense among "Hindus" from different parts of the subcontinent, that they all belonged to the same India-wide socio-religious system — a conviction that was also implicit in much of the missionary preaching and propaganda in the earlier nineteenth century.

All of these developments led to widening public discussion and protest and the mobilization of large numbers of "Hindus." How far was defense of "the Hindu system" and opposition to the measures as discussed above motivated by religious as distinct from social considerations? To what extent did these numerous and deep-seated challenges to the status quo raise Hindu awareness of their dharma as a religious as well as a social phenomenon?

The various episodes centered on fear of conversion were of primary importance to middle- or higher-caste "Hindus" who, among other things, were concerned with pollution and loss of status. Nevertheless, the practice of *sati*, the right to inherit ancestral property, the neglect of Hindu rituals because of defection to Christianity — all involved specifically "religious" issues or practice. In this respect religious concerns never seemed to be far from the surface. Furthermore, it was the specifically religious or doctrinal issues that the middle- and high-caste converts to Christianity continued to emphasize. These considerations prompted their conversion and led to their separation from parents and Hindu society. In this situation, immediate families, relatives, and other "Hindus" must have been made more acutely aware of belief and doctrinal difference as an important factor distinguishing "Hindus" from Christians.

---

64. C. A. Bayly, *Empire and Information: Intelligence Gathering and Social Communication in India, 1780-1870* (Cambridge, 1996), esp. chs. 5 and 6.

New Methods of Defense and Propagation

The same feelings of resentment and fear of conversion that heightened Hindu awareness and encouraged a greater sense of the need for unity increased pressure for more modern and effective institutional organizations, for the adoption and refinement of new and more permanent methods of defense and propaganda.

One significant approach was to try to facilitate reconversion. This involved the formal readmission of Hindu apostates into Hindu society. In the first half of the nineteenth century many of these apostates were high-caste young men who had been baptized into Christianity and broken caste and were seeking a return to the Hindu fold. As the number of converts of this type increased, so did pressure for measures that would facilitate their readmission into Hindu society. Existing prescriptions not only were complex but were believed (erroneously) to be designed primarily for those who had broken caste rules rather than for those who had left Hindu society altogether.[65] They also included forms of atonement sufficiently severe as to dissuade converts who had become dissatisfied with Christianity from seeking readmission.

In 1844 a controversy in Bombay involving the readmission of Shripat Sheshadri, a twelve-year-old Brahman boy, who was baptized and had eaten forbidden food, received widespread publicity throughout India. In spite of the fact that the boy's case was taken up and strongly supported by Hindu liberals, "a party not great in numbers, but strong in learning, wealth and influence," they made no headway in the face of opposition from Bombay and Benares Brahmans.[66] Pressure for change was, however, gradually increasing, especially in Calcutta where the number of high-caste converts was almost certainly greater than in western India. In 1851 a meeting of between three hundred and one thousand mainly conservative and high-caste "Hindus" was convened in Calcutta to reconsider the rules of readmission.[67] After lengthy discussion the meeting ended in indecision. Later in the same year, the Society for the Deliverance of Hindu Apostates was established with the object of reintroducing into society "those young men who by the evil counsels and wills of the missionaries may become Christians."[68] As a result of these devel-

65. J. F. T. Jordens, "Reconversion to Hinduism: The Shuddi of the Arya Samaj," in *Religion in South Asia: Religious Conversion and Revival Movements in South Asia in Medieval and Modern Times,* 2nd ed., edited by G. A. Oddie (Delhi, 1991), p. 216.

66. Jordens, "Reconversion to Hinduism," pp. 215-16; *Bombay Guardian* (13 June 1851).

67. Ali, *Bengali Reaction,* p. 97.

68. Ali, *Bengali Reaction,* p. 100.

opments, further public debate, and consultation with pandits in all the seats
of sacred learning in Benares, new rules of readmission were drawn up and
applied. It was this reshaping of the rules of readmission that then became the
precedent for Dayananda's more radical and systematic policy of *shuddhi* in
the Punjab and the northwest provinces.[69]

A second and well-known measure of defense was to adopt and develop
the Christians' own techniques of organization and propaganda in order to
contain and defeat their purpose. One of the earliest of these organizations in
South India was the Society for Diffusing the Philosophy of the Four Vedas.
According to the Rev. George Pettitt, whose work was affected by the operations of the society in Tinnevelly, the association:

> held mock Christian service, substituting their Puranas for the Bible, and
> giving an exposition of their slogans (verses) and their stories of the
> gods; retailing also to their hearers arguments against Christianity, and
> every kind of scurrility and abuse that they could gather from infidel au-
> thors. . . . They constructed it appears, a doxology and benediction in im-
> itation of those used in the Christian Church, introducing the names of
> Brahma, Vishnu and Siva, as we do those of the Holy Trinity. They also,
> like their auxiliaries in Tinnevelly, got up petitions to the Government
> against Missionary operations; and they afterward commenced a series
> of publications in Tamil poetry, burlesquing Christianity, and exhorting
> the Hindoos to be stedfast in their own time-honoured religion.[70]

Techniques and methods based on Christian models were adopted or further
developed by other Hindu organizations in Madras (for example by the
Hindu Tract Society established in 1887),[71] in the Punjab, and in other parts
of India, including Bengal where the Tattvabodhini Sabha sent out its own
"missionaries" and published Christian-type tracts and pamphlets in order to
attack and undermine the efforts of Christian missionaries.

A third way of coping with missionary criticism was to deny that certain
"objectionable" scriptures, ideas, or customs were actually a part of "Hinduism": to excise carefully the corrupted parts and rearrange boundaries. In his
writings in English, published primarily for European consumption,

---

69. Jordens, "Reconversion to Hinduism," pp. 216-30.

70. George Pettitt, *The Tinnevelly Mission of the Church Missionary Society* (London,
1851), pp. 255-56.

71. G. A. Oddie, "Anti-Missionary Feeling and Hindu Revivalism in Madras: The
Hindu Preaching and Tract Societies, c 1886-1891," in *Images of Man: Religion and Historical Process in South Asia*, edited by Fred W. Clothey (Madras, 1982).

Rammohan Roy drew a distinction between "the real Hindooism" and the "superstitious practices" that deformed "the Hindoo religion" and that had nothing to do with "the pure spirit of its dictates."[72] While it is likely that Rammohan Roy held these views even before he came into contact with Christian missionaries, in some other instances Hindu reaction, including the attempt to draw similar distinctions between the authentic faith and its corruptions, was clearly a result of missionary pressure and criticism of Hindu belief and practice. Early examples of this were the controversies and doctrinal changes introduced in the Tattvabodhini Sabha, and subsequently the Brahmo Samaj, after the death of its founder in 1833.

As Ali has so convincingly shown, these debates over the issue of the Vedas as the Sabha's source of authority, and the Sabha's subsequent decision to change its policy, were a direct result of missionary arguments and pressure.[73] The missionaries not only argued that the Vedas could not provide a rational basis for the Sabha's faith and teachings on monotheism but held that, on the contrary, and in direct contradiction to the Sabha's own teachings, they upheld "a system of gross Pantheism" and idol worship. The society's founder, Devendranath Tagore, who journeyed to Benares to consult the pandits, became convinced that the Vedas did, in the main, inculcate idolatry and that it was no longer possible to base the doctrine of monotheism upon them. The Vedas were abandoned, and, in subsequent years, the basis of religious authority in the Sabha and the Brahmo Samaj (which members of the Sabha formally joined in 1859) became reason and nature.

While the Brahmos' rejection of the Vedas as a source of religious authority was an extremely radical and unusual measure even among reformers, there was a broader concern among Hindus about certain forms of more popular practice that, it was felt, needed to be exorcised and placed outside the boundaries of "real Hinduism." A determination to jettison idol worship and systems of popular religion, a trend apparent in the policies of the Brahmo and Arya Samajes, is also reflected in the comment of Western-educated Hindus generally who, like the leaders of these societies, also feared the ridicule of Christian critics. For example, one of the reasons why the elites became increasingly opposed to the practice of hook swinging (the custom of being suspended or swung from hooks) was because it discredited "the Hindu religion" in the eyes of others.[74] The *Sungbad Purnachandroday,* a Ben-

72. *A Defence of Hindoo Theism* (Calcutta, 1817), in *EW,* pt. 2, p. 84.

73. Ali, *Bengali Reaction,* ch. 1.

74. Geoffrey A. Oddie, *Popular Religion, Elites and Reform: Hook-Swinging and Its Prohibition in Colonial India, 1800-1994* (Delhi, 1995), ch. 5.

gali daily and one of the organs of the Dharma Sabha, joined with other newspapers in urging reform. The editor's main argument was that while the *charak puja* festival was "a part of Hinduism," which was commanded in scripture, there was no authority in the *sastras* for the *sannyasis* "to pierce themselves as they do with iron spears, or run hooks into their backs, etc." The paper, which had long been involved in attempts to defend "Hinduism" from the assaults of Christian missionaries, declared that the continued adherence of lower-class Hindus to these "cruel" rites was doing much "to lessen the glory of the faith they profess" and was giving just grounds "to those who are hostile to Hinduism." Likewise, in the Madras Presidency there was concern lest the custom be used to discredit "Hinduism." Hindu-controlled newspapers and prominent individuals throughout the region argued that there was no way in which hook swinging and other acts of "barbarism" could be considered a part of authentic Hindu tradition.

Assimilation of Christian Ideas

All of these strategies as outlined above illustrate the process whereby tradition is changed as a result of attempts to defend what were seen as "the fundamentals." It is also important to recognize that not all Hindu attitudes towards Christianity were defensive or negative. On another level, a slow transformation was taking place in Hindu attitudes partly out of a sense that Christianity had something to offer. For example, very few higher-caste "Hindus" converted to Christianity; and yet Protestant missionary influence, especially through the mission school system, was probably considerable. One estimate is that, in 1901, 35 percent of all students in colleges (excluding the professional and technical colleges) were studying in Protestant institutions.[75] Alongside this statistic is the sense of rapport and affection that sometimes developed between the Hindu student and his Christian teacher or "guru." This relationship encouraged the transmission of Christian ideas and produced many more "inquirers" and covert Christians than may be apparent at first sight.[76]

A detailed investigation of the unobtrusive and informal ways in which Christianity, or different aspects of the Christian faith, influenced the perception and outlook of Hindu youth (and others) is beyond the scope of this

75. Julius Richter, *A History of Missions in India*, translated by Sydney H. Moore (Edinburgh, 1908), p. 320.

76. See Geoffrey A. Oddie, *Hindu and Christian in South-East India: Aspects of Religious Continuity and Change, 1800-1900* (London, 1991), pp. 142-43.

study. There is, however, evidence of a Christian influence that profoundly affected Hindu reformers and other leading "Hindus" in their own personal religious life and development. Examples are Keshub Chandra Sen's deeply felt sense of "sin" and unworthiness,[77] Rajnarayan Basu's Bengali works, "shot through with Victorian moralism,"[78] Ramakrishna's reverence for Christ,[79] and M. G. Ranade's regular Bible reading and preaching from biblical texts on repentance and love at meetings of the Prarthana Samaj.[80] In these circumstances, the main concern was not polemics or how Christian ideas or methods might be turned against Christianity but rather the way in which Christian teachings and insights seemed to enhance the Hindus' own spiritual growth and understanding. This type of change in the life of individuals was already reshaping Hindu tradition, and it needs to be considered alongside reforms and other innovations that were introduced in order to defend "Hinduism" from its assailants.

Missionaries and Contending Hindu Views of Hinduism

One of the complications of missionary influence was its ambiguous and contradictory effect. While one effect of missionary campaigns was to drive "Hindus" closer together in self-defense, in other instances the effect of missionary comment and activity was to consolidate division or even to drive "Hindus" further apart.

Debates and interaction with missionaries, such as religious disputes during the precolonial era, could have the effect of sharpening theological and other differences within the so-called "Hindu system." This is apparent in controversies and public disputations between the missionaries and "Hindu" opponents. One example was the encounter between Dr. John Wilson of the Free Church of Scotland and a pandit named Morobhat Dandekara in Bombay in the 1830s.[81] While Dandekara was a person "about whom nothing is

77. See especially Keshub Chunder Sen's lecture, "The Disease and the Remedy," in his *Lectures in India* (Calcutta, 1954), pp. 271-92.

78. William Radice, "Tremendous Literary Rebel: The Life and Works of Michael Madhusudan Datta (1824-73)," D.Phil. thesis, University of Oxford, 1986, p. 181.

79. See Hal W. French, "Reverence to Christ through Mystical Experience and Incarnational Identity: Sri Ramakrishna," in *Neo-Hindu Views of Christianity*, edited by Arvind Sharma (Leiden, 1988), pp. 66-81.

80. G. A. Oddie, *Social Protest in India: British Protestant Missionaries and Social Reforms, 1850-1900* (Delhi, 1979), p. 4.

81. Young, *Resistant Hinduism*, pp. 26-27; also Rosalind O'Hanlon, *Caste, Conflict*

known," it is clear, from the summary of the debate, that he was a Vaishnavite, who was probably more interested in defending his own particular tradition and therefore consolidating difference than he was in promoting a broader, more inclusive concept of "the Hindu tradition." In his study of Vishnubawa Brahmachari and polemics in Bombay in 1857, Frank F. Conlon leaves the reader in no doubt that Vishnubawa, like Dandekara, was very concerned with his own distinctive theological and sectarian perspective.[82] According to Conlon, Vishnubawa claimed to have obtained his insights "in visions from the god Dattatreya, the goddess Parvati, and the medieval philosopher Shamkara." While Vedanta philosophy and *bhakti* devotion "provided the inspiration," the particular kind of *bhakti* Vishnubawa espoused differed from that of many other "Hindus." Vishnubawa's concerns were, therefore, not with defending an inclusive, India-wide "Hindu faith" but with preserving something very much more particular within an Indian world of competing religious tradition.

These occurrences illustrate the way in which missionary pressure helped to consolidate existing differences. Developments elsewhere, however, suggest that, in some cases, the ultimate effect of missionary activity was more radical, creating an even greater gulf between "conservatives" and those who were struggling to modernize or reshape some form of Hindu tradition. An illustration of this latter trend toward greater division and fragmentation is Rammohan Roy's reaction to missionary attacks on "idolatry," the effect of which was to strengthen his determination to distance himself from the more common Hindu views of Hinduism. His sense of hurt and outrage, especially at Joshua Marshman's comments that he participated in the worship of "false gods" represented in "impure fables," almost certainly fueled his desire for reform, strengthening his resolve to demonstrate that "real Hinduism" did not include a worship of idols and other "superstitious practices." In his *Second Defence of the Monotheistical System of the Vedas* he explained that being a Brahman, and therefore one of a class of people who usually worshipped idols, he had suffered "the disgrace and ridicule" to which Brahmans had subjected themselves by the worship of idols "very often under the most shameful forms."[83] Instead of uniting with "Hindus" of different shades of opinion,

---

and Ideology: Mahatma Jotirao Phule and Low Caste Protest in Nineteenth-Century Western India (Cambridge, 1985), p. 65.

82. Frank F. Conlon, "The Polemic Process in Nineteenth Century Maharashtra. Vishnubawa Brahmachari and Hindu Revival," in *Religious Controversy in British India: Dialogues in South Asian Languages*, edited by Kenneth W. Jones (Albany, N.Y., 1982), pp. 5-26.

83. *A Second Defense of the Monotheistical System of the Vedas in reply to an apology for the present state of Hindoo worship* (Calcutta, 1817), in *EW*, pt. 2, pp. 109-10.

however, he appears to have separated himself still further from many of his own countrymen, taking pains to point out to his "European friends" as well as Indian readers that "the superstitious practices" that deformed the Hindu religion had nothing to do with "the pure spirit of its dictates."[84]

The effect of missionary criticism of the Bengal Tattvabodhini Sabha's reliance on the Vedas has already been noted. The decision to abandon the Vedas as the basic source of authority, like Rammohan Roy's publications, had the effect of driving "Hindus" still further apart. The Brahmos, influenced by the force and logic of the missionaries' case, moved still further from their roots in indigenous tradition.

Last, but not least, was the effect of missionary activity in stimulating the rise of organizations diametrically opposed to each other. The rise of reform associations (encouraged by missionary enterprise) led to the formation of conservative organizations dedicated to the defense of the status quo. The effect of reform associations in creating further tensions within "Hinduism" has been highlighted by Kenneth W. Jones in his work on religious developments in the Punjab and northern India, where he refers to the increasing activity of Sanatana Dharma Sabhas in opposition to the Arya Samaj and other associations attempting to change or reform what was perceived as the orthodox faith.[85] By helping to promote an atmosphere of change and reform, the missionaries were, therefore, one of the parties that were, at least indirectly, responsible for increasing the levels of anxiety in conservative circles and, as a result of this mounting concern, increasing conflict between the "Hindus" themselves.

The pressure of the missionary movement on "Hindus" to sink their differences and fight the common foe has, therefore, to be balanced against the evidence that, in certain circumstances, missionary pressure was moving others in the opposite direction, toward a more combative and confrontational approach. What then can be said about Hindu feeling and self-perception? What was the impact on Hindu divisions and the prospect of unity?

Fear of conversion and of the consequences of a government-missionary alliance was a powerful factor that served to mobilize large numbers of people and to make the missionaries' idea that "Hinduism" was one unified "national" religion more of a reality. The dissenters, including Rammohan Roy and his followers, were very few in number. The rise of the Western-educated

84. *A Defence of Hindoo Theism in Reply to the Attack of an Advocate for Idolatry at Madras* (Calcutta, 1817), in *EW*, pt. 2, p. 84.

85. Kenneth W. Jones, *Socio-Religious Reform Movements in British India* (Cambridge, 1989), pp. 77-82; J. N. Farquhar, *Modern Religious Movements in India* (Delhi, 1967), pp. 316-24.

elites, the growth of the newspaper industry, and improvements in communication began to affect life especially in the urban areas. Anxieties about conversion encouraged the incidence of public meetings, and the cry that "Hinduism" or Hindu dharma was in danger was reported widely in the press.

Not only was there a growing feeling of being Hindu in a religious sense, but the idea of what that meant was also changing. Some, like Ranade, felt that being a good Hindu was to adopt some of the ideas and practices reflected in Victorian religion and the Christian faith. Some began to draw a clearer distinction between what was generally acceptable and what was not, between, for example, "the real Hindooism" and popular belief and practice. This way of thinking became increasingly popular among elites because of missionary criticism and the way in which new and more narrow definitions of "Hinduism" helped to preempt the missionary onslaught on "Hindu" cruelty and superstition. Last and clearly apparent in the first half of the nineteenth century was the idea that, whatever constituted "the Hindu religion," "Hinduism," or "Hindu dharma," "Hindus" were free to modernize in the sense that they could and should imitate and adopt Protestant missionary methods of organization and propaganda. This idea was increasingly influential among leaders of all shades of Hindu religious opinion, even before the outbreak of the mutiny and civil rebellion in 1857.

Developments in the Second Half of the Nineteenth Century

Most of the evidence and examples illustrating the role of Protestant missionaries in the formation of Hindu views of "Hinduism" have been drawn from material relating to the period before the events of 1857. This was the author's deliberate decision partly because there does seem to be a difference between the religious situation before and after 1857, and because the complex strands of missionary and other influence in the later period are even more involved and difficult to disentangle than those of the earlier period. If the precise effects of Protestant missionary ideas and activity on Hindu awareness and self-perception in the period before the upheavals of 1857 are difficult to ascertain with any degree of certainty, their impact in the latter part of the nineteenth century is still more problematic.

Whatever the complexities of the latter period, however, one thing is already clear: Protestant missionaries no longer played such an important part in developing Hindu religious awareness as they did from about 1800 to 1857. Any estimate of missionary influence on Hindu thinking about "Hinduism" would need to take account of the fact that some missionaries were beginning to question their own dominant paradigm of the one universal and all-encompassing Brahmanical system. Second, the threat of a combined government missionary assault on Hindu religion receded as the new government of India reverted to a more neutral position, taking greater care not to be perceived as associating with missionary operations. Third, there is some evidence that missionaries were becoming less inflammatory and more tactful in their techniques of evangelism.[86] While, on the one hand, the impact of missionary activity in raising Hindu consciousness and awareness of "Hinduism" as their own unified and sacred "religion" was declining in importance, other nonmissionary influences were beginning to operate more strongly in the same direction, reinforcing the idea that the vast majority of India's people shared in the same religious tradition. Among these developments was the advent of more inclusive forms of Hindu revivalism, such as Vivekananda's movement in which he incorporated popular, as well as philosophical, traditions in the idea of "Hinduism." Also significant was the emergence of nationalism, including a search for a unifying national ethos in Hindu religion and culture, and the introduction of the census of India, which classified over 70 percent of the population as Hindus and, therefore, followers of "Hinduism." A more precise estimate of the influence of Protestant missionary thought and activity, alongside the effect of these and other developments, in raising levels of Hindu religious awareness in the latter half of the nineteenth century will have to await further research and consideration.

86. K. A. Ballhatchet, "Some Aspects of Historical Writing on India by Protestant Christian Missionaries During the Nineteenth and Twentieth Centuries," in *Historians of India, Pakistan and Ceylon,* edited by C. H. Philips (London, 1961).

CHAPTER EIGHT

Receding from Antiquity:
Hindu Responses to Science and Christianity on the Margins of Empire, 1800-1850

RICHARD FOX YOUNG

Traditional Hinduism has not reached out for the West. It has not been driven by the zeal of proselytization and discovery, and by the urge to understand and master foreign cultures. . . . Even with reference to foreigners in India — the Muslims and other invaders — Hindu literature . . . presents us for the most part with a tradition of silence and evasion. There is no sign of active theoretical interest, no attempt to respond to the foreign challenge, to enter into a "dialogue" — up to the period around 1800.[1]

As early as the 1880s, nearly all school children in India could be expected to know, like their counterparts in Europe, America, and Japan, certain scientific "facts" about our planet, its sphericity, diurnal rotation, and revolution through space around a stationary sun. Whether a pupil took tuition from English-speaking instructors at prestigious metropolitan institutions or from rustic schoolmasters of impoverished villages, the dominant cosmology being taught was what we now call Copernicanism.[2] Even though India resisted

1. Wilhelm Halbfass, *India and Europe: An Essay in Understanding* (Albany, N.Y., 1988), p. 437.
2. The Copernican system of astronomy was heliostatic: it was premised upon the sun being immobile at a point near, but not necessarily at, the center of the universe. Here

many of the social changes that accompanied the development of science in the West, one could by this time openly espouse the structure of the universe in heliocentric terms and still be recognized as an upstanding, orthodox Hindu (or Buddhist) without experiencing an identity-threatening crisis of cognitive dissonance. Scientific cosmology had become a religiously neutral, culturally relative datum of mundane knowledge.[3]

Copernicanism was not entirely unknown, but its advocates were few and mainly of non-Indian origin (including, *inter alia,* missionaries, European travelers, traders, and colonial administrators). The cosmological wrappings of Christianity often elicited as much contempt, consternation, and controversy as the package of religious doctrines inside.[4] Considering that astronomy relates to observable phenomena normally taken for granted (not least of which is the apparent motion of the sun), it was unsurprising that dialogue with the West commenced in the empirical domain of science, not the transempirical domain of ethics, soteriology, and theology. Of all the sciences since antiquity, astronomy has proven time and again to be extraordinarily capable of leaping over cultural boundaries, seldom, of course, without provoking dismay at its broader implications. For India of the early nineteenth century, these were as disturbing as they had been for Europe.

The deceptively simple Copernican basics elicited vigorous objections from almost all learned communities of Brahmans and monks, no less than from traditionally educated higher castes and the Buddhist laity. The centerpiece of the Western system of the heavenly spheres, Copernicanism was dismissed as preposterous.

The idiom in which Indians of the nineteenth century expressed their bewilderment at the notion of a circular earth rotating on its axis through space

---

I take Copernicanism in the broad sense of heliocentrism. See Bernard Cohen, *Revolution in Science* (Cambridge, Mass., 1985), p. 495.

3. For a highly sophisticated socio-metric study of contemporary scientific knowledge, see Gauhar Raza et al., *Confluence of Science and Peoples' Knowledge at the Sangam* (New Delhi, 1996), pp. 29-33, 166-68. Based on extensive surveys at the Kumbh and Ardha Kumbh *melas* at Allahabad in the 1980s and 1990s (augmented by urban population cohorts in New Delhi), the study found that three-quarters of the interviewees knew the correct shape of the earth. The researchers concluded that such knowledge had become "an integral component of the cultural belief system."

4. On the response to Christianity, see Richard Fox Young, *Resistant Hinduism: Sanskrit Sources on Anti-Christian Apologetics in Early Nineteenth-Century India* (Vienna, 1981); Richard Fox Young and Subramanium Jebanesan, *The Bible Trembled: The Hindu-Christian Controversies of Nineteenth-Century Ceylon* (Vienna, 1995); Richard Fox Young and G. P. V. Somaratna, *Vain Debates: The Buddhist-Christian Controversies of Nineteenth-Century Ceylon* (Vienna, 1996).

echoed that of critics among the Indian astronomers of antiquity, such as Varāhamihira, author of the sixth-century A.D. *Pañcasiddhāntika.* This treatise propounded the view of the earth as a spherical body, stationary in the void without any support, around which other celestial bodies revolved. Varāhamihira did not claim, as had Āryabhaṭa earlier, that earth was also a planet revolving on its axis. Against this view, he asks how hawks could return to their nests if the world was spinning east to west.[5] In the nineteenth century, critics were still concerned about the hawks flying above the earth, but Copernicanism conjured up even more terrifying visions of terrestrial movement than the writings of Āryabhaṭa. Indians, who found reassuring confirmation of earth's immobility in the fact that hawks did return to their nests, were not unlike Europeans of the pre-Galileo and Newton era. In the face of stereotypical objections such as these, articulated by Indians or Europeans, Copernicanism came across as unempirical, hypothetical, and irrational. Perhaps for that reason, it was eminently discussible as a prelude to arguing about dharma in Hinduism or grace in Christianity.[6]

If the cosmology of nineteenth-century India had been that of the astronomers of antiquity, whose systems approximated (and in some cases surpassed) the model set forth in the second-century A.D. *Almagest* of Ptolemy, Copernicanism might have received a more sympathetic hearing than it did. Cosmology, however, was derived mainly from other sources to which a high religious authority was ascribed, particularly the Hindu *Purāṇas.* Since one question raised here concerns the processes by which popular Indian cosmology was demythologized, a brief survey of Purāṇic perspectives is pertinent.

According to the *Purāṇas* earth occupies the center of the universe, and its nearest neighbors are the sun and moon (in that order). What of the shape and contour of earth itself? How was India situated in its own imagination in relation to the world beyond its natural boundaries? The following passage from a contemporaneous European observer, Lancelot Wilkinson, maps the globe in a characteristically Purāṇic idiom:

5. O. Neugebauer and David Pingree, *The Pañcasiddhāntika of Varāhamihira* (Copenhagen, 1970-71), p. 109. I am grateful to Prof. S. R. Sarma of Aligarh Muslim University for clarifying my understanding of Varāhmihira's objections to Āryabhaṭa. See also Paul K. Feyerabend, *Realism, Rationalism and Scientific Method: Philosophical Papers* (Cambridge, 1981), 1:179-81.

6. For an early example of the Evangelical utility of astronomy see the letters of Jacobo Fenicio (1584-1632), an Italian Jesuit at the court of Calicut in Kerala (Jarl Charpentier, "The Livro da Seita dos Indios Orientais of Jacobo Fenicio," *Bulletin of the School of Oriental and African Studies* 2 [1921-23]: 742-48).

The followers of the Puráns . . . maintain that the earth is a circular plane, having the golden mountain Merú in its centre; that it is . . . surrounded by a sea of salt-water . . . that this salt sea is encompassed by a second dwip of two lakhs of yojans in breadth, and it again by a sea of sugar-cane juice of the same width. . . . The seas are of fermented liquor, ghí [clarified butter], milk, dhaí [curd] and sweet-water.[7]

Europeans in metropolitan India, who thought that Purāṇic cosmology could be easily debunked, began to contradict the charming symmetry of a world few Indians ventured out to see. Against the background of the *Purāṇas* the opening lines of a Bengali-language textbook on geography by the British Baptist W. H. Pearce (1794-1839), published by the Calcutta School Book Society in the mid-1820s, would have evoked disbelief: "The surface of the globe," Pearce wrote, "is divided into land and water, and the water occupies twice the extent of the land. All the water in the ocean contains salt."[8] As late as the 1850s, it was still argued in all seriousness by an indigenous supporter of the Buddhist variant of the Purāṇic paradigm that European sailors who boasted of circumnavigating the world had actually sailed in circles because they were drunk, even though they managed to return to their home ports. The source of this was an educated Sinhalese proctor working in a British police court in southwest Ceylon.[9] His tale was symptomatic of an underlying xenophobic bias against the knowledge of outsiders, especially knowledge that was not religiously neutral.[10]

Considering that early nineteenth-century India did not yet know the precise location of the sun and moon in relation to the earth, or that of Britain, the colonial power, in relation to itself, how was the horizon of its cosmological awareness broadened? What effect did the new, demythologized

7. Lancelot Wilkinson, "On the Use of the Siddhantas in Native Education," *Journal of the Asiatic Society of Bengal* 3 (1834): 504-5. Purāṇic accounts of the earth vary. That cited here draws mainly from the *Bhāgavata*. For a wider selection, see Ludo Rocher, *The Purāṇas, A History of Indian Literature*, vol. 2, fasc. 3 (Wiesbaden, 1986), pp. 130-31.

8. Michael Laird, *Missionaries and Education in Bengal, 1793-1837* (Oxford, 1972), p. 104.

9. Young and Somaratna, *Vain Debates*, p. 94.

10. Buddhists in South Asia took longer than Hindus to assimilate Copernicanism, probably because their variant of the Purāṇic cosmology was articulated authoritatively in the Pali canon. In Ceylon, Brahmans of the Jaffna peninsula bitterly contested the veracity of Copernicanism in the 1830s. See Young and Somaratna, *The Bible Trembled*, pp. 49-68. Sinhalese Buddhists, in contrast, fought against Copernicanism (especially Newton's laws of celestial motion) well into the century. For the Buddhist-Christian debate at Panadure in 1873, see Young and Somaratna, *Vain Debates*, pp. 173-75.

cosmological paradigm have on the self-identity of India? The assimilation of Copernicanism had enormous implications for certain communities of learned Hindus, for colonial educational policy, and for our own understanding of the distinctively Indian and European ways of "receding from antiquity."

Was, then, the assimilation of Copernicanism a breakthrough to modernity or a breakdown of tradition? Did the demise of Puranic cosmology rock the foundations of a pervasive form of living Hinduism? Did the separation of religion and science entail the transvaluation of empirical knowledge at the expense of religious certainty? Are there historical grounds on which to base the claim that Copernicanism "would not have created the controversy in South Asia that it did in Europe"?[11] Was Hinduism better prepared to meet this challenge? Was the "motive force" behind the introduction of Copernicanism invidious and "far from scholarly"?[12] Was the mathematical basis of Copernicanism useful to the "arithmetic of imperialism"?[13] Did a learned person who was "Copernicanized" become a "subaltern of science"?[14] Had the introduction of Copernicanism in the colonial milieu "blunted the possibility of evolving perspectives rooted in the indigenous intellectual and cultural heritage"?[15]

Some of the best materials for exploring these issues come from Malwa in central India during the first half of the nineteenth century. Consisting of printed books, manuscripts, and other documents in English, Hindi, Marathi, and Sanskrit, they reveal certain facets of the changes that were occurring far from metropolitan centers. It was, of course, in those centers that new ideas flooded into India like a tidal wave. Malwa, with Bhopal (a Muslim princely state) as its political center, was not at this time British administered. As a whole, the region was located on the margins of empire: Bombay, the closest presidency, was a good distance away. Clustered in and around Malwa, however, were towns and cities — Jaipur and Ujjain to the west, Benares and Mathura to the north and east — where the Indian astronomy of antiquity once flourished. As a result, Malwa's *joṣīs* and *bhaṭṭas* (astrologer-astronomers) were still renowned for the reliability of their almanacs. As recently as the eighteenth century under Sawai Jai Singh of Jaipur, whose realm included Malwa, the region

11. Susantha Goonatilake, *Aborted Discovery: Science and Creativity in the Third World* (London, 1984), pp. 60-61.
12. Gauri Viswanathan, *Masks of Conquest: Literary Study and British Rule in India* (London, 1989), p. 28.
13. Deepak Kumar, *Science and the Raj, 1857-1905* (Delhi, 1995), p. 189.
14. Kumar, *Science and the Raj*, p. ix.
15. Kumar, *Science and the Raj*, p. 227.

was a meeting ground for Indian, Islamic, and European traditions of astronomy. Unfortunately for science, no new school of thought was established to institutionalize the studies to which the raja contributed a much needed impetus.[16] Having come only recently under British influence, Malwa had no English-medium schools worth mentioning. The system of patronage, moreover, that sustained its learned communities had not yet been totally disrupted as in Bengal. Reforms in land ownership and the revenue collection in Eastern India had deprived its pandits of their traditional sources of income. Forced in droves to Calcutta in the 1790s, they often found more remunerative employment under the British financiers of Oriental scholarship than from indigenous patrons.[17] Malwa, therefore, seems ideal for learning more about the interplay of religion, science, and colonialism.

Adversarial Science

The fulcrum of change that helped lever traditional science in Malwa into a new phase of vitality was not initially Copernicanism, circulating in printed works or by word of mouth, although in time that would become the case. On the contrary, it was an individual, Lancelot Wilkinson (1805-41) of the Bombay Civil Service. Born in Cumbria in the north of England, Wilkinson's Indian career, which began after graduation in 1824 from the East India Company college at Haileybury, was mainly spent in the diplomatic corps as a Resident representing British sovereignty in the princely states of Rajputana and central India. Bhopal was his longest assignment, and it is said that, were it not for his untimely death, he would have been appointed to the Council in Bombay. Pragmatic visionary, Evangelical sympathizer, disinterested patron of charitable endeavors, ardent but obscure advocate of a constructive or practical Orientalism, C. A. Bayly has aptly described him as a "subaltern of Orientalism."[18] Wilkinson was all this and more. Beatified by his European admirers as a modern-day patron saint of Indian astronomy, he once admitted that among his Indian acquaintances he was known as the *yavanāchārya*, a title that honored him as an equal of the Greeks and other Westerners who

16. Kumar, *Science and the Raj*, p. 30.
17. Ruth Gabriel, "Learned Communities and British Educational Experiments in North India, 1780-1830," Ph.D. dissertation, University of Virginia, Charlottesville, 1979, p. 184; David Kopf, *British Orientalism and the Bengal Renaissance: The Dynamics of Indian Modernization, 1773-1835* (Calcutta, 1969), pp. 68-69.
18. "Orientalists, Informants and Critics in Benares 1790-1860," unpublished manuscript. Also see Bayly's *Empire and Information* (Cambridge, 1996), pp. 257-60.

had gone to India in antiquity with knowledge that indigenous scholars assimilated into their own scientific systems.[19]

Accolades aside, Wilkinson was a minor figure overall in the colonial service. The power factor is often overrated in current research on "colonial science" when coercion, overt or covert, is adduced as the primary factor that explains the diffusion and "authorization" of European science.

Wilkinson is remembered for one classically imperial act of mathematical measurement, namely, the mapping of Kotah, a princely state in Rajputana adjacent to the colonial realm. The project was about to commence when he was gazetted to the Hadoti Agency, where Rāj Rānā Madhu Singh was indignant that his territories were about to be surveyed. Rightly surmising that the real intent might be annexation, Madhu Singh ordered the surveyors to return to Delhi. Wilkinson intervened and convinced the Rāj Rānā to rescind the order, quoting a passage from the twelfth-century A.D. *Siddhāntaśiromaṇi* of Bhāskara II. The passage (v. 34 of the section on globes), which contains a formula for determining latitude and longitude, is very technical. This, however, was practical knowledge from India's own antiquity that Madhu Singh recognized as being in his best personal and political interests. Kotah had had a long history of cultivating astronomy and could boast of a still-functioning observatory in the ramparts of the fort opposite the palace. The passage had come to Wilkinson's attention while he was being initiated into the arcana of the venerable *Siddhāntaśiromaṇi* (of which even the most competent *joṣīs* were often ignorant), by a certain Vaijnāth, the Rāj Rānā's *purohita* Brahman. If the mapping of Kotah gave a fillip to empire, it also afforded Wilkinson his first opportunity for invoking antiquity in order to affect modernity.[20]

Wilkinson was by no means the first Orientalist to study Indian astronomy, through texts or intermediaries. Among the British, there had been Robert Chambers, Samuel Davis, William Jones, H. T. Colebrooke, and James Prinsep. Before the Orientalists, there had been numerous missionaries and continental scholars, some of whom had never set foot in India. Early observers of Indian astronomy spoke eloquently about its achievements, but by late seventeenth century, when European self-definition vis-à-vis India focused increasingly on

19. West Bengal State Archives (Calcutta), Miscellaneous Volume of Applications from Different Schools for Pecuniary Aid from the Committee, 1834-1840, Wilkinson to General Committee of Public Instruction, Camp Goolana, 15 January 1835.

20. Unless otherwise specified, all references to Wilkinson in Malwa are based on John Muir's *Brief Notice of the Late Lancelot Wilkinson of the Bombay Civil Service* (London, 1853); Wilkinson's "On the Use of the Siddhantas" (1834) and documents in the Oriental and India Office Collections [OIOC] (London). For personal details, I am grateful to Teddy Relph and Nicholas Dent.

the superiority of its own scientific and technological accomplishments, ambivalence, condescension, and even hostility had set in. In the perspective that became typical of many, ancient Indian astronomy developed a high level of sophistication around the twelfth century A.D. (the time of Bhāskara II) but then began to stagnate. Astrologers, almanac-makers, and other Indians of the late eighteenth and early nineteenth centuries who, in the European view, should at least have had a passing knowledge of the first principles of astronomy, impressed them as being singularly ignorant and, what is worse, disinterested in, or contemptuous of, the ostensibly more advanced systems of the West.[21]

Among the Orientalists who studied astronomy, derisive attitudes toward the contemporary state of scientific knowledge prevailed. Samuel Davis, for example, an outstanding scholar who enjoyed excellent relations with learned pandits, wrote a pioneering study of the Benares observatory built by Sawai Jai Singh of Jaipur in the eighteenth century. He could, however, only recommend the study of Indian astronomy to his compatriots as a pursuit to "amuse themselves" with "curious information."[22] Another pioneer of Indian astronomy was William Jones: "In sciences," he said, "it must be admitted that the Asiatics, if compared with Western nations, are mere children."[23] By 1788, two years later, Jones's Eurocentric bias had been significantly reconsidered. The following passage tells of an encounter with a pandit (probably from Nuddea, a center of Brahmanical learning in Bengal) who, like Wilkinson's Vaijnāth, was a rare specialist in the astronomy of antiquity, which is called *jyotiḥśāstra* in Sanskrit:

In our conversations with the Pandits, we must never confound the system of the Jyautishicas, or mathematical astronomers, with that of the Pauranicas, or poetical fabulists; for to such a conclusion alone we must impute the many mistakes of Europeans on the subject of Indian science. A venerable mathematician of this province, named Ramachandra . . . visited me lately at Crishnonagar. . . . "The Pauranics," he said, "will tell you, that our earth is a plane figure studded with eight mountains, and surrounded by seven seas of milk, nectar, and other fluids; that the part which we inhabit, is one of seven islands . . . that a God riding upon a huge elephant, guards each of the eight regions."[24]

21. Michael Adas, *Machines as the Measure of Men* (Ithaca, 1989), p. 57.
22. Cited in Adas, *Machines*, p. 106.
23. Cited in Satpal Sangwan, "European Impressions of Science and Technology in India (1650-1850)," in *History of Science and Technology*, edited by G. Kuppuram and K. Kumudamani (Delhi, 1990), 5:100.
24. William Jones, "On the Antiquity of the Indian Zodiac," *Asiatic Researches* 2 (1788).

Unfortunately, the venerable Rāmacandra, obviously an exceptionally learned individual, never again appears in Jones's writings.[25] And, like Jones, other Orientalists of this racially unpolarized era, who mixed freely with Indians of all descriptions in the performance of their duties, rarely encountered the truly learned. For the most part Orientalists were scholars whose curiosity seldom went beyond the realm of antiquity.

Many scholars were even convinced that shopkeepers and moneylenders were the only surviving repositories of mathematical knowledge apart from the often elusive figures who compiled the local almanacs *(pañcāṅga).*[26] Wilkinson, too, hobnobbed with "Jain banyas" and "opulent Márwári merchant bankers," with whom he discussed the cosmology of the *Purāṇas,* but his circle of informants was wider than most. When most Orientalists deplored the "debasement" of scientific learning, Wilkinson recognized pragmatically that the astronomical literature of antiquity might prove useful for the renewal of indigenous science. Indian astronomy in his view could, with exposure to Western astronomy, evolve into Copernicanism. He also believed that the revitalization of Indian astronomy would necessarily have a unsettling effect on popular belief in the Hindu *Purāṇas,* which were full of risible "puerilities."

The late second and early third decades of the nineteenth century, in which Wilkinson's views on the renewal of Indian science were formulated, were years of Governor-General William Bentinck's administration. It is no surprise, then, that Wilkinson met with indifference from official policymakers and that his work in Malwa came to naught insofar as the Calcutta-based General Committee of Public Instruction was concerned. Six months after a seminal article, "On the Use of the Siddhantas in the Work of Native Education," appeared in the *Journal of the Asiatic Society of Bengal* (his

---

25. The surname of Jones's Rāmcandra was Sabhāpati. Rāmcandra's son "Kaleedas Pundit" taught *jyotiḥśāstra* on the basis of the *siddhāntas* at Serampore College. Kaleedas worked closely with Joshua Marshman in preparing *Jyotiṣa ebang Golādhyāya* (1818) for teaching astronomy and geography (Sunil Chatterjee, archivist at Serampore College, personal communication). In 1824 six students were taught by Kaleedas, "who this year added the Newtonian system to their own" (*Friend of India* 7 [1824]: 57). Kaleedas's connection with the College, however, was terminated soon afterward. An obituary described him as "without question the greatest Hindoo astronomer in Bengal." His former patrons, however, added the symptomatic caveat that "he was, notwithstanding, a rigid, if not a bigoted Hindoo."

26. Henry Warren, Madras Civil Service, cracked the mysteries of the "native" almanac *(pañcāṅga)* with the assistance of a local informant. His interests were practical. The Company needed to understand the ways in which Indians reckoned time and calculated eras. See Young and Jebanesan, *Bible Trembled,* p. 57.

only major publication on science) the Anglicist-Orientalist controversy ended in a Pyrrhic victory for the Anglicist party. After raging for years in metropolitan circles, the issue was, for the time being, decided by the governor-general's endorsement of the Macaulay Minute of 1835. Wilkinson's article outlined a strategy with a characteristically Orientalist rationale for using the traditional systems of Indian astronomy known as *siddhāntas*.[27] Concluding with a reference to himself as too "blind an admirer [of Sanskrit and the vernacular languages] to have any influence with the admirers of English who have now the dispensation of all the patronage in the Educational Department," Wilkinson persisted in pestering the authorities with detailed reports about his activities. Over time, the experiments conducted in Malwa drew considerable attention, being often cited by W. H. Macnaghten and H. T. Prinsep, the main dissenters on the General Committee of Public Instruction; by Brian Hodgson, the British Resident at Kathmandu known for his inveterate opposition to Anglicist policies; and by the Serampore missionaries in their weekly newspaper, *The Friend of India*. In memoranda, tracts, and editorials, the results of Wilkinson's labors were seen as the best proof that Indian science could flourish without recourse to English-medium education, if only it were developed on the basis of an already existing, indigenous corpus of scientific text.[28]

Wilkinson's appeal to the developmental potential of an existing corpus of scientific texts in Sanskrit could not have come at a more opportune time in the view of his Orientalist sympathizers. The Serampore Baptists were especially enthusiastic, even though their own efforts on behalf of science in the vernaculars were beginning to falter. Founded in 1818, their college had once accorded a prominent place to Indian science in its heavily Sanskritized curriculum. Lālla's eighth-century A.D. treatise, for example, had been used for teaching astronomy. By the early 1820s, however, English was becoming attractive even to this stronghold of Orientalism where few students proved capable of mastering *wissenschaftliches* Sanskrit despite intensive tutoring by competent pandits. John Mack (1797-1845) of Edinburgh, who taught chemistry at the college, was typical of second-generation missionaries who, unlike

---

27. See Kopf (*British Orientalism*, p. 278) contrasting Orientalists and Anglicists: "Orientalists advocated syncretic schemes for self-help according to one's own value system, whereas Anglicists were less sympathetic to traditional values and more convinced that no real change was possible without radical assimilation to the British style of life."

28. As an exemplar of science education in the indigenous languages, Wilkinson was repeatedly invoked by Brian Hodgson, the most ardent critic of the Anglicists among the Orientalists. See his often-reprinted polemic, *On the Education of the People of India* (Serampore, 1835). This was originally a series of letters to *Friend of India*.

their predecessors, doubted whether any Indian language, classical or vernacular, could accommodate modern scientific terms and concepts. *Kimiyāvidyār Sār* (1834), his flawed but pioneering attempt at making chemistry intelligible in the medium of Bengali, was an unreadable mishmash. To this day chemistry is still called in most Indian languages by its Sanskrit name, *rasāyana*. Among the earlier missionary Orientalists, only William Yates (1792-1845), a Calcutta Baptist who had brought out a good portion of the Bible in Sanskrit, applied his expertise to practical education in a work on natural science, the *Padārthavidyāsāra* (1834), also in Sanskrit. Elsewhere in Bengal during these years, innovative curricular changes in science education, at Hindu College and Sanskrit College, where comparative studies of Indian and Western texts had once aroused considerable interest,[29] were discontinued because of interference from the General Committee of Public Instruction. English had the upper hand in other metropolitan centers besides Calcutta although philanthropic individuals, including "native gentlemen," not just European civil servants like Wilkinson, could be found almost everywhere devoting their energies to popular education, in the "useful sciences."[30]

Many Europeans adopted an adversarial stance over science. They associated it with their inflated sense of the West's "cultural advancement and creative potential" and its preeminence in technology.[31] This was especially true of certain missionaries, who as a bloc were by no means solid advocates of Orientalist schemes where education was concerned. The curricula of Christian schools tended to be weighted more toward science, Indian or Western, than that of schools funded or subsidized out of the Company treasury; but the Serampore model of heavily Sanskritized education was on the wane, and

---

29. Gabriel, *Learned Communities,* p. 203; Kopf, *British Orientalism,* pp. 54-55.

30. Bālgangadhār Śāstrī Jambhekār of Bombay (1810-46), an example of an indigenous science popularizer, was in contact with the Malwa circle. On Jambhekar see Rosalind O'Hanlon, *Caste, Conflict, and Ideology: Mahatma Jotirao Phule and Low Caste Protest in Nineteenth-Century Western India* (Cambridge, 1985), pp. 90-95. On Yesudas Ramacandra of Delhi (1821-80) see S. Irfan Habib and Dhruv Raina, "The Introduction of Scientific Rationality into India: A Study of Master Ramchandra — Urdu Journalist, Mathematician and Educationalist," *Annals of Science* 46 (1989): 597-610. Ramcandra, a Christian convert and mathematical prodigy, disseminated Western science in Urdu in the 1830s. As a corrective to Habib and Raina's emphasis on scientific empiricism in bringing Ramacandra to Christianity, see Avril Powell, *Muslims and Missionaries in Pre-Mutiny India* (Richmond, 1993), pp. 206-25; and her "Processes of Conversion to Christianity in Nineteenth Century North-Western India," in *Religious Conversion Movements in South Asia: Continuities and Change, 1800-1900,* edited by Geoffrey A. Oddie (Richmond, 1997), pp. 15-55.

31. Adas, *Machines,* p. 33.

aggressively Anglicist biases were evident, or even dominant, in almost all Christian institutions. Internalizing demeaning Anglicist rhetoric about their supposedly under-par civilizational achievements, Indian students often chafed at the constraints of a society that had not yet separated science from the domain of religion. One graduate of Alexander Duff's Scottish Free Church Institution in Calcutta tore the cosmology of the *Purāṇas* to shreds in an angry diatribe couched in the Baconian idiom of "the Idols of the Theatre." Demanding the overthrow of dogma, superstition, and tradition, he argued that, in Hindu society, freedom of inquiry on any subject, the exercise of one's own mind, and thinking and judging for one's own self are not only wholly unpracticed but "are thought to amount to a crime."[32]

In Bombay, John Wilson (1804-75), like Duff another Scottish educator but respected for his Orientalist scholarship, drew upon modern science for a stinging critique of popular Hinduism in a prolonged, multi-round debate with Morabhaṭṭa Dandekar, himself a *joṣī*. Wilson's *Second Exposure of Hinduism* (1834) is in certain respects the strangest of books, full of section headings such as "Meteorological Objections to Hinduism," "Anatomical Objections to Hinduism," and "Botanical Objections to Hinduism." The reason why science was now being wielded as a weapon was that Morabhaṭṭa, a less naive *joṣī* than such men were reputed to be, had raised a few scientific conundrums of his own, in an earlier tract, aware that science was not altogether one-sided in favor of Christianity. If, for example, the star of Bethlehem had come so near the earth that it loomed over the Savior's birthplace like a beacon, would not our planet have been consumed by its heat? "Is it not unreasonable," he asked, "that religion and astronomy should be thus opposed to one another?" Morabhaṭṭa also ridiculed, as irrational, the belief that Jesus had ascended bodily into heaven: "Don't Christians understand gravity?"[33] Wilson's exposures of Hinduism were typical of tracts, pamphlets, and broadsides that had a profound influence on relations between Christians and Hindus.

The Paradigm Shift in Malwa

The typical Evangelical sympathizer in the Company's service performed his duties neutrally with respect to Hinduism but involved himself privately in

32. Anonymous, "Physical Errors of Hinduism," *Calcutta Review* 11 (1849): 399.
33. Cited in John Wilson, *A Second Exposure of the Hindu Religion: in Reply to Narayana Rao of Satara Including Strictures on the Vedanta* (Bombay, 1834), pp. 114, 117.

charitable endeavors, often helping Christian schools and other missionary institutions in metropolitan centers and the provinces. Wilkinson was atypical. It can even be argued that his sympathies were more Orientalist than Evangelical. His perspectives on Indian science, however, were deeply imbued with Christian principles. As the British Resident in Bhopal, Wilkinson resided at Sehore, a military cantonment-administrative center since the time of the Marathas, where a small community of Brahmans maintained traditional systems of knowledge at the Śihūra Saṃskṛta Pāṭhaśālā. Although little is known about the Pāṭhaśālā before he became its patron, it may have originated as a satellite community of *jyotiḥśāstra* scholars who flourished in the region under Sawai Jai Singh in eighteenth-century Jaipur. Some scholars contend that the Copernican theory may have been known to Indian scholars at the time of Jai Singh.[34] Wilkinson found no evidence of it when he arrived in Malwa around 1827. Science was at a low ebb, and the scope of instruction in vernacular *pāṭhaśālās* was generally limited to basic literacy and arithmetic that was useful to the shopkeepers and moneylenders despised by Europeans. Sanskrit *pāṭhaśālās* were fewer and catered to a predominantly Brahmanical clientele, offering grammar as the core curriculum. Advanced students might go on to study late medieval texts such as the *Grahalāghava* and *Tithīcintāmaṇi*, which taught them how to prepare almanacs and practice prognosticative astrology.

Like their counterparts everywhere, including those in metropolitan centers, the pandits of Malwa perpetuated science within a system that was sustained in part by an inertia in learned traditions. Additionally, they enjoyed relatively fewer opportunities for access to modern scientific knowledge than their counterparts in Bombay, Calcutta, and Madras. The inertia evident in Indian science, however, cannot be fully explained by recourse to socioeconomic and political analysis of the unsettled conditions prevailing throughout India at the time. For a more comprehensive understanding, one must also consider that *jyotiḥśāstra*, like grammar (*vyākaraṇa*), was a *vedāṅga*, one of the auxiliary branches of Vedic studies, the very eye of the Veda and therefore a superior science. As such, astronomy had for most pandits — just as other branches of sacred learning — a dogmatic, perfected, and self-sufficient character. As described by Wilhelm Halbfass, *vedāṅga* literature manifested neither an "empiricist" openness for future additions or

34. On the acceptance of Copernicanism during the reign of Sawai Jai Singh, see Kumar, *Science and the Raj*, pp. 19-24; and Sreeramula Rajeswara Sarma, "Sanskrit as Vehicle for Modern Science: Lancelot Wilkinson's Efforts in the 1830s," *Studies in History of Medicine and Science* 14 (1995-96): 189-90. Sarma doubts that Sawai Jai Singh's influence was discernible in Malwa and that his impact on Jaipur itself was of lasting significance.

"corrections," nor a willingness to make "explicit adjustments to 'current historical situations' or 'current states of knowledge.'"[35]

The question, then, of whether the science we find in the *vedāngas* was static or progressive is notoriously complex. If science is defined as a form of critical inquiry dealing with "truth" as a set of testable hypotheses within a framework of epistemology that presupposes the existence of objective reality, the canonization of *jyotiḥśāstra* would therefore appear to immobilize authentic scientific inquiry, just as the angry young Brahman of Duff's Scottish Church Institution alleged. In antiquity, however, Indian astronomy had obviously been receptive to the global flow of knowledge. As an Orientalist steeped in the study of Jones and others who had revealed the connections between India and the West, Wilkinson knew this to be true but faulted the Purāṇic "Idols of the Theatre" for bringing the process of scientific inquiry to a grinding halt. In convincing his pandits that science could be revitalized by divorcing it from the *Purāṇas,* he proved to be pragmatic and radical and above all extremely effective: as in the affair at Kotah, he invoked tradition to affect modernity. It was Wilkinson himself who first expounded the *Siddhāntaśiromaṇi* at Sehore, through intermediaries who subsequently became informal advocates of Copernican astronomy. According to his own account, only two before him in the whole of Malwa had acquired a specialized knowledge of *jyotiḥśāstra,* Vaijnāth and Jinchand, who had been his teachers. By the time of his death in 1841, however, more than twenty *joṣīs* would join his advocate corps and disseminate heliocentric astronomy as an organic outgrowth of the old, geocentric variety. Students, including some from noble families in Rajputana, began flocking to the *pāṭhaśālā* in Sehore. One of them, a Brahman boy from Maharashtra named Nṛsiṃha Deva-Parāñjpe, later became the first professor of Indian and Western astronomy at the Benares Sanskrit College (where he became better known as Bāpūdeva Śāstrī).

While Wilkinson's expanding circle of pandits may have regarded him adoringly as an idealized *yavānachārya,* he saw himself more as a pragmatic visionary whose programmatic approach to the renewal of Indian science depended, in his own words, on the "dexterous use of blind and prejudiced veneration for authority." The repositories of that authority were the much neglected *siddhāntas,* known by name but studied by a dwindling few, Jones's Rāmacandra, for example, or Vaijnāth, of Kotah, and Jinchand, of Ajmere. Wilkinson invoked antiquity in order to affect modernity. The response he elicited was symptomatic of science in the process of being separated from re-

35. Halbfass, *India and Europe,* pp. 393, 253.

ligion. Pandits began to see the indigenous traditions of science, in contrast and even opposition to Purāṇic cosmology, as being relevant to the observable world, of being updatable, supplementable, and open to insights from the outside world without prejudice to the integrity of antiquity. In short, the creative potentialities of the *siddhāntas* were being recognized in Sehore.

The first of Wilkinson's pandits to respond to his overture was Soobajee Bapoo (in Devanagari Subājī Bāpu or, more precisely, because of his South Indian origin, Subbāji Bāppu), "a man of wonderful acuteness, intelligence, and sound judgment." Until Wilkinson's death, Soobajee was always the foremost advocate of Copernicanism in the Sehore Pāṭhaśālā. Described as a "Tailingi" (from Telangana), he had entered his patron's service as a tutor in Sanskrit when Wilkinson was assigned to the court of Berar in Chanda (Chandrapur), in today's Maharashtra near the border with Andhra Pradesh. A Telugu-speaking Brahman, Soobajee was fluent in Marathi and, like his forebears, a ritualist who served the god Rāmacandra, at the temple in Chanda. From Berar he followed Wilkinson in his official peregrinations from one princely state to another ending in Bhopal, including the stay at Kotah where his mentor was introduced to the ancient texts of *jyotiḥśāstra* by Vaijnāth. Although Soobajee did not record how he disentangled himself from the cosmology of the *Purāṇas,* which in his case would have been that of the *Bhāgavata,* Wilkinson was obviously instrumental, using what he in turn had learned from the *rājpurohit* of Madhu Singh. The outcome of Soobajee's return to tradition was described by his *yavanāchārya* as a *volte-face* symptomatic of conversion experiences:

> [After eight years] he was lost in admiration when he came fully to comprehend all the facts resulting from the spherical form of the earth, and when the retrogressions of the planets were shewn to be so naturally to be accounted for on the theory of the earth's annual motion, and when he reflected on the vastly superior simplicity and credibility of the supposition that the earth had a diurnal motion, than that the sun and all the stars daily revolve round the earth, he became a zealous defender of the system of Copernicus. He lamented that his life had been spent in maintaining foolish fancies, and spoke with a bitter indignation against all those of his predecessors who had contributed to the wilful concealment of the truths that once had been acknowledged in the land.[36]

36. Unless otherwise specified, references to Soobajee's life and labors come from the colophons of his writings; a letter by Wilkinson in the *Journal of the Asiatic Society of Bengal* 6 (1837): 401-2; and Wilkinson's official correspondence, mainly in the Oriental and India Office Collections (London).

Soobajee did become a zealous disciple, but of whom? Copernicus or Bhāskara? Examining his writings one is hard put to say which attracted him more. Wilkinson thought the former, although the latter seems more likely. Soobajee himself declared, with an almost religious conviction, that he was a *bhakta* (devotee) of Bhāskara.[37] In this connection, the title of Soobajee's main work, the *Siddhāntaśiromaṇiprakāśa* (Bombay, 1836) is itself suggestive. Splitting the compound into its components, it can be rendered as *An Illumination* [of Bhāskara's] *Siddhāntaśiromaṇi (The Crest Jewel of Astronomical Systems).* This would imply that Soobajee saw himself not as an innovator but an improver, one of Francis Bacon's "merchants of light" whose role was to keep his society informed of scientific developments in the world at large. Bernard Cohen argued that Copernicus did not regard *De Revolutionibus Orbium Coelestium* as a radical rupture with the past but simply an improvement on the *Almagest* of Ptolemy.[38] Soobajee likewise regarded the *Siddhāntaśiromaṇi* as a paradigmatic text of antiquity fundamentally congruent with the current state of astronomy in the West. In this perspective, what transpired in Sehore was renewal — not revolution.

The *Siddhāntaśiromaṇiprakāśa* mainly consists of straightforward siddhantic mathematical astronomy with Copernican heliocentrism added to it, the whole being tersely argued in heavily Sanskritized, *wissenschaftliches* Marathi. It is, however, also a treatise shrouded in theology. Like European astronomers who prefaced their works with citations from the Bible in praise of the Creator's handiwork, Soobajee, a *Vaiṣṇava* whose faith contained a nuance of nondualistic Vedanta, commenced the *Siddhāntaśiromaṇiprakāśa* with a paean to Lord Bhagavān. Shifting to a more Purāṇic idiom, he paid tribute to the Brahmāṇḍa, the immense cosmic egg of Brahmā, from which material reality emerged. After this devotional prelude, among the standard arguments adduced on behalf of heliocentrism one, in particular, involves a peculiar line of reasoning: Soobajee claims that if the universe is geocentric, the whole Brahmāṇḍa would revolve around the earth, because the sun is the yolk of the cosmic egg. A universe like this would indeed be very wobbly. He argues, therefore, that it would be more rational to posit the sun as the yolk of the cosmic egg and center of the solar system instead of earth. To make sense of this, one should note that, according to Indian cosmology, the Brahmāṇḍa is of limited extent, unlike the open universe of modern Western cosmol-

37. Soobajee identifies himself as a *bhakta* of Bhāskara *(bhāskarabhakta)* in the first line of the *Bhūgolamabhitobhramaṇabhramabhaṅgi,* a four-folio preface to the Sanskrit version of the *Siddhāntaśiromaṇiprakāśa* (Baroda Oriental Research Institute, ms. no. 6177).

38. Cohen, *Revolution in Science,* pp. 107, 115.

ogy.[39] The argument reveals Soobajee's continuing captivity to religion as an astronomer and highlights his failure to attain the full autonomy of scientific inquiry. Taking the Brahmāṇḍa literally as an objective reality and not merely as a metaphor of cosmic immensity, he had to save it from being discarded along with everything else that the heliocentric theory appeared to place in jeopardy.[40]

Thus, although dogma still exercised a degree of constraint over Soobajee's willingness to accommodate Copernicanism, it was a limitation that pertained only to the section of the *Siddhāntaśiromaṇiprakāśa* devoted to astronomy *(khagol)*. The section on geography *(bhūgol)* exemplifies a wholesale abandonment of the Purāṇic "Idols of the Theatre" that even the science of antiquity itself had not attained. In the realm of geography, as David Pingree points out, there had been since the time of the *Paitāmahasiddhānta* an attempt to break away from Puranic cosmology, but also a reluctance to depart altogether from it. The astronomers of antiquity would have no truck with the flat-earth model of the *Purāṇas,* but they did concede that its geography retained a certain validity. The problem was resolved by redistributing *Jambudvīpa*, the six surrounding concentric continents, Mount Meru, and the various oceans around a globe, which took the place of the Purāṇic circular plane. The classic articulation of reconciled Purāṇic-siddhāntic geography was that of Lālla's eighth-century A.D. *Śiṣyadhīvṛddhidatantra*, which influenced all succeeding astronomers, including Bhāskara II. "As far as the astronomers were concerned," Pingree observes, "that is where the matter rested."[41]

Voicing "bitter indignation," Soobajee went further than the astronomers of antiquity and vigorously denounced the "poetical fabulists" (as Jones had called them) who expounded the geography of the *Purāṇas* as dogmatic, superstitious, and tradition bound. Although there were precedents in the science of antiquity for resisting the more fanciful aspects of Purāṇic cosmology, it is the European explorers of the Age of Discovery whom Soobajee held up as exemplars of the spirit of empirical inquiry. In the *Siddhāntaśiromaṇiprakāśa* we find Columbus, Magellan, da Gama, Cook, and even Capt. James Ross, who attempted a passage from Europe to Asia via the Arctic Ocean, por-

---

39. See the note in the Wilkinson-Bapudeva translation of the *Siddhāntaśiromaṇi* (Osnabrück, 1981 [reprint of the 1861 edition]), p. 138, by Bapudeva himself, who had studied under Soobajee before taking his post in Benares.

40. Copernicus insisted, on Aristotelian grounds and by trivializing "unhelpful" evidence, that in a perfect, God-created universe, planets must move in perfect circles.

41. David Pingree, "The Purāṇas, and Jyotiḥśāstra. Astronomy," *Journal of the American Oriental Society* 110 (1990): 278-80.

trayed not as drunken sailors but as pioneers of an observationally based science. They put the stay-at-home Indians to shame for refusing to cross the oceans out of fear of having their ritual purity compromised. Not only do we find in the *Siddhāntaśiromaṇiprakāśa* a willingness to make "explicit adjustments to current historical situations and current states of knowledge," we see in Soobajee's enthusiasm for the Western methodology of science an emerging critique of the social environment for doing science "the Western way" in the context of India.

Defending the Paradigm

Among the many accolades and rewards reaped by Soobajee for writing the *Siddhāntaśiromaṇiprakāśa* was one from Lord William Bentinck, the governor-general whose endorsement of the Macaulay Minute turned the tide of Indian education in favor of the Anglicists: a silver ink stand surmounted by a pandit holding a globe. There were also *sanads* (affidavits) in Sanskrit and English from Calcutta, guaranteeing him safe passage through British territories in recognition of his contribution to disseminating "useful knowledge." In a semiotic perspective, what message might the gift of an ink stand convey? The "authorization" of "colonial" science? The "empowerment" of an emerging member of an elitist "native" establishment that would impose the knowledge of the powerful few upon the hapless and powerless masses? While some interpreters might be inclined to think so, Bentinck's gift was at worst a thoughtless put-down: at the time, children received similar gifts from their parents after completing their years of study, few or many, in traditional *pāṭhaśālās*. Equally significant is this, that Orientalist achievements were not lost even on the Anglicists. Were we to stop here, however, the indigenous dynamics of the revitalization of science in Malwa would be overlooked. Revitalization, after all, entailed a knowledge that no amount of colonial authority invested in Residents or in governors-general could ever "authorize," in any simplistic sense, as if Indians were witless and hapless victims unable to think for themselves. Only Soobajee himself and like-minded pandits in the Sehore advocate corps, who had responded to Wilkinson's invocation of antiquity to affect modernity, could authorize new knowledge in terms that made cultural as well as political sense. When Soobajee received the governor-general's gesture of approbation, there were some among his contemporaries who began to address him deferentially as "rājā śrī." In the indigenous establishment outside Sehore, however, were others — the Purāṇic rearguard, who found the *Siddhāntaśiromaṇiprakāśa* critique of traditional astronomical dogmas too harsh and alienating to be tolerated in silence. We hear of their reactions and of their intention to conduct face-to-face debates (*śāstrārthas*) in a self-effacing comment by Wilkinson on the overall success of his efforts on behalf of the revitalization of Indian science beyond the confines of his own circle:

> With all my care to carry along with me the convictions and concurrence of the people in what I teach, I have so far failed — the published and unpublished writings of my pundits and scholars, have been the subjects of constant attacks from the learned of Poona, Nagpore, Oojain, Sagar and Benares. Many long and warm discussions have been maintained, not between me and the learned men of these places, but between my pundits and the learned men of these places: the most bigoted of whom utterly forgetful of the fact, that their Jyottishu shastru [sic] has been pronounced to be the eye of the Vedas, and itself a Vedanga — have announced a bann of excommunication against all who study the Siddhants, and Astronomy.[42]

Although the "bann of excommunication" sounds onerous, its impact on the popularity of the Śihūra Saṃskṛta Pāṭhaśālā appears to have been minor. Soobajee was never "outcasted" for his espousal of heliocentrism or his association with Wilkinson. Clearly, however, Soobajee was assailed on more than one front. A Vaiṣṇava *gosāīn* of Mathura, for instance, summoned him to a public debate (which, if it occurred, was not recorded). The *Siddhāntaśiromaṇiprakāśa* was also attacked by certain *joṣīs* of Pune in a manuscript to which a lithographed rejoinder was issued. The reactions from Mathura and Pune can be differentiated along several lines.

Without more "explicit" evidence, one can only surmise that Wilkinson was correct in claiming that the *gosāīn*'s objections to the *Siddhāntaśiromaṇiprakāśa* were an expression of "the rancor of the feelings with which any enmity towards, or attack on, the infallibility of Vyas-jee, is regarded by orthodox Hindus."[43] To make sense of this, it should be noted that a total of six *gosains* residing at Mathura (or, more correctly, Vrindāvan) presided over the sacred precincts of Kṛṣṇa in this vicinity, which were held in especially high esteem by Kṛṣṇa Caitanya's followers in Bengal. Which of the six *gosāīns* took

---

42. All references to the affair of the Mathura *gosāīn* are from the preface of Wilkinson's edition of Bhāskara's *Gunitadhia* [*sic*] (Calcutta, 1842).

43. Edward Dimock, "Doctrine and Practice among the Vaiṣṇavas of Bengal," in *Krishna: Myths, Rites, and Attitudes,* edited by Milton Singer (Honolulu, 1966), p. 42.

umbrage at Soobajee's comments on Puranic cosmology is unknown, but certain *gosains* devoted their entire lives to studying the *Bhāgavatapurāṇa*, which the *Vaiṣṇavas* of Bengal venerated most of all. If one of the *gosāīns* became offended, it was probably because Soobajee, himself a *Vaiṣṇava*, appeared to undermine the *Bhāgavata*'s authority by extracting passages from it that demonstrated the incommensurability of Purāṇic cosmology with modern astronomy. Edward Dimock's account of the status ascribed to the *Bhāgavata* by the *gosāīn* community founded by Jīva Gosvāmin helps explain why Soobajee aroused such wrath:

> Jīva Gosvāmin . . . categorically rejects all the traditional types of theological proofs and arguments (pramāṇa) except that of śabda (word) — direct revelation. Among the texts that fall into this category of revelation, the primary ones are the Vedic texts and the Purāṇas. Of these two types of texts . . . the Purāṇas, are the higher: they are the completion (purāṇa) of the Vedas. And, of all the Purāṇas, the Bhāgavata is the greatest; it reveals all the Vedas, all itihāsa (tradition), and all the Purāṇas, it is Vyāsa's own commentary on his Brahmasūtra, which others hold to be itself the ultimate revelation of truth.[44]

In this perspective, it becomes clearer why the *Siddhāntaśiromaṇiprakāśa* was found by its critics to be in conflict with the absolute, all-encompassing authority attributed to the *Bhāgavata* by the *gosain* community. Soobajee, in a roundabout way of defending "poetical fabulists," did so by shunting them out of the domain of science into the realm of religion. That is to say, he argued that it was the *gosains* who abused the *Bhāgavata*, making it out to be the fount of empirical "truth." Devotional love, with Lord Bhagavān as its object, was why the *Bhāgavata* and other *Purāṇas* should be valued. Having become at Sehore a *bhakta* (devotee) of the astronomer Bhāskara did not imply that Soobajee had ceased to be a *bhakta* of Lord Bhagavan, which he had been at the temple of Rāmacandra, in Chanda, along with his forebears.

Rightly read, the *Siddhāntaśiromaṇiprakāśa* was a systematic attempt, by no means irreligious, positivistic, or scientistic, to disentangle science from religion so that each could attain its respective end. Thus, one finds in the text a dichotomizing terminology: religious knowledge is *jñān*, scientific knowledge is *vijñan* (a usage that has become standardized in contemporary languages). As observed above, the *Siddhāntaśiromaṇiprakāśa* was nonetheless a devotional text shrouded in theology. Vyāsa was not traduced but simply put

---

44. Pingree, "Purāṇas and Jyotiḥśāstra," p. 280.

in his proper place. Regarded by tradition as the original propounder of the *Bhāgavata* and other sacred literature, the bard was extolled as a poet *(kavi)* but not deprecated, marginalized, or trivialized because he was not a Bhāskara or Copernicus. Soobajee admitted and affirmed that listening to the *Bhāgavata* being recited, one could be overwhelmed with awe at the ways in which Lord Bhagavān disports himself in his timeless life; God's divinity *(aiśvārya)*, attributes *(guṇas)*, and power *(śakti)* could be more deeply appreciated; and the Brahmaṇḍa, the material embodiment *(sthal svarūp)* of the deity, could become an even greater marvel. Science, however, was not to be learned from Vyāsa. If the "poetical fabulists" did not consult the *siddhāntas* when they propounded the *Purāṇas,* neither did astronomers need to consult the *Purāṇas* when composing the *siddhāntas.* For a deeply devotional person who was less able to disengage himself from Purāṇic cosmology than his rhetoric might imply, this was a trifle too disingenuous, but it was the mentality science engendered. In the West astronomers had done likewise. Johannes Kepler, for example, prefaced his *Harmonies of the World* (1619) by reminding readers that when he spoke of the "heavens" he was referring to the universe, not the empyrean, the abode of God and the blessed dead, "which no corruption will ever touch."

The response of the Pune *joṣīs* to the *Siddhāntaśiromaṇiprakāśa* was less inquisitorial than that of the Mathura *gosāīns* who prohibited the study of the *siddhāntas* just as the Catholic Church in Europe had put *De Revolutionibus* on the Index Librorum Prohibitorum in 1616. The first to rise in defense of Purāṇic cosmology was Bābā Joṣī Roḍiye, a former professor of *jyotiḥśāstra* at the Pune Sanskrit College, who attacked Soobajee in the *Avirodhaprakāśa* [Illumination of Non-contradictoriness], a manuscript in Sanskrit that was never published (much to Bābā Joṣī's disadvantage). The complete text has, however, been preserved in Soobajee's rebuttal of it, also in Sanskrit, the *Avirodhaprakāśaviveka,* which was lithographed in Bombay in 1837.

The arguments adduced by the two parties are too technical to survey in detail, but the approach of Bābā Joṣī to Copernican heliocentrism was to reassert the cosmology of the *Purāṇas* without demonstrating their compatibility with the *siddhāntas* as Lālla, Bhāskara and other astronomers had done in antiquity. Fighting for the received cosmology, come what may, was symptomatic of a Hindu variety of scriptural fundamentalism comparable to the advocacy of creation science among conservative Christians today. It was a reaction to modernity that had, in fact, been emerging since at least the eighteenth century. The *joṣīs* of Pune withdrew from the *siddhāntas* into the shelter of the *Purāṇas* by insisting on transempirical truth as the only valid source of empirical knowledge about the world. Soobajee stirred them up, but vocif-

erous denial was Bābā Joṣī's response to modernity. One had a way of returning to tradition by restoring rationality to science; the other returned to tradition by hiding behind it.

The *Avirodhaprakāśa,* in Soobajee's view, was a revenant of the same anti-
progressive mentality from which he had already been released. It did, however, pose questions that were not easily answered. The toughest were
epistemological.[45] In contrast to the *Siddhāntaśiromaṇiprakāśa,* which advocated a transformation of Indian science into modern science by accommodating the Western emphasis on empiricism, Bābā Joṣī flatly denied that sense
perception *(pratyakṣa)* can be an authoritative source of knowledge
(pramāṇa) — an argument that was necessary if the transempirical veridity of
Purāṇic cosmology was to be affirmed. He demonstrated that empirical observation is an unsound basis for science through two instances of visual decep-
tion, one natural and the other artificial. In the first instance, it was claimed
that the reflection of Dhruva, the pole star situated above Mount Meru, appears in the water below, by which the eye is deceived into thinking that a second pole star exists on the opposite side of the earth. In the second instance,
Bābā Joṣī denounced the telescope into which the British (called *yavanas* in the
Sanskrit text and *Ingrej lok* in the Marathi introduction) invited the witless to
gaze at the heavens in order to convince them of their theory that the moon is
closer to the earth than the sun. As in Europe, where Galileo's discovery of Jupiter's moons provoked a backlash from skeptics who doubted the reliability
of instruments, Bābā Joṣī objected that the moon is magnified when seen
through the telescope (and therefore appears to be closer to the earth than previously believed). What is worse, the telescope not only distorts vision, it can
even conjure images of things that have no real existence.

Bābā Joṣī, then, was as wary of the European *yavanas* as he was of sense
perception. Soobajee and others who advocated the use of astronomical instruments *(jyotiṣayantra)* as a tool for empirical science were as deceived.
Sense perception was not to be trusted. Nor was the mathematical astronomy
of the *siddhāntas* more attractive to Bābā Joṣī than the observational astronomy of the West. Be the truth empirical or transempirical, its basis had to be
an *āpta,* an individual of impeccable reliability.

Anticipating criticisms like these from orthodox opponents, Soobajee had
gone out of his way in the *Siddhāntaśiromaṇiprakāśa* to cite passages from the

45. *Avirodhaprakāśa* adduces one argument reminiscent of the drunken-sailor genre
of popular objections to the sphericity of the earth: the continent of Jambudvipa is round,
and navigators who sail around it or along it therefore assume that the earth itself must be
a globe.

siddhāntas that place non-Indians, especially those who are learned in the sciences, in a more congenial light than was ordinarily the case in the Indian xenological tradition.[46] In the literature of India, foreign peoples were often referred to as *mlecchas* (barbarians) or *yavanas* (lit., Ionians or Greeks but generally applied to persons of non-Indian, usually Islamic or Western, origin). Both terms had variable connotations, from neutral to derogatory. A derogatory connotation was ordinarily evident when the absence of dharma existed. Among the neutral usages, some of the most interesting occurrences are found in contexts where the attainments of foreigners in the sciences were seen as offsetting the obloquy to which they were otherwise subjected. One such passage from the sixth-century A.D. Br̥hatsaṃhita of Varāhamihira reads as follows: "Since the yavanas deserve respect as men of science, even though they are mlecchas, all the more is respect owed to a brahmin astrologer who is ritually pure." The same citation appeared also in Soobajee's *Avirodhaprakā-śaviveka* and another like it: "One should acknowledge whatever is reasonable, even if it comes from the mouth of a child." A truly remarkable dictum inscribed in the same text goes even further (whether following a maxim of Indian gnomic literature I do not know): Where people of profound knowledge are concerned, there is no differentiation of status [*jātyādi*, "caste," etc.].

Should Soobajee's contribution to the reinvigoration of science be considered less notable for having been the response of a Hindu to a European *yavana* who invoked antiquity in order to affect modernity? The argument thus far has been that this was not the case: such interactions, after all, were always symptomatic of learned communities, Indian or not, which never flourished in isolation. Indeed, after what we have seen of the tenacious defense of tradition by the *joṣīs* of Mathura and Pune, one wonders how science ever progresses, in any society, without collaboration between people of different cultures on the basis of some egalitarian creed. In a hostile environment, assailed on all sides by irate *gosāīns* and *joṣīs*, Soobajee's pronouncements on the suspension of caste distinctions in the practice of science were indeed radical and perhaps unprecedented. It would appear, however, from the material introduced below, that he saw himself, in Baconian idiom, as a "merchant of light" who mediated influences from abroad — but with a certain wariness about becoming tainted in the process by those aspects of the outside world that were unacceptable within the structure of his own society. Soobajee's vision was, as we shall see, not so wide as to include a science-induced leveling of the

---

46. On the Indian xenological tradition, see Aloka Parasher, "Attitudes towards the Mleccha in Early Northern India up to c. AD 600," *Indian Historical Review* (1987): 1-30; and Halbfass, *India and Europe,* pp. 172-96.

caste hierarchy or an integration of the diverse cultures in which people of science pursue the same truths. In his view, the exchange of knowledge between India and the outside world would not impinge upon transempirical verities if it were conducted on the basis of dharma.

Lines around the Dharma

If science and technology in this era were becoming as important as religion to the European self-identity vis-à-vis India, dharma was still the Indian measure of Europe, not its heliocentric theory or telescopes. Soobajee was not a hidebound traditionalist, but his affirmation of modernity was not uncritical. Limits there were, and the longer he associated himself with Wilkinson, the more insecure his identity as a Hindu became. His patron may have been a *yavana* who deserved respect as a man of science, but their relationship must have been problematic. One wonders at the concessions they must have made to each other's sensibilities in order to collaborate so fruitfully over a number of years. Wilkinson could invoke antiquity, but did he adhere to the norms of European gastronomic culture and bring pollution into the Śihūra Saṃskṛta Pāṭhaśālā? Did meeting his mentor to compare the *Purāṇas* and *siddhāntas* with Copernicanism defile Soobajee's purity and necessitate a ritual ablution? It can only be surmised that this was how the exchange of knowledge affected their behavior.[47] What is certain is that Wilkinson's agenda for India was based on ideals that would not only transform its sciences but also reform its social and religious institutions. How far did Soobajee concur with those ideals? Where was the line drawn?

In the idiom of his contemporaries, Wilkinson's social agenda for India revolved around a cluster of practices "abhorrent to civilized morality," including suttee *(sati)*, thuggee, and especially female infanticide. In Kotah, where he had studied the *siddhāntas* with Vaijnāth, he became an effective advocate for the suppression of infanticide, which was practiced by several Rajput clans. Not only did he persuade Madhu Singh to allow his realm to be surveyed, in 1833 he also convinced the Rāj rānā to suppress the "murder" of girls by providing their fathers with dowries for the intended victims once they reached a marriageable age (dowry being one among many factors behind infanticide).[48] Wilkinson mentions that a work in Sanskrit by Soobajee condemning

47. Halbfass, *India and Europe,* p. 260.
48. For analysis of the social interactions between missionaries and pandits, see Young, *Resistant Hinduism,* and Young and Jebanesan, *Bible Trembled,* esp. p. 138 for an ac-

infanticide in Rajputana was once in circulation. I would conjecture that Wilkinson prevailed upon his pandit to consult the texts of Hindu law *(dharmaśāstra)* and compare them with the practices of the locality for the purpose of issuing a *vyavasthā* (legal opinion), as was commonly done by pandits attached to Company courts. What effect, if any, the *vyavasthā* may have had on Madhu Singh remains unknown. Nevertheless, "a learned Brahman of Nagpore," another of Wilkinson's wide circle of acquaintances, found Soobajee's invocation of the laws of antiquity a meaningful precedent for his own treatise on a related issue concerning women. In 1841, the year of his death, Wilkinson brought out an English summary of the work, *On the Second Marriages of Widows,* which saw in the *śāstras* no impediment to the remarriage of women. A similar tract by Soobajee himself, entitled *Punarvivāha* [Remarriage], had reached the same conclusion. This was published even before the *Siddhāntaśiromaṇiprakāśa* by Bālgangādhār Śāstrī Jambhekār, a progressive Hindu professor of natural science at Elphinstone College, in his weekly, the *Bombay Darpan.*[49] These discussions, one should note, transpired some fifteen years before the passage of the Hindu Remarriage Act of 1855.

With comparatively few exceptions from their earliest contacts with India, Europeans have experienced its social hierarchy as an intolerable rigidity. Wilkinson, who likewise considered caste in Malwa to be an arch evil, felt his antipathy to it most keenly when the Mathura *gosāīn* issued his "bann of excommunication" against all who studied the *siddhāntas,* the very texts on which he had pinned his hopes for the renewal of Indian science. Although it seems unlikely that the brouhaha over the *Siddhāntaśiromaṇiprakāśa* resulted in a serious crisis for the Sehore Pāṭhasālā, most of the students were Brahmans, and the possibility of being "outcasted" would have been unnerving. As in the mission schools, which often broke up or closed down because the "embryonic meritocracy" they fostered came into conflict with the principles of a dharmocratic society, so in the Pāṭhaśālā a feeling of being vulnerable must have been always evident.[50] Caste, then, in Wilkinson's perspec-

---

count of an orthodox pandit who daily purified himself of ritual pollution after assisting in a Bible translation. Wilkinson's defense of the eating of beef is on record: West Bengal State Archives (Calcutta), Misc. Vol., Applications for Pecuniary Aid from the Committee, 1834-1840, Wilkinson to GCPI, General Committee of Public Instruction, Camp Goolana [*sic*], 15 January 1835.

49. I have been unable to locate Soobajee's *Punarvivāha.* A companion piece, *Punarvivāha Prakaraṇa,* perhaps by a pandit of the Sehore circle, has been reprinted from the same issue of the *Bombay Darpan* (15 August 1837) in M. Josi and S. Sahasrabuddhe, eds., *Darpaṇ Saṅgraha* (Bombay, 1946), pp. 32-50.

50. Laird, *Missionaries and Education,* p. 115.

tive, stifled the renewal of Indian science and inhibited the exchange of knowledge.

Wilkinson acquired from a *samnyāsin* of Malwa the text of an indigenous, anti-Brahmanical critique of the institution of caste known as the *Vajrasūcī* [Thunderbolt Ax], which tradition attributed, mistakenly, to Aśvaghoṣa, a first-century B.C. or A.D. Buddhist. The text seemed ideal for Wilkinson's purposes. The *Vajrasūcī* applied a withering, analytical logic to the concept of Brahmanhood, reducing it to an absurdity. The author's method was to pose questions like following: "Tell me, first of all, What is Brahmanhood? Is it life, or parentage, or body, or Wisdom, or the way, or acts, i.e., morality *(karam)*, or the Vedas?" When Wilkinson discovered that Brian Hodgson, for whom he was to become an exemplar of the Orientalist cause, had already published the translation, in 1829, from which the quotation above was cited, he reprinted the complete version in 1839 with an introduction of his own. In Soobajee, however, the *Vajrasūcī* met an unforeseen opponent, and for the first time pandit and patron found themselves at odds. Wilkinson himself recounted in a letter from Sehore to Hodgson, dated 11 May 1835, how Soobajee reacted to the *Vajrasūcī*'s aspersions upon his Brahmanhood:

> Your translation of the Buddhist Disputation on Caste has amused me mightily. It is intrinsically excellent. My shastree who was with me when I got your letter, listened to my version of it into Maratha with the utmost uneasiness. . . . He was obliged to acknowledge the truth of all it contained. Indeed, he is anything but an orthodox Hindoo now. But still his eye glistened with anger when he heard the arguments expounded and all the long buried animosities of the Brahman for the [Buddhist] were evident in him.[51]

Thus, in Soobajee's view, science may have had an empirical basis, and the Buddhists, being behind the Hindus on that score, could be told their science

51. The letter is in the archives of the Royal Asiatic Society (London) in an undated album donated by Hodgson's daughter. In the same album another letter, dated Sehore, 11 September 1837, tells that other pandits in the Wilkinson circle responded to the *Vajrasūcī* more favorably than Soobajee: "I am very much obliged to you for the copy of the Wujra Soochi. It is a most excellent piece of close and sound argument. Nothing could be better. I have two or three learned men about me, so far enlightened, or perhaps so much annoyed by the reflections of their ignorant friends upon their new doctrines, that they are quite delighted with this attack on their own Brahmanism. They have not only taken copies for themselves, but have also been lending copies of it to their learned orthodox friends, who have been provoking them by attacks on their abandonment of Vyas' system of the world."

was absurd, but the dharma transcended the empirical by virtue of being re-vealed knowledge rooted in the Vedas. An alliance against it by a Buddhist and a Christian had to be resisted. For his part, Wilkinson adhered to the principle of free inquiry and printed the *Vajrasūcī* with a commentary by Soobajee, the *Laghuṭaṅka* [Little Chisel], an abbreviation of a larger work, the *Bṛhaṭṭaṅka* [Big Chisel].[52]

Short as it is, the *Laghukaṅka's* sixty pages in traditional commentarial style are replete with copious citations from law, epics, and the *Purāṇas*. The tone throughout was that of *bissigkeit* (biting sarcasm).[53] Halbfass found the philosophical basis for its defense of Brahmanhood in the idea that caste *(varṇa)* is "prior to all behavior" as a universal inherent in the nature of real-ity.[54] Even so, Soobajee's retorts on the *Vajrasūcī's* acerbic logic were often po-lemical witticisms without a basis in philosophy: "A donkey, even a good one, can never become a horse"; "A mongrel that thinks itself a lion, won't be able to roar, no matter how hard it tries"; and so forth.

At a more serious level, Soobajee introduced into the *Laghuṭaṅka* a curi-ous discussion of the social status and soteriological entitlements of the *yavanas,* who, by implication, included Wilkinson. The *Vajrasūcī* did not compel him to broach a sensitive topic like this, but doing so enabled him to assign a rationale to the role he played in a world structured by another dharma. Obviously the bonds of patronage called for caution and restraint. Nevertheless, the *Laghuṭaṅka* makes a radical departure from traditional In-dian xenology. While there was no getting around the fact that the British who had overrun India were indeed *yavanas,* one could in good conscience serve them because the *kṣatriya* kings who had patronized learned communi-ties were now a relic of the past. This, after all, was the Kali yuga, a time of de-cline and dharmic disorder. Citing a gnomic verse attributed to Manu, "To feed one's elderly parents, a faithful wife, and an obedient son, one will com-mit a hundred sins," Soobajee exculpated himself from the sin that would otherwise accrue to conduct like his in another age. Such a defense would have been specious had he not taken refuge in the underlying concept of

52. Highly regarded in missionary circles of the era, the *Vajrasūcī* was translated into regional languages as diverse as Bengali and Tamil. See O'Hanlon, *Caste, Conflict, and Ide-ology,* pp. 225-27, for the impact of the Wilkinson-Hodgson edition on Jotirao Phule, a leader in the early Dalit movement in Maharashtra.

53. Albrecht Weber, "Über die Vajrasuchi (Demantnadel) des Açvaghosha," *Abhandlungen der Königlichen Akademie der Wissenschaften zu Berlin, Philologisch-historische Klasse* (1859): 210.

54. Wilhelm Halbfass, *Tradition and Reflection: Explorations in Indian Thought* (Al-bany, N.Y., 1991), p. 377.

āpaddharma, which permitted breaches of the Brahmanical code if the circumstances were extenuating.

As for the foreigners with whom he associated, Soobajee explained that they could not help being *yavanas* for the most natural of reasons: the climate of the land they inhabited. Soobajee was aware that in some regions the days were short and the nights long, summers cool and winters frigid. In places marked by extreme cold, a *yavana* could hardly be expected to perform the morning and evening *saṃdhyā* rituals in icy water. Even though *yavanas* were ritually impure and were thus undifferentiated in terms of social hierarchy, Lord Bhagavan did not despise them. On the contrary, God had descended among them as an *avatāra* to bring them a scripture *(śāstra)* in their own language. This revealed his nature in a way that was appropriate to theirs. What better proof could there be that the ferment in Malwa was making an impact on deeply entrenched biases as its eyes on the world beyond itself were being opened by the newly revitalized astronomy and its collateral science, geography?

Far from being totally depraved, *yavanas* in Soobajee's view could aspire to godliness within certain limitations. A consistent thrust of the *Laghuṭaṅka,* however, is that nothing besides dharma makes a Brahman a Brahman — neither religious knowledge *(jñāna)* nor scientific knowledge *(vijñāna).* Brahmanhood, therefore, was not a metaphor signifying high attainments. On the contrary, Soobajee held to the belief that Brahmanhood, at birth, is intrinsic to some and extrinsic to others; although it might be forfeited, it can never be acquired. Nothing much was new here, except the application. *Yavanas,* accordingly, may be men of science, but knowing science does not make them Brahmans. In the egalitarian environment promoted by Wilkinson, the threat posed to established identities must at times have seemed severe. Nevertheless, in returning to antiquity Soobajee rediscovered not only an authentic tradition of science but also a solid basis — his own Brahmanhood — for his involvements with the *yavanas* who were helping him affect modernity. Scientific knowledge, by virtue of being nonsacred, could thus be shared with all. With a refortified sense of himself, Soobajee roamed freely through the world of science outside India as a "merchant of light." If, then, the *Laguṭaṅka* erected a barrier between Hindus and non-Hindus, it was at least a permeable one that allowed for exchange and interaction.

Discordant Concord

Soobajee was by no means the only liminal figure in the Sehore Pāṭhaśālā whose quest for balance in the act of straddling contrasting worlds of science and religion has attracted little attention. There was also Somanātha Vyāsa (1807-90) of Śājāpur, a town near Gwalior. A Nāgar Brahman whose ancestors had migrated from Gujarat, Somanātha was less a man of science than Soobajee, but he was remarkably well informed and by no means uninterested. His expertise was Sanskrit grammar and literature, which he began teaching at the Pāṭhaśālā in 1839, where he remained until resigning in 1857, the year of the "Mutiny," to become a *saṃnyāsin*. Somanātha was a prolific scholar whose works — thirty-six are preserved in manuscript repositories in Baroda and Ujjain — range across a variety of fields.[55] The earliest of these, and the only one that predates his tenure at Sehore, is the *Āryāvaravarṇinī* of 1829, a piece of belletristic writing on the deeds of Rāma. Religion was foremost among the subjects that attracted his attention, and Somanātha returned spontaneously and repeatedly not to antiquity but to the presence and virtues of his *iṣṭadevatā* (chosen deity). Among other major works appearing over the years, including more than a few that were composed after his renunciation, are the following: a work of philosophy, the *Kalpalatā;* a commentary on the *Rāmagītā,* the concluding section of the *Adhyātmarāmāyaṇa;* the *Advaitapadyabhasya,* a work on devotional love extolling Rāma as the highest manifestation of the nondual Brahman; and the *Bhaktimuktāvali,* a work in the same vein asserting the primacy of devotional love over philosophy as the most effective means for apprehending the transpersonal Brahman as Rāma, who in turn is identical with Śiva, Viṣṇu, and all other deities. Were we to compile a profile based on his writings, it would be that of a learned *bhakta,* capable, like Soobajee, of admiring Bhaskara and other astronomers, but even more of being enraptured by God, the divine Rāma to whom he was deeply devoted without also being a sectarian zealot.

No sooner had Somanātha started teaching at Sehore than a book came to his attention about a religion centered on a different *iṣṭadevatā,* that of his *yavana* mentor Wilkinson. This was a work of Christian apologetics, the *Mataparīkṣā* or *The Examination of Religions,* as its English subtitle in the 1839 edition reads. A pretentious work, it exemplifies the dry, intellectual arguments of Paleyan, "evidential" theology, originally intended as an antidote to the skeptical philosophy of David Hume but still popular among Evangelicals in the colonies even though it would soon fall from grace in Britain. The author, John Muir (1810-82), who was later to earn a reputation as one of the

55. Somanātha Vyāsa's manuscript writings in Sanskrit came to my attention through the kind assistance in Ujjain of Prof. Shrinivas Rath (Vikram University), Dr. Balkrishna Sharma, and Dr. Kailasnarayan Sharma (both of the Scindia Oriental Institute). Prof. Rajendra Nanaviti and Dr. Siddharth Yeshwant Wakankar of the Baroda Oriental Research Institute were equally helpful.

century's finest Sanskritists, was at the time, like Wilkinson, an official in the Company's service. Somanātha's defense of Hinduism, the *Mataparīkṣāśikṣā* [A Lesson for the Mataparīksā], was an exposition of one symptomatic way, among others, that Hindus have found meaningful for resolving the dilemmas of religious plurality. In a sense, it is to religion what the *Siddhāntaśiromaṇiprakāśa* was to science. That is to say, just as Soobajee had resolved the apparent contradictions in the domain of empirical truth between Indian and Western astronomy by positing an underlying unity of congruence in the *siddhāntas,* Somanātha resolved the contradictions in the realm of transempirical truth between Hinduism and Christianity by positing a unity of congruence in godhood, that of his *iṣṭadevatā* Rāmā. This discussion will be limited to the content of the *Mataparīkṣā* and *Mataparīkṣāśikṣā* that sheds light on Somanatha's self-identity as a Hindu in a *paṭhaśālā* where ideas were in constant ferment as a result of the activities of the *yavanas,* who were not only Orientalists but also Christians.[56]

Muir's *Mataparīkṣā* pivots around the contention that the transempirical origin of the "true" religion can be confirmed or disconfirmed by human reason. Several criteria were adduced for this purpose, miracles and martyrdoms in particular. Hinduism and Christianity were then "tested" against these criteria, and only the author's faith was found to hold up under "impartial" scrutiny. For Somanātha this was all risible. Muir's perspective on the "practical utility" of Hinduism, however, placed him in more of a quandary. Like virtually all European treatises on India at the time, whether Christian or not, the *Mataparīkṣā* debunked the cosmology of the *Purāṇas* in a few cursory strokes. It did, nonetheless, intend to conciliate, not alienate. Thus, Bhāskara I was singled out as an exemplar of scientific rationality to offset the impression that Europeans were biased in favor of their own magisterial scientists.[57] What was given, however, was also taken away: for, Muir then made a point of his own self-identity as a product of the Enlightenment by claiming that Hinduism impeded progress in useful knowledge and practical matters by denying reality to the *vyavahārika* world — the world of empirical transactions in-

---

56. The introduction of Somanātha Vyāsa into this discussion enables me to rectify an error of long standing. In *Resistant Hinduism* (1981), I conflated Somanātha with Soobajee Bapoo. This was partly due to the fact that the writings of Somanātha had not yet attracted scholarly attention by manuscriptologists. Similarities between the writings of the two are attributable to both being in the same Sehore Pāṭhaśālā and exposed to Wilkinson's ideas.

57. Muir, introduced to the achievements of Bhāskara II by Wilkinson, avidly supported the Śihūra Saṃskṛta Pāṭhaśālā and was the anonymous author of the *Brief Notice of the Late Lancelot Wilkinson of the Bombay Civil Service* (1853).

habited by human beings. In short, the *Mataparīkṣā* conjured up an image of India as a madhouse of naked, meditating gymnosophists, unlike industrious, Christian Britain.

Muir's portrayal of India and the debatable philosophical assumptions underlying it were not directly contradicted by Somanātha even though his father had become a *sannyāsin* and he himself would as well. Rather, he was simply unimpressed, unlike some in the second half of the century (Dayānanda Sarasvatī, for example) who ransacked the Vedas for prefigurements of modern inventions. *Yavanas* were undeniably clever, skilled mechanics; endowed with *cāturya,* they knew how to apply science to technology. They built steamships *(uṣmapota)* for the Ganges and flying machines (*ākāśayāna-yantra;* hot-air balloons?) for the sky; wise in *nītiśāstra,* their administration was competent and the economy well oiled. Wisdom could come from the mouth of babes, as Soobajee had admitted, but in religion *yavanas* were immature. They looked for contrariety where there was congruence, just as there was between the sciences of India and Europe. As for science, in certain respects they were even behind. Their minds were clouded by the dogma that creation occurred in the recent, chronological past, compared with the eons and cycles of the *sanātana* (eternal) dharma. How could a civilized people be so parochial? How could they be so unaware of the timelessness of existence? This he attributed to karmic hindrances: for their imaginations to be so primitive, *yavanas* must have been brute creatures (*paśu;* lit., "animals") in their previous lives.

The *Mataparīkṣāśikṣā* is mostly an elaborate plea for recognition of the unity *(aikya)* and compatibility *(avirodha)* of Hinduism, Christianity, and all other religions on the basis of a concord of function rather than a concord of doctrine. Discord is not denied but simply subordinated to an unspecified, underlying identity of purpose. This was certainly anticipatory of the symptomatic perspectives of neo-Hinduism that were then emerging elsewhere in response to India's encounter with the exclusivism of Europe. In Somanātha's idealized image, Hinduism has a superior status because of its capacity for transcending the rigid boundaries of Christianity. Unlike the *Siddhāntaśiro-maṇiprakāśa* however, which resolved the apparent conflict between the *siddhāntas* and Copernicanism, the *Mataparīkṣāśikṣā* does not attempt to systematically reconcile Christianity with Hinduism. The two treatises nonetheless agree in asserting the existence of various overriding unities. At one point in the *Siddhāntaśiromaṇiprakāśa* for instance, Soobajee reflected on the undeniable fact that in some respects the *siddhāntas* did not mesh neatly with Copernicanism. A quotation from the *Śivamahimnastava* [The Praise of Śiva's Glory] was chosen to smooth over the difficulty by making the point that in the end all cosmologies amount to the same limited human efforts at comprehending a reality defying comprehension: "Some philosophers say the universe is eternal; others that the universe is perishable; still others, that this composite universe is both eternal and non-eternal. Even though I am bewildered by all this speculation, I am unashamed to sing your praise, for I cannot hold my tongue."

In the *Mataparīkṣāśikṣā*, Somanātha likewise resolved the dilemmas of religious plurality by bursting into exuberant inclusivistic adoration of the divine, to which, despite being a *bhakta* of Rāma, he did not attach a particular name but rather a multiplicity of names:

> He who is the atman in all things, the true Lord, who is honored as the Buddha in Buddhism, the Jina in Jainism, Christ in Christianity, Allah in Islam; he who is honored as Arka, Prathameśa, Śakti, Girīśa, Śrīśa and other gods in the Vedas, tantras, Purāṇas, and other scriptures — He is the One who is to be worshipped!

One can extrapolate from the *Siddhāntaśiromaṇiprakāśa* and the *Mataparīkṣāśikṣā* a symptomatic view that would become prominent later in the century among neo-Hindus in metropolitan India. If Europe had a wide view of science and technology, India had a wider view of religion, one that could embrace science and technology as well. This realization emerged from self-discovery vis-à-vis Europe in response to the "imagining" of India by Orientalists and Christians and, in turn, engendered an "imagining" of Europe by learned Hindu pandits. Now, however, the tables were turned. Instead of merely being "merchants of light," the passive recipients of outside influences, Soobajee and Somanātha were empowered by their encounter with Europe and thus engaged in dispensing transempirical illumination in and through religion. As ever, the dharma continued to be the resilient foundation of their identity.

Comprehending Sacred Madness

The revitalization of the study of astronomy was at best a merely transitional phase in the modernization of Indian science, although of intrinsic historical interest. It did not inaugurate a new era of Indian science. After Soobajee, very few pursued siddhāntic studies as if they might contribute to the progress of science. When the patronage ran dry, the entire Wilkinsonian project ground to a halt. The *siddhāntas* were treated as monuments of antiquity, full of "curious information" for the "amusement" of scholars European and Indian, but peripheral to the "real" science overrunning India.[58] In a comparative perspective, however, one finds deeper affinities with Europe than might be expected. As different as they were, Kepler could not resist the blandishments of the *Almagest*, just as Soobajee could not resist those of the *siddhāntas:*

> I am free to give myself up to the sacred madness, I am free to taunt mortals with the frank confession that I am stealing the golden vessels of the Egyptians, in order to build of them a temple for my God, far from the territory of Egypt. If you pardon me, I shall rejoice; if you are angered, I shall bear up.[59]

The temple of astronomical scholarship that Soobajee attempted to build in Malwa may have been made of "golden vessels" from Europe, not Egypt, but it was, like Kepler's, a temple dedicated to God in the form of Lord Bhagavān. In this "sacred madness" we find a reflection of the mentality that the exchange of knowledge between antiquity and the present, Europe and India, engendered.

If the foregoing discussion is valid at all, it now makes rather poor sense to dismissively categorize Soobajee, and others like him, as "subalterns of science." Indeed, given C. A. Bayly's naming of Wilkinson as a "subaltern of Orientalism," one might wonder whether hierarchy and power relationships affect scientific exchanges in any simplistic manner that can be called "colonial science" — as if Western hegemony explains everything. I would not dispute the contention that the West became hegemonic in the sciences, but it becomes obvious from the evidence given here that one task of the historian may be to contest the claim that this was always so and that hegemony was necessarily incompatible with the survival of traditional science. One supportable inference is that hegemony cannot be synchronized with the sociopolitical and economic domination of India by the British. Where science is concerned, one must take into account the difference between India in the early nineteenth century and India by the end of the century, or at least the 1880s. The educational infrastructure in the first half of the era was inadequate to enforce a totalistic regime of science, much less "colonial science," as

58. It can be said, however, as R. S. Sarma has argued in "Sanskrit as Vehicle for Modern Science," pp. 189-99, that Wilkinson's work was carried on by former students, chief of whom was Bapudeva Śāstrī, and that the modern study of India's exact sciences started in Sehore.

59. J. Mortimer Adler, ed., *The Harmonies of the World* (Chicago, 1952), p. 1010.

an invidious tool of social mobilization and political control. Although the initial stage of such a system might have been evident in the early metropolitan centers, it was a long way to Malwa. Everywhere, moreover, one must take into account the phenomenon of "cognitive lag." Heliocentrism had been kicked around, as it were, well before Europe overran India, but without being assimilated, not because no one was there to impose it, but rather because learned communities affected modernity by invoking antiquity. At least for the pandits of Malwa, there could be no conversion of the present without a conversion of the past.

For all its attractiveness Malwa was perhaps less symptomatic of the whole than simply the exception that proves the rule. The "colonization" of science was anyway already proceeding apace elsewhere in India, and Malwa would soon be engulfed by it. What is more, a narrow focus on astronomy imposes rather arbitrary limits on exploring the "arithmetic of empire." Unlike biology and chemistry, which had direct applications to the colonial agrarian economy, astronomy and the other exact sciences had comparatively little commercial practicality. Modern astronomy, in short, was a science that the colonial authorities could afford to ignore. A silver ink stand from the governor-general should not mislead us. Copernicanism was assimilated because learned communities came to see it as a more comprehensive, more rational paradigm than the one they had received from antiquity. With this understanding and within these limitations, the material from Malwa is sufficient for us to query certain perspectives in the literature on "colonial science," especially its more sweeping generalizations about India's responses to science, Christianity, and even the "colonization" of the Indian mind itself.

We can dispense with the notion that assimilation of the Copernican heliocentric theory "would not have created the controversy in South Asia that it did in Europe."[60] As a Sanskrit maxim says, if one grain of rice is found to be undercooked, the whole pot should be put back on the fire. Copernicanism was more readily accepted by India than Europe, of that there is no doubt, but not with open arms and unfeigned delight. In Malwa there was no dearth of antagonism, contempt, and incredulity, although the seams of India's society were not pulled apart by the new cosmology to the same extent as Europe's. The foundations of religion may not have toppled, but they were rocked. It remains to be seen, however, whether or not the relatively rapid assimilation of Copernicanism in South Asia, and the impetus it gave to the separation of science from religion, can be sufficiently explained by the presuppositions of Hinduism. By the same token, one can question whether re-

60. Goonatilake, *Aborted Discovery,* pp. 60-61.

Receding from Antiquity

sistance to Copernicanism in Europe should be attributed to Christianity, as such, or to the Aristotelianism underlying it. The implication that religion in South Asia, or religion anywhere, would have welcomed its own compartmentalization seems dubious at best. The answer may lie more in the likelihood that all religions have been forced in varying degrees to acquiesce to science and accommodate its epistemology and methodology.

In a study like this, which draws on stray fragments of history to reconstruct a micro-relationship of collaboration, interaction, and self-differentiation, much can be learned, despite the missing elements that might affect the overall picture. Whatever the gaps, enough has been recovered from the past to indicate that Malwa experienced at least a temporary renewal of science and not a precipitous decline. I am, therefore, unable to agree with Deepak Kumar that the colonial milieu "blunted the possibility of evolving perspectives rooted in [the] indigenous intellectual and cultural heritage."[61] On the contrary, it could be that the downward spiral began before the onset of colonialism and that astronomy in the new milieu was drawn out from isolation and reintegrated with the larger world of science, as it had been during antiquity. If this was so, did the assimilation of Copernicanism in the first half of the nineteenth century differ intrinsically from the assimilations of Babylonian, Greek, and Islamic astronomy because it occurred under colonial conditions? I suggest that in the *Siddhāntaśiromaṇiprakāśa* Soobajee articulated his own symptomatic perspective on what is now called "colonial science."

A View from the Vortex

Within the parameters of patronage, Soobajee maintained, fortified, and even broadened his self-identity as a Hindu, a Brahman, and a scholar of science. That he was not doing "European" science, overawed by Copernicus, subordinated or constrained by Wilkinson, is an inference supported by the materials introduced. In this same connection Malwa may provide a context for reflection on a suggestive possibility put forth by Wilhelm Halbfass:

> Eastern and Western "cultures" can no longer meet one another as equal partners. They meet in a Westernized world, under conditions shaped by Western ways of thinking. . . . But is this factually inescapable "universality" the true telos of mankind?[62]

61. Kumar, *Science and the Raj,* p. 227.
62. Halbfass, *India and Europe,* p. 440.

If Soobajee's adjustments to the "universality" of Westernization seem even more intriguing than his mentor's Orientalist fascination with India while remaining at the same time committed to the particularity of his own tradition, it is also true that Soobajee's adjustments were more limited than those of his contemporaries who regarded a more complete merger with Europe to be in India's best interests. One of these was "Onkar Bhut" (Oṃkār Bhaṭṭ), an Audambar Brahman of Aṣṭa (near Sehore) whose forebears had migrated to Malwa from Gujarat. Onkar was a practicing *joṣī* (astrologer) until being inducted by Wilkinson into the Śihūra Saṃskṛta Paṭhaśālā, where he became an ardent advocate of Copernicanism and, like Soobajee, the recipient of a silver ink stand from Governor-General Bentinck. Onkar's *Bhūgolsār* [An Epitome of Geography] was lithographed around the same time as the *Siddhāntaśiromaṇiprakāśa* in 1836 (no copy in existence, however, appears to be older than the 1841 edition of the Agra School Book Society). This work differs from Soobajee's in several important respects. Purāṇic cosmology, for instance, is treated as the product of "poetical fabulists" who used the material world as metaphors of divinity *(aiśvārya),* but these are bluntly denounced as lies *(jhūṭ)* insofar as they describe objective realities — Soobajee had not gone so far as that. On the whole, the *Bhūgolsār* is less shrouded in theology than the *Siddhāntaśiromaṇiprakāśa,* and its compartmentalization of religion is more thorough.

Unlike Soobajee, Onkar was overawed by Europe, its magisterial scientists, and the observational methods they employed. The transvaluation of empiricism by the British made them a veritable master race: "Because the sahibs *(sahib log)* see things with their own eyes, what they say about astronomy is authoritative knowledge *(pramāṇa)* based on sense perception *(pratyakṣa).* They never write anything without seeing for themselves. But the Hindus believe in their sacred books blindly and without reason *(upapatti).*" About this streak of Positivism in Onkar, an observation by Gauri Viswanathan seems apropos. Viswanathan has rightly observed that in the self-identity of people like Wilkinson, who exemplified Europe in India, "Western empiricism was invested with extraordinary religious power."[63] Irfan Habib and Dhruv Raina[64] have further observed that empiricism was sometimes simplistically

---

63. Viswanathan, *Masks of Conquest,* p. 98. "We are thoroughly convinced that it is by actual measurement and actual inspection, by the measuring-rod, the theodolite and the telescope, that the Puranic idol is to be demolished. . . . In introducing the European astronomy, we come with no human authority, but with the authority of the very God of truth, and show His signature and His seal impressed upon the book of the universe." Extract from an anonymous review of Wilkinson's Sehore experiment, which the author found to be too gradual; see "The Astronomy of the Hindus," *Calcutta Review* 1 (1844): 288.

64. Habib and Raina, "The Introduction of Scientific Rationality," p. 601.

associated with Christianity and could even become an inducement to conversion. Such may have been the case with Yesudas Ramacandra, a renowned mathematician of Delhi and a contemporary who was in certain respects Soobajee's polar opposite, although both were popularizers of science for the masses.

One model for understanding how local scientific paradigms are dismantled in a colonial milieu is that of Shigeru Nakayama, who emphasizes the role of institutional diffusion. Nakayama argues that, unlike the West that exhibits a sequence from breakthrough (e.g., heliocentricity) to informal advocacy, followed by eventual magisterial recognition by professors, faculties, and universities, the order in colonial societies is the reverse: institutions first gain control over students who then assimilate the paradigm, which is subsequently disseminated among the masses informally.[65] While this model works in other situations,[66] it cannot account for the paradigm shift in Malwa. Wilkinson began exercising some degree of control over the Śihūra Saṃskṛta Pāṭhaśālā when he became its patron, but the school did not then have pandits who were acquainted with the *siddhāntas*. It was taught to them by an individual who happened to be the British Resident. Does that necessarily make this "colonial science" in the invidious sense of that expression? Not necessarily. In Malwa, the sequence was first a breakthrough, then informal advocacy, followed by magisterial recognition. The last step in the sequence, which is yet to be discussed, exemplifies the final, irretractable dethronement of Purāṇic cosmology. This occurs in the period immediately after Soobajee vanishes from the records because of the death of Wilkinson. Attention then shifts to the protégé of the protégé, Bāpūdeva Śāstrī (1821-90).

Bāpūdeva Śāstrī, earlier known as Nṛsiṃha Deva-Parāñjpe, a Cittapāvaṇa Brahman from Maharashtra, came as a young man to the Śihūra Saṃskṛta Pāṭhaśālā where he studied the *siddhāntas*. Not only was Bāpūdeva a mathematical prodigy, but he was socialized into Western science at an age when his mind was supple and able to make the transition from Purāṇic cosmology without a traumatic experience of intellectual dissonance. As Wilkinson observed: "My Pundits are all now admirers of English science, but they became so after years of discussion. He got all his doubts of the truths of the Pooranic system, &c. removed by them, as a boy." By the time Bāpūdeva was ready to leave the Pāṭhaśālā, certain events had occurred in the institutionalization of science that catapulted him to the front ranks of Indian education. In 1844,

65. Shigeru Nakayama, *Academic and Scientific Traditions in China, Japan, and the West* (Tokyo, 1984).
66. Young and Jebanesan, *Bible Trembled*, pp. 49-68.

John Muir, author of the *Mataparīkṣā,* became acting principal of the Benares Sanskrit College. The College was then in the doldrums, and a drastic reorganization was being considered. One action taken by Muir that can be construed unequivocally as an act of colonial science was to "interdict" the teaching of astrology and substitute in its place the *siddhāntas* and Western astronomy. In this regard, the Benares Sanskrit College was far behind similar institutions in the metropolitan centers where European influence was greater. In the 1820s, for instance, the Orientalist H. H. Wilson had recommended the same reform but met with a rebuff from the college pandits.[67]

Under Muir's administration, the change in curriculum at the Sanskrit College was affected by appointing Bāpūdeva upon a recommendation from Wilkinson (who had earlier been lobbying for his protégé) as the professor of mathematics and *jyotiḥśāstra.* Although it was claimed by a prominent Christian Brahman of Benares, Nīlakaṇṭh Goreh (1825-85), who converted around the same time, that Bāpūdeva was "afraid to hear about our religion lest he become a convert to it too [i.e., in addition to Copernicanism]," he remained a Hindu and straddled the colonial worlds of science and religion with even more aplomb than his mentor Soobajee. With many translations from Sanskrit into English and from English into Hindi to his credit, Bāpūdeva's rewards and accolades, including the distinction of being made a Companion of the Order of the Indian Empire in 1878, make Soobajee's silver ink stand look rather paltry in comparison.[68]

Halbfass's observation that "India has discovered Europe and begun to respond to it in being overrun and objectified by it" is a penetrating insight. How did those who were swept into the vortex of the dramatic changes occurring in Indian science, religion, and society perceive what was happening around them? Among the sources I have explored, none is better for isolating a symptomatic response than the *Siddhāntaśiromaṇiprakāśa.* The author, after all, was swept into the vortex himself. The extract I adduce is not found in

67. Sangwan, "European Impressions of Science," p. 87.

68. Here I draw primarily on Muir, *Brief Notice of the Late Lancelot Wilkinson,* pp. 8-10; William Smith, *Dwíj: The Conversion of a Brahman to the Faith of Christ* (London, 1850), p. 46; and Baldeva Upādhyāya, *Kāśī ki pāṇḍitya-paramparā* (Varanasi, 1994), pp. 187-99. For Muir's account of his reorganization of the Benares Sanskrit College, see OIOC (London), North-West Provinces, Lieut.-Governor's Proceedings in the General Dept., April-June 1844, Range 214.63, no. 59. Muir there states that it was on the recommendation of Wilkinson that Bāpūdeva was appointed. For the recommendation itself, see West Bengal State Archives (Calcutta), General Committee of Public Instruction, Benares College and Seminary, vol. 4, 1 January 1840; 8 September 1842, Wilkinson to Thomas Wise, GCPI, Sehore, August 1841. Wilkinson begins as follows: "I have one youth who is a splendid Sanskrit scholar, perfectly acquainted with the Siddhants."

the Marathi text of 1836; it occurs in a polyglot version in Sanskrit, Hindi, and his "native" Telegu, which was published the following year in Madras. The idiom, imagery, and metaphors articulate in a compact synthesis how the numerous forces of colonialism brought into being what we now call "colonial science." The following passage, which comes from the Hindi appendix, is cast in the standard format of popular didactic works, that of a dialogue between a pupil *(śiṣya)* and a teacher *(guru)*:

> PUPIL: The *siddhāntas* of Hindu astronomy are very ancient. The sahibs acquired them from various places around the country. So how come their ideas [about astronomy] are more highly developed than ours? Why is that?
>
> GURU: After the sahibs went out to see the whole world for themselves, they returned and settled in each of the places they had seen, having been very careful to record the latitude and longitude. That's why their ideas [about astronomy] are so highly developed. Besides, whoever puts a lot of effort into his labour makes a good profit from it. The cotton we cultivate in India, the sahibs carry back to their own country, spin it, and make it into cloth *(kapṛā)*. When the cloth is brought back to India, everybody goes wild about it. There's a market for their cloth *(kapṛā)* now, but none for our cloth *(vastra)*. Just like they took the cotton, the sahibs took home the astronomical texts *(siddhānt granth)* they found in Arabia [Arbusthān], Greece [Yūnān], India, and other countries for study. They put a lot of effort into making our astronomy better than it was before — like they did our cotton.[69]

An echo of begrudging admiration is also evident here. The Indian astronomy of antiquity, which suffered the same fate as the Indian agrarian economy, declined for the same reasons: Europe made a better product — although it was made with Indian raw material and Europe controlled the market to boot.

There was more to Soobajee's perspective on the "colonization" of science than wounded feelings, however. For the word "cloth" in English he employed two in Hindi. When he spoke of "their cloth," the word was *kapṛā*, and when he spoke of "our cloth," the word was *vastra*. Both words come down to the same thing in plain Hindi and English, but semiotically the meanings are

---

69. For an alternative reading of this passage, see Gyan Prakash, *Another Reason: Science and the Imagination of Modern India* (Princeton, 1999), pp. 64-68. My analysis differs diametrically from his.

worlds apart. Ever since the Lancashire mills began to mass produce it, *kaprā* has had an ordinary, work-a-day quality as the material of clothing for worldly activity. *Vastra*, in contrast to *kaprā*, is not merely the local product; it is a material made into seamless, unstitched garments, undefiled by foreign hands, fit for wearing by Brahmans and appropriate for offering to the deities enshrined in temples. *Vastra* carries associations of the sacred that *kaprā* does not.[70] If the metaphor holds and expresses what Soobajee truly felt, then what the European "colonization" of Indian science did was transform the science of astronomy, which had been imbued with a sacred quality, into a science that was secular but also an improvement over the science of antiquity. One might return to the past, but not remain there; if one did, science would not be science but nostalgia.

70. For historical-anthropological analysis of the place and meaning of "cloth" in Indian society, see C. A. Bayly, "The Origins of Swadeshi (Home Industry): Cloth and Indian Society," in *The Social Life of Things: Commodities in Cultural Perspective,* edited by Arjun Appadurai (Cambridge, 1986), pp. 285-321. On Indian markets and British cloth, see Sumit Gupta, "The Handloom Industry of Central India: 1825-1950," *Indian Economic and Social History Review* 26 (1989): 297-305.

CHAPTER NINE

"Pillar of a New Faith": Christianity in Late-Nineteenth-Century Punjab from the Perspective of a Convert from Islam

AVRIL A. POWELL

Convert Theology in Northwest India

This study examines the ways in which a convert to Christianity from Islam, a former Sunni *'alim,* attempted to strengthen the Christian faith of other Urdu-reading Christian converts in the thirty-year period following his own Christian baptism and ordination in the Punjab in the mid-1860s. He retained his Muslim name, "'Imad ud-din,"[1] "pillar of the faith," after baptism, because it was perceived to be as aptly symbolic of his new role within the Christian community as it had been of the role ascribed to him by his Islamic education and his family's reputation for Islamic scholarship in the community into which he was born. His active and highly public life within the North Indian church certainly made him a "pillar" of the nascent Punjabi Christian community during the volatile last quarter of the nineteenth century. The ordination of 'Imad ud-din thrust him into a situation of strident public disputation not only between Christianity and Islam, but among spokesmen for the various revivalist movements that were emerging within the Muslim, Hindu, and Sikh communities of the Punjab region.[2]

---

1. Transliterated "'Imad ud-din" here, rather than the more consistent "'Imad al-din," because it was the spelling he used for his English publications.

2. Kenneth W. Jones, *Socio-religious Reform Movements in British India* (Cambridge, 1989); Barbara Metcalf, *Islamic Revival in British India: Deoband, 1860-1900* (Princeton, N.J., 1982); A. A. Powell, *Muslims and Missionaries in Pre-Mutiny India* (London, 1993).

'Imad ud-din from the outset was greatly valued by the European and American missionaries because of his powers of communication with all these claimants and, in particular, for his eagerness to carry the Christian message in the Urdu language, not only back into the mosque and *madrassa* circles in which he had been born, but also out into the urban bazaars and *mahallas* inhabited by the humbler strata of Muslim Urdu-speaking Punjabis. For more than thirty years, from 1866 until his death in 1900, 'Imad ud-din was tireless in the preaching of Christianity and in the writing of evangelical tracts and biblical commentaries for just such audiences and readers.

Some aspects of 'Imad ud-din's interaction with the Muslims of North India have been told elsewhere. These concern, first, the process through which he finally accepted Christianity following long years of spiritual struggle within the parameters of Sunni and mystical Islam and, second, the significance of his postbaptismal critique of the character and life of the prophet Muhammad.[3] The confrontational aspects of his approach to his former colleagues among the *'ulama*, for which he was increasingly criticized by missionaries as well as by spokesmen for other faiths, will not be explored in detail here. Center stage will be given to the separate though interrelated question of how he chose to present and transmit his own new certainty of the truth of Christianity both to fellow converts and to those he referred to as his "brothers and sisters" among less highly educated Punjabi Muslims. Although there has been some study of the relationship between Christian "convert theology" and Hindu theology and philosophy, very little attention has been paid to "Muslim Christian theology," at least as it emerged in the Indian rather than the Middle Eastern environment. This study of a particularly prolific convert's writings is a contribution to that end.

Before turning to the Reverend Maulvi 'Imad ud-din's understanding of Christianity, the salient characteristics of some precedents and parallels that have been suggested in the earlier studies of others, particularly in the context of converts from Hinduism, will be briefly indicated. A number of such studies have suggested a paradigm whereby "convert theology" might be placed in an appropriate relationship to "Western" modes of exposition of Christianity on the one hand, and to the convert's culture and religion of birth on the other. Particularly influential in its exploration of this paradigm was Robin Boyd's *India and the Latin Captivity of the Church: The Cultural Context of the*

---

3. A. A. Powell, "Processes of Conversion to Christianity in Nineteenth-Century North-Western India," in *Religious Conversion Movements in South Asia: Continuities and Change, 1800-1900*, edited by Geoffrey A. Oddie (London, 1997), pp. 15-55; and idem, "William and John Muir as Catalysts for Scholarly Responses to Evangelical Discourse in North-Western India," NAMP Position Paper.

Gospel (Cambridge, 1974).[4] A more recent study of some "new voices offering a counter-theology," has continued the metaphor of "captivity," positing that "historically, Indian Christian thinking has in the last four or five centuries been strongly influenced by, if not been somewhat imprisoned in, Western Christian ways of expression." When Indian theology finally "broke out" from its Western mold during the last hundred years, it was only to almost immediatcly find itself entrapped in a form of "Sanskritic captivity." Underlying this conclusion is the observation that "the pioneers of Indian Christian thinking, with their liberal education, evolved their theology as an apologetic response within the context of Indian nationalism and Hindu renaissance."[5] From this perspective late-nineteenth-century responses to Christ by those Hindus, such as Vivekananda and Radhakrishnan, who showed a sympathetic interest but did not convert are placed in the context of a reaffirmation of Vedantic monism in which Christ is interpreted only as a single manifestation of Vedanta, on a par with many other such manifestations.[6] The "existing and dominant Sanskritically-based theology" of Vedanta nevertheless continued to structure convert theology among those Hindus who did adopt Christianity and then preached it in the renaissance climate of which they were a part.

Some work on Nilakhanta Goreh and on K. M. Banerjea is suggestive of the ways in which these two Indian Christians might be placed in the context of concepts of "Western" and "Sanskritic" captivities in their own expositions of Christian teaching.[7] Nilakhanta Goreh, a Maratha Brahman who first encountered Christianity in Benares, at first reacted strongly against it, as 'Imad ud-din would also do a few years later. Contact with Evangelicals in order to refute them subsequently resulted in his baptism as "Nehemiah" and in his turning from writing against Christianity to publishing on its behalf, and in criticism of Hindu philosophy. The complexity of this convert's relationship both to the religion of his birth and to the religion he adopted is reflected in his seeming total intellectual rejection of Hinduism; yet he continued with lifelong doubts about Christianity and an increasing preference for the modes of being a "Christian sannyasin," which were closest to the meditative paths of being Hindu. Although his judgments on Hinduism remained "unsparingly harsh," a searching study discerns that "he was never

---

4. Also, R. H. S. Boyd, *An Introduction to Indian Christian Theology,* rev. ed. (Madras, 1975 [1969]).

5. R. S. Sugirtharajah and Cecil Hargreaves, *Readings in Indian Christian Theology I* (London, 1993), pp. 1-2.

6. Sugirtharajah and Hargreaves, *Readings,* p. 7.

7. Boyd, *Introduction,* pp. 40-57, 280-87.

quite at ease either in his disbelief of Hinduism or in his newfound Christian faith."[8]

Krisna Mohan Banerjea, a Bengali Brahman who was baptized under Alexander Duff's influence in Calcutta, did not seem to suffer from the kind of doubts experienced by Nilakhanta, and, as 'Imad ud-din would do, he played an active role as an ordained minister in preaching Christianity and publishing on evangelical themes. Yet Banerjea's gradual move from a mode of "Western evangelical" preaching of Christianity, which was very close to that of his missionary mentors in the Bengal of the 1840s and 1850s, to the conviction of his last twenty years (ca. 1865-85) that Vedic sacrifice could be seen as prefiguring and being fulfilled in Christ's sacrifice seems a particularly instructive example of "engrafting on," rather than "captivity of," one tradition by the other.[9]

It seems that converts to Christianity who subsequently took up an evangelistic role usually chose to preach to audiences consisting predominantly of members of their own birth community, as indeed 'Imad ud-din did. It may be possible to generalize this tendency to include patterns of conversion from, and into, other religious communities in the Punjab. Muhammad 'Umar, for example, a Muslim convert to the Arya Samaj, subsequently preached Arya doctrines to predominantly Muslim audiences.[10] In contrast, there are some interesting cases of North Indian converts to Christianity who opted to evangelize other communities. Prominent examples are the North Indian converted Hindus, Ram Chandar and Tara Chand, who, after Christian baptism in the mid-nineteenth century, chose to address Muslim audiences and readers in the Delhi region through the medium of the Urdu language. "Master" Ram Chandar might be regarded as a special case, having spent many years before baptism in the Islamic and Urdu environment of the Anglo-Oriental Delhi College. Such Christian spokesmen as these should perhaps be seen as the exceptions which prove the rule. Their significance in the context of 'Imad ud-din's Christian witness lies in their lifetime interaction with him as founding and fellow members of the Punjab Native Church Council, and in numerous collaborative translation projects.

Dramatically different was the path of those numerically few, yet highly

8. Richard Fox Young, *Resistant Hinduism: Sanskrit Sources on Anti-Christian Apologetics in Early Nineteenth-Century India* (Vienna, 1981), pp. 169-72.

9. See esp. K. M. Banerjea, *The Arian Witness: or Testimony of Arian Scriptures in Corroboration of Biblical History and the Rudiments of Christian Doctrine* (Calcutta, 1875); idem, *The Relation between Christianity and Hinduism* (Calcutta, 1881).

10. Muhammad 'Umar took the name Alakhdari under which he published in Urdu on the Vedas. See S. and H. Vidyalankar, *Arya Samaj Ka Itihas* (New Delhi, n.d.), pp. 41-42.

influential, converts from Hindu or Sikh backgrounds who, although they espoused Christianity and even accepted ordination, chose to adopt evangelistic modes of exposition that drew not from Sanskritic and Brahmanical sources and models but from *sannyasi* paths of devotionalism. In the Punjab region the outstanding example (still an eleven-year-old boy when 'Imad uddin died in 1900) was "Sadhu" Sundar Singh, a Sikh, who in 1904, when still only about fifteen, had a vision of Christ that impelled him to seek immediate baptism in the community he had previously denounced, and whose Bible he had publicly burnt. Yet, in so doing he rejected entirely "Western" modes of Christian thought and behavior, stating significantly that "Indians do need the Water of Life, but not in the European cup." For the rest of his short life he remained a "Christian sadhu," adopting an ecstatic form of preaching to present Christianity to remote hill peoples in a devotional idiom more akin to some indigenous expressions of religious fervor than to the sermons being preached in the missionary churches of the Punjab.[11] Some attention has been paid recently to the theology of another Christian *sannyasi*, a Bengali, later named Brahmabandab Upadhyay (1861-1907), who after baptism in 1881 as an Anglican found space within the Catholic Church to become what Rabindranath Tagore described as "a Roman Catholic ascetic yet a Vedantin."[12] He is remembered as "a pioneer in exploring creative ways of relating Christian faith with the culture, tradition, philosophy and genius of India."[13] Nehemiah Goreh, though he was to remain within "Western" institutional orders, also belonged in some respects, as suggested above, with the "Christian *sannyasin*" converts. These few examples indicate that the forms of inculturation among converts of Hindu birth in northern India were much more varied than the term "Sanskritic captivity" immediately suggests.

The appropriate and complementary questions to ask of Muslim-Christian ordinands would seem to be, first, how far were they, too, captives, and in what forms, of the styles of Western evangelicalism that they experienced before or after their baptisms. Second, how far were they influenced, consciously or subconsciously, by socio-religious and political movements within the wider Islamic world, both historical and contemporary, and par-

---

11. C. F. Andrews, *Sadhu Sundar Singh: A Personal Memoir* (London, 1934); A. J. Appasamy, *Sundar Singh: A Biography* (London, 1958).

12. Julius J. Lipner, "A Meeting of Ends? Swami Vivekananda and Brahmabandhab Upadhyay," in *Swami Vivekananda and the Modernization of Hinduism*, edited by William Radice (New Delhi, 1998), pp. 61-76; Timothy C. Tennent, *Building Christianity on Indian Foundations: The Theological Legacy of Brahmabandhav Upadhyay* (Delhi: ISPCK, 2000).

13. Felix Wilfred, *Beyond Settled Foundations: the Journey of Indian Theology* (Madras, 1993), pp. 19-20, 24-36.

ticularly within North India, in formulating their own representations of Christianity for the guidance of other converts from Islam. Such "Indo-Islamic" underpinnings or influences might include popular forms of Sufism in northwest India and the attack from within "reforming" *'ulama* circles upon "custom-laden" Islam; current reinforcement of the textual basis of the Islamic faith and concomitant "return" movements; the emergence of "Islamic modernism" and a consequent redebating of the place of "reason" in Islam; and, finally, the proclaiming in the Punjab of a new prophet of Islam, in the person of Mirza Ghulam Ahmad, the founder of the Ahmadiyya community, who was regarded as a heretic by other Sunni Muslims and who was particularly disturbing to Christians because of his claim to be Masih (the Messiah) in his "second coming." Some of these contextual processes will be examined below. The newly baptized 'Imad ud-din's preaching of Christianity in Amritsar began and continued simultaneously with the appearance in the public arena of most of these fissiparous and newly competitive modes of being a "true" Sunni Muslim. More long-standing among North Indian Muslims in the region of his birth and education was persistent internal debating over the legitimacy and efficacy of mystical modes of religious questing. Such contests had come to a head earlier in the nineteenth century as a result of the preaching against *bid'at* (innovation) of the Tariqa-i Muhammadiyya (miscalled the "Wahhabi") movement. Examination of the methods of evangelization and reinforcement he chose to adopt will therefore reveal not only the extent of 'Imad ud-din's own "evangelical captivity" but also how much he owed to, or rejected from, his own past spiritual life as a Muslim *'alim* in a period of highly contested interpretation of Islamic priorities. A brief consideration of the path of his own spiritual quest up to the point of baptism, and of his sudden elevation to a position of leadership in the Punjab "native church," sets the scene for an examination of these influences.

Sunni, Sufi, and Faqir Stages in 'Imad ud-din's Religious Quest

Among the very few Muslims who converted to Christianity in northwest India, there was a significant number from *ashraf* backgrounds. A notable figure was 'Abd al-Masih, the only convert who had been baptized as a direct result of Henry Martyn's pioneering evangelism of North Indian Muslims at the beginning of the nineteenth century.[14] Although 'Abd al-Masih had died shortly before 'Imad ud-din's birth, the latter referred to him in his memoirs as repre-

14. Powell, "Processes of Conversion," pp. 31-36.

senting the starting point of Christian influence among *ashraf*[15] Muslims in the region, for it was in the bazaars of the old city of Agra, where 'Abd al-Masih had baptized a small flock of Indian Christians thirty years earlier, that 'Imad ud-din first heard about Christianity in the mid-1840s. The circumstances of 'Imad ud-din's family life and education have been fully discussed elsewhere.[16] It is sufficient to emphasize here, first, the role of his family in the pious and learned concerns of the Sunnis of his birthplace, Panipat, and, in particular, his family's long-standing connection with the shrine in Panipat of the four-teenth-century Sufi saint, Bu 'Ali Qalandar. Second is his experience as a col-lege student on the fringes of an influential circle of Sunni *'ulama* in Agra. For several years he attended the Agra Anglo-Oriental government college, from whose number emerged the first defenders of Islam against the persistent at-tacks on the life of the Prophet by some newly arrived Christian missionaries. Third, and most important for the purposes of this particular study, however, is the nature of the Evangelical enterprise, witnessed, but strongly rejected in his youth, which was undertaken in Agra by these German Pietist missionar-ies, who had been educated in the Basel Mission Seminary in Switzerland but who were writing and preaching in Agra under Church Missionary Society (CMS) Anglican auspices. He despaired that neither his Sunni mentors nor the Christian missionaries were able to provide answers for his own spiritual needs. The significance to his own subsequent preaching as a Christian con-vert of the long period in the 1850s when 'Imad ud-din completely abandoned the formal demands of the faith in which he had been brought up in order to experiment in the jungles of North India with some extreme ascetic practices will be discussed below. During this period, he felt, as he later recorded, that he might end his life as a Faqir, far removed from the urban, educated circles in which he had been brought up.

'Imad ud-din has left us a detailed account of this phase of his tormented spiritual search. He reached a state of such deep despair that he was con-vinced that "there was no true religion in the world at all."[17] By different paths he had then reached the agnostic position professed by some Hindu students during Calcutta's "renaissance" era. Finally, he abandoned his quest, and after returning to his home in Panipat, decided to settle in Lahore, the capital of the then British-administered Punjab. Through the good offices of an elder brother, who was in the British education service, he obtained a post

---

15. "Noble," indicating well-born and respectable. More precisely in India it refers to those Muslims who claimed descent from the Sayyids, Shaikhs, Mughals, and Pathans.

16. See esp. Powell, "Processes of Conversion," pp. 36-42.

17. 'Imad ud-din, *Waqi'at-i 'Imadiyyah*, 2nd ed. (Ludhiana, 1874), p. 9.

in a new government teacher-training college. That within two years he accepted baptism seems to have been the result of a long-term process begun as a student in Agra but brought to this particular conclusion, he said, through discussions with a British officer with whom he worked in the education service. He also said he had been influenced by the rereading of the same books and tracts that he had despised while he was at college. Among those that helped to shape his own future exposition of Christianity were the apologetic works on Islam and Christianity of Karl Pfander, the initiator in Agra of missionary-Muslim controversy. He had returned to Pfander's books in an attempt to confute a Muslim fellow student from his Agra days, one Maulwi Safdar 'Ali, who had informed him that, under Nehemiah Goreh's influence, he had accepted Christian baptism.[18] Anger and incredulity at Safdar 'Ali's act of apostasy appear to have brought 'Imad ud-din to a climactic emotional state. Although apparently suddenly, but actually after many years' struggle, he made a public acceptance of Christianity, the faith that, from his youth, he had very openly denounced. A two-year period of voracious study of the Urdu Bible, and of Urdu missionary tracts comparing Islam and Christianity, had preceded his request for baptism.

Baptism and Church Leadership

Within two years of his baptism by Robert Clark, a leading Punjab missionary, 'Imad ud-din was ordained and quickly put to work to preach in Urdu to bazaar audiences that had hitherto seemed resistant to missionary influence. His missionary mentors in the CMS had accelerated his ordination, not normally permissible until several years after baptism, because they recognized the useful part a scholar such as 'Imad ud-din might play in public contestation with the local Sunni 'ulama. From the late 1860s until the mid-1870s he was particularly prolific, publishing a stream of tract literature, initially criticisms of Islam, but later works on doctrine and biblical commentary intended for Indian converts. He also took a leading role in public debates with Muslims, who included Deobandi specialists in hadith ("traditions") scholarship, Aligarh modernists and rationalists, and, at a later stage, Ahmadi "heretics." In the latter two cases he took on the leaders themselves, namely, Sir Sayyid Ahmad Khan and Mirza Ghulam Ahmad. He played a leading part, along with Tara Chand, another recent convert, in the estab-

18. Powell, "Processes of Conversion," pp. 40-41. Safdar 'Ali published an explanation of the reasons for his own conversion: *Niyaz Namah* (Allahabad, 1867).

lishment of the Punjab Native Church Council, which for the first time empowered Indian converts with a limited but significant voice in church affairs in northwest India.[19] For the remainder of his life Western missionaries and local Christians had recourse to him for advice and collaboration, particularly in translating and publishing works in Urdu. As a result of these literary activities he "may well be regarded as the founder-member of the Punjab Religious Book Society," the main channel of transmission of Christian religious literature in this region.[20] The highest accolade to his achievements was an invitation to attend the Parliament of Religions in Chicago in 1893. Unlike Vivekananda, the well-known Hindu delegate at the Parliament, however, 'Imad ud-din did not travel to America. The ostensible reason was that in his old age he seldom moved out of the Punjab, but a feeling that he was not fluent enough in English probably also influenced the decision. This former *'alim* had managed nevertheless, in spite of much initial hostility to his baptism, to maintain a reputation in the Punjab as a "man of God," irrespective of his change of religious community. Although his father, wife, children, and several brothers followed him into baptism, he seems to have remained in communication with many scholarly Muslim families of the region.[21] Because he managed to maintain some influence and standing in the community of his birth, 'Imad ud-din provides a particularly insightful perspective on "Indian Christianity" as it developed in its interface with "Indian Islam."

'Imad ud-din's Representation of Christianity to Indian Muslims

Some comments will be offered here on 'Imad ud-din's perceptions of Christianity. These are based mainly on some of the many devotional and explanatory works he composed for Indian converts and on his tracts for the evangelization of Indian Muslims. The half-dozen or so treatises and

---

19. The Native Church Council in the Punjab was the first to be established in North India (1877) by the CMS, which delegated to it some responsibilities for appointing, transferring, and fixing the salaries of Indian clergy. It became a forum for urging, with little success, that Indian ordinands in the CMS should be granted equal status with Western missionaries. Its members sought common ground with Indian Presbyterian clergy in the region. See John C. B. Webster, *The Christian Community and Change in Nineteenth-Century North India* (Delhi, 1976), p. 234; *Report of the Second Meeting of the Punjab Presbyterian Conference* (Ludhiana, 1880), esp. pp. 37-40.

20. *A Short History of the Punjab Religious Book Society,* p. 7.

21. Powell, "Processes of Conversion," pp. 41-42.

tracts drawn on here are a representative selection from his nearly thirty publications.[22]

In many cases it is difficult to separate 'Imad ud-din's own contributions from those of his foreign mentors. This is mainly because many tracts were jointly written, while others, though composed by him, were then translated and edited by the foreign missionaries. Consequently, considerable modification of his original drafts probably took place. He tended to be overmodest in his deference to his Western mentors. He was quoted in one report as holding that "the Native Church is not sufficiently advanced to act independently whether in making translations or analyses or collections of matter." "Hindustani people," he said, "have not the knowledge of other times and countries to prepare books of commentary, history and biography."[23] Speaking specifically of his work on the Urdu biblical commentaries, he emphasized that Clark "caused me to write four books in which the major portion of the work was his. It was mine to write, and here and there I interpolated some subject matter, but it was his part to bring the material from the books of the bygone great."[24] Another colleague, H. U. Weitbrecht, who was generally skeptical about the achievements of the "native church," commented on what he perceived as "an absence of theological initiative" in the "Native Christian mind."[25] Thus while 'Imad ud-din's skills were undeniable in the sphere of controversial works for Muslim readers, Weitbrecht considered that his role in writing in tandem with Clark was limited to putting the commentaries

22. The following are drawn on here: (a) his autobiographical works: various updates and translations of *Waqi'at-i 'Imadiyyah* [Incidents in the Life of 'Imad ud-din], 1st ed. (1866); 2nd ed. (Ludhiana, 1874); e.g., *A Mohammedan brought to Christ; being the Autobiography of a Native Clergyman in India*, 2nd ed. (Lahore, 1870); Ernest Hahn, trans., *The Life of the Rev. Mawlawi Dr. 'Imad ud-din Lahiz* (Vaniyambadi, 1978); (b) works of Christian exposition: *Tahqiq al-Iman* [Investigation of Faith: A Defense of Christianity], 1st ed. (1866); 2nd ed. (Allahabad, 1870); *Manana?* [Who am I?: A Sermon on Matt. 16:13] (n.d.); *Khun Se Mua'afi* [Atonement through Blood] (n.d., ca. 1874); *Asar-i Qiyamat* [Signs of the Resurrection] (Lahore, 1870); *Haqiqi 'irfan* [The True Knowledge: 12 separately published monthly pamphlets in support of particular Christian doctrines] (1868-69); and (c) tracts in response to the "new Islam" of Sayyid Ahmad Khan, notably pt. 1 of *Tanqid al-Khiyalat* [A Criticism of Thoughts, Entitled "Reason As a Spiritual Guide"] (Allahabad, 1882).

23. Quoted in section on "Preparation of Books," in Dr. Brodhead and Dr. Murdoch, *Conference on Urdu and Hindi Christian Literature Held at Allahabad, 24th and 25th February 1875* (Madras, 1875), p. 16.

24. 'Imad ud-din in the journal, *Makhzan-i Masihi*, cited in Henry Martyn Clark, *Robert Clark of the Panjab: Pioneer and Missionary Statesman* (London, 1907), pp. 297-98.

25. H. U. Weitbrecht, *A Descriptive Catalogue of Urdu Christian Literature, with a Review of the Same* (London and Lahore, 1886), pp. xxx-xxxi.

into "an Urdu form . . . with additions and illustrations."[26] Two of the Western missionaries who worked closest with him disagreed strongly, commenting soon after his ordination on his "originality and independence of thought."[27] His school friend, Safdar 'Ali, in a review of his contribution to the commentaries, gave a very different assessment, enthusing over 'Imad uddin's contribution that "we who are Urdu speakers may rightly deem them our Indian 'Scott's Commentaries.'"[28] Accurate attribution of authorship within such works remains problematic, as it does with many collaborative efforts between Western and Indian authors in which significant indigenous inputs often remained anonymous. Evangelical scholar-administrators as well as missionaries seldom gave sufficient credit to their informants and collaborators. Attempts will be made, nevertheless, mainly on the basis of his tracts and lectures, to identify both what 'Imad ud-din adopted from his missionary mentors and what he retained from his turbulent Islamic past.

Unlike many of the prominent ordinands from Hinduism in other parts of northern India, such as Banerjea and Goreh, 'Imad ud-din never fully mastered English. He was valued by the missionaries because of his education and reputation as an *'alim* and for his skills in Arabic and Persian as well as in Urdu. Throughout his life he was referred to within the Christian community as the "maulwi sahib." All his original publications were in Urdu, some of which Clark and other missionaries translated into English, mainly for publication in missionary journals in Britain. Significantly, after his first few publications, he abandoned the format and style favored for theological disputation by earlier Muslim controversialists. Most *'ulama* of the first half of the century had prided themselves on a highly Persianized Urdu style, which incorporated Arabic quotations and a complex syntax. Most of 'Imad ud-din's Christian tracts were expressed, in contrast, in a very simple Urdu. He seems to have adopted, deliberately, the style of earlier missionary tracts, even though the missionaries themselves were attempting by then, rather paradoxically, to emulate the *'ulama's* own ornate Persianized style. The missionaries advocated this practice to increase receptivity, as they thought, among learned Muslim readers who would otherwise despise their publications as "ignorant." As 'Imad ud-din had published nothing apart from history and geography textbooks for schoolchildren before his baptism, it is difficult to assess whether he made a conscious decision to simplify his style in order to

26. Weitbrecht, *Descriptive Catalogue*, p. xxx.
27. Church Missionary Society Archives [hereafter CMSA]: CI1/069/84a. Quoted in R. Clark to CMS, Amritsar, 27 March 1868.
28. "An Urdu Review of an Urdu Commentary," *Church Missionary Intelligencer* [hereafter *CMI*] (August 1898), p. 600.

be more accessible to a non-*ashraf* Punjabi readership, or whether he was anyway less practiced than, for instance, his eldest brother, the well-known literary critic, Maulawi Karim al-din, in the traditional modes of writing still favored in *ashraf* circles in North India. It is difficult to assess to what extent the simplicity of his style reflected broader trends in the evolution of Urdu prose, as in the works of leading literary figures such as Sayyid Ahmad Khan and the novelist Nazir Ahmad, rather than a conscious decision to write simply for a barely literate readership.[29] There is certainly a suggestion, in the preface to his *Tawarikh-i Muhammad* [History of Muhammad], that he deliberately intended to address the growing numbers of Urdu-reading Muslims whom he felt were excluded from the high Perso-Arabic culture of his erstwhile colleagues among the *ashraf* classes.[30]

At all events, Maulwi Safdar 'Ali, the Muslim class fellow from his Agra college days, whose own apostasy from Islam and Christian baptism seemingly influenced 'Imad ud-din's own conversion, certainly implied some criticism of traditional modes of prose writing in praising his friend's religious tracts as "not written in the sapless, dry language of the would-be mullah, nor in that of the pedagogue or pedant. The style is simple, natural, polished, terse, yet attractive. . . . All is clear, concise, and to the point."[31] A missionary reviewer, E. M. Wherry, an influential American Presbyterian, also remarked on 'Imad ud-din's "plain and terse form."[32] Some Western missionaries in the Punjab later expressed some reservations about signs of "aggression" and "dogmatism" in 'Imad ud-din's publications. Most would, however, continue to regard 'Imad ud-din as the one among them best placed to make an impact on Urdu-reading Muslims at this particular juncture in their history, because of his inner knowledge and experience as a respected *'alim*.

One of the most insistent characteristics of 'Imad ud-din's publications was a preoccupation with the time and the place in which he was writing, and with the supposed needs of some communities, newly categorized, in British census terms, as "religious." While millenarian concerns were implicit and often overt in most Evangelical preaching, some particular features of 'Imad ud-din's Punjab environment probably reinforced them.[33] When, in the

29. For the "simple" and "direct" characteristics of modern prose as it developed in the second half of the nineteenth century see Muhammad Sadiq, *A History of Urdu Literature* (London, 1964), p. 245.

30. 'Imad ud-din, *Tawarikh-i Muhammadi,* 2nd ed. (Amritsar, 1878), pp. 4-5.

31. "An Urdu Review of an Urdu Commentary," *CMI* (August 1898), pp. 597-600.

32. E. M. Wherry, *The Muslim Controversy: A Review of Christian Literature in the Urdu Language* (London, 1905), p. 35.

33. On "premillennial" and "postmillennial" features of evangelical eschatology in

1880s, in a town a few miles from 'Imad ud-din's own missionary station in Amritsar, a hitherto insignificant Muslim, one Mirza Ghulam Ahmad, began to preach to fellow Sunnis to follow his own calling as *mahdi,* messiah and even prophet, the millenarian projection took on a competitive aspect. This increased when the Mirza's followers institutionalized themselves as the Ahmadiyya movement. For ten years before the public emergence of the Ahmadi prophet, 'Imad ud-din had been expounding a Christian projection of future events in the region. His tracts are imbued with a sense of immediate crisis: he identified the period from 1850 to 1875 as a distinct new epoch, during which Christianity, its preaching now eased by colonial expansion in the region, had belatedly been made known to the peoples of northern India. His mentor, Robert Clark, had been identifying "signs" of the readiness of this region for Christianity since shortly after the British annexation of the Punjab.[34] The effects, 'Imad ud-din was convinced, would be made evident "within the next one or two generations," when, he anticipated, "all India will pass through a vast change."[35] He frequently reminded his readers that "the inhabitants of Hindustan" were at last fully receptive to the Christian message because "the Gospel has now been here for a long time."[36] The millenarian tone was strongest in his tract on the "signs" of the proximity of the Resurrection, newly manifest in "this the nineteenth century of our Lord."[37] This theme underlay many of his other publications, which also emphasized North India as the precise location to which "the disciples of the (former) disciples have brought the word of God."[38] The question "Who am I?" asked by Christ of his disciples he therefore addressed "to all the people of this country."[39] Muslims who prevaricated and responded that they were prepared to wait until Christ's Second Coming to become convinced of his real identity were simply mistaken. Christians, he urged, wanted to share the cer-

---

the nineteenth century see D. W. Bebbington, *Evangelicalism in Modern Britain* (London, 1989), esp. pp. 81-86.

34. In 1853 Clark had identified the drying up of the Euphrates as a sign that the newly discovered lost tribes of Israel (the Afghan tribes he encountered in the Peshawar region) were about to be led back to the land of Canaan: the CMS should speed up the process by opening a mission in Peshawar (Birmingham University Library, CMSA: CI1/069/2, Robert Clark to Henry Venn, Peshawar, 23 December 1853).

35. 'Imad ud-din, *The Results of the Controversy in North India with Mohammedans* (Amritsar, March 1875). Published as a pamphlet, n.d., pp. 4-6. Also published in *CMI* (September 1875).

36. 'Imad ud-din, *Manana?* p. 5.

37. 'Imad ud-din, *Asar-i Qiyamat,* p. 1.

38. 'Imad ud-din, *Haqiqi 'irfan* I, p. 1.

39. 'Imad ud-din, *Manana?* p. 3.

tainties of the gospel message with them immediately.[40] Although his target readers were often recent converts to Christianity, especially some former fellow Sunnis, he specified in his earlier tracts that Brahmo Samajists, Unitarians, and "ignorant Hindus" all needed to listen. In his later publications he noted, in addition, Arya Samajists, the "rationalist" followers of Sayyid Ahmad Khan, and the by then rapidly growing and actively missionary Ahmadi community, as categories of readers requiring separate attention. Tracts for specific times, places, and groups, with appropriate modifications to reflect the changing sectarian composition of the Punjab over the thirty years of his public utterances, were 'Imad ud-din's particular contribution to his mission's program of evangelization.

Discussion of some of the most significant characteristics of 'Imad ud-din's contribution follows under three headings, bearing in mind the concepts of "Western" and "Sanskritic" captivity discussed above in respect to Hindu Christian theology: (i) the extent to which he adopted or modified the apologetic of his European and American mentors in his own critique of Islam and understanding of Christianity; (ii) the relationship of his own long Sufi quest for truth to his subsequent understanding of Christianity; and (iii) his response to what he called the "New Islam," when, from the mid-1870s onwards, Islamic reform movements were felt to be proving more successful among North Indian Muslims than he was in his preaching of the "new Christianity."

The Influence of Western Missionaries and Evangelical Theology on 'Imad ud-din's Writings on Christianity

The Mentors

'Imad ud-din enjoyed very close relations with some of the most outstanding leaders of the post-1857 generation of Protestant missionaries in northwest India, most of whom belonged to the Anglican missionary society, the CMS. This society had been the first to encourage interchanges with Muslim leaders in northwest India. Among the CMS missionaries in the Punjab, Robert Clark, whom he called his "spiritual father," probably had the most direct influence upon him, through conversations during his preparation for baptism and ordination, and as a result of their long residence together in Amritsar. Dying within a few months of each other in 1900, they were buried side by

---

40. 'Imad ud-din, *Manana?* p. 8.

side in the "native" churchyard. Maulwi Safdar 'Ali's view was that his school friend had received all his "teaching, training and blessing" in matters of faith from Clark.[41] Other Amritsar missionaries to whom 'Imad ud-din was close included Rowland Bateman, Thomas Wade, and William Keene.[42] He was also very close to a British official, Henry E. Perkins, the son of a Society for the Propagation of the Gospel (SPG) missionary, who collaborated with 'Imad ud-din on various translations while he was still serving the Raj as a Deputy Commissioner. Perkins subsequently gave up government service to become, first, an honorary CMS assistant in Amritsar and, then, an ordained missionary.

Because the CMS and American Presbyterian missionaries in the Punjab enjoyed unusually fraternal relations, 'Imad ud-din was able to seek the latter's company also. He had close contact with Charles Forman, head of the American Presbyterian mission in Lahore. Forman, who had been resident in the Punjab since 1848, was a prolific publisher of Urdu tracts on doctrinal themes. At the time of 'Imad ud-din's baptism in 1866 the CMS had not yet opened a mission station in the city. It was thus Forman's church that 'Imad ud-din had attended for the first two years of his life as a Christian, while he was still employed in the education service in Lahore.[43] John Newton, an American Presbyterian who wrote mainly in Punjabi, was acknowledged by 'Imad ud-din as having been "the means of solving many of my religious difficulties."[44]

Particularly significant was 'Imad ud-din's long-standing "brotherhood" with Thomas Valpy French, founder of the Lahore Divinity School, who subsequently became the first bishop of Lahore and who remained in the Punjab until 1888. When 'Imad ud-din had first heard the CMS-led Christian critique of Islam in Agra, French, also very young at that time, and new to India, had been teaching in St. John's College, a Christian college he had founded to counteract the influence of the secular government college, where 'Imad ud-

41. "Urdu Review," p. 599. Clark's "hortatory and devotional" works in Urdu included *Rah-i Nijat* [Way of Salvation, "a collection of scripture passages on Christian truths"] (Ludhiana, 1875).

42. He had long and close contact with Keene, who appreciated his "mental culture and love of study" (*Proceedings of the CMS, for 1869-70*, p. 126).

43. Forman's tracts include: *Wafat-i Masih* [The Death of Christ] (Ludhiana, 1867); *Shakuk-i Kifarah* [A Reply to Objections on the Doctrine of the Atonement] (Ludhiana, 1873); *Bayan-i Faraqlit* [About the Paraclete], 2nd ed. (Ludhiana, 1875).

44. 'Imad ud-din, *Autobiography*, 2nd ed. (London, 1870), p. 18. See Newton's "Essay on Preaching to the Heathen," *Report of the Punjab Missionary Conference Held at Lahore in December and January, 1862-63* (Ludhiana, 1863), p. 5, in which he urged that preaching should be confined to the Word of God and should avoid the "subtleties of philosophy."

din was first a student, and later a teacher of Urdu. Rather reluctantly, French had agreed to be Karl Pfander's partner in public debates with the local *'ulama*. He was probably already aware of the young 'Imad ud-din, particularly as it is known from the latter's autobiography that he had by then been schooled to preach in the royal mosque against just such missionaries as French and Pfander.[45] Some fifteen years later, after 'Imad ud-din's baptism, French's correspondence confirms that the two became very close spiritually. 'Imad ud-din, who was under Clark's direct tutelage at Amritsar, had been ordained too early to benefit from enrollment in French's new theological college for prospective Indian pastors, which opened in 1870 in Lahore. He did not, therefore, experience the rigor of the divinity school's first syllabus. Although the lectures were in Urdu, students read the Old Testament in Hebrew and the New in Greek, as well as having lectures on the Greek and Latin Fathers. Yet French soon turned to him for advice concerning the college courses, during a period when the majority of the divinity students happened to be converts from Islam.[46] The depth of the "brotherhood" that then developed between them was demonstrated when, on his final departure from Lahore in 1888, French invited 'Imad ud-din to spend a week in meditation with him in an isolated hut on the banks of the river Beas. Their approaches to the evangelization of Muslims were initially very different, for French had long abandoned the "controversial" methods favored by his Agra partner, Pfander, whose mantle 'Imad ud-din at first chose to adopt. Yet French's personal influence seems to have run very deep and was probably an important factor in 'Imad ud-din's decision to abandon controversial methods in the early 1870s in order to take up evangelistic work in a mode more akin to that favored by French himself.[47] 'Imad ud-din reported this resolve very decisively: "For eight years I have been engaged in laying before Mohammedans their sad condition . . . but now I wish to devote the rest of my days in showing them the mercies of God; that is, I wish to show them the excellency of the holy teaching of the Gospels, their mysteries, and the hidden treasures which Christ has revealed to his faithful servants."[48] At almost the same date French

45. 'Imad ud-din certainly knew French by sight, although his memory when reminiscing in old age was vague on the precise chronology of the relationship (e.g., Rev. Herbert Birks, *The Life and Correspondence of Thomas Valpy French: First Bishop of Lahore*, 2 vols. [London, 1895], 2:111).

46. T. V. French, journal, 14 November 1870, in Birks, *Life*, 1:218.

47. French of 'Imad ud-din: "We seem quite brothers," 22 December 1887, in Birks, *Life*, 2:117.

48. 'Imad ud-din, annual report on Amritsar, *Proceedings of the CMS for 1872-73* (London, n.d.), pp. 85-86.

was urging, in a conference paper on "preaching to Muhammadans," the abandonment of "the arena of logic, metaphysics etc," appealing instead for "works of a less controversial and more devotional and spiritual cast" that should be preached by a "class of native Evangelists, Christian Yogees."[49] He clearly envisaged his *murid*, 'Imad ud-din, as one such "Christian yogi."

However, when 'Imad ud-din was first thrust into bazaar preaching and tract publishing in 1866 without any formal training in Christian theology, it was Karl Pfander's methodology and emphases that he adopted both in his enthusiasm for public debating with Muslim leaders and in his stream of publications on both "controversial" and expository themes. The German Pietist Karl Pfander's *Mizan al-Haqq* [Balance of Truth] was regarded throughout the nineteenth century and continues to be considered more than a century later as the classic exposition of Evangelical Christianity for Muslims.[50] 'Imad ud-din had been part of a circle of *'ulama* who, in Agra in the early 1850s, had attempted its refutation, in the course of which several books had been published in Urdu that became as important to Muslim apologetics throughout the Islamic world as the *Mizan* was to Evangelical apologetic. Having come full circle in his own religious evolution, from preacher of Islam to preacher of Christianity, 'Imad ud-din chose to draw on the *Mizan al-Haqq* very extensively when commencing his own Christian mission in the mid-1860s. This is demonstrated most fully in his *Tahqiq al-Iman* [Investigation of the Faith], which he published in 1869, soon after his ordination, in order to vindicate a change of faith that was being scorned as apostasy by his erstwhile colleagues among the *'ulama* class.[51] The greater part of the *Tahqiq* was thus concerned with many of the "controversial" issues that had been characteristic of much Western writing on Islam from earliest times. These included criticism of the character of Muhammad and attempts to disprove his claim to prophethood. The final section of the *Tahqiq*, in which he turned to "a discussion of the Christian religion," provides a basis, in the early stages of his own writing, for assessing his relationship to the evangelicalism of his Western mentors, notably to that of Pfander and French.

---

49. *Report of the General Missionary Conference, Held at Allahabad, 1872-73* (London, 1873), pp. 58-64.

50. Written in German in Armenia in 1829 and first published in Persian in 1835. The first Urdu edition was published in Mirzapur in 1843. There have been many subsequent editions in most of the languages of the Muslim world. It was reprinted and published again in Arabic and English in Germany in the 1980s. See Powell, *Muslims*, pp. 139-42; 296-8.

51. *Tahqiq al-Iman*, 2nd ed. (Allahabad, 1870); 4th ed. (Lahore, n.d).

The Message

His appeal in the *Tahqiq,* as in much of his street preaching, sermonizing, and tract writing, was, like Pfander's, to Christianity as the fulfillment of human "spiritual needs." The Bible "reveals the secrets of the heart" (a favorite phrase of his) and "changes the heart of man," transforming him into a pure and humble person. Many of his other tracts and sermons have the same emphasis. Like Pfander, 'Imad ud-din represented those who had not yet recognized the gravity of their plight as living in "dense darkness."[52] Christianity alone is capable of bestowing "spiritual life" on man and leading him out of his state of darkness. Although such desperate "need" must first be acknowledged by the individual, its fulfillment is then entirely within God's gift: "I believe that to obtain, or even to increase, spiritual life is not within the scope of man's effort, either for himself or for his friend. It is the work of the most High God. He puts this life into men. He nourishes it and makes it grow. Its existence and development is of His power and will."[53]

Throughout his writings he emphasized that spiritual fulfillment can only be realized through acceptance that God sent Christ to save mankind. Thus, "the spiritual life exists and increases by that power and energy, which comes forth from Christ the Lord, and which works in and upon our souls."[54]

Knowledge of fulfillment and salvation by this means, and proof of its power, 'Imad ud-din constantly reminded his readers and hearers, were to be found only in the Bible. This one-time *maulwi,* a former spokesman for those *'ulama* who had led the charge of *tahrif* ("corruption" of the text of the Bible) against Pfander and French, had been completely transformed through his own conversion into an upholder of the inspiration of every verse of every book of both testaments of the Bible. Although such a complete *volte face* may seem surprising, it was one experienced by most of the handful of scholarly Muslims who made the same leap of faith from Islam to Christianity. Seemingly there was at this stage no *serai,* or resting-house, en route to a full and unequivocal acceptance of the literal authority of the text they had once scorned. 'Imad ud-

52. 'Imad ud-din, paper in panel "Preaching to Muhammadans," *Report of Conference, Held at Allahabad, 1872-73* (Allahabad, 1873), p. 52.

53. 'Imad ud-din, paper read to Punjab Native Church Council, December 1879, on "The best means of deepening the spiritual life of the Church." Cited in Robert Clark, *A Brief Account of Thirty Years of Missionary Work of the Church Missionary Society in the Punjab and Sindh: 1852 to 1882* (Lahore, 1883), pp. 191-92. Translated by 'Imad ud-din's friend, C. J. Rodgers.

54. 'Imad ud-din, paper read to Punjab Native Church Council, December 1879, on "The best means of deepening the spiritual life of the Church." Cited in Clark, *Brief Account,* pp. 191-92.

din's mentors among the Punjab missionaries would have certainly reinforced his newly adopted certainty that the "word" of the Urdu Bible then circulating in northwest India was indeed the "Word of God" on which his own faith now rested. For with the exception of French, who from his Oxford student days had been open to the work of the "milder" biblical critics, most of the Punjab missionaries chose to ignore or reject the findings of "Higher Criticism." Among the American Presbyterians, notably Charles Forman, ideas about the Bible were formed by the theological teaching of their own Princeton educations. The received teaching of the Bible was not open to question, derived as it was held to be "from an infallible scripture which provided the divine standard according to which all truth must be judged."[55] This theological standpoint, John Webster has shown, remained dominant among missionaries appointed to North India until at least the 1890s.[56] Many of the German and British missionaries of the CMS missions in the region were equally staunch supporters of the plenary inspiration of very word of the Bible.[57] 'Imad ud-din's closeness to the more theologically liberal Thomas French may have occasioned some questioning of the received wisdom, but, if so, this did not intrude into his public utterances. Consequently, his tracts and sermons for Indian Christians were always centered on exposition and proof from specific passages of both testaments. 'Imad ud-din first followed, and then sublimated, the preferred practices of his local mentors. *Manana?* [Who am I?], based on Matthew 16:13, and *Khun Se Mu'afi* [Atonement through Blood], based on Exodus 12, were both written in the mid-1870s after he had abandoned controversial methods in favor of demonstrating instead "the excellence of the holy teaching of the Gospels." They exemplify his particular mode of detailed textual exposition. The attention he began to pay at this time also to a genre of composition with which he had earlier experimented, the biblical *tafsir,* or commentary, confirms his resolution to make the "Word" of revelation more accessible to relatively poorly educated Urdu-reading converts to Christianity.[58] Other projects he embarked

---

55. Webster, *Christian Community,* pp. 30-40.

56. Webster, *Christian Community,* pp. 32-36.

57. For Anglican attitudes in Britain, see Richard Fox Young, "Revelation in Hinduism and the Rise of Heretical Views about Biblical Inspiration among mid-Victorian Broad Churchmen," in *Zeitschrift für Missionswissenschaft und Religionswissenschaft,* 67 (1983): 237-45, 296-305.

58. He contributed to four commentaries: *Tafsir-i Mukashafat* [Revelation of St. John] (Lahore, 1870), based on E. B. Elliott's *Horae Apokalypticae; Khazanah al-Asrar: Injil-i Matti Ki Tafsir* [Treasury of Secrets: Commentary on St. Matthew's Gospel] (Lahore, 1875); *Tafsir-i Kitab-i 'Amal* [Commentary on the Book of Acts] (Punjab Committee of SPCK, 1879). The fourth was on the Pentateuch.

on, which show a similar concern with detailed biblical interpretation, include his *Lughat al-Kalam* [Biblical Dictionary, ca. 1888], and his *Kawaif al-Sahaif* [Companion to All the Books of the Bible, ca. 1885].

'Imad ud-din's purpose in emphasizing the teachings of both Testaments was to convey certain doctrinal essentials, acceptance of which he believed was necessary before the spiritual truths of Christianity could be opened up to any seeker. The first of these was belief in Christ's sonship and divinity, historically the main obstacle to Muslim comprehension of Christianity. According to 'Imad ud-din's credo, the nature of the godhead was to be accepted, as urged by Pfander, simply as one of the divine mysteries *(asrar)*, inexplicable by, but not in conflict with, man's reason. Thus, "the eye of his [a Christian's] soul should rest all his days upon his Saviour. He should fix his attention on that inexhaustible spring of perfection, the mystery God manifest in the flesh."[59] The process of salvation through Christ's mediational atonement for the sins of all mankind was thus a main theme of several of his tracts and sermons for both Christian and Muslim readers. In the first two tracts of his *Haqiqi-'irfan* series, written very soon after his own ordination, he explained the Christian understanding of Adam's sin, its consequences for the rest of mankind, and Christ's incarnation and crucifixion as the "second Adam." *Manana?* a sermon on Christ's question to his disciples shortly before the Crucifixion, consisted of a detailed exposition of Jesus' identity as "the Christ, the son of the living God," in fulfillment of Old Testament prophecies of the Messiah. The problematic first verse of Psalm 110, which had earlier caused the Agra *'ulama* to scoff at Pfander, he expounded here as the key to the understanding of Christ's two natures, divine but also human.[60] In further tracts he explained other aspects of the Christian understanding of salvation that converts from Islam always found particularly difficult: notably, in *Khun Se Mu'afi*, the necessity for atonement through the sacrifice of the incarnate Christ. The imminence of the final resurrection of the souls of all believers (which he urged in *Asar-i Qiyamat* [Signs of the Resurrection]), made possible through Christ's atonement for men's sins, he also based on the fulfillment of biblical signs. The doctrine of the Trinity *(taslis)*, perceived in Islam as *shirk* (association in the godhead), and therefore decried as heresy by all Muslims, he did not attempt to prove from the Bible as some of his prede-

59. "'Imad ud-din to Punjab Native Church Council, December, 1879," in Clark, *Brief Account,* p. 193.

60. He recounted the Jews' answer to "Whose son is Christ?" (Matt. 22:24): "He is Daud's (David's) son," based on Psalm 132:11, to which Jesus had replied citing Psalm 110:1: "The Lord said unto my Lord, sit thou at my right hand, until I make thine enemies thy footstool." *Manana?* pp. 19-22.

cessors, including Pfander, had done. This ultimately most difficult doctrinal belief he presented simply as a divine mystery, essential to the unfolding of the Christian salvation process. If inexplicable in terms comprehensible to man, it was no more irrational, he suggested, than Muslim adherence to the "necessity" of *wahadat* (divine unity). His critique of what he considered to result in the captivity of many Muslims by "rationalist" apologetics will be considered below in the context of "Islamic Modernism."

Apart from the seemingly intractable problem of explaining the Trinity, 'Imad ud-din found the text of the Bible to constitute the sufficient and essential basis for the acceptance of all other Christian doctrines. His mode of explanation of spiritual truth included constant recourse to citation of examples of miracles and prophecies from both Testaments. Three of the twelve monthly tracts that constituted his *Haqiqi-'irfan* series consisted of lists of prophecies from the Old Testament and of miracles from the New. The *Asar-i Qiyamat* pointed out "signs" of the coming resurrection of souls, which were based on biblical prophecies. Such emphases seem to reflect a number of unrelated influences. First, as John Webster has shown, Protestant theology had retained, alongside a new emphasis on spiritual criteria, a strong reliance, favored particularly in the eighteenth century, on "evidential" proofs of the truth of Christianity.[61] The theological teaching imbibed in the early nineteenth century by Scottish evangelicals similarly bore the mark of post-Enlightenment "arguments from reason" alongside new revivalist, more fully spiritual imperatives.[62] Among Anglican and German Pietist missionaries in North India too, evidential arguments maintained a subsidiary role throughout the nineteenth century. Thus Henry Martyn and Karl Pfander both chose to place the occurrence of miracles and fulfillment of prophecies high in their lists of "tests of truth."[63] William Paley's works on Christian "evidences," available in various Urdu translations by the time of 'Imad ud-din's conversion, were drawn on widely by many missionaries.[64] 'Imad ud-din's exposition remained firmly within this post-Enlightenment tradition of "evidences." He was probably also influenced by the place such arguments had taken in debates between Muslims and Christians, in which apologists on both sides had asserted the "superiority" of particular claims to agency in the performing of miracles or in the fulfilment of prophecies. When he turned, in

61. Webster, *Christian Community*, p. 31.

62. For some Hindu responses to the Scot John Muir's proffering of arguments from miracles see Fox Young, "Revelation," pp. 296-99.

63. Powell, *Muslims*, pp. 89-90, 140-41.

64. E.g., Sayyid Kamal al-din Haidar, trans., *Marifat-i Tabi'i* (Delhi, 1848), a translation of Paley's *Natural Theology*.

the 1870s, from debating with Muslims to writing for Indian Christians, the evidential strand remained very prominent in 'Imad ud-din's exhortations. His particular emphasis on biblical prophecies also reflected his preoccupation, already noticed above, with a conviction that the spread of the gospel to the Punjab, and to India generally, presaged the fulfillment of "signs" that the whole world was about to turn to Christianity in anticipation of the apocalypse. His commentary on Revelations and his tract on the "signs of the Resurrection" convey, in particular, his sense of the urgency of this message.

In his pastoral role among Indian Christians, during more than thirty years at the CMS church in the old city of Amritsar, and as an itinerant evangelist, 'Imad ud-din reinforced the lifestyle incumbent on those seeking to follow the "spiritual life" he had delineated in his tracts. The thrust of his preaching was to read the Bible, to recognize shortcomings in the spiritual life, to repent, and to seek the certainty of obtaining eternal life through demonstrating faith in the "living Christ." The rituals and practices of the low Anglican Church into which he had been ordained he emphasized as necessary observances, stressing, particularly, conformity to Anglican notions of the keeping of the "Lord's Day."[65] Yet he also urged Indian Christians to find time for the periods of private prayer and meditation during which he himself sought the invigoration of a faith that never seemed to waver once he was baptized. We turn now to consider the relationship between his meditative devotions as a Christian and his prebaptismal initiation into, and struggle with, Islamic mysticism.

Christianity and Islamic Mysticism

The perceptions of Christianity put forward by Indians who were formerly Hindus has shown both the extent of "Sanskritic captivity," or appropriation, among intellectual theologians and the preference of some very influential individuals for *sannyasi* modes of being Christian. If there is a parallel to the latter to be found among converts from Islam it might be sought in influences from Islamic mysticism and from Sufi modes of expression and practice. The only widely known example of an experience of this kind among North Indian Muslims is John Subhan's long journey from discipleship within the Qadari order of Sufis during his boyhood in Calcutta to his teaching role, first

65. Paper on "Lord's Day Observance," given to 8th annual meeting of the Punjab Native Church Council, 28-29 December 1884 (*Proceedings of the CMS for 1883-84* [London, n.d.], p. 110).

among Roman Catholics in Agra, and later in the Methodist Church of North India and the Henry Martyn School of Islamics in Lahore, where in the 1920s and 1930s he explained Sufism to Christian readers with the benefit of his former "insider" perspective as a Qadiri Sufi.[66] 'Imad ud-din's history suggests that he had been in a position to have been an earlier transmitter of such insights, for, like many other Sunni Muslims in North India, he had combined close adherence to the legal requirements of the *shari'at* with initiation into a number of Sufi orders. He had close links with Sufi circles both in his hometown of Panipat and, during his student days, in Agra. He was particularly attached to the followers of Shaikh Bu 'Ali Qalandar in Panipat[67] and to the *dargah* in Delhi of the great Chisti saint, Nizam al-din Auliya. He often visited the Chisti shrine at Fatehpur Sikri, near Agra. In his autobiographical accounts he described the anguish of his efforts to find a *shaikh,* no matter where, whose path would offer him full spiritual satisfaction. To this end he had moved gradually from the formal Sufi orders, such as the Chistis, to increasingly esoteric forms of physical and mental meditative practice. After he had abandoned Islam, he described his long sojourn with mystics whose "esoteric science," as he termed it, he endeavored to imbibe:

> I meditated and practised abstinence. I performed *dhikr* loudly and silently. I sat in seclusion with closed eyes and mentally began to write the word "Allah" on my heart. While at the graves of the saints I meditated, hoping for illumination from their graves. I attended the Sufi assemblies, confidently gazing upon the faces of the Sufis, anticipating a flow of light from their direction. Through their intercession I constantly besought union with God.[68]

He finally abandoned the mosques and *khanqahs* of his youth to seek his goal among faqirs meditating in the forest and desert regions of northwest India. He placed his reliance on one particular guide who gave him a book whose teachings promised that "the outcome of this [pathway] is union with God." The guide warned him, he said, "tell no one its secret. It contains every eternal

66. John Subhan, *Sufism: Its Saints and Shrines* (Lucknow, 1938); idem, *How a Sufi Found His Lord: An Autobiography of the Rev. John A. Subhan of the Henry Martyn School* (Lucknow, ca. 1942).

67. Sharif al-din Bu 'Ali Qalandar (d. 1324) was a Chisti initiate who left the order to seek God through ascetic discipline. He was initiated into the Qalandari order, his own teachings passing down through his letters to a disciple. His *urs* draws a strong popular following in Panipat and Karnal. See Subhan, *Sufism,* pp. 312-14.

68. Subhan, *Sufism,* pp. 5-6.

bliss." He followed its instructions, treasuring it so much that "while on my travels I slept during the night with it close at hand and whenever I felt ill at ease, I clasped it to my breast to pacify my heart."[69] After his baptism 'Imad ud-din related to Christian audiences the state of mental and physical collapse that followed years in such lonely practices, his total state of despair, and his settling in Lahore. Among the Indian Christian community in the Punjab in the late nineteenth century, he was probably the only former Muslim who had traveled such distances, both in the company of initiates into the Chisti and other orders, and with wandering *qalandars*. His friend and fellow convert, Maulawi Safdar 'Ali, confirmed that during this time 'Imad ud-din had reached "the state of *Sukr*" ("intoxication") in which he became "beside himself, because of the contemplation of God, lost in meditation."[70] Such accounts suggest that after baptism 'Imad ud-din's forms of Christian witness would probably reflect some of the meditative modes of this long period of spiritual struggle.

On the contrary, 'Imad ud-din seems to have reacted very strongly against all Sufi modes of devotion once he had accepted Christianity. Some of his writings suggest he was even more disparaging of the Sufi masters whom he considered to be "ignorant" and "unscrupulous" than were most foreign missionaries. As late as the Edinburgh Conference of 1910 some missionaries continued to regard Sufis simply as pantheists, often as charlatans.[71] Among the few early-nineteenth-century Evangelicals who had made any study of Islam through close contact with Muslims, only Henry Martyn seems to have been interested in understanding and explaining differences between Sufi and Christian paths towards spiritual knowledge.[72] By the time of 'Imad ud-din's baptism, however, some missionaries in other regions of India, particularly those working among Hindus, were becoming sensitive to possible parallels between the nature of *bhakti* devotionalism and the "working of the Spirit" in Christian devotionalism.[73] Some missionaries in the Punjab were also beginning to urge that attention should be paid to Sufis who, they felt, would be more open to evangelism than other Muslims. French, indeed, urged the Allahabad Conference of 1872-73 to nurture "a class of native Evangelists,

---

69. Subhan, *Sufism*, p. 7.

70. Safdar 'Ali, review article, published in *CMI* (August 1898), p. 598.

71. Chapter on Islam, "Report of Commission IV: The missionary message in relation to non-Christian religions, World Missionary Conference, 1910," Edinburgh, London, and New York, n.d), pp. 124, 146.

72. Henry Martyn, "Third Tract on the Vanity of the Sofee System, and on the Truth of the Religion of Moses and Jesus."

73. See Boyd, "Christianity as Bhakti Marga," in *Introduction*, pp. 110-18.

Christian Yogees of a type and stamp as yet almost unprecedented" for the task of preaching to Muslims.[74] He reminded his audience of Sufi responsiveness to Henry Martyn in Shiraz more than sixty years earlier. 'Imad ud-din's school friend and fellow convert, Maulwi Safdar 'Ali, read a paper at the same conference, in which he identified "certain sects among the Muhammadans, which are known as Sufis, Mashaikhs, Faqirs and Darwishes," living in many parts of India, to whom "our efforts should be directed."[75] There were numerous such communities of Sufis in the Punjab, he said, particularly in the western districts. Safdar 'Ali then gave an account of extreme Sufi austerities in terms remarkably similar to 'Imad ud-din's representation of his own period of meditation in the jungles. Their so-far unsatisfied spiritual longings, Safdar 'Ali suggested, made Sufis ready to listen to the gospel, for God has "in his wondrous wisdom caused very much of his Holy Law to reach them, and produced in their hearts a constant and deep conviction of sin and ignorance." Mian Sadiq Masih, 'Imad ud-din's colleague in the Punjab Mission, also an ordained convert from Islam, reported a few years later that the engrafting of Christianity onto a Sufi root was currently taking place in a village near Amritsar where the lifestyle of some "Christian faqirs" was proving, he found, an "excellent influence" on others.[76]

Yet 'Imad ud-din's own paper to the Allahabad Conference betrayed no hint of French and Safdar 'Ali's sense of Sufi commonality with Christian devotionalism. The little he did write on Sufism after his baptism tended to be unsympathetic in tone. In his many accounts of his prebaptismal spiritual struggles he referred to the efforts of some former Sufi friends to "entrap" him in the esoteric form of knowledge known as *tasawwuf* (mysticism). The *Taftish al-Auliya*, on "the origin of Sufi saints," which he wrote near the end of his life, was an examination of various facets of Sufi history and current practice.[77] It was later deemed by H. U. Weitbrecht, a missionary colleague, to be "an interesting work, useful for those who have to deal with Sufis."[78] It was, however, extremely unsympathetic to the current preoccupations of the various Sufi *khanaqas* and their *pirs* in northern India, asserting among many points of criticism that mysticism originated in the Vedas, not in the Qur'an, and that those who practiced *tasawwuf* were *mulhids* (heretics), not Mus-

74. T. V. French, in panel "Preaching to Muhammadans," p. 64.
75. Safdar Ali, in panel, "Preaching to Muhammadans," pp. 56-57.
76. 'Imad ud-din, annual report on Amritsar, *Proceedings of the CMS for 1880-81* (London, n.d.), pp. 86-87.
77. 'Imad ud-din, *Kitab Taftish al-Auliya* (Religious Book Society, 1889). I am grateful to Tim Green and John Wooley for help in obtaining this rare tract.
78. For Weitbrecht's review see, *Descriptive Catalogue* (1902), pp. xiv, 70.

lims.[79] In spite of his dismissal of mysticism as un-Islamic, however, 'Imad ud-din made a strong distinction between the first generations of Sufis who settled in North India in the time of Shaikh Muin al-din Chisti, whose books he acknowledged "do contain some things which are truly spiritual," and the later and contemporary Sufi *tariqahs,* which he felt had entirely lost any "true" spirituality.[80] "Nowadays," he affirmed, "they are only sufi in name," a view he supported with accounts of saint worship at the tombs of *pirs,* and *pirzadas* who had become as worldly as *jagirdars* and *zamindars.*[81] In an earlier account he had also conceded that Sufism "had its origin in the spiritual aspirations of Mohamedans of bygone days who were really seekers after truth," but not so the Sufi "deceivers" of his own day, he insisted, whose enticements could only result in "calamity."[82] The stressing of contrasts between earlier ages of genuine spiritual inquiry and a present age of alleged religious charlatanism was characteristic of the writings of other religious reformers, both Hindu and Muslim, who, like Ram Mohan Roy, perceived the accretions of subsequent ages to result in the contamination of pristine concepts and impulses. 'Imad ud-din thus concluded that Sufism in its present deceptive forms had nothing to offer the contemporary inquirer. Far from accepting any influences, or seeking to "engraft" Christian devotionalism onto a Sufi root, in the manner of Sadhu Sundar Singh's later inculturation of his Christian beliefs, 'Imad ud-din denied any validity to non-Christian mystic paths. His purpose in continuing to examine and explain particular movements, both old and new, within Islam, whether mystical or rationalist, was merely to inform other Christians about them, the better to resist any superficial attraction they might present.

In spite of these strong disavowals, some latent Sufistic assumptions no doubt affected, at least at a subconscious level, the ways in which he chose to present the gospel. For example, when faced with the difficult problem of explaining how a man might become one of the "sons of god" through the coming of the Holy Spirit, he drew on both Sufi terminology and personal experience, explaining that after a long process of self-denial, patient suffering, and good works, "evil begins to leave that man," so that his soul "becomes fenced in the habitation of divine radiance: then the eyes of his mind are opened;

79. See 'Imad ud-din, *Kitab Taftish al-Auliya,* pp. 1-13, 160-64.

80. The views expresssed in the *Kitab Taftish al-Auliya* reinforce the disparagement of Sufism expressed in his autobiography over twenty years earlier. Hahn, *Life,* p. 5; compare with John Subhan's much more sympathetic perceptions of the state of Indian Sufism in the 1930s, in *Saints,* p. 5, passim.

81. 'Imad ud-din, *Kitab Taftish al-Auliya,* pp. 161-62.

82. Hahn, *Life,* p. 5.

then with his spiritual eyes, with the aid of the Divine Word, he begins to see something of his own inner faults, of God's holiness, of the instability of this world, and the worth and value of the world to come, and his true discernment begins to be enlightened."[83]

Such language can, of course, be found in the Gospels, and in Patristic sources, without necessarily supposing any Sufistic vestiges, yet 'Imad ud-din's particular rapport with Indian inquirers seems to have owed part of its success to his instinct for couching mystical and abstract concepts in appropriate Urdu forms. His repeated robust denials of his own prebaptismal spiritual quest nevertheless distinguish 'Imad ud-din's quest very strongly from Sundar Singh's quest to inculturate the Christian message into indigenous forms of devotionalism, and from the empathy later shown by John Subhan for the Islamic mysticism of his own prebaptismal stage.

'Imad ud-din's Views on the Relations between "Revelation and Reason" in the Context of the "New Islam"

'Imad ud-din kept a watchful, if critical, eye on all movements within Sunni Islam in the Punjab and its neighboring provinces. A fellow missionary, E. M. Wherry, commented shortly after 'Imad ud-din's death that he was "a progressive student of all the religious movements in India and especially of those among his former co-religionists."[84] 'Imad ud-din's views on one of the most influential of those new movements will be considered here in order to test how far he had moved over the years in his critique of the use of reason as a proof or buttress of truth, and to assess the store that he finally set on the Bible, in contrast to the Qur'an, as a corpus of uniquely revealed truth.

The emergence, in the vicinity of his own missionary station very soon after his own baptism and ordination, of a number of movements within Islam that he deemed to be "rationalist" made for some very polarizing interchanges. Accounts of these help to sharpen any conclusions that may be drawn on 'Imad ud-din's relations with his former co-religionists. The most significant new movement was the emergence from among the scholarly circles of northwest India of a Muslim government servant who was ready to make his own judgments on the sources both of Islam and of Christianity. Sayyid Ahmad Khan's commentaries on the Bible and the Qur'an antagonized many Sunni

83. 'Imad ud-din, *Haqiqi 'irfan*, tract 2, "Showing how Christians are grafted into Jesus Christ the second Adam," p. 26.
84. Wherry, *Muslim Controversy*, p. 36.

'ulama and were responsible, along with his other writings on religious issues, for the emergence of a new school of interpretation. This was later deemed to have introduced a "modernist" methodology into the study of Islam.

A second movement arose even closer to Imad ud-din's mission station in Amritsar. In the 1880s, Qadiyan, a small town a few miles from Amritsar, became the center of a new movement, initiated by one Mirza Ghulam Ahmad, a local Sunni *'alim.* By the time of 'Imad ud-din's death a decade later, the Ahmadiyya was one of the fastest-growing religious movements in northern India and a local competitor to Christian evangelicalism. This movement, too, 'Imad ud-din criticized for its alleged "rationalist" apologetic. It represented enough of a threat to the prospects of Christian evangelism, he thought, to cause him to engage in debates with its founder and to write a critical tract.[85] His relations with the Ahmadis are important,[86] but discussion here will be limited to his published responses to Sayyid Ahmad Khan's "new rationalism."

'Imad ud-din was certainly in agreement with many contemporary Sunni theologians, as well as with some British observers of the North Indian religious scene, in characterizing Sayyid Ahmad Khan's exposition of Islam as a contrived effort to make revelation conform to human reason or, as he called it, to "simple reason."[87] Yet if Sayyid Ahmad's views on Islam had been disseminated ten or fifteen years earlier, while 'Imad ud-din was still struggling to realign himself within Sunni Islam, he may well have felt some attraction. This possibility was raised by E. M. Wherry in a review of 'Imad ud-din's ensuing critique of Sayyid Ahmad's religious works. "The author tells us," he reported, "that when he first read the statements of Sir Sayud Ahmad he remembered that he had been a Mussalman, and the thought came to him that possibly in leaving Islam he might have misjudged the religion of his fathers."[88]

85. For an analysis of a debate between a Christian convert from Islam and Mirza Ghulam Ahmad, at which 'Imad ud-din was present in his old age, see A. A. Powell, "Contested Gods and Prophets: Discourse among Minorities in Late Nineteenth-Century Punjab," *Renaissance and Modern Studies* 38 (1995): 38-59.

86. 'Imad ud-din was surely mistaken in denouncing, as he did, the Ahmadiyya movement for its alleged rationalism. Its real danger to Evangelical Christianity was rather the Mirza's claim to be the Messiah, Jesus, in his Second Coming, as well as the *mahdi,* thus challenging, or even appearing to "fufill," Christian eschatology. The impact of the Ahmadiyya on 'Imad ud-din's Christology has its own interest, but no copy of his tract on Ahmadi beliefs has as yet been found. The brief comments here rely on E. M. Wherry's detailed summary of its contents (*Muslim Controversy,* pp. 57-66) and on journal reports of his relations with the community.

87. 'Imad ud-din, "Results," p. 3.

88. Wherry, *Muslim Controversy,* p. 40.

That he ultimately harbored no such regrets and continued to write highly critical comments on Sir Sayyid's standpoint reflected more than anything else his distaste, like that of many Sunni critics, for the pragmatic rationalism and secularism that he found in Sayyid Ahmad's understanding of Islam, for, in his view, "the New Islam of Sir Sayud Ahmad Khan is not only not the Islam of the Qur'an, but is a combination of the rationalism of the Brahmo Samaj and the teachings of that secular scholarship, which has always arrayed itself against true religion."[89]

In a report to the CMS 'Imad ud-din explained that he had felt "compelled" to resume the writing of "controversial books," which he had by then gladly abandoned, because of his fear that Sayyid Ahmad's efforts "were becoming a very great obstacle in the way of weaker Christians."[90] In preparation, he set about reading all of Sayyid Ahmad's publications on religion. In the report he drew mainly from only two of these for his own published response, for as soon as the first part of Sayyid Ahmad's own commentary on the Qur'an was published in 1880, 'Imad ud-din started to prepare a critique of the rationalist assumptions that he felt underpinned his Qur'anic exegesis. He responded also to some statements that the Sayyid had made several years before in the first issue of his journal, *Tahzib al-Akhlaq*, concerning the sufficiency of human reason for adjudging truth.[91] He planned twelve tracts but completed only the first four, which, though linked by a common title, *Tanqid al-Khiyalat* or "A Criticism of Thoughts," were published separately during 1882 and 1883. The third and fourth tracts were concerned mainly with contesting Sayyid Ahmad's "thoughts" on revelation and inspiration, but the first two[92] challenged Sayyid Ahmad's views on the sufficiency of human reason to identify truth and the harmony of nature with revealed truth. Many other *'ulama* had already criticized Sir Sayyid on similar grounds, denouncing in particular his view that "the testimony of nature" is sufficient for determining the truth of a "Book of God."[93] They had also scorned the idea that Sayyid Ahmad, a former British government servant, who lacked the formal education of an *'alim*, should pontificate on questions of faith.

Although 'Imad ud-din was always prepared to concede considerable

---

89. Wherry, *Muslim Controversy*, p. 40.

90. Annual report on Amritsar, *Proceedings of the CMS for 1881-82*, p. 99.

91. *Tahzib al-Akhlaq* [Mohammadan Social Reformer] I (1870).

92. Tract 1 of the *Tanqid al-Khiyalat* was subtitled *Aya 'aqal insani ke sawa insan ke lie ko'i aur rahnma bhi hai ya nahin?* [Whether or not there is any other guide for mankind except for reason?]; Tract 2, *Qadim aur jadid Islam* [The old and the new Islam].

93. Sayyid Ahmad Khan to Nithar Ahmad, 1880, as cited in Christian W. Troll, *Sayyid Ahmad Khan: A Reinterpretation of Muslim Theology* (New Delhi, 1978), pp. 296-97.

scope to "reason" in assisting people to decide the practical problems of human existence, he denied it any role in resolving ultimate questions. Among these he listed questions on the creation of the universe, the nature and attributes of God, the identity of the soul, and the character of life after death. On these, he insisted, only God's own revealed "Word" could inform. In his rebuttals of Sayyid Ahmad he was simply redirecting, for a new polemical purpose, the same views he had often expressed about the priority of revelation over reason in his many homiletic tracts written for Indian Christians. The new challenge represented by Sir Sayyid merely drew from him some new formulations of a stance he had consistently upheld throughout his postbaptismal life. He objected, in particular, that allowing unlimited scope to human reason would give free rein to individuals, notably to Sayyid Ahmad, a mere secular scholar, to exercise their own judgments in spheres where even those learned in the religious sciences were out of their depth. "Truth" would be made relative by being left, in Sayyid Ahmad's hands, to the subjective judgment and impaired intellectual capacity of mere human beings.

'Imad ud-din was clearly concerned that the plausible case put forward by the Sayyid, which was proving attractive to the youth of the Muslim service class, might also appeal to some Muslims who might otherwise have been drawn to Christianity. He ignored any mention of the conciliatory steps Sayyid Ahmad had recently been taking toward Christian teaching, which were at the time being noticed with interest and considerable approbation and optimism by some of his Western observers. In his *Commentary on the Holy Bible,* for example, Sayyid Ahmad had disputed the claim of many Indian *'ulama,* that the Bible had suffered textual "corruption." Rather, he supported the much more conciliatory view that some Jews and Christians had unwittingly altered some of the meanings of the text merely in the process of recitation. Clearly the conciliatory tone of Sayyid Ahmad was inconvenient to 'Imad ud-din. He chose to emphasize instead that, far from "repairing" or "restoring" the "old building" of Islam, the Sayyid was building a completely new edifice on a basis of pragmatic rationalism. In his view, the "new Islam" of the modernists was entirely different from the "old." As it was based on new foundations, it was no longer "Islam," and neither Muslims nor Christians should pay any heed to the Sayyid's religious teachings.[94]

In spite of his efforts, 'Imad ud-din's tracts on Sayyid Ahmad's theology seem to have made little impact in Muslim circles. They triggered no replies either from the Sayyid or from others. They serve nevertheless the purposes

---

94. 'Imad ud-din, "Results," p. 3. There is some evidence, however, that 'Imad ud-din appreciated Sayyid Ahmad's educational agenda (*Mohammedan Converts,* p. 10).

of this study as they reinforce some of the conclusions drawn from his other tracts on specific Christian teachings: his firm rejection of the Sayyid's rational readings from "nature," reiterated in this new context that the ground of his own faith in Christianity was his confidence in the Word of God revealed in Scripture, to the understanding of which human reason was entirely subordinate.

Conclusion

During the second half of the nineteenth century a dominant concern of missionary conferences was how to acquire and train a "native agency" that would be more successful than the foreign missionaries had so far proved in achieving an effective rapport with potential converts. 'Imad ud-din was extolled throughout his long ministry and after his death as the model, *par excellence,* of just such a successful "native agent." He maintained the physical appearance of a *maulwi* and was addressed as such. He always spoke and wrote in Urdu and chose to live within the old city of Amritsar, in close touch with his Christian congregation, but also with non-Christians of all communities. He maintained that it was possible and appropriate to follow indigenous customs without jeopardizing the Christian message, and he was criticized by some missionaries for keeping his own wife, also a convert, in *parda.* His role within the organization of the native church was strenuous and multifaceted, including ministry to the Amritsar congregation, itinerant evangelism, and representation and leadership through the Punjab Native Church Council. He and others considered that his outstanding legacy to the nascent Punjab church would prove to be his writings, "constructive as well as destructive," for which he received in 1884 the first Lambeth doctorate in divinity to be awarded to an Indian convert. The annual reports of the CMS Mission in the Punjab described him proudly as a "lecturer and writer on theological subjects."[95] On his death a colleague commented that he "left a mass of material which will be more and more valuable as time goes on."

The verdict of history is rather more complex. The expansion in the numbers of converts during the late nineteenth-century phase of "mass movements" in the Punjab occurred not in the urban bazaars where 'Imad ud-din debated and preached, but in villages on the periphery of the province where his Urdu tracts must have remained unread by the mainly illiterate low castes and outcastes who sought baptism. By the second decade of the twentieth

95. *Proceedings of the CMS for 1881-82,* p. 95.

century his particular emphases in preaching and writing would no longer be so favored by his missionary successors in a new climate in which Christians sought complementarity and points of contact between Christianity and other religions, rather than 'Imad ud-din's first mode of interchange, through controversy, or his second, through stress on the uniqueness of the Christian revelation as conveyed in the "Word" of the Bible.

Where then should the evangelism of this "pillar" of Christianity in the Punjab be placed on the spectrum of modes of interchange ranging from various degrees of acculturation to complete inculturation of the Christian message? How useful in assessing this is the concept of "captivity" by either the theological understandings and methods of his Western mentors or his own notion of his youthful "entrapment" within, but subsequent escape from, both scholastic and mystical modes of understanding and practicing Islam? The preceding discussion suggests that the answers will remain equivocal in the case of 'Imad ud-din. In spite of the evidence of indigenization noted above, particularly in his successful transposition of the Gospels into Urdu, the messages thereby transmitted have been shown to be those preached by the first generation of European evangelists in northwest India, without any concessions to more recent biblical scholarship. If he was affected over time by his contacts with Bishop Thomas French, he had already been molded theologically by his reading of Karl Pfander, whose precritical stance he adhered to resolutely. In spite of his own long journey along various Sufi paths, 'Imad ud-din claimed to owe very little to his Islamic past. In moving from a dogmatic understanding of the Qur'an to an equally literalist adherence to the "Word" of the Bible, little place was left for any vestigial sympathy for his former creed, which he now perceived as a pathway on which any seeker must forever remain lost in darkness. The historical sequence of the Christian and Islamic revelations of course render illogical the kind of "fulfillment" relationship through which K. M. Banerjea was suggesting a new positive relationship between Christianity and the Vedic legacy, through the continuity of the principle of sacrifice. Thus, shortly after 'Imad ud-din's death, a missionary Islamicist would question rhetorically, "How can that which denies the whole essential and particular content of the message be said to prepare for Him?"[96] Though retaining as much of the lifestyle of an Indian Muslim as he deemed consistent with the profession of Christianity, 'Imad ud-din firmly rejected any support from the Islamic message. He rejected even the one dimension of the two faiths that others deemed a possible pathway to a more positive relationship, that of mystical devotion. The reason may lie in the

96. W. H. T. Gairdner, *The Reproach of Islam* (London, 1909), p. 311.

depth of his personal disillusion with all forms of Islamic mysticism after a decade spent in vainly trying to find spiritual satisfaction within the parameters of Sufism. If he rejected his own Sufi heritage, he also rejected the attempts, which began partway through his Christian ministry, of Muslims to come to terms with both modern science and Christianity through the rationalist and conciliatory routes proposed by Sir Sayyid Ahmad Khan. 'Imad ud-din, in responding to Sir Sayyid, chose to stress the differences, not the common ground, between the Islamic and Christian concepts of the relation between revelation and reason in respect to their conformity to evidences displayed in "nature."

In a tribute to 'Imad ud-din some fifty years after his death, the historian of the Punjab Religious Book Society, which had published many of his tracts, attributed to him the fulfillment of a wish to channel "the water of Life, but not in your Western pan," through his contribution to the dissemination of Christian literature in the Urdu language.[97] This was the self-same metaphor that had also been attributed to Sadhu Sundar Singh, expressed by him as "Indians do need the Water of Life, but not in the European cup."[98] These two Punjabi Christians, 'Imad ud-din and Sundar Singh, no doubt perceived their roles as evangelists in very different ways. The *sannyasin* singing devotional songs to Christ in the mountains of Tibet, where Sundar Singh died a mysterious death in the late 1920s, is much the more remembered in the Punjab today. Yet, 'Imad ud-din, certainly a "pillar" of his new community, had gained by more conventional missionary means a considerable local reputation during his own lifetime as one of the "chosen vessels"[99] for the transmission of the Christian message in his Punjab homeland.

97. *A Short History of the Punjab Religious Book Society*, p. 7.
98. Cited in Sugirtharajah and Hargreaves, *Readings*, p. 76.
99. The metaphor of Rajaiah D. Paul's *Chosen Vessels: Lives of Ten Indian Christian Pastors of the Eighteenth and Nineteenth Centuries* (Serampore, 1961).

CHAPTER TEN

Missionaries and Print Culture in Nineteenth-Century Assam: *The* Orunodoi *Periodical of the American Baptist Mission*

JAYEETA SHARMA

"A monthly Paper, devoted to Religion, Science, and General Knowledge." That was what the *Orunodoi* declared itself to be, the agency through which the American Baptist Mission would deliver components of "enlightenment" to the population of Assam, as monthly installments in print in their own language. The *Orunodoi* was the most prominent product of the first printing press established in Assam,[1] the American Mission Press, from 1846-80. Almost a century after its inception, a contributor to a contemporary Assamese journal remarked that local villagers were still in the habit of referring to any periodical paper that they came across by what they regarded as its generic name — an "Orunodoi."[2]

The proposition that the American Baptists should venture into a new frontier in northeast India had been initially mooted by East India Company officials who, ever since its annexation in 1826, had been attempting to bring

1. "Assam" here refers to the northeastern part of the Indian subcontinent, which had come under British rule from 1826 onward and encompasses the present-day states of Assam, Meghalaya, Nagaland, and Mizoram in the Indian Union. "Assam Valley" is the term commonly used in the missionary papers of the period and refers to the Brahmaputra valley in the present-day state of Assam. The Naga hills district in British Assam is the modern state of Nagaland.

2. Jnandabhiram Barua, *Those Bygone Days* (Awahon, 1929). (Incidentally, the writer's father, Gunabhiram Barua, and his uncle Anandaram Dhekial Phukan had been two of the most significant indigenous contributors to, and supporters of, the *Orunodoi*.)

order to this region that had a huge diversity of ethnic groups at different stages of technology and culture. The administrators' invitation to missionaries, initially addressed to the Serampore Baptists and passed on by them to their American counterparts, was testimony to their hope that they would buttress the efforts of the handful of colonial administrators in "elevating the character of the people" of this new territory.[3] The American Baptists, however, initially regarded their Assam field as a foothold enabling further penetration into previously inaccessible parts of Southeast and Central Asia, which lay beyond the mountainous boundaries of this region. The people of the Upper Assam hills, the Khamti and Singpho, were said to be related to the Shan of northern Burma, among whom the Americans had established their first foreign missions from 1814. Sadiya, their first base in Assam, was envisaged as the doorway to an estimated 170 million people in Asia believed to use variants of the same language that the missionaries had already learned in Burma.[4] A Shan Mission, initiated on a small scale in Assam in 1836 but eventually extending over China and Central Asia, was the grandiose target that the American Baptist Foreign Mission Board planned.

As the discrepancies between such expectations and the reality of the new field became apparent, however, the mission had no option but to modify these plans drastically. The unilingual Shan-speaking field it had hoped to find proved to be a chimera, with the geographical and cultural distance between Assam and the territories beyond its hills making the pan-Asian project an impossibility. Instead, even within the province itself, the Baptists were faced with the necessity of learning a large variety of dialects (mostly belonging to the Tibeto-Burmese language family) and transposing them from oral into written forms before any scriptural dissemination could be undertaken. As they acquired more information about the region, doubts arose about the viability of their base. Sadiya was a remote area sparsely populated by imperfectly "pacified," preliterate "tribal" people. The missionaries learned that the plains below were inhabited by a settled agriculturist, caste Hindu population communicating in a single language with a written tradition. By 1841 it was decided to abandon all that the mission had done there so far for a more inviting prospect, the relatively "civilized" territory of the Assam Valley. Nathan Brown reported to the Home Board, justifying the abandonment of their ongoing projects near Sadiya, such as Miles Bronson's work among the Namsang Nagas: "It has long been in doubt whether . . . while there are so

3. H. K. Barpujari, *The American Missionaries and Northeast India (1836-1900): A Documentary Study* (Guwahati, 1986), p. 93.

4. F. S. Downs, *The Mighty Works of God* (Guwahati, 1971), p. 17.

many inviting fields among the Assamese, it is the duty of any brother to devote his life to the study of a language . . . spoken only by a few thousands of people."[5] The plains, with their majority of inhabitants using the Assamese language (of the Indo-European family, like Bengali and other Indic vernaculars with Sanskrit roots) appeared to be much more promising than the many preliterate tongues of the "tribal" groups among whom they had struggled so far. "The Assamese are a most encouraging and inviting field; they are in great measure a civilised people. . . ."[6]

This essay examines the interaction of these American missionaries with indigenous society in the context of colonial modernity and print culture as the entry points of a new sensibility in nineteenth-century Assam. First, it traces the American Baptist missionaries reorienting their "civilizing mission" as well as their views on indigenous society in the light of their experiences in the Assam valley. Second, it examines the *Orunodoi,* the vehicle through which they sought to relay the paper's message to a high-caste Assamese-speaking gentry, and the discrepancies between the paper's intent and its reception. Contrary to the expectations of the periodical's promoters, there was a deliberate and selective appropriation of its contents by the majority of these readers, with the religious component of the "enlightenment" that it was designed to achieve being mostly ignored in favor of more general "knowledge" that could serve their own concerns about regenerating indigenous cultural and social mores. Third, it discusses the modalities of missionary interaction with another section of Assam's population, preliterate "tribal" people living in hill territories, among whom quite another response was forthcoming, with most aspects of an "improving" agenda being adopted, and Christianity eventually becoming the predominant faith. Its objective is to show how the divergent backgrounds and cultural levels of such differing groups within indigenous society brought into being very different reactions to this "civilizing" project, which in turn influenced its own assumptions and strategies.

A fundamental principle of the Baptist philosophy was that the Word should reach people in their own language. This was no easy task in a region with such diverse cultures, even after the missionaries had discarded their initial erroneous assumptions. By 1841 the American Baptists had decided to convey their message through that language which seemed to have the greatest numbers of adherents in the region, the mother-tongue of its caste Hindu inhabitants, known as the Assamese. Their initial tours led them to conclude

5. Letter from Bronson to Peck, 1841, in Downs, *Mighty Works,* pp. 251-52.
6. Letter from Bronson to Peck, 1841, in Barpujari, *American Missionaries,* pp. 251-52.

that though "as many dialects are spoken . . . as were heard at Jerusalem on the day of Pentecost . . . each of the tribes has a language of its own, while the Assamese is the common medium [of trade]."[7] This conclusion was to set the activities of the American Baptist mission apart from the linguistic policy that the colonial state had adopted. The Ahom kingdom of Assam had come under British rule in 1826 after the First Burmese War, and had been incorporated into the Bengal Presidency. In 1836 the new regime ruled that administrative convenience would be best served by using Bengali as a standard language for the entire Presidency, disregarding the local languages and dialects in use throughout its huge territorial reach. In areas such as Assam, with no previous history of common administration with the other parts of the presidency, this decision produced a considerable amount of upheaval for the local population. Proceedings in courts and schools in Assam were henceforward to be conducted in Bengali rather than in Assamese. A justification put forward was that the latter was but one of the former's many local variants. The American Baptist mission did not follow this directive, however, either in its educational endeavors or in the printed literature it was introducing into the province. Even their brief experience in their new field had convinced the missionaries that Assamese was a different language and that Bengali was totally incomprehensible to the common people. By interacting in Assamese, the American Baptists saw the advantage of stepping into the vacuum left by the British state in sponsoring a strange language for use in its institutions:

> I believe that so long as the courts and schools are in Bengali, there will be the greatest impediment to the education and improvement of the people. If missionaries should adopt Bengali, as the means of communicating religious truth, everyone would doubt them. . . . [Therefore] we have by every means in our power endeavoured to make ourselves acquainted with the people, and by daily familiar intercourse acquire their language, so as to be able to communicate to them in the most direct manner the blessings of science and Christianity.[8]

The lack of official support for an indigenous language and literature until after 1874, when Assam was constituted as a separate Chief Commissioner's Province, meant that until then the products of its sole printing press, the Mission Press at Sibsagar, retained prominence as examples of a new "litera-

---

7. Journal of Nathan Brown, 1841, in Barpujari, *American Missionaries*, p. 77.
8. Letter from Bronson to Halliday, Lt. Governor of Bengal, in Barpujari, *American Missionaries*, pp. 135-41.

ture of print" in the region's vernacular. From 1846 it was through their *Orunodoi* periodical that the missionaries sought to disseminate their new print culture of Christian devotion and modern information:

> Its object is to kindle and foster a spirit of inquiry. Whenever the missionary sets up his tent, his first business is to set up that instrument to which the nations of Europe are so greatly indebted for whatever superiority they enjoy over the ancient world. Hence, even when we are not able, as in the case of the present mission, to notice a large accession of converts, we are still certain that the elements of improvement are quietly and vigorously at work.[9]

The periodical's masthead declared it to be "a monthly Paper, devoted to Religion, Science, and General Knowledge." This clearly was attuned to the Evangelical project of using "useful knowledge" to promote "godly society." Reformist sentiment in the first half of the century had furthered this agenda by distributing pamphlets studded with facts and moral and religious sentiments, initially in Europe and America, and then beyond. This dissemination of printed knowledge came to be a particularly significant accompaniment of colonial rule, one that was eagerly taken advantage of by elite Indians seeking greater acquaintance with the new order. C. A. Bayly sees this as a new information movement, although one confined to the upper classes.[10] In regions such as Assam, on the periphery of the state's "civilizing" efforts, it was through agencies such as missionaries that this "useful knowledge" made its belated appearance. "A store of wisdom *(gyan bhandar)*" — the *Orunodoi* was described thus by an upper-caste reader, in his article "What are the advantages for Assamese people in reading the *Orunodoi?*" in its October 1855 issue. The Baptist monopoly over the new technology of print meant that a discourse on modernization and identity among the region's nascent intelligentsia would emerge through the pages of its only discussion forum, the *Orunodoi,* alongside the periodical's intended agenda of disseminating the Christian faith.

As with the general run of such missionary periodicals, the *Orunodoi* carried out its improving project by linking Christian literature with apparently secular and objective facts, from accounts of the working of nature to the differential progress of human societies.[11]

9. *Baptist Missionary Magazine* [hereafter *BMM*], September 1846, p. 290.
10. C. A. Bayly, *Empire and Information: Intelligence Gathering and Social Communication in India, 1780-1870* (Cambridge, 1996), pp. 215-16.
11. See Rosalind O'Hanlon, *Caste, Conflict and Ideology: Mahatma Jotirao Phule and*

Such headings appear as, Turko-Russian hostilities; War in China; Revolution in Spain; Telegraph from Calcutta to Bombay. . . . Illustrated articles on Astronomy, Geography and natural history conveyed useful and needed instruction, while temperance, veracity, self-reliance, family government and other appropriate themes received attention. Through its columns, Christian hymns, translations of psalms, the Pilgrim's Progress, a brief history of the Apostles found their way into heathen homes, where Christian scriptures in their usual form, could not have been admitted.[12]

Apart from such artfully scattered morsels of preaching, there were other ways of combining secular information and religious propaganda. A series on astronomy was meant to take care of both. As the Mission's report stated:

[T]he Assamese, Brahmins as well as others, think it impossible to measure the distance of an inaccessible object. [From the articles on western science] they learn, for instance, that lightning and thunder are connected as the flash of a cannon and the report of it, while, according to the shasters, the thunder only proceeds from the clouds, while the lightning is caused by the darts of Indra. From the errors of the shasters on these . . . points, the people will readily see that they are only the work of man.[13]

This strategy, introduced during the 1830s by the Orientalist Lancelot Wilkinson in the Central Provinces, of spreading accurate scientific knowledge was continued by the American missionaries in Assam, partly as a laudable end in itself and partly to ridicule Puranic cosmology and thus its Brahman guardians.[14]

As far as its most important objective of religious propaganda was concerned, a good beginning seemed to have been made by the mission in the Assam plains, with a handful of converts coming in from the Assamese-speaking population during the decade of the 1840s. This was regarded only as a step toward more lofty objectives, as the missionaries were looking to a

---

Low Caste Protest in Nineteenth-Century Western India (Cambridge, 1985), pp. 50-87, for an analysis of similar missionary periodicals in Western India.

12. "Annual Report Assam, 1838," *BMM*, 1839, p. 145.

13. "Report of the American Baptist Mission to Assam, 1845," *BMM*, August 1846, p. 256.

14. Richard Fox Young, *Resistant Hinduism: Sanskrit Sources of Anti-Christian Apologetics in Early Nineteenth-Century India* (Vienna, 1981), p. 82.

very different constituency from the handful of lower-caste villagers who had initially joined them. They made no secret of their hopes of eventually winning over the most influential section of the Assamese, the high-caste gentry, who had a near monopoly of educational opportunities and formed the bulk of the *Orunodoi's* reading public. This hope, encouraged perhaps by the highly publicized conversions of some young *Babus* from a similar social background in Bengal, had also influenced the mission in its move from the hills near Sadiya to the small towns of Guwahati, Sibsagar and Nagaon, in the heart of the Assam Valley. This was the area where, before the British advent, the Ahom kingdom had its epicenter, and many gentry families, now in administrative posts under the British, were based there. The handful of high schools and courts dating from the first years of colonial rule were concentrated in this area and attracted the well-born, educated youths the missionaries hoped to wean away from traditional beliefs. After the remote, sparsely populated, and densely forested tracts where they had spent their first years, such a relatively "civilized" part of the region seemed to offer better scope for "improvement." "The principal government of the district is invested in this court, which brings together the most active, learned and intelligent part of the people . . . the population is a reading one."[15] The *Orunodoi's* initial focus on enlightenment through religious exhortations and secular truths gradually began to be supplemented by contributions from its indigenous reading public, reflecting their concerns about education, language, and the social regeneration of Assam. Instead of the piecemeal attacks on various native superstitions by missionaries in earlier issues, there were now passionately argued polemics on social reform, mostly from the pens of natives themselves. In 1858 the Foreign Secretary of the Board was informed:

> Our paper is now in its 13th year and is regarded by Young Assam at least, as one of the institutions of the province. . . . A brief sermon or exhortation, a chapter of church history, a chapter of the Life of Mohammad, . . . of the history of Bengal, . . . of the life of Luther, a geographical article, a chapter of Isaiah, together with the news of the month, contributions on various topics such as the marriage of widows, duties of wives, duties of parents, from Christian and other contributors, make up each monthly number.[16]

15. Journal of Barker, 1840-42, in Barpujari, *American Missionaries*, pp. 33-36.
16. Letter from Whiting to Peck, 1858, in Barpujari, *American Missionaries*, p. 158.

An active role had originally been envisaged within the *Orunodoi* for a single category of native contributor, the newly converted Assamese Baptist. "We require a medium through which the talents of our converts may be called out and find development. They cannot write books, but they can write articles which will be the alternative and [be] beneficial to the native public."[17] The first convert baptized by the Americans, Nidhi Levi Farwell, seemed to epitomize the realization of these hopes. An orphan, from a low-caste background, he had lived with Nathan Brown since his childhood, and was baptized in 1841, at around eighteen years of age. He was the most visible of the Assamese Christian writers, with at least two or more pieces in almost every *Orunodoi* issue. It does seem significant that the most striking characteristic of the *Orunodoi's* language and orthography in its first few decades — that is, its use of a colloquial variant approximating as far as possible the spoken vernacular of the common people — was displayed most prolifically in the writings of this individual from a non-literati background. Nidhi was far removed in terms of caste status and social position from Assam's indigenous gentry, many of whom espoused a literary style closer to a "high" Sanskritized model and took issue with the *Orunodoi* over its use of everyday idiom.[18] His first signed article, in 1846, was about the discovery of printing, tracing a teleology of progress for the English nation through its use. Appropriately enough, his piece resounded with praise of this invention having been brought to Assam by the Americans, and its positive impact there. "Formerly, apart from the gentle folk, the ordinary people were not able to acquire reading, but now they are engaging in it, and acquiring wisdom thereby."[19] A later essay attributed the "wisdom" of the American and British people in modern times to their spirit of inquiry, and it appealed to "all the people of Assam, whether gentle or ordinary" to promote education, which would ultimately make "our land Assam praiseworthy in front of others."[20] Apart from Nidhi's prolific output, however, the bulk of the Assamese converts did not manage to fill the role envisaged for them as writers, attributable perhaps to the fact that despite the mission's educational initiatives, these new members, mostly from unlettered backgrounds, were unable to attain the anticipated degree of competence. Instead, it was quite another class of native, with another set of concerns, that was joining Nidhi on those pages.

17. Letter from Brown to Danforth, 1850, in Barpujari, *American Missionaries*, p. 157.

18. Hemchandra Barua, "Introduction," in *Hemkosha or An Etymological Dictionary of the Assamese Language*, edited by P. R. T. Gurdon and Hemchandra Barua (Goswami, 1901).

19. "Discovery of the Printing Press — N.L.," *Orunodoi*, March 1846, pp. 23-24.

20. "Wisdom — N.L.," *Orunodoi*, February 1847, pp. 14-16.

Any attempt to read the mentalities of the various sets of people interacting with the *Orunodoi* is complicated by the fact that while the missionaries have copiously documented their actions and motivations, there is hardly any possibility of similarly accessing the minds of the Assamese converts of the period. Despite the education that the mission schools imparted to them, the poverty and class position of the Assamese converts did not enable them to enter the nascent public sphere that the *Orunodoi* was initiating. Almost their sole representative in terms of written matter is Nidhi Levi Farwell, and he too was remarkably reticent as far as personal documentation was concerned. It is possible, however, to infer from his use of a colloquial idiom and his frequently expressed wish for "ordinary people" to acquire wisdom that his vision of the periodical's audience did not altogether collude with that of its missionary sponsors. The "ordinary people" whom he addressed were not the intended audience of the missionaries, who were well aware that "not one in a hundred of the common people" could read the products of their press.[21] The intentions behind running such a native paper were quite clear:

> The *Orunodoi* . . . was established by a vote of the whole mission after full discussion and deliberation. [It] has been considered . . . as one of the most powerful instrumentalities for gaining access to the mind of the Assamese, and nothing we have ever done has created such an interest among them. . . . We can reach a portion of the more influential part of the people in no other way. They have too great a contempt for our scriptures and religious books to read them until we can dissipate their prejudices and engender a sense of enlightenment. They will receive and read the paper and by this medicine a curiosity will be existed to know . . . our religion.[22]

Despite Nidhi's appeal to "gentle as well as ordinary people," the enlightenment that the *Orunodoi* hoped to distribute was not, in the first instance, targeted toward the latter.

It was the literate, "influential," "higher class" of the Assamese people whom the missionaries were anxious to convert. This was, of course, similar to the attitudes taken by Christian missions in other parts of India with an, often expressed, profound distrust of the motivation behind the conversion of lower classes. Various studies have drawn attention to the missionary ob-

21. "Annual Meeting of Assam Mission, *1850*," BMM, May 1852, pp. 132-34.
22. Letter from Brown to Danforth, 1850, in Barpujari, *American Missionaries*, pp. 156-57.

session, in their first few decades of work, with converting Brahmans and the deferential attitude toward them.[23] The optimism engendered by even the slightest overture from a "higher class" of native after the long years of effort expended upon the *Orunodoi* makes these hopes fairly clear. Mrs. Bronson anticipated winning over

> two pundits . . . representative men of . . . the educated Assamese. One is an old Brahmin, deeply read in Sanskrit. . . . He seems to be like one of old, anxious to bow in the house of his god for appearance' sake, while in his heart he worships the only living and true God. The other is a representative of young Assam. He is bound hand and foot by the chains of custom and caste, like the old man, but he seems to have a conviction that there is truth in the new religion, and that he must seek for it.

These contacts with various upper-class individuals impelled her to write that "we have never felt more encouragement in our work than now."[24]

This hopefulness seems somewhat misplaced. It certainly points to a considerable gap between the type of flock the Baptist missionaries gathered and what they aspired to, at least until they entirely reorganized their priorities some time later. In spite of their optimism for the "educated Assamese," the few converts they had made (there were fifty Assamese Christians by 1858, after twenty-five years put in by twenty-two missionaries) were almost all from a low-caste, unlettered background. They were largely dependent upon the mission for sustenance, as their previous occupations usually came to an end in the face of social ostracism. For instance, Kolibor, one of the early converts, was a washerman who was subsequently taken on as a preacher by the Sibsagar church. Others, such as Kandura, the son of a blind beggar, entered into the new faith through an education in the Orphan Institution. The usual channels for mobility within the colonial regime seem to have been fairly restricted for such educated native Christians from humble backgrounds compared with their counterparts from upper-caste, gentry families, a far greater proportion of whom were appointed to government jobs. For the Assamese Christians of this period, the ultimate government job in reach seems to have been that of a clerk or school inspector. None of them managed to obtain the more coveted and lucrative revenue collectorate jobs that almost every native

---

23. See Anthony Copley, *Religions in Conflict: Ideology, Cultural Contact and Conversion in Late-Colonial India* (Delhi, 1997); also D. B. Forrester, *Caste and Christianity: Attitudes and Policies on Caste of Anglo-Saxon Protestant Missions in India* (London, 1980).

24. Letter from Mrs. Bronson, 1865, in Barpujari, *American Missionaries*, p. 213.

youth of "good" family was taking up in these years, very often stepping into posts earlier held by family members. Dick Kooiman has pointed out the perilous job prospects for educated native Christians of humble background in the princely state of Travancore,[25] but matters were not much better for such converts even under a British administration, given its unwillingness to upset the indigenous status quo. Peasant society in Assam, though lacking strong landlord-tenant ties, had a powerful substitute in the patronage links maintained by the Vaishnava *satras* or monasteries that dotted the countryside, with their tithe-paying disciples spanning different castes. Such links with spiritual preceptors were as difficult to break for the peasants as for the gentry and, even more than the ubiquity of caste, may account for the very scanty harvest the mission achieved among the Assamese population and the frequent complaints of "backsliding" among those who did enter the mission compound.

For almost three decades most of the missionaries retained hopes for a respectable variety of converts, drawn from the class providing its reading public. From their private papers, it also seems that in these early decades, it was only from this class that they felt sure of an intellectual acceptance of their creed, as opposed to what they regarded as the materialistic motives of the lower echelons. At the same time, a filtration theory was often adhered to, with the supposition that higher-class converts would gradually invite emulation by their subordinates. The reality, however, was that not one of their first generation of Assamese converts was from those higher reaches of indigenous society. Indeed, this failure probably contributed to the relative lack of hostility toward the mission. Despite missionary complaints of priestly hostility, there does not seem to have been much active animus displayed by the heads or *gosains* of the *satras* against their activities. Indeed, among the names of *Orunodoi* writers and subscribers can be found a few members of the *satras*.[26] Assamese society of the plains was characterized by a spiritual dominance exerted by these *gosains*. It was only the "tribal" people settled in ecologically peripheral zones such as the hills surrounding the Assam valley who were mostly outside the ambit of this *satra* culture. Once the first few years of the *Orunodoi* had shown that despite its occasional fulminations against indigenous "superstitions" and its Christian teachings, it was not making inroads into the religious constituencies of the *satras*. The periodical came to be re-

25. Dick Kooiman, *Conversion and Social Equality in India: The London Missionary Society in South Travancore in the Nineteenth Century* (New Delhi, 1989).

26. Kinaram Dutta, from the Kamalabari Satra, List of Subscribers, *Orunodoi*, November 1853; and Krishnakanta Adhikar Gohain, from Kamalabari Satra, *Orunodoi*, October 1849.

garded with tolerance for its patronage of the Assamese language. As far as their silence on its religious message is concerned, Richard Fox Young's contention that this was typical of many Hindus and part of their refusal to recognize other faiths, as fully accredited Dharmas in opposition to their own, has to be kept in mind.[27] By 1871 the most powerful indigenous religious institution in Assam, the Auniati Satra, had set up its own Dharma Prakash Press and initiated periodicals of its own, such as the *Axom Bilasini* and the *Axom Tara,* dealing with religious and general questions.[28] This can be interpreted as a reaction to, and perhaps even an imitation of, the new kind of cultural patronage that the missionaries had provided, and monopolized, for a while. The trickle of printed Assamese books from other presses that began to make their appearance in subsequent years were mostly versions of Vaishnava scriptures, with print culture enabling such wide dissemination of cheap copies of the teachings of Assam's *Bhakti* preachers for the first time.

Unlike the strong language they used during itinerant preaching, the missionaries did try to be fairly circumspect in their polemics within the *Orunodoi.* "The whole influence of the priests and the Hindu religion is to keep the people in ignorance. The most effective way of defeating the purpose of the Brahmins is, not to attack them personally, but to enlighten the masses."[29] However, there was an occasional skirmish when the periodical did give offense by going too far in its criticisms. There is a vivid instance from 1867, when the editor reacted angrily to a rumor that the Chief Commissioner was dying due to a curse put on him by the Gosain of the Auniati Satra. His stinging condemnation of the ignorance of a public that laid credence to such powers for their priests was accompanied by equal scorn for allegedly godly personages who encouraged such beliefs. The next issue, however, cooled matters somewhat, with a disclaimer of any such curse in a letter from the Gosain. The editor added a fairly conciliatory footnote to this but could not resist pointing out that the Gosain had disclaimed possession of any miraculous powers, contrary to the assertions of his deluded disciples. Feelings had run high and the controversy did not end there. Subsequently, we find Nidhi Farwell defending the editor's rebukes and expressing revulsion at what he described as the "shame-inducing" tone of the correspondence from the Gosain's followers.[30] Such incidents do indicate that not all the *Orunodoi's* readers were able to pass over any criticism of indigenous institutions, and

27. Fox Young, *Resistant Hinduism,* p. 141.

28. H. K. Barpujari, ed., *The Comprehensive History of Assam,* 5 vols. (Guwahati, 1993), 5:231.

29. "Annual Meeting of Assam Mission, 1850," *BMM,* May 1852, pp. 132-34.

30. *Orunodoi,* March and April 1867.

that a mental gap had opened up between an individual such as Nidhi and his countrymen who regarded their spiritual preceptors as omniscient beings.

Nonetheless, it does seem that many regular readers had a very different attitude toward the only source of modern "knowledge" in their tongue. "It is a matter of great shame that in a land where the ranks of persons who have its welfare in mind are extremely scanty, if an attempt is made to deal with the country's problems, every obstacle is put in their way."[31] In a letter from Babu Gunabhiram Barua, we find him bemoaning that:

> our countrymen do not sufficiently appreciate the invaluable work done by the *Orunodoi*. They have never had the opportunity in the past of coming across the kind of weighty matters which it has made available now, every month. . . . We must not miss the opportunity to thank the sahibs who have taken out this paper. . . . O respectable people of Assam, all those who are cultured and well-off, do try to benefit from the store of wisdom contained in it.

It is interesting to compare the very different kind of audience that the humbly born Nidhi and the patrician Gunabhiram were reaching out to, with their fairly similar rhetoric. While Nidhi's hopes were for the upliftment of "ordinary people," Gunabhiram was addressing his own class, the same social elite that the missionaries wished to reach. As far as this main target of "Young Assam" was concerned, the *Orunodoi* seems to have become an indispensable part of their socialization into colonial modernity with their assimilation into a reading, subscribing, and corresponding public. From 1854 onward, hardly an issue appeared without articles and long letters from such native contributors, with themes and concerns very different from the mainly religious pieces that Nidhi and a few other converts were producing. On the whole, most of these contributions came from that section of Assamese society that clearly supported the *Orunodoi* as a window into a new world of modern knowledge, while simultaneously appropriating it, through their own pieces, to further their project of revitalizing language, education, and social norms.[32] The missionary project served for them as a harbinger of broad cultural change, without necessarily succeeding in its own objective of bringing about religious conversions.

The name *Orunodoi* means "Dawn" or "Sunrise." Such a trope of darkness to light appears frequently in the names of vernacular periodicals, expressive

---

31. *Orunodoi*, October 1855.
32. *Orunodoi*, October 1855.

of the main objective behind this genre of nineteenth-century literature. This trend started in Bengal with the *Samachar Chandrika, Prabhakar,* and *Divakar;* found place in Western India with the *Jnanodoy;* and was continued in Assam toward the later part of the century with the *Orunodoi* and its successors — *Asom Tara, Chandradoi,* and others, all names centering around images of light. (Incidentally, the name *Arunodoy* was not only given to another Bengali Christian periodical but also was the title of Baba Padmanji's conversion account in Marathi.)[33] Missionary publishers shared this vision of a civilizing enlightenment through print, with their religious input as its most significant component. What they do not seem to have anticipated, however, was an audience exercising its own agency within the process of reading by selectively appropriating the contents of this literature. From the missionary's point of view, such partial dissemination of their message into their readers' conceptual world was highly unsatisfactory. A significant gap existed between what their periodicals were intended to convey and what they actually did, in accordance with the selective and willed way in which texts have to be seen as being appropriated by their readers.[34] In the context of nineteenth-century Assam, the reading public's own agenda decreed an acceptance, as far as the *Orunodoi* was concerned, of its project of general knowledge and language regeneration, but not of the religious message that its editors envisaged as its primary task. The premise of moving from darkness to light did come to be a generally held belief among the "influential classes" who were the periodical's target audience, but not its corollary that Christianity provided the sole entry point. These readers therefore participated enthusiastically in the *Orunodoi's* enlightening project but re-created it within the context of their own priorities to serve as a discussion forum for their own central concerns of cultural and social regeneration. For "progress-minded" members of the Assamese gentry, the process of re-creating themselves as a "modern" intelligentsia expressing itself in its own language was facilitated by the *Orunodoi.* It is significant that in the praise of the periodical from natives there is no mention among their eulogies of its contents, the religious sections of which were clearly seen as irrelevant to their own project of "civilization." By the 1870s, with official patronage for the Assamese language reinstated, the Mission Press ceased to be the sole purveyor of its print culture.

Around the same time, some members of the mission were attempting to move beyond the Assamese Hindu community where progress was so slow

---

33. O'Hanlon, *Caste, Conflict and Ideology,* p. 67.

34. Roger Chartier, *Cultural History: Between Practices and Representations,* trans. Lydia G. Cochrane (Cambridge, 1988), pp. 40-42.

and its harvest so limited. For a new generation of missionaries in the 1870s, a shift in priorities was obvious, with the *Orunodoi* being issued very irregularly until its final demise around 1880. The barren harvest from the plains was blamed, in retrospect (in 1891), on the innately "conservative" character of the people. "Their history proves them to have been always . . . timid of innovation. When the Mohammadan faith spread like a flood over Southern Asia, it never gained a strong foothold here. . . . This extreme conservatism has been one of the chief hindrances to the progress of missions."[35] Newcomers at the mission were now turning full circle back to earlier attempts at claiming the preliterate "tribes" of the region, with Edward Clark resuming work among the Nagas in 1871-72. The mission had brought a halt to Bronson's work among the Namsang Nagas near Sadiya in its first decade because it doubted whether a few thousand "uncivilized" people would merit the effort required to learn and reshape their obscure dialect into a written language suitable for the Scriptures. While the enthusiasm for enlightenment displayed by "Young Assam" had raised expectations, the lag in actual conversions made caste ties seem an insurmountable obstacle in the plains. Condemnations of caste were perhaps to be expected at this stage as a scapegoat for missionary failure in gaining converts and also as an index of the hidebound attitudes the missionaries had to overcome.[36] Only a hundred or so Assamese Christians comprised the plains church after decades of effort. The once daunting prospect of learning new languages in order to reach the Naga hill people became a more attractive one and held out the prospect of being among "non-idolaters" with "no distinctions of caste, or priesthood."[37] Positive experiences with other unlettered communities such as the Kols, who had been brought into Assam as indentured plantation labor, was encouraging. Another hill people, the Garos, had come into the Baptist orbit in the 1860s, their representatives themselves seeking out the Guwahati mission and going back as native preachers to spread the word of a new God in their villages.[38] The long-abandoned venture to the Nagas in the hills was restarted when it became clear that "our missions seem to have been more successful among the aboriginals proper."[39]

These hills in Assam were inhabited by diverse groups of "aboriginal" people who adhered to localized worship traditions and lived by hunting or shifting cultivation, not by intensive agriculture as on the plains. The ecologi-

35. R. D. Grant, "Report of the Committee on Missions in Assam," *BMM*, 1891, p. 203.

36. Copley, *Religions in Conflict*, p. 11.

37. *Mission to the Assamese: Fifty-fourth Annual Report, BMM*, July 1868, pp. 254-55.

38. *Mission to the Assamese: Fifty-fourth Annual Report, BMM*, July 1868, pp. 254-55.

39. M. C. Mason, "The People of Assam," *BMM*, September 1880, pp. 327-29.

cal situation had enabled them to retain such localized cultures outside the more homogenized traditions that had spread through more accommodating regions of the Indian subcontinent. Over the centuries, as Indo-Aryan communities had pressed outward from the Gangetic plains, they not only cleared forest tracts and disseminated agricultural technology but also absorbed "aboriginals" into a caste system while imparting to them the essentials of Vedic religion and culture. Later, Buddhism and Islam followed similar trajectories, operating not so much through religious conversions as through cultural reorientation, and into settled modes of life. By the time a British colonial regime appeared, much of the previously forested regions of the subcontinent had been turned over to settled agriculture, and their inhabitants now identified themselves in terms of such religious traditions with lettered cultures.[40] This continued in the case of some groups, such as the Mishing, who were still acquiring the status of *satra* disciples well into the twentieth century.[41] The efforts of Christian missions in such areas proved conspicuously less successful than those in the peripheral regions and among groups that such acculturations had bypassed.

One of these regions was the Naga hills district of Assam. From the 1870s the American Baptists gradually transferred their energies into such terrain, abandoning their earlier partiality for a filtration policy of winning over the influential, "civilized" Hindu gentry of the plains. There, these missionaries had been working against indigenous lettered traditions that were able to appropriate elements from projects such as the *Orunodoi* without committing themselves to aspects seen as incompatible with their own beliefs. The plains' intelligentsia engaged itself in "regenerating" its own culture so as to successfully respond to the challenges posed by colonial modernity. Christianity did not appear as an essential clearing house in this project for them. For others it was possible to identify with notions of reform applied to indigenous traditions, as by the Brahmo sect that Gunabhiram Barua joined. Others again were able to apply new ideas to a regional *Bhakti* tradition and stay within what was depicted as a continuum of indigenous dissent and reform. As in western India, a new periodical press articulated a crisis in legitimacy that brought into being a small but vocal group of social reformers, who were able to select from a wide variety of ideas in the formation of their own independent critiques of Hindu society.[42] At this level missionary propaganda proved

40. Richard Eaton, "Conversion to Christianity among the Nagas," *Indian Economic and Social History Review* (January-March 1984): 1-44.
41. Jatin Mipun, *The Mishings of Assam* (New Delhi, 1993), pp. 56-60.
42. O'Hanlon, *Caste, Conflict and Ideology,* pp. 50-87.

successful, but, contrary to expectations, it did not mean automatic acceptance of Christian tenets by readers.

By the later decades of the nineteenth century, missionary methods were being revamped to meet the needs of new targets, with the Home Board acceding to the opinions of the Baptists in the field and revising its earlier assumption that schools could only be auxiliary to preaching. Anthony Copley's instancing of conferences from 1872 onward, where education had overtaken itinerant preaching as the preferred strategy, seems indicative of a general rethinking about missionary methodology.[43] This was gradually accompanied by an acceptance of the potential for success among low-caste and "tribal" people in different parts of India. The Judson Centennial discussions in 1914, reviewing a century of American Baptist foreign missions, felt bound to conclude that in almost all their fields most converts had come from the "poorer and thus less intelligent classes."[44] This changed strategy was only possible, however, with the free hand given by the colonial state. Despite misgivings among certain officials, by the end of the century British administrative policy accepted missions as intermediaries for "indirect rule" in the hill territories of northeast India where revenue could hardly meet even bare administrative costs. Since the only viable returns would be "souls," the missions came to enjoy a monopoly over literacy and health facilities that had never been possible in the plains. The Baptists in Assam had long believed in "improvement of civilization" for these tribes as being conditional upon eroding their "perfect independence of feeling."[45] This was now possible, with a chance to provide a "civilizing" infrastructure for the Nagas. Since government policy also dictated minimal contact with other agencies (through regulations such as the Inner Line System), missionaries represented the state and the accoutrements of modernity that now entered the Naga villagers' autonomous world. Richard Eaton argues that this was the context within which the rapid shift from a localized oral cosmology to a universalistic religion was brought about by the missionaries through their literature and schools. While earlier beliefs, limited in time and space, came to seem increasingly irrelevant in the wider context of the present, the Nagas were able to identify some of their powerful forces of nature with the all powerful Creator to whom they were introduced. The incorporation of Naga ritual terms by the missionary scriptural translations smoothed the process of transition.

43. Copley, *Religions in Conflict*, p. 23.
44. Howard B. Grose and Fred P. Haggard, eds., *The Judson Centennial, 1814-1914* (Boston, 1914), p. 6.
45. Letter from Bronson to Jenkins, July 1840, in Barpujari, *American Missionaries*, p. 260.

In the Assam plains, though print culture had been pioneered by the mission, it developed against an existing infrastructure of a literate gentry and a written tradition and thus merely served the interests of a modernizing gentry. The situation in the hills, whether for the Welsh Presbyterians in the Khasi Hills or the American Baptists among the Garos, Nagas, and Mizos, was very different. The shift to literacy was itself mediated through the missionaries and their message of Christian "improvement." The general information and social debates on which the *Orunodoi* had concentrated were no longer in vogue. Scriptural and pedagogical texts in newly enscripted "tribal" languages for the missionary schools came to comprise the majority of their publications. In the plains, another periodical, the *Dipti,* ultimately succeeded the *Orunodoi,* but its readership was now entirely made up of the small constituency of Assamese Christians.

CHAPTER ELEVEN

The Santals, Though Unable to Plan for Tomorrow, Should Be Converted by the Santals

MARINE CARRIN AND HARALD TAMBS-LYCHE

Introduction

In the later decades of the nineteenth century, two Scandinavian missionaries, Lars Skrefsrud and Hans Peter Börresen, tried to create a Santal National Church. To an unusual degree for missionaries, they tried to respect tribal custom,[1] but their universalist ideas of acceptable Christian behavior, tinged as they were with rather parochial traits of Scandinavian Pietism, eventually led them to distrust their newly converted priests and catechists. Conceiving of the Santal as simple savages, they never left their converts to work out their own ideas of Christianity. Though devoted to education, they did not want to spoil the innocence of the Santals with bookish learning. They were not theologians and treated Western recruits to the mission with skepticism. In brief, their experience led them to mistrust everybody but themselves. The project of a National Church for the Santals faded as its founders aged, and it died with them. Their Santal collaborators, some of whom are known through their own writing, never got a chance to influence the development of the church.

---

1. For Santal ethnography see, e.g., W. G. Archer, *The Hill of Flutes: Life and Poetry in Tribal India: A Portrait of the Santals* (London, 1974); M. Carrin-Bouez, *La fleur et l'os: Symbolism et ritual chez les Santal* (Paris, 1986); R. Parkin, *The Munda of Central India* (Delhi, 1992).

The Santals in the Nineteenth Century

The Santals, who speak a language of the Munda family, inhabit Chota Nagpur and neighboring districts of Bengal, Bihar, and Orissa. Today they number some four and one-half million. For centuries they had been in contact with neighboring Hindu populations, and, like other tribals, they were integrated into the princely states of northern Orissa. They seem to have had little contact with the market economy of the Mughal Empire, however, and money was peripheral to their economy. Later, like other populations bordering on Bengal, the Santals were confronted, from the early nineteenth century, with the market economy[2] — through cash cropping and wage labor on plantations, and through wage labor on major public works such as the railways.[3] These economic changes contributed to the destruction of their traditional economy[4] in spite of government measures, instituted from time to time, to protect them from encroachment on their lands. The forebears of the people among whom the missionaries worked migrated to the present Santal Parganas on British initiative to clear land for indigo planting and so alleviate pressure on the land. The emergence of a tribal working class and the exploitation it suffered largely explain the various rebellions among tribals of the region from 1820 onward.[5]

Among the most important of the rebellions was that of 1855-56, led by the charismatic leaders, Sidhu and Kanhu. The Santals attacked merchants and planters, and, though the Santals were suppressed, their courage and integrity won them respect from British officers. Not all the results of the rebellion were negative for the Santals. The Santal Parganas became a non-regulated area under a Special Commissioner, exempted from certain Bengal

2. See K. S. Singh, "Colonial Transformation of Tribal Society," *Economic and Political Weekly* 29 (1978): 1221-31.

3. The impact was uneven geographically and socially. Hunter, for example, notes the role of conflicts between "rich" and "poor" Santals in the 1855 rebellion (T. Ray, *Santal Rebellion: Documents* [Calcutta, 1983], p. 72).

4. The Santals may have been hunters and gatherers at an early date, as the Birhors still are, but they were practicing shifting cultivation when British rule was established in Bengal. See S. C. Roy, *The Birhors* (Ranchi, 1925); *Journal of Francis Buchanan Kept during the Survey of the District of Bhagalpur in 1810-11*, ed. C. E. A. W. Oldham (Patna, 1930), pp. 12-64.

5. The Bhils rose in the 1820s, the Kols in 1829-33, and the Santals in 1855-56, but there were many other cases, big and small, up to the present, where the Santals were highly active in the movement for a separate Jharkhand state. See M. Carrin, "Les tribus de l'Inde: repli identitaire et mouvements insurrectionnels," in *L'Inde contemporaine*, edited by C. Jaffrelot (Paris, 1996); C. A. Bayly, *Indian Society and the Making of the British Empire* (Cambridge 1988), p. 174.

laws. This left considerable responsibility with traditional Santal chiefs.[6] Yet the memory of defeat was still strong when the missionaries arrived in 1867, and some Santals still doubted the religious powers that had inspired Sidhu and Kanhu. Had the *bongas,* the tribal divinities, been corrupted by foreign gods or sorcerers? Was it the British who sent them that white man, carrying a Bible and having ten fingers on each hand symbolizing his powers, who appeared to their leaders assuring them of immunity to the bullets of the white man? Did this figure represent one of the earlier missionary efforts?

Similar factors may have led to the Kherwar movement, which broke out in 1871-72.[7] Further activity followed between 1876 and 1879. Successive Kherwar leaders, combining Hindu elements with the dream of a golden age, tried to re-create the lost Santal kingdom. Skrefsrud fought the movement from the start and denounced the leaders, but he underestimated the appeal of the movement, which became the most dangerous rival for the missionary enterprise.

The Scandinavian Missionaries and Their Background

The Moravian Pietists were established in Denmark and Norway during the early eighteenth century, but revival in Norway really started with Hans Nielsen Hauge,[8] whose activity spanned the years of the Napoleonic wars. A layman, Hauge opposed the Lutheran State Church's legal monopoly on preaching. His imprisonment for several years did not stay the spread of his books and pamphlets that circulated in enormous numbers during the period. Hauge enjoyed strong support, and the authorities were handicapped in their actions against him by the isolation from Denmark due to the British blockade. From Hauge, the Norwegian Church inherited a strong low-church and evangelical movement,[9] nurturing Skrefsrud, the leading figure of the mission we describe, who is still seen as one of its heroes. Born near Lillehammer in 1840, he came from the class of rural artisans that, free of the ties that

6. At times, however, administrators reintroduced certain Bengal laws (Archer, *Hill of Flutes*). Skrefsrud consistently fought for the application of Santal customary law.

7. Kherwar is an old name for the Santals. The term *saph hor* in this context refers to reform of Santal custom according to Hindu ideas of purity, while at the same time fighting Hindu landlords and moneylenders.

8. E.g., D. Kullerud, *Hans Nielsen Hauge* (Oslo, 1996); E. Molland, "Haugianere," in *Aschehougs konversasjonsleksikon,* 16 vols. (Oslo, 1969), 8: 672.

9. See E. Molland, *Fra Hans Nielsen Hauge til Eivind Berggrav* (Oslo, 1951); Carl Fr. Wislsff, *Norsk Kirkehistorie, III* (Oslo, 1971).

bound sharecroppers to the landlords, fostered several interesting men during this period.

Skrefsrud started off badly, going to jail for burglary in 1861.[10] In prison he read voraciously — Novalis, Kierkegaard, Swedenborg — and taught himself English, German, and Latin. He had a strong experience of grace and decided to become a missionary. The missionary academy in Stavanger[11] refused him on account of his past. Through the mediation of a leading Moravian he went to Berlin, with introductions to Hans Peter Börresen, a Dane, chief mechanic at a locomotive factory, whose home had become a haven for Scandinavian Evangelicals. Börresen came from the workman's area at the Copenhagen dockyards, but it was after moving to Berlin for work that he experienced a religious awakening. He married Caroline Hempel, daughter of the works' manager, a member of the Pietist milieu centered on the Bethlehem Church, where J. E. Gossner[12] had been the pastor. The Börresens wanted to become missionaries, and it was Skrefsrud who inspired them to go with him to India. They all then studied at the "mission school" that Gossner had founded, and it was the Gossner Missionary Society[13] that sent them to Bengal. Skrefsrud arrived there in 1864 and the Börresens in 1865.

Association with the Gossnerians was to be brief, however. One reason was the Prusso-Danish war of 1864, though rumors also spoke of an indecently close relationship between Mrs. Börresen and Skrefsrud.[14] Conflicts

10. The shop he burgled belonged to Mr. Fagstad, a close friend of Skrefsrud's later father-in-law. These two were to found the committee of support at Lillehammer, urged on by Fagstad's daughter, Klara, at one time a candidate for Skrefsrud's remarriage after his first wife's death. Lunde, the head of the committee, was Klara's employer and married to the sister of Skrefsrud's wife. The director of the jail, too, became one of Skrefsrud's supporters.

11. This institution, founded in 1842, is still very active. It belongs to the Norwegian Missionary Society, which is Lutheran and close to the State Church.

12. J. E. Gossner (1773-1858), a Catholic priest, was defrocked in 1817 because of his Protestant views. In 1820 he was called to Russia by Alexander I, then returned to Germany when Orthodox circles reaffirmed themselves after the Tsar's death. From 1829 he was the pastor of the Bethlehem Church.

13. Gossner founded his missionary society in 1836. Highly evangelical in spirit, it did not insist on theological training but expected its missionaries to fend for themselves and convert the heathen with a minimum of financial support. The society's first missionaries went to India in 1839.

14. This accusation was repeated, notably by the Norwegian missionary Pahle, sacked by Skrefsrud and Börresen in 1883. He also accused them of enriching themselves at the cost of donors and Santals. The "Pahle affair" was probably the worst crisis in the mission's history. Hertel and the Lillehammer committee were Skrefsrud's strongest supporters during this crisis. See J. Nyhagen, *Santalmisjonens historie*, 3 vols. (Oslo, 1990, 1990, 1992), 2:112-22.

also arose between the Gossner society in Berlin and its representatives in India at this time.[15]

A Baptist Mission to the Santals

Skrefsrud and the Börresens, who had to return to Calcutta, did not give up the idea of missionary work. They developed links with the Baptists, partly through lodging with a Baptist family. They also saw Kol tribals working on the riverfront and were impressed by these people. Perhaps they were influenced by the contrast, perceived by some contemporaries, between the tribal — a "noble savage" — and the "degenerate" Hindus.[16]

The Baptists had already shown some interest in the Santals. R. Leslie had started working at Monghyr in 1824, but he returned to England in 1841. By then the American Baptists were well established on the Orissa coast and had worked among the Santals since 1838. The most eminent of them was J. Phillips, who produced a Santal grammar. Then, in 1850, the Church Missionary Society (CMS) started a work at Bhagalpur.[17]

Among the Calcutta Baptists was R. Johnson,[18] recently converted and ea-

---

15. This was largely a generational conflict. The older missionaries reacted strongly against the criticism of the young, who, after Gossner's death, had received more substantial training. This ultimately led to a schism. The supporters of the older missionaries joined the Anglican Church; see M. E. Gibbs, *The Anglican Church in India* (London, 1972), pp. 239-40.

16. Bayly notes the views of the ethnologist Sir Walter Elliott (Madras Civil Service), who stressed tribal "democracy" and love of freedom, citing Santal behavior during their rebellion. Major Jarvis, praising Santal bravery, had said: "They were the most *truthful* set of men I ever met, brave to infatuation" (Susan Kaufman Bayly, "'Caste' and 'Race' in the Colonial Ethnography of India," in *The Concept of Race in South Asia*, edited by P. Robb [Delhi, 1997], pp. 165-218, esp. pp. 192-93). For the "effeminate" Bengalis, see, e.g., D. Kopf, "The Universal Man and the Yellow Dog: The Orientalist Legacy and the Problem of Brahmo Identity in the Bengal Renaissance," in *Aspects of Bengali History and Society*, edited by R. van M. Baumer (Honolulu, 1975); and I. Chowdhury-Sengupta, "The Effeminate and the Masculine," in *The Concept of Race in South Asia*, edited by P. Robb (Delhi, 1997), pp. 282-303.

17. Their missionary, Dröse, contacted the Santals in 1852, but he did not speak Santali, and the real work among the Santals started in 1861-62. For various missions to the Santals see Nyhagen, *Santalmisjonens historie*, 1:49-70.

18. Johnson's leg was mauled by a tiger when his gun failed. Börresen, who chased the tiger by singing hymns, felt that Johnson should have trusted his God, not his gun. This soured their relations. Then, when Johnson's wife died, he left. He continued missionary work, however, making an abortive attempt to itinerate in Afghanistan, where he was saved only by official intervention (Nyhagen, *Santalmisjonens historie*, 1:164-67, 176-80).

ger to be a missionary. Aided by the Calcutta branch of the Baptist Missionary Society (BMS), Johnson, Skrefsrud, and the Börresens established their mission station Ebenezer at Benagaria, near Rampur Ghat in the Santal Parganas, in 1867. In their Evangelical enthusiasm, Johnson and the Scandinavians bothered little about theological differences. Skrefsrud, however, decided to rebaptize himself in 1868, a move that became an embarrassment later when the mission sought Lutheran support. The Börresens remained Lutherans throughout.[19]

Compared to many missionary efforts in India, the mission was off to a good start: by 1873 there were 275 converts.[20] The first Santal catechists, Siram and Birju, were recruited in 1870.[21] Two other converts, Hatia and the woman Hinduma, showed their zeal in converting others.[22] Yet there was also resistance: the chiefs feared that the new religion would destroy the distinctive character of the Santals, defined as their custom, *colon*.[23]

Skrefsrud proudly describes two large assemblies of chiefs that he organized,[24] where it was agreed that the converts should lose none of their rights in the community. He was empowered to marry converts in 1873. He remained anxious to avoid schism between Christians and non-Christians although their relations were sometimes conflictual. Religious difference did break marriages. This was embarrassing to the missionaries who, in spite of respecting marriages with non-Christians, tended to impose their own moral view of marriage as a lifelong commitment.

Skrefsrud's strategy was to convert the chiefs with whom he identified,[25] trying, with some success, to imitate their oratory skills in Santali. His lin-

---

19. Skrefsrud retained his doubts about infant baptism, but Hertel convinced him to change his views, as shown by their correspondence. Skrefsrud finally declared his adherence to Lutheran doctrine. Börresen seems to have had no objection to the Baptist practice, nor to the later change. Stadsbiblioteket, Aarhus, Hertel Letter Collection (hereafter HLC), several letters, esp. May to November 1879. Relevant correspondence is also found in the Royal Library, Copenhagen, *DMS collection,* while Olav Hodne (*L. O. Skrefsrud Missionary and Social Reformer among the Santals of Santal Parganas: With Special Reference to the Period between 1867 and 1881* [Oslo, 1966], pp. 151-60) also refers to the Copy Book at Dumka of letters sent from the field. (We have not yet had access to this source.)

20. Indian Home Mission to the Santals (hereafter IHM), Fifth *Annual Report* [hereafter *AR*], 1872-73.

21. IHM, Fourth *AR,* 1871-72.

22. Hodne, *Skrefsrud,* p. 168.

23. Traditional authority rests on this concept of *colon,* thus underpinning both ethnic conscience and the position of the chiefs.

24. IHM, Fifth *AR,* 1872-73.

25. Skrefsrud writes of this strategy in several of his early letters to Hertel, up to 1881 (Stadsbiblioteket, Aarhus, HLC).

guistic aptitude stood him in good stead here. Matru Pargana, however, the most influential of the local chiefs, obtained his fellow chiefs' consent to expel the missionaries and to exclude converts from the tribe. The British feared trouble, and Matru was imprisoned. After eight months in jail he was seriously ill. Skrefsrud succeeded in healing him and in converting him in the process. The conversion, in January 1873, marked a new stage in the missionary enterprise.

Success and Separation from the Baptists

The year 1874 was one of drought and famine. Börresen obtained authorization to supervise irrigation works and preached to the thousands of Santal workers employed there. Aided by the zeal of the converts, the mission baptized sixteen hundred new Christians that year. Yet there was severe criticism in the press *(The Times; The Englishman)* of the missionaries profiting from distress to convert poor people. P. O. Bodding, Skrefsrud's successor, explained much later that the Santals believed the drought was due to the wrath of God, and so, conscious of their fault in ignoring Him, they wanted to change their religion.[26]

By the end of the year there were about two thousand adult converts with some four thousand children (whom the mission did not baptize). Santal Christians formed a sizeable and influential, though localized, community. The mission territory was divided into parishes, each with a Santal pastor as its head. (These, however, had no formal ordination.)

The success of the mission awoke interest in India, Britain, and Scandinavia.[27] It was still a Baptist enterprise,[28] but stresses and strains began to be felt, and there began a drawn-out and conflictual process of separation. Briefly explained, Johnson had left because of ill-health, and the Baptists were skeptical of financing a mission led by Lutherans, who were getting jealous of their independence from the BMS. They broke with the Baptists, who felt that

26. IHM, Fifty-second *AR*, 1919-20.
27. In India, there is strong support in the Evangelical milieu, where Börresen was making fund-collecting tours. In Britain, the main supporter was Dr. Graham of Edinburgh, a friend of Alexander Duff. In Denmark, L. Hertel became aware of the mission through an article in *The Times*.
28. It was called the Indian Home Mission to the Santals (IHM). The BMS in Calcutta supported it both morally and financially and expected it to be run as a Baptist mission, though it was organizationally separate from the BMS (Hodne, *Skrefsrud*, pp. 71-138, and esp. pp. 117-22, where the link to the BMS is discussed).

Skrefsrud had made away with their investments and buildings. The key document here was the Trust Deed, whereby the mission and its property belonged to the Santal National Church, with Skrefsrud, the Börresens, and a couple of their British friends as the trustees.[29]

In spite of these conflicts, the mission continued to grow. From 1874 to 1878 they baptized some two thousand adults; then, adding the baptism of children, they performed some twenty-five hundred to three thousand baptisms a year until 1882. In comparison to other missions, this was an impressive record, and these were years of great optimism. The break with the Baptists led them to seek funds elsewhere, first among Evangelicals in India, then in Britain, in Scandinavia, and, later, among Norwegians in America. But these new links undermined the independence of the missionary-trustees, as we shall see.

The committees in Britain were important mainly in the early years. Central here was Dr. Graham of Edinburgh. Scots Presbyterians seem to have supported the mission more than English Evangelicals. The network overlapped, however, with that of the Evangelicals in India.

An Independent Mission: The Projected Santal National Church

From the start, Skrefsrud and the Börresens showed their concern for the culture and traditions of the Santals. The converts kept their Santal names, and there was no attempt to Westernize their dress. Pastors and missionaries did not wear gowns, reflecting a tradition where laymen preach and priests have no special status. Instead of infant baptism, Skrefsrud tried to Christianize the traditional name-giving ceremony *(janam chatiar)*,[30] which was combined with baptism when the mission turned toward Lutheranism. The church did not use bells but drums to call believers to services and meetings. The goal was to build a Santal National Church, independent of the Baptists as well as of the Scandinavian churches, a church that the Santals would one day take over themselves. There was not much concern with defining a theological base for this church, apart from references to the earliest, original, or "apostolic church." "We have not started," said Skrefsrud during a visit to

29. These trustees were the lawyers Robert Allen (who had been responsible for the deed) and his brother T. T. Allen, both based in Calcutta (Hodne, *Skrefsrud,* p. 125).

30. The traditional ritual consists of a first haircut and of anointing the head with oil. The child is named and presented to the *bongas.* In the Christian ritual, the child is presented in church. The libation of rice beer in the traditional rite was dispensed with by the missionaries.

Sweden, "by teaching Luther's or any other catechism, but tried to get them on their knees, in prayer. . . . It was only when they had felt the spiritual life in their hearts, that we have started to teach them."[31] The liturgy used remained simple though somewhat original until 1894: at the end of the service the congregation would declare its adherence to the apostolic beliefs, without specifying further.[32]

Such a church hardly needed theologians to preach. "I am convinced," wrote Börresen to Graham in 1883, "that the ability to preach, to lead the Church, to associate with Christians as well as Heathens, letting oneself be led by the Holy Spirit, were much more important than any qualification — dry and rigid — of a University." Börresen assured Graham there was no lack of young Santals ready to take on the responsibilities of a pastor.[33]

Skrefsrud wanted the projected church to be simple, suited to the requirements of a people still regarded as "primitive." What the projected church needed, then, was independence — guaranteed juridically by the Trust Deed — to develop its own national character.

His concern for the people led him, like many missionaries, to defend their juridical rights. Skrefsrud went further than most, participating with the Deputy Commissioner, Wood, in preparing (1872-79) the *Regulation Land Settlement*.[34] In 1880, he wrote to the press *(Statesman; Friend of India)* to present to the government demands that the Santals themselves had formulated. He also wrote a memoir on Santal customary law, which was used in reforming the juridical system of the Santal Parganas. In 1890 he reported that a certain *zamindar* had torn down a small house built on his land by the mission for evangelizing purposes: "The reason," says Skrefsrud, "is of course easily understood — he knew well, that he can not treat the Santals as he liked, when we were there." The mission complained to the magistrate, and the *zamindar* was fined.[35] Skrefsrud's pleas for better protection against usury and land encroachment did not bear fruit, however, until 1919, with passage of the Bengal Tenancy Act.

Almost from the beginning the missionaries organized village schools subsidized by government funds, and there were almost a hundred in 1882-83.[36]

31. Letter (published in Göteborgs *Weckoblad*), 18 October 1883, cited by Hodne, *Skrefsrud*, p. 193.

32. Hodne, *Skrefsrud*, pp. 194-95.

33. Börresen to Graham, 10 March 1883, in *Dahkwala* 7 (1883): 102.

34. The first settlement was rather incomplete, but it was continued by others such as McPherson. It was completed in 1910 (Hodne, *Skrefsrud*, p. 253).

35. Twenty-third *AR*, 1889-90.

36. Fifteenth *AR*, 1882-83.

They also started boarding schools at Benagaria, the one for girls being the responsibility of Mrs. Börresen. They taught in Santali, using teaching materials prepared chiefly by Skrefsrud. A conflict over teaching in Bengali led to the departure of Ernst Heuman, later Bishop of Tranquebar, who wanted the schools to conform to the official system. Skrefsrud and Börresen preferred to provide elementary education in Santali for the greatest possible number of people.

Santal Ethnicity and the Mission

Skrefsrud's work in describing and codifying Santal customs was important in making the British recognize the cultural specificity of the Santals, whose ethnic identity was in no way a creation of the colonial period. This is clear not only from their Austro-Asiatic language but from the whole semantic complex of their ritual language, religion, kinship, and oral literature.[37] This specificity is essentially unchanged over the large area where Santals are found and regardless of the degree of organizational integration with other groups.[38] The distinction between tribe and caste may of course have been elaborated by colonial discourse. While Santals have been for centuries neighbors to Hindu populations and have accepted cultural loans from them, texts as well as praxis reveal a conscious effort on their part to maintain their own distinct cultural identity and their refusal of caste hierarchy.

Like many missionaries, Skrefsrud and Bodding translated the Scriptures. Skrefsrud also translated Luther's catechism and wrote a grammar that was a considerable improvement on Phillips's earlier attempt. He collected more than twelve thousand words for a Santal dictionary, completed and published many years later by P. O. Bodding. Skrefsrud translated hymns too, but he also wrote his own hymns in Santali, using traditional Santal tunes. Then, in 1887, he published the *Horkoren Mare Hapram Ko,* a collection of Santal myths and traditions. This material was not to be forgotten, and Skrefsrud even introduced it in the mission schools as part of national tradition, though Bodding later withdrew it. No doubt, Skrefsrud hoped the *bongas,* like Norwegian gremlins and trolls, would soon become folklore: he may not have realized that this had taken centuries in the Norwegian case.[39]

37. Carrin-Bouez, *La fleur et l'os,* and articles by the same author.
38. G. Haaland, "Cultural Content and Ethnic Boundaries," in *The Ecology of Choice and Symbol,* edited by R. Grönhaug, G. Haaland, and G. Henriksen (Bergen, 1991), pp. 155-79.
39. In their collection of folk tales, 1840, Asbjörnsen and Moe note that some of their informants actually believe in these supernatural beings (*Norske Folkeeventyr,* 2 vols. [Oslo, 1982]). Yet Norway was Christianized in A.D. 1030.

In 1890, Skrefsrud started a Christian monthly magazine in Santali, *Hor Hoponren Pera,* which continues today.[40] It was a journal intended for popular education. In its pages, Norway figures prominently, with Hauge and the Norwegian low-church tradition presented as a model of civilization for the Santals.

Through his literary work, Skrefsrud had created a viable tradition of writing in Santali. This legacy probably remains as important, in the long run, as the minority of Santal Christians.[41]

The Santals' Role in Their Own Church

Converts were co-opted into the missionary enterprise from the beginning. Catechists were named from 1870; "pastors" were made responsible for a district from 1874; and the first ordinations took place in 1876. They were Siram Soren, one of the first converts, and Birju. There were councils, and there was the institution of elders, borrowed from Pietist communities in Europe. This also implied a certain delegation of responsibility. Elders not only guided communities of converts but also itinerated.

The missionaries were struck by the democratic traditions of the Santals, and in their letters they stressed the contrast between the Santals and the hierarchical Hindus. Santal custom includes assemblies at several levels, where all Santal men (but not women) are free to speak and participate in decisions. This is particularly clear with regard to the village community, but less so in clan matters.[42] Skrefsrud was fascinated by the discourse he found in these meetings. The compatibility between tribal and Evangelical community structures enabled him, in fact, to create a series of substitutes for tribal institutions although it became clear, later, that the new ideology was in fact seen to undermine tribal custom in the eyes of the converts.

40. It did, in fact, disappear from 1906 to 1920, but it then reappeared as the *Hor Pera.*

41. Not all Santals use the roman script introduced by Skrefsrud. In 1953, Raghanath Murmu invented a Santal ideogrammatic script, now used in education and in newspapers mainly in Orissa. The roman script is chiefly used by the Christians of the Santal Parganas. See M. Carrin-Bouez, "De la langue au discours," *Langage et Société* 35 (1986): 67-91; "Retour au bosquet sacré, réflexion sur la réinvention d'une culture adivasi," *Pūrūsartha* 23 (2002).

42. According to the creation myth, the twelve clans are equal, but later narratives introduce status differences between them. The segmentation into about 160 subclans is accounted for in myths emphasizing the authority of the elders (J. Gausdal, *The Santal Khuts* [Oslo, 1960]; Carrin-Bouez, *La fleur et l'os*).

Thus the *kulhi durup*,[43] a traditional intervillage meeting of a *Pargana*,[44] was transformed into a monthly assembly of believers. To respect tradition, chiefs still presided at these meetings, but the transformed meeting differed from the original in several ways. Thus, while the latter allowed individuals to contest the authority of the chief, the Christian *kulhi durup* became rather a consultative forum where local ideas were presented to the leaders of the mission, that is, to the missionaries themselves. Skrefsrud, who hunted with the chiefs and kept their company, was delighted when they offered him the title of *Pargana*. At other occasions *Kerap* (Skrefsrud) was believed to possess the powers of the *jan guru*, the anti-sorcery priest or witchfinder. There was a contradiction here: the man who wanted to build democracy was himself a man who would be king.

The Role of the Early Converts: The Story of Hatia

One of the first converts, Hatia, died in 1881. He was often called the dreamer. Börresen wrote in his obituary that he had

> remarkable dreams, which were fulfilled, and it was one of them that led to his conversion. The Devil cult of the Heathen was never able to satisfy him, so he had let go of it a long time before he became a Christian. In his longing for the unknown God, he dreamt one night that a man came to tell him to go out into the fields, where a message would be brought to him. This he should take to the white men who had settled nearby.

What he found was a leaf from a hymnbook; he was soon converted. Hatia, wrote Börresen,

> was highly concerned that others should share with him in the Grace that he had experienced, and so he went around everywhere preaching the joyful Evangiles, like the disciples and the original Christians in the days after Pentecost. Starting by announcing in his own village what the Lord had done for him, he then went to others further abroad, and became, if we remember rightly, the instrument of converting 16 families. He . . . left

43. The term actually means "sitting in the village street." Traditionally, matters of village settlement were discussed there, but also a wide range of other problems. Matters of the hunt or the forest are formally excluded. Today, the term is sometimes used for a "sit-down" type of political demonstration.

44. A word that translates into the chief of twelve villages as well as the district itself.

his property to the care of his brother, while he now spent all his time and effort in preaching the Grace of God. His needs were but few and small, and since he was highly respected among Christians and Heathens alike, he was welcomed everywhere. He was continually travelling and became Börresen's companion on all the latter's voyages, and in this way he became well acquainted with the Evangiles. . . . When we were walking across the hills and dales . . . he often broke into laughter from pure joy and expressed his burning desire soon to be taken home to Jesus. In the year of famine he was one of our most energetic preachers.[45]

In 1878 Hatia was made head of the colony of emigrants to Murshidabad District, where he stayed until 1881. Then he returned to Ebenezer, where he spent his time visiting and preaching to Hindus and Muslims of the area. He was always welcome, Börresen continued:

Whereas the European Missionary, when preaching to Hindus and Muslims, tries in the most philosophic language . . . Hatia came to them with the simple Gospel and without demonstrations, but was himself living and true proof of everything he said; and as fellow Indians they realised more fully the power of his words.[46]

Börresen reported on how Hatia died fully and truly convinced of his salvation: "When we gather the Elders for council," he recalled, "we see numbers of dear faces among them, who, like Hatia, have dedicated themselves wholly to the Lord. . . . Thus our missionaries, as so many others saw themselves as planting the seed that would bear manifold fruit." But, as Börresen could see, these men were now old, "and we often look at them with some apprehension . . . for we doubt very much, that we may again have such powerful witnesses of the Lord."[47]

The Report of 1881-82

The fourteenth annual report for the year 1881-82, when the mission had become independent and missionary optimism was running high, shows that the Santals occupied important positions in the structure of the nascent

45. *Dahkwala* 8 (1882): 6-7.
46. *Dahkwala* 8 (1882): 6-7.
47. *Dahkwala* 8 (1882): 8-9.

church. In that year Skrefsrud left for his second visit to Europe. Mrs. Börresen also went to visit her children, so only Börresen was left at Ebenezer. Before Skrefsrud left, he and Börresen accompanied a large number of converts to Assam, where the mission had obtained lands to found a new Christian colony.[48] They were joined by a Danish missionary, Jensen, but in March 1881 he went home on sick leave. A fresh Norwegian recruit, Bunkholdt, had arrived, but he was not yet given the charge of a station, assisting here and there to learn his task.[49]

Although 1881-82 was an exceptional year, this was probably when Santal participation in the running of the missionary enterprise reached its height. Practically alone, Börresen had to stay at Ebenezer, and thus the Santals themselves had to do the evangelizing work. Börresen increased the number of Santal assistants, adding eight new elders, and so the total became forty men and six women. They met every fortnight, discussing the means of evangelizing the country. "We are not ashamed," said Börresen, of "speaking our minds freely and openly one to another, when we perceive something wrong with the Elders."[50] If the first "we" was collective, was it true of the second also? While there is a certain ambiguity between a collective we and one more like the majestic use of the pronoun, Börresen was no racist. He appreciated the success of his Santal assistants as fully as he criticized any return to idolatry. If he stressed the simplicity of their teaching, he knew that most priests would make the same criticism of himself, as happened later when Skrefsrud tried to convince the Danish Church that it should make Börresen a bishop.[51]

In the year 1881-82 all the out-stations of the mission were led by Santals. There were six of them, to which two new ones were added during the year. Then there was the new colony in Assam, which a Danish doctor adminis-

---

48. The mission had obtained lands in Assam to alleviate land hunger among the Santals and to create an ideal community where the converts would be physically removed from their heathen past. But the neighboring tea estates found the colony a source of cheap labor, and the situation only improved partly when the mission bought an estate (M. Carrin-Bouez, "Le Paradis dans les jardins du thé," *L'homme* 27.2-3 [1988]: 199-212).

49. This was common practice in the early years. Later, new recruits were given a particular task from the start. The early practice shows the pains the pioneers took to see that new missionaries would fit into their setup. The Pahle affair and the example of Heuman shows that this was no easy task.

50. *Dahkwala* 8 (1882): 10.

51. The attempt revealed Börresen's "extreme simplicity" to the dismay of High Churchmen and Grundtvigians, yet Skrefsrud and Hertel almost succeeded in convincing the Danish Church. However, the low-church supporters of the mission in Norway and Sweden protested against the idea of having a bishop — an office they knew only too well from their own churches (Nyhagen, *Santalmisjonens historie,* 2:164-80).

tered, but where the Santal pastor Siram ministered to the migrants' spiritual needs. There was, then, a considerable devolution of responsibility to the Santal pastors, catechists, and elders. the Santals took care of day-to-day worship and church affairs. Certainly, at this date, the missionaries, and Börresen in particular, were earnest when they spoke of a church that the Santals would one day be capable of running themselves.

Contradictions

If Börresen was trusting the Santals, Skrefsrud defended Santal culture and even went native to a point, but he never ceased to fight tribal religion: "I put my fingers into everything that can bring down the *bongas*, and raise Thakur in every consciousness," he wrote to his Danish supporter, Hertel, in 1879, telling him how he had destroyed an altar to the *bongas*, which a converted chief had allowed to be built in his village.[52] Though writing down the traditions of the old cults, he insisted they should be dead and remembered only as folklore.

Skrefsrud argued for the word *Thakur* to translate the Christian God, since he believed it was a Santal word, though they also used it for Shiva.[53] In one version of the Santal creation myth, Thakur had destroyed humanity but, at the request of Maran Buru, had saved one Santal couple.[54] Later, Thakur introduced caste by dividing humanity by *jāt* ("birth"). In several stories, Thakur is confused with Jom Raja — a Santalization of Yama, the Hindu god of death. Thakur, then, is an ambiguous term. Even Sidhu and Kanhu, leading the rebellion, claimed to act on Thakur's orders.

Skrefsrud was hardly aware of how deeply the *bongas* pervade the feelings of Santals; they even fall in love with their deities. *Bongas* could become divine spouses, bestowing visions and powers on their human companions. In one account a man possessed daily by a female *bonga* fell madly in love with her. He was taken to the missionaries, who tied him up, then taught him to read and write. He was no more a Santal, concluded the story, since he had escaped from his *bonga*.[55] Skrefsrud also neglected another belief: that every Santal would become a *bonga*, three generations after his death.

52. Letter, 9 October 1879, *Dahkwala* 1 (1880): 15-16.

53. L. O. Skrefsrud, *What Is the Correct Term for God in Santali?* (Benares, 1876).

54. Maran Buru, "great mountain," is the chief among the Santal *bongas*. See M. Carrin-Bouez and S. Bouez, "Le mythe de création Santal," *Asie du sud-est et monde insulindien* 5 (1974).

55. *Bonga bapla reak'katha*, Oslo University Library Ms. Div., Santalia, M.8, 1448, vol. B.

Not surprisingly, when Skrefsrud asked the Santals to write down their traditions, they responded to Christian ideas in their own way.[56] In one story, an old woman, recently converted, wanted to go to Paradise to meet Jesus. When she arrived before the gates of Heaven, two guards *(sipahi)* told her to go away. Yet she insisted, only to hear Thakur himself declare that her time had not yet come. She had no right to decide for herself, said the terrible voice. The woman fell down and found herself in her own village, where her children were drinking to celebrate her funeral. They teased her about this *Isor Baba* (Jesus) whom she had not even seen, and they told her instead to walk into the forest, where the *bongas* would be waiting for her. Next morning she did so, and after that she was not seen again. She must have become a witch, felt the villagers, since nobody wanted her.[57] Now, according to the story, people tell this tale whenever anybody wants to meet Isor Baba.[58] Many Santals, then and now, seem to be disappointed that the missionaries were unable to show them Jesus in person: "Why should he not take a human *rup* just one time?" asked one of Carrin's informants.

Skrefsrud mounted a strong campaign against the use of rice beer[59] and alcohol made from the *mohua* flower,[60] especially from 1872 to 1875. Coming from a country where evangelism was becoming identified with teetotalism, he also realized how rice beer was symbolically central to most "heathen" rites. To drink was thus to associate with the devil in more ways than one, but the symbolic significance of rice beer makes it particularly difficult to ban.

Having fun *(raskau)* is a fundamental value in Santal culture; Santals find the Hindus stuffy. Dancing, drinking rice beer, flirting, and making sexual jokes are all part of their culture — none of which was acceptable to the missionaries. Wanting to replace tribal ontology by the belief in heaven and hell, the missionaries failed to see that these categories meant little to the Santals, who saw no point in moral conduct as a means to gain benefits after death. To the missionaries, the Santals seemed carefree, and gradually the idea that they were "unable to think of tomorrow" began to turn up more frequently in

56. M. Carrin-Bouez, "L'apparition de l'écrit et la naissance du récit chez les Santal," in *Vers des sociétés pluriculturelles* (Paris, 1987).

57. A Santal saying affirms "witches are women who have been unable to find a place in other people's eyes" (M. Carrin-Bouez, "Celles qui sont sorties du regard," *Cahiers de Littérature Orale* 39-40 [1996]: 157-74).

58. *Mittan budhi reak' katha,* Santalia, N, 1469.

59. Rice beer libations are used to formalize any kind of contract, as also in most sacrifices (M. Carrin-Bouez, "La biére de riz santal," *Information sur les Sciences Sociales* 26.3 [1987]: 611-32).

60. The *mohua* flower is seen as the essence of possession.

Skrefsrud's letters. In 1890, he reported the following answer to his exhortations to turn to Christ: "Although we do not believe in our gods any more, and although we were convinced that Christianity was the only true religion — yet we feel no inclination to become Christians, as we can not conceive of any other kind of happiness than eating and drinking, getting drunk and dancing and altogether living a sensuous life."[61]

This brings us to the Santal conception of work. In one myth, death is described as a labor camp, where Jom Raja, king of death, directs the recently deceased to make new human beings out of the bones of those long-since dead. Hammer and nails are used, and the workers are driven hard by a *chaukidar*, just as when Santals were working for the British.[62] Moreover, in the Santal myth of creation, work and death enter the world together.[63]

It was certainly not, as the missionaries realized from the beginning, that the Santals were unwilling to work. In the context of collective enterprises, such as building a church, the missionaries praised their converts' energy and goodwill. Rather, it was in the long run that the puritan view of work butts against the Santal view: the Santals do not like drudgery.

Doubts and Discouragements

Most of the contradictions were present from the start, but in letters and reports these problems were minimized during the first phase, when conversions were numerous and progress was evident. The Mission Report of 1881-82 may be seen as the apogee of this period. During the 1880s doubts and reservations were sometimes expressed as the number of new conversions decreased. Thus the 1889-90 report speaks of indifference, but then notes that distress and drought had led the Santals to come to the mission. There follows an apologetic defense against critics who speak of "rice-Christians,"[64] concluding: "We must thank God, that there were such things as poverty, cares and suffering — else, we fear, very few, if any, would seek after God."[65] Proof was the case of the young man who "baptize[d] himself" in mockery — "look at me, how quickly

---

61. Twenty-third *AR*, 1889-90, p. 5.

62. *Hanapuri reak' katha*, Santalia, M 8, 1448, vol. L.

63. See M. Carrin-Bouez, "Rethinking Female Participation in Tribal Labour in Chotanagpur and Bengal," in *Dalit Movements and the Meanings of Labour in India*, edited by P. Robb (Delhi, 1993), pp. 150-58.

64. This was the accusation made in 1874, after the famine and conversions that year. This criticism, from less "successful" colleagues, seems to be still felt fifteen years later.

65. Twenty-third *AR*, 1889-90, pp. 2-3.

I shall become a Christian, and yet enjoy life" — yet died in agony the same night. "God is not mocked," concluded the report.[66]

By the late 1890s a certain despondency was apparent: "What we miss now, is the first, hotly burning love of the first Christians," wrote Skrefsrud in 1897, "Now we have many who sleep, and even quite a few who must be seen as the enemies of the Cross of Christ. . . ."[67] Later he lamented the passing of the "golden age" of the mission.[68] Certainly, from a Santal point of view, conversion to Christianity had not brought a return to the golden age that Sidhu and Kanhu had dreamed about. Any attendant advantages of Christianity had been marginal to their situation.

While the number of European missionaries increased throughout the 1880s and 1890s,[69] the place of the Santals in what was to be their own church diminished. Ostensibly, the missionaries were disappointed by their Santal pastors and catechists. One case they referred to was that of Sibu Besra. In 1881-82, as a catechist, he was in charge of a station. We hear of a considerable number of baptisms, and Sibu's eagerness was praised.[70] In 1884, he was ordained. He distinguished himself as a writer of hymns. In 1892, he was put in charge of evangelization in the Sultanpur area and managed two thousand conversions in a few years. Skrefsrud and Bodding decided to place a European at Sultanpur to help him, but Börresen wanted to leave the initiative to the Santals. By the late 1890s Sibu had been removed from his post, and most of his converts had returned to the tribal religion.[71] The missionaries said he had proved unable to bear his own success. Did he play a role that the missionaries wanted to keep for themselves? Sibu's case seems typical: three more ordained Santal pastors were sacked in the space of a few years.[72] Important posts were no longer left to Santals.

The Santal pastor Siram had been given spiritual charge over the Assam colony. There was no criticism of Siram, who kept his post until his death in 1894, but he had no Santal successor. From 1896 the Norwegian missionary,

---

66. Twenty-third *AR*, 1889-90, pp. 8-9.

67. Santalen, 1897, p. 188.

68. Thirty-fourth *AR*, 1901-2, p. 17.

69. This is clear from the annual reports. In 1882-83 there were five Europeans, four of them missionaries, though three of them were away that year. By 1889-90 the number of Europeans had grown to nine. The numbers grew steadily from then on, until there were about a hundred Westerners in 1947. The number of Santals did not increase in proportion.

70. *Dahkwala* 8 (1882): 16.

71. Nyhagen, *Santalmisjonens historie*, 2:195-96.

72. J. Gausdal, *Santalmisjonens historie paa misjonsmarken* (Oslo, 1937), pp. 314-15.

Bunkholdt, led the colony both administratively and spiritually. The Santals, wrote Skrefsrud, were "like children" and "unable to think of tomorrow."[73]

The Increasing Importance of the Support Committees

Contributing to this change in the leadership of the church was an increasing dependence on the Scandinavian countries. The factions and trends, different in each of the three Scandinavian countries, can only be sketched here.

In Denmark, the *primus motor* was the young pastor, Ludvig Hertel. Having read about the mission in the *Times,* he wrote to Skrefsrud, offering his assistance. Hertel was a Grundtvigian, that peculiar national-liberal strain of Danish Christianity that owed some of its popular support to feelings aroused by the war with Prussia in 1864. Hertel's father had been a priest in South Jutland, then lost to Germany. The liberal Grundtvigian sometimes clashed with the Pietist Inner Mission, closer to Börresen's social milieu, and with the High Church, but he struggled to defend the Santal Mission against all comers while maintaining links with all three camps of Danish Christianity. Hertel founded the journal *Dahkwala,* which at first reached all the Scandinavian countries, and he maintained a voluminous correspondence with Klara Fagstad and the Lillehammer Committee.

In fact, when Skrefsrud returned to Norway, he found that Hertel had prepared the ground for him. Apart from Lillehammer, strong support groups had been formed in Drammen and in Christiania (Oslo). There, the core was a low-church group that had known Skrefsrud since members were visiting prisoners at the time of his confinement. None of them wanted to head the Christiania Committee, however, so they turned to Dr. Nissen, a left-wing medical doctor, who had helped to organize the first strike of female workers and also worked among prostitutes. Later, he was a founder of the Social Democrat Party. He soon left mission work, however, when the Liberal victory and the introduction of parliamentarism produced a schism between the Committee's main constituents, the Low Church and the radical Left.[74]

The Swedes lost interest when Heuman left the mission. In Denmark, support waned after Hertel's death, while the National Church idea that had inspired the Grundtvigians became less and less important to the mission. Nor-

---

73. Skrefsrud uses this characterization of the Santals earlier (letter to Hertel, 9 October 1879; *Dahkwala* 1 [1880]: 15-16). Yet here, the tone is full of optimism: Santal simplicity will be the stuff from which true believers are made.

74. Nissen's role was ambiguous during the Pahle affair, which probably hastened his break with the mission.

wegian-American developments broadly paralleled those in the home country.[75] Today's concern for the Santal mission is overwhelmingly Norwegian with a significant Norwegian-American participation: its supporters are low-church and still somewhat at odds with Lutheran orthodoxy.

The supporters of the mission are still Lutherans, however, and new missionaries, who joined from the 1880s onward, had theological training. They looked askance at the loose theology of the founders; as Börresen's simplicity was replaced by a more formal approach, the mission examined more closely the quality of conversions. This, too, may be why Santal pastors and catechists, whose training was rudimentary to say the least, were no longer seen as real collaborators.

These tendencies were strengthened by the death of the founders, Börresen in 1901, Skrefsrud in 1910, and Caroline Börresen in 1914. Bodding,[76] who sometimes hinted at the "not exactly Lutheran" practices of the founders, became sole trustee and head of the mission at Skrefsrud's death. He introduced the liturgy of the Norwegian State Church in 1913, but he was surrounded by younger missionaries whose main allegiance was to the support committees. Their training did not include British law, however, and they failed to understand the meaning of the Trust Deed, which had no parallel in Norwegian law. They felt the mission should belong to the supporters who paid for it, and the fact that the mission legally belonged to the Santal National Church made little sense to them. When Bodding, in 1922, handed over the mission to the Norwegians, he was giving away Santal property, but it was in his right, as sole trustee, to do so.

From then on the mission was led from Norway. To Gausdal, in 1927, the time had come to discuss the role of the Santals in what would ultimately become again their own church. He was opposed by Rosendal, the head of the mission, who saw the Santals as immature and irresponsible. Gausdal may be

---

75. For more detail, see Nyhagen, *Santalmisjonens historie*, 2:210-29, 374.

76. P. O. Bodding (1865-1938) was Skrefsrud's favorite and chosen successor. He assisted in the literary and linguistic work and continued it after Skrefsrud's death (Hodne, *Skrefsrud*, pp. 223-31). His five-volume *Santal Dictionary* (Oslo, 1932-36) is the *sine qua non* of Santal studies, and his three-volume *Santal Folk Tales* (Oslo, 1925-27) is a major work. What led Bodding to give up leadership of the mission was his third marriage, which proved to be bigamous. After the death of his first wife he married Börresen's daughter, Ingeborg, in 1897, but she soon ran away to the Nepal frontier with the mission's Muslim coachman. Bodding thought her dead when he married Christine Larsen, a doctor and female missionary, in 1922, but Ingeborg's sister, married to Bishop Heuman of Tranquebar, had recently received letters from her sister (see Nyhagen, *Santalmisjonens historie*, 3:89-103). The mission banned Bodding from evangelization but gave him a stipend to continue his ethnographic and literary work.

seen, here, to represent the voice of the future as well as the memory of the past. Yet Rosendal's views, so typical of colonial society in the 1920s, prevailed.[77] Only by 1950 did the Santal church again become independent of the mission, and it was only in 1958 when a Santal finally became its head.

77. See Nyhagen, *Santalmisjonens historie*, 3:414-39.

CHAPTER TWELVE

Christian Missionaries and Orientalist Discourse: Illustrated by Materials on the Santals after 1855

PETER B. ANDERSEN AND SUSANNE FOSS

This chapter criticizes the concept of latent Orientalism and the assumption of a generalized hegemonic imperialism behind all Western scholarship on India, as claimed by Ronald Inden. The argument is illuminated by historical material concerning colonial administration and Christian missions among the Santals. The situation of the Santals, who have been ascribed "tribal" status, demonstrates a situation of double "otherness": Santals were viewed as "other" people, both to the colonial power and to the indigenous majority. This chapter seeks to show that Inden's assumption that all Indians represented a simple otherness to the colonial power is an untenable simplification.

The lively discussions on Orientalism initiated by Edward W. Said's homonymous book have opened new lines of research by stressing that the notion of the "Orient" put forward by the colonial powers was a hegemonic concept that allowed the colonial powers to master the subjugated peoples through classification.[1]

1. See Edward W. Said, *Orientalism* (Harmondsworth, 1995 [1st ed., 1978]). Said's critique of Orientalism, i.e., Oriental studies, has been developed by Ronald Inden for India; see his "Orientalist Constructions of India," *Modern Asian Studies,* 20.3 (1986): 401-46; and

Our special thanks to Dr. Morten Warmind (Dept. of History of Religions, Copenhagen) and Birgitte Städe for discussion and inspiration; to the participants in the Workshop on Orientalism, organized by Stein Tönnesson at the Nordic Institute for Asian Studies, Copenhagen, 1995; and to participants in a seminar organized by Gunnel Cederlöf and Beppe Karlsson at Uppsala, where an earlier version of this paper was presented.

As is well known, Said uses Gramsci's concept of cultural hegemony, that is, a political, moral, and intellectual dominance based on some degree of general acceptance or consent, passive or active, in society. Yet whereas Gramsci expanded Lenin's use of the term, so that it also covered the formation of a general consensus, it may be important to note that he put forward his considerations as part of a revolutionary strategy against the political hegemony. Said's use of the term hegemony refers solely to how a system of political power creates (or constructs) a general acceptance of its own interests.

An excellent example of this from the world of fiction is to be found in Salman Rushdie's *The Satanic Verses*. There the manticore explains Saladin Chamcha's transformation to a goat:

> "The point is," the manticore continued, "Are you going to put up with it?" Saladin was still puzzled. The other seemed to be suggesting that these mutations were the responsibility of — of whom? How could they be? — "I don't see," he ventured, "who can be blamed. . . ."
>
> The manticore ground its three rows of teeth in evident frustration. "There's a woman over that way," it said, "who is now mostly water-buffalo. There are two businessmen from Nigeria who have grown sturdy tails. There is a group of holidaymakers from Senegal who were doing no more than changing planes when they were turned into slippery snakes. . . .
>
> . . . "The point is," it said fiercely, "some of us aren't going to stand for it. We're going to bust out of here before they turn us into anything worse. Every night I feel a different piece of me beginning to change. I've started, for example, to break wind continually. . . . I beg your pardon . . . you see what I mean? By the way, try these," he slipped Chamcha a packet of extra-strength peppermints. "They'll help your breath. I've bribed one of the guards to bring a supply."
>
> "But how do they do it?" Chamcha wanted to know.
>
> "They describe us," the other whispered solemnly. "That's all. They

Imagining India (Cambridge, Mass., 1992). Raymond Schwab's study on the Oriental renaissance, *The Oriental Renaissance: Europe's Rediscovery of India and the East 1680-1880* (New York, 1984 [1st ed., 1950]) was the study that inspired Said's book. The impact of the Orientalist studies on the colonialized peoples is becoming an integrated part of scholarship; see, for instance, Carol A. Breckenridge and Peter van der Veer, "Orientalism and the Postcolonial Predicament," in their edited *Orientalism and the Postcolonial Predicament: Perspectives on South Asia* (Philadelphia, 1993); Erik Reenberg Sand, "Nogle træk af indiensreceptionen i Vesten og Danmark i nyere tid," in *Indiske Religioner i Danmark, Chaos*, 21, edited by Peter B. Andersen and Erik Reenberg Sand (København, 1994), pp. 4-29.

have the power of description, and we succumb to the pictures they construct."[2]

In Rushdie's book, Chamcha is an Indian-born actor who succumbs to the power of description in London, the capital of the former colonial power. Within the novel's fictional framework Chamcha succumbs to classification in a very real way, and in some respects Rushdie's book deals with the ideological subjugation of migrants to the United Kingdom.

In what follows we demonstrate that the general conditions are not that simple, and, as far as the specific circumstances are concerned, we argue against the assumption of a simple dissipation of a hegemonic ideology from the top of society toward the lower strata. In the quotation from Rushdie's novel, it is implicitly assumed that "they" have the power to define and to, so to say, execute the definition. And "they" participate in a general plan with the deliberate intention to dominate. Whether those conditions are fulfilled is not specified in Rushdie's novel, and in a scholarly argument it would need qualification.

We will try to illustrate the implications of those qualifications with examples of classifications and definitions of so-called tribal peoples in India, concentrating on the Santals. The notion of tribes in India is particularly suitable for illuminating the discussion on Orientalism because the tribes in India have been defined in opposition to the Hindus. This opens an opportunity to get behind the commonly accepted opposition between Westerners and Hindus that has dominated the discussion on Orientalism in India.

The scholar whose work has come closest to the ideas expressed in Rushdie's novel is Ronald Inden. Other scholars have distinguished between two different points of view. The first is that of the so-called "Orientalists,"[3] who found great spiritual values in the religious heritage of India, a point of view still prevalent in much philological research on India. The other was that of those colonial administrators who were unsympathetic to the spiritual heritage of India and argued for a linguistic and educational Anglification of India. Ronald Inden argues, however, that the difference between these two points of view is confined to their evaluation of India, while both agree that India is dominated by irrational religious powers, Hinduism and caste.

Inden argues that the observations and interpretations of Westerners

2. Salman Rushdie, *The Satanic Verses* (London, 1988), pp. 167-68.

3. In this Indian context "Orientalist" refers to those scholars and administrators who argued for administrating India by means of Indian languages and law; see David Kopf, *British Orientalism and the Bengal Renaissance: The Dynamics of Indian Modernization, 1773-1835* (Berkeley, 1969).

working in Indian studies are governed by unconscious factors that he terms the "episteme" of Indology. He writes: "Indological discourse, I argue, holds (or simply assumes) that the essence of Indian civilization is just the opposite of the West's. It is the irrational (but rationalizable) institution of 'caste' and the Indological religion that accompanies, Hinduism."[4] According to Inden, the Hinduism of Indologists is not a religion that can be accounted for in relation to some kind of social reality. It is a pure construct made up by the Indologists.

He continues:

> Human agency in India is displaced by Indological discourse not only onto a reified State or Market but onto a substantialized Caste. This has entailed several consequences for the Indological construction of India. It has necessitated the wholesale dismissal of Indian political institutions, and especially of kingship. To give this construct of India credibility, the depiction of Indian thought as inherently symbolic and mythical rather than rational and logical has also been required. Finally, it has been necessary for Brahmanism or Hinduism, the religion considered to be the justification of caste, to be characterized as essentially idealistic (i.e. apolitical).[5]

Inden criticizes Indological studies for being too essentialistic, searching first for an essence and only then constructing a representation of India in accordance with that essence. This is only possible because the discipline acts in a dreamlike unreal state where hidden instincts govern what the Indologists consider realities. In fact Inden describes the process with a terminology encountered in Freudian interpretation of dreams. The factual knowledge (the manifest context) is adapted in the dream by condensing and repressing until secondary revision ultimately takes over. This causes several elements that, when a person is awake, are distinguished as different (the manifest context) to appear as identical in the dream. However, one element in a dream can correspond to several elements when awake. After a short summary of Freud's theory of dreams, Inden notes that reality has been transformed into the unrecognizable. "Parts appear as wholes (synecdoche), associated elements appear as the entities with which they are asso-

---

4. Most of the argument here is directed toward Inden's essay "Orientalist Constructions," p. 402, not his later, more elaborate book *Imagining India*. Although the book's major qualities are its insights into the history of Indology, it leaves those problems we raise in this critique unsolved.

5. Inden, "Orientalist Constructions," pp. 402-3.

ciated (metonymy), and ideas are expressed not in their own form but in analogical form (metaphor)."[6]

As Inden sees it, Indology is related to a manifest context at several levels. At the first level, Indology is merely "descriptive"; at a higher level of recognition it is "interpretive"; and at the last level it is "explanatory." Consequently it should only be at the highest level that Indology was comparable to the dream state, but Inden argues that already the selection of elements for description is governed by hidden urges. The urge that is decisive for the total picture is the imperialism of the colonial power that leads to the creation of a "hegemonic" picture of India.[7] Here the circle is complete, and the colonial power continues the invasions of India begun at the time of Alexander, and subdues the dreaming, unpolitical India, which disintegrates into local castes that have never tried to create any political system on their own. Consequently Inden can write about "the nineteenth-century scholar and imperialist" as being generally representative of Indological research.[8]

Inden's account is rich with new observations, and it leads toward a fruitful reinterpretation of the history of research on India. Nevertheless, we think that his generalization that any kind of Western research on India since the eighteenth century has been an imperialistic (or perhaps postimperialistic) project is untenable. If Inden were right, one could say that he himself has taken over an imperialistic point of view when he writes on India as a unity, but we can imagine that Inden feels he has transgressed the imperialistic restrictions of Indology. This thought illustrates some of the problems of Inden's presentation of Indology. It is not possible to put it in a form that lends itself to falsification. Even if Inden were right in his general approach to Indology, his generalizations would need some other kinds of qualification when they lump the views of the sociologist Max Weber, the economist Karl Marx, and the colonial administrator James Mill in the same formula and view all of them as being determined by Hegel's idea of India; Marx and Weber cannot be considered as imperialists in any simple meaning of the word. A discussion along these lines would not, however, do justice to the very high abstraction of Inden's theoretical work. It would be more relevant to see how it is possible to elaborate his theory in a way where the problems can be circumscribed.

---

6. Inden, "Orientalist Constructions," p. 413, with further reference to Freud.

7. The essence of Indology would be an adequate term, but Inden does not use it in this context.

8. Inden, "Orientalist Constructions," p. 420.

The Background of Inden's Theoretical Position

Inden recognizes his debt to Said, who in turn developed the theories and methods of Michel Foucault. Said sees Orientalism as a discourse in Foucault's sense of the concept, and Inden follows Said's interpretation and use of the concept. Foucault sees discourses as ways of speaking and conceptualizing the world. They form the framework of logical possibilities for statements of any kind (spoken, written, painted, and so on), and whoever speaks or acts within a certain discourse is caught within the limitations and possibilities set by the discourse. Since the discourse produces knowledge and what is perceived as being "the truth," the discourse in fact produces or creates reality. Speakers within a specific discourse re-create that very same discourse among themselves, often on a subconscious level. Foucault does not separate discourse from action — action is an integrated part of the concept of discourse. Since all knowledge is produced by discourse and discursive practices, there is no such thing as "true knowledge" or "objective reality" — reality is whatever is produced by the discourse. This interpretation of discourse also means that Foucault does not differentiate between objective "knowledge" and ideological "politics" — it is all part of and produced by discourse. Discourse itself has no specific political (e.g., Marxist or imperialistic) content. Within the same discourse it is possible to fight out political confrontations for opposing interests. The discourse only determines the framework for what it is possible to think and formulate, but it does not determine the outcome of conflicting interests between different opponents.

In his own use of the discourse as an analytical framework, Foucault stuck to a manifest level of analysis where he considered the acts or statements, that is, what was actually said or done. He stressed that the reason to

> isolate, in relation to the language and to thought, the occurrence of the statement/event, it is not in order to spread over everything a dust of facts. It is in order to be sure that this occurrence is not linked with synthesizing operations of a purely psychological kind (the intention of the author, the form of his mind, the rigour of his thought, the themes that obsess him, the project that traverses his existence and gives it meaning) and to be able to grasp other forms of regularity, other types of relations.[9]

9. Michel Foucault, *The Archaeology of Knowledge & the Discourse on Language* (New York, 1972), pp. 28-29 (French original, 1969).

This is exactly one of the important differences between Foucault and Said. Whereas Foucault insists on analyzing discourse at the manifest level, Said introduced an analytical level of material hidden beneath the manifest level of analysis. He termed this level "latent discourse" or latent Orientalism, and by this he means an unconscious psychological absolute distinction between the Orient and the West. In his analyses latent Orientalism is at the same time used to interpret statements or events as part of descriptions, and as part of explanations of the statements and events.

Inden employs the concept of discourse in accordance with Said rather than with Foucault, and Inden's introduction of a psychological approach to the interpretation of the material is even beyond the overt methodology in the work of Said. Inden and Said agree in acknowledging the importance of the individual as an historical actor and here they are both in opposition to Foucault, who did not recognize the individual author/actor as being of any analytical interest.

Discourses and Discourses

Instead of assuming the existence of a subconscious stratum under the manifest discourse as Inden proposes, one can adopt other approaches directed toward the manifest texts and at the same time attempt to keep track of how relevant notions are formed by the language. This approach keeps track of the background of the authors or speakers and the social background they address, but the analysis takes its point of departure in the manifest formulations and by inductive forms of generalized statements about the social and cultural stipulations behind those formulations.

In a European context the Dutch scholar van Dijk is well known for this kind of investigation of press coverage of minorities in Europe.[10] At a general level van Dijk tries to demonstrate how a majority may define cultural "others" through its way of speaking about them. At a certain level this is parallel to the analysis of Said and Inden since they also investigate how one group conceptualizes other groups. The difference is found at the level of analysis. Said and Inden investigate long spans of time and general cultural and political currents, whereas van Dijk examines a limited amount of material over a short period of time. The analysis of van Dijk concerns the specific usage of language in expressions about the object of a text, *in casu* the

---

10. Teun A. van Dijk, *Communicating Racism: Prejudice in Thought and Talk* (Newbury Park, Calif., 1987).

ethnic minorities, and through his analysis of a number of related texts he points to some general tendencies. One of van Dijk's points is that a close linguistic analysis of a statement makes possible a recognition of the nonformulated parts of the statement. In the European context the method allows van Dijk to identify discriminatory strategies in the media even where discrimination in the press is forbidden in accordance to political correctness or by the law. Even though political correctness is not as disseminated in India as in Europe and the United States, it is still a relevant approach when analyzing the Indian media. What is more important is that the method keeps the specific usage in focus. This enables the scholar to avoid assumptions about a subconscious strata of discourse and to demonstrate how discourse may define minorities as "others," different from the majority population, even if it is difficult to identify specific discriminatory words in the statement. Such a specific linguistic analysis may also help in uncovering whether there exists only a single discourse about certain matters in a society at any given point of time.

Inden states that his analysis identifies a unified and general discourse in colonial India, but he emphasizes that it was also present in precolonial times just as it is found today, and he explains its existence by referring to a subconscious imperialism. Contrary to Foucault, Inden does not recognize the existence of different opinions and ideas within the same discourse, which according to Foucault is often the case. As already mentioned, a discourse in Foucault's sense does not indicate any kind of agreement within a population or society at a given point in time. To Foucault a discourse is a way of speaking or describing the world, and it defines *how* different opinions can be argued. It is this general aspect of the discourse that constitutes the reality or the truth, and in this respect a certain discourse is restricting for all groups within a given society.

For Foucault it is not possible to speak about a reality in any objective sense since the reality is created as part of the discourse. In the quotation from the *Satanic Verses,* and in the theories of Said and Inden, discourse also shapes reality, but the perspective is different from Foucault's because there is an intention behind the discourse. The businessmen from Nigeria grow sturdy tails, and, when the colonized peoples are described as without political agency, they lose whatever political agency they may once have had.

As already indicated, we think that this is to take a theory covering elements of a construction of realities too far. This point may be exemplified by the growth of the concept of tribalism and the classification of the Santals as tribals in nineteenth-century India. Since our discussion is part of a general argument against the way Said and Inden analyze discourses, it would be possible to sustain our argument with practically any example. The reason for selecting the so-called tribes is that they are considered "others" in several ways, both to the Europeans and to the Hindus, and the material thus makes it easy to recognize the problems of general statements about a hegemonic discourse toward the others as a single unit.

First, the concept of tribalism will be introduced with a note on how it can be said to constitute a discourse. Second, whether that discourse is governing the actions of people at all is considered. Last, it will be possible to argue whether the discourse is imperialistic in certain ways or not.

The Notion of "Tribal"

The origin of the notion of tribal in Indian anthropology is quite obscure. It is true that the theories of Indian villages, whether they were proposed by Karl Marx, Henry Sumner Maine, or B. H. Baden-Powell, addressed the antique concept of *tribus,* but they discussed settled Hindus in comparison with Indo-European groups in Europe.[11] This has very little relevance for the distinction between Hindus and tribals that gradually has become common in Indian anthropology. Here the term tribe came to designate peoples on a lower level of civilization than the Hindus or members of other higher kinds of religions. In H. H. Risley's survey of *Tribes and Castes of Bengal,* published in 1891, he offered a thorough theoretical argument on the origin of caste and a systematic description of the different institutions within the castes. The terminology concerning tribes seems, though, to have been introduced as an *ad hoc* designation for non-Hindus.[12] Sometimes this term may just have been used for endogamous groups that could not be included among the Hindus. The reasons may have varied. In surveys such as Risley's the main reason may have been that other Hindus did not accept them as such. That left open the opportunity for the group under consideration to propagate a Hindu identity, sometimes with success. This led Risley to identify a number of Hindu castes as semi-Hinduized tribes or, in those cases where the tribal concept was given priority, as tribes who had become semi-Hinduized (hereby indicating that they were one step further away from being accepted as Hindus). Often the decisive factor in Risley's argument was

11. See Inden, *Imagining India,* pp. 134-72.
12. H. H. Risley, *The Tribes and Castes of Bengal, Ethnographic Glossary* (Calcutta, 1981 [1891]), 1:xv-xviii.

race or language and not what we today would consider religious or cultural traits.

In this way a group could be classified as caste or non-caste. From a modern perspective this classification might be in harmony with their religious confession or in conflict with it. Risley and other contemporary anthropologists considered religion and social organization as so intimately interwoven that they did not try to introduce two different and independent systems of classification. Some of the Christian missionaries, though, had other interests underlying their understanding of the tribals, as will be shown below.

Before Risley's survey there had been more than a hundred years of contact with the involved "tribal" groups after the East India Company took over the collection of revenue for the Great Mughal in Bengal (including major parts of the present-day Bihar, Jharkhand, and Orissa) in 1765. In Bengal the largest "tribal" group was that of the Santals with whom the British came into contact during the 1790s. At that time they inhabited an area around the borders of the present-day states of Orissa, Jharkhand, Bihar, Madhya Pradesh, and West Bengal; and at a later point a great number of them migrated northward to an area in the present-day Jharkhand that came to be known as Santal Parganas. As noted in the discussion of Risley, there could, at times, be doubt as to whether individual groups should be considered as tribes or as Hindus, but, with the exception of some irresolute statements from the 1790s, there was general agreement that the Santals were to be considered as tribals.[13]

When one consults the early sources on the Santals, it becomes evident that their classification as tribals colored the observations of their culture among administrators as well as missionaries. There were also major differences between the two groups — tribals and Hindus — as will be demonstrated.

The Missionaries on the Santals

The first Christian mission among the Santals was initiated in 1824 but soon ceased. It was later taken up again, and records from 1841 make it clear that missionary activity had been going on for some years. In his diary for the afternoon of 10 February 1841, the missionary Jeremiah Phillips compares the Santals very favorably to the Hindus:

13. See, for instance, L. S. S. O'Malley, *Bengal District Gazetteers: Santal Parganas* (Calcutta, 1910).

Hearing that there would be a large dance some three or four miles off, and as most of our villagers had gone, we determined to go also. On our way we overtook a company of men, women and children, dressed in their nicest cloth[e]s, singing and skipping about in the most delightful manner. On arriving at the spot, we found some six hundred people assembled in a circular enclosure, in the centre of which a few leaves of the *sarl* tree were placed upon some rough images of elephants, horses, crocodiles, etc. Around these were some two hundred women, while in the outer part of the circle a large company of musicians, followed by the men, were marching round at a varied pace, the weaker sex in the centre more leisurely. The scene was pleasant to witness; it is so seldom that we see anything like activity, that we delight to gaze even upon a dance. The highest bliss to which an Oriya [*viz.*, a Hindu] aspires is to stuff himself till he can eat no more, and then lie down to sleep in the sun. This constitutes his happiness here, and in his opinion will constitute his happiness hereafter. But here appears to be a very different people. Wherever we have been, we have found the women mingling with the men, in their labours and in their recreations; and they do not appear to be considered inferior. The consequence is they look like human beings — they respect themselves.[14]

The missionaries varied in their enthusiasm for the Santals, but they generally agreed with the administrators that the tribals were fundamentally different from the Hindus. Their agreement, however, was determined by widely different approaches to the study of the tribes. The administrators worked from a evolutionary theory of society where the tribals represented a low step in the development of religions, mostly animism focused on fertility rituals. The missionaries, however, had a theory of an original High God; and to them the tribals represented isolated groups of people who had preserved traces of an original monotheism according to natural law, or who could perhaps even remember the original revelation of God.

These different approaches are evident in their studies of the *karam* festival among the tribals. The evolutionist approach is represented by Risley and the Indian anthropologist S. C. Roy,[15] and inserted in a general theoretical framework by the Cambridge anthropologist James George Frazer.[16] Frazer

14. Quoted from W. J. Culshaw, *Tribal Heritage: A Study of the Santals* (London, 1949), p. 161.

15. Sarat Chandra Roy, *The Mundas and Their Country* (Calcutta, 1921); idem, *Oraon Religion and Customs* (Delhi, reprint 1985).

16. James George Frazer, *Aftermath: A Supplement to The Golden Bough* (London,

used the ritual acts in the *karam* festival as evidence for his interpretation of an old Greek ritual, "The Gardens of Adonis," as one of fertility.

The missionaries were seldom interested in the rituals in the *karam* festival or the mythological explanations that accompanied them. Their aim was to collect myths of creation because they wished to find a native god who could be identified with the Christian God in their translations of Christian texts into Santali. Seeing that those stories told during the festival were introduced by myths of creation, the missionaries concentrated on collecting those parts of the stories. The Danish missionary Rasmus Rosenlund explained those collections as a search for

> One great God, creator or primordial father, who stands out completely from and over the crowd of spirits. . . . This great God is conceived as a good, benevolent being, but besides he resembles the picture of God in the European deism, he is a "Deus Otiosus," who once created the world, and since then has not interfered in the course of events.[17]

Rosenlund succeeded in finding all those elements in the Santal god Thakur, who "is not charged with frightening or disgracing mythological elements,"[18] and Rosenlund could conclude that "the theory of an original Monotheism is not more unscientific than the insistence that the primitive man cannot think the thought about God the Creator."[19]

This High God who did not receive any sacrifices did not resemble the godhead that evolutionists found in the rites of fertility. Different solutions have been suggested, but they have usually not addressed the problem in the general theories and only focused on the name of the god or whether he had originated among the tribals or the Hindus. In other words, two different theories led the missionaries and the administrators to differentiate between tribes and Hindus as far as their social organization, culture, and religion were concerned.

In considering whether this debate between the missionaries and the administrators indicates the existence of a discourse, it is possible to put forward several arguments both for and against such a proposition. Said and Inden seldom specify which requirements a discourse must satisfy before it

---

1966 [1st ed., 1936]), pp. 130-31; idem, *The Golden Bough: A Study in Magic and Religion, Abridged Edition* (London, 1974 [1922]), pp. 450-51.

17. Reassumes Rosenlund, *Fra Santalistan, Missionsstudiebog,* 2nd ed. (København, 1949), p. 115.

18. Rosenlund, *Fra Santalistan, Missionsstudiebog,* p. 115.

19. Rosenlund, *Fra Santalistan, Missionsstudiebog,* p. 118.

can be considered as such. It is worth mentioning that both operate with the concepts of hegemonic epistemes (Inden) or hegemonic discourses (Said and Inden), thereby indicating that the discourses have reached some degree of general acceptance at the various levels of society. This demand is met by the notion of tribes.

Foucault is reluctant to define exactly what he means by a discourse, but the concept of tribalism easily meets his demands for speaking of discursive formations as systems of dispersion between a number of statements that can be defined by a regularity.[20] One can surmise that he would have supported the notion of tribes in nineteenth-century Indian anthropology as a discursive formation since it is specific to the period and came to signify certain groups of people. One may further add that it is to a very high degree a product of classification that Foucault pointed to as one of the most powerful conditions of knowledge in the seventeenth and eighteenth centuries. In this period the world was analyzed through establishing taxonomies and classifications. Natural history, with Linnaeus as one of the important representatives, is an example of the way discourse was formed in this period, and all scientific knowledge evolved through this classificatory discourse.

As to our argument we think that it is proper to accept the agreement between missionaries and administrators on the notion of tribes in twentieth-century India as a discursive formation. There are, however, major problems when it comes to interpreting the meaning of the discursive formation in the history of India.

Unconscious Imperialistic Mission *versus* Manifest Imperialist Opposition against Mission

The agreement between missionaries and administrators could, of course, be seen as another example reflecting an unconscious collaboration between missionaries and administrators in their common imperialistic project, as it might be argued along the lines of Ronald Inden; or even as manifest evidence of collaboration between missionaries and administrators, as has supported by some historians and sociologists.[21] A collaboration undoubtedly

20. Foucault, *Archaeology of Knowledge*, p. 38.

21. This, in general terms, is K. M. Pannikar's point; see *Asia and Western Dominance* (London, 1970 [1953]). Pannikar's views, in accord with the theological historian of Christian mission, Stephen Neill, were that "the only notable successes of the missions in recent years have been obtained when they could rely on the superior force of the western nations, or at least on the artificial aura of prestige by which the western man was sur-

existed during some periods of the British Empire in India,[22] and at times it was also specifically used by missionaries to the Santals when they argued for support from the government for their social work.

One illuminating instance of such manifest imperialism among missionaries to the Santals will be considered here. It concerns an attempt to shape a docile native through Christian teachings. This position was articulated by a missionary of the British Church Missionary Society (CMS), Rev. Droese, just after the Sepoy Mutiny of 1857, when he was arguing for government support for the Schools for the Santals, which had been recently established by the CMS after the Santals own rebellion, the *Hul* of 1855.[23]

Rev. Droese felt that the Mutiny would "inaugurate a new era in connexion with Christian Missions in India" because "the attention" had

> been called to the subject, before too much disregarded by people in general, both at home and in this country; the evident bearing of the spread of Christianity upon the safety and happiness, if not the very continuance of Europeans in this land; the evident regard shewn by natives in many places to Missionaries above every other European; the now palpable fact, that there are many native Christians in the country; the generally excellent conduct of those Christians all through the late fearful struggle.[24]

The imperialistic emphasis is clear from his eagerness to forward the spread of Christianity solely as a means of repression of the population; and in his continuation he reports that he sees that government officers as well as others now "obtain native Christians for officers and employments which, it

---

rounded in the colonial period" (*Colonialism and Christian Missions: Foundations of the Christian Missions* [London, 1966], p. 13). Even Neill had to admit that Pannikar recognized the good that the Christian missions have done and stressed that formalized collaboration between the British imperialists and the missions was only found in limited periods and areas. Neill himself is much more elaborate in his summary of the "attitude of unfriendliness towards missions, which never entirely ceased to exist as long as British rule was maintained in India" (*Colonialism and Christian Missions,* p. 99). For the purpose of our argument Neill's problematization of agency behind Pannikar's argument is more important (p. 14).

22. Bent Smidt Hansen, *Afhængighed og Identitet: Kulturmødeproblemer i forbindelse med dansk mission i Sydindien mellem de to verdenskrige* (Aarhus, 1992).

23. The Church Missionary Society, *The Fifty-Eighth Report of the Calcutta Corresponding Committee of the Church Missionary Society* [hereafter CMS, *Report*], 1856 and 1858.

24. CMS, *Report,* 1859, pp. 2-3.

is felt, cannot be so safely entrusted to any others of the native population."
All elements that "have combined to give Christian Missions a new *status* in
public estimation, and a new footing in the land different from what they
held before."[25]

In spite of these observations it was still necessary for the Rev. Droese to
fight the educational policy of the local (British) commissioner of Bhagalpur,
a Mr. Yule, who did not see conversion to Christianity as a relevant goal for
education and had already established a local school with a Hindu teacher.[26]
So Droese had to defend his position in letters to the commissioner's superiors, where he argued that it was

> better to leave the Santhals uneducated, than educate them by means of
> teachers who [it] must be feared, may become willing tools of designing
> men averse to British rule. . . . Why should a Christian Government set
> up heathen schools, that is schools where a heathen teacher without
> Christian supervision is allowed to influence the minds of the chil-
> dren?[27]

Droese argues for a strategy to construct a hegemony in the Gramscian
understanding of the term, as he intends that his schools shall produce common interests between the Santals taught and the government. Interestingly,
the very existence of this attack on Hindu teachers in government schools indicates the lack of any discourse as some government officers, such as Yule,
seemingly conceptualized the situation in a terminology that did not even fit
with the terminology Droese selected to put his case.

Ultimately Droese did get the grant for the Church Missionary Society's
schools from the government, although the existing government school was
allowed to continue for some time. In the following years the reports of the
Church Missionary Society tell of progress for the schools among the Santals
in spite of the fact that they had continuous problems with the Hindu teacher
at the government school: "a heathen Bengalee, [who] has tried his utmost to
vilify the Mission schools and to prejudice the minds of the people against
Christian instruction."[28]

As far as discourses are concerned, one finds the Rev. Droese's conceptual-
ization of the Santals as tribals. This is evident again some years later when

25. CMS, *Report,* 1859, pp. 2-3.

26. J. S. Jha, *Education in Bihar 1813-1859* (Patna, February 1979), pp. 349-57.

27. General Department, General Branch, Prog. No. 127, 11 February 1858, quoted in
Jha, *Education in Bihar,* p. 353

28. CMS, *Report,* 1958, pp. 75-76.

the Santals' very low level of civilization is used to explain the poor progress of pupils in the schools:

> [The schools] are attended by about 300 boys. These Schools being so to say, the very beginning of Educational and Missionary work among a race but just rising out of the condition of savages, cannot be expected to teach more than the very rudiments of learning. Reading, Writing, and Arithmetic is all the secular knowledge as yet aimed at in our Sonthal Schools. In order to convey to the minds of the boys religious instruction, the more advanced read the Gospels, and all have to learn by heart Bible passages, the Ten Commandments, and Christian Hymns, in Hindee.[29]

In this passage the Rev. Droese's estimation of the Santals is indeed low and paternalistic. He credits himself, and other civilized people, with a knowledge of which they can only hope to convey the rudiments to the Santals who are unable to act on their own behalf, in relation to learning, because they are impeded by being near to savagery.

So even though Droese, like so many other missionaries, much preferred the Santals to the Hindus, it is evident that he considered them to be almost uncivilized, and that he was fundamentally in agreement with the classification of them as tribals and "others" to the Hindus.

The Hegemonic Account That Led to Mobilization against the Hegemonic Power

There can be little doubt that Inden would have termed Droese's view of the Santals an hegemonic account. As Inden has argued in another context, "given this, it was only 'natural' for European scholars, traders, and administrators to appropriate the power of Indians . . . to act for themselves. This they have done since the formation of Indological discourse made it possible."[30] But, as far as the Santals and the so-called tribes of India are concerned, we think that the course of events has taken quite a different direction, and we hope to identify where Inden's argument goes "wrong." The problem with the argument is that it assumes the possibility of depriving a people (in this case the Santals) of agency simply by the *intention* of depriving them of agency

29. CMS, *Report*, 1860, pp. 42-43.
30. Inden, "Orientalist Constructions," p. 403.

(for a certain kind of political action, i.e., revolution). This difficulty arises because of the way Inden uses the term "hegemony": he does not investigate the communication of hegemonic concepts.[31] We will test our assumption in the particular case of the Santals.

Evidence for the Existence of Common Discourses

It is evident that the classification of the administrators and missionaries has been developed through time in accordance with the general political and social development in India, and that those peoples who were classified as tribals have adopted the designation as a self-designation. In this respect the notion of tribes versus Hindus forms a discourse as both groups are defined as opposing "others," and the terminology seems to be generally accepted by all groups.

Since the 1860s a number of social movements among the Santals have demanded *Santal raj,* "power to the Santals." This demand was perhaps first made by the Kherwar movement, which tried to unite a number of tribes and low castes by claiming a common origin. The movement emphasized the ways in which these groups were different from the Hindus who were designated *diku,* a word that in Santali denotes any kind of stranger or foreigner, but is usually used to designate those groups of Hindus considered to be exploiters.

During the Indian fight for independence the tribals in Central India united under the emblem of "indigenous." They translated this to the "Indian" word *adivasi* (or *adibasi* in Bengali, Hindi, Oriya), meaning "indigenous" or "original inhabitant." This designation was generally accepted by the Congress and most of the other national parties during the 1930s.

After independence when a word to designate "tribes" was needed to designate those groups who would be the recipients of positive discrimination, it was decided to use a term with less symbolic content: "scheduled tribes." The term "schedulement" in itself means nothing more than that the tribes are recorded on an authorized list.

It is evident that the notion of tribe governs the discourse and that all shades of the political spectrum, from the national parties to minority groups among the Santals and other "tribes," address the political issues in terms of tribal policy. At the state level there has been agitation for the creation of a new constituent state carved out of existing states to form a "Forest State" for

---

31. From a theoretical point Gramsci included the communication of hegemony in his investigation.

the Adivasis. This agitation has sometimes met with support from the national parties, and whether the state is termed *Jharkhand,* a name still popular among most of its adherents, or is termed *Vana Chal,* as recently put forward by the Bharatiya Janata Party–led national government in Delhi, the names evoke aboriginal themes. The present state of Jharkhand was cut out of the southern parts of Bihar in 2000.

Even if parts of their "indigenousness" have originated in a colonial and, later, a national discourse that spoke to the people classified as tribals, it is evident that those addressed had a voice of their own. From the Kherwars to the Adivasis [Adibasis] or the Scheduled Tribes, the people so classified joined the discourse and spoke on their own behalf from their own position within the structure created by the discourse.

Since 1871, when the first census took place, every census operation has been accompanied by agitation regarding which questions the census should contain, and whose representations have framed, as well as being framed by, the discourse. For the individual Santal, the census operations provided an opportunity to develop one's own understanding of ethnic and religious identities within the limits of the framework.

In the early censuses the Santals were only enumerated: the actual counting was left to the village leaders who made knots on different colors of strings indicating the sex of the inhabitants. Later on when a separate question on religion was included, it transpired that a number of Santals considered themselves to be of Hindu confession. As far as confessional status is concerned, in about 1961 only a very small percentage of the Santals claimed other religions. From that time on there has been a continuous movement in confession from Hinduism toward two other categories: either "other religions" or "Christian." In the census of 1981 about 20 percent of the Santals were reported as belonging to "other religions," and the number of Christians had tripled over the previous twenty years. The most substantial change, however, has been in the category called "other religions," which seems to indicate a tendency toward embracing some kind of aboriginal religion, a change that may well be connected with the agitation for a Jharkhand state.[32] This aboriginal religion is very different from the animism-like aboriginal religions that were imagined by the colonial administrators. The trend can be interpreted as a form of tribal mobilization that indicates that the concept of being tribal has come to include a religion distinct from Hinduism.

32. Peter B. Andersen, "Santalerne — en minoritet på 5 millioner mennesker," in *Aktører versus staten — De folkelige, sociale og politiske bevægelsers relationer til staten* (Copenhagen, 1997), pp. 80-94.

Discourses, Imperialistic or Classificatory?

To return to the question — whether the texts show evidence that the administrators and the Christian missions in India are part of a common, corporate, imperialistic discourse — we have argued that they are not. Christian missions cannot be characterized as having been deliberately imperialistic in any simple meaning of the word, and the texts even show evidence of opposition from the colonial administrators to the missionary project. An example of this is the case of the (British) commissioner of Bhagalpur, Mr. Yule, who opposed government support to schools run by the CMS.

The texts seem to indicate that the colonial administrators and the Christian missionaries were pursuing different ideological and political goals, and that it is an untenable simplification to consider them as simply part of the same imperialistic project. In fact, we did not find evidence of any unified imperialistic discourse.

We did, however, find that the administrators and the Christian missionaries were using the same concepts and categories in describing the peoples of India. The letters of the Rev. Droese show that he conceptualized the Santals within the terminology created by the great classificatory project of the nineteenth century, designating them as tribals, and that he was thereby part of the generally accepted discourse on Indian society during his time. This is an important point, since it shows that the discourse identified by Inden — a basic distinction between Westerners and Indians — can and should be differentiated. The texts show that the categorization of peoples has at least three levels: Westerners are perceived and described as opposed to Indians, and the latter are divided into different categories where Hindus are opposed to other categories such as the Santals.

In the analysis of the concept of tribe we found that there is evidence of the creation of a discourse since nearly all the parties involved seem to be addressing the situation through that very same terminology: tribal versus nontribal. The designation "tribal" is used by the administrators and the missionaries alike and is soon used by everybody, including the tribals themselves. The term "tribal" is accepted by both majority and minority, by the designators and the designated. The designated even begin to use the concept themselves in their self-designation, as distinct from the majority of Indians.

As far as agency is concerned, one should not assume that the peoples who are called, and indeed come to call themselves, tribal are necessarily either more or less suppressed by the colonial power or by the majority *because* of the tribal designation. On the contrary, the very designation used by representatives of the colonial power to categorize certain Indian peoples, for instance, the Santals, is used by these peoples in a political struggle for cultural, social, and economic rights. The discourse defines how every group in society is able to think and talk about themselves and others. It is important to note, however, that this does not deprive people of their potential to act. The texts suggest that the tribes do act along the lines defined by the discourse. The discourse governs the forms and ways of agency possible in the situation, but it does not preclude people from agency itself.

CHAPTER THIRTEEN

Glimpses of a Prominent Indian Christian Family of Tirunelveli and Madras, 1863-1906: Perspectives on Caste, Culture, and Conversion

E. M. JACKSON

The Satthianadhan family is unusual in being able to trace its descent and tradition of ordained service through the female line to Diego, ordained in the Danish Lutheran Mission, Tranquebar, in 1741, and in arranging marriages across the lines of caste and culture in every generation to the present day. This study focuses on Annal Arokium, daughter of the Rev. John Devasahayam of Kadachapuram, pioneer of women's education in Madras; her convert husband, the Rev. William Thomas ("W.T.") Satthianadhan, who was presented to Queen Victoria and proposed as the first Indian bishop in 1878; their son Professor Samuel Satthianadhan (1860-1906); and his successive wives, Krupabai, a Maratha Brahman convert (1862-94), and Kamala, a Telugu Brahman (1880-1947). All were outstanding literary figures, making a unique contribution to the development of English literature and Tamil education.

The Satthianadhan family are an exceptionally distinguished dynasty in terms of their contribution to the growth of the Anglican Church in South India, to

This chapter is based on research in Tamilnadu in 1994 and the CMS Archives, University of Birmingham. The work was facilitated by grants from St. Martin's College, Lancaster, and J. Sainsbury's, which is acknowledged with gratitude.

315

the history of the ecumenical movement and the Church of South India, to the development of education in India, especially for women, to literature, and to the policy-making of the Indian National Congress and the first governments after independence.[1] For the purposes of this chapter, however, a line will be drawn after the death of Samuel Satthianadhan in 1906, rather than continuing to Padmini Sengupta, Bishop Sundar Clarke, and Dr. Satthianadhan Clarke.

Krupabai Satthianadhan's first novel, *Kamala: A Story of Hindu Life* (Madras, 1894)[2] describes how her heroine, the only child of a Brahman *sannayasi* (renunciant) and a runaway Brahman heiress, goes as a child-bride to the Brahman quarter of the local town. Mistreated by her in-laws, she learns from her cousin Ramchander the true circumstances following her father's death. Her estranged husband dies shortly after her infant daughter's death, and, finally, she is seen devoting herself to "unselfish works of charity."[3]

There is more than an echo of George Eliot in the story, not surprisingly since Krupabai studied and admired her works, including, presumably, *Middlemarch*. Eliot also wrote from the perspective of a young idealist. Kamala, like Krupabai herself, was intensely patriotic but achieved far more, in practical terms, than her heroine, Dorothea Brooke. Unlike Eliot's heroine, Kamala cannot bring herself to defy convention when she is widowed. Like any respectable woman from the "twice-born" castes, her life is forever bound up in her husband's dharma (as laid down in the Laws of Manu), and she cannot accept Ramchander's offer of marriage and live "happily ever after."[4] As in *Middlemarch*, the old world is passing away, but it is far from clear what will replace that world. Likewise, in Kamala Satthianadhan's sto-

1. Padmini Sengupta, *Portrait of an Indian Woman* (Calcutta, 1956). Professor Samuel Satthianadhan himself, by virtue of his post at Presidency College, Madras, and as Vice-President of the YMCA of India, influenced the development of higher education in India.

2. The original title, 1894 edition, was *Kamala: A Story of Hindu Life*. For a recent edition see C. Lokugé, ed., *Kamala: The Story of a Hindu Life by Krupabai Satthianadhan* (Delhi, 1998) [hereafter *Kamala*], pp. 34, 86.

3. *Kamala*, pp. 156, 171. Lokugé feels the phrase may be inspired by a visit Kamala made to Pandita Ramabai's boarding school for young widows, but the phrase could equally have come from the *Bhagavadgita*. Gavin Flood, *An Introduction to Hinduism* (Cambridge, 1996), p. 176; J. L. Brockington, *The Sacred Thread* (Edinburgh, 1993), p. 124.

4. *Kamala*, p. 157. W. T. Satthianadhan reported to Bishop Gell in 1867 that there were no former caste Hindus in his congregation who wanted to remarry, and the question of the remarriage of widows, taken as a yardstick of adherence to caste, simply had not arisen. See Frederick Gell, *Inquiries by the Bishop of Madras regarding the removal of caste prejudice and practices in the native church of South India* (Madras, 1865), p. 5.

ries,[5] there is an expressed anxiety that traditional Sanskrit learning will disappear, and with it, moral values and even Indian culture itself.

George Eliot wrote *Middlemarch* in order to explore how a modern Teresa of Avila would react to the England of the Great Reform Act of 1832. Krupabai's heroine derives little comfort from trying to emulate Sita, or Savitri;[6] and Ramchander, after oscillating for years between life as an ascetic practicing herbal medicine and his obligations as manager of the family estates, finally decides where his duty lies.[7]

In the 1998 edition of *Kamala,* the editor, Chandani Lokugé applied a modern feminist perspective. She thereby signaled the author's importance in producing a genuine Indian heroine and for thus pioneering a new genre of literature in India. It is equally possible, however, to see the novel as a Dickensian type: an exposure of social conditions, an indictment of Brahmanical culture and caste, and a lament for unfulfilled lives. Kamala's father's search for enlightenment ends only in death. Her mother dies when Kamala is two because the family is too far from a doctor when she is suddenly taken ill. Her husband, Ganesh, has done no more with his Western education than procure a dead-end office job. Sai, the courtesan, who might be cast as the principal villain of the story, who alienated the affections of Kamala's husband, is pitied for allowing Western education to corrupt her. Sai longs for children and respectability despite her cherished "independence." Kamala's mother-in-law loses her son despite all her machinations. The ill-treated child-brides slave for their in-laws and yet eventually grow up to be like their mothers-in-law, and so on. Kamala and Ramchander each pay a terrible price in suffering before they find serenity and meaning in life. At one point Kamala's position as a rejected wife is such that she contemplates suicide, but then she spots her baby daughter gurgling and reaching out for the stars on a beautiful moonlit night. That sight gives her hope and strength not to flee to her father, as tradition would require, but to go and confront her father-in-law concerning his erring son and to shame her husband into changing his behavior. To her deepest regret Ganesh dies, a victim of that great scourge cholera, before there can be a reconciliation. Even as he

5. S. Satthianadhan and K. Satthianadhan, *Stories of Indian Christian Life* (Madras, 1898), p. 54.

6. For the way in which Hindu girls are urged to emulate these heroines, see V. Narayanan, "Hindu Perceptions of Auspiciousness and Sexuality," in *Women, Religion and Sexuality: Studies on the Impact or Religious Teachings on Women,* edited by J. Becher (Geneva, 1990; Philadelphia, 1991), pp. 69-72.

7. *Kamala,* pp. 125, 156. In rejecting her marriage she embraces self-immolation like Sita; her integrity is vindicated while Ramchander emulates Ram in following his dharma.

dies, she blames herself, and the author allows no hint of just deserts for infidelity.

Caste and culture are inextricably linked in Kamala's story. Krupabai's telling of a story in which the heroine shares some of the same traits of her own mother, a Marathi Brahman convert to Christian faith, was partly autobiographical. In her anguish at losing her own child, Kamala relives Krupabai's own bereavement. Nevertheless the dilemmas faced by these characters are not resolved by conversion. The redemptive feature of the novel is rather her beloved India. Krupabai's most exquisite writing is devoted to describing the glories of the Deccan countryside, the changing seasons, the breathtaking scenery of the western *ghats,* and even the beauty of the people themselves, whatever their caste. Chandani Lokugé attributes it to the influence of Tennyson.[8] Her imagery and emotion resemble rather the writings of her contemporaries, the Marathi Brahman Christian poet Narayan Vaman Tilak and his wife Lakshmibai,[9] or one of the greatest poets of the nineteenth-century Bengal, Michael Madhusadhan Seal.[10] When wracked by doubt and anxiety about "God"[11] and their needs to fulfill personal dharma, the characters sense the numinous in nature. The Lord is not Krishna the charioteer on the battlefield, revealing eternal truths to them as to Arjuna in the *Bhagavadgita,* but is a voice within. They turn to the Divine within the parameters of Hindu philosophical traditions, but there is always an unresolved tension between renouncing worldly materialistic values for this spiritual quest and the felt value of good works and kindly deeds.

Kamala has a transcendent quality about her, a Christ-like nobility in suf-

8. *Kamala,* p. 12.

9. Lakshmibai Tilak, *I Follow After* (Ahmednagur, 1925); P. S. Jacob, *The Experiential Response of N. V. Tilak* (Madras, 1979); J. C. Winslow, *Narayan Vaman Tilak: The Christian Poet of Maharashtra* (Calcutta, 1923).

10. Born in the Jessore area (present-day Bangladesh) and educated initially at the General Assembly's Institution in Calcutta, he was converted by Gopinath Nandi and baptized 4 January 1833. Rated more highly than the Tagore family by the Calcutta intelligentsia I knew during the 1980s, even in translation his poetry is distinguished by its remarkable lyricism.

11. While it is not wholly appropriate to use the English term "God" in a Hindu context, Tamil spirituality has been greatly influenced by the eleventh-century philosopher Ramanuja's concept of qualified nondualism, so that many may believe in a personal Being to whom one can direct love and devotion. Many Christian converts, including several members of the Satthianadhan family, came from this tradition. See S. S. Raghavachar, "The Spiritual Vision of Ramanuja," in *Hindu Spirituality:* vol. 1, *Vedas through Vedanta,* edited by Krishna Sivaram (London, 1989); K. P. Aleaz, *Christian Thought through Advaita Vedanta* (Delhi, 1996); *Kamala,* pp. 106-7, 148.

fering, but her all too human craving for love, chronic abuse-induced lack of self-esteem, and naivete preclude too close a comparison. Lokugé criticizes Krupabai for her occasional Evangelical use of a derogatory epithet, but some Brahmans criticize "idol worship," more in the tradition of Ram Mohun Roy than Carey, Marshman, and Ward.[12]

It is important to remember that Hindus do not practice their religion in the way that Catholics are held to do in popular discourse: simply by "having their being" they are Hindu, the embodiment of their caste and culture. Characters in Satthianadhan fiction, not surprisingly therefore, are conscious that this eternal dharma governs their whole outlook on life, every action in every single day, and their eternal destiny, and they distinguish their approach from that of the poor misguided Christians whom they encounter. Conversion is therefore seen as a total disaster, a family pollution, an aberration that may mean an individual's doom but certainly involves cultural alienation. For this reason also, conversion to Christianity may involve intellectual conviction, or Quaker-type convincement, but for the convert it is primarily a *bhakti* experience, involving the experience of the love of God and devotion to Jesus, come what may.[13]

If Hindus belong to a world-faith community that derives from the Indian religious traditions and is held together by culture, language, and shared values based on a common understanding of revelation and spiritual experience, the sense of belonging to a local community is still a core experience, be it the extended family, the *jāti* (lit.: "birth-group"; caste or subcaste) or the village,[14] not least because it is these groups that, by their ability to inflict sanctions on the dissident, enforce orthopraxy. Typically, in the Satthianadhan stories, characters identify themselves or are identified by their *jāti* and devotional tradition, Shaiva or Vaishnava, as they themselves do in their autobiographical writings. This sense of identity is reinforced by knowledge of the Vedas. It should be noted that the Satthianadhans — "W.T." (who was the convert formerly known as "Thiruvengadam"), his son Samuel, and his

12. See Ram Mohun Roy, "A Translation of an Abridgement of the Vedanta, or Resolution of the Most Celebrated and Revised Work of Brahmanical Theology, Establishing the Unity of the Supreme Being, and that He Alone is the Object of Propitiation and Worship," private publication, Calcutta, 1816, quoted in *The Circular Letters of the Serampore Mission* (in-house publication of the Baptist Serampore Mission), Archives, Carey Library, Serampore College, Srirampur, West Bengal. Also reproduced in S. Collett, *The Life and Letters of Raja Ram Mohun Roy* (Calcutta, 1962).

13. Satthianadhan and Satthianadhan, *Stories of Indian Christian Life*, pp. 46, 137.

14. A good illustration can be found in F. Mohani, *My Village, My Life: Nanpur: A Portrait of an Indian Village* (London, 1973).

daughters-in-law, Krupabai and Kamala Satthianadhan — were knowledge-able in the Sanskrit scriptures, while Annal Arokium, his wife, clearly had access to Tamil sacred writings. Like many missionary writers they refer vaguely to "the Hindu *sastras*" as defining revelation even when this is, at least from the context of the reference, more likely to be from the Laws of Manu or from Sankara's commentaries. Commitment to the education, classical and modern, of Hindu women is not only a subtext in their writings but also the professional occupation of generation after generation of Satthianadhan women.[15] Padmini Sengupta (nee Satthianadhan) even wrote a biography of the reformer, Pandita Ramabai.[16]

Members of the Satthianadhan family corresponded with their friends in English, edited their own journals in English, and published a variety of works in English as well as in Tamil. Clearly, use of any language can shape thought and identity. Cultural alienation or marginalization was a very sensitive issue in the family. W. T. Satthianadhan became angry when he found himself being treated like some exotic bird for wearing Indian attire in England. Similarly, Samuel and Kamala Satthianadhan made complaints against missionaries who discriminated against Indians who, for whatever reason, chose European clothing.[17] From the family tree provided by Bishop Sundar Clarke, W. T. Satthianadhan's great-grandson, it is clear that from his grandparents' generation onward, a number of family cousins married English or French citizens and settled in Europe. His elder sister married a Swiss domiciled in India. He himself has children in Australia. Notorious for his little paperback book, *Let the Indian Church Be Indian,* and for wearing *khadi jibba* and *lunghi* with only a pectoral cross to distinguish him from a DMK (Dravida Munetra Kazhagam) politician, Bishop Sundar Clarke was surprised when in 1994 he discovered that his great-grandfather, in the 1880s, had taken a much more radical line than he himself in arguments for a self-governing and self-financing Indian National Church.[18] Perhaps because the Satthianadhans oscillated,

15. *Kamala,* pp. 43, 59, 100; Krupabai Satthianadhan, *Saguna: A Story of Native Christian Life* (Madras, 1895) [cited henceforth as *Saguna*], pp. 199-231; see also C. Miller, *Female Education in Southern India* (Madras, 1878).

16. Padmini Sengupta, *Pandita Ramabai Saraswati* (Madras, 1970).

17. Satthianadhan and Satthianadhan, *Stories of Indian Christian Life,* pp. 62, 219. W. T. Satthianadhan to Rev. Gray (28 February 1879), University of Birmingham, Church Missionary Society [CMS], South India. W. T. Satthianadhan, C12/o 211/1-42.

18. Interview (March 1994). CMS, South India, W. T. Satthianadhan, "on the native church": Letter to Rev. Gray (26 February 1879): "The Native Church in South India," a paper given to the General Missionary Conference (Allahabad, 1872-73). See J. Barton, A. Brodhead, and J. Murdoch, eds., *Report of the General Missionary Conference held at Allahabad, 1872-73* (London; Madras, 1873).

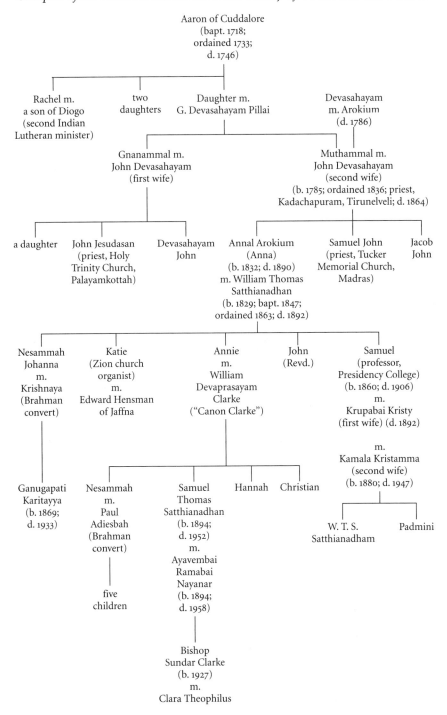

from generation to generation, between attitudes of Westernization (Anglicization) and Indianization (or what they viewed as "Indian" traditions), their changing stances on styles can be seen as a paradigm for what happened in many Indian families, Hindu and Christian. They were acute observers of the Indian scene, and social critics. Hence it should come as no surprise, when in a bookstore, to find on sale alongside *Kamala, The Story of a Hindu Life,* a volume titled *Dalits and Christianity* by W. Satthianadhan Clarke.[19]

In terms of the family tradition and spiritual heritage the Satthianadhan family is interesting because of its matrilineal, if not matriarchal, character. A succession of matriarchal women stoutly maintained their Christian heritage while marrying first-generation converts. In the case of Samuel Satthianadhan, however, this trend was reversed. When he died suddenly of a heart attack, at the World Student Christian Federation meeting in Tokyo in 1906, however, his widow, Kamala Satthianadhan, did not look to her relatives for support for herself and her two young children. According to her daughter Padmini, Kamala followed the family tradition of strong independent women and took a post as Sanskrit tutor to a *rani*.[20]

Annal Arokium, wife of W.T., was the daughter of John Devasahayam,[21] a district missionary and the first Indian Anglican clergyman to hold such a charge. She had been a pupil at Miss Giberne's school for girls. Miss Giberne was a missionary who had arrived in Kadachapuram in 1842 after four years' service with the Female Education Society in Colombo, Ceylon (Sri Lanka). She served in Tinnevelly (1842-48) and then in Madras (1852-62), and after ill health forced her to retire to England, charge of her schools was eventually handed over to her former pupil, Anna. By then, however, Anna had become Mrs. W. T. Satthianadhan.[22] It was Caroline Giberne who had Anglicized her name. "Anna" had originally been christened "Annal Arokium" — or "child of grace."

Annal's father came from a respectable trading Vaishnava family of Mayavaram, which had long been an outpost of the Royal Danish Mission that was based in Tranquebar. Born in 1785 to Christian parents, he found his

19. W. Satthianadhan Clarke, *Dalits and Christianity* (Delhi, 1998), based on his Harvard Ph.D. dissertation.

20. Sengupta, *Portrait of an Indian Woman.* Kamala Satthianadhan also edited an influential ladies magazine, in which some women leaders of the pre-Independence Indian National Congress, such a Sarojini Naidu, put their articles.

21. S. A. John, *A Brief Memoir of the Revd John Devasagayam, First Native Minister of the Church of England in South India* (Madras, 1895).

22. I am indebted to Meline Nielsen of the Orchard Learning Centre, University of Birmingham, for drawing my attention to a scrapbook by Miss Caroline Giberne. It was donated to the Selly Oak Colleges' Library by Miss Giberne's niece, Helen Neave, nee Pearson.

vocation through the influence of C. S. John, his Pietist-Lutheran missionary teacher (1747-1813), after whom he had been named. Subsequently he had taught in Tamil Christian schools, helped administer them, and also engaged in evangelistic work. In 1830, as German Lutheran missionaries gradually gave way to Church Missionary Society and Society for the Propagation of the Gospel (both Anglican) missionaries, he was ordained deacon in Madras by the short-lived Bishop Turner. When C. T. E. Rhenius went into schism in 1836, John Devasahayam remained loyal to Bishop Corrie and was ordained priest in the ensuing reorganization.[23]

Annal Arokium had grown up within a mission compound. Through her maternal grandmother she was the great-granddaughter of Aaron, the first Tamil Evangelical to be fully trained and ordained to the ministry in 1727.[24] Although she had four brothers, two of whom were to become prominent as clergymen, it was Annal who accompanied her father on his tours around to village congregations of his "parish."[25] Like many a "heroine" in a Victorian novel, she married her father's handsome curate.

William Thomas Satthianadhan after his ordination, as part of his clerical garb, wore a large turban and a long, knee-length tunic-coat (modeled on an *achkhan* or *sherwani,* such as that worn by Muslim gentry). Born in Sinthapathurai, Tirunelveli, and named Thiruvengadam at birth, he was reared in a strict Naidu family of Vaishnava devotion and was sent to the CMS secondary school in Palayamkottai at the age of thirteen. There he came under the influence of an outstanding blind teacher; and after three years he became a convinced Christian. His suspicious family tried to hasten his long-arranged marriage, but he had fled on the night before the wedding, claiming that a divine voice had called him. The missionaries who sheltered him sent

23. Brilliant and controversial, Robert Caldwell considered Rhenius one of the ablest, most clear-sighted and practical missionaries to India. C. T. E. Rhenius's letters and journals are preserved in the CMS Archives, the University of Birmingham, England. Rhenius could not accept the use of a Book of Common Prayer in the churches he had founded. Some of his colleagues joined the London Mission Society mission in Nagarcoil but most of his supporters were reconciled after his death in 1839. See M. E. Gibb, *The Anglican Church in India 1600-1970* (Delhi, 1973), pp. 101-2, 134-37; Paul Appasamy, *A Centenary History of the CMS in Tinnevelly* (Palamcottah, 1925); and George Pettit, *A History of the Tinnevelly Mission of the Church Missionary Society* (London, 1851).

24. Aaron was the son of Sockananda Pillai, a Vellālar Cuddalore merchant, baptized in 1718 by Ziegenbalg. See J. G. Fenger, *A History of the Tranquebar Mission* (Madras, 1906), p. 122; E. Arno Lehmann, *It Began in Tranquebar* (Madras, 1956), p. 149.

25. Appasamy, *History of the CMS*, pp. 106, 116-20; E. Stock, *A Centenary History of the Church Missionary Society* (London, 1899), 2:179; Gibb, *Anglican Church in India*, p. 145; and S. Satthianadhan, *Sketches of Indian Christians* (Madras, 1896).

him to Megnanapuram hoping that the veteran missionary, John Thomas, could protect him. Dragged before the district magistrate by his family, who maintained he was only fourteen, he convinced the court he was of age to know his own mind. At his baptism in 1847, he changed his name. Two years later he married Annal Arokium and became one of those lowliest of church workers, a "catechist" or "mission agent" (at seven rupees a month). In 1855, he entered Doveton College, Madras. There he won a gold medal for his examination results in 1857. This English-medium education laid the foundations for his later literary work. Further academic success was preempted by a summons to service from the CMS. Going to a remote village in North Tirunelveli, he joined one of the remarkable evangelistic teams ever assembled, led by a man of prayer, the former Cambridge don, Thomas Ragland.[26]

The North Tinnevelly Itineracy, as it was known, was directed at an area where the CMS had had little success. Nor were the Evangelical missionaries who camped, preached, or directed operations much more successful. Of crucial importance for this new effort, however, was the way it was organized by Indian co-workers themselves. These were not "foreign" agents but young volunteers sent for a month each and supported by Christian churches in South Tirunelveli. Such activities gave Indian Christians renewed confidence, of the kind they had once possessed in the 1790s and 1820s, that they could organize and fund their own evangelistic efforts. The Itineracy as such continued until 1940. W.T. kept a journal from which it is clear he grew in confidence. Shattered though he was by Ragland's early death followed by those of C. Every and M. Baerenbruck, he was comforted by David Fenn's friendship.

The Itineracy had a remarkable impact on women. A Welsh-style, almost Pentecostal form of revival broke out among schoolgirls. Anna Satthianadhan was a young mother with demanding "under fives." She had no time to write journals; yet, it seems, she was often called out at short notice, sometimes at night, to calm hysterical girls, steady the converts, soothe anxious relatives, or organize prayer groups and Bible studies. In later years these girls were to marry Christian converts and provide a vital element of congregational leadership. Another extraordinary feature of the North Tinnevelly Itineracy seems to be the impact made on the goldsmiths' *jāti* in Sivakasi, an ancient market town dominated by a famous Shaiva temple. There is no simple explanation as to why so many women from this very respectable community were converted. They seem to have formed some sort of secret or un-

---

26. S. Satthianadhan, *The Rev. W. T. Satthianadhan B.D., A Brief Biographical Sketch by S. Satthianadhan, to which is Appended the Story of a Conversion by Krupabai Satthianadhan* (Madras, 1893).

derground church of largely unbaptized believers. While their menfolk knew about their devotion to Christ, they tolerated their faith so long as their facade of "Hindu" tradition was preserved. There was a long tradition, prevalent in some villages, of underground *bhakti* cults, inspired by a charismatic leader, in which the devotees could ignore social norms such as distinctions of caste and gender. This movement persists to this day, but by its very nature has proved resistant to academic research.[27] When the Satthianadhans moved to Madras in 1862-63, they drew on these experiences in their work to create an independent Evangelical church.

W. T. Satthianadhan was called to Madras when two Evangelical missionaries wished him to have an independent charge. He was assigned two churches: one, John Pereira's, was an old, predominantly Anglo-Indian congregation originally founded for servants and their families; and the other, created in 1843, was strategically sited in Chintadripet, on the edge of Napier Park, at the head of a street of traditional houses in the gold merchants' quarter. Although returns for the former show year on year increases, the latter was to develop into a large and prestigious Tamil church. Renamed Zion Church, it is today almost a family chapel, full of monuments to W.T.'s descendants. Successive generations of Satthianadhans held the charge; for years his daughter Katie was the organist. It was ideally situated for evangelizing educated caste Hindus.[28]

With difficulty and much patience, Anna Satthianadhan developed schools for caste Hindu girls and began *zenana* visiting. Her report for the Madras *Christian Observer*, April 1865, ends with the words:

27. Gibb, *Anglican Church in India*, pp. 159-62; Stephen C. Neill, *A History of Christianity in India, 1707-1858* (Cambridge, 1985); F. J. Dhanasekharan, "The North Tinnevelly Itineracy," M.Th. thesis, UTC Library, Bangalore, 1988; A. Wingate, "The Secret Christians of Sivakasi, Tamilnadu: One Pattern of Conversion in a South Indian Town," *Religion and Society* 33.1 (March 1986): 73-87, further discussed in his *The Church and Conversion: A Study of Recent Conversions to and from Christianity in the Tamil Area of South India* (Delhi, 1997), pp. 139-50.

28. In 1865 Zion Church had 207 baptized persons, 18 unbaptized, and 87 communicants. John Periera's had 76 baptized and 42 communicants according to a *Report* dated 13 December 1867. In 1867 there were 298 baptized members in the two congregations, and 94 communicants, the drop in the number of communicants being due to migration and possibly W.T.'s stand on caste. In 1868 there were 282 members and 116 communicants. W.T. claims to have baptized 101 adults, and admitted 27 to communion in a decade's ministry. In 1879 there were 397 baptized members, 176 communicants, and 30 baptized that year. The transient nature of the congregation, the result of migration in search of work, makes it difficult to assess progress. University of Birmingham UK. CMS Archives. CMS South India. W. T. Satthianadhan. C12/o 211/1-42.

If God be pleased to use us in any measure as instruments in His hands, not only in diffusing the blessings of Christian education in this large city, and in sowing the seeds of religion in the young hearts of these dear little ones, but also in raising our poor countrywomen from the depth of degradation in which they are sunk and carrying light into their dark dwellings and bringing them to knowledge of Him whom to know is eternal life, and whose favour is better than life, we very well have cause to magnify and adore the love and grace of Christ throughout eternity.[29]

Stripped of Victorian verbiage and pious spirituality, this paragraph reveals how connections were made between education and evangelism in bringing enlightenment and liberation to secluded, high-caste Hindu girls, both in the "here-and-now" and in eternity, a matter seen as affecting the Satthianadhans' own salvation.

With so much at stake, both in theological and in personal terms, one can understand W.T.'s 1877 refusal to move back to Palayamkottai. Even so, acting as head of the little seminary there and as chairman of a mission district, together with the impossibility of working under Bishop Sargent and the damage such a move would do to his sons' education, would have been reasons enough. In his letter to the CMS, he added:

But the difficulty is increased when we take into consideration the large and important work in which my wife is engaged. She has six girls' schools, four of which are for Hindu girls, in all comprising 400 children, and the number of zenanas under her charge is 45, the result of her own voluntary efforts. She moves among the highest native ladies in this city as she does among the Europeans, and exercises a great influence for good. Were she to leave Madras and go to Megnanapuram or Kadachapuram or even to Palamcottah [Palayamkottai], her influence and usefulness would be greatly removed. Besides I think I may state, though at risk of supposed egotism, that the whole family is bearing a humble part in representing the Native Church of the CMS both to Europeans and to natives residing in this city in a manner, I trust, not unworthy of the great society to which they have the honour to belong.[30]

29. Birmingham, Selly Oak Colleges Library, Giberne Papers, Orchard Centre. These are uncatalogued.

30. Letter to Rev. Gray (2 April 1872). CMS Archives. CMS South India. W. T. Satthianadhan. C12/o 211/1-42.

This statement reflects some prejudice against "native Christians" both on the part of the English ecclesiastical establishment that for decades had excluded them from government services, and on the part of high-caste Hindus. Indian Christians, in some measure, were held to be renegades who imperiled the communal stability of the Raj, or from the Hindu point of view, a source of pollution and adharma — immorality and misfortune. It also reflects the priority the family gave to women's education, the four surviving Satthianadhan daughters becoming involved in their turn.

Almost immediately after this exchange, agitation mounted to have W.T. and four colleagues from itineracy days made assistant bishops for the Tirunelveli diocese. The area was vast, and the ailing Bishop Sargent needed co-adjutors. The situation was also complicated. At this time the expanding diocese of Tinnevelly had two bishops: Edward Sargent representing the Evangelical (CMS) interest and Robert Caldwell, the Tamil linguist and scholar, representing the Anglo-Catholic (SPG) tradition. Caldwell was nearing retirement. A further problem, within the Anglican establishment, was the fact that until 1876 there were legal obstacles to the consecration of any Indian bishop. W.T. himself did not want to see an Indian bishop appointed, neither himself nor anyone else. He did not wish to see any Indian lording it over the church in the way the Anglican bishops did, being paid by the colonial government. He wanted bishops to be paid salaries that Indian churches could realistically afford, and he wanted them to have an altogether more humble lifestyle.[31]

Whether or not W.T. was prepared to go to Bishopstowe, Palayamkottai, there was opposition to him. Coming from a "Shudra" caste background, it was alleged he would not be acceptable within a predominantly Nadar Christian community, such as made up most of the churches in Tirunelveli.[32]

31. Gibb, *Anglican Church in India*, p. 216. Gibb quotes a letter from Bishop Gell objecting to the Satthianadhans leaving Madras on the grounds that Mrs. Satthianadhan was irreplaceable. This view is at variance with her statement (p. 254) that the "CMS still hankered after the consecration of an Indian bishop. Apparently, somewhat to Sargent's surprise, he discovered that Satthianadhan, a Shudra of Palayamkottah, would not be acceptable to a predominantly Nadar church." In an undated address, in the UTC Archives, Bangalore: *The Missionary or Pastor, adapting himself in India to the Peculiarities of Native Thought*, W.T. confronted the issue unflinchingly, telling these European candidates for ordination that their work would be vitiated in India if they did not treat all races equally under God and show respect where respect was due in Tamil society.

32. On Nadars within the Tinnevelly Church, see R. Caldwell, *Records of the Early History of the Tinnevelly Mission* (Madras, 1881), pp. 71-100; Neill, *History of Christianity in India*, p. 216; Duncan Forrester, *Caste and Christianity* (Richmond, 1980), p. 84. On Caldwell's own contribution to the development of Nadar consciousness, as manifest in

Whether or not he was aware of a latent caste and social prejudice or any whispering campaign is unknown. He certainly was vehement in objecting to the racism he encountered within the church, the mission, and the state. At this point he and his wife visited Britain for six months to promote the cause of female education. At the Annual Meeting of the British and Foreign Bible Society in London in 1878, the Satthianadhans met Bishop Adjai Crowther, the Yoruba bishop on the Niger who had found favor with an earlier generation of CMS administrators, especially the great Henry Venn, but was at this time being harassed and persecuted by a younger generation of missionaries and administrators.[33]

In London the Satthianadhans were presented to Queen Victoria. They were probably also being closely scrutinized with a view to episcopacy; but the view appears to have prevailed that the Crowther experiment was a failure and should not be repeated in South India. Gibb, the historian of the Church of England in India, insists that W. T. Satthianadhan was not made Bishop of Tinnevelly because Bishop Gell of Madras could not think of any way to replace Mrs. W. T. Satthianadhan. Mrs. Satthianadhan was a close friend of Gell's sister, the most active member of the Madras Committee of Church of England's Zenana Mission Society (CEZMS), which was by now funding Mrs. Satthianadhan's schools.[34] Bishop Gell served from 1861-99, even longer than Bishop Wilson of Calcutta (1830-58). Had he been the one to die or retire and had he not been predeceased by W. T. Satthianadhan, it is possible that there might have been a further challenge to the colonial establishment of the Church of England, and to the views held by the colonial or white clergy who might not have been willing to accept ordination from an Indian bishop.[35]

W. T. Satthianadhan was no stranger to caste prejudice. In a letter to C. G. Fenn in May 1865, he wrote that although its spirit is dying away, the forms of caste feeling still exist among members of the educated classes, who feared

---

their conferences (1935, 1940, 1952), see Hugald Grafe, *History of Christianity in India*, vol. 4/2: *Tamilnadu in the 19th and 20th Centuries* (Bangalore, 1990), p. 212.

33. J. B. Webster, *The African Churches among the Yoruba, 1888-1922* (Oxford, 1964), p. 11. The connection with the Crowther case is made by Rev. J. Barton in a letter quoted in Satthianadhan, *The Revd. W. T. Satthianadhan*, p. 43.

34. Gibb, *Anglican Church in India*, p. 216. Minutes and Correspondence of the Church of England Zenana Missionary Society (CEZMS) are to be found in the United Theological College, Bangalore, South India.

35. Gibb, *Anglican Church in India*, p. 343. For Azariah's reaction see John R. Mott, *World Missionary Conference* (Edinburgh, 1910), 9:315; S. Billington Harper, *In the Shadow of the Mahatma: V. S. Azariah and the Travails of Christianity in British India* (Richmond, 2000), pp. 159, 163.

the loss of respect of their orthodox countrymen if they did not conform to caste protocols. He quoted, with approval, a speech by the university's chaplain, the Rev. Richards, asserting that education "would end that fearful system of caste which darkens the whole land today holding the masses in the most abject thralldom and crushing every upward exchange of natives."[36] Responding to a question about caste in the Church, however, he mourned that there were those in Madras who "boast more of their caste than of their Christianity." As a prime example, he cited the "Jaffna Christians" of Madras.[37] Most of them were able men, university graduates in science and philosophy, holding high government offices. Some he felt were ignorant of "the ABC of Christianity"; others were Christians connected to "the Leipzig Society," the Lutheran society that had succeeded the Royal Danish or Tranquebar Mission (and its affiliated SPCK missionaries). W. T. Satthianadhan lamented the seeming impossibility of uniting Christians within a single community when some retained caste feelings while others had no caste *(dalits)* or rejected their caste background. However, unwittingly contradicting himself, he also found no sectarian feeling among native Christians but a growth of cooperation in the Body of Christ. His early observations were borne out by evidence in letters and reports of later years.[38]

To demonstrate that the revival in North Tinnevelly had been genuine, W. T. Satthianadhan took pains to note that catechists who previously would not have allowed a European missionary in their houses lest they were to become defiled now welcomed such a person with enthusiasm.[39] It seems clear that Satthianadhan's approach to the observance of caste practices within the church was at one with the approach of American Congregationalist missionaries in Madurai, his hometown, who saw caste as diametrically opposed to the gospel and fostered "love feasts" within congregations as a device by which to

36. CMS South India. C12/0 211/1-42.

37. Jaffna Christians in Madras, originally Sri Lankan Tamils who were educated in institutions of the CMS and the American Board of Commissioners for Foreign Missions and who had migrated to the city in search of better professional positions, seem to have been upwardly mobile. W.T.'s daughter, Katie, married Edward Hensman, one of many from this community who had gravitated into the Zion Church in such numbers that, by the 1960s, it had become known as the "Jaffna Church" of Madras. Interview with a long-standing member of the congregation (March 1994). *Annual Report,* July 1865, Question 6: CMS Archives. CMS South India. C12/0 211/1-42.

38. Grafe, *Christianity in India,* vol. 5.2, p. 113. My own interviews with families living in Lalgudi (small town near Tiruchinopoly, the model for the fictional Malgudi) in 1985 substantiated his findings that people became Lutheran rather than break caste. My own experience in India 1979-86 witnessed the prevalence of caste in the church.

39. CMS Archives. South India. C12/0 211/1-42. Journal entry (31 May 1860).

test the sincerity of conversions.[40] Satthianadhan's solution to problems of caste observance, both inside and outside the church, was conciliatory and constructive. Rather than engaging in head-on confrontations, he placed confidence in creating a culture of education, voluntary work, and economic self-help. The education of caste girls was a key part of this strategy, even though a total enrollment of only 650 girls in *zenana* and related schools in 1865 would have been but a small fraction of the total high-caste female population of Madras. From minutes of meetings of the CEZMS's Madras Committee, referred to above, one can see that there was a difficulty. Efforts to increase the number of high-caste girls in *zenana* schools were frequently disrupted, and sometimes ceased, when European missionaries returned to Europe or when local voluntary workers moved away, as happened when Krupabai Satthianadhan moved to Ootacamund, or when another Indian Christian lady-worker had to move because her husband had been transferred to another station.[41] Nevertheless, for W. T. Satthianadhan, it was this voluntary effort that was extremely important.

While self-government and self-finance were keys to W.T.'s entire strategy for the church in India, he could be very critical of the CMS for the haste with which they attempted to implement money-saving devices. In conference paper after conference paper, he advocated changing the system of recruiting, employing, and paying Indian clergy so as to attract more graduates.[42] One key element in his work was to encourage a rapid mushrooming of educational clubs and religious societies. This was viewed as a means for India's Christians not only to improve their minds and lives but also to explain their faith. On many occasions, he and his friends gave talks of general interest, with a subtext that conveyed the Christian message. To this end, he built a lecture hall and endowed it with a library. In the 1870s he founded the Satya Vedam Society (True Scripture or True Veda Society) as a way to counter activities of the Tamil Veda Society. The Tamil Veda Society attempted to reclaim educated Tamils for a reformed Hinduism, through more flexible, less "churchy" ways than were being employed by the Brahmo Samaj. Both Keshub Chunder Sen and Mary Carpenter, the Unitarian educationalist, had visited Madras and had influenced Madras leaders. In work that he and his friends did, Satthianadhan

40. Kamala Satthianadhan, however, in a story published after W.T.'s death, pointed out the unfairness of American missionaries removing the insignia of caste and then criticizing converts who felt they had lost their culture and had adopted European dress and ways.

41. UTC Archives, Bangalore, CEZMS. Minutes, vol. 1 (entries for 20 August 1884 and 25 September 1884). In the latter entry the Madras Bishop spoke highly of Krupabai Satthianadhan's work and of the difficulties of finding someone to take her place.

42. See, for example, Barton, Brodhead, and Murdoch, *Report*, pp. 250-58.

presaged the work of the Young Men's Christian Association (YMCA). Established in Madras (in 1892) after Satthianadhan's, the YMCA was embraced by Samuel Satthianadhan, and he represented it at international events.

More modestly, Anna created the Half Anna Society from her girls' meetings. This was so-called because each girl, if she could, contributed two pice to a fund for charitable work and for spreading the gospel. Piecing together their stories from her letters, one can with justification apply the words of S. Radhakrishnan that Padmini Sengupta applied to Kamala Satthianadhan:

> India in every generation has produced millions of women who have never found fame, but whose daily existence has helped to civilise the race, and whose warmth of heart, self-sacrificing zeal, unassuming loyalty and strength in suffering, when subject to trials of extreme severity are among the glories of this race.[43]

Anna Satthianadhan had strong views on child nurture. In 1878 her recipe for a happy family (of whatever faith) had been published in a small but highly popular book. Entitled *The Good Mother*,[44] it purports to be a series of letters from an experienced mother who has reared a number of children to a new mother who is overwhelmed by her responsibility, which includes responsibility for her child's eternal salvation. A by no means perfect Christian family was presupposed by Anna Satthianadhan. Many of her illustrations were drawn from her visits to Hindu families, from her attempts to encourage mothers to adopt sensible healthy and hygienic practices, and from popular moral stories. Many of her stories seem to come from Tamil proverbs, such as:

> A son who does not help his mother is worthless to all
>   men.
> She reared her child with meat, while she ate bones.
> Will not the creeper bear the weight of its fruits?
> A child that will not obey its mother is like a rag in a dog's mouth.
> He considers his mother the goddess of ill-luck and his wife the goddess of good luck.[45]

43. S. Radhakrishnan, *Religion and Society,* 2nd ed. (London, 1948), pp. 197-98 as quoted by Sengupta, *Portrait of an Indian Woman,* p. x.

44. A photocopy of the Kannada version printed at the Wesleyan Press (Mysore, 1928), was very kindly lent to me by the archivist of UTC, Bangalore, and admirably translated into English for me by the Rev. Dr. Joseph Basappa.

45. Hermann Jensen, *Tamil Proverbs: A Classified Collection* (Madras, 1897 [reprinted Delhi, 1982]).

There is a sense in which the book reads like a social worker's casebook. The author usually balanced each example of good practices with one of tragic mistakes. It is fascinating to see, from the references to towns and villages in Tamilnadu, how widely she had traveled in an era of primitive public transport. Presumably the examples were drawn from many years of experience. Her work provides a vivid picture of life in small-town India during the 1870s, and many of the issues raised are as pertinent today as they were then. As such, they depict recognizable dilemmas.

In many ways, Mrs. W. T. Satthianadhan lived in advance of her time. She was unconditionally opposed to corporal punishment, advocating taking an offending child aside and sending it to bed, and resorting to reasonable persuasion, with no supper as the ultimate sanction! Hitting a child, she felt, could only encourage it to hit others and to believe that violence is right. She warned parents about demanding too much from their children. Yet, at the same time, she repeatedly stressed the dangers of spoiling children, especially boys, of not giving them medicine (with fatal consequences), of letting them play with dangerous objects, and of showing disrespect to others. Lying and stealing clearly had to be nipped in the bud, as any little fib could lead to worse deceptions. More serious was any situation in which a mother deceived her own child — such as saying that she was going to the well when, in fact, she was going to shop; or promising her children mangoes if they would behave themselves while she is out shopping when, in fact, the mango season had not yet arrived. Even worse was any failure to love one's children or any failure to take time for having fun with them.

Throughout, Anna sought to strike a balance between the interests of mother and those of the child, or husband, or family, between one child and other children, or between favoring boys and favoring girls. Such advice was timeless and would strike a chord with any mother, in any place or any time. Her letters on a mother's authority, by which she harmonized Christian with Hindu beliefs, were balanced by letters on a mother's duties and a mother's mistakes. In one paragraph she insisted that although a mother held primary responsibility, she should not allow her husband to escape all responsibility by claiming that domestic affairs were a woman's concern. Indeed, each mother was obliged to strive to get her husband to share responsibility when he was at home. Insisting that the nurture of each child in knowledge of God was what really mattered most, she argued that it was each parent's task to help a child to face death without fear. Anna Satthianadhan herself died an exemplary or "holy" death, without fear, in October 1890.[46] Her husband was

---

46. Satthianadhan, *Stories of Indian Christian Lives*, p. 45. Stock (*Centenary History*,

devastated and found it difficult to continue without her. Less than two years later, in February 1892, he too succumbed to a chest infection. He died in Palayamkottai after a visit to his birthplace in order to ascertain the security of his inheritance. Much of this was bequeathed for the continuation of evangelistic work among his own people.

In her second book, *Saguna*, Krupabai incorporated her own experience of coming to Madras to study medicine, of being met at Madras Central Station by W.T., and of living within his family for a year. Krupabai was the daughter of the Rev. Haripant Kristy, a notable Maratha Brahman convert. She described how the Satthianadhan family's youngest son, of whose existence she had been but dimly aware, returned from Cambridge after his graduation, and how their romance rapidly developed. In fact, the Satthianadhans blessed this intercaste marriage, but the couple's life together did not last long. Krupabai's health not only prevented her from studying in Britain but worsened, so that she had to abandon her ambition of being a *zenana* doctor or of emulating Pandita Ramabai by establishing a home school for high-caste child widows. She died in 1892, shortly after the death of her infant son. Most of her work was published posthumously by her husband. Samuel Satthianadhan then had an arranged marriage to Kamala Krishnamma, daughter of Oruganti Sivarama Krishnamma.[47]

Unlike Krupabai, Kamala's childhood had not been happy. Brought up by her maternal step-grandmother, she had managed to liberate herself through acquiring literacy and education. Indeed, she had only agreed to the marriage on condition that she would still be free to complete a B.A. degree. After she achieved this in 1898, she went on to become the first Indian woman to acquire an M.A. With her husband's support she soon published her first collection of stories. These reflected the culture clash that converts experienced. Her writings, in some measure, anticipated the outlook and style of R. K. Narayan — with vignettes of Indian Christian life and with themes of conversion repeated in a variety of anecdotal forms that are quite similar. After doubts about life have taken root in a young person's mind, a prolonged intellectual struggle occurs followed by a crisis situation, such as an impending

---

3:460) quotes an obituary (undated) in *The Hindu:* "Her simplicity of character, her self-sacrificing love and care for others, her single-hearted devotion to her work have attracted the notice of all with whom she came in contact. She occupied a unique place in the Native Christian Church in Madras."

47. Krishnamma's maternal grandfather, Ratnamgaru, was also a Telugu Brahman convert who had come under the influence of Robert Noble of Masulipatnam. See John Noble, *A Memoir of the Rev. Robert Turlington Noble, Missionary to the Telugu People of India* (London, 1853).

marriage, that precipitates a decision. This decision was usually free from influence or intervention by any foreign missionary. Dreams and visions, however, could play a role in such a decision. While, invariably, the family of a convert would be alienated, this alienation could later be followed, often many years later, by a family reconciliation. Loneliness, as a result of alienation, could become an acute problem, and a convert could also suffer lapses in faith. Each of these stories presented readers with a complete portrait of Indian life, conveying details of conversion, conflicts, and negotiation over caste and culture. They also mirror the experiences of W. T. Satthianadhan, as found in both his own accounts and Krupabai's "docudrama" account of his life published together with posthumous tributes to him.[48] Those new converts who were reclaimed by their families suffered in ways reminiscent of teenagers caught up in new religious movements during the late twentieth century who then had to be "deprogrammed" by their relatives. No attempt was made, in any of these conversion narratives, to gloss over the failures and sometimes dire fates of individuals whose subsequent lives were filled with suffering and tortured experience.[49]

One might ask how or why the Satthianadhan women could write such powerful stories while their men, especially W.T. and his son Samuel, wrote voluminous amounts of nonfiction. This distinction can be found even within the contents of W.T.'s literary newspaper and Kamala's magazine, *The Indian Ladies' Magazine,* 1901-13. More importantly, what is the extent to which, a century later, their vision of the future has been realized?

Many Indian women are now highly educated; but their opportunities are constrained by limitations imposed by caste and class. Caste remains as central an issue today — in church, society, and state. These pioneering women can be accorded some share of the credit for opening up debates on such matters. While intercaste marriage is still largely limited to the rarified upper-class levels of society, even within the church, both Christian doctrine and the Indian constitution formally condemn negative discrimination on the basis of caste.[50] Despite increased affluence and eclecticism among Christians of India, religious and social identity and culture are still hotly debated. If any-

48. Satthianadhan, *Revd W. T. Satthianadhan,* pp. 24-27; British and Foreign Bible Society Archives, University of Cambridge, *Bible Society Monthly Reporter* 10.28 (2 September 1878).

49. Satthianadhan, *Revd W. T. Satthianadhan,* pp. 25-6. There is, however, an account of a reverse situation in which a Hindu bride named Radha is kidnapped by her Christian brother-in-law and not allowed to return to her Hindu home. This is found in *Saguna,* ch. 4.

50. Satthianadhan and Satthianadhan, *Stories of Indian Christian Life.*

thing, the gulf between urban and rural cultures is wider than ever. As economic dependence persists, both nationally and in local churches, the kind of self-confidence displayed by the Satthianadhans is now at least as prevalent. One question remains: whether, in empirical terms, one can ever describe such a thing as "total" conversion and, if so, whether "caste" feelings and prejudices that have "washed over" into church life in India, and remain so prevalent within Indian Christian culture, are relevant to questions about conversion.[51] An inverted form of this question can be found in *dalit* struggles for abolition of caste prejudice in our own day. To what degree is conversion simply a change of direction or a "turning" from one perspective to another, with far too many converts failing to apply the radical critique of the gospel to the presuppositions of caste, culture, and social status?[52] For Evangelicals, such as the Satthianadhans, apart from the metaphysical or supernatural dimension of salvation, the conversion experience itself brought great personal joy and fulfillment, whatever its costs may have been.

51. For comparisons, see F. Gell, *Inquiries by the Bishop of Madras regarding the removal of caste prejudices and practices in the Native Church of South India* (London and Madras, 1868), p. 5.

52. The situation should be viewed in the context of W.T.'s comment in his *Six Months in England* (Madras, 1978) that in England, despite Christianity being a "holy" religion that strikes at the roots of evil, there were constant warnings against pickpockets, and that many "Christians" were unconverted nominal Christians.

CHAPTER FOURTEEN

Social Mobilization among People Competing at the Bottom Level of Society: The Presence of Missions in Rural South India, ca. 1900-1950

GUNNEL CEDERLÖF

One major feature of late-nineteenth- and early-twentieth-century South Indian history is the growth of broad-based social and popular movements. At a time when business and industrial enterprises expanded and the market grew, political space opened up for new groups in society. Caste affiliation was often, though far from always, important in mobilization, particularly so as the colonial state made caste classificatory in public records and important for the recruitment to civil and military service. Organizations often corresponded to one or more associated castes, and movements had political, cultural, and religious forms. Some of the movements confronted the state, others, an opposing or a superior community.[1]

Among the lowest sections in society, among the untouchable castes,[2]

1. On the expansion of caste associations see, for example, Narendra Subramanian, *Ethnicity and Populist Mobilization: Political Parties, Citizens and Democracy in South India* (Delhi, 1999), pp. 96-101; Sekhar Bandyopadhyay, *Caste, Protest and Identity in Colonial India: The Namasudras of Bengal, 1872-1947* (Richmond, 1997), ch. 2; Susanne Bayly, *Caste, Society and Politics in India from the Eighteenth Century to the Modern Age* (Cambridge, 1999), pp. 160-62, 237; Geoffrey Oddie, *Hindu and Christian in South East India* (London, 1991).

2. The terms to denote members and castes of the lowest social strata in society follow that of the contemporary documents; in general, this means that "untouchable" will be used for the period up to approximately the 1930s and "scheduled caste" for the subsequent period. Terms like "harijan" or "depressed classes" rarely occur in the sources consulted.

336

mobilization often took the form of community- or kinship-based conversion to either Christianity or Islam. When people turned to Christianity, as a rule, Protestant missions were approached. A number of studies of "mass movements" deal with the strivings among these communities for social and economic uplift, identity, self-esteem, and recognition as full human beings. Missions have been seen both as a means for the untouchables to reach social goals and as a place where downtrodden people found relief.[3]

In the case of the rural history of the Coimbatore district in South India's highlands, previous generalizations about mobilization among the untouchable castes do not seem to fit. Here the movement to seek baptism and encounters with mission workers (pastors, evangelists, Bible women, missionaries) involved two major communities and a handful of members from other, smaller communities. This study concerns the two larger communities: the Madhari and the Paraiyar. The former is the largest of the untouchable caste communities in the district, 206,162 persons according to the 1921 Census, or 9.3 percent of the population. The Paraiyar is the second largest community, approximately half the size of the Madhari. Both communities found their major sources of income, in the main, as landless agricultural laborers.[4]

From 1910 to 1970 approximately fifty thousand people, most of them members of the Paraiyar and Madhari communities, converted to Christianity.[5] The two major castes — the Paraiyar, locally known as the Adi Dravida, and the Madhari — however, regarded each other with mutual contempt and never joined together in one common conversion movement. While arguing between themselves about who occupied the higher of the two lowest levels in the social hierarchy, they competed for chapels and visits from local pastors.

3. See further Henriette Bugge, *Mission and Tamil Society* (Surrey, 1994); Duncan Forrester, "The Depressed Classes and Conversion to Christianity," in G. A. Oddie, ed., *Religion in South Asia* (New Delhi, 1991); Dick Kooiman, *Conversion and Social Equality in India: The London Missionary Society in South Travancore in the 19th Century* (New Delhi, 1989); G. A. Oddie, "Missionaries as Social Commentators: The Indian Case," in Robert Bickers and Rosemary Seton, *Missionary Encounters: Sources and Issues* (Surrey, 1996).

4. Among the Paraiyar, a substantial group migrated seasonally to the nearby tea estates in the hills to labor for up to ten months a year. The Madhari were the local leather workers. In the Coimbatore district they were Telugu-speaking; however, in most parts of Tamilnadu the leather workers were Tamil and were known as Chakkiliyar.

5. London, School of Oriental and African Studies, Wesleyan Methodist Missionary Society [MMS], Report of the Trichinopoly Mass Movement Commission 1935, in South India Provincial Synod 1936, app. IX, pp. 68-69, 101; Tamil Evangelical Lutheran Church, the pastorates of Mandiripalayam, Palladam, and Tiruppur, baptismal records; Gunnel Cederlöf, *Bonds Lost: Subordination, Conflict, and Mobilisation in Rural South India c. 1900–1970* (Delhi, 1997), p. 171, table 5:1 (based on the Census of India).

If one of the two communities in a village converted, as a rule the other would remain hostile to the mission. In some exceptional cases, a mission built two chapels in the same village, one for the Paraiyar and the other for the Madhari. It was unthinkable for them to enter and worship in the same chapel.[6] This situation might well be explained in terms of taboos and caste perceptions, but for this region, historical evidence reveals another story that suggests other lines of explanation.

As has been widely recognized, mission archives include reports and correspondence that reflect life at the local, village level to a much higher degree than colonial and government archives do.[7] Critics have argued that documents relating to missions focus only on church matters — the inauguration of a chapel, the number of newly baptized, and so on.[8] The point has some relevance, but important differences between the mission archives need to be observed. In the Coimbatore district, two Protestant missions received converts from the Paraiyar and the Madhari communities. Those were the Wesleyan Methodist Missionary Society (MMS) and the Church of Sweden Mission (Evangelical Lutheran, CSM). Comparing the records of these two missions, a striking difference becomes evident.

In general the MMS reports reflect a situation where the Methodists planned and worked systematically, surveying the local region for the numbers of members of the converting communities, listing their subcastes, and recording the kinship groups of the different castes and subcastes. Missionaries strove not to baptize anyone of a particular community in a village until all members of that group were willing to convert, and they tried not to leave the region until all, or as many as possible, had become members of the church.[9] In their reports to London, they wrote much of the "growing har-

6. When this happened, the missionaries described it as extraordinary. Examples of villages having two Evangelical Lutheran chapels are Devanampalayam and Kuppandampalayam. Church of Sweden Mission Archives [hereafter CSMA], Uppsala MBa 1956:152/56, p. 2; Karunagarapuri Mission station [hereafter KMs], Karunagarapuri Annual Report 1936.

7. See, for example, J. D. Y. Peel, "Problems and Opportunities in an Anthropologist's Use of a Missionary Archive," in *Missionary Encounters: Sources and Issues*, edited by Robert A. Bickers and Rosemary Seton (Richmond, 1996), pp. 74-78.

8. See Dick Kooiman, *Conversion and Social Equality in India: The London Missionary Society in South Travancore in the 19th Century* (New Delhi, 1989), pp. 4-7. He criticizes the missionaries for the narrowness of their records. When such a critique is directed exclusively to the mission material, it can be taken lightly since all kinds of material carry a bias and need critical treatment.

9. MMS, Annual Report 1925, p. 45; MMS, South India Provincial Synod 1940, p. 113. See also Geoffrey Oddie on the importance of kinship ties for the spread of Christian con-

vest" and the encouraging ways in which the converts endured suffering, thus revealing "the glory of God in the lives of His disciples." However, they rarely give details about the conflicts and the conflicting parties that would shed light on the causes of this suffering. For example, a missionary might report burnt-down houses of the Paraiyar and a court case but give no information about the cause of the conflict or whether it was solved in court. The overriding impression from reading the MMS documents is that missionaries had a need to convince their home office about the success of their work in India — a need that may have stemmed from both moral and financial concerns.[10]

In contrast to the Methodists, after some years (mainly between 1927 and 1931) of keeping the Madharis out, largely through lack of resources, the Swedish Lutherans seem to have opened up for all who came with "sincere motives." This soon resulted in an overwhelming workload. Although they often commented on it, the CSM does not seem to have systematically followed the "community- or caste-trail," in order to reach as many as possible, and the MMS workers were rather irritated by the "free-lance pioneer work" of the CSM among the untouchables in their neighborhood.[11] In their reports to Uppsala, subdivisions of castes are systematically mentioned by only one of the mission workers, an Indian pastor whose working methods to some extent corresponded with those of the Methodists.[12] In contrast to the MMS reports, those of the CSM are filled with problems that the missionaries were facing. These were generally not their own private problems but those of their "flock," members of the Paraiyar and, in particular, the Madhari communities. The common criticism of mission archives — that they only report church matters — does not apply to these records. On the contrary, a large number of reports and letters describe village life and local conflicts. Villages and individuals are named, events are dated, and several subsequent reports follow a course of events. When these reports are used to complement government reports and oral material (interviews, observations, etc.), the life of a

---

version in the Thanjāvur and Tiruchirapalli districts in the 1880s and 1890s (*Hindu and Christian in South East India* [London, 1991], p. 156).

10. For example, in the village of Sulliporikkipalayam "riots" were said to have taken place between the Madhari and the Goundar (dominant landowners) communities. Madhari men were arrested, a court case was filed, and houses were burned to the ground. After this brief description, the author concludes that all Madharis remained Christian. MMS, South India Provincial Synod 1936, p. 132; MMS, South India Provincial Synod 1943, p. 112.

11. MMS, Correspondence, Trichinopoly Chairman, Minutes of the Standing Committee, Dharapuram, 6 April 1938, paragraph 4.

12. CSMA, MBa 1927:243, p. 8; CSMA, MBa 1941:362, pp. 1-2.

complex local society is revealed. Terms such as "conversion movement," "converts," and so on, where members of the untouchable castes are grouped into one category, are not useful unless local social divisions, including those among the different untouchable or scheduled castes, are considered together with an understanding of the different local contexts.

Mobilization among the untouchable castes in rural Coimbatore, in terms of conversions, formed not *one* but at least two distinct movements, in the sense of having different members, means, and goals. Both communities, however, could be described as "subaltern" from the overall societal level to that of the village where both communities related to the same superior caste. The Madhari alone would make a particularly good case study of the struggles of an oppressed, subaltern community, but it would not throw much light on the differences between them and the Paraiyar, especially in terms of mobilization. The aim here is to consider some of the general features and forms of mobilization within the two communities during the first half of the twentieth century in an attempt to shape an argument about the conditions for social mobilization among people competing at the bottom level of rural South Indian society.

Several scholars have addressed the topic of mobilization among the lowest sections or classes in society. One of the original driving forces of the Subaltern Studies project, headed by Ranajit Guha, was to bring out the autonomous history of the people or the peasants to show their contribution to Indian history in its own right. In contrast to colonialist and bourgeois-nationalist elite history, subaltern history would reveal the politics of the people. Guha has written extensively on the conscious actions of rioting peasants and the rationality of the peasant uprisings and insurgency in India.[13]

David Hardiman's seminal study on the *adivasi* (tribal) mobilization in south Gujarat in the 1920s brought political and religious aspects of a popular movement together.[14] In this region a socio-religious movement, which eventually turned into a political one, evolved among the different tribal communities. This movement took religious forms, and the message, which was basically social-reformist in character, was delivered through spirit mediums giving voice to a goddess. Hardiman uses the term "Adivasi," thus emphasizing that common interests superseded community barriers; at the same time he argues that the term has a special relevance in India and that it is free from

13. Ranajit Guha, *Elementary Aspects of Peasant Insurgency in Colonial India* (Oxford, 1983); and Ranajit Guha, "The Prose of Counter-Insurgency," in *Writings in South Asian History and Society*, edited by Ranajit Guha, Subaltern Studies 2 (Oxford, 1983), pp. 1-42.

14. David Hardiman, *The Coming of the Devi* (Oxford, 1995 [1st ed., 1987]).

the "evolutionist connotations" attached to the term "tribal." His aim was to write a history from a perspective of the Adivasi group and to refrain from explaining the movement as a product of superstitious beliefs or as an elite mobilization of tribals.[15]

"Resistance" is a concept that has attracted analyses of strategies to counter the forces of domination and exploitation of the lowest classes in society. James Scott, in *Weapons of the Weak*, drew attention to a debate about the everyday, hidden resistance of the poor where resistance by the subordinate may take the form of evasion, sabotage, slander, false compliance, and other means that avoid direct confrontation with authority. For the peasants,

> their safety may depend on silence and anonymity; the kind of resistance itself may depend for its effectiveness on the appearance of conformity; their intentions may be so embedded in the peasant subculture *and* in the routine, taken-for-granted struggle to provide for the subsistence and survival of the household as to remain inarticulate.[16]

An absence of organized movements against elites should not therefore be viewed as a lack of resistance.

Scott's work has been much debated. His contention that the presence of resistance is evidence of a nondominated culture of the subordinate — an ideology that the hegemonic ideology cannot influence — resembles the Subaltern Studies' argument about subaltern autonomy.[17] Douglas Haynes and Gyan Prakash, however, question this distinction between culture and behavior, between struggle and submission. Such a distinction implies that, when peasants show deference to landlords, they are deliberate and calculating, while, argue Haynes and Prakash, such acts are actually "influenced by a logic that accepts the larger structures of landholding and political power as unalterable facts." They argue for an analysis that brings the concept of everyday resistance inside the field of power.[18]

The social construction of dominance and subordination is central also in the work of David Mosse, though from a different perspective. He strongly criticizes arguments for the existence of an autonomous cultural sphere that is independent of a dominant culture. Mosse concentrates his efforts on the

15. Hardiman, *Coming of the Devi*, pp. 1-17.

16. James C. Scott, *Weapons of the Weak: Everyday Forms of Peasant Resistance* (New Haven, 1985), p. 29 and pp. 289-303 for "What is Resistance?"

17. In Scott's critique of Gramsci; see Scott, *Weapons of the Weak*, ch. 8.

18. Douglas Haynes and Gyan Prakash, *Contesting Power: Resistance and Everyday Social Relations in South Asia* (Delhi, 1991), pp. 10-11.

tensions and conflicts that exist within an overall culture and draws conclusions about long-term continuity in history. He argues for the continuity of a regional, in this case South Indian, culture embracing members of all religions. Caste is prominent in his discussion, and he outlines a caste order where dominance and power or where subordination and dependence rest on both religion and politics (purity and power). It is within caste that dominance is expressed in village politics. The continuity that Mosse recognizes, however, may seem submerged when cultural and religious differences are stressed. But when social and political mobilization among scheduled castes (*harijan* in Mosse's terminology) takes place, it is often articulated through the manipulation of the institutions and symbols that define subordination. Thus, in Ramnad district, in the state of Tamilnadu, the *harijans* used their membership in the Roman Catholic Church to raise their caste status and to gain political power. Christianity became "embedded" in the indigenous, social, and religious order.[19] In a later publication, Mosse further develops his work on caste strategies and human action. Here the cultural consensus he argues for, even though characterized by certain inertia, should not be understood as static. Conflicts can be strong and people socially mobile; however, conflicts still take place within the South Indian culture. In their strategies for social and political upward mobility, the Catholic *harijans* in Ramnad employed new identities, "projecting themselves as Christians, Scheduled Castes," and manipulated those identities in order to maximize access to material and political resources and to promote their interests and caste honor.[20]

These different debates and their implications for the analysis have a bearing on the analysis that follows of mobilization in the Coimbatore district.

Securing Laborers in the Coimbatore Highlands

The Paraiyar caste was one of the three major untouchable or scheduled castes in the Tamil country. In spite of low social position, it was a caste surrounded by myths about its members' physical strength and close contacts with the untamed spirits of the dark forests. It appears that, both in the late

---

19. David Mosse, "Caste, Christianity and Hinduism: A Study of Social Organisation and Religion in Rural Ramnad," D.Phil. thesis, University of Oxford, 1986, pp. 89, 100, 107, 513-14.

20. The *harijans* that Mosse has studied belong to the Pallar caste. David Mosse, "Idiom of Subordination and Styles of Protesting among Christian and Hindu Harijan Castes in Tamil Nadu," *Contributions to Indian Sociology* 28.1 (1994): 68; Cederlöf, *Bonds Lost*, pp. 8-10, 12-13.

eighteenth century and again in the late nineteenth, after a period of harden-ing control over the group by their employing landowners, the Paraiyar were able to mobilize and organize regionally.

David Washbrook emphasizes the comparative advantages they gained in the times of war during the late eighteenth century. The demand for their la-bor grew, both as agricultural workers and as soldiers, on both sides in the war between the British and Mysore State. This gave the Paraiyar an opportu-nity to bargain for better remuneration. In the case of the agricultural labor-ers a substantial part of their pay was often given as an advance, in the form of a share of the harvest, when the laborer was taken on by the landowner on a yearly basis. When the British gained control over South India, land was set-tled, and the Paraiyar became more dependent. The system of taking on la-borers by the giving of an advance appears to have become "oppressive." The advance became a debt to the landlord that was almost impossible to repay, and, when landed property was institutionalized by the courts, "non-real rights, such as claims to grain shares, were not enforceable at law." Agricul-tural wages were determined by the laws of supply and demand. Thus, the la-borers lived at the mercy of the landowners.[21]

In the later part of the nineteenth century, however, the Paraiyar began again to move. At that time laborers were urgently needed on various estates, in mines, and on railway-construction sites in South and Southeast Asia and in East and South Africa. Following the Slavery Abolition Act (1843) and the Penal Code (1861), the growing demand for laborers led to large-scale migra-tions in which the Paraiyar became one of the more predominant communi-ties. The important employers from the Coimbatore district were the estate owners in the hills surrounding the highlands to the north, west, and south of the district and the expanding spinneries, textile mills, and market places in the towns. It was common for the adult males in the family, sometimes to-gether with their wives, to stay on the estates during the working season, leav-ing children, some adult women and the elderly behind. In this way families gained incomes both from work on the large estates and from local agricul-tural labor, and this generally enabled the estate owners to keep wages low. Another work possibility was employment "with the British," as it was often called, in the railway system, and as drivers, butlers, cooks, and so on.[22]

21. David Washbrook, "Land and Labour in Late Eighteenth-Century South India: The Golden Age of the Pariah?" in *Dalit Movements and the Meaning of Labour in India,* edited by Peter Robb (Oxford, 1993), pp. 78-85.

22. Net immigration of Indian laborers, most of them coming from the Madras Presidency, has been estimated to 1,451,319 between 1843 and 1903. See Benedicte Hjejle, "Slavery and Agricultural Bondage in South India in the Nineteenth Century," *Scandina-*

Increasing mobility among the Paraiyars helped to facilitate the growth of political mobilization within the community at the turn of the century. This was a period when social, political, and cultural movements grew in the Presidency as a whole. The term Adi Dravida was adopted by several castes who were influenced by the Dravidian movement and pronounced a self-conscious identity as "original Dravidians." This term became an alternative name for Paraiyar in the Coimbatore highlands.

In contrast to the Paraiyar, the Madhari community does not seem to have gained from the growing demand for laborers outside the villages, nor are there any indications of a politicization of the community. Rather, members of this community appear to have become more tied to the villages and their farms, even at a time when industries expanded in the towns and estates were established in the hills. Barbara Evans's study of the tea estates in the Nilgiri Hills shows the existence of two separate labor flows in the district, one to the towns and their factories and the other to the estates. This was the result of different labor-recruitment methods and the preexisting socio-economic order of labor. She found that there were obstacles to the lower stratum of the labor force finding work in the towns. Potential industrial laborers were reported to have bribed their way into the factories, and workers who were already established recommended their relatives for vacancies. Poor members of the dominant local Goundar community would rather seek industrial employment than have to move to the rainy and cold estates. At the same time sheer poverty was an obstacle to the landless untouchable laborers doing the same.[23] In addition, one should note that the flow of laborers to the estates, largely members of untouchable castes, was not an even mix of various untouchable castes. One major caste was largely missing — the most numerous in the Coimbatore district of the untouchable castes — the Madhari. The reason for this cannot be traced to the labor-recruitment preferences of the estate labor-contractors but to the organization of labor and the prevailing social hierarchies in the villages.

The Coimbatore district of the late nineteenth and most of the twentieth century became known for its cotton and textiles. Earlier, in the eighteenth century, Mysore State imported textiles from these highlands. The Mysore Wars put an end to such trades, and it took some effort to reintroduce the crop into the district. By the turn of the century the scale and methods of cot-

---

vian *Economic History Review* 15.1, 2 (1967): 103, table 1; Barbara Evans, "Constructing a Plantation Labour Force: The Plantation-Village Nexus in South India," *Indian Economic and Social History Review* 32.2 (1995): 172-74; Christopher John Baker, *The Politics of South India 1920-1937* (Cambridge, 1976), pp. 184, 187; Cederlöf, *Bonds Lost*, pp. 98-99.

23. Evans, "Plantation Labour Force," pp. 172-74.

ton cropping and weaving of cloth had changed. More important than cotton, however, was cattle raising. The Goundar community was famous for its high-quality breeds, and Fredric Nicholson, writing the *Manual of the Coimbatore District* in the 1880s, estimated the number of horned cattle in the district to be around 900,000.[24]

A cattle breeder needs a leather worker, both for his skills and because working with dead animal products — flaying the skin, tanning the hides, and stitching leather items — was restricted by taboos. Neither a Goundar nor a Paraiyar nor a member of any other community would consider doing the job. This put the Madhari in a crucial position vis-à-vis the Goundar cattle breeder. At the same time, when the cultivation of cotton expanded and the high-yielding Cambodia variety was introduced on the farms between 1900 and the 1910s, the need for irrigation grew.[25] Coimbatore is a dry district. The highland plateau is situated in a rain shadow, shielded by the Western Ghats from the southwest monsoon and lacking sufficient rivers to divert in order to irrigate the fields. Thus, farming is dependent on deep-dug wells. From 1902 to 1916, the area of cultivated land watered by well irrigation was around 300,000 acres. In 1917, an upward trend began. The area increased to over 400,000 acres by 1922-24, and after 1926 the acreage of land under well irrigation stabilized at that level.[26]

The wells were worked by a pair of oxen hauling water from the well into the irrigation canal and then, backing up the slope to the edge of the well, letting the bucket drop back into the water again. The *kavalai* technique was simple but efficient and brought tons of water out of the wells. The water was drawn for three to four hours in the morning and a similar period in the late afternoon.[27] The bucket and its outlet were made of copper and leather. For this work, as a rule, a Madhari man was employed. Therefore, during the expansion of cash crop cultivation, the Madhari community played a central part.

Arrangements for the employment of agricultural labor had the same appearance as those of the early nineteenth century. An advance was given, ap-

24. The number of cattle can be compared to the size of the population in the district. In 1881, it was estimated to 1,657,690 persons (Census of India 1881, Part I, Table II; F. Nicholson, *Manual of the Coimbatore District* [Madras, 1887], p. 243, n. 46).

25. A. R. Cox, ed., *Gazetteer of the Coimbatore District,* vol. 2 (Madras, 1933), pp. 149, 161; N. Ganesamurthi, "Economic Survey of a South Indian Village — Perumanallur," *Madras Agricultural Journal* 23.7 (1935): 272.

26. Government of Madaras, *Season and Crop Report,* 1902/3-1933/4.

27. For a colorful description of the *kavalai,* see Oriental and India Office Collections, London District Officers' Collection, Downing Collection, Diary, 10 December 1937.

proximately ten rupees in the 1930s,[28] and the laborers had rights in a share of the produce of the village and rights in water, shelter, and clothes at the time of major festivals, and they could count on protection from the Goundar. However, the historical context and local situation within which this labor contract operated in the early twentieth century changed. This form of labor was called *pannaiyal* (*pannai* meaning "farm," *al* meaning "laborer"; in the colonial documents these laborers were often called "permanent farm servants"). Employing *pannaiyal* appears to have provided the farmer with a high degree of flexibility. It involved a one-year contract where formal and informal customary rules seem to have worked together in such a way that the farmer could take on laborers for long periods, even for several generations. Advances that were not repaid on time, at the end of the year, turned into an inheritable debt. At the same time, the farmer could dismiss laborers after a one-year contractual term.[29]

The *pannai* system was not the only network that kept the laborers in the villages. The informal side of the relationship between Goundar and Madhari may also be explained by the term *urimai* (lit., ownership, liberty, claim for right, wife, slave and the services of a bondservant — a term with judicial connotations), explained by a Lutheran missionary as a customary contract "half way to slavery" that included drum-beating at Hindu festivals and "other dubious things as part of their ordinary duties." Old Madhari, living in today's rural Coimbatore, define *urimai* from the perspective of the security it rendered them, as the laborer's right to a share of the harvest that could not be denied.[30] Brenda Beck describes a similar system in her study of the Coimbatore highlands. Though giving a slightly ideal-type impression, her work reveals a system in a village where castes are hierarchically ranked and ordered according to their relationships in production (those relating to agriculture making up a special category). Each caste possesses different defined rights and carries different duties. At the top of the hierarchy is the Goundar community; at the bottom, the Madhari.[31]

28. Ganesamurthi, "Economic Survey," pp. 270-71, 277.

29. CSMA, MBa 1931:224, p. 14; P. Gopalaratanam, "Rural Studies — Madathupalayam Village, Coimbatore District," *Madras Agricultural Journal* 19.12 (1931): 523; Hjejle, "Slavery and Agricultural Bondage," p. 100; Dharma Kumar, *Land and Caste in South India: Agricultural Labour in the Madras Presidency during the Nineteenth Century* (New Delhi, 1992), p. 75; Venkatesh B. Athreya, Göran Djurfeldt, and Staffan Lindberg, *Barriers Broken: Production Relations and Agrarian Change in Tamil Nadu* (London, 1990), pp. 133, 241.

30. CSMA, FaR A IV:4, Jothipuram 1956; *Tamil Lexicon*. See also, for example, Interview, Arulpuram, 26 January 1995.

31. Brenda Beck, ed., *Peasant Society in Konku: A Study of Right and Left Sub-Castes*

In this way, the labor of the Madhari as *pannaiyal* was interwoven with, and worked to reinforce, the social hierarchy of the village and Goundar superiority within it. Thus, the dependence between the two communities, though uneven, was mutual.

Two Movements for Conversion

In 1913, Methodist missionaries in Dharapuram received the first converts from the Paraiyar community. Relatives had converted further south in Ramnad, having approached the London Missionary Society. Hearing about the advantages of conversion, a group among the Sangu (conch shell) subcaste of the Paraiyar community decided to approach the nearest missionaries, who happened to be Methodists.[32] In 1924 the first baptisms were reported by the Lutheran missionaries in Tiruppur and Pollachi, places miles apart and further west in the highlands. The baptismal records show that they were Adi Dravida (Paraiyar), most likely relatives of the Sangu Paraiyar living around Dharapuram.[33]

A common description of the Paraiyar converts by the missionaries was that they were keen to improve their social and economic status and anxious to uphold barriers between themselves and those whom they considered to be "lower," in particular the Madhari community. However, in contrast to the far fewer converts of some other low castes, the Koravar and the Valayar, they did not keep moving between different churches and missions in order to secure a better "deal" from the missionaries.[34]

In 1925 the first members among the Madhari community living near the town of Udamalpet also asked Methodist missionaries for baptism. The first Madhari conversions were recorded by the Lutheran missionary in Palladam in 1931. Udamalpet town is situated in the southeastern part of the highlands, while Palladam lies at the heart of it. Just like the Paraiyar, the Madhari came as a village group. All members, or the major part of the community, in a specific village would make a joint decision to approach some local pastor or missionary with their request. Since two different kinship groups, or subcastes, of the same community rarely lived in the same village, the mission

---

in South India (Vancouver, 1972), pp. 42-49, table 1.2, pp. 44-47. The table showing the ranking of castes is based on an interview from 1966.

32. *The Foreign Field of Wesleyan Methodist Church,* July 1927, p. 232.

33. CSMA, MBa 1924:141; Tamil Evangelical Lutheran Church, Tiruppur Baptismal Records.

34. CSMA, MBa 1947:393, p. 1.

records indicate that the movement spread not only within the community but within a kinship group or subcaste of the community. The most reliable information about this is to be found in the reports of the Indian Lutheran pastor, mentioned above, and in the MMS reports.[35]

The missionaries' judgments about the Madhari community bear no resemblance to those of the Paraiyar. The Madhari were described as more tied to the villages, and their financial situation, as more precarious. Furthermore, they were said to be ignorant and low in morale.[36] It appeared to be impossible to establish mission village schools, which worked fairly well among the Paraiyar, in the Madhari *cheris* since the children were needed for work and, as a rule, were mortgaged for a year at a time to the Goundar landowner to pasture his cattle and collect manure.[37] One might expect such a community to do its utmost to gain material benefits from conversion. Compared to the Paraiyar, Koravar, and Valayar communities, however, the Madhari do not seem to have been in a position to bargain. They may have joined the church in the hope of getting a well of their own, but in most cases an offer from the evangelist appears to have been their only alternative to the status quo. The Catholic church did not work in the rural Tiruppur-Palladam region, and to "go to the Harijans," that is, to ask for government help as Scheduled Caste Hindus, implied a level of organization and a possibility of moving from the village, traits that could not be attributed to the Madhari in general.[38]

When both Paraiyar and Madhari people began to make contacts with pastors, evangelists, or missionaries, the response from the dominant landowners in the region, mostly Goundar but sometimes Naidu/Naicker, came immediately. Stones were thrown, cattle were killed, sheds were burnt, and — the most common reaction — laborers were denied access to water or work and, thus, from their *urimai* rights in the village. Without water and work,

35. MMS, *Annual Report*, 1925, p. 25; CSMA MBa 1932:145, 3, 1932:146, 3; CSMA, Unsorted documents, Correspondence, Coimbatore, 1929-33, J. Sandegren to the Church Council, draft; Tamil Evangelical Lutheran Church, Palladam Baptismal Records, vol. 1; SKMT 1931:22, extracts from letters by missionary Frykholm (24 July 1931 and 3 September 1931).

36. CSMA, MBa 1932:145, p. 3; MMS, South India Synod Minutes, Meeting of the District Synod of the Trichinopoly District, 2-10 January 1935, App. E, "Mass Conversion Movement Report," p. 5.

37. *Cheri* means a settlement of an untouchable community in the village. Andrén Collection, Karunagarapuri Annual Report 1937; CSMA, MBa 1953:545, p. 1.

38. In order to avoid "rice Christians," the CSM introduced a number of fees: one rupee per married couple for baptismal instruction, another rupee for baptism. One rupee was at the time (the 1940s) equal to a day's income. KMs, Karunagarapuri Annual Report 1948; CSMA, MBa 1949:489, p. 2.

their means of survival were removed together with their legitimate identification with the village. The situation resembles that described by Geoffrey Oddie in his article on missionaries as social commentators. He states that the Protestants spent most of their time among people who tended to represent a challenge to the power and status of the traditional, landed, and commercial classes. Conflicts between missionaries and landlords occurred. Missionaries regarded landlords as "an obstacle to the spread of the Christian Gospel," and conversions among the laborers made the landlords fear they would lose control over them.[39]

In the Coimbatore district, it was not always the presence of a mission that caused the conflict; sometimes mission workers were caught up in local conflicts in which some members of their congregation had become embroiled.[40] The roles assumed by the mission workers were mainly those of diplomats. In documents and interviews, they consistently expressed their wish to avoid conflicts with the local authorities. One missionary, working in the district from 1944 to 1953, used to explain to the Goundar village leader: "We do not want to change the order of the village, the labourer shall continue to labour for you. We just want to evangelize and establish congregations." With some exceptions, missionaries in both missions never strove to start a social revolution, but the fact that they began to repay *pannaiyal* debts and argue the case of Madhari laborers against their employers in court, outside the domains of the village, spoke a different language to the Goundars.[41]

Goundar reactions seem to have been less violent when members of the Paraiyar community converted than when Madharis converted. Madhari conversions culminated in the 1930s and early 1940s, years that correspond with an overwhelming number of reports about "persecution" of the Madhari congregation members in the villages.[42] To understand this difference, one needs to consider the organization of agriculture.

Between 1900 and 1930, the number of *pannaiyal* grew. These were years

39. Andrén Collection, Biskopsvisitation, Karunagarapuri 16-18 March 1937; SKMT 1938:4, pp. 86-87; CSMA, Unsorted documents, CSM in India 1941, p. 23; CSMA, MBa 1953:547; Geoffrey Oddie, "Missionaries as Social Commentators: The Indian Case," in *Missionary Encounters: Sources and Issues,* edited by Robert A. Bickers and Rosemary Seton (Richmond, 1996), p. 200.

40. See, for example, the case of Manickapuram in Cederlöf, *Bonds Lost,* pp. 203-6.

41. Interview, Bertil Envall [former CSM missionary], 12 October 1995; CSMA, MBa 1941:362, p. 3; CSMA, Sorted documents, box 9:A, Appendix, The Minutes of the Meeting of the Economic Uplift Committee, 22 August 1946.

42. CSMA, Sorted documents, box 9:A, Appendix, The Minutes of the Meeting of the Economic Uplift Committee, 22 August 1946; Tamil Evangelical Lutheran Church, the pastorates of Tiruppur, Palladam, and Mandiripalayam, Baptismal Records.

with strong competition for labor between agriculture, industry, and estates. On the farms, there were already well-established, close relations between the Goundar farmers and the Madhari leather workers in an economy based on cattle and on the need for laborers with skills in leather work for managing irrigation. Therefore, Madhari were the laborers that Goundar farmers preferred to take on as *pannaiyal*.[43] A situation of labor scarcity is often one where laborers find ways to negotiate higher wages or to choose between different employers and trades. While the Paraiyar were able to take advantage of expanding opportunities, however, nothing indicates that the Madhari could realize the same opportunities and leave the villages.

Some similar features in Madhari and Paraiyar mobilization in the villages may be observed. Both movements originated from outside the highlands and spread into the district via the relatives of converted Paraiyar and Madhari communities in the adjoining Tiruchirapalli and Ramnad districts. These movements can be further understood by considering the growing mobility in general among untouchable or scheduled castes in the Madras Presidency from the late nineteenth century onward. For the Paraiyars, this connection is fairly obvious, while in the case of the Madharis it may have come about in a more indirect way. The Paraiyar, being more mobile, had greater opportunities to meet people outside the villages and to be influenced by the social and political movements in the towns and on the estates. Visits to marketplaces held out similar possibilities for Madharis. The growth of *pannaiyal* between the 1880s and the 1930s does not seem to have been just a matter of tying down laborers in a situation of competing interests. It is reasonable to view it in the light of the growing political awareness among the laboring castes.

Long before the 1930s, Paraiyars had broken away from tight village control. It is reasonable to assume that the Goundar farmer did not want the Madhari to do the same. The ties inherent in *pannai* contracts served to control more than a labor force; they were also part of the control of the Madhari community in the village. Any mobilization among the Madhari would therefore be met by strong Goundar opposition. Thus, a major difference between the two communities was the level of mobility allowed to them and their different positions within different structures and systems of agricultural labor.

43. Cox estimates the proportions between permanent and casual laborers to be one-third of the former and two-thirds of the latter. These figures do not consider the fact that the wives and other adult persons of the *pannaiyal*'s household were expected to give preference to work for the *pannaiyar* (farmer) and, thus, were included in the *pannai* system. See Cox, *Gazetteer of the Coimbatore District*, p. 149; Christopher John Baker, *An Indian Rural Economy 1880-1955: The Tamilnad Countryside* (Oxford, 1984), p. 209; Ganesamurthi, "Economic Survey," pp. 271-72, 277.

The Paraiyar showed clear intentions of improving their social and economic status as part of their reasons for conversion, while the Madhari appear to have had other aims for letting the mission workers into their *cheris*. As a rule, until the 1950s the local Indian pastors of the Tamil Evangelical Lutheran Church were of a high caste. When they entered the living quarters of people from untouchable castes in the villages, they broke with social codes. No Goundar or member of any other community in the village would consider entering the *cheri* or the home of a Madhari. Building a chapel in the *cheri,* even of the simplest quality, meant providing the congregation with a house to enter when they worshipped, a place that resembled the village temple but did not reinforce the village hierarchy. New ceremonies and new songs were introduced, processions were held, and, at baptism, converts received new names and wore white shirts. In cases where the Goundar were not hostile, they were invited as honored guests and even contributed financially to the Christian festivals.[44] Accepted or not, converted Madharis were no longer identified only with leather and as the laborers of the Goundar, as the lowest on the social scale. They were also acknowledged and recognized as having a new identity, that of Christian, which was an identity derived from outside and beyond village control.

The Indian high-caste pastors, to some extent perhaps more than the foreign missionaries, were received with regard to their social (including caste) status. As educated visitors who showed appropriate respect, they could not be thrown out. When a pastor or missionary took a case to court, where a Madhari laborer had been ill-treated, such an act was a challenge to local power and to the authority of the Goundar as the community that enforced law in the village. This may also help to explain why the *pannaiyal* system survived into the 1950s, long after the system had ceased to be economically the most profitable alternative for a farmer.[45] The mission worker appeared as an authority with his own "power base" outside the village; he could, in certain matters, match Goundar authority. In the long term, the Goundar was the stronger party, but, for the Madhari, the mission worker represented a chance to break Goundar control without having to leave the village. To find protection from arbitrary exercises of power by the Goundar appears to have been

44. KMs, Karunagarapuri Annual Report 1934; CSMA, Unsorted documents, CSM in India 1941, p. 2, MBa 1952:547, p. 7

45. During the years of severe drought, in 1947-53, the share of *pannaiyal* of the total agricultural labor force dropped from one-third to 5 percent, thereafter to stay at this level (Cox, *Gazetteer of the Coimbatore District,* p. 148; *Agricultural Labour Inquiry: Report on Intensive Survey of Agricultural Labour Employment, Underemployment, Wages and Levels of Living,* 1954, Ministry of Labour, vol. 1, *All India,* p. 258; Cederlöf, *Bonds Lost,* pp. 120-22).

an important reason for turning to the mission workers. To the Madhari it was a matter of survival.

The fact that the Madharis were so tied to the villages most probably worked to reinforce the kinship character of the conversion movement since they lacked many opportunities to meet other laborers where, hypothetically, a community-based conversion movement or a broad-based agricultural labor movement, or the like, could have emerged.

Mobilization and Power

The introduction to this chapter summarized the contributions of James Scott, David Mosse, and David Hardiman on different perspectives of the issue under discussion. Hardiman's approach is to hear the voice of the Adivasi as subordinates of colonial authority, and (as for the whole Subaltern Studies project) to make the Adivasi the subject of the history in which they are a part. Thus, he questions writings where the history of "tribals," the simple people of the forests, or their "development," begins when "high civilisations," in this case the British colonial power, enter their area. In short, he challenges the stereotyped ideas about people living on the margins or outside the colonial state domains. He also focuses on religious beliefs as expressions of aspiration for a better life here and now. These are hopes that may take many forms, of which religion is only one.[46]

Hardiman places special emphasis on the use of the term Adivasi, which he uses to include all the Adivasi (tribal) communities. His aim is not to attach a label to them but to focus on the collective identity that grew from being oppressed. This oppression grew when the capitalist, colonial power made exploitation of the Adivasi possible, and, according to Hardiman, when they lost access to the forest, their lands became heavily taxed, and they became indebted to moneylenders and, eventually, became landless laborers for Parsi landlords. Hardiman describes the Adivasi society in precolonial India as an economically stratified society. Wealthy Adivasi communities contracted poorer Adivasi laborers, but these relations were not exploitative, he argues. Oppression emerged when Parsi landlords could utilize options open under colonial rule. In this situation, a collective awareness of being oppressed, an "Adivasi consciousness," grew, and a movement followed.[47]

The use of such an inclusive term as "Adivasi" seems to serve Hardiman's

46. Hardiman, *Coming of the Devi*, pp. 10-11.
47. Hardiman, *Coming of the Devi*, pp. 1-17.

purposes well. It can be compared with the present-day usage of Dalit to include all scheduled castes. If the aim is to study how a mixed but united group struggles against a state, caste, or class that possesses much power and has hegemonic ambitions, encroaching on the physical and mental sphere of the disadvantaged, then an inclusive term serves the purpose. However, it does not facilitate a study of inner conflicts within the Adivasi community.

While Hardiman emphasizes a relative isolation among the Adivasis, that is, a culture of their own, Mosse builds his argument on an assumption of South Indian society as embraced by *one* culture, irrespective of religion or caste. No one acts outside this culture, and all conflicts and collective action take place within and in accordance with it. It is tempting to apply the last statement to interpret the actions of Madhari and Paraiyar converts, while it is somewhat more difficult to find an autonomous culture and the united consciousness that Hardiman problematizes (unless one can speak of several parallel consciousnesses, a strategy which corresponds badly with Hardiman's basic assumptions).

To speak about a collective identity of Madharis is to speak about a multi-layered identity: kinship, caste, leather worker, *pannaiyal*, musician, in some cases Christian, Telugu-speaking, guardians of a princess (according to a myth of their origin), and so on.[48] Some of these "layers" relate only to the Madhari community of the village, some to the caste in the highlands, some to all Telugu-speaking castes, some to the village power structure or to an individual landowning family, some to the mission, and so forth. Several derive from an identification with being an acknowledged part of the entire village community, and it cannot be said that these characteristics were less important to the Madhari than were those derived from their community. It is even more difficult to find a common Madhari or a common Paraiyar identification. When they interacted they were competitors.

In *The Coming of the Devi*, Hardiman stresses the role of capitalist, colonial intrusion into Adivasi territory as conducive to the escalating oppression of the group and the forming of a common Adivasi identity. This may lead to an underestimation of conflicts within the Adivasi group that may have worked to shape the Devi movement. In contrast, Mosse places a strong emphasis on a cultural *longue durée*, the cultural continuity in which the forms and means of domination and power had been reproduced over several centuries in South India. In his analysis there is, rather, a risk that this emphasis underestimates the influence of the fundamental economic changes in social

48. Of course, such "layers" can also be observed within the group: gender, family, division of labor, generations, official and ritual offices, etc.

relations in the late nineteenth and early twentieth centuries. The cultural consensus Mosse argues for dates back to the Vijayanagara Empire of the fourteenth to the sixteenth centuries. From this period onward, dominance in Ramnad was not based on land but derived from holding political and military office. From the mid-nineteenth century, at the time when dry-land cash cropping was introduced, however, the basis for political dominance began to change. During the next hundred years, as a result of a caste order that was not based on territory and land, the old basis for political power, the opportunity for economic domination was eroded under British colonial rule. It followed that new opportunities opened up for the *harijans*. Mosse emphasizes that the forms for domination among both the old and new elites were similar, and lists what he calls a number of "idiosyncratic factors" on which domination was based: credit, financial skill, employment, industry, skilled deployment of patronage, strategic marriage, and inheritance.[49]

Mosse's findings about Ramnad are interesting. Paradoxically, however, his position means both an emphasis on qualitative changes in production and, at the same time, a reduction of the implications of capitalism to merely the introduction of new crops and the turning of land into a marketable commodity. The possibilities for *harijans* to gain greater access to land are explained by a logic of caste-based, political power relations. In this process, the old power holders did not realize the growing importance of possessing land as a means to political influence since they were tied by an old logic of the reproduction of status and power. Mosse's work provokes further questions. One concerns the role of the economy in Ramnad, which, until the late nineteenth century, to a significant extent was based on cattle. (This generally reduces the importance of owning land compared to an economy based on the cultivation of land.) What was the role of such an economy in the formation and reproduction of a social order where domination became based on military rank and status? Second, considering the changing social and economic power relations in the late nineteenth century, the question arises whether the cultural code — culture itself — did not change accordingly and, hence, culture can be regarded as a constantly changing process.[50]

In the Coimbatore district, the fast-growing industrial enterprises that were established from the late nineteenth century had very different effects on the Paraiyar and Madhari communities. For the Paraiyar, it meant increas-

49. Mosse, "Caste, Christianity and Hinduism," pp. 89, 107, 513-14.
50. See further B. G. Karlsson, *Contested Belonging: An Indigenous People's Struggle for Forest and Identity in Sub-Himalayan Bengal* (Lund, 1997), pp. 276-79 and his reference to Sherry Ortner, "Theory in Anthropology since the Sixties," *Comparative Studies in Society and History* 26.1 (1984): 143.

ing opportunities to break with local relations of domination, while for the Madhari the results were an increased control of their group. With more opportunities to meet across kinship and community borders, the Paraiyar show a growing political awareness and strong ambitions to further improve their economic and social position. When a situation of labor scarcity occurred at the turn of the century, the Paraiyar were already involved in seasonal migration to the estates while there was a constant and subsequently growing demand for the Madhari leather work at the farms.

To enquire into the dominant ideology of the villages in the Coimbatore district from the early twentieth century until the present means, to a great extent, to discover its institutionalized practices rather than its norms and ideas. Ideology is thereby manifest in terms such as *urimai* and *pannai,* and in the information provided by Brenda Beck, as well as in rules of behavior and such hierarchical ranking as in the ordering of the different participants in ceremonial processions in village rituals. All these procedures and rituals are aimed at expressing a situation where society works smoothly, "as it should," and all members participate with their different abilities to the benefit of everyone. It reflects a situation that is considered to be "normal." The sets of norms they express may be hidden in everyday language and practices to such an extent that they are taken for granted as a result of life-long socializing processes. Thus, a dominant ideology works to conceal contradictions, whether they are structural inequalities or antagonistic interests. As pointed out by Scott and others, a lack of open conflict is not the same as a lack of conflict. In cases where new converts were punished by being deprived of their rights and means of livelihood, the unequal structural relationship between them and the dominant Goundar community, which had been until then hidden, was suddenly laid wide open. The Goundar were at the top of the socioeconomic hierarchy of the village and wielded their power; the converts' only power lay in their refusal to yield. In such circumstances, the Madhari community chose to appeal to an authority based outside the domains of village power, the mission worker. This was sometimes as dramatic as it may sound, but (similar to Scott's findings) resistance to Goundar threats often turned into a stubborn, silent group of laborers waiting for the Goundar to realize that *they* were *his* only opportunity in the running of his farm. A decision not to provoke the village authorities should not be understood as submissive backwardness, but as the only rational thing for laborers, without alternative means of income or protection, to do.

There is a myth that is often told by old Madhari women. When asked the question, Who are the Madhari? the women will generally relate a tale about themselves as once having been the guardians of a princess. The king,

Tirumalai Naiyak (a sixteenth-century emperor), had asked the Madhari to guard his daughter during the rites performed at her first menstruation. As described by the women, the rites resemble those the Madhari perform for their daughters. In these, the maternal uncle has a central role, which can be compared to that given to the Madhari in the myth. Thus, in the myth, the Madhari describe themselves as closely related to the supreme power.[51] This is not a myth of submission. It reflects ideas of the Madhari that run counter to the dominant ideology of the village.

There are also many jokes told in the backyards of the Paraiyar and the Madhari settlements, grim humor, one could say. For example, an old woman showed how the Goundar used to pour water down her throat when she asked for something to drink. As a Madhari, she was not allowed to use the Goundars' well or touch their drinking vessels. So, the woman kneeled and bent her head backwards. But when she related this, the younger men started to tease her and asked why she did not demand to have water poured into her hands. She laughed and replied, "Why should I? They served me like a queen. I let them do it so that I could rest myself and just open my mouth!"[52]

Do cultures or ideologies of the subordinate develop in relation to a dominant, hegemonic culture and ideology or is there a "hegemony-free zone" among the subordinate where an ideology can develop within an autonomous sphere of its own? The two examples just cited, are, of course, ripped out of their contexts. They serve, however, to make a point. Neither of them would have been heard in the main village among other communities. A Madhari or Paraiyar man would not dare to utter them and a Goundar man would find them too ridiculous to even mention. However, in the *cheris* they make sense. It was with some pride that the Madhari women related their origin. They can be proud of their heritage. Also, to ridicule the landlords, unmask their high-caste, offensive behaviors, "demystify their ideology," in the words of Scott, reveals a distance between the thinking of the subordinate and that of the dominant communities. At the same time, the myth, told in the 1990s, makes sense as it puts the power relations of the village into question, and, in that sense, as it relates to power. Most likely it has no roots in the main village or its dominant ideology, but in a sphere of consciousness existing in the *cheris*. But the existing dominant power structure and ideology are what allow both myths and jokes to make sense at the time when they are told.

51. Interview, Mandiripalayam, 31 January 1995.
52. Interview, Arulpuram, 26 January 1995.

CHAPTER FIFTEEN

From Pentecostal Healing Evangelist to Kalki Avatar: The Remarkable Life of Paulaseer Lawrie, alias Shree Lahari Krishna (1921-1989) — A Contribution to the Understanding of New Religious Movements

MICHAEL BERGUNDER

Discussion of the encounter between Hinduism and Christianity is still widely treated at the level of theological debate only.[1] The area of popular religion is a rather neglected subject of scholarly research, though it is here that an amazing mutual exchange between the two religions took place.[2] Many are

1. Kaj Baago, *Pioneers of Indigenous Christianity* (Madras, 1969), pp. 1-11; Felix Wilfred, "Zeitgenössische Strömungen in einigen Hauptbereichen der Theologie in Indien," in *Theologiegeschichte der Dritten Welt, Indien*, edited by F. Wilfred and M. M. Thomas (München, 1992), pp. 321-33.

2. See, for example, Sigfrid Estborn, *Our Village Christians: A Study of the Life and Faith of Village Christians in Tamilnadu* (Madras, 1958); Carl Gustav Diehl, *Church and Shrine: Intermingling Patterns of Culture in the Life of Some Christian Groups in South India* (Uppsala, 1965); P. Y. Luke and John B. Carman, *Village Christians and Hindu Culture: Study of a Rural Church in Andhra Pradesh, South India* (London, 1968); Herbert E. Hoefer, *Churchless Christianity: A Report of Research Among Non-baptised Believers in Christ in Rural and Urban Tamilnadu, India, with Practical and Theological Reflections* (Madras, 1991); David Mosse, "Catholic Saints and the Hindu Village Pantheon in Rural Tamil Nadu," *Man* 28 (1994): 1-32; Michael Bergunder, "Wenn die Geister bleiben . . . Volksreligiosität und Weltbild" in *Es begann in Halle . . . Missionswissenschaft von Gustav Warneck bis heute*, edited by Dieter Becker and Andreas Feldtkeller (Erlangen, 1997), pp. 153-66.

unaware that out of Indian Christianity new indigenous religious movements had developed, which have embraced many Hindu beliefs and rituals.[3] An example of this remarkable phenomenon is the Manujothi Ashram founded by Paulaseer Lawrie.[4]

Lawrie's Early Years

As is the case with most of the religious charismatics, it is not easy to establish the historical facts about Lawrie's early life. There are few independent sources and the biographical stories told by Lawrie himself and his followers are inseparably interwoven with hagiographical patterns. Nevertheless, some dates and events seem to be quite certain.

Rasaiah Paulaseer Lawrie was born on 24 February 1921 in Letchmi Estate, Munnar (Kerala),[5] which was where his mother's family lived. Although his father was working in Ceylon, as a secretary in a company, and his family was to live there also, in accordance with South Indian tradition, he, the first child of his family, was delivered at the maternal home.

Lawrie was raised in Ceylon for some years, but it seems that in the second half of the 1920s his mother left Colombo with her children and settled in

---

3. For example, on Nattu Sabai, see M. Thomas Thangaraj, "The History and Teachings of the Hindu Christian Community Commonly Called Nattu Sabai in Tirunelveli," *Indian Church History Review* 5 (1971): 43-67. On Pratyaksha Raksha Deiva Sabha, see W. S. Hunt, *The Anglican Church in Travancore and Cochin 1816-1916*, 2 vols. (Kottayam, 1920/1933), 2:235; Stephen Fuchs, *Godmen on the Warpath: A Study of Messianic Movements in India* (New Delhi, 1992), pp. 236-38; Saju, *Kerala Pentekosthu Charithram* [Malay] (Kottayam, 1994), pp. 49-51. On Yuyomayam, see Hunt, *Anglican Church*, 2:93, 159-68, 191-92; and Werner Hoerschelmann, *Christliche Gurus: Darstellung von Selbstverständnis und Funktion indigenen Christseins durch unabhängige, charismatisch geführte Gruppen in Südindien* (Frankfurt am Main, 1977), pp. 152-55. On Bible Mission, see K. Devasahayam, "The Bible Mission," *Religion and Society* 29 (1982): 55-101; P. Solomon Raj, *A Christian Folk Religion in India: A Study of the Small Church Movement in Andhra Pradesh, with a Special Reference to the Bible Mission of Devadas* (Frankfurt am Main, 1986); and P. Solomon Raj, "Father Devadas and the Story of a Folk Church in India," *Dharma Deepika* 1 (1995): 61-68.

4. Empirical data were collected during stays at the ashram in summer 1994 and summer 1998. For some findings see Michael Bergunder, *Die südindische Pfingstbewegung im 20. Jahrhundert Eine historische und systematische Untersuchung*, Studies in the Intercultural History of Christianity, vol. 113 (Frankfurt, 1999), pp. 150-54. For an earlier but not fully reliable account of the ashram see Hoerschelmann, *Christliche Gurus*, pp. 308-85.

5. Devaaseer Lawrie, *Days of the Son of Man, Tree of Life, Tenth Incarnation of Lord Narayana* (Manujothi Ashram, 1996), p. 81.

Nazareth (Tamilnadu). His father stayed in Ceylon and came only for short periods to visit his family on the mainland. In Nazareth the family belonged to the Society for the Propagation of the Gospel although it is reported that Lawrie's father had close contacts with the Salvation Army in Colombo.[6] After school, Lawrie attended St. John's College at Palayamkottai and finished intermediate class. For his further studies he went to Ceylon to obtain the London "matric" certificate from Wesley College, Colombo. In about 1940, he began his B.A. studies at Madras Christian College, Tambaram.[7] It seems that he soon abandoned these studies and tried to join the army, but his father prevented him. So, he went back to his studies and joined St. Xavier's College, Palayamkottai. His studies were interrupted, however, as he involved himself in some anti-British activities and had to return to Ceylon again in 1942 to avoid persecution by the colonial administration. After that, he never resumed his college education; instead he started to work as a stenographer on a tea estate in Ceylon.

Under the influence of one of his colleagues, who most probably belonged to an indigenous Pentecostal Church called Ceylon Pentecostal Mission,[8] Lawrie came to a personal conversion connected with a healing experience. He gave the exact date of his conversion as 2 June 1943,[9] and one can assume that he also received immersion baptism at that time, presumably in the Ceylon Pentecostal Mission. During his time in Ceylon, however, Paulaseer Lawrie remained a member of the Anglican Church like his father and mother, who also lived in Ceylon by then.

There is ample evidence that Lawrie was a good sportsman in the years before his marriage. At least, there are certificates that prove his successful participation in regional athletic tournaments in the 1940s. All through his life he was very conscious of these achievements and often referred to them, realizing that hardly any other Pentecostal evangelist had any kind of athletic career.

After his conversion Lawrie changed jobs and became a secretary in a larger mercantile company at Colombo city. In 1947 he married a woman from Tamilnadu, and in 1948 his first son, Daya Eevu, was born. It is said that at the end of 1948, his nine-month-old son was taken severely ill with diphtheria. In their desperation the Lawries made a religious vow. In a major hagiographical biography this is described as follows:

---

6. L. D. Dale, *The Lightning from the East* (Alcoa, Tenn., 1973), pp. 14-15.

7. Lawrie, *Days*, p. 80, with copies of certificates that prove that he was a student at Madras Christian College in 1941 and 1942.

8. The history of South Indian Pentecostalism is broadly documented in Bergunder, *Die südindische Pfingstbewegung*.

9. Dale, *Lightning*, p. 19.

One morning Bro. Lawrie and his wife went to the Anglican Church —
St Michael & All Angels — and cried and prayed to the Lord, that if He
would heal their son, they would spend their lives in India for His work.
The next day, to the amazement of the doctors, the child was healed!
Faithful to the promise he made to his Lord, Brother Lawrie resigned his
lucrative job in Ceylon which had brought him so much popularity.[10]

Religious vows in the case of severe illness of a child are quite common in
popular Indian Christianity, but the parents normally promise to dedicate the
child, if healed, to the Christian ministry, and not to pledge themselves for the
ministry. So it is not really clear if this account is a later interpretation of the
incident. Moreover, in the following years Lawrie never tried to enter into
full-time Christian work, which is what is understood when a person promises to dedicate himself to the ministry. However, as will be quoted below, he
later refers to that vow as a real promise for full-time ministry. In 1949 Lawrie
returned to India with his family, and finally, after short interludes in a firm at
Madurai and at the Yercaud Tea Estate, he obtained a permanent post as secretary to the superintendent at the Christian Medical College in Vellore.

The Making of a Pentecostal Evangelist

It was probably immediately after his return to India that Lawrie came into
contact with the newly arrived missionaries of the Assemblies of God in
Tamilnadu, the Edwards family. How this happened is a matter of speculation,[11] but evidence suggests that Lawrie was closely connected with the Edwards. According to the Pentecostal teachings, Lawrie received the baptism of
the Holy Spirit with speaking in tongues in March 1952.

It is typical for Pentecostal churches in India, which are zealous toward
missions, to place constant psychological pressure on young converts to dedicate themselves to full-time ministry. So it was in the newly formed congregations of the Assemblies of God, where American missionaries urgently
needed Indian co-workers. Lawrie's report that he got a severe diphtheria in
1953 and that he had a vision in which he was shown that he had to give up his
job and enter into full-time ministry in order to receive healing must be
placed in that context:

10. Dale, *Lightning*, p. 20.
11. Cf. that at the same time another person from Nazareth, Y. Jeyaraj, joined the Assemblies of God at Shengottai (cf. Bergunder, *Die südindische Pfingstbewegung*, pp. 74-75).

That night [when he was laying in a hospital in critical condition] I had a vision of a great train with a countless number of carriages full of dead bodies, [and] maimed and sick people. Carriage after carriage with dead bodies were added. My soul came out of my body and I saw Jesus Christ, and He spoke to my soul, "Do you remember the promise you made four years ago, when your son was suffering from the same disease?" I said "Yes Lord, I promised to serve you all my life with my wife in India.["] Then he asked me, "Have you done so?" I said "No". Then He commanded, "I require your entire life and your wife's too." Then I asked, "What about feeding my wife and three children?" The Lord replied, "Leave that to me. I will look after you all if you will believe me." In an awe inspiring voice Jesus Christ said, "Decide between these two — your life today, or your promise that you will serve me fully with your household." Then I wept and said "Heal me Lord. We will serve Thee forever." The Lord healed me instantly. Then I saw a vision of a train with many cars and all compartments filled with living people of all colours and races; and the train was driven by a gruesome person. Compartment after compartment were being dropped off into a pit of fire. Then Jesus put His arm on me and commissioned me and said, "Son, I am sending you to them. Do not bother if they listen or not. I will judge them by your words. I have blessed your hand like the rod of Moses and will take you all over the world".[12]

This particular kind of vision and promise, where healing from a deadly disease can only be achieved by the dedication to the full-time ministry, is very common in the testimonies of Pentecostal evangelists in India.[13] As a stereotype, one has to be very cautious in accepting it as an historical fact. Lawrie, however, claims this visionary experience to be the real starting point of his evangelistic ministry, and shortly after he was discharged from the hospital he resigned his job (in October 1953) to enter full-time ministry.

Probably immediately after his resignation, Lawrie joined the Southern Asia Bible College at Bangalore, run by the Assemblies of God.[14] It seems, however, that he dropped out soon after. Though it is not clear why he stayed at Southern Asia Bible College for a short time only, this fits with the general impression that, from the beginning, Lawrie was heading for a career as an

12. Dale, *Lightning*, p. 22.
13. Bergunder, *Die südindische Pfingstbewegung*, pp. 189-92.
14. Kurt Hutten, *Seher, Grübler, Enthusiasten: Das Buch der traditionellen Sekten und religiösen Sonderbewegungen*, 14th ed. (Stuttgart, 1989), p. 219.

evangelist and had no interest in pastoral work. Moreover, he even tried to follow a strict transconfessional line, consciously keeping his membership with the Church of South India.[15] Thus, he deviated from the prevailing pattern for an Indian Pentecostal minister at the time, and became the prototype for modern Pentecostal healing evangelists like D. G. S. Dhinakaran.[16] Maybe Lawrie got inspiration from W. M. Branham, the famous American healing evangelist who visited Bombay for a healing crusade in 1954.[17] Lawrie managed to participate in Branham's Bombay crusade, and later on, Branham played a crucial role in the further growth of Lawrie's ministry.

During the second half of the 1950s Lawrie developed into quite a popular independent evangelist who had his headquarters first at Nazareth and, from 1957 onward, at Nagarcoil. He was preaching in both Pentecostal and mainline churches alike, and he even visited Ceylon for two long evangelistic campaigns in 1955 and 1956.[18] From those visits we have a letter of one A. P. Guruswamy from the Evangelical Fellowship of Ceylon, which gives a good impression of the character of Lawrie's ministry:

> Bro. Lawrie was specially used of God for casting out evil spirits from devil-possessed folk. Some healings were spectacular. Bro. Lawrie is a humble man of God with a simple message which readily appeals to the unsophisticated Tamil folk. His emphasis was placed rightly on Salvation; praying for the sick was incidental. . . . Bro. Lawrie's sermons were simple, forthright, and convincing. His telling illustrations, drawn from everyday life, helped to build up the faith of the crowds who came to hear him.[19]

The Great Success

The year 1959 marked a turning point. In that year Lawrie managed to obtain an invitation for an International Conference on Healing of the Order of St. Luke at Glasgow. After the conference was over he traveled through Europe,

15. Dale, *Lightning*, p. 30.
16. M. Bergunder, "'Ministry of Compassion': D. G. S. Dhinakaran — Christian Healer-Prophet from Tamilnadu," in *Christianity Is Indian*, ed. R. E. Hedlund (New Delhi, 2000), pp. 158-74.
17. C. Douglas Weaver, *The Healer-Prophet, William Marrion Branham: A Study of the Prophetic in American Pentecostalism* (Macon, Ga., 1987), p. 51.
18. Dale, *Lightning*, p. 24.
19. Dale, *Lightning*, p. 25. The letter can be considered as authentic.

and, in 1960, he went to the United States in spite of great financial difficulties. In the United States he met many prominent Pentecostal evangelists and church leaders in the hope that they would become interested in sponsoring his ministry in India, but nobody came forward,[20] with the exception of William Marion Branham, the man he had already met through the Bombay crusade in 1954.

The Branham of 1960 was not the same as the Branham of 1954. In the late 1950s he had become more outspoken about his peculiar doctrinal stand. In his early years Branham had tried to equivocate on doctrinal questions in order to avoid conflicts and to preserve his standing as a broadly accepted healing evangelist.[21] When Lawrie met Branham in April 1960, Branham received him well, but he urged Lawrie to accept the "Oneness" doctrines and become baptized in the name of Jesus Christ, and, indeed, Lawrie did accept Oneness Pentecostalism and was baptized at the Branham Tabernacle.[22]

That Lawrie ended up as a Branhamite seems rather accidental since reportedly he also tried to associate himself with other Pentecostal ministries. Before he met Branham he went to Springfield, Missouri and expressed his readiness to join the Assemblies of God. The denominational leaders turned down his request, however, as they were not willing to accept him without consulting their missionaries in India.[23] Lawrie also contacted evangelists such as Oral Roberts and T. L. Osborne, but nobody seemed to be ready to support his ministry. (He later helped in organizing the Indian visit of the Oral Roberts Youth Team in 1961.) He even contacted Evangelicals such as the editors of *Herald of His Coming* and Robert Walker from the Christian Life Missions.[24] Lawrie's requests for help were often turned down in a very humiliating manner. So, there also seem to be some psychological reasons for Lawrie becoming a Branhamite.

After his return to India in 1960 Lawrie continued his ministry in the way he had before, but with one difference: suddenly he became extraordinarily successful. Although Lawrie had returned as a Oneness Pentecostal and, moreover, a Branhamite, he did not stress doctrinal questions when he continued his evangelistic ministry in India, nor did he contact other Oneness churches, which were already present there. Furthermore, he did not give up his official membership with the Church of South India, and, for nearly two

20. Dale, *Lightning*, pp. 43-46.
21. David Edwin Harrell, Jr., *All Things Are Possible: The Healing and Charismatic Revivals in Modern America* (Bloomington, 1975), p. 163.
22. Cf. Dale, *Lightning*, pp. 45-46; Lawrie, *Days*, p. 81.
23. Dale, *Lightning*, p. 43.
24. Dale, *Lightning*, p. 44.

years, he even managed to get the firm support of David Chellappa, then bishop of Madras Diocese of the Church. Only when his followers became more numerous did tensions with the established churches arise, so that the Madras bishop had to withdraw his assistance in the later half of 1962. Nevertheless, like the early Branham, Lawrie always tried to soften conflicts with the churches, and he was very careful to dispel suspicions that he might purposely form his own church organization. In one of his magazines from 1964, for instance, it is clearly stated:

> Bro. Lawrie is not building any denomination as [is] commonly misunderstood by so many. The numerous prayer groups and few assemblies which are functioning in various centres are simply the meeting places of people who have been touched by God, and who gather for fellowship with others of like faith, wait on God, offer praises to Him and pray with a burden for the propagation of the Gospel throughout India. No material help is given to these prayer groups or assemblies by Bro. Lawrie and no control over them is exercised by him. They are encouraged to look for themselves. He simply tells them to be completely dependent on God alone and to be led by the Holy Spirit in everything as he himself is.[25]

It seems that Lawrie's transconfessional strategy was not without results, because, despite growing opposition, the doors to the churches never entirely closed. In the years between 1960 and 1967 Lawrie became the first famous Indian healing evangelist of stature and the role model for all others to come.

The salient feature of Lawrie's ministry was that he claimed a healing power without limits, as can be illustrated by the following report in one of his magazines:

> As the time of the meeting draws near every day vast crowds from all walks of life begin to pour in and in a short time the grounds are jammed to capacity — a unique feature unheard of in history. . . . It is strange to notice that as Bro. Lawrie gets on the platform and begins to deliver Holy Spirit-anointed messages, even a child stops crying and there is pin-drop silence. It is evident that a supernatural power — the power of our Lord and God Jesus Christ — falls on the people and keeps them attentive and responsive. As this power begins to fall on the people, men and women bound by evil spirits stir out from their places in

---

25. *The Eleventh Hour* 2.1 (January-April 1964): 3.

the crowd and come running to the platform. As they approach the platform, the Holy Spirit controls them and allows the meeting to proceed without disturbance. At the end, these demon-possessed people are delivered by God through the mass prayer or individual prayer offered by Bro. Lawrie.[26]

Notwithstanding this kind of exaggerated report, the extraordinary success of Lawrie's "Mass-Salvation-Healing Campaigns" is confirmed by many unbiased or even critical witnesses.[27] Big Pentecostal crusades in India up to that time were mainly staffed with foreign speakers. Before Lawrie, there had been only a few important Indian evangelists of the evangelical type, namely, Sadhu Sundar Singh, Bakht Singh, and N. Daniel. No one before had drawn such crowds as Lawrie did.

Claiming the Branham Legacy

Lawrie showed no particular interest in doctrines during his time as a successful healing evangelist. However, he baptized people only in the name of Jesus Christ, and all the prayer groups that were established around him were maintained to Oneness doctrines.[28] Moreover, Lawrie's growing international contacts were mainly confined to Branhamites such as Ewald Frank from Freie Volksmission in Krefeld (West Germany) who came to India in 1965 to participate in Lawrie's meetings.[29] Lawrie, however, changed his outward show of strict transconfessional strategy after he got a second opportunity to travel overseas. It was on an invitation of Ewald Frank that he went to Europe in April 1967. At that time the Branhamites worldwide were in a state of confusion. After the sudden death of Branham at the end of 1965, the Branhamites were puzzled about what his appropriate legacy would be. As Lawrie spent many months among Branhamites during his second overseas trip, he naturally became involved in the whole issue.

First, Lawrie preached for nearly four months in assemblies of Branhamites in Germany, Switzerland, and Austria. Then he went to the United States in September 1967. In the Americas he made extensive visits to Branham as-

26. *The Eleventh Hour* 2.1 (January-April 1964): 2.

27. Cf. Hoerschelmann, *Christliche Gurus*, p. 317.

28. A. Christopher Asir, "A Historical Survey of the Sectarian Church Groups in the C.S.I. Diocese of Tinneveli in the 20th Century," B.D. thesis, United Theological College, Bangalore, 1975, p. 72.

29. Dale, *Lightning*, p. 68.

semblies and even undertook an evangelistic excursion to the West Indies and the South American Caribbean Coast. During his preaching tours Lawrie was much acclaimed by many Western Branhamites, but back in India, he suddenly experienced a severe setback of his ministry. Apparently he was not able to revive his former success and could no longer draw crowds as large as before.[30]

The reasons for this are difficult to discern. Maybe there was some increasing agitation against Lawrie by mainline and Pentecostal churches, which became more aware of his doctrinal background. Or maybe Lawrie himself changed his priorities, started to get interested in the Branham legacy, and became more outspoken on doctrinal matters. Probably it was both. Lawrie himself gave the following explanation:

> I found out that the world has deceived me, led me falsely and treacherously hid from me the truth of eternal separation and death spiritually. I returned to India with God and His Word and lost all popularity as I refused to walk with the crowd and people of the day. . . . The Lord dealt with me severely in India and I was despaired of life for certain things around and happenings at home and so on.[31]

In 1969 Lawrie received a invitation to visit a Branhamite conference in the United States. This trip would turn his ministry around. When Branham died in a car accident in December 1965 his followers tried to find meaning behind his unexpected death. The discussions focused mainly on one point: Who was Branham? The only common view shared by all Branhamites was the notion that the end of the world was near. Apart from this, there were conflicting views about the true nature and identity of Branham. Whereas many considered Branham simply as the returned prophet Elijah (Mal. 4:23) and so the forerunner of Christ's Second Coming to restore the original apostolic faith, others went much further, and a small minority even identified Branham as a new incarnation of Jesus Christ.[32] As their beliefs about the identity of Branham differed, so also did their expectations about the future.

In the midst of this doctrinal confusion, several persons claimed to be the chief interpreter of Branham's message, or even to be the only successor for continuing his ministry.[33] Lawrie became one of those who claimed the leg-

30. Hoerschelmann, *Christliche Gurus*, p. 318; Dale, *Lightning*, p. 73.

31. Paulaseer Lawrie, *Son of Man: Message to the Bride,* Thunder Series, No. 1 (Manujothi Ashram, 1970), p. 39.

32. Weaver, *Healer-Prophet*, p. 156.

33. Weaver, *Healer-Prophet*, pp. 159-63.

acy of Branham when he visited the United States in 1969 at a time when many Branhamites hoped that something would happen to clarify the legacy of their dead leader. According to Branham, every three-and-a-half years new things will occur in the course of the so-called divine dispensations.

In this tense atmosphere some American Branhamites observed miraculous light phenomena during the time when Lawrie was preaching. These particular people were convinced that Branham had prophesied that Jesus Christ would come again as a human being, and they thought that Lawrie was the man through whom this would happen. It is said that 21 July 1969, one hour before the American astronauts landed on the moon, was when this remarkable event occurred. Lawrie was at this time staying in Chicago. In the words of one who was a very close American disciple at the time:

> Immediately Bro. Lawrie felt himself transformed into two persons — one Jesus Christ and the other himself — yet fused into one within the mighty presence of the power of God. This being a unique experience, Bro. Lawrie feels the inadequacy of words whenever he tries to express it, and he always fails. He attempts to explain it by standing close to someone and going through the motion of his hands to show people how it was, and again he fails. It is difficult for anyone to fully grasp the glorious act of God or fully understand the significance of it either. It is a godly act foretold by [the] Lord Jesus when He walked this earth 2000 years back; and down [through] the ages mankind had misconstrued it in their imagination, that when it did happen quite different to their pet conception, they were not able to comprehend the superb act of God.[34]

Soon after this revelation Lawrie returned to India. Since 1964 the headquarters of his evangelistic activities had been at the Manujothi Ashram near Tirunelveli (Tamilnadu). Now, Manujothi Ashram also became the world-wide center of the new ministry in which Lawrie was mainly involved in spelling out the implication of his being Jesus Christ, and in which he revealed new teachings to specify his claim, year after year. In accordance with his new identity, he also changed his preaching style from revival preaching to doctrinal teaching. He never tried to give comprehensive and systematic doctrines, however, so that most of his teachings are full of contradictions and shrouded by dark passages. This is partly because, as in the case of Branham, most of his books are mere transcriptions from his recorded speeches.

---

34. Dale, *Lightning*, p. 76.

Waiting for the End of the World

To gain acceptance among Branhamites it was of utmost importance that Lawrie show that his new doctrine was indeed nothing more than the proper fulfillment of Branham's prophecies. Soon after his return to India, he published a collection containing words of Branham that were selected to prove his claim.[35] From that time on, the prevailing model of interpretation was that Branham meant to Lawrie what John the Baptist meant to the biblical Jesus. Branham was thought to be the forerunner who prepared his followers for the advent of Christ in the person of Lawrie.

Great efforts were made to propagate the new message among Branhamites in the whole world. In India, from the prayer groups that were related to Lawrie, some twenty-five accepted this new revelation.[36] Others, who had been in fellowship with Lawrie before, rejected his claim immediately, or after some time, and became independent Oneness Churches, but there was no organized joint action against Lawrie among his former followers. In the West, however, a fierce opposition arose headed by Ewald Frank, the former close friend of Lawrie and the most influential Branhamite in Europe at this time.[37] In a circular letter in December 1970, Frank made his complete separation from Lawrie public and denied all the latter's new teachings. In March 1971 he even visited Lawrie in India to confront him personally, but with no result. Then Frank wrote an open letter to all Branhamites in India, Europe, and North America to warn them about Lawrie.

Frank was unable to stop many Western Branhamites from accepting Lawrie's teachings, and eventually some Europeans and Americans moved to India. More than fifty German-speaking people from Europe and nearly thirty from North America joined the Manujothi Ashram during the summer of 1971. Unlike the hippie drop-outs who were usually on the way from the West to India, these were well-settled, lower-middle-class people, quite a few over fifty years of age. Some came as families with young children. They gave up their jobs, sold all their belongings, and booked the next flight to India. In Germany, this exodus did not go unnoticed by the "yellow" press. Several newspapers even sent special correspondents to India, and the Manujothi Ashram was featured in the German headlines during this period.[38]

Up to 1972 Lawrie had gathered about six hundred Indians and more than

35. Cf. L. D. Dale and Deva Eevu Lawrie, *Gleanings from "The Spoken Word,"* Revised Edition (ca. 1970).

36. Lawrie, *Son of Man,* p. v.

37. Cf. *Materialdienst der EZW* 34 (1971): 59-60, 200-203.

38. Cf., e.g., *BILD,* 13 July 1971, p. 5; *BUNTE,* 5 April 1973, pp. 59-65, 154.

one hundred foreigners in three centers. Most of the Indians stayed at Tuticorin, the foreigners and a few Indians stayed at Manujothi Ashram, and some close co-workers of Lawrie lived at Gandhinagar, a suburb of Tirunelveli. The people did not simply want to stay with Lawrie to be near to the Lord Jesus Christ, but, as Lawrie claimed that he had come down to earth to gather the bride and prepare her for the "soon to come" rapture, they desired to make sure they were on the right side when the world came to an end. Indeed, time was thought to be very short. According to Branham's three-and-a-half-year period, the rapture was expected to take place in 1973, and the end of the world another three and a half years later in 1977.[39]

People who wanted to join the ashram had to sign a "New Covenant To Be Made With God Almighty (Oath of Allegiance to the Lord Jesus Christ)" and take communion for the last time. Excerpts from the New Covenant read as follows:

> I . . . henceforth take the Lord Jesus Christ to be mine own. I promise to receive Him as my Husband and give myself to Him, . . . I believe that the Lord Jesus Christ has come down in this world in pillars of cloud, flaming eyes and the voice of thunders from the East. . . . I believe with my whole heart that Brother William Marrion Branham was a real prophet of God and Forerunner of the Ministry which is now in full swing to take the Bride off the earth before the onset of tribulation. Now that I take this last communion, I also promise that I will no more partake in any communion service of any group or denomination since I have come into the New Bride Covenant which sets me free from all bondage.[40]

To his bride Lawrie gave so-called end-time messages in which he progressively elaborated his teachings. Though he adapted many of Branham's doctrinal positions, especially the rigid concept of predestination and emphasis on eternal security,[41] Lawrie created an independent doctrinal framework. As a central idea, he considered himself to be the "Son of Man" prophesied in the Bible as the Second Coming of Christ. One of his followers explains it as follows:

---

39. Hoerschelmann, *Christliche Gurus*, p. 341.

40. Paulaseer Lawrie, *It Is Possible to Overcome Death in This Generation or the Feast of the Tabernacles*, Thunder Series, No. 2 (Manujothi Ashram, 1971), pp. 74-75; Hoerschelmann, *Christliche Gurus*, p. 354.

41. For the main teachings of Branham, see Weaver, *Healer-Prophet*, pp. 121-26.

The second coming of Christ was a coming of His, but all the time Jesus refers to it as the appearing of the Son of Man. The second coming is a spiritual coming where Jesus himself is manifested. Therefore it was the plan of God to come and tabernacle in the body of a man . . . Hebrews 10:5. . . . In accordance with this, God came down and tabernacled in the body of Bro. Lawrie.[42]

As a result, all passages in the Bible that mention the "Son of Man" were thought to hint at Lawrie and never at the Jesus of the New Testament whose human nature is denied completely: "Actually, to be plain, just like God appeared to Abraham and dined with him, Jesus was a Theophany very close to human being, and He was in this world for nearly 30 years."[43]

At that time, however, Lawrie did not bring this kind of docetism to all Christological consequences because the focus was entirely on Lawrie as the first real godly incarnation in a human being according to the biblical prophecies. Lawrie even claimed to be a descendant from King David, stating that the Nadar caste to which he belonged got its name from Nathan (Luke 3:31) and that it was part of the scattered Jewish tribe of Judah.

According to the said schedule, the gathered bride expected the rapture in 1973, but no visible event took place among them in that year.[44] However, Lawrie claimed that this did not mean it had not actually happened:

But we believe God's Word, although we don't see anything happen. By that, we open the tap for the tremendous power to flow into our lives. Our belief on the Word opens the power of God. We believe first and then we see. If you don't believe that the rapture has already taken place, you are an unbeliever.[45]

Lawrie claimed that the bride was actually raptured in 1973, that she was gathered now, and that the period of the "Son of God" had started, even though a visible transformation into heavenly bodies had not happened yet. As a further sign of the new status of his followers in the ashram, they celebrated the Sabbath every Saturday from the beginning of 1974 onward, instead of the Christian Sunday. According to Lawrie this was not regarded as a mere return

42. V. Jothipackiam, in Dale, *Lightning,* pp. 98-99.
43. Paulaseer Lawrie, *The Secret of Rapture,* Thunder Series, Nos. 4, 5, 6 (Manujothi Ashram, 1972), p. 346.
44. Hoerschelmann, *Christliche Gurus,* pp. 341-46
45. Paulaseer Lawrie, *Heavenly Canaan,* Thunder Series, No. 7B (Manujothi Ashram, 1973), p. 246.

to Jewish customs: "That sabbath is different. That sabbath makes us walk in our own righteousness."[46]

In 1973 Lawrie had introduced a new ministry. He appointed one German and one American follower as the so-called "two witnesses" who should testify to the world about Lawrie and open the door for more people to be saved. The words of the two witnesses read as follows:

> Now, my Beloved, don't be shocked. . . . [T]o partake in the rapture is no more possible for you. The rapturing church is now about to get ready for the changing of their physical bodies into immortal bodies. . . . God in His amazing grace, has still a second way of salvation, provided in His plan for you beloved ones,[47] . . . God goes back to His original plan for Israel once again. The reason you cannot join the Bride this side of the 1000 year reign is that you must fulfill the Scriptures. . . . But the 144,000[,] although they do not come up in the Bride, they will gladly fulfill their positions, . . . [t]hey receive the same spirit that was poured out on the Bride, and come under the same word.[48]

So the two witnesses had to call and to gather the 144,000 from all over the world who were to be with Lawrie when he and his bride would come to Mount of Olives of Jerusalem in the year 1977 to start his reign of the millennium as the messianic son of David. The predicted end of the world in 1977 did not happen. In the same year the foreigners, unexpectedly, did not get visa extensions and had to leave India. So, the ministry of Lawrie experienced its most severe crisis, but it did not disappear.

The Kalki Avatar

Naturally, when nothing happened, Lawrie's entire claim to be the returned Jesus Christ was questioned. Unfortunately there is very little information available about the years immediately following 1977. The existing information hints that Lawrie first explained the problem as some small delay, or something like that.[49] Nevertheless, from 1980 onward, Lawrie started to reinterpret the old predictions. He wrote in 1980:

46. Paulaseer Lawrie, *The Revelation of the Lord God* (Manujothi Ashram, 1974), p. 344.

47. Dale, *Lightning*, pp. 124-25.

48. Dale, *Lightning*, p. 127.

49. Hutten, *Seher*, p. 220.

These are hard days and a "birth-pangs" moment. Many questions arise after 1977. Is this message true and how long are we to wait? For people on God's Word, waiting is a "gift" through redemption. They will believe everything what God has said. These are also days when people will just follow the majority whether they be wrong or right, . . . But in our experience, we know that the minority can be and mostly always are right.[50]

It seems clear that many of Lawrie's followers had already left by this time, and that the two witnesses probably did not stay very long after 1977.[51] Quite a few of his foreign believers, who had to return home in 1977, did not break with him, however, and maintained the contact with Manujothi Ashram. Many of his Indian followers also retained their belief in Lawrie.

Moreover, in subsequent years people with a Hindu background began to join the ashram as new believers because Lawrie modified his teachings toward a universal approach that attracted non-Christians. Over time Lawrie redefined his legitimacy in a very broad manner, claiming that his ministry was not only the fulfillment of Christianity but also of all other religions.

This broadening of his appeal was not completely unexpected. As early as 1974, Lawrie had come into contact with followers of Mutthukutty Swamy, a nineteenth-century Hindu reformer from the Nadar caste. Mutthukutty Swamy is regarded as a Vishnu *avatar,* and his followers believe that he will be resurrected and come back a second time to judge the world and establish a "world of *dharma.*"[52] It seems that some of his followers were inclined to identify Lawrie as the returned Mutthukutty Swamy, and Lawrie responded positively to them:[53] "God gave them [i.e., the Hindus] a prophet called Mutthukutty 150 years ago. Through him the end time message of the present day is made more clear than even through Prophet Branham."[54] It seems, however, that not many followers of Mutthukutty Swamy actually joined Lawrie in the 1970s.

In the 1980s Lawrie went further down this line, and studies on different Hindu scriptures, such as the *Bhagavadgita* and several *Puranas,* were published to prove the legitimacy of Lawrie as the Kalki *avatar* who had come

---

50. Paulaseer Lawrie, *Stumbling Block* (Manujothi Ashram, 1980), p. 1.

51. Paulaseer Lawrie, *The Travailing Woman and the Man Child, Revelation ch. 12* (Manujothi Ashram Tabernacle, 2 March 1980), p. 6 (mimeo).

52. C. Rajamani, "The Cult of Mutthukkutty Swamy," M.Th. thesis, United Theological College, Bangalore, 1981, p. 56.

53. Lawrie, *Revelation,* esp. pp. 458-91.

54. Lawrie, *Revelation,* p. 470.

down to earth, but Lawrie no longer predicted any date for the end of the world:

> Thus, from the knowledge of Vedic Scriptures, from prophetical books of the Hindu religion and also other faiths (such as Buddhism, Islam, Sikhism, prophecy of William Marrion Branham) and the Holy Bible, we conclude that the Kalki Maha Avatar advented Himself on February 24th 1921 in Lakshmi Tea Estate in Munnar, Kerala State of South India.[55]

Although Lawrie started to refer to all kinds of messianic traditions in different religions, which he got to know, he focused on Hindu scriptures. Because of that, his new universal message appealed mainly to Hindus, and his Hindu followers began to call him Shri Lahari Krishna. Leaflets were printed that did not contain anything that referred to the Christian background of the ashram. The following example gives an impression:

> Think seriously! Your fame or prosperity or pride regarding your colour, caste, creed, religion[,] wealth, traditions and ceremonies can never save you from the oncoming terrible destruction[.] Go on your knees and plead with God to reveal to you himself, in His final Maha Avatar. . . . Prostrate yourself at the Lotus-feet of Lord Narayana, who has come down in the glorious name Lawrie (Lahiri) and having His Pathi, in the following blessed, holy land (India) to get His endless, life-giving blessings.[56]

In the 1980s Lawrie also started to teach a new doctrine of the so-called "Supreme Sacrifice" (Tamil *aatipali*) that is based on a cosmological mythology. Supreme Sacrifice became a central teaching. According to this doctrine the supreme God *(paramapurusha)* "offered Himself as a sacrifice before His children to prove that He is a Living God. He was tested when He was given power to give His life and take it back."[57] This idea is explicitly taken from *Purusasuktam,* the famous Vedic myth of creation through a cosmic sacrifice.[58] Furthermore, Lawrie equated this sacrifice of the *paramapurusha* with

---

55. Ram D. Prasad, *Kalki Maha Avatar* (Odaimarichan, Tamilnadu, 1990), p. 20.
56. Paulaseer Lawrie, *His Is the Paramathma* (leaflet, no date [ca. 1985]) (capitalization reduced by the author).
57. Devaaseer Lawrie, *The Seven Thunders of Lord God Almighty Lahari Krishna Opens the Seven Seals* (Manujothi Ashram, 1998), p. 244.
58. *Rigveda* 10:90. See also Prasad, *Kalki,* p. 36.

the sacrificial death of Jesus Christ. Biblical passages about the sacrificial death of Jesus Christ were now interpreted as belonging to the Supreme Sacrifice before the foundation of the world. The creation of the world, as it is described in Genesis, was therefore an event that took place later, and so lost its soteriological importance. Even the first sin was now located at the time of the Supreme Sacrifice, when Lucifer rebelled during the sacrificial act. Moreover, predestination now meant that only the persons who took part in the Supreme Sacrifice would obtain salvation and would believe in Lawrie.

Although the Bible was still a much-quoted book, nearly all Christian doctrines received a new interpretation. Shortly before his death, Lawrie, adopting a popular Muslim conviction, went so far as to insist that it was not Jesus who died on the cross but Judas. It must be remembered that Lawrie had already started to deny that Jesus was a real human being when he proclaimed himself as the "Son of Man." This "Judas doctrine" could also be seen as a late consequence of his docetism. Lawrie's death in 1989 was interpreted not as a human death but as glorification:

> Now, after preaching this doctrine for the past twenty years (hidden since the foundation of the world) and revealing the deep hidden truths (secrets) from all the Scriptures, Shri Lahari Krishna ascended to Heaven on February 24, 1989, without our knowledge, yet fulfilling the Scriptural prophecies of Kalki Maha Puranam. Now, we are awaiting eagerly His glorious return to earth as the King of Heaven and Earth for the purpose of judgement.[59]

With the death of Lawrie a real crisis developed. Among his three sons a struggle for the leadership in the ashram arose, and they even went to court. At present, it is not clear what the legacy of Lawrie will be, but the ashram still has many followers. During the moon-landing festivities in July 1998 at least one thousand participants from all over India went to the ashram to stay for several days.

Conclusion

Lawrie went a long way to end up as the Kalki *avatar*, and he did it through a constant progression of religious synthesis. He created a new religious movement that seems to be quite unique in its composition, although none of its

59. Prasad, *Kalki*, pp. 9-10.

ingredients is without parallels in other religions. Manujothi Ashram is a messianic universalistic religion originating from Indian Christianity.

Religious universalism is very common in India, but not among Indian Christians, who keep a clear distance from the surrounding religions despite some cautious attempts to integrate certain Hindu ideas into a contextual theology. Messianism is, in spite of some striking cases,[60] a rather rare phenomenon to the Indian tradition; moreover, it is widely considered to be connected with nativism and not with universalism.[61] Its unique combination makes Manujothi Ashram an interesting case for further research from the perspective of comparative religion. Through it a broader understanding of the encounter between Christianity and Hinduism in India may be possible.

60. Fuchs, *Godmen.*

61. Wilhelm Emil Mühlmann, *Chiliasmus und Nativismus: Studien zur Psychologie, Soziologie und historischen Kasuistik der Umsturzbewegungen,* 2nd ed. (Berlin, 1964); Bryan Wilson, *Magic and Millenium: A Sociological Study of Religious Movements of Protest among Tribal and Third-World Peoples* (London, 1973).

CHAPTER SIXTEEN

Praising Baby Jesus in
Iyecupiran Pillaittamil

PAULA RICHMAN

For centuries the image of Baby Jesus has played a crucial role in Christian piety. The significance of venerating the infant Jesus in Europe started in the early Middle Ages and received new momentum in the twelfth and thirteenth centuries when Cistercians and Franciscans emphasized the theme. In Tamil literary tradition a long-standing devotional genre of poetry, called the *pillaittamil*, also emphasized the veneration of an extraordinary child. Several Tamil Christian poets found the *pillaittamil* an appropriate literary genre for expressing their love of Jesus.[1] This chapter focuses on one of them, Arul Cellatturai, who published *Iyecupiran [Lord Jesus] Pillaittamil* in 1985.[2]

1. See, for example, Cāminātapiḷḷai, *Cēcunātar Piḷḷaittamiḷ* (Madras, 1864). For a more recent one, to the Virgin Mary, see S. Tamas, *Mariyaṉṉai Piḷḷaittamiḷ* (Tañcai, 1972), published by the author.

2. On 27 July 1991 in Tiruchirappalli, I interviewed Mr. Arul Cellatturai, who was accompanied by Rev. Fr. Soosaimanickam from the Catholic press that published the book. In this chapter all quotations without footnotes come from my conversations with the poet; those in the text followed by page numbers in parentheses are from Arul Cellatturai, *Iyēcupirāṉ Piḷḷaittamiḷ* (Tiruchirappalli, 1985). In addition to the poem considered here, his other writings include a *patikam* on Mother Mary (1984); *Velaṇkaṇṇip Patirruppattu*, on Mary as worshipped in the Virgin Mary shrine in Nagore (1987); and a

A slightly different version of "Praising Baby Jesus in *Iyecupiran Pillaittamil*" appeared as pp. 158-77 in Paula Richman's *Extraordinary Child: Poems from a South Indian Devotional Genre* (Honolulu: University of Hawai'i Press, 1997) and has been reprinted here with their kind permission.

In a *pillaittamil,* the poet assumes a maternal voice to praise an extraordinary being (deity, prophet, saint), envisioning him or her in the form of a baby. The *pillaittamil* genre produced a corpus of diverse and sophisticated poetry over many centuries. Although the genre began within the Tamil Hindu literary tradition in the twelfth century, in the nineteenth century Muslim and Christian poets adopted it as well.[3]

In writing *Iyecupiran Pillaittamil* [henceforth *IPPT*], Cellatturai self-consciously set out to compose a *pillaittamil* that would achieve several goals. Inspired by the beauty of ancient (largely pre-Sanskritic) Tamil poetry, he wanted to write a poem excluding words and poetic imagery that came from Sanskrit, English, and other non-Tamil sources. At the same time, he sought to make a place in the *pillaittamil* tradition for the world of technology.

Cellatturai is a registered senior technical member of the Institution of Engineers. After teaching for five years as an engineering instructor at St. Joseph's College in Tiruccirappalli, followed by three years at St. Joseph's Industrial School, he has worked for more than two decades at Bharata Heavy Electrical Limited as a foreman in the Human Resource Development Centre. As an engineer and a person fascinated by science, he wanted to praise the Lord as creator of the mysteriously complex and beautiful patterns of nature. Even though most of the commonly used words in his scientific training were English, in his poetry he translated them into Tamil as a way of displaying the richness of its linguistic resources.

Finally, he explicitly identified his *pillaittamil* as a way to teach the greatness of Lord Jesus and to inform people of various religious persuasions. In consonance with the movement to indigenize expression of the Christian faith in Tamilnadu, Cellatturai portrayed Baby Jesus as a Tamil child. In this way, he hoped to show people how Lord Jesus could enter their religious lives in a familiar form. Cellatturai's composition process and the circumstances of the poem's first recitation demonstrate how his *pillaittamil* sought to transcend conventional boundaries by bringing together lovers of Tamil literature in general, pious Christians, and those whose lives center around scientific and technical training.

---

poem in honor of his wife. On the *pillaittamil* genre and other *bhakti* poetry addressed to children, see Kenneth Bryant's study of devotion to Baby Krishna in the Hindi poetry of Surdas, *Poems to the Child God: Structures and Strategies in the Poetry of Sūrdās* (Berkeley, 1978); for the nature and early history of the *vatsalya* tradition, see Lynn Marie Ate, "Periyālvār's *Tirumoḻi,* a Bala Kṛṣṇa Text from the Devotional Period in Tamil Literature," Ph.D. dissertation, University of Wisconsin–Madison, 1978, pp. 92-96.

    3. For a history of the genre, see Paula Richman, *Extraordinary Child: Poems from a South Indian Devotional Genre* (Honolulu, 1997).

Praising a Child in *Paruvams*

The name of the genre, a compound of *pillai* and *tamil,* testifies to the centrality of the subject of childhood. *Pillai* means "child" or "baby," and so the
title can be understood and translated simultaneously as "Tamil [poetry] for
a child" and "Tamil [poetry] to a child."[4] *Pillaittamil* writers do more than
adopt the role of parent; they take on a maternal voice in particular.[5] Although poets envision, address themselves to, and praise an extraordinary
child, they also praise the grown child's powerful and salvific acts. Each verse
of a *pillaittamil* juxtaposes praise of the baby with praise of the adult. Thus
the poet can express closeness to a chosen deity, conceived of as accessible and
responsive to the affection of his mother, while simultaneously praising the
adult deity's awesome and miraculous powers.

Each verse of a poem occurs in one of ten carefully sequenced *paruvams,*
or sections. The ten *paruvams* of a *pillaittamil* function in ways that might be
seen as analogous to the classical Indian system of musical *ragas.* The well-
trained listener knows the mood associated with each *raga* and the notes of its
required scale. Although the performer begins with the scale of the *raga* and
takes it as the musical foundation of the composition, true artistry reveals itself in the performer's ability to improvise within the *raga.* This structured
creativity brings delight to musically sophisticated listeners. Each of the
paruvams, like each of the *ragas,* provides a structure within which invention
flourishes.

A *paruvam* takes as its subject matter a specific childhood activity:[6] for example, a child giving the mother a kiss, a little girl bathing in the river, or a little boy beating a toy drum. Each *paruvam* possesses a name, usually based on
a key word in the *paruvam*'s assigned activity. For example, the *paruvam*
where the mother asks the child for a kiss bears the name "kiss" *(muttam);* the
paruvam where the girl bathes in the river is named "playing in the water"
(nīrāṭal); and the *paruvam* where the boy beats a drum is called "little drum"
(ciṟuparai). The final phrase of each verse in a given *paruvam,* which I have
called a "refrain," functions to specify the *paruvam.* The refrain is a short consistent phrase with which all the verses in that *paruvam* close, such as "clap

---

4. Other less frequently used names for the genre include *piḷḷaikkavi* [poetry of/for
the child], *piḷḷaippāṭṭu* [songs of/for the child], and *piḷḷaittirunāmam* [the sacred name of/
for the child].

5. See Richman, *Extraordinary Child,* ch. 9 for the implications of a male poet assuming a female voice.

6. See Richman, *Extraordinary Child,* ch. 1 for a review of the secondary literature
on the development of the *paruvam* structure.

your hands" or "beat your little drum." A *pillaittamil* usually contains ten verses in each *paruvam*, so an entire poem usually contains about 100 verses.

The *paruvam* structure provides the organization and sequencing of a *pillaittamil*. Because the term *paruvam* carries with it the sense of growth, one might expect the *paruvams* to form a sequence of child development, with the activity in each *paruvam* becoming more difficult, requiring increasingly mature mental and physical skills. Some developmental thrust occurs in the sequence of the *paruvams*, but that development is also crosscut by literary and religious elements that have also shaped the *paruvam* structure.

The first *paruvam*, for example, provides a ritual entrance into the *pillaittamil*. In this "protection" *(kāppu) paruvam*, the poet requests divine assistance to guard the child from danger. Each verse in this *paruvam* appeals to a different deity to watch over the tiny infant. Within the internal logic of the *pillaittamil*, the protection *paruvam* enables the mother to enlist a set of powerful divine protectors for her infant; apparently, the more gods that protect the child, each with his or her special powers, the better. From the perspective of the *pillaittamil* poet as well, these multiple entreaties for protection prove crucial; they begin the poem auspiciously and allow the poet to praise (and himself receive merit from) deities besides the one to whom he addresses his *pillaittamil*.

Tamil literary tradition interprets the second and third *paruvams* variously. The meaning of the second *paruvam*'s name, *ceṅkīrai*, has been interpreted in several ways, but the favorite explanation breaks it into *cen*, "red," and *kīrai*, "vegetable greens." Imagine vegetable greens whose stalks, when young, have a slightly reddish tinge (for example, beet and rhubarb stalks) and which, when small and tender, sway gently in the breeze. Most *ceṅkīrai* verses depict some kind of gentle undulating movement on the part of the baby. *Paruvam* three, *tāla* (tongue), always includes the refrain *talelo*, an onomatopoeic lullaby sound equivalent to English "la la la." Some scholars argue that this *paruvam* encourages the child to move its tongue and prattle, an explanation that accounts for the word "tongue" in the *paruvam* name.

Next follow three *paruvams* that need little exegesis. In the fourth *paruvam*, *cappāṇi*, the mother asks the child to clap its hands. The fifth *paruvam* asks for a kiss *(muttam)*. The sixth *paruvam*, called *vārāṇai*, or the variant title *varukai*, both of which mean "coming," depicts the mother calling the child to come hither.

In *pillaittamil* tradition, the seventh *paruvam* stands out as the most challenging *paruvam*, with great scope for creativity. In this "moon" *(ampuli) paruvam*, the mother addresses the lunar sphere shining in the sky, asking it to come play with her baby. Poets take this *paruvam* in a literal way, and, in order to entice the moon to come and provide companionship for the child, they employ a number of rhetorical strategies, including threats, bribes, and even arguments about the compatibility of the moon and the baby because of their similarities.

The first seven *paruvams* remain constant in all *pillaittamils,* but the last three *paruvams* differ in notable ways. Most important, the *paruvam* system branches into two types, depending upon the sex of the child. These last three *paruvams* also vary in order because poets have not always sequenced them in the same order over time.

Of the three *paruvams* in the male branch, two *paruvams* are rather straightforward. In the *ciruparai* (little drum) *paruvam,* the speaker encourages the boy to beat on his drum. In a similar *paruvam, cirutēr* (little chariot), the speaker tells the boy to drive his toy chariot. The most unusual *paruvam* for males bears the name *cirril* or "little house(s)." Unlike all the other *paruvams* in the *pillaittamil* genre, the poet adopts not the maternal voice but that of a little girl, or group of little girls, playing in the sand by the seashore. The girls entreat the little boy not to destroy their tiny houses, which they have built with such care. Most *pillaittamils* to little girls ask them to bathe in the river, play jacks, and swing on a swing.

Although the *paruvam* arrangement provides a fairly rigid structure for the composition of a *pillaittamil,* the content of the verses remains relatively open to the imagination and choices made by the poet. Intriguingly, the genre's conventions seem to have nurtured literary invention. It is precisely this combination of creativity and structure that attracted Arul Cellatturai to the genre.

How the Poem Came to Be Written and Published

Despite Cellatturai's training and employment in the field of engineering, writing poetry played a large role in his life. His father encouraged his son's literary education, and, under the guidance of a guru, he studied selected classical texts. He tremendously admired Sangam poetry, wishing that the poetry of his own time were more like the ancient verses. After studying thoroughly the techniques of poetic composition, he began writing poetry in the 1960s and showing it to his guru for correction. A turning point occurred in 1974 when, as Cellatturai describes it, his guru "was adorned with Ponnadai [a shawl of honor] on the public dais by the Bishop." Once his guru had attained public recognition as an outstanding poet, Cellatturai felt inspired to undertake more ambitious poetic enterprises of his own.

Cellatturai was deeply influenced in his writing style by the literary magazine *Thenmozhi* [Words of Honey], in which various present-day poets wrote in the Sangam style. He recalls what an inspiration it was to discover the magazine: "I sighed with relief. I felt hopeful that it was possible to continue the literary work which had ceased to exist long back." From this point on, he sought to practice the principles set out in the *Tanittamil Iyakkam* [Only Tamil Movement/ Pure Tamil Movement], particularly as set out in the writings of G. Devaneya Pavanar. That is, the movement sought to emulate the "unadulterated Tamil" of the ancient period, before it had been diluted by semantic borrowings from Sanskrit, Persian, and, more recently, English.

Cellatturai's motivation to write a *pillaittamil* arose from a religious vow. His family consisted of two boys and a girl, but he and his wife deeply wanted another son and prayed daily for a little boy *(kuṭṭi tampi):* "I also made a personal vow that I would offer a pillaittamil to child Jesus if a male child was born," recalls Cellatturai. The parents, indeed, "were blessed by God" with a little boy whom they loved very much. So Cellatturai set out to write a *pillaittamil* to Baby Jesus.

Cellatturai prepared for writing in two ways. As he now had a growing infant in his home, he observed his son closely in preparation for his *pillaittamil* writing: "God had given me a very good chance to study all the gestures and habits of a little child. I did so and was prepared to write." As a result, he felt comfortable assuming the voice of a mother: "Whatever she [his wife] feels as mother is known to me," he said. He also read every *pillaittamil* he could find, 228 *pillaittamils* at various libraries and private collections, which steeped him in the *pillaittamil* tradition.

Cellatturai worked steadily on his poem. Every moment of free time was precious, so he used his daily forty-minute bus ride to the office for composition. The poem took him exactly ten months to write, the period that ancient Indian texts take to be the time between conception and birth. When he finished his composition, he went to Mukkombu, the dam site on the river Kaveri where it branches into three streams. Under a huge banyan tree there, from early morning to late evening, he gave the first recitation and explication of the full poem for two friends, one Hindu and the other Catholic. This, he said, was his version of the traditional debut recital *(araṅkerram).*

At the time that Cellatturai completed the poem, he was attending Bible classes at St. Paul's Seminary in Tirunelveli. He asked his professor, Rev. Dr. Fr. Hieronymus, whether it would be possible to publish his work. The priest convinced those in the seminary administration to act as patron for the poem's publication at a nearby Christian press. The publishers printed one thousand copies of the book, which were almost entirely sold out by 1990.

Public libraries in Tamilnadu purchased three hundred copies, and the others were sold through direct orders.

The finished product received a book-releasing celebration, a type of ceremony often held for works of traditional poetry.[7] The ceremony welcomes a new book into the world and establishes it in a community of appreciative readers. Organizers of the ceremony invite guests to witness the book receiving honor from prominent people.[8] The person deemed worthy of receiving the first copy was Arul Thiru Lambert Miranda Atikal, Director of St. Joseph Theological College, Tiruccirappalli, an influential representative of the institution that supported the poet early in his career. Several people gave words of blessing, including the widely acclaimed poet Mariyatacu (the name means "Servant of Maria") and the Secretary of "The Three Tamils Sangam," an organization active in promoting classical and classically inspired Tamil literature.

On a more mundane level, the ceremony also advertised the book, targeting appropriate markets. The ceremony for Cellatturai's book, organized by his publisher, took place in the city's Tamil Sangam, a pan-Tamilnadu literary association that promotes traditional Tamil poetry. The audience of Tamil literary savants, people active in Catholic education and publishing, friends, and the poet's family members created a community for the new work of poetry and expressed their appreciation of its excellence by participating in the ritual. The book's reception, thus, began with a ceremony that helped it to cross boundaries of Tamil reading communities. Clearly the poem had a wider audience than just the Tamil Catholic community.

Why a *Pillaittamil* to Jesus?

Cellatturai chose to write in the *pillaittamil* genre for specific reasons after much careful thought. In our interview he stressed that particular genres are appropriate for depicting certain kinds of activity and expressing particular emotions. Among the available genres, which was most appropriate for con-

7. For an analysis of the book-releasing ritual in Tamil culture see Paula Richman and Norman Cutler, "A Gift of Tamil: On Compiling an Anthology of Translations from Tamil Literature," in *Between Languages and Cultures: Translation and Cross-Cultural Texts*, edited by Anuradha Dingwaney and Carol Maier (Pittsburgh, 1996).

8. The invitation to the ceremony highlights the key actors in the events. Bishop Rev. Thomas Antakai Avarkal released the first copy of the book. On the invitation to the ceremony not only do Catholic titles of status (Bishop, Reverend) precede his given name; it is followed by Tamil literary titles of veneration (Antakai, "preeminent," and the honorific Avarkal).

veying the endearing activities of childhood and the poet's love toward Jesus? Cellatturai quickly ruled out certain genres for the praise of Lord Jesus: "Other genres, like *ulā, kōvai, kuṟavanji,* etc. are not acceptable to Christ because of their inclination towards sex." Although he used the English term "sex" here, he glossed it with the traditional Tamil phrase *akapporuḷ,* a term dating from the ancient period of Tamil literature, meaning "the subject matter of love." According to the poetic taxonomy used by classical authors, poetry fell into two categories: *akam,* "inner," deals with the intimate feelings of lovers and families and *puṟam,* "outer," deals with the public realm of court life, warfare, and praise of generous donors. Poems dealing with *akam* often possess an erotic tone that Cellatturai felt inappropriate for depiction of Jesus.[9]

This tendency to avoid eroticism also shaped his decision to address his *pillaittamil* to Jesus rather than to Mother Mary. Although several Christian poets had written *pillaittamils* to Mary, Cellatturai felt that doing so would either compromise the image of Mother Mary or the spirit of the *pillaittamil* genre. He noted, "In the church we make adoration to Mary because of her implicit obedience to the word of God and because she was the mother of Christ. We do not attribute to her personal beauties." He explained further that *pillaittamils* to females (especially in the last three *paruvams*) expatiate on the sensual beauty of the girl. In contrast, "There are limitations on *varṇaṉai* [description] regarding Mary Mother."[10]

Cellatturai wrote praise of Jesus as a *baby* because of the universal appeal of children, as he comments: "Everybody is fond of children and in every society there is a special place for children. Children amuse other members of

9. The genres to which he refers fall under the rubric of *ciṟṟilakkiyam* (also called *pirapantam* or *prabandham*). The three he rejected have prescribed subject matter that he considers inappropriate for glorification of Jesus: e.g., *ula* is a genre in which, by poetic prescription, the poet describes the hero going in procession through a city. Upon seeing him, women of all ages fall in love with him. The poet should explain in detail, with a tone of eroticism, the sensual allure of these women and how they feel attracted to the hero. Cellatturai rejected such genres. He mentioned one genre from the *pirapantam* classification that would be appropriate for the praise of Jesus: the *āṟṟuppaṭai,* in which the poet lauds holy places. Not all Christian Tamil poets would agree with Cellatturai's attitude toward many *pirapantam* genres. For example, Vedanayakam Sastriar wrote *Bethlehem Kuṟavanji* in the *kuṟavanji* genre with erotic content. For an overview of these genres, see Kamil Zvelebil, *Tamil Literature,* vol. 10, fasc. 1, in *A History of Indian Literature,* edited by Jan Gonda (Wiesbaden, 1974), ch. 5.

10. Note that Cellatturai is *not* claiming that it would be impossible to write a *pillaittamil* to Mary. (There are several to her.) He is saying that it would be impossible to write one to her that maintained the traditions of erotic imagery associated with the *pillaittamils* to females that have earned the highest literary praise, while staying within the constraints of Christian propriety.

the family." So, he felt that a poem about a child would give particular pleasure to readers. Cellatturai also admired the creative scope of the *pillaittamil*
genre. Commenting that it challenged his imagination to envisage the childhood of Jesus in the Tamil land, he said, "If Jesus were born again in
Tamilnadu, these are the feelings he would have."

Personal as well as poetic reasons led him to write to Jesus as a baby. He
noted: "Adult Jesus is always kept in a high elevated position; [but] there is no
fear to approach child Jesus." He could even address Lord Jesus as a baby with
the non-honorific grammatical forms used only for children or intimate
friends.[11] Further, the very *paruvam* structure bestowed upon him the opportunity to share his life with that of Jesus: "I wanted to walk hand in hand with
him *(varukai)*, I wanted to play with him *(cirril)*, I wanted kisses from him
(muttam), I wanted to put him in the cradle and sing for him *(tāla)*. Altogether I wanted to enjoy the nature of Lord Jesus as baby." Note that in
Cellatturai's "little house" verse (translated below) he portrays the little girls
as inviting Baby Jesus to join them in play. Cellatturai, thus, sees the *paruvams*
of the *pillaittamil* as a means of envisioning a close and loving relationship
with his God.

Theology and Technology

Cellatturai's experiences led him to awareness of both the constraints and
freedoms of writing a *pillaittamil*. Interestingly, some aspects of the protection *paruvam* irked him because he found them theologically unnecessary.
The *paruvam* might be appropriate for Hindu tradition, but it did not really
square with Christian doctrine. As he put it, "I am convinced that the Son of
God himself protects everyone." Further, he noted that since the Father and
the Son are one, protection does not seem necessary because the baby in his
poem can surely protect himself.

Nonetheless, since *pillaittamil* tradition requires a protection *paruvam*, he
set out to write one. Still, he felt a poetic tension between the multiple deities
of Hindu *pillaittamils* and the monotheism of Christianity:

> Regarding the first *paruvam*, namely *kāppu paruvam*, it is customary to
> pray to various gods according to Hindu mythology. There is a wider
> range of choice. But for me there was only one choice, to pray to God

11. As he said, "I can even call him in the single person [a grammatical form indicating familiarity and intimacy, rather than honor and distance], like *vā*, *nāta*, etc."

the Father, to protect the child Jesus. Since he is above all, I could not find anyone except the Father to protect him. This limitation was a constraint for me.

One could say that as a poet he felt his style was constrained in this *paruvam* because he had limited options for filling the protection niches. Such minor constraints, however, did not interfere with Cellatturai's overall sense of the elasticity of the genre. Although his extensive reading did not uncover any previous examples of *pillaittamils* that had dealt adequately with the marvels of modern technology, he took it for granted that he was free to focus on the topic. He recalled, "I found that the modern contemporary world of science and technology was not depicted in any of the literature I studied. There is no representative of my living, my world, in the [*pillaittamil*] literature." So, in his poem he strove to encompass his daily work world based on engineering technology, either by using familiar Tamil words or by coining his own Tamil words to describe various scientific terms, as this verse shows:

IPPT 52 (come 2)

Lamps burn because of water
and light shines inside the water.
Even wind cannot attack them.

All the sheets of paper turn into books
through linotype.
Tape recorders speak Tamil.

Speech comes from the sky
and favorite songs come.
Scenes spread on the wide screen.
Speedy arrow-boilers even touch the moon and return.

Night lamps burn without oil.
Spring water deep in the earth rises.
There is even artificial rain.
Medicine accomplishes transformations.

All sorts of machines develop
to calculate beyond the mind's ability
and change history.

Source of knowledge,
who encompasses all these things,
making people look to the sky in wonder,
to my rejoicing heart, come.

Practice balancing on your toddling feet,
like honey-dripping lotus petals.
Son of the loving God, come.

Cellatturai expresses a wonder at the miracles of modern science that remains deeply rooted in his belief in God, the God who made all these miraculous inventions possible. The tone of this verse suggests that appreciation of these electric and mechanical breakthroughs bears witness to the greatness of a supreme deity who is, simultaneously, a cute little boy balancing uncertainly on his two feet.

Lest his audience miss the significance of some of the amazing inventions he describes in the verse, Cellatturai provides his own annotations at the end of the poem, which I have translated in full, complete with his additional remarks in parentheses and my own clarifications in square brackets:

> *lamps burn because of water:* (connecting electricity with water [hydroelectric power]) electric lamps burn.
> *light shines inside the water:* it shines unceasingly in the water that runs by the flower garden at the Anicut Dam. [The Anicut Dam site has a park lit by electric lights underwater.]
> *linotype:* as soon as you strike it, the letter is transformed into print (Linotype).
> *tape recorders:* tape which makes a sound recording (Tape recorder).
> *scenes on the wide screen:* film (Cinima [Cinema]).
> *arrow-boilers: rakkettu* [rockets].
> *spring deep in the earth:* tube wells, water tube wells.
> *medical transformation:* transforming, performing surgery (transplantation).
> *calculating machines: calkulettar* [calculator], *kampyuttar* [computer].

These annotations act as a bridge between Cellatturai's world of engineering and the linguistic resources of Tamil. He has coined some of the terms he uses for mechanical devices, and so he explains them in his notes. In other places, his annotations provide the widely used English term that has been transliterated into Tamil (e.g., *kampyuttar* for computer), but he does not use those transliterated terms in his text because he has committed himself to writing in "Tamil only." Rather than lose his reader, though, he will give the more familiar English term so they can see how the device can be expressed using only Tamil words. The annotations also act as an educational device to inform or remind readers of the scientific advances that have been made in the last few decades. By incorporating verses and annotations into his poem, he brings his world of technology into the *pillaittamil* tradition.

Making the Poem Accessible

As Cellatturai himself admitted, his *pillaittamil* is written not for a popular audience but for literary connoisseurs: "I cannot expect a layman to read my book. Even general literary readers may not find it convenient to read." So, he feels that the more he can aid people in reading his work, the more he can carry out his goal of providing religious education. He considers the composition of his poem "not only an act of devotion" but also "a way in which I pass on information [about Jesus] to non-Christians." He feels that this book will help others to appreciate Jesus, noting that all three of the Tamil savants who wrote forewords to his *pillaittamil* were non-Christians, and yet, "all the three have admired the good qualities of my Lord Jesus." Because Cellatturai knows of the diverse experiences that members of his audience bring to his poem, he provides readers with an elaborate explanatory apparatus: preface, introduction, and literary information compiled in charts.

Even before the poetry begins, the front matter in the book suggests ways of understanding Cellatturai's motivation in writing the poem. Prefatory remarks written by admirers suggest particular ways to savor certain aspects the poem. For example, the Rev. Dr. Fr. Hieronymous's preface advises the reader to put Jesus in a local context, a perspective in keeping with recent trends to indigenize Christian symbols and practice in South India:

> The custom of Tamils is to rejoice and speak sweetly of a baby, praising its excellence, putting on ornaments, a *tilak* [an auspicious mark on the forehead] and collyrium [eye decoration]. The world knows that once upon a time Lord Jesus, the holy Son of God, who is capable of being born anywhere, was born in the country of Judea. . . . *Iyecupiran Pillaittamil* is an attempt through literary imagination to draw out, according to the tradition of *cirrilakkiyam* and Tamil grammar, all the ways in which, if Jesus came and was born in our sweet Tamil country now, our mothers would adorn and praise him. (p. 3, front matter, my translation)

Extrapolating from the theological idea that an omnipotent God is capable of sending his son to earth anywhere, the Rev. Hieronymous takes the poem to be the author's attempt to envision Jesus born in Tamilnadu and nurtured as a Tamil infant.

After Hieronymous's comments come several appreciative essays by non-Christian Tamil literary scholars, all of whom provide "testimony" of the poem's worth: a secular intellectual, a Hindu savant, and the Secretary of the Tamilnadu Government Culture and Development Department. Cellatturai also presents his own guide to his work, including a concise description of the subject matter of each *paruvam*, classification of types of imagery used, a summary of electrical and technological subjects to which he alludes (e.g., rockets, remote control, orbits of electrons, velocity of light), as well as an enumeration of biblical passages to which he refers.

After the front matter comes Cellatturai's introductory essay, in which he explains what he sees as the theological significance of his *pillaittamil* to Baby Jesus. Noting that every year on 25 December people celebrate the Lord's birth as a baby, he suggests that, in a sense, at Christmas time Jesus is born annually, again and again, all over the world. Cellatturai sees his *pillaittamil* as the logical outcome of this continuing celebration of Baby Jesus: "He [Jesus] continues to be born every moment in the mind of his devotees as they think of him, singing a *pillaittamil*." For this reason, Cellatturai argues that praising the Lord as a baby in a *pillaittamil* is quite an appropriate act of devotion (p. 10).

Some verses also come complete with the poet's footnotes and explanations, including biblical references. Cellatturai follows verse 61 with his own systematic gloss of the verse that exceeds the verse itself in length. The exegesis is numbered to highlight how many similarities there are between the moon and Jesus. He took pride in the fact that he had been able to discern an impressive number of similarities between Jesus and the moon: "To my own astonishment I have shown 8 similarities in the first verse and 5 similarities in the second verse, 13 in total, which is a record in the history of pillaittamil." So that the reader can see what Cellatturai takes as the religious authority for his poetry, I provide a translation of verse 61 and the complete exegesis that Cellatturai has put immediately after it.[12]

---

12. He labels it *pirippurai,* "gloss of separate [sections]." This label refers to the commentarial technique of dividing the poetry into components and then glossing words and explaining their meaning, as opposed to an alternate technique of focusing on the overall verse as a unit and providing exegesis of it in its entirety.

Verse 61 (moon 1): Similarity

Since you receive light
from another source,

since you rise high in the sky
while many people watch,

since you receive life again
even though your body dies,

since you remove the darkness of the world
with your light,

since you conceal your vast form
in a round white shape,

since you bear a blemish,

since those who read stars seek you,

since you are appropriate for supplicants/night blossoms,

and since the hero of my poem,
the Lord born of the Virgin
who is conceived through the Holy Spirit,
is like you,

Moon in the beautiful sky,
you should quickly agree
to play joyously and happily
with the one who is entwined with Tamil poetry,
flowing like a waterfall.

Moon, come to play.

1. *Receiving light from another source*
moon: from the sun
Lord Jesus: from the Holy Father

2. *Rising high in the sky while many people watch*
moon: At the sea harbor many people watch each white moon rising on
   (full moon) day.
Lord Jesus: On the fortieth day after he returned to life, many people came
   to see him ascend into the sky (Luke 24:51; Mark 16:19).

3. *Receiving life again even though the body died*
moon: appearing again after the dark moon (new moon)
Lord Jesus: reviving on the third day after death (Rev. 1:18; 2:8)

4. *Removing the darkness of the world with your light*
moon: removing outer darkness
Lord Jesus: removing inner darkness

5. *Concealing your vast form in a round white shape*
moon: making it appear that he has a round white form, when in truth his
   form is a large planetary sphere
Lord Jesus: hiding his large body in the round white wafer of communion

6. *Bearing a blemish*
moon: bearing the blemish called "hare"
Lord Jesus: his body bearing the stains (sins) of the world (1 Kings 2:24)

7. *Those who read the stars seeking you*
moon: Those who do celestial research for prediction (astrologers) seek to
   calculate the waxing moon and waning moon.
Lord Jesus: Those who watched the sky (shepherds) in the eastern direction sought him at birth.

8. *Being appropriate for supplicants/night blossoms [pun]*
moon: appropriate for making the night-blossoming lotus bloom
Lord Jesus: appropriate even for poor people

The numerical organization of his exegesis of the verse highlights his
quantitative triumph; the mathematical approach provided one way for an
engineer to distinguish himself in the moon *paruvam*. When asked why he
added the extensive gloss at the end of his verse, Cellatturai answered, "I can't
convey fully precisely what I want to convey if people don't understand."

In other verses, Cellatturai also makes his poetry attractive to readers by
linking Christian imagery with the glories of the Tamil heritage. In several re-

frains he describes how the sounds of Tamil and divine compassion overflow with sweetness (v. 36). In verse 70 he even portrays a tottering Jesus clasping the hand of Mother Tamil (Tamil envisioned as a mother). He draws his reader into his religious vision by linking Jesus with Tamil literary culture.

Verse 31, upon which Cellatturai's book's cover is based, provides the clearest example within the poem of "Tamilizing" the depiction of Jesus. In this verse, Cellatturai provides a poetic conceit that idealizes childish play and the surprises of the natural world. The verse depicts endearing Baby Jesus in a rural setting, observing the events around him. When he sees an irritated cock digging the ground in search of pearls, the toddler rips his string of pearls from his neck and throws them at the cock. The rest of the verse traces the results of this single action. One of the pearls hits a ripe mango, which plunges into the pond and throws up drops of water. When the peacock, who dances beneath the monsoon clouds, sees the water, he mistakes it for rain and begins to prance. Baby Jesus views its dance with glee and claps in appreciation.

The image that Cellatturai chose for the front cover, based on this verse, may be seen as emblematic of his larger enterprise. It depicts a small baby dressed and bejeweled in the traditional Tamil style (necklace, garland, anklets, armbands, and a *tilak*), watching a cock and a peacock on a lush green bank near a mango tree. Cellatturai told me that he deliberately chose a Tamil landscape with Tamil features. Jesus looks Tamilian, not Mediterranean or Near Eastern, and resembles Baby Krishna. Even more striking, however, is the baby's resemblance to Murukan, especially because of the prominence of the peacock in the drawing. The peacock appears often in Tamil poetry as the vehicle of youthful Murukan, a deity who is especially popular in South India. As Clothey notes, Murukan is considered the quintessential Tamil deity.[13] Cellatturai said he placed Baby Jesus near the peacock because it would link his God with a familiar Tamil figure. This cover picture can be seen then as encapsulating a major motivation of Cellatturai's poem: to indigenize Jesus by envisioning him as a Tamil baby, through the use of a Tamil literary genre, made accessible to the reader through annotation and familiar poetic conceits.

Cellatturai's composition also demonstrates how dramatically poetic structures influence expressions of religious devotion over time. Because the *pillaittamil* must contain ten specific *paruvams,* poets shape their compositions according to the framework of particular activities, no matter what the particular mythic or legendary tradition of the poet's community is. For ex-

---

13. Frederick Clothey, *The Many Faces of Murukan: The History and Meaning of a South India God* (The Hague, 1978).

ample, Cellatturai writes protection verses because you cannot have a *pillaittamil* without them. Thus, his *pillaittamil* provides an example of how literary conventions can shape the construction of religious expression.

Tamil Hindus and Christians (as well as Muslims, although that topic lies outside the scope of this study) express feelings of devotion by composing in the same genre, even though they inflect it in their own ways. That Hindus and Christians with differing concepts of divinity, notions of virtuous behavior, and ideas of religious community write in the same literary genre suggests the adaptability and scope possible in the *pillaittamil*'s seemingly restrictive *paruvam* structure. Viewing the *pillaittamil* as a multi-religious genre helps us to understand Indian religion as a phenomenon that encompasses many different strands, many of which share and exchange certain literary modes of expression.

Translations of Selected Poems from *IPPT*

IPPT 5 (protection 5): Addressed to God the Father

Manna from heaven
and cool water from the mountain
you gave to people
as soon as they asked.

Descending from heaven
taking form on earth
Jesus was born
as the Son of Mary.

The Holy Child from heaven,
bless him with goodness in life
and the arts,
beautiful in form.
Shower from heaven
a rain of flowers,
O God worshipped
by all who live.

a rain of flowers: The celestials in heaven are believed to send a downpour of blossoms when an especially auspicious event takes place on earth.

Praising Baby Jesus in Iyecupiran Pillaittamil

IPPT 31 (clap 1)

A cock pecks out pearls
from a heap of spilled emeralds.
Peering, he stands tall and dissatisfied,
scratching them with his feet.

You see this and drive him away, hurling at him
the strand of pearls from your neck.
Then you clap your hands, happily.

As the strand hits him, its pearls fly off
and snap the stalks of a bunch of ripe mangos.
When the mangos drop into the pond,
water scatters.

A peacock with brilliant eyes in its tail
lives in the cool grove.
He thinks the drops are rain from the sky
and dances.

Seeing his mistake, you clap your tender hands
and rejoice.
Our Lord, the color of radiant burnished gold,
graciously clap your hands.

Our Lord, who is a storehouse that opens with a knock,
graciously clap your hands.

his mistake: According to Indian poetic convention peacocks dance when the monsoon rains come. This peacock mistakes the falling pearls for rain drops.
opens with a knock: Reference to Luke 11:9-10.

IPPT 36 (clap 6)

There are so many atoms in a fraction
of one eight-hundredth of a split sesame seed!

There are so many wide worlds far far away
that we cannot reach, no matter how we try!

How is it that the binding force of electrons changes,
and electricity flows?

How does the black bee live inside the *ottu* mango nut
and still find food to nourish itself?

How does flowing water change state
into steam and snow?

How did the radiant ascetic
come here and live?
Is it easy to explain?

You, whose Father holds the wealth of flowing Tamil,
clap your hands!
You, whose sweet tender words of Tamil resonate,
clap your hands!

radiant ascetic: Kōlamātavaṉ, literally "handsome great ascetic," is a term for
Lord Jesus. Acts of intense asceticism are said to generate an attractive glow
from the heat *(tapas)* they produce.

IPPT 63 (moon 3): Difference

You look like a pearl,
but a single smile from my Master surpasses that.

You rise high in the sky,
but have you ever crossed the sky
and seen lofty heavens like my Lord?

You get smaller when your form shrinks,
but my Master has never decreased like you.

You appear in one direction and disappear in the opposite one,
but he defeats you by going in all eight directions.

Only half of the time you wander
and then you remove the darkness outside,
but all the time, he remains inside us.

Don't you know his nature is superior to yours?
Why do you still hesitate?

With this young offshoot of God,
joined with budding and sprouting Tamil,
Moon, come to play.

With the Son of God,
seated on the right side of Gracious God,
Moon, come to play.

eight directions: north, northeast, east, southeast, south, southwest, west, north-west.
young offshoot of God: literally, "a leaf bud of God." The little child is compared to the tender, soft beautiful bud of a leaf. The child is also linked with the tenderness and richness of the Tamil language, which has grown and flourished.

IPPT 66 (moon 6): Giving

Curing the sickness that afflicts us,
driving out the demons who seize us,
destroying all our misery,
he is the Lord.

His touch cures the hunchback,
the blind, and the deaf.
Praising him enough
for the deeds he can perform is difficult.

A woman who suffered never-ending sickness was cured
the moment she touched the end of his robe.
With one hand, he raised the officer's daughter.

When you touch his body, he will remove your blemish.
Who will be your companion as you orbit?
Choose the company of the Pure One.

Is there any relish equal to the pleasure
of touching his radiant, glittering body
treasured in the minds of the pure ones?
With the child of the Lord who gives eternal life,
come to play.

With the Son of God,
seated at the right side of gracious God,
Moon, come to play.

Poet's own footnotes accompanying the verse:
Casting out spirits (Matt. 8:28-34; Mark 5:1-20; Luke 8:26-39)
Healing the hunchback, blind, and deaf by his touch (Luke 7:22)
Ending the longtime illness (Mark 5; Luke 8)
Raising the officer's daughter with a touch of the hand (Mark 5; Luke 8)
The Lord who gives eternal life (John 6:68)

***IPPT* 76 (little house 6)**

Our mother is your mother.
Our father is your father.
You are our precious soul, right?
In our world, who else is kind?

You said you are the salt
in the surging ocean waters.
You declared you are the shining light.

We simple ones want to place
soft white rice in your mouth.

Come, we'll play in the little houses,
fixing them with fine sand from the Kauvery River.

Our Lord and our King
with a straight scepter,
don't destroy our little houses.

Holy One who flows with clear honeyed Tamil,
don't destroy our little houses.

your father: since Christians view God as father and the Virgin as mother, all people are children of these parents. So these girls tell Baby Jesus that he is their brother and shouldn't knock down their little houses.
salt . . . shining light: biblical references from Matt. 5:13-14
King with a straight scepter: in classical Tamil tradition, a king with a straight scepter rules fairly. A king's scepter is said to become crooked when he acts unjustly.

Index

Aaron, 75, 81, 321, 323
Acts of Thomas, 35
Adi-Dravida, 29, 337, 344, 347
Adivasi, Adibasi (aboriginal or tribal people), 1, 27, 28, 31, 59, 270, 311-12, 340, 341, 352-53
Aesop Fables, 119, 125
Africa, 6, 30, 116, 118
Agents, agency, 234, 313; of change, 25; divine, 18; human, 19, 298; mission, 16, 25, 71; native agents, 74, 75, 79, 84, 91, 253; of Westernization, 104
Agra, 43, 64, 229, 230, 237, 238, 241, 242, 245; Anglo Oriental Government College in, 229; Roman Catholics in, 245; School Book Society of, 218
Ahmad Khan, Sir Sayyid, 230, 234, 235, 236, 249, 250-51, 252, 253, 255
Ahmad, Mirza Ghulam, 228, 230, 235, 250
Ahmad, Nazir, 234
Ahmadi community, 236
Ahmadiyya movement, 235, 250
Ahom kingdom, Assam, 259, 262
Ajmere, 196
Akbar, 169
Al-din, Nozam Auliya, 245
Al-din, Maulwi Karim, 234
Al-Masih, Abd, 228-29
Alburquerque, Alfonso d', 134-35, 137, 138

Alcohol, 45, 289
Aleppa, 86, 90
Alexander the Great, 62, 299
'Ali, Maulwi Safdar, 230, 233, 234, 237, 246, 247
'Ali, Muhammad Mohar, 168, 176
'Ali Qalandar, Shaikh Bu, 229, 245
Aligarh, 230
'Alim (Muslim teacher/scholar), 223, 228, 231, 233, 234, 250, 251
Allah, 214
All-Indian Muslim League, 47
Allahabad Conference, 246, 247
Almanacs, almanac-makers, 191, 195
Alphonso (Alfonso) I, 135
America, Americans, 8, 13, 14, 22, 26, 37, 48, 59, 116, 118, 231, 257, 260, 363
American Baptist mission, 27, 256, 257, 258, 259, 265, 270, 271, 272, 273, 278, and high caste, 264; press, 256; and science, 261
American Baptist Foreign Mission Board: Shan mission, 257, 262
American Baptist Home Mission Board, 264, 272
American Congregationalist Mission (Madurai), 329
American Marathi Mission, 60
American Pentecostals, 360

Chiefs, 276, 279, 280, 285

China, 6, 33, 38, 43, 257

Chistis (a Sufi order), 245, 245, 246

Chola kingdom, 36

Cholera epidemic, 317

Chota Nagpur, 275

Christ, 240; divinity of, 242; and salvation, 242; as Savior, 242. *See also* Docetism; Doctrine; Salvation; Trinity

Christian (catechist), 75

Christian, meaning of, 3, 4-5

Christian elites, 22, 28, 36-37, 153

Christian Life Missions, 363

Christian Mandate, 5

Christian Medical College, Vellore, 360

Christian missions, 9; and health, 58, 80, 272, 360; and publishing, 255, 256, 260, 269, 273, 284. *See also under* Education *and* Missionaries

Christian Observer, 325

Christian yogi, yogees, 239, 247

Christianity: stereotypes of, 1, 5-6

Christianity in the East, 38-39, 131

Christianity in India, 1-2, 34; attacks on, 39, 55; and caste, 13-14, 21, 22, 104; and class, 22; and colonialism, 7, 9, 49; criticism of, 7; Eastern, 38-39; Indian and European tension, 41; indigenous expressions of, 227-28; and indigenous social structure, 342; institutions of, 3; misconceptions about, 5; and missionary colonialism, 11; and modernism, 150; "new," 236; non-Western, 6, 38; and religions in India, 332. *See also* Caste; Church; Colonial *and under individual denominations and missions*

Christians, 145, 146, by birth; and colonialism, 2; and caste, 13-5

Christo Samaj (Hindu-Christian sect), 21

Christo Seva Sangh (Christian Service Society), 21

Church and state [British], 11, 56-57, 58, 144, 145, 151, 154, 155, 170, 327; and chaplains, 55; collaboration, 170-71, 307, 308, 313; and endowments, 58, 144, 308, 309; and foreign missionaries, 58-59; and hostility between, 54-56; intervention in conflicts, 169-70; and patronage, 144; and the persecuted, 55; and race, 54, 56, 57; and support for other religions, 57-8. *See also under* Caste, Education, Patrons

"Church" and state [Muslim]: Akbar's model, 169; Aurangzeb's model, 169

Church Missionary Society (CMS), 16, 25, 46, 56, 143-46, 148, 149, 150, 151, 165, 166, 167, 229, 230, 236, 237, 241, 244, 251, 253, 278, 308, 309, 313, 323, 324, 326, 327, 328, 330; and Indian clergy, 330; and Syrian Christians, 144

Church of England, 328; rites of, 142

Church of England Zenana Mission, 328, 330. *See also* Zenana

Church of South India, 46, 316, 362, 363

Church of Sweden Mission (Lutheran), 29, 338, 339, 347, and Madharis, 339, 347; methods of, 339; and Paraiyars, 339, 347; problems of, 339

Citizenship, 169

"Civilizing mission," 258, 260

Claphamites, 52

Clark, Edward, 270

Clark, Robert, 230, 232-33, 235, 236, 238

Clarke, Bp. Sundar, 316, 320, 321

Clarke, Dr. Satthianadhan, 316

Clergy, Indian. *See under* Indian missionary workers

Clorinda, 51

Cochin, 25, 40, 41, 134, 137, 138, 139, 141

Cohen, Bernard, 198

Coimbatore, 29, 337; and British, 343; cattle-raising, 345; highlands, 342-44; industry, 343, 344-45, 354-55; missions in, 338, 340, 345, 347; rural history, 337, 343, 345-47. *See also under* Caste; Labor; Madhari; Paraiyar

Colebrooke, H. T., 189

Colombo, Ceylon, 322, 358, 359; Wesley College, 359

Colonial discourse, 283. *See also* Discourse; Foucault; Inden; Said

Colonial hegemony, 93. *See also* Hegemony

Oomen, George, 152
Ootacamund, 330
Oppression, 352, 353
Ordain, ordination, 42, 50, 75, 227, 230, 236, 242, 280
Oriental scholarship, 155, 158, 188
Orientalism, 88, 295, 297, 300, 301. *See also* Said, Edward W.
Orientalist, 28, 155, 189, 190, 194, 208, 214, 215, 218, 261
Orientalists, 93, 101, 191, 297
Orissa, 171, 275, 278, 304
Orphans' institutions, 97, 265. *See also* Serfoji
Orthodox Christians, 10. *See also* Thomas Christians; Syrian Christians
Orunodoi, 27, 256, 258, 260, 261-71; and history, 262; and Islam, 262; and modern knowledge, 268; progress, 263; and religion, 260-61; and science, 261; and upper class readership, 260, 262; and useful knowledge, 260
Osborne, T. L., 363
Oslo, 292
"Other," "Otherness," 89, 157, 295, 301, 310
Outcasting, outcaste, 150, 201, 203, 207

Padmanji, Baba, 269
Padroado Real, 23, 40, 44, 46, 135, 136
Pagan practices, 136. *See also* Heathen; Idols; *and under* Festivals
Pakistan, 47, 60
Palayamkottai, 51, 323, 326, 327, 333, 359
Paley, William, 243
Palladam, 347
Pallar Christians, 15
Pandit (learned Hindu, teacher), 64, 69, 119, 165, 176, 178, 190, 192, 195, 196, 197, 201, 208, 214, 219, 265
Pandya, Vikrama Aditha, 43
Panipat, 229, 245
Pannaiyal, 346, 349, 350, 351, 355
Paraiyar, 1, 30; Aangu Paraiyar, 347; caste, 342, 353, 356; Christians, 13, 15, 83, 130; and Madhari compared, 337, 349, 350, 354-55; mobilization of, 343, 344
Parambil Tume. *See* Mar Thoma I

Paravas, 43-44
Parda (*purdah*, seclusion), 253
Parliament, 55, 127, 157
Parliament of World Religions (Chicago), 21, 231
Parsee, Parsees, 128
Parsi landlords, 352
Pastors. *See* Indian missionary workers; *Kattanas*
Partition of India, 47
Pathasala (society of scholars), 196, 197, 201, 206, 207, 210, 211, 218, 219
Patrons, patronage of learning, 188, 197, 206, 208, 209, 217, 219. *See also* Serfoji; Wilkinson, Lancelot
Patron-client relationships, 130. *See also under* Caste
Paulinius a Sancto Bartholomaeo (alias Vesdin/Wessdin), 68-69
Pavanar, G. Devaneya, 381
Pearce, W. H., 186
Penal Code, 343
Pentecost, Day of, 3
Pentecostal, 2, 22, 30; evangelists, 361; healing evangelists, 362; teachings, 360; testimonies, 361. *See also* Oneness Pentecostalism
Pentecostal church: and American missionaries, 360; in Ceylon, 359; in India, 360, 366. *See also* Assemblies of God
Perkins, Henry E., 237
Perron, Anquetil du, 68
Persecution of Christians, 36, 39, 51-52, 55, 80, 135, 137, 145, 147, 170, 348, 349
Persia, 6, 33, 36, 38, 39; Christians in, 36, 38; church in, 131; language of, 50, 233
Perso-Arabic culture, 234
Petitions, 15, 171-72. *See also* Memorials
Pettitt, Rev. George, 175
Pfander, Karl, 230, 237, 238, 239, 240, 242, 243, 254
Phillips, Jeremiah, 278, 283, 304
Physics, 119
Piazzi, Giuseppe, 112
Pietist, Pietists, 47, 120, 277, 284, 292; German, 47, 95, 96, 103, 117, 120, 229, 243, 323; of Halle, 124; of Inner Mission, 14;

Ramachandra, Yesudas, 219
Ramakrishna, 178
Ramnad, 43, 55, 342, 350, 354
Rampur Ghat, 279
Ranade, M. G., 178, 181
Rao, Rani Pavathi, 147
Rapture, 369, 270, 371
Rayappan, 51
Real Hinduism, 162
Rebellions, 275. *See also* Indian mutiny
Reconversion, 174
Religions, unity of, 214
Religious charismatics. *See* Lawrie,
    Paulaseer; Singh, Sadhu Sundar
Religious movements: indigenous, 21,
    236, 267, 358. *See also under* Islam
Religious universalism, 375
Renaissance, 115
Resistance, forms of, 341, 355. See also
    Mobilization
Rhenius, C. T. E., 323
Rice beer, 289. *See also* Alcohol
"Rice Christians," 290
Richards, Rev., 166
Riots. *See* Hul; Kerwar; Sepoy; Tinevelly;
    also Rebellions
Risley, H. H., 303, 304, 305
Rites, 136, 177; Church of England, 142;
    Hindu, 166, 173; Latin, 136, 137, 138, 144;
    Naga, 272; Nayar, 134; Syriac, 136, 137,
    138
Ritual, 37, 131, 144, 166, 173; authority, 140;
    domestic, 132; and purity, 131, 200, 205,
    206, 210. *See also* Brahmans
Roberts, Oral, 363; Youth Team of, 363
Robinson, Thomas, 122
Rodiye, Baba Josi, 203-4
Rogerius [Roger], Abraham, 48, 66
Roman Catholic Church, 10, 12, 16, 23,
    40-47, 55, 74, 75, 77, 95, 143, 203; and
    caste, 16; and Christians in Kerala, 136;
    converts to Protestantism, 74-75, 77;
    mass movements and, 23, 43; and Syr-
    ian Orthodox, 136. *See also under* Por-
    tugal
Rome, 41, 42, 142; arrogance of, 144. *See
    also* Jesuits

Roman Empire, 33, 35
Rosendal, Remus, 293-94, 306
Ross, Captain James, 199
Roth, Heinrich, 64; grammar of, 65-66,
    67
Rottler, Johann Peter, 95, 102
Roy, Ram Mohan (Rammohan), 101, 162,
    163, 168, 169-70, 175, 179, 180, 248, 319
Roy, S. C., 305
Royal Asiatic Society, London, 102
Royal Danish Halle Mission. *See* Halle
Rushdie, Salman, 296

Sabbath, 370-71
Sacraments, 18. *See also* Baptism; Eucha-
    rist; Marriage; Ordain/Ordination
Sacred madness, 214-15
Sacrifice: Christian, 5, 374; Hindu, 166,
    373; Supreme Sacrifice, 374; Vedic, 226
Sadiya, Assam, 257, 262, 270
Sagas, 34, 35
Saguna, 333. *See* Satthianadhan, Krupabai
Said, Edward W., 295, 300, 301, 302, 306-7
St. Francis Xavier, 23, 43-44
St. John's College, Lahore, 237
St. John's College, Palayamkottai, 359
St. Joseph's Theological College,
    Tiruccirappalli, 377, 382; industrial
    school, 377
St. Paul's Seminary, Tirunelveli, 381
St. Peter (apostle), 34, 42
St. Thomas (apostle), 34-35, 42, 46, 130
St. Xavier's College, Palayamkottai, 359
Sajapur, 211
Salvation, 12, 240, 242, 243. *See also* Savior
Salvation Army, 22, 359
Sanatana Dharma Sabhas, 180
Sangam poetry, 30, 45, 380-81, 382
Sanneh, Prof. Laman, 3
Sannyasi (ascetic, religious mendicant),
    45, 211, 227, 255, 316; Christian, 225, 227;
    devotionalism, 227
Sanskrit College (Benares), 193
Sanskrit, 50, 62, 63-69, 90, 216; beauty of,
    63; Europeans and, 62, 69; grammar, 2,
    65-69; learning, 317; metric stanzas, 65;
    missionaries and, 62-69; sacred lan-

Trinity, doctrine of, 242, 243
Tuljaji, King of Tanjore, 95
Turner, Bp. [of Madras], 323
Tweeddale, Marquis of, 58, 170-71

Udayamperur, 37, 40
Ujjain, 187, 211
'Ulama (Muslim scholars, teachers), 224, 228, 230, 233, 238, 239, 240, 242, 250, 251, 252
'Umar, Muhammad, 226
Unitarian, Unitarians, 236, 330
Untouchables, 16, 27, 59, 150, 152, 337, 340, 342
Upadhyaya, Brahmabandab, 21, 227
Uplift, 150, 337
Urdu, 2, 223, 224, 226, 231, 233, 238; Bible, 230, 241; Bible commentaries, 224, 230, 232, 241; press, 231; tracts, 224, 230, 253; translations from, 233
Urimai, 346, 355
Useful Knowledge, 200, 212

Vaijnath, 196, 206
Vaishnavite-Saivite dispute, 150, 160
Vaisnava, vaishnava, 179, 198, 266, 267, 319, 322, 323
Valayar caste, 347, 348
Van Dijk, Teun A., 301-2
Varanasi. *See* Benares
Vatican, 137
Vatican II, 20
Veda, Vedas (Hindu sacred scriptures), 45, 53, 104, 166, 176, 180, 202, 209; Christianity as true Veda, 164
Vedic sacrifice, 226; scripture, 373; studies, 195
Vellalar Christians, 12, 13, 15
Vellalars, 51, 83, 146; mutiny, 171
Vellore, 43; Christian Medical College, 360; mutiny, 171
Velu Thampi insurrection, 141
Vesdin/Wessdin. *See* Paulinius
Victoria, Queen of England, 315, 328
Vijayanagara empire, 354
Villages of Refuge, 52
Viswanathan, Gauri, 218

Vivekanda, 225, 231
Von Stietencron, Heinrich, 156
Vopadeva, 65, 67
Vyasa, Somanatha, 211, 212, 213, 214

Wade, Thomas, 237
Wahhabi, 228
Walker, Robert, 363
Walther, Cristophe Theodorius, 88
Ward, William, 56, 157, 319
Washbrook, David, 343
Weber, Max, 299
Webster, John, 241, 243
Weitbrecht, H. U., 232, 247
Welfare societies, 52
Welsh Presbyterians, 273
Wesley College, Colombo, 359
Wesleyan Methodist Mission Society, 29
West, Western, Westerners, 1, 6, 7, 8, 9, 26, 31, 59, 60, 313
Western education, educated, 96, 173, 180. *See also under* Medicine; Science
Westernization, 218, 322
Wherry, E. M., 234, 249, 250
Widow burning, 57
Widows and literature, 88
Wilberforce, William, 57, 127
Wilkinson, Lancelot, 185, 188-89, 191-93, 195, 196-98, 200, 201, 206-8, 209, 211, 212, 214, 215, 217, 218, 219
Wilkinson, Michael, 165
Wilson, Bp. Daniel [of Calcutta], 14, 328
Wilson, H. H., 220
Wilson, Rev. John, 178, 194
Wink, André, 160
Women: and Christianity, 322, 324-25. *See also* Breast cloth dispute; Female Education Society; Female infanticide; Marriage; *Zenana*
Word of God, 2, 3, 235, 241, 252, 253. *See also* Gospel
World Council of Churches, 19, 20
World Missionary Conference (Edinburgh), 21, 246
World Student Christian Federation, 322
Worth, Rev. C. F., 167